DICTIONARY OF
LAW

third edition

P.H. Collin

PETER COLLIN PUBLISHING

Third edition published 2000
reprinted 2001, 2002

Second edition published 1992
First published in Great Britain 1986
as *English Law Dictionary*

Published by Peter Collin Publishing Ltd
32-34 Great Peter Street, London, SW1P 2DB

British Library Cataloguing-in-Publication Data

A catalogue record for this book is available from the British Library

ISBN 1-901659-43-7

Text computer typeset by PCP
Printed and bound in Finland by WS Bookwell
Cover artwork by Gary Weston

Preface to the first edition

This dictionary provides the user with the basic vocabulary used in British and American law. The subject matter covers criminal, civil, commercial and international law, dealing with situations as different as the solicitor's office, the courtroom, and the prison. The level of language ranges from the very formal (including many Latin terms) to prison slang.

The 6,000 main words and phrases are explained in simple English. Very many examples are given to show the words and phrases used in context, and many of the more difficult phrases are also defined in clear and simple English. Words which pose particular grammatical problems have short grammar notes attached, giving irregular verb forms and plurals, together with notes on constructions and the differences between British and American usage. Many words also have comments of a more general nature, referring to the judicial system, or to particular points of law.

We would like to thank many people who helped in the compilation and checking of this dictionary, in particular Stephen Baister who brought his trained legal mind to bear on the text and provided many valuable expert comments.

Preface to the second edition

The text of the first edition has been completely updated, removing certain items which were only peripherally connect to legal matters, and inserting much new material, in particular relating to legislative processes.

Preface to the third edition

The text of the dictionary has again been completely revised, and now includes over 7,500 main words and phrases including many items from European Union law. The changes in the British civil procedures which came into effect in early 1999 have also been incorporated.

Because the pronunciation of some specialized words can cause problems, we have added the phonetic transcription of all the main words, using the International Phonetic Alphabet.

Phonetics

The following symbols have been used to show the pronunciation of the main words in the dictionary.

Stress has been indicated by a main stress mark ($'$), but these are only guides as the stress of the word may change according to its position in the sentence.

Vowels		*Consonants*	
æ	back	b	buck
ɑː	harm	d	dead
ɒ	stop	ð	other
aɪ	type	dʒ	jump
aʊ	how	f	fare
aɪə	hire	g	gold
aʊə	hour	h	head
ɔː	course	j	yellow
ɔɪ	loyalty	k	cab
e	head	l	leave
eə	fair	m	mix
eɪ	make	n	nil
ə	abroad	ŋ	bring
əʊ	float	p	post
əʊə	lower	r	rule
ɜː	word	s	save
iː	keep	ʃ	shop
ɪ	fit	t	take
ɪə	near	tʃ	change
u	supreme	χ	loch
uː	pool	θ	theft
ʊ	book	v	value
ʌ	shut	w	work
		z	zone
		ʒ	measure

Aa

A [eɪ] *first letter of the alphabet;* **Class 'A' drugs:** = cocaine, heroin, crack, LSD, etc.; **category 'A' prisoners** = prisoners who are dangerous, and would be a danger to the public if they escaped from prison; **Schedule A** = schedule to the Finance Acts under which tax is charged on income from land or buildings; **Table A** = model articles of association of a limited company set out in the Companies Act, 1985; **'A' shares** = ordinary shares with limited voting rights

A1 [ˈeɪ ˈwɒn] *adjective* **(a)** best; *we sell only goods in A1 condition* **(b) ship which is A1 at Lloyd's** = ship which is in best condition according to Lloyd's Register

A.B.A. [ˈeɪ ˈbiː ˈeɪ] = AMERICAN BAR ASSOCIATION

abandon [əˈbændən] *verb* **(a)** to give up, not to continue; **to abandon an action** = to give up a legal action **(b)** to leave (something, a person); *he abandoned his family and went abroad; the crew abandoned the sinking ship*

> COMMENT: abandoning a child under two years old is a notifiable offence

abandonment [əˈbændənmənt] *noun* **(a)** act of giving something up voluntarily (such as the right to a property); **abandonment of a claim** = giving up a claim in a civil action **(b)** act of leaving someone or something

abate [əˈbeɪt] *verb* **(a)** to remove or stop a nuisance **(b)** (i) to reduce (a legacy); (ii) *(of a legacy)* to be reduced (because there is not enough money in the estate to pay it in full)

abatement [əˈbeɪtmənt] *noun* **(a)** removal or stopping of a nuisance; **noise abatement** = stopping someone who is making an unpleasant loud noise; *a noise abatement notice was served on the club* **(b)** reducing a legacy or legacies, where the deceased person has not left enough money to pay them all in full **(c) tax abatement** = reduction of tax

abator [əˈbeɪtə] *noun* person who abates a nuisance

abduct [əbˈdʌkt] *verb* to take (someone, especially a woman or child) away by force; *the bank manager was abducted at gunpoint; the robbers abducted the heiress and held her to ransom*

abduction [əbˈdʌkʃn] *noun* notifiable offence of taking someone (especially a woman or child) away by force

abductor [əbˈdʌktə] *noun* person who takes someone away by force

abet [əˈbet] *verb* to encourage someone to commit a crime; **aiding and abetting** = offence of helping and encouraging someone to commit a crime (NOTE: **abetting - abetted**)

abeyance [əˈbeɪəns] *noun* **(a) this law is in abeyance** = this law in not being enforced at the present time **(b)** situation where there is no owner of a piece of land

ABH [ˈeɪ ˈbiː ˈeɪtʃ] = ACTUAL BODILY HARM

abide by [əˈbaɪd ˈbaɪ] *verb* to obey (an order or a rule); *he promised to abide by the decision of the court; she did not abide by the terms of the agreement*

ab initio ['æb ɪ'nɪʃɪəʊ] *Latin phrase meaning* 'from the beginning'

abjuration [æbdʒu'reɪʃn] *noun* act of abjuring

abjure [əb'dʒʊə] *verb US* to swear not to bear allegiance to another country

abnormal [æb'nɔːməl] *adjective* not normal, not usual

abode [ə'bəʊd] *noun* residence, the place where someone lives; **right of abode** = right to live in a country

abolish [ə'bɒlɪʃ] *verb* to cancel or to remove (a law, a rule); *the Chancellor of the Exchequer refused to ask Parliament to abolish the tax on alcohol; the Senate voted to abolish the death penalty*

abolition [æbə'lɪʃn] *noun* act of abolishing; *to campaign for the abolition of the death penalty*

abortion [ə'bɔːʃn] *noun* ending of a pregnancy before the natural term

> COMMENT: illegal abortion is a notifiable offence

abrogate ['æbrəgeɪt] *verb* to end (a law or a treaty)

abrogation [æbrə'geɪʃn] *noun* ending (of a law or a treaty)

abscond [əb'skɒnd] *verb* to go away without permission; not to return to the court after being released on bail; to escape from prison; *he was charged with absconding from lawful custody*

absence ['æbsəns] *noun* not being at a meeting or hearing; **in the absence of** = when someone is not there; *in the absence of the chairman, his deputy took the chair; the trial took place in the absence of the defendant; she was sentenced to death in her absence;* **leave of absence** = being allowed to be absent from work; *see also* IN ABSENTIA

absent ['æbsənt] *adjective* not at a meeting or hearing; *(in the armed forces)* **absent without leave (AWOL)** = being away from duties without the permission of a superior officer

absentee [æbsən'tiː] *noun* person who is not able to attend a meeting or hearing

absolute ['æbsəluːt] *adjective* complete or total; **absolute discharge** = letting a convicted person go free without any punishment; **absolute monopoly** = situation where only one producer or supplier produces or supplies something; **absolute privilege** = privilege which protects a person from being sued for defamation (such as an MP speaking in the House of Commons, a judge making a statement in judicial proceedings); **absolute title** = land registered with the Land Registry, where the owner has a guaranteed title to the land (absolute title also exists to leasehold land, giving the proprietor a guaranteed valid lease); *see also* DECREE, FORECLOSURE

absolutism ['æbsəluːtɪzm] *noun* political theory that any legitimate government should have absolute power

absolutist ['æbsəluːtɪst] *adjective & noun* (person) who believes in absolutism; (system) where the government has absolute power

abstain [æb'steɪn] *verb* to refrain from doing something (especially voting); *sixty MPs abstained in the vote on capital punishment*

abstention [æb'stenʃn] *noun* **(a)** refraining from doing something (especially voting); *the motion was carried by 200 votes to 150, with 60 abstentions* **(b)** *US* situation where a federal court may refuse to hear a case and passes it to a state court which then becomes competent to decide in the federal constitutional issues raised

abstract ['æbstrækt] **1** *noun* short form of a report or document; *to make an abstract of the deeds of a property;* **abstract of title** = summary of the details of the ownership of a property which has not been registered **2** *verb* to make a summary

abuse 1 [ə'bjuːs] *noun* **(a)** using something wrongly; **abuse of power** = using legal powers in an illegal or harmful way; **abuse of process** = suing someone in bad faith, without proper justification or for malicious reasons; **drug abuse** = being mentally and physically dependent on taking a drug regularly **(b)** rude or insulting words; *the prisoner shouted abuse at the judge* **(c)** bad treatment (usually sexual) of a person; *child abuse*; *sexual abuse of children* **2** [ə'bjuːz] *verb* **(a)** to use something wrongly; **to abuse one's authority** = to use authority in an illegal or harmful way **(b)** to say rude words to (someone); *he abused the police before being taken to the cells* **(c)** to treat someone badly (usually in a sexual way); *he had abused small children*

abut (on) [ə'bʌt] *verb (of a piece of land)* to touch another property (NOTE: **abutting - abutted**)

ACAS ['eɪkæs] = ADVISORY CONCILIATION AND ARBITRATION SERVICE

ACC ['eɪ 'siː 'siː] = ASSISTANT CHIEF CONSTABLE

accept [ək'sept] *verb* **(a)** to take something which is being offered **(b)** to say 'yes', to agree to something; *she accepted the offer of a job in Australia*; *he accepted £200 for the car*; **to accept an offer conditionally** = to accept provided that certain conditions apply

acceptable [ək'septəbl] *adjective* which can be accepted; *the offer is not acceptable to both parties*

acceptance [ək'septəns] *noun* **(a)** one of the main conditions of a contract, where one party agrees to what is proposed by the other party; **acceptance of an offer** = agreeing to an offer (and therefore entering into a contract); **we have his letter of acceptance** = we have received a letter from him accepting the offer; *see note at* CONTRACT **(b)** act of signing a bill of exchange to show that you agree to pay it

accepting house [ək'septɪŋ 'haʊs] *noun* firm which accepts bills of exchange (i.e. promises to pay them) and is paid a commission for this

acceptor [ək'septə] *noun* person who accepts an offer

access ['ækses] **1** *noun* **(a)** right of the owner of a piece of land to use a public road which is next to the land; *he complained that he was being denied access to the main road* **(b)** **to have access to something** = to be able to obtain or reach something; **to gain access to something** = to reach or to get hold of something; *access to the courts should be open to all citizens*; *the burglar gained access through the window* **(c)** right of a child to see a parent regularly, or of a parent or grandparent to see a child regularly, where the child is in the care of someone else; **access order** = court order allowing a parent to see a child where the child is in the care of someone else, such as the other parent in the case of a divorced couple **(d)** *(in the EU)* **right of access to a solicitor** = the right of anyone who is in police custody to see a solicitor in private to ask advice **2** *verb* to call up (data) which is stored in a computer

accession [ək'seʃn] *noun* **(a)** joining something; **Treaty of Accession** = treaty whereby the UK joined the EC **(b)** taking up a position; **accession to the throne** = becoming King or Queen

accessory [ək'sesəri] *noun* person who helps or advises someone who is committing a crime; *(formerly)* **accessory after the fact** = person who helped a criminal after the crime had been committed; **accessory before the fact** = person who helped a criminal before the crime was committed

accident ['æksɪdənt] *noun* something unpleasant which happens by chance (such as the crash of a plane); **industrial accident** = accident which takes place at work; **accident insurance** = insurance which will pay when an accident takes place

accidental [æksɪ'dentl] *adjective* which happens by accident; *a case of accidental death*

accommodation [əkɒmə'deɪʃn] *noun* **(a)** money lent for a short time **(b)** something done to help someone; **to reach an accommodation with creditors** = to agree terms for settlement; **accommodation address** = address used for receiving messages but which is not the real address of the company; **accommodation bill** = bill of exchange where the drawee signing is helping another company (the drawer) to raise a loan; it is given on the basis of trade debts owed to the borrower; **accommodation maker** = person who signs a promissory note for no fee, but who expects to lend the creditor money

accomplice [ə'kʌmplɪs] *noun* person who helps another to commit a crime or who commits a crime with another person

accord and satisfaction [ə'kɔːd ənd sætɪs'fækʃn] *noun* (i) payment by a debtor of (part of) a debt; (ii) the performing by a debtor of some act or service which is accepted by the creditor in full settlement, so that the debtor can no longer be sued

accordance [ə'kɔːdəns] *noun* **in accordance with** = in agreement with, according to; *in accordance with your instructions we have deposited the money in your current account*; *I am submitting the claim for damages in accordance with the advice of our legal advisers*

according to [ə'kɔːdɪŋ 'tʊ] *preposition* as someone says or writes; *according to the witness, the accused carried the body on the back seat of his car*; *the payments were made according to the maintenance order*

accordingly [ə'kɔːdɪŋli] *adverb* in agreement with what has been decided; *we have received your letter and have altered the contract accordingly*

account [ə'kaʊnt] **1** *noun* **(a)** invoice, a record of money paid or owed; *please send me your account or a detailed or an itemized account*; **accounts payable** = money owed to creditors; **accounts receivable** = money owed by debtors; **action for an account** = court action to establish how much money is owed by one party to another; *(copyright law)* **account of profit** = assessment showing how much profit has been made on the sales of goods which infringe a copyright or patent, because the plaintiff claims the profit made by the defendant **(b)** *(in a shop)* arrangement which a customer has with the shop to buy goods and pay for them at a later date (usually the end of the month) **(c)** customer who does a large amount of business with a firm and has a credit account with that firm **(d) the accounts of a business** *or* **a company's accounts** = detailed record of a company's financial affairs **(e) bank account** *US* **banking account** = arrangement to keep money in a bank **(f)** *(Stock Exchange)* period of credit (usually fourteen days) at the end of which all people who have traded must pay for shares bought **(g)** notice or attention; **to take account of the age of the accused** *or* **to take the accused's age into account when passing sentence** = to pass a certain sentence because the accused is very old or very young **2** *verb* **to account for** = to explain and record a money deal; *to account for a loss or a discrepancy*

accountability [əkaʊntə'bɪləti] *noun* being accountable or responsible

accountable [ə'kaʊntəbl] *adjective* (person) who has to explain what has taken place, who is responsible for something; *if money is lost, the person at the cash desk is held accountable*; *the group leader will be held accountable for the actions of the group*

accountant [ə'kaʊntənt] *noun* person trained in keeping or drawing up accounts, arranging systems of accounts; **Chartered Accountant** = accountant who has passed the professional examinations and is a member of the Institute of Chartered Accountants

accounting [əˈkaʊntɪŋ] *noun* preparing the accounts of a business; **false accounting** = notifiable offence of changing, destroying or hiding financial records for money

accredited [əˈkredɪtɪd] *adjective* **(a)** (agent) who is appointed by a company to act on its behalf **(b)** (ambassador) who is appointed by a country to represent it in another country; *he is accredited to the United Nations* (NOTE: you are accredited **to** a country or an organization)

accretion [əˈkriːʃn] *noun* enlargement of a piece of land by natural causes (as when the course of a river changes)

accrual [əˈkruːəl] *noun* slow increase by addition; **accrual of interest** = automatic addition of interest to capital

accrue [əˈkruː] *verb (of interest or dividends)* to increase and be due for payment at a later date

accumulate [əˈkjuːmjəleɪt] *verb* to grow larger by adding

accusation [ækjuːˈzeɪʃn] *noun* act of saying that someone has committed a crime

accusatorial procedure
[ækjuːzəˈtɔːriəl prəˈsiːdʒə] *noun* procedure in countries using common law procedures, where the parties to a case have to find the evidence themselves; *compare* INQUISITORIAL

accuse [əˈkjuːz] *verb* to say that someone has committed a crime; to charge someone with a crime; *she was accused of stealing £25 from her boss*; *he was accused of murder*; *of what has she been accused? or what has she been accused of?* (NOTE: you accuse someone **of** a crime)

accused [əˈkjuːzd] *noun* **the accused** = person or persons charged with a crime; *all the accused pleaded not guilty; the police brought the accused into the court; the accused said she regretted what she had done* (NOTE: can be singular or plural: **the six accused all pleaded guilty**)

acknowledge [əkˈnɒlɪdʒ] *verb* **(a)** (i) to accept that something is true; (ii) to admit that a debt is owing; **acknowledged and agreed** = words written on an agreement to show that it has been read and approved **(b)** to confirm that (a letter) has been received; **to acknowledge service** = to confirm that a legal document (such as a claim form) has been received

acknowledgement [əkˈnɒlɪdʒmənt] *noun* act of acknowledging; **acknowledgement of service** = document whereby a defendant confirms that a claim form or other legal document has been received and that he intends to contest the claim

COMMENT: the defendant must file an acknowledgement of service within 14 days of service, and serve the acknowledgement on the claimant. If the defendant does not file an acknowledgement of service, the claimant may obtain a default judgment

acquit [əˈkwɪt] *verb* to set a person free because he or she has been found not guilty; *he was acquitted of the crime*; *the court acquitted two of the accused* (NOTE: **acquitting - acquitted** Note also that you acquit someone **of** a crime)

acquittal [əˈkwɪtəl] *noun* act of acquitting someone of a crime; *after his acquittal he left the court smiling*

COMMENT: there is no appeal against an acquittal, and a person who has been acquitted of a crime cannot be charged with the same crime again

act [ækt] **1** *noun* **(a)** statute which has been approved by a law-making body (in Great Britain, by Parliament); **Act of Parliament** = decision which has been approved by Parliament and so becomes law; **Community act** = legal act of the European Community which has force of law; **Companies Act** = British Act which rules how companies should do their business; **Finance Act** = annual Act of the British Parliament which gives the government power to raise taxes as proposed in the budget (NOTE: use **under** when referring to an Act of Parliament: **a creditor seeking a receiving order under the Bankruptcy Act; she does not qualify under section 2 of the 1979 Act**) **(b) act of God** = natural disaster which you do not expect to happen, and which cannot be avoided (such as a storm or a flood) (NOTE: acts of God are usually not covered by an insurance policy) **2** *verb* **(a)** to work; *to act as an agent for an American company*; *to act for someone or to act on someone's behalf* **(b)** to do something; *the lawyers are acting on our instructions*; **to act on a letter** = to do what a letter asks to be done

> COMMENT: before an Act becomes law, it is presented to Parliament in the form of a Bill. See notes at BILL

acte clair ['ækt 'kleə] *noun* (*in the EU*) French legal term meaning that a legal question is clear and there can be no doubt about it

action ['ækʃn] *noun* **(a)** thing which has been done; **to take action** = to do something **(b) court action** = civil case in a law court where a person files a claim against another person (NOTE: in general, **action** has now been replaced by **claim**); **letter before action** = letter written by a lawyer to give a party the chance to pay his client before he sues; **action in personam** = court case in which one party claims that the other should do some act or should pay damages; **action in rem** = court case in which one party claims property or goods in the possession of the other; **action in tort** = case brought by a claimant who alleges he has suffered damage or harm caused by the defendant; **to take legal action** = to begin a legal case (such as to instruct a solicitor or to sue someone); *action for libel or libel action*; *to bring an action for damages against someone*; **chose in action** = personal right which can be enforced or claimed as if it were a property (such as a patent or copyright); **civil action** = case brought by a person or company (the claimant) against someone who is alleged to have harmed them (the defendant); *US* **class action** = legal action brought on behalf of a group of people;

criminal action = case brought usually by the state against someone who is charged with a crime; **personal action** = (i) legal action brought by a person himself; (ii) common law term for an action against a person arising out of a contract or tort

actionable ['ækʃnəbl] *adjective* (writing, speech or act) which could provide the grounds for bringing an action against someone; **torts which are actionable per se** = torts which are in themselves sufficient grounds for bringing an action without the need to prove that damage has been suffered

active ['æktɪv] *adjective* working, busy; **active partner** = partner who works in the firm

activist ['æktɪvɪst] *noun* person who works actively for a political party (usually a person who is in disagreement with the main policies of the party or whose views are more extreme than those of the mainstream of the party); *the meeting was disrupted by an argument between the chairman and left-wing activists*; *party activists have urged the central committee to adopt a more radical approach to the problems of unemployment*

actual ['æktʃuəl] *adjective* real; **actual bodily harm (ABH)** = assault which causes injury to the victim; *(insurance)* **actual loss** *or* **damage** = real loss or damage which can be shown to have been suffered; **actual total loss** = loss where the thing insured has been destroyed or damaged beyond repair; **actual notice** = real knowledge which someone has of something; **actual value** = real value of something if sold on the open market

actuarial [æktʃu'eəriəl] *adjective* calculated by an actuary; *the premiums are worked out according to actuarial calculations*; **actuarial tables** = lists showing how long people of certain ages are likely to live, used to calculate life assurance premiums

actuary ['æktʃuəri] *noun* person employed by an insurance company to calculate premiums

actus reus [ˈæktəs ˈreɪəs] *Latin phrase meaning* 'guilty act': act which is forbidden by the criminal law, one of the two elements of a crime; *compare* MENS REA; *see note at* CRIME

addict [ˈædɪkt] *noun* **drug addict** = person who is physically and mentally dependent on taking drugs regularly

addicted [əˈdɪktɪd] *adjective* **addicted to alcohol** *or* **drugs** = being unable to live without taking alcohol or drugs regularly

addiction [əˈdɪkʃn] *noun* **drug addiction** = being mentally and physically dependent on taking a drug regularly

additional member [əˈdɪʃənəl ˈmembə] *noun* electoral system used in Germany, where half the parliament is elected by the first-past-the-post system, and the other half by a party list system, giving additional members to represent each party's national vote

address [əˈdres] **1** *noun* **(a)** details of number, street and town where an office is or where a person lives; **address for service** = address where court documents (such as pleadings) can be sent to a party in a case **(b)** formal speech; *in his address to the meeting, the mayor spoke of the problems facing the town*; **humble address** = formal communication from one or both Houses of Parliament to the Queen; **address of thanks** = formal speech, thanking someone for doing something (such as thanking a VIP for opening a new building, thanking the Queen for reading the Queen's Speech); **debate on the address** = debate after the Queen's Speech at the Opening of Parliament, where the motion is to present an address of thanks to the Queen, but the debate is in fact about the government's policies as outlined in the Queen's Speech **2** *verb* **(a)** to write the details of an address on an envelope, etc.; *an incorrectly addressed package* **(b)** to speak to; *the defendant asked permission to address the court*; *the Leader of the Opposition will address the meeting* **(c)** to speak about a particular issue; *he then addressed the question of government aid*

to universities; **to address yourself to a problem** = to deal with a particular problem; *the government will have to address itself to problems of international trade*

adduce [əˈdjuːs] *verb* to bring before the court; **to adduce evidence** = to bring evidence before a court

adeem [əˈdiːm] *verb* to remove a legacy from a will because the item mentioned no longer exists (as when the person who made the will sells the item before he dies)

ademption [əˈdempʃn] *noun* removing a legacy from a will, because the item concerned no longer exists

adequate [ˈædɪkwət] *adjective* large enough; **to operate without adequate cover** = to act without being protected by insurance; *he made adequate provision for his wife* = in his will he left his wife enough money to live on

ad hoc [ˈæd ˈhɒk] *Latin phrase meaning* 'for this particular purpose'; **an ad hoc committee** = a committee set up to study a particular problem; *see also* STANDING

ad idem [ˈæd ˈaɪdem] *Latin phrase meaning* 'in agreement'

adjective law [ˈædʒektɪv ˈlɔː] *noun* law which refers to legal practices and procedures

adjoin [əˈdʒɔɪn] *verb* (*of a property*) to touch another property; *the developers acquired the old post office and two adjoining properties*; *the fire spread to the adjoining property*

adjourn [əˈdʒɜːn] *verb* to stop a meeting for a period; to put off a legal hearing to a later date; *to adjourn a meeting*; *the chairman adjourned the tribunal until three o'clock*; *the meeting adjourned at midday*; *the appeal was adjourned for affidavits to be obtained*; **the hearing was adjourned sine die** = the hearing was adjourned without saying when it would meet again; **the House stands adjourned** = the sitting of the House of Commons is adjourned and will resume on the following day

adjournment [ə'dʒɜːnmənt] *noun* **(a)** act of adjourning; time when a meeting has been adjourned; *the adjournment lasted two hours*; *the defendant has applied for an adjournment* **(b)** act of ending a sitting of the House of Commons, House of Lords, House of Representatives or Senate, which will reconvene on the following day; **motion for adjournment of the debate** = motion to adjourn a debate (which has the effect of killing the motion being debated); **motion for the adjournment of the House** = motion to adjourn a sitting until the following day; **adjournment debate** *or* **debate on the adjournment** = debate in the House of Commons on a motion to adjourn the sitting, used by backbench MPs to raise points of particular interest to themselves; **adjournment sine die** = adjournment without fixing a date for the next meeting (used in the US Congress to end a session); *US* **adjournment to a day certain** = motion to adjourn a sitting of Congress to a certain stated day

adjudicate [ə'dʒuːdıkeıt] *verb* to give a judgment between two parties in law; to decide a legal problem; *to adjudicate a claim*; *to adjudicate in a dispute*; *magistrates may be paid expenses when adjudicating*; **he was adjudicated bankrupt** = he was declared legally bankrupt

adjudication [ədʒuːdı'keıʃn] *noun* act of giving a judgment or of deciding a legal problem; **adjudication order** *or* **adjudication of bankruptcy** = order by a court making someone bankrupt; **adjudication tribunal** = group which adjudicates in industrial disputes

adjudicator [ə'dʒuːdıkeıtə] *noun* person who gives a decision on a problem; *an adjudicator in an industrial dispute*

adjust [ə'dʒʌst] *verb* to change something to fit new conditions, especially to calculate and settle an insurance claim

adjuster [ə'dʒʌstə] *noun* person who calculates losses for an insurance

company; **average adjuster** *or* **loss adjuster** = person who calculates how much is due to the insured when he makes a claim under his policy

adjustment [ə'dʒʌstmənt] *noun* act of adjusting; slight change; **average adjustment** = calculation of the share of cost of damage or loss of a ship

adjustor [ə'dʒʌstə] *noun* = ADJUSTER

ad litem ['æd 'laıtəm] *Latin phrase meaning* 'referring to the case at law'; **guardian ad litem** = person who acts on behalf of a minor who is a defendant in a court case

administer [æd'mınıstə] *verb* **(a)** **to administer justice** = to provide justice; **to administer an oath** = to make someone swear an oath **(b)** to organize, to manage; *he administers a large pension fund* **(c)** to give someone a medicine, a drug; *she was accused of administering a poison to the old lady*

administration [ədmını'streıʃn] *noun* **(a)** **the administration of justice** = providing justice **(b)** organization, control or management, especially the management of the affairs of someone who has died; **letters of administration** = document given by a court to allow someone to deal with the estate of a person who has died without leaving a will or where the executor appointed under the will cannot act (NOTE: not used in the singular); **administration bond** = oath sworn by an administrator that he will pay the state twice the value of the estate being administered, if it is not administered in accordance with the law; **administration order** = order by a court, appointing someone to administer the estate of someone who is not able to meet the obligations of a court order **(c)** government; *the Act became law under the previous administration*; *she was Minister of Education in the last administration*

administrative [əd'mınıstrətıv] *adjective* referring to administration;

administrative law = laws which regulate how government organizations affect the lives and property of individuals; **administrative tribunal,** *US* **administrative hearing** = tribunal which decides in cases where government regulations affect and harm the lives and property of individuals

administrator [əd'mɪnɪstreɪtə] *noun* **(a)** person who arranges the work of other employees in a business so that the business functions well **(b)** person appointed by a court to represent a person who has died without making a will or without naming executors, and who is recognized in law as able to manage the estate

administratrix [əd'mɪnɪstrətrɪks] *noun* woman appointed by a court to administer the estate of a person who has died

Admiralty ['ædmərəlti] *noun* British government office which is in charge of the Navy; **Admiralty Court** = court (part of the Queen's Bench Division) which decides in disputes involving ships; **Admiralty law** = law relating to ships and sailors, and actions at sea

admissibility [əmɪsə'bɪləti] *noun* being admissible; *the court will decide on the admissibility of the evidence*

admissible [əd'mɪsəbl] *adjective* (evidence) which a court will admit or will allow to be used; *the documents were not considered relevant to the case and were therefore not admissible*

admission [əd'mɪʃn] *noun* **(a)** allowing someone to go in; *there is a £1 admission charge; admission is free on presentation of this card; free admission on Sundays* **(b)** making a statement that you agree that certain facts are correct, saying that something really happened **(c)** *(in civil cases)* admitting by a defendant that a claim or part of a claim by the claimant is true; *when a party has made an admission in writing, the other party can apply for judgment on that admission*

admit [əd'mɪt] *verb* **(a)** to allow someone to go in; *children are not admitted to the bank; old age pensioners are admitted at half price* **(b)** to allow someone to practise as a solicitor; *he was admitted in 1989* **(c)** to allow evidence to be used in court; *the court agreed to admit the photographs as evidence* **(d)** to agree that an allegation is correct; to say that something really happened; *he admitted his mistake or his liability; she admitted having stolen the car; he admitted to being in the house when the murder took place* (NOTE: **admitted - admitting.** Note also that you admit **to** something, or admit **having done** something)

adopt [ə'dɒpt] *verb* **(a)** to become the legal parent of a child who was born to other parents **(b)** to agree to (something); to accept (something) so that it becomes law; *to adopt a resolution; the proposals were adopted unanimously*

adoption [ə'dɒpʃn] *noun* **(a)** act of becoming the legal parent of a child which is not your own; **adoption order** = order by a court which legally transfers the rights of the natural parents to the adoptive parents; **adoption proceedings** = court action to adopt someone **(b)** act of agreeing to something so that it becomes legal; *he moved the adoption of the resolution*

adoptive [ə'dɒptɪv] *adjective* **adoptive child** = child who has been adopted; **adoptive parent** = person who has adopted a child

> COMMENT: if a child's parents divorce, or if one parent dies, the child may be adopted by a step-father or step-mother

ADR = ALTERNATIVE DISPUTE RESOLUTION

adult ['ædʌlt] *noun* person who is eighteen years old, who has reached majority

adulteration [ədʌltə'reɪʃn] *noun* adding material to food for sale, which makes it dangerous to eat or drink

adulterous [ə'dʌltrəs] *adjective* referring to adultery; *he had an adulterous relationship with Miss X*

adultery [ə'dʌltri] *noun* sexual intercourse by consent between a married person and someone of the opposite sex who is not that person's spouse; *his wife accused him of committing adultery with Miss X*

ad valorem ['æd və'lɔːrem] *Latin phrase meaning* 'according to value'; **ad valorem duty** *or* **ad valorem tax** = tax calculated according to the value of the goods taxed

advance [əd'vɑːns] **1** *noun* **(a)** money paid as a loan or as a part of a payment which is to be completed later; *to receive an advance from the bank*; *an advance on account*; *to make an advance of £100 to someone* **(b) in advance** = early; before something happens; *to pay in advance*; *freight payable in advance* **(c)** early; *advance booking*; *advance payment*; *you must give seven days' advance notice of withdrawals from the account* **2** *verb* **(a)** to lend (money); *the bank advanced him £10,000 against the security of his house* **(b)** to increase; *prices generally advanced on the stock market* **(c)** to make something happen earlier; *the date of the hearing has been advanced to May 10th*

advancement [əd'vɑːnsmənt] *noun* money or goods given by a parent to a child which the child would inherit in any case if the parent died; **power of advancement** = power of a trustee to advance funds from a trust to a beneficiary

advantage [əd'vɑːntɪdʒ] *noun* something useful which may help you to be successful; **to learn something to your advantage** = to hear news which is helpful to you, especially to hear that you have been left a legacy; **obtaining a pecuniary advantage by deception** = offence of deceiving someone so as to derive a financial benefit; *(in the EU)* **social advantage** = advantage within society which is given to a person (such as a bus pass to an OAP, special loans to families

with many children, etc.); **tax advantage** = special tax reductions accorded to certain classes of taxpayers, such as the low paid, which must be extended to workers who are not nationals of the country

adversarial [ædvə'seəriəl] *adjective* **adversarial politics** = way of conducting political affairs where opposing sides always attack each other, and create an atmosphere of tension; **adversarial procedure** = ACCUSTORIAL PROCEDURE

adversary ['ædvəsəri] **1** *noun* opponent, the other side (in a court case) **2** *adjective* **adversary procedure** = ACCUSATORIAL PROCEDURE

adverse ['ædvɜːs] *adjective* **(a)** contrary, which goes against one party; **adverse possession** = occupation of property (such as by squatters) contrary to the rights of the real owner **(b) adverse party** = the opponent, the other side (in a court case); **adverse witness** = hostile witness, a witness called by a party, whose evidence goes unexpectedly against that party and who can then be cross-examined by his own side as if he were giving evidence for the other side **(c) adverse outcome** = the result of medical or surgical treatment which is not what was expected, and makes the patient's condition worse

advert [əd'vɜːt] *verb* to refer to; *this case was not adverted to in Smith v. Jones Machines Ltd*

advice [əd'vaɪs] *noun* **(a) advice note** = written notice to a customer giving details of goods ordered and shipped but not yet delivered; **as per advice** = according to what is written on the advice note **(b)** opinion as to what action should be taken; **to take legal advice** = to ask a lawyer to advise about a problem in law; **counsel's advice** = opinion of a barrister about a case; *we sent the documents to the police on the advice of the solicitor or we took the solicitor's advice and sent the documents to the police*

advise [əd'vaɪz] *verb* **(a)** to tell someone what has happened; *we are advised that the* *shipment will arrive next week* **(b)** to suggest to someone what should be done; *we are advised to take the shipping company to court*; *the solicitor advised us to send the documents to the police*

advise against [əd'vaɪz ə'genst] *verb* to suggest that something should not be done; *the bank manager advised against closing the account*; *our lawyers have advised against suing the landlord*

adviser *or* **advisor** [əd'vaɪzə] *noun* person who suggests what should be done; *he is consulting the company's legal adviser*; **financial adviser** = person or company which gives advice on financial problems for a fee

advisory [əd'vaɪzəri] *adjective* as an adviser; *he is acting in an advisory capacity*; **an advisory board** = a group of advisers *GB*; **the Advisory Conciliation and Arbitration Service (ACAS)** = government body which assists in settling industrial and employment disputes

advocacy ['ædvəkəsi] *noun* (i) skill of pleading a case orally before a court; (ii) support for a cause; *his advocacy of the right of illegal immigrants to remain in the country*

advocate 1 ['ædvəkət] *noun* **(a)** person (usually a barrister or solicitor) with right of audience in a court as the representative of a party in a case; *fast track trial costs include the cost of a party's advocate in preparing the case and appearing in court*; **employed advocate** = person employed to plead in court (as, for example, a Crown Prosecutor) **(b)** *US* lawyer **(c)** *(in Scotland)* barrister; **Faculty of Advocates** = legal body to which Scottish barristers belong **2** ['ædvəkeɪt] *verb* to suggest (a course of action)

Advocate General ['ædvəkət 'dʒenrəl] *noun* **(a)** one of the two Law Officers for Scotland **(b)** **Judge Advocate-General** = lawyer appointed by the state to advise on all legal matters concerning the army **(c)** *(in the European Court of Justice)* one of eight independent members forming part of the European

Court of Justice, along with the 15 judges, who summarizes and presents a case to the judges to assist them in coming to a decision (NOTE: the plural is **Advocates General**)

> COMMENT: the position of the Advocates General is equal to that of the fifteen judges in the European Court of Justice; their role is to give careful advice on legal matters

advowson [əd'vaʊsən] *noun* right to nominate a person to be a parish priest

affair [ə'feə] *noun* **(a)** business, dealings; *are you involved in the copyright affair?*; *his affairs were so difficult to understand that the lawyers had to ask accountants for advice* **(b)** adulterous relationship, a sexual relationship where one party (or both parties) is married to someone else; **to have an affair with someone** = to commit adultery

affection [ə'fekʃn] *noun* love (for another person); *see also* ALIENATION

affidavit [æfi'deɪvɪt] *noun* written statement which is signed and sworn before a solicitor, judge, JP, commissioner for oaths, etc., and which can then be used as evidence in court hearings

affiliation [əfili'eɪʃn] *noun* **affiliation order** = court order which makes the father of an illegitimate child pay for the child's maintenance; **affiliation proceedings** = court case to order the father of an illegitimate child to provide for the child's maintenance

affirm [ə'fɜːm] *verb* **(a)** to state that you will tell the truth, but without swearing an oath; *some of the new MPs affirmed, instead of swearing the oath of allegiance* **(b)** to confirm that something is correct

affirmation [æfə'meɪʃn] *noun* **(a)** (i) statement in court that you will say the truth, though this is not sworn on oath; (ii) written statement which a deponent affirms is true (similar to an affidavit, but not sworn on oath) **(b)** statement by an MP, showing his allegiance to the Queen (when he does not wish to take the Oath of Allegiance on religious or other grounds)

affirmative [əˈfɜːmətɪv] *adjective* meaning 'Yes'; **the answer was in the affirmative** = the answer was 'Yes'; *US* **affirmative action** = policy of avoiding discrimination against groups in society who have a disadvantage (such as handicapped people, etc.) (NOTE: the British equivalent is **equal opportunity**)

affix [əˈfɪks] *verb* to attach something (such as a signature) to a document

affray [əˈfreɪ] *noun* public fight which frightens other people

COMMENT: a person is guilty of affray if he uses or threatens to use unlawful violence towards another, and his conduct is such that a reasonable person who happened to be present might fear for his safety

aforementioned [əfɔːˈmenʃənd] *adjective* which has been mentioned earlier; *the aforementioned company*

aforesaid [əfɔːˈsed] *adjective* said earlier; **as aforesaid** = as was stated earlier

aforethought [əˈfɔːθɔːt] *adjective* **with malice aforethought** = with the intention of committing a crime (especially murder)

a fortiori [ˈeɪ fɔːtiˈɔːraɪ] *Latin phrase* meaning 'for a stronger reason'; *if the witness was present at the scene of the crime, then a fortiori he must have heard the shot*

after the event [ˈɑːftə ði ɪˈvent] *adjective* **after the event insurance policy** = policy to cover the recovery of costs in case of failure in a case where a conditional fee arrangement is applied

age [eɪdʒ] *noun* number of years someone has lived; *see* CONSENT, DISCRIMINATION

agency [ˈeɪdʒənsi] *noun* **(a)** (i) arrangement where one person or company acts on behalf of another person in contractual matters; (ii) office or job of representing another company in an area; *they signed an agency agreement or an agency contract* **(b)** branch of government; *the Atomic Energy Agency*; *a counter-intelligence agency*

agenda [əˈdʒendə] *noun* list of things to be discussed at a meeting; *the committee meeting agenda or the agenda of the committee meeting*; *after two hours we were still discussing the first item on the agenda*; *the Secretary put finance at the top of the agenda*

agent [ˈeɪdʒənt] *noun* **(a)** person who represents a company or another person in matters relating to contracts; **land agent** = person who manages a farm or large area of land for someone **(b)** person in charge of an agency; *advertising agent*; *estate agent*; *travel agent*; **commission agent** = agent who is paid by commission, not by fee **(c)** person who works for a government agency, especially in secret; **secret agent** = person who tries to find out information in secret about other countries, other governments or other armed forces

Agent-General [ˈeɪdənt ˈdʒenrəl] *noun* official representative of a provincial government of a Commonwealth country in another Commonwealth country; *the Agent-General for Quebec in London*

agent provocateur [ˈæʒɒn prəvɒkəˈtɜː] *French words meaning* 'agent who provokes': person who provokes others to commit a crime (often by taking part in it himself) in order to find out who is not reliable or in order to have his victim arrested

aggravated [ˈæɡrəveɪtɪd] *adjective* made worse; **aggravated assault** = assault causing serious injury or carried out in connection with another serious crime; **aggravated burglary** = burglary where guns or other weapons are used; **aggravated damages** = damages awarded by a court against a defendant who has behaved maliciously or wilfully

aggravating circumstances [ˈæɡrəveɪtɪŋ ˈsɜːkʌmstænsɪz] *noun* circumstances which make a crime worse

aggravation [ægrə'veɪʃn] *noun* something (usually the carrying of a weapon) which makes a crime more serious

aggrieved [ə'griːvd] *adjective* (party) who has been damaged or harmed by a defendant's actions

AGM ['eɪ 'dʒiː 'em] = ANNUAL GENERAL MEETING

agree [ə'griː] *verb* (a) to approve; *the figures were agreed between the two parties*; *terms of the contract are still to be agreed* (b) to say 'yes', to accept; *it has been agreed that the lease will run for twenty-five years*; *after some discussion he agreed to our plan*; *the bank will never agree to lend the company $250,000* (c) to agree to do something = to say that you will do something (NOTE: you agree **to** or **on** a plan or agree **to do** something)

agree with [ə'griː 'wɪθ] *verb* (a) to say that your opinions are the same as someone else's (b) to be the same as; *the witness' statement does not agree with that of the accused*

agreed [ə'griːd] *adjective* which has been accepted by everyone; *an agreed amount*; *on agreed terms* or *on terms which have been agreed upon*

agreement [ə'griːmənt] *noun* document setting out the contractual terms agreed between two parties, contract between two parties where one party makes an offer, and the other party accepts it; *written agreement*; *unwritten* or *verbal agreement*; *to draw up* or *to draft an agreement*; *to break an agreement*; *to sign an agreement*; *to witness an agreement*; *to reach an agreement* or *to come to an agreement on prices* or *salaries*; *an international agreement on trade*; *collective wage agreement*; *an agency agreement*; *a marketing agreement*; **blanket agreement** = agreement which covers many different items; **exclusive agreement** = agreement where a company is appointed sole agent for a product in a market; **shareholders' agreement** = agreement showing the rights of

shareholders in a company; **agreement in principle** = agreement with the basic conditions of a proposal; **gentleman's agreement,** *US* **gentlemen's agreement** = verbal agreement between two parties who trust each other

COMMENT: a gentleman's agreement is not usually enforceable by law

aid [eɪd] **1** *noun* help; **Legal Aid** = British government scheme whereby a person with very little money can have legal representation and advice paid for by the state; **to pray in aid** = to rely on something when pleading a case; *I pray in aid the Statute of Frauds in support of the defendant's case* **2** *verb* to help; **to aid and abet** = to help and encourage someone to commit a crime

aiding and abetting ['eɪdɪŋ ənd ə'betɪŋ] *noun* offence of helping and encouraging someone to commit a crime

a. k. a. ['eɪ 'keɪ 'eɪ] = ALSO KNOWN AS

al. [æl] *see* ET AL.

aleatory [æli'eɪtəri] *adjective* not certain; which carries a risk; **aleatory contract** = bargain (such as a wager) where what is done by one party depends on something happening which is not certain to happen

alia ['eɪliə] *see* ET ALIA, INTER ALIA

alias ['eɪliəs] **1** *noun* name which you take to hide your real name; *the confidence trickster used several aliases* **2** *adverb* otherwise known as, using the name of; *John Smith, alias Reginald Jones*

alibi ['ælɪbaɪ] *noun* plea that a person charged with a crime was somewhere else when the crime was committed

alien ['eɪliən] *noun* person who is not a citizen of a country; *(in the UK)* person who is not a UK citizen, not a citizen of a Commonwealth country and not a citizen of the Republic of Ireland; **resident alien** = alien who has permission to live in a country without having citizenship; **undesirable alien** = person who is not a citizen of a country, and who the government considers should not be allowed to stay in the country; *she was declared an undesirable alien and deported*

alienation [eɪliəˈneɪʃn] *noun* **(a)** the transfer of property (usually land) to someone else **(b) alienation of affection** = making one of the partners in a marriage stop loving the other

alieni juris [eɪliˈenaɪ ˈdʒuːrɪs] *Latin phrase meaning* 'of another's right': a person (such as a minor) who has a right under the authority of a guardian; *compare* SUI GENERIS

alimony [ˈælɪməni] *noun* money which a court orders a husband to pay regularly to his separated or divorced wife; **alimony pending suit** *or* **pendente lite** = money paid by a husband to his wife while their divorce case is being prepared; *see also* PALIMONY (NOTE: in British English this is usually referred to as **maintenance**)

> COMMENT: can occasionally be applied to a wife who is ordered to support her divorced husband

all [ɔːl]; **on all fours with** = exactly similar to; *this case is on all fours with Donoghue v. Stevenson*

All England Law Reports (All E.R.) [ˈɔːl ˈɪŋlənd ˈlɔː rɪˈpɔːts] *plural noun* reports of cases in the higher courts

allegation [ælɪˈgeɪʃn] *noun* statement (usually in evidence) that something has happened or is true

allege [əˈledʒ] *verb* to state (usually in evidence) that something has happened or is true; *the prosecution alleged that the accused was in the house when the crime was committed*

allegiance [əˈliːdʒəns] *noun* obedience to the State or the Crown; **oath of allegiance** = (i) oath which is sworn to put the person under the orders or rules of a

country, an army, etc.; (ii) oath sworn by all MPs before they can take their seats in the House of Commons (or alternatively they can affirm); *all officers swore an oath of allegiance to the new president*

All E. R. [ˈɔːl ˈiː ˈɑː] = ALL ENGLAND LAW REPORTS

allocate [ˈæləkeɪt] *verb* **(a)** to divide (something) in various ways and share it out **(b)** *(of a court)* **to allocate a case to a track** = to decide which track a case should follow; *before allocating a case, the court needs to have all the necessary information*; *the court may allocate a case to a track of a higher financial value*

allocation [æləˈkeɪʃn] *noun* **(a)** dividing a sum of money in various ways; *allocation of funds to research into crime* **(b)** *(of a court)* deciding which track a case should follow; *the allocation of a case to a particular track has implications for the speed with which the case will be processed*; **allocation hearing** = court hearing where the court hears statements from the parties to a case and decides which track the case should follow; **allocation questionnaire** = form to be filled in by each party to a claim, to give the court information to allow it to allocate the case to a particular track; **notice of allocation** = official letter from a court, telling the parties to which track their case has been allocated **(c) share allocation** *or* **allocation of shares** = spreading a small number of shares among a large number of people who have applied for them

allocatur [ælɒkæˈtuːə] *Latin word meaning* 'it is allowed': court document confirming the amount of costs to be paid by one party to another after a court action

allocution [ˈælɒkjuːʃn] *noun* *US* request by the judge to a person who has been found guilty, asking him if he wants to say anything on his own behalf before sentence is passed

allot [əˈlɒt] *verb* to share out; **to allot shares** = to give a certain number of shares to people who have applied for them (NOTE: **allotting - allotted**)

allotment [ə'lɒtmənt] *noun* **(a)** sharing out funds by giving money to various departments **(b)** giving some shares in a new company to people who have applied to buy them

allow [ə'laʊ] *verb* **(a)** to say that someone can do something; *the law does not allow you to drive on the wrong side of the road*; *begging is not allowed in the station*; *visitors are not allowed into the prisoners' cells* **(b)** to give (someone) time or a privilege; *the court adjourned to allow the prosecution time to find the missing witness*; *you are allowed thirty days to pay the fine* **(c)** to agree, to accept legally; *to allow a claim or an appeal*

allow for [ə'laʊ 'fɔː] *verb* to give a discount for, to add an extra sum to cover something; *delivery is not allowed for* = delivery charges are not included; **allow twenty-eight days for delivery** = calculate that delivery will take at least 28 days

allowable [ə'laʊəbl] *adjective* legally accepted; **allowable expenses** = expenses which can be claimed against tax

allowance [ə'laʊəns] *noun* **(a)** money which is given for a special reason; *travel allowance or travelling allowance*; **cost-of-living allowance** = addition to normal salary to cover increases in the cost of living **(b)** **personal allowances** = part of a person's income which is not taxed; *allowances against tax or tax allowances* **(c)** proportion of money removed; *to make an allowance for legal expenses or an allowance for exchange loss*

alteram ['ɔːltərəm] *see* AUDI

alteration [ɔːltə'reɪʃn] *noun* change made to a legal document, such as a will, which usually has the effect of making it invalid

alternative [ɔːl'tɜːnətɪv] *noun* & *adjective* (something) which takes the place of something else; **pleading in the alternative,** *US* **alternative pleading** = making two or more pleadings which are mutually exclusive; *see also* SERVICE BY AN ALTERNATIVE METHOD

alternative dispute resolution (ADR) [ɔːl'tɜːnətɪv dɪs'pjuːt rezə'luːʃn] *noun* various methods which can be used to settle a dispute without going to trial

alternative vote (AV) [ɔːl'tɜːnətɪv 'vəʊt] *noun* system of voting used in Australia, where voters show their preferences on the ballot paper by marking candidates with numbers 1, 2, 3, 4, etc.; if a candidate does not get 50% of the votes, the votes for the candidates with the lowest polls are redistributed to the candidates shown as second preferences on their papers, and so on, until a candidate gets 50%; *see also* SECOND BALLOT

ambassador [æm'bæsədə] *noun* person who is the highest level of diplomat representing his country in another country; *she is the wife of the Spanish Ambassador*; *our ambassador in France*; *the government has recalled its ambassador for consultations*

ambassadorial [æmbæsə'dɔːriel] *adjective* referring to an ambassador; *the ambassadorial Rolls-Royce*

ambassadress [æm'bæsədres] *noun* **(a)** woman ambassador **(b)** ambassador's wife

ambiguity [æmbɪ'gjuːti] *noun* **(a)** being ambiguous **(b)** words which are ambiguous; **latent ambiguity** = words in a contract which can mean two or more things, but which do not appear to be misleading at first sight

ambiguous [æm'bɪgjuəs] *adjective* (words) which can mean two or more things, which can be misleading; *the wording of the clause is ambiguous and needs clarification*

ambulatory [æmbjʊ'leɪtəri] *adjective* (of a will) which only takes effect after the death of the person who made it

> COMMENT: writing a will does not bind you to do what you say you are going to do in it. If in your will you leave your car to your son, and then sell the car before you die, your son has no claim on the will for the value of the car

amend [ə'mend] *verb* to change; *please amend your copy of the contract accordingly*

amendment [ə'mendmənt] *noun* **(a)** change made in a document; *to propose an amendment to the draft agreement*; *to make amendments to a contract* **(b)** *(civil law)* change made to a statement of case (this can be done before the particulars of claim are served) **(c)** change proposed to a Bill which is being discussed in Parliament

amends [ə'mendz] *plural noun* **to make amends** = to do something to compensate for damage or harm done; **offer of amends** = offer (by a libeller) to write an apology

American Bar Association (ABA) [ə'merɪkən 'bɑː əsəusi'eɪʃn] *noun* association of lawyers practising in the USA

amicus curiae [ə'maɪkəs 'kjuəriaɪ] *Latin phrase meaning* 'friend of the court': lawyer who does not represent a party in a case but who is called upon to address the court to help clear up a difficult legal point or to explain something which is in the public interest

amnesty ['æmnəsti] **1** *noun* pardon, often for political crimes, given to several people at the same time; **general amnesty** = pardon granted to all prisoners **2** *verb* to grant convicted persons a pardon; *they were amnestied by the president*

anarchic *or* **anarchical** [ə'nɑːkɪk *or* ə'nɑːkɪkl] *adjective* with no law or order; *the anarchical state of the country districts after the coup*

anarchism ['ænəkɪzm] *noun* belief that there should be no government or control of people by the state

anarchist ['ænəkɪst] *noun* person who believes in anarchism

COMMENT: anarchism flourished in the latter part of the 19th and early part of the 20th century. Anarchists believe that there should be no government, no army, no civil service, no courts, no laws, and that people should be free to live without anyone to rule them

anarchy ['ænəki] *noun* absence of law and order, because the government has lost control or because there is no government; *when the president was assassinated, the country fell into anarchy*

ancestor ['ænsestə] *noun* person living many years ago from whom someone is descended; **common ancestor** = person from whom two or more people are descended; *Mr Smith and the Queen have a common ancestor in King Charles II*

ancient lights ['eɪntʃənt 'laɪts] *plural noun* claim by the owner of a property that he has the right to enjoy light in his windows, which light must not be blocked by a neighbour's buildings

ancillary [æn'sɪləri] *adjective* which gives help or support; **ancillary relief** = financial provision or adjustment of property rights ordered by a court for a spouse or child in divorce proceedings

animus ['ænɪməs] *noun* intention; **animus cancellandi** = the intention to cancel; **animus furandi** = the intention to steal; **animus manendi** = the intention to stay (in a place); **animus revocandi** = the intention to revoke (a will) (NOTE: when used to mean 'with the intention of', use **animo:** **animo revocandi** = with the intention of revoking a will)

annexe *or* **annex** **1** ['æneks] *noun* document added or attached to a contract **2** [ə'neks] *verb* **(a)** to attach (a document) **(b)** to take possession of a territory which belongs to another state and attach it to your country, so taking full sovereignty over the territory; *the island was annexed by the neighbouring republic*; *the war was caused by a dispute over the annexing of a strip of land*

annexation [ænek'seɪʃn] *noun* act of annexing a territory

annual ['ænjuəl] *adjective* for one year; **Annual General Meeting (AGM),** *US*

Annual Meeting = meeting of the shareholders of a company which takes place once a year to approve the accounts; **annual return** = form to be completed by each company once a year, giving details of the directors and the financial state of the company; **on an annual basis** = each year

annually ['ænjuəli] *adverb* each year; *the figures are revised annually*

annuitant [ə'njuːitənt] *noun* person who receives an annuity

annuity [ə'njuːəti] *noun* money paid each year to a person, usually as the result of an investment; *he has a government annuity* or *an annuity from the government*; *to buy* or *to take out an annuity*

annul [ə'nʌl] *verb* (i) to cancel, to stop something having any legal effect; (ii) to declare that something never existed or that something never had legal effect; *the contract was annulled by the court*; *their marriage has been annulled* (NOTE: annulling - annulled)

annullable [ə'nʌləbl] *adjective* which can be cancelled

annulling [ə'nʌlɪŋ] **1** *adjective* which cancels; *annulling clause* **2** *noun* act of cancelling; *the annulling of a contract*

annulment [ə'nʌlmənt] *noun* act of cancelling; **annulment of adjudication** = cancelling of an order making someone bankrupt; **annulment of marriage** = ending of a marriage, by saying that it never existed

annum ['ænəm] *see* PER ANNUM

answer ['ɑːnsə] **1** *noun* **(a)** reply, a letter or conversation coming after someone else has written or spoken; *I am writing in answer to your letter of October 6th*; *my letter got no answer* or *there was no answer to my letter*; *I tried to phone his office but there was no answer* **(b)** formal reply to an allegation made in court, especially defence made by a respondent to a divorce petition **2** *verb* **(a)** to speak or

write after someone has spoken or written to you; **to answer a letter** = to write a letter in reply to a letter which you have received; **to answer the telephone** = to lift the telephone when it rings and listen to what the caller is saying **(b)** to reply formally to an allegation made in court; **to answer charges** = to plead guilty or not guilty to a charge; **the judge ruled there was no case to answer** = the judge ruled that the prosecution or the claimant had not shown that the accused or the defendant had done anything wrong

answerable ['ɑːnsrəbl] *adjective* having to explain why actions have been taken, being responsible for one's actions; *he is answerable to the Police Commissioner for the conduct of the officers in his force*; *she refused to be held answerable for the consequences of the police committee's decision* (NOTE: you are answerable **to** someone **for** an action)

ante ['ænti] *Latin adverb meaning* 'which has taken place earlier' or 'before'; **status quo ante** = the situation as it was before

antecedents [ænti'siːdənts] *plural noun* details of the background of a convicted person given to a court before sentence is passed

antedate [ænti'deɪt] *verb* to put an earlier date on a document; *the invoice was antedated to January 1st*

anti- ['ænti] *prefix* against; *an anti-drug campaign*; *the anti-terrorist squad*

anticipation [æntɪsɪ'peɪʃn] *noun* doing something before it is due to be done

anticipatory [æntɪsɪ'peɪtəi] *adjective* done before it is due; **anticipatory breach** = refusal by a party to a contract to perform his obligations under the contract at a time before they were due to be performed

anti-trust ['ænti'trʌst] *adjective* which attacks monopolies and encourages competition; *anti-trust laws* or *legislation*

Anton Piller order ['æntɒn 'pɪlə 'ɔːdə] *noun* order by a court in a civil case allowing a party to inspect and remove a defendant's documents, especially where the defendant might destroy evidence (NOTE: since the introduction of the new Civil Procedure Rules in April 1999, this term has been replaced by **search order**)

COMMENT: so called after the case of *Anton Piller K.G. v. Manufacturing Processes Ltd*

AOB ['eɪ 'əʊ 'biː] = ANY OTHER BUSINESS

a posteriori ['eɪ pɒsteri'ɔːraɪ] *Latin phrase meaning* 'from what has been concluded afterwards'; **a posteriori argument** = argument based on observation

apparent [ə'pærənt] *adjective* which can be seen; **apparent defect** = defect which can be easily seen; **heir apparent** = heir who will certainly inherit if a person dies before him

appeal [ə'piːl] **1** *noun* asking a higher court to change a decision of a lower court; asking a government department to change a decision; *the appeal from the court order or the appeal against the planning decision will be heard next month*; *he lost his appeal for damages against the company*; **she won her case on appeal** = her case was lost in the first court, but the appeal court said that she was right; **appeal against conviction** = asking a higher court to change the decision of a lower court that a person is guilty; **appeal against sentence** = asking a higher court to reduce a sentence imposed by a lower court; **Appeal Court** *or* **Court of Appeal,** *US* **Court of Appeals** = civil or criminal court to which a person may go to ask for a sentence to be changed and of which the decisions are binding on the High Court and lower courts; **Lord of Appeal in Ordinary** = one of the eleven lords who sits as a member of the House of Lords when it acts as a Court of Appeal **2** *verb* to ask a government department to change its decision or a high law court to change a sentence; *the company appealed against the decision of the planning officers*; *he has appealed to the Supreme Court* (NOTE: you appeal **to** a court or **against**

a decision; an appeal is **heard** and **allowed** or **dismissed**)

COMMENT: in the majority of cases in English law, decisions of lower courts and of the High Court can be appealed to the Court of Appeal. The Court of Appeal is divided into the Civil Division and the Criminal Division. The Civil Division hears appeals from the County Court and the High Court; the Criminal Division hears appeals from the Crown Court. From the Court of Appeal, appeal lies to the House of Lords. When the remedies available under English law are exhausted, it is in certain cases possible to appeal to the European Court of Justice. For many countries (especially Commonwealth countries) appeals may be heard from the highest court of these countries by the Privy Council

appear [ə'pɪə] *verb* **(a)** to seem; *the witness appeared to have difficulty in remembering what had happened* **(b)** *(of a party in a case)* to come to court; **failure to appear** = not coming to court (the case may continue in the absence of one of the parties, but not when both fail to appear) **(c)** *(of a barrister or solicitor)* to come to court to represent a client; *Mr A. Clark QC is appearing on behalf of the defendant*

appearance [ə'pɪərəns] *noun* act of coming to court to defend or prosecute a case; **to enter an appearance** = to register with a court that a defendant intends to defend an action; **entering** *or* **entry of appearance** = lodging by the defendant of a document in court to confirm his intention to defend an action

appellant [ə'pelənt] *noun* person who appeals, who goes to a higher court to ask it to change a decision or a sentence imposed by a lower court

appellate [ə'pelət] *adjective* referring to appeal; **appellate committee** = committee of the House of Lords which considers appeals and reports on them to the House; **appellate court** = APPEAL COURT; **appellate jurisdiction** = jurisdiction of a court to hear appeals; *if the ECJ tries to decide if a national court's decision to* *refer a case to it is correct, then the ECJ is exercising a form of appellate jurisdiction*

> COMMENT: applications can now be dealt with by telephone (a 'telephone hearing'); urgent applications can be made without making an application notice

appendix [əˈpendɪks] *noun* additional text at the end of a document; *the markets covered by the agency agreement are listed in the Appendix; see Appendix B for the clear-up rates of notifiable offences* (NOTE: plural is **appendices**)

apply [əˈplaɪ] *verb* **(a)** to ask for something, usually in writing; *to apply for a job; to apply for shares; to apply in writing; to apply in person; my client wishes to apply for Legal Aid; he applied for judicial review or for compensation or for an adjournment;* **to apply to the Court** = to ask the court to make an order; *he applied to the Court for an injunction* **(b)** to affect, to touch; *this clause applies only to deals outside the EU; the legal precedent applies to cases where the parents of the child are divorced*

applicant [ˈæplɪkənt] *noun* **(a)** person who applies for something; *an applicant for a job or a job applicant; there were thousands of applicants for shares in the new company* **(b)** person who applies for a court order

application [æplɪˈkeɪʃn] *noun* **(a)** asking for something, usually in writing; *application for shares; shares payable on application; application for a job or job application;* **application form** = form to be filled in when applying; *to fill in an application form for a job or a job application form;* **letter of application** = letter in which someone applies for a job or applies for shares in a new company **(b)** act of asking the Court to make an order; *his application for an injunction was refused; solicitors acting for the wife made an application for a maintenance order;* **application notice** = document by which an applicant applies for a court order; the notice must state what type of order is being sought and the reasons for seeking it (NOTE: the phrase **applications made without notice being served on the other party** is now used instead of **ex parte applications**)

appoint [əˈpɔɪnt] *verb* to choose someone for a job; *to appoint James Smith to the post of manager; the government has appointed a QC to head the inquiry; the court appointed a receiver* (NOTE: you appoint a person **to** a job or **to do** a job)

appointee [əpɔɪnˈtiː] *noun* person who is appointed to a job

appointment [əˈpɔɪntmənt] *noun* **(a)** arrangement to meet; *to make or to fix an appointment for two o'clock; to make an appointment with someone for two o'clock; he was late for his appointment; she had to cancel her appointment;* **appointments book** = desk diary in which appointments are noted **(b)** being appointed to a job; **on his appointment as magistrate** = when he was made a magistrate; **letter of appointment** = letter in which someone is appointed to a job **(c)** **power of appointment** = power given to one person (such as a trustee) to dispose of property belonging to another **(d)** job; **legal appointments vacant** = list in a newspaper of legal jobs which are vacant

apportion [əˈpɔːʃn] *verb* to share out (property, rights or liabilities) in proportion; *costs are apportioned according to projected revenue*

apportionment [əˈpɔːʃnmənt] *noun* sharing out of (property, rights or liabilities)

appraise [əˈpreɪz] *verb* to make an estimate of the value of something

appraiser [əˈpreɪzə] *noun* person who appraises something

apprehend [æprɪˈhend] *verb* (*formal*) **(a)** to understand; *I apprehend that you say your client has a reference* **(b)** to arrest; *the suspect was apprehended at the scene of the crime*

apprehension [æprɪ'henʃn] *noun* *(formal)* arrest (of a person)

appropriate 1 [ə'prəupriət] *adjective* suitable, which fits; *is a fine an appropriate punishment for sex offences?* **2** [ə'prəuprieɪt] *verb* **(a)** to take control of (something) for one's own use; *the town council appropriated the land to build the new municipal offices* **(b)** to take something for a particular use, such as taking funds from an estate to pay legacies to beneficiaries

appropriation [əprəupri'eɪʃn] *noun* allocating of money for a particular purpose, such as for distributing parts of an estate to beneficiaries; **appropriations committee** = committee which examines government expenditure

approval [ə'pru:vlə] *noun* **(a)** agreement; *to submit a budget for approval*; **certificate of approval** = document showing that an item has been approved officially **(b) on approval** = sale where the buyer pays for goods only if they are satisfactory

approve [ə'pru:v] *verb* **(a) to approve of** = to think something is good **(b)** to agree to something officially; *to approve the terms of a contract*; *the proposal was approved by the board*; *the motion was approved by the committee*

approved school [ə'pru:vd 'sku:l] *noun* old name for a school for young delinquents

appurtenances [ə'pɜ:tɪnənsɪz] *plural noun* land or buildings attached to or belonging to a property

appurtenant [ə'pɜ:tɪnənt] *adjective* connected to, belonging to

a priori ['eɪ praɪ'ɔ:raɪ] *Latin phrase meaning* 'from the first'; **an a priori argument** = reasoning based on ideas or assumptions, not on real examples

arbitrate ['ɑ:bɪtreɪt] *verb* to settle a dispute between parties by referring it to an arbitrator instead of going to court (usually used in building, shipping or employment disputes); *to arbitrate in a dispute*

arbitration [ɑ:bɪ'treɪʃn] *noun* settling of a dispute by an outside person or persons, chosen by both sides; *to submit a dispute to arbitration*; *to refer a question to arbitration*; *to take a dispute to arbitration*; *to go to arbitration*; **arbitration agreement** = agreement by two parties to submit a dispute to arbitration; **arbitration award** = ruling given by an arbitrator; **arbitration board** *or* **arbitration tribunal** = group which arbitrates; **industrial arbitration tribunal** = court which decides in industrial disputes; *to accept the ruling of the arbitration board*; *see also* ACAS

arbitrator ['ɑ:bɪtreɪtə] *noun* person not concerned with a dispute who is chosen by both sides to try to settle it; *an industrial arbitrator*; *to accept or to reject the arbitrator's ruling*

argue ['ɑ:gju:] *verb* **(a)** to discuss something about which there is disagreement; *they argued over or about the price*; *counsel spent hours arguing about the precise meaning of the clause*; *the union officials argued among themselves over the best way to deal with the ultimatum from the management* **(b)** to give reasons for something; *prosecuting counsel argued that the accused should be given exemplary sentences*; *the police solicitor argued against granting bail* (NOTE: you argue **with** someone **about** *or* **over** something)

argument ['ɑ:gjumənt] *noun* **(a)** discussing something without agreeing; *they got into an argument with the judge over the relevance of the documents to the case*; *he sacked his solicitor after an argument over costs* **(b)** (speech giving) reasons for something; *the judge found the defence arguments difficult to follow*; *counsel presented the argument for the prosecution*; *the Court of Appeal was concerned that the judge at first instance had delivered judgment without proper argument* (NOTE: can be used without **the**)

arise [ə'raız] *verb* to happen, to come as a result; *the situation has arisen because neither party is capable of paying the costs of the case*; *the problem arises from the difficulty in understanding the VAT regulations*; **matters arising** = section in an agenda, where problems or questions which refer to items in the minutes of the previous meeting can be discussed (NOTE: arising - arose - arisen)

aristocracy [ærıs'tɒkrəsi] *noun* people of the highest class in society, usually people with titles such as Lord, Duke, etc.; *the aristocracy supported the military dictatorship*

aristocrat ['ærıstəkræt] *noun* member of the aristocracy; *many aristocrats were killed during the revolution*

arm's length ['aːmz 'leŋθ] *noun* at **arm's length** = not closely connected; **to deal with someone at arm's length** = to deal as if there were no connection between the parties (as when a company buys a service from one of its own subsidiaries); *the directors were required to deal with the receiver at arm's length*

armourer ['aːmərə] *noun* *(slang)* criminal who supplies guns to other criminals

arraign [ə'reın] *verb* to make the accused person appear in the court and to read the indictment to him or her

arraignment [ə'reınmənt] *noun* reading of the indictment to the accused and hearing his plea

arrange [ə'reınʒ] *verb* **(a)** to put in order; *the office is arranged as an open-plan area with small separate rooms for meetings*; *the files are arranged in alphabetical order*; **arrange** **the** **documents in order of their dates (b)** to organize; *the hearing was arranged for April*; *we arranged to have the meeting in their offices*; *she arranged for a car to meet him at the airport* (NOTE: you arrange **for** someone to do something or you arrange **for** something to be done)

arrangement [ə'reınʒmənt] *noun* **(a)** way in which something is organized; *the company secretary is making all the arrangements for the AGM* **(b)** settling of a financial dispute, especially by proposing a plan for repaying creditors; *to come to an arrangement with the creditors*; **deed of arrangement** = agreement made between a debtor and his creditors whereby the creditors accept an agreed sum in settlement of their claim rather than make the debtor bankrupt; **scheme of arrangement** = agreement between a company and its creditors whereby creditors accept an agreed sum in settlement of their claim rather than force the company into insolvency

arrears [ə'rıəz] *plural noun* money which is owed, but which has not been paid at the right time; *to allow the payments to fall into arrears*; **in arrears** = owing money which should have been paid earlier; *the payments are six months in arrears*; *he is six weeks in arrears with his rent*

arrest [ə'rest] **1** *noun* **(a)** act of taking and keeping someone legally, so that he can be kept in custody and charged with a crime; **a warrant is out for his arrest** = a magistrate has signed a warrant, giving the police the power to arrest someone for a crime; **under arrest** = kept and held by the police; *six of the gang are in the police station under arrest*; **citizen's arrest** = right of a private person to arrest without a warrant someone who he suspects has committed a crime; **house arrest** = being ordered by a court to stay in your own house and not to leave it; *the opposition leader has been under house arrest for six months*; **summary arrest** = arrest without a warrant **(b)** **arrest of judgment** = situation where a judgment is held back because there appears to be an error in the documentation **2** *verb* **(a)** to hold someone legally so as to keep him in custody and charge him with a crime; *two of the strikers were arrested*; *the constable stopped the car and arrested the driver* **(b)** to seize a ship or its cargo

arrestable offence [əˈrestəbl əˈfens] *noun* crime for which someone can be arrested without a warrant (usually an offence which carries a penalty of at least five years' imprisonment)

arrest warrant [əˈrest ˈwɒrənt] *noun* warrant signed by a magistrate which gives the police the power to arrest someone for a crime

COMMENT: any citizen may arrest a person who is committing a serious offence, though members of the police force have wider powers, in particular the power to arrest persons on suspicion of a serious crime or in cases where an arrest warrant has been granted. Generally a policeman is not entitled to arrest someone without a warrant if the person does not know or is not told the reason for his arrest

arson [ˈɑːsən] *noun* notifiable offence of setting fire to a building; *he was charged with arson*; *during the riot there were ten cases of looting and two of arson*; *the police who are investigating the fire suspect arson*; an arson attack on a house = setting fire to a house

arsonist [ˈɑːsənɪst] *noun* person who commits arson

article [ˈɑːtɪkl] *noun* (a) product or thing for sale; *a black market in imported articles of clothing* (b) section of a legal agreement; *see article 8 of the contract* (c) articles of association, *US* articles of incorporation = document which regulates the way in which a company's affairs are managed; **articles of partnership** = document which sets up the legal conditions of a partnership; *he is a director appointed under the articles of the company*; *this procedure is not allowed under the articles of association of the company* (d) articles = time when a clerk is working in a solicitor's office learning the law; **to serve articles** = to work in a solicitor's office to learn the law (NOTE: officially this is now called a **training contract,** though the old term is still used); **articles of indenture** = contract by which

a trainee craftsman works for a master for some years to learn a trade (e) *US* articles of impeachment = statement of the grounds on which a public official is to be impeached

articled [ˈɑːtɪkld] *adjective* articled clerk = clerk who is bound by contract to work in a solicitor's office for some years to learn the law (NOTE: officially now called a **trainee solicitor,** though the old term is still used)

artificial person [ˈɑːtɪfɪʃl ˈpɜːsən] *noun* body (such as a company) which is a person in the eyes of the law

ascendant [əˈsendənt] *noun* parent or grandparent of a person (NOTE: the opposite, the children or grandchildren of a person, are **descendants**)

aside [əˈsaid] *adverb* to one side, out of the way; **to put aside** *or* **to set aside** = to decide not to apply a decision, to decide to cancel an order, judgment or a step taken by a party in proceedings; *the arbitrator's award was set aside on appeal*

ask [ɑːsk] *verb* (a) to put a question to someone; *prosecuting counsel asked the accused to explain why the can of petrol was in his car* (b) to tell someone to do something; *the police officers asked the marchers to go home*; *she asked her secretary to fetch a file from the managing director's office*; *the customs officials asked him to open his case*; *the judge asked the witness to write the name on a piece of paper*

ask for [ˈɑːsk ˈfɔː] *verb* (a) to say that you want or need something; *he asked for the file on 1992 debtors*; *counsel asked for more time to consult with his colleagues*; *there is a man on the phone asking for Mr Smith*; **to ask for bail to be granted** = to ask a court to allow a prisoner to be remanded on bail (b) to put a price on something for sale; *they are asking £24,000 for the car*

assassin [əˈsæsɪn] *noun* murderer of a public figure

assassinate [ə'sæsɪneɪt] *verb* to murder (a public figure)

assassination [əsæsɪ'neɪʃn] *noun* murder of a public figure

assault [ə'sɒlt] **1** *noun* crime or tort of acting in such a way that someone is afraid he will be attacked and hurt; *he was sent to prison for assault*; *the number of cases of assault or the number of assaults on policemen is increasing*; *see also* BATTERY (NOTE: as a crime or tort, assault has no plural; when it has a plural this means 'cases of assault'); **2** *verb* to attack someone; *she was assaulted by two muggers*

> COMMENT: assault should be distinguished from battery, in that assault is the threat of violence, whereas battery is actual violence. However, because the two are so closely connected, the term 'assault' is frequently used as a general term for violence to a person. 'Aggravated assault' is assault causing serious injury or carried out in connection with another serious crime. The term 'common assault' is frequently used for any assault which is not an aggravated assault

assay [ə'seɪ] *noun* test (especially of gold or silver) to see if a metal is of the right quality; **assay mark** = hallmark, a mark put on gold or silver items to show that the metal is of correct quality

assemble [ə'sembl] *verb* **(a)** to put something together from various parts; *the police are still assembling all the evidence* **(b)** to come together or to gather; *the crowd assembled in front of the police station*

assembly [ə'sembli] *noun* **(a)** coming together in a group; **freedom of assembly** = being able to meet as a group without being afraid of prosecution; **unlawful assembly** = notifiable offence when a number of people come together to commit a breach of the peace or any other crime **(b)** group of people who come together to discuss political problems, to pass laws; **the Assembly of the European Community** = the European Parliament;

the General Assembly of the United Nations = meeting of all the members of the United Nations to discuss international problems, where each member state has one vote (NOTE: many national legislatures are called 'National Assemblies' in English)

assemblyman [ə'semblimən] *noun* member of an assembly

assent [ə'sent] **1** *noun* **(a)** agreement to something; **Royal Assent** = formal passing of a Bill into law to become an Act of Parliament; *(in the EU)* **assent procedure** = procedure by which the approval of the European Parliament is necessary before legislation can be put into law **(b)** notification by a personal representative that part of an estate is not needed for the administration of the estate and can be passed to the beneficiary named in the will (the assent can be given verbally or in writing and applies to personal property and real estate) **2** *verb* to agree to something; *the executor assented to the vesting of the property to the beneficiary*

assess [ə'ses] *verb* to calculate the value of something, especially for tax or insurance purposes; *to assess damages at £1,000*; *to assess a property for the purposes of insurance*

assessment [ə'sesmənt] *noun* calculation of value; *assessment of damages*; *assessment of property*; *tax assessment*; **assessment of costs** = assessment of the costs of a legal action by the costs judge (NOTE: since the introduction of the new Civil Procedure Rules in April 1999, this term has replaced **taxation of costs**)

assessor [ə'sesə] *noun* expert who can help a judge in a particularly difficult case

asset ['æsɪt] *noun* thing which belongs to company or person, and which has a value; *he has an excess of assets over liabilities*; *her assets are only $640 as against liabilities of $24,000*; **concealment of assets** = hiding assets so that creditors do not know that they exist; **capital assets** *or* **fixed assets** = property or machinery which a company owns and uses in its business; **current assets** = assets used by a company in its ordinary work (such as materials, finished goods, cash); **fictitious assets** = assets which do not really exist, but are entered as assets to balance the accounts; **frozen assets** = assets of a company which cannot be sold because someone has a claim against them; **intangible assets** = assets which have a value, but which cannot be seen (such as goodwill, a patent or a trademark); **liquid assets** = cash, or bills which can be quickly converted into cash; **personal assets** = moveable assets which belong to a person; **tangible assets** = assets which have a value and actually exist (such as furniture, jewels or cash); **asset value** = value of a company calculated by adding together all its assets

assign [ə'saɪn] *verb* (a) to give or transfer; *to assign a right to someone*; *to assign shares to someone*; *to assign a debt to someone* (b) to give someone a piece of work to do; *he was assigned the job of checking the numbers of stolen cars*; *three detectives have been assigned to the case*

assignee [əsaɪ'niː] *noun* person who receives something which has been assigned

assignment [ə'saɪnmənt] *noun* (a) legal transfer of a property or of a right; *assignment of a patent or of a copyright*; *assignment of a lease*; **deed of assignment** = agreement which legally transfers a property from a debtor to a creditor (b) document whereby something is assigned (c) particular job of work; *we have put six constables on that particular assignment*

assignor [ə'saɪnə] *noun* person who assigns something to someone

assigns [ə'saɪnz] *plural noun* people to whom property has been assigned; **his heirs and assigns** = people who have inherited his property and have had it transferred to them

assist [ə'sɪst] *verb* to help; *the accused had to be assisted into the dock*; **assisted person** = person who is receiving Legal Aid

assistance [ə'sɪstəns] *noun* help; *litigants who receive assistance under the Legal Aid scheme*; **financial assistance** = help in the form of money

Assizes *or* **Assize Courts** [ə'saɪzɪz or ə'saɪz 'kɔːts] *plural noun* old name for what is now the Crown Court

associate [ə'səʊʃieɪt] **1** *adjective* joined together with something; **associate company** = company which is partly owned or controlled by another; **associate director** = director who attends board meetings, but does not enjoy the full powers of a director; *US* **Associate Justice** = ordinary member of the Supreme Court (not the Chief Justice) **2** *noun* person who works in the same business as someone; *in his testimony he named six associates*; **associate of the Crown Office** = official who is responsible for the clerical and administrative work of a court **3** *verb* to mix with or to meet (people); **she associated with criminals** = she was frequently in the company of criminals

associated [ə'səʊʃieɪtɪd] *adjective* joined to or controlled by; *Smith Ltd and its associated company, Jones Brothers*

association [əsəʊʃi'eɪʃn] *noun* (a) group of people or of companies with the same interest; *trade association*; *employers' association*; **freedom of association** = being able to join together in a group with other people without being afraid of prosecution; **guilt by association** = presumption that a person is guilty because of his connection with a guilty person (b) **articles of association** = document which regulates the way in which a company's affairs are managed (such as the appointment of directors and rights of shareholders); **memorandum of association** = document setting up a limited company, giving details of its aims, the way it is financed and its registered office (c) *(in prison)* time when prisoners can move about and meet other prisoners

assure [ə'ʃʊə] *verb* to insure, to have a contract with a company where if regular payments are made, the company will pay compensation if you die or suffer harm or damage; **the assured** = the person whose interests are assured, who is entitled to the benefit in an insurance policy

assurance [ə'ʃʊrəns] *noun* insurance, agreement that in return for regular payments, one party will pay another party compensation for loss of life

assurer *or* **assuror** [ə'ʃʊərə] *noun* insurer, company which insures

> COMMENT: **assure** and **assurance** are used in Britain for insurance policies relating to something which will certainly happen (such as death or the end of a given period of time); for other types of policy use **insure** and **insurance**

asylum [ə'saɪləm] *noun* (a) hospital for people who are mentally ill (b) safe place; **to ask for political asylum** = to ask to be allowed to remain in a foreign country because it would be dangerous to return to the home country for political reasons

at issue ['æt 'ɪʃuː] *see* ISSUE

attach [ə'tætʃ] *verb* (a) to fasten, to join; *I am attaching a copy of my previous letter; attached is a copy of my letter of June 24th* (b) to arrest (a person or a property)

attaché [ə'tæʃeɪ] *noun* person who does specialized work in an embassy abroad; *a military attaché; the government ordered the commercial attaché to return home*

attachment [ə'tætʃmənt] *noun* (a) holding a debtor's property to prevent it from being sold until debts are paid; **attachment of earnings** = legal power to take money from a person's salary to pay money, which is owed, to the courts; **attachment of earnings order** = court order to make an employer pay part of an employee's salary to the court to pay off debts (b) **warrant of attachment** = warrant which authorizes the bailiff to arrest a person in contempt of court

attack [ə'tæk] **1** *verb* (a) to try to hurt or harm someone; *the security guard was*

attacked by three men carrying guns (b) to criticize; *MPs attacked the government for not spending enough money on the police* **2** *noun* (a) act of trying to hurt or harm someone; *there has been an increase in attacks on police or in terrorist attacks on planes* (b) criticism; *the newspaper published an attack on the government* (NOTE: you attack someone, but make an attack on someone)

attacker [ə'tækə] *noun* person who attacks; *she recognized her attacker and gave his description to the police*

attainder [ə'teɪndə] *noun* **bill of attainder** = obsolete way of punishing a person legally without holding a trial, by passing a law to convict and sentence him

attempt [ə'tempt] **1** *noun* (a) trying to do something; *the company made an attempt to break into the American market; the takeover attempt was turned down by the board; all his attempts to get a job have failed* (b) trying to do something illegal, to commit an offence (NOTE: attempt is a crime even if the attempted offence has not been committed) **2** *verb* to try; *the solicitor attempted to have the charge dropped; he was accused of attempting to contact a member of the jury*; **attempted murder** = notifiable offence of trying to murder someone

attend [ə'tend] *verb* to be present at; *the witnesses were summoned to attend the trial*

attendance [ə'tendəns] *noun* being present; **attendance centre** = place where a young person may be sent by a court to take part in various types of sport or do hard work as a punishment

attention [ə'tenʃn] *noun* careful thought; *for the attention of the Managing Director; your orders will have our best attention*

attest [ə'test] *verb* to sign (a document such as a will) in the presence of a witness who also signs as evidence that the signature is real

attestation [æte'steɪʃn] *noun* signing a document (such as a will) in the presence of a witness to show that the signature is genuine; **attestation clause** = clause showing that the signature of the person signing a legal document has been witnessed

COMMENT: the attestation clause is usually written: 'signed sealed and delivered by ... in the presence of ...'

attorn [ə'tɜːn] *verb* to transfer

attorney [ə'tɜːni] *noun* (a) person who is legally allowed to act on behalf of someone else; **letter of attorney** = document showing that someone has power of attorney; **power of attorney** = official power giving someone the right to act on someone else's behalf in legal matters; *his solicitor was granted power of attorney* (b) lawyer; **attorney-at-law** = old title for a barrister

Attorney-General [ə'tɜːni'dʒenrl] *noun* (a) *GB* one of the Law Officers, a Member of Parliament, who prosecutes for the Crown in certain cases, advises government departments on legal problems and decides if major criminal offences should be tried (b) *US* head of legal affairs in a state or federal government

COMMENT: in the US Federal Government, the Attorney-General is in charge of the Department of Justice

attributable [ə'trɪbjʊtəbl] *adjective* which can be attributed

attribute [ə'trɪbjuːt] *verb* to suggest that something came from a source; *remarks attributed to the Chief Constable*

auction ['ɔːkʃn] **1** *noun* selling of goods where people offer bids, and the item is sold to the person who makes the highest offer; **to put something up for auction** = to offer an item for sale at an auction; **mock auction** = sale where gifts are given to purchasers or where only certain purchasers are allowed to make bids **2** *verb* to sell to the person who makes the highest offer; *the factory was closed and the machinery was auctioned off*

auctioneer [ɔːkʃə'niːə] *noun* person who conducts an auction

audi alteram partem ['aʊdi 'ælterəm 'paːtəm] *Latin phrase meaning* 'hear the other side': a rule in natural justice that everyone has the right to speak in his own defence and to have the case against him explained to him

audience ['ɔːdiəns] *noun* **right of audience** = right to speak to a court, which can be used by the parties in the case or their legal representatives; *a barrister has right of audience in any court in England and Wales* (NOTE: solicitors now have right of audience in some courts)

audit ['ɔːdɪt] **1** *noun* examination of the books and accounts of a company; *to carry out an annual audit*; **external audit** *or* **independent audit** = audit carried out by an independent auditor; **general audit** = examining of all the books and accounts of a company; **internal audit** = audit carried out by a department inside the company; **Audit Commission** = independent body which examines the accounts of local authorities, which ensures that money is spent legally and wisely, and checks for possible fraud and corruption; **National Audit Office** = independent body, headed by the Comptroller and Auditor-General, which examines the accounts of government departments **2** *verb* to examine the books and accounts of a company; *to audit the accounts*; *the books have not yet been audited*

auditor ['ɔːdɪtə] *noun* person who audits; *the AGM appoints the company's auditors*; **Comptroller and Auditor-General** = official whose duty is to examine the accounts of ministries and government departments; he heads the National Audit Office; **external auditor** = independent person who audits the company's accounts; **internal auditor** = member of staff who audits a company's accounts; *(in the EU)* **Court of Auditors** = group of 15 experts who are appointed to examine the European Community's financial affairs, both its income and its expenditure

autarchy ['ɔːtɑːki] *noun* situation where a state has total power over itself, and rules itself without outside interference

autarky ['ɔːtɑːki] *noun* situation where a state is self-sufficient, and can provide all its needs without outside help

authenticate [ɔː'θentɪkeɪt] *verb* to show that something is true

authenticity [ɔːθən'tɪsəti] *noun* being genuine; *the police are checking the authenticity of the letter*; *an electronic signature confirms the authenticity of the text*

authoritarian [ɔːθɒrɪ'teərɪən] *adjective* acting because of having power; **authoritarian regime** = government which rules its people strictly and does not allow anyone to oppose its decisions

authoritarianism [ɔːθɒrɪ'teərɪənɪzm] *noun* theory that a regime must rule its people strictly in order to be efficient

authoritative [ɔː'θɒrɪtətɪv] *adjective* which has the force of law; *courts in Member States cannot give authoritative rulings on how Community law should be interpreted*

authority [ɔː'θɒrəti] *noun* **(a)** official power given to someone to do something; *he has no authority to act on our behalf*; *she was acting on the authority of the court*; *on whose authority was the charge brought?* **(b) local authority** = section of elected government which runs a small area of a country; *a court can give directions to a local authority*; *a decision of the local authority pursuant to the powers and duties imposed upon it by the statutory code*; *the Bill aims at giving protection to children in the care of a local authority* **(c)** the **authorities** = the government, those who are in control your behalf

authorization [ɔːθəraɪ'zeɪʃn] *noun* **(a)** official permission or power to do something; *do you have authorization for this expenditure?*; *he has no authorization to act on our behalf* **(b)** document showing that someone has

official permission to do something; *he showed the bank his authorization to inspect the contents of the safe*

authorize ['ɔːθəraɪz] *verb* **(a)** to give official permission for something to be done; *to authorize payment of £10,000* **(b)** to give someone the authority to do something; *to authorize someone to act on*

authorized ['ɔːθəraɪzd] *adjective* permitted; **authorized capital** = amount of capital which a company is allowed to have, according to its memorandum of association; **authorized dealer** = person or company (such as a bank) which is allowed to buy and sell foreign currency

automatism [ɔː'tɒmətɪzm] *noun* defence to a criminal charge whereby the accused states he acted involuntarily

autonomous [ɔː'tɒnəməs] *adjective* (region) which governs itself; *an autonomous regional government*; *the former Soviet Union was formed of several autonomous republics*; **semi-autonomous** = (state) with a limited amount of autonomy

autonomy [ɔː'tɒnəmi] *noun* self-government, independence or freedom from outside control; *the separatists are demanding full autonomy for their state*; *the government has granted the region a limited autonomy*

autopsy ['ɔːtɒpsi] *noun* examination of a dead person to see what was the cause of death

autrefois acquit ['əʊtrəfwæ ə'kiː] *French phrase meaning* 'previously acquitted': plea that an accused person has already been acquitted of a crime with which he is charged

COMMENT: there is no appeal against an acquittal, and a person who has been acquitted of a crime cannot be charged with the same crime again

autrefois convict ['əʊtrəfwæ kɒn'vɪkt] *French phrase meaning* 'previously convicted': plea that an accused person has already been convicted of the crime with which he is now charged

AV ['eɪ 'viː] = ALTERNATIVE VOTE

available [ə'veɪləbl] *adjective* which can be used, which is ready to be used; *the right of self-defence is only available against unlawful attack*

aver [ə'vɜː] *verb* to make a statement or an allegation in pleadings (NOTE: **averring - averred**)

average ['ævrɪdʒ] **1** *noun* **(a)** number calculated by adding together several figures and dividing by the number of figures added; *the average for the last three months or the last three months' average*; *sales average or average of sales*; **on average** = in general; *on average, $15 worth of goods are stolen every day* **(b)** sharing of the cost of damage or loss of a ship between the insurers and the owners; **average adjuster** = person who calculates how much is due to the insured when he makes a claim under his policy; **general average** = sharing of the cost of the lost goods by all parties to an insurance; **particular average** = situation where part of a shipment is lost or damaged and the insurance costs are borne by the owner of the lost goods and not shared among all the owners of the shipment **2** *adjective* **(a)** middle (figure); *average cost of expenses per employee*; *the average figures for the last three months*; *the average increase in prices* **(b)** not very good; *the company's performance has been only average*; *he is an average worker* **3** *verb* to produce as an average figure; *price increases have averaged 10% per annum*; *days lost through sickness have averaged twenty-two over the last four years*

averager ['ævrɪdʒə] *noun* person who buys the same share at various times and at various prices to give an average price

averment [ə'vɜːmənt] *noun* statement or allegation made in pleadings

avoid [ə'vɔɪd] *verb* **(a)** to try not to do something; *the company is trying to avoid bankruptcy*; *my aim is to avoid paying too much tax*; *we want to avoid direct competition with Smith Ltd*; **to avoid creditors** = to make sure that creditors cannot find you so as not to pay them (NOTE: you avoid something or someone or avoid **doing** something) **(b)** to make something void; to quash a sentence; *to avoid a contract*

avoidance [ə'vɔɪdəns] *noun* **(a)** trying not to do something; *avoidance of an agreement or of a contract*; **tax avoidance** = trying (legally) to pay as little tax as possible; *see also* EVASION **(b)** confession to a charge, but suggesting it should be cancelled

award [ə'wɔːd] **1** *noun* decision which settles a dispute; *an award made by an industrial tribunal*; *the arbitrator's award was set aside on appeal*; **arbitration award** = ruling given by an arbitrator **2** *verb* to decide the amount of money to be given to someone; *to award someone a salary increase*; *to award damages*; *the judge awarded costs to the defendant*; **to award a contract to a company** = to decide that a company will have the contract to do work for you

AWOL ['eɪwɒl] = ABSENT WITHOUT LEAVE

aye [aɪ] = YES; **the ayes lobby** = division lobby in the House of Commons, where MPs pass if they are voting for the motion; **the Ayes have it** = the motion has been passed; *see also* DIVISION

Bb

B [biː] *second letter of the alphabet;* **Class 'B' drugs** = amphetamines, cannabis, codeine, etc.; **category 'B' prisoners** = less dangerous prisoners, who still have to be guarded carefully to prevent them from escaping; **Schedule B** = schedule to the Finance Acts under which tax is charged on income from woodlands; **Table B** = model memorandum of association of a limited company set out in the Companies Act, 1985; **'B' shares** = ordinary shares with special voting rights

back [bæk] **1** *noun* opposite side to the front; *the conditions of sale are printed on the back of the invoice; please endorse the cheque on the back* **2** *adjective* referring to the past; **back interest** = interest not yet paid; **back rent** = rent owed; **back taxes** = taxes which have not been paid; **back wages** *or* **back pay** = wages which are owed to a worker **3** *adverb* in return; *he will pay back the money in monthly instalments; the store sent back the cheque because the date was wrong; he went back on his promise not to see the girl* **4** *verb* **(a) to back someone** = to help someone financially **(b) to back a bill** = (i) to sign a bill promising to pay it if the person it is addressed to is not able to do so; (ii) to support a Bill in Parliament

back benches [ˈbæk ˈbenʃɪz] *noun* seats in the House of Commons, behind the front benches, where ordinary members of parliament sit

backbencher *or* **backbench MP** [bækˈbenʃə *or* bækˈbenʃ ˈempiː] *noun* ordinary Member of Parliament who does not sit on the front benches (and is not a government minister or a member of the Opposition shadow cabinet)

backdate [bækˈdeɪt] *verb* to put an earlier date on a cheque or an invoice; *backdate your invoice to April 1st; the pay increase is backdated to January 1st*

backer [ˈbækə] *noun* **backer of a bill** = person who backs a bill

background [ˈbækgraʊnd] *noun* **(a)** past work, experience or family connections; *the accused is from a good background; can you tell us something of the girl's family background?* **(b)** past details; *he explained the background to the claim; the court asked for details of the background to the case; I know the contractual situation as it stands now, but can you fill in the background details?*

backsheet [ˈbækʃiːt] *noun* last sheet of paper in a legal document which, when folded, becomes the outside sheet and carries the endorsement

bad [bæd] *adjective* not good; **bad debt** = debt which will never be paid; **in bad faith** = dishonestly

bail [beɪl] **1** *noun* (i) releasing an arrested person from custody after payment has been made to a court on condition that the person will return to face trial (NOTE: the American equivalent is **pretrial release**) (ii) payment made to a court to release an arrested person; *to stand bail of £3,000 for someone; he was granted bail on his own recognizance of £1,000; the police opposed bail on the grounds that the accused might try to leave the country;* **police bail** = bail granted by the police from police custody; **he was remanded on bail of £3,000** = he was released on payment of £3,000 as a guarantee that he would return to the court to face trial; **to jump bail** = not to appear in court after having been released on bail; **bail bond** = signed document which is given to the court as security for payment of a judgment **2** *verb* **to bail someone out** = to pay a debt on behalf of someone; *she paid £3,000 to bail him out*

bailee [beɪˈliː] *noun* person who receives property by way of bailment

bailment [ˈbeɪlmənt] *noun* transfer of goods by someone (the bailor) to someone (the bailee) who then holds them until they have to be returned to the bailor (as when leaving a coat in a cloakroom or at the cleaner's)

bailor [beɪˈlɔː] *noun* person who transfers property by way of bailment

Bailey [ˈbeɪli] *see* OLD BAILEY

bailiff [ˈbeɪlɪf] *noun* **(a)** *GB* person employed by the court, whose responsibility is to see that documents (such as summonses) are served, and that court orders are obeyed; *the court ordered the bailiffs to seize his property because he had not paid his fine* (NOTE: the American equivalent is a **marshal**) **(b)** *US* deputy to a sheriff

balance [ˈbæləns] **1** *noun* **(a)** amount to be put in one of the columns of an account to make the total debits and credits equal; **credit balance** = balance on an account showing that more money is owed or has been paid by someone than is due or has been received by him or her; **debit balance** = balance in an account showing that more money is owed to or has been received by someone than is owed or has been paid by him or her **(b)** rest of an amount owed; *you can pay £100 deposit and the balance within sixty days* **(c)** **bank balance** = state of an account at a bank at a particular time **(d)** **balance of mind** = good mental state; **disturbed balance of mind** = state of mind when someone is temporarily incapable of

rational action (as because of illness or depression); *the verdict of the coroner's court was suicide while the balance of mind was disturbed* **2** *verb* **(a)** to calculate the amount needed to make the two sides of an account equal; *I have finished balancing the accounts for March* **(b)** to plan a budget so that expenditure and income are equal

balance sheet [ˈbæləns ˈʃiːt] *noun* statement of the financial position of a company at a particular time, such as the end of the financial year or the end of a quarter; *the company balance sheet for 1997 showed a substantial loss*; *the accountant has prepared the balance sheet for the first half-year*

ballot [ˈbælət] **1** *noun* **(a)** election where people vote for someone by marking a cross on a paper with a list of names; **ballot paper** = paper on which the voter marks a cross to show for whom he wants to vote; **ballot box** = sealed box into which ballot papers are put; **postal ballot** = election where the voters send their ballot papers by post; **secret ballot** = election where the voters vote in secret **(b)** selecting by taking papers out of a box; *the share issue was oversubscribed, so there was a ballot for the shares* **2** *verb* to take a vote by ballot; *the union is balloting for the post of president*

ballot-rigging [ˈbælətˈrɪɡɪŋ] *noun* illegal arranging of the votes in a ballot, so that a particular candidate or party wins

ban [bæn] **1** *noun* order which forbids someone from doing something, which makes an act against the law; *a government ban on the sale of weapons*; *a ban on the copying of computer software*; **to impose a ban on smoking** = to make an order which forbids smoking; **to lift the ban on smoking** = to allow people to smoke **2** *verb* to forbid something, to make something illegal; *the government has banned the sale of alcohol*; *the sale of pirated records has been banned*; **banning order** = court order to stop someone from going to a certain place (NOTE: **banning - banned**)

banish ['bænɪʃ] *verb* to send (someone) to live a long distance away (usually out of the country, or to a distant part of the country) as a punishment; *he was banished for ten years*

banishment ['bænɪʃmənt] *noun* being banished

bank [bæŋk] **1** *noun* business which holds money for its clients, which lends money at interest, and trades generally in money; **central bank** = main bank in a country (usually controlled by the government), which controls the financial affairs of the country by fixing main interest rates, issuing currency and controlling the foreign exchange rate; **clearing bank** = bank which clears cheques by transferring money from the payer's account to another account **2** *verb* to deposit money into a bank or to have an account with a bank

bankable ['bæŋkəbl] *adjective* (paper) which a bank will accept as security for a loan

bank account ['bæŋk ə'kaunt] *noun* account which a customer has with a bank, where the customer can deposit and withdraw money

bank draft ['bæŋk 'drɑːft] *noun* cheque payable by a bank

banker ['bæŋkə] *noun* person who carries on the business of a bank; **banker's draft** = cheque payable by a bank

bank holiday ['bæŋk 'hɒlɪdeɪ] *noun* a weekday which is a public holiday when the banks are closed (in legal cases, this includes Good Friday)

bank note *or* **banknote** ['bæŋknəut] *noun* piece of printed paper money (NOTE: American English is **bill**)

bank statement ['bæŋk 'steɪtmənt] *noun* document showing payments into and out of a bank account

bankrupt ['bæŋkrʌpt] **1** *adjective & noun* (person) who has been declared by a court not to be capable of paying his debts and whose affairs are put into the hands of a trustee; *he was adjudicated or declared bankrupt*; *a bankrupt property developer*; *he went bankrupt after two years in business*; **certificated bankrupt** = bankrupt who has been discharged from bankruptcy with a certificate to show he was not at fault; **discharged bankrupt** = person who has been released from being bankrupt; **undischarged bankrupt** = person who has been declared bankrupt and has not been released from that state **2** *verb* to make someone become bankrupt; *the recession bankrupted my father*

> COMMENT: a bankrupt cannot serve as a Member of Parliament, a Justice of the Peace, a director of a limited company, and cannot sign a contract or borrow money

bankruptcy ['bæŋkrʌpsi] *noun* state of being bankrupt; *the recession has caused thousands of bankruptcies*; **bankruptcy notice** = notice warning someone that he faces bankruptcy if he fails to pay money which he owes; **bankruptcy petition** = petition to the Court asking for an order making someone bankrupt; **bankruptcy proceedings** = court case to make someone bankrupt; **adjudication of bankruptcy** *or* **declaration of bankruptcy** = legal order making someone bankrupt; **criminal bankruptcy** = bankruptcy of a criminal in the Crown Court as a result of crimes of which he has been convicted; **criminal bankruptcy order** = order made against someone who has been convicted in the Crown Court of an offence which has resulted in damage above a certain sum to other identified parties; **discharge in bankruptcy** = being released from bankruptcy; **to file a petition in bankruptcy** = (i) to apply to the Court to be made bankrupt; (ii) to ask for someone else to be made bankrupt

> COMMENT: the term bankruptcy is applied to individuals or partners, not to companies. For companies, the term to use is 'insolvency'

Bankruptcy Court ['bæŋkrʌpsi 'kɔːt] *noun* court which deals with bankruptcies

banns [bænz] *plural noun* declaration in church that a couple intend to get married; *to publish the banns of marriage between Anne Smith and John Jones*

bar [bɑː] **1** *noun* **(a) the Bar** = (i) the profession of barrister; (ii) all barristers or lawyers; **to be called to the bar** = to pass examinations and fulfil certain requirements to become a barrister; **the Bar Council** = the ruling body of English and Welsh barristers; **the American Bar Association (ABA)** = the ruling body of American lawyers **(b)** rails in a court, behind which the lawyers and public have to stand or sit; **prisoner at the bar** = prisoner being tried in court, the accused **(c) the Bar of the House** = (i) line across the floor of the House of Commons, behind which people who are not members can stand to present petitions or to be questioned; (ii) rail across the floor of the House of Lords, behind which people who are not peers can stand; *he appeared in person at the Bar of the House*; *at the State Opening of Parliament MPs go to the House of Lords and stand behind the bar to hear the Queen's Speech* **2** *verb* to forbid something, to make something illegal; *he was barred from attending the meeting*; *the police commissioner barred the use of firearms*

bareboat charter ['beəbəut 'tʃɑːtə] *noun* charter of a ship where the owner provides only the ship, not the crew, the fuel or the insurance

bargain ['bɑːgɪn] **1** *noun* **(a)** agreement between two parties (such as when one sells and the other buys something) **(b)** thing which is cheaper than usual; **bargain hunter** = person who looks for cheap deals **(c)** sale of one lot of shares on the Stock Exchange; **bargains done** = number of deals made on the Stock Exchange during a day **2** *verb* to discuss a price for something; *you will have to bargain with the dealer if you want a discount*; *they spent two hours bargaining about or over the discount*

bargaining ['bɑːgɪnɪŋ] *noun* act of discussing a price, usually wage increases for workers; **(free) collective bargaining** = negotiations between employers and workers' representatives over wages and conditions; **bargaining power** = strength of one person or group when discussing prices, wage settlements, etc.; **bargaining position** = statement of position by one group during negotiations; **plea bargaining** = arrangement where the accused pleads guilty to some charges and the prosecution drops other charges or asks for a lighter sentence

baron ['bærən] *noun (slang)* prisoner who has power over other prisoners because he sells tobacco and runs other rackets in a prison

barratry ['bærətri] *noun* **(a)** criminal offence by which the master or crew of a ship damage the ship **(b)** *US* offence of starting lawsuits with no grounds for doing so

barrier ['bæriə] *noun* thing which stops someone from doing something, especially sending goods from one place to another; **customs barriers** *or* **tariff barriers** = customs duty intended to make trade more difficult; **to impose trade barriers on certain goods** = to restrict the import of certain goods by charging high duty; **to lift trade barriers from imports** = to remove restrictions on imports

barrister ['bærɪstə] *noun* lawyer (especially in England) who can plead or argue a case in one of the higher courts

---

COMMENT: in England and Wales, a barrister is a member of one of the Inns of Court; he or she has passed examinations and spent one year in pupillage before being called to the bar. Barristers have right of audience in all courts in England and Wales, that is to say they have the right to speak in court, but they do not have that right exclusively. Note also that barristers were formerly instructed only by solicitors and never by members of the public; now they can take instruction from professional people such as accountants. Barristers are now allowed to advertise their services. A barrister or a group of barristers is referred to as 'counsel'

base ['beɪs] **1** *noun* **(a)** lowest or first position; **base costs** = general costs of a case, which apply before any percentage increase is assessed; **base rate** = interest rate set by a central bank, such as the Bank of England's Monetary Policy Committee, used as a basis for calculating the interest rates of other banks; **base year** = first year of an index, against which later years' changes are measured **(b)** place where a company has its main office or factory, place where a businessman has his office; *the company has its base in London and branches in all European countries*; *he has an office in Madrid which he uses as a base while he is travelling in Southern Europe* **2** *verb* **(a)** to start to calculate or to negotiate from a position; *we based our calculations on last year's turnover*; **based on** = calculating from **(b)** to set up a company or a person in a place; *the European manager is based in our London office*; *our foreign branch is based in the Bahamas*; *a London-based sales executive*

basic ['beɪsɪk] *adjective* **(a)** normal; **basic pay** *or* **basic salary** *or* **basic wage** = normal salary without extra payments; **basic rate tax** = lowest rate of income tax **(b)** most important; **basic commodities** = ordinary farm produce, produced in large quantities (such as corn, rice, sugar) **(c)** simple, from which everything starts; *he has a basic knowledge of the market*; *to work at the cash desk, you need a basic qualification in maths*

basics ['beɪsɪks] *plural noun* simple and important facts; **to get back to basics** = to start discussing the basic facts again

basically ['beɪsɪkli] *adverb* seen from the point from which everything starts

basis ['beɪsɪs] *noun* **(a)** point or number from which calculations are made; *we have calculated the turnover on the basis of a 6% price increase* **(b)** general terms of agreement, general principles on which something is decided; *we have three people working on a freelance basis*; **on a short-term** *or* **long-term basis** = for a short or long period; *he has been appointed on a short-term basis*

bastard ['baːstəd] *noun* illegitimate child, a child born to an unmarried mother (the child now has certain rights to the property of its parents)

baton ['bætn] *noun* large stick used to hit people with; *the crowd was stopped by a row of policemen carrying batons*; **baton charge** = charge by police using batons against a mob

baton round ['bætən 'raʊnd] *noun* thick bullet made of plastic fired from a special gun, used by the police only in self-defence (NOTE: also called a **plastic bullet**)

batter ['bætə] *verb* to hit someone or something hard; *the dead man had been battered to death with a hammer*; *police were battering on the door of the flat*; **battered child** *or* **battered wife** = child who is frequently beaten by one of its parents, wife who is frequently beaten by her husband

battery ['bætri] *noun* crime or tort of using force against another person; *compare* ASSAULT

beak [biːk] *noun (slang)* magistrate

bear [beə] *verb* **(a)** to pay (costs); *the company bore the legal costs of both parties* **(b)** **to bear on** = to refer to, to have an effect on; *the decision of the court bears on future cases where immigration procedures are disputed* (NOTE: **bearing - bore - borne**)

bearer ['beərə] *noun* person who holds a cheque, certificate or bond; **the cheque is payable to bearer** = is paid to the person who holds it, not to any particular name written on it; **bearer bond** = bond which is payable to the bearer and does not have a name written on it; **bearer cheque** = cheque which entitles the person who has it to be paid

bearing ['beərɪŋ] *noun* effect; **to have a bearing on** = to refer to, to have an effect on; *the decision of the court has a bearing on future cases where immigration procedures are disputed*

beat [biːt] **1** *noun* area which a policeman patrols regularly; **the constable on the beat** = the ordinary policeman on foot patrol **2** *verb* **to beat a ban** = to do something which is going to be forbidden by doing it rapidly before the ban is enforced (NOTE: **beating - beat - has beaten**)

beforehand [bɪ'fɔːhænd] *adverb* in advance; *the terms of the payment will be agreed beforehand*

behalf [bɪ'hɑːf] *noun* **on behalf of** = acting for (someone or a company); *I am writing on behalf of the minority shareholders*; *she is acting on my behalf*; *solicitors acting on behalf of the American company*

belli ['beliː] *see* CASUS BELLI

bellman ['belmən] *noun (slang)* criminal who specializes in stopping burglar alarms and other security devices

bench [benʃ] *noun* **(a)** place where judges or magistrates sit in court; **bench of magistrates** = group of magistrates in an area; **to be up before the bench** = to be in a magistrates' court, accused of a crime; **he is on the bench** = he is a magistrate; **bench warrant** = warrant issued by a court for the arrest of an accused person who has not appeared to answer charges; **Queen's Bench Division** = one of the main divisions of the High Court; **Masters of the Bench** = senior members of an Inn of Court **(b) the back benches** = two rows of seats in the House of Commons, behind the front benches, where ordinary Members of Parliament sit; **the front benches** = two rows of seats in the House of Commons, facing each other with the table between them, where government ministers or members of the opposition Shadow Cabinet sit; **the Opposition front bench** = (i) the seats for the Opposition Shadow Cabinet; (ii) the members of the Shadow Cabinet; **the government front bench** *or*

the **Treasury bench** = (i) the seats where the members of the government sit; (ii) the members of the Cabinet; *an Opposition front bench spokesman asked why the Government had been so slow in investigating the affair*

Bencher ['benʃə] *noun* one of the senior members of one of the Inns of Court

benefactor ['benɪfæktə] *noun* person who gives property or money to others, especially in a will

benefactress ['benɪfæktrəs] *noun* woman who leaves property or money to others, especially in her will

beneficial [benɪ'fɪʃl] *adjective* **beneficial interest** = interest of the beneficiary of a property, shares or trust, which allows someone to occupy or receive rent from a property, while the property is owned by a trustee; **beneficial occupier** = person who occupies a property but does not own it; **beneficial owner** = true or ultimate owner (whose interest may be concealed by a nominee); **beneficial use** = right to use, occupy or receive rent from a property which is owned by a trustee

beneficiary [benɪ'fɪʃəri] *noun* **(a)** person who is left property in a will; *the main beneficiaries of the will are the deceased's family* **(b)** person whose property is administered by a trustee

> COMMENT: in a trust, the trustee is the legal owner of the property, while the beneficiary is the equitable owner who receives the real benefit of the trust

benefit ['benɪfɪt] **1** *noun* **(a)** money or advantage gained from something; *the estate was left to the benefit of the owner's grandsons* **(b)** payments which are made to someone under a national or private insurance scheme; *she receives £50 a week as unemployment benefit*; *the sickness benefit is paid monthly*; *the insurance office sends out benefit cheques each week*; **death benefit** = money paid to the family of someone who dies in an accident at work **2** *verb* **to benefit from** *or* **by**

something = to be improved by something, to gain more money because of something

Benjamin order ['bendʒəmɪn 'ɔːdə] *noun* order from a court to a personal representative, which directs how an estate should be distributed

bent [bent] *adjective (slang)* corrupt, stolen or illegal; **bent copper** = corrupt policeman; **bent job** = illegal deal

bequeath [bɪ'kwiːð] *verb* to leave (property, but not freehold land) to someone in a will; *he bequeathed his shares to his daughter*

bequest [bɪ'kwest] *noun* giving of property, money, etc. (but not freehold land), to someone in a will; *he made several bequests to his staff*

> COMMENT: freehold land given in a will is a **devise**

Berne Convention ['bɜːn kən'venʃn] *noun* international agreement on copyright, signed in Berne in 1886; *see also the comment at* COPYRIGHT

> COMMENT: under the Berne Convention, any book which is copyrighted in a country which has signed the convention is automatically copyrighted in the other countries. Some countries (notably the USA) did not sign the Convention, and the UCC (Universal Copyright Convention) was signed in Geneva in 1952, under the auspices of the United Nations, to try to bring together all countries under a uniform copyright agreement

best evidence rule ['best 'evɪdəns 'ruːl] *noun* rule that the best evidence possible should be produced, so an original document is preferred to a copy

bestiality [besti'æləti] *noun* buggery with an animal

bet [bet] **1** *noun* amount deposited when you risk money on the result of a race or on a game; *the horse came in last, and he lost his bet* **2** *verb* to risk money on the result of something; *he bet £100 on the result of the election*; *I bet you £25 the accused will get*

off with a fine; **betting duty** *or* **tax** = tax levied on betting on horses, dogs, etc.

betray [bɪ'treɪ] *verb* to give away a secret; *he betrayed the secret to the enemy*; **to betray your country** *or* **a friend** = to give away your country's or your friend's secrets to an enemy

betrayal [bɪ'treɪəl] *noun* **betrayal of trust** = acting against something with which you have been entrusted

beyond [bɪ'jɒnd] *preposition* further than; **it is beyond question that** = it is certain that; **beyond reasonable doubt** = almost certain proof needed to convict a person in a criminal case

BFP ['biː 'ef 'piː] *US* = BONA FIDE PURCHASER

bi- [baɪ] *prefix* twice; **bi-annually** = twice a year; **bi-monthly** = (i) twice a month; (ii) every two months, six times a year

bias ['baɪəs] *noun* leaning towards, favouring one party in a case; **likelihood of bias** = possibility that bias will occur because of a connection between a member of the court and a party in the case

biased ['baɪəst] *adjective* (judge or juror) who favours one of the parties in a case

bicameral [baɪ'kæmərəl] *adjective* (legislature) which has two chambers or houses; *the United States has a bicameral legislative assembly, composed of the House of Representatives and the Senate*

bicameralism [baɪ'kæmərəlɪzm] *noun* system of government where there are two houses of parliament, one senior to the other (NOTE: the two chambers are usually referred to as the **Upper and Lower Houses**; systems with only one chamber are called **unicameral**)

bid [bɪd] **1** *noun* **(a)** offer to buy something at a certain price (especially at an auction); **to make a bid for something** = to offer to buy something; **to put in a bid for something** *or* **to enter a bid for something** = to offer to buy something **(b)** offer to do some work at a certain price; *he* *made the lowest bid for the job* **(c)** *US* offer to sell something at a certain price; *they asked for bids for the supply of spare parts* **(d) takeover bid** = offer to buy all or a majority of shares in a company so as to control it; **to make a takeover bid for a company** = to offer to buy a majority of the shares in a company; **to withdraw a takeover bid** = to say that you no longer offer to buy the majority of the shares in a company **2** *verb (at an auction)* **to bid for something** = to offer to buy something; **he bid £1,000 for the jewels** = he offered to pay £1,000 for the jewels (NOTE: **bidding - bid**)

bidder ['bɪdə] *noun* person who makes a bid; **the lot was sold to the highest bidder** = to the person who had offered the most money

bigamy ['bɪgəmi] *noun* notifiable offence of going through a ceremony of marriage to someone when you are still married to someone else; *compare* MONOGAMY, POLYGAMY

bigamist ['bɪgəmɪst] *noun* person who is married to two people at the same time

bigamous ['bɪgəməs] *adjective* referring to bigamy; *they went through a bigamous marriage ceremony*

bilateral [baɪ'lætərəl] *adjective* (agreement) between two parties or countries; *the minister signed a bilateral trade agreement*; **bilateral contract** = contract where the two parties each have duties to the other; *see also* UNILATERAL

bilaterally [baɪ'lætərəli] *adverb* between two parties or countries; *the agreement was reached bilaterally*

bilking ['bɪlkɪŋ] *noun* offence of removing goods without paying for them, or of refusing to pay a bill

bill [bɪl] **1** *noun* **(a)** written list of charges to be paid; *the salesman wrote out the bill*; *does the bill include VAT?*; *the bill is made out to Smith Ltd*; *the builder sent in his bill*; *he left the country without paying his bills*; **to foot the bill** = to pay the costs

(b) list of charges in a restaurant; *can I have the bill please?*; *the bill comes to £20 including service*; *does the bill include service?*; *the waiter has added 10% to the bill for service* **(c)** written paper promising to pay money; **bill of exchange** = document which orders one person to pay another person a sum of money **(d) bill of health** = document given to the master of a ship showing that the ship is free of disease; **bill of indictment** = (i) draft of an indictment which is examined by the court, and when signed becomes an indictment; (ii) *US* list of charges given to a grand jury, asking them to indict the accused; **bill of lading** = list of goods being shipped, which the shipper gives to the person sending the goods to show that the goods have been loaded **(e)** *US* piece of paper money **(f) bill of sale** = (i) document which the seller gives to the buyer to show that the sale has taken place; (ii) document given to a lender by a borrower to show that the lender owns the property as security for the loan **(g)** draft of a new law which will be discussed in Parliament; *the house is discussing the Noise Prevention Bill*; *the Finance Bill had its second reading yesterday*; **Private Member's Bill** = Bill which is drafted and proposed by an ordinary Member of Parliament, not by a government minister; **Private Bill** = Bill relating to a particular person, corporation or institution; **Public Bill** = ordinary Bill relating to a matter applying to the public in general, introduced by a government minister **(h)** *US* **Bill of Rights** = those sections (the first ten amendments) of the constitution of the United States which refer to the rights and privileges of the individual **2** *verb* to present a bill to someone so that it can be paid; *the builders billed him for the repairs to his neighbour's house*

COMMENT: a Bill passes through the following stages in Parliament: **First Reading, Second Reading, Committee Stage, Report Stage** and **Third Reading.** The Bill goes through these stages first in the House of Commons and then in the House of Lords. When all the stages have been passed the Bill is given the Royal

Assent and becomes law as an Act of Parliament. In the USA, a Bill is introduced either in the House or in the Senate, passes through **Committee Stage** with public hearings, then to general debate in the full House. The Bill is debated section by section in **Second Reading** and after being passed by both House and Senate is engrossed and sent to the President as a **joint resolution** for signature (or veto)

bind [baɪnd] *verb* to tie or to attach (someone) so that he has to do something; *the company is bound by its articles of association; he does not consider himself bound by the agreement which was signed by his predecessor; High Court judges are bound by the decisions of the House of Lords*

binder ['baɪndə] *noun* **(a)** stiff cardboard cover for papers; **ring binder** = cover with rings in it which fit into special holes made in sheets of paper **(b)** *US* temporary acknowledgement of a contract of insurance sent before the insurance policy is issued (NOTE: the British English for this is a **cover note**)

binding ['baɪndɪŋ] *adjective* which legally forces someone to do something; *this document is legally binding or it is a legally binding document*; **the agreement is binding on all parties** = all parties signing it must do what is agreed; **binding precedent** = decision of a higher court which has to be followed by a judge in a lower court

bind over ['baɪnd 'əʊvə] *verb* **(a)** *GB* to make someone promise to behave well and not commit another offence, or to return to court at a later date to face charges; *he was bound over (to keep the peace or to be of good behaviour) for six months* **(b)** *US* to order a defendant to be kept in custody while a criminal case is being prepared

bind-over order ['baɪnd'əʊvə 'ɔːdə] *noun* court order which binds someone over; *the applicant sought judicial review to quash the bind-over order*

birth [bɜːθ] *noun* being born; **he is British by birth** = he has British nationality because his parents are British; **date and place of birth** = day of the year when someone was born and the town where he was born; **birth certificate** = document giving details of a person's date and place of birth; **concealment of birth** = offence of hiding the fact that a child has been born

black [blæk] **1** *adjective* **(a)** **black market** = buying and selling goods in a way which is not allowed by law; *there is a lucrative black market in spare parts for cars; you can buy gold coins on the black market; they lived well on black-market goods*; **to pay black market prices** = to pay high prices to get items which are not easily available; **black marketeer** = person who sells goods on the black market **(b)** **black economy** = work which is paid for in cash or goods, and therefore not declared to the tax authorities **2** *verb* to forbid trading in certain goods or with certain suppliers; *three firms were blacked by the government; the union has blacked a shipping firm*

blackleg ['blækleg] *noun* worker who goes on working when there is a strike

black letter law ['blæk 'letə 'lɔː] *noun* (*informal*) emphasizing the fundamental principles of law, as opposed to discussion of possible changes to the legal system to make it more perfect

black list ['blæk 'lɪst] *noun* list of goods, people or companies which have been blacked

blacklist ['blæklɪst] *verb* to put goods, people or a company on a black list; *his firm was blacklisted by the government*

blackmail ['blækmeɪl] **1** *noun* notifiable offence of getting money from someone by threatening to make public facts about him which he does not want revealed or by threatening violence; *he was charged with blackmail; they got £25,000 from the managing director by blackmail; she was sent to prison for blackmail* **2** *verb* to threaten someone that you will make public facts about him or to do violence to him unless he pays you money; *he was blackmailed by his former secretary*

blackmailer ['blækmeɪlə] *noun* person who blackmails someone

Black Maria ['blæk mə'raɪə] *noun (informal)* van used by the police to take prisoners from one place to another

Black Rod ['blæk 'rɒd] *noun* (Gentleman Usher of the) Black Rod = member of the Queen's staff in the Houses of Parliament, who attends all meetings of the House of Lords, but can only enter the House of Commons with the permission of the Speaker

COMMENT: like the Sergeant at Arms in the Commons, Black Rod is responsible for keeping order in the House. His best-known duty is to go from the Lords to summon the Commons to attend the opening of Parliament and hear the Queen's Speech

blag [blæg] *noun (slang)* robbery by an armed gang

blanche [blɑːnʃ] *see* CARTE

blank [blæŋk] **1** *adjective* with nothing written; **a blank cheque** = a cheque with the amount of money and the payee left blank, but signed by the drawer **2** *noun* space on a form which has to be completed

blanket ['blæŋkɪt] *noun* **blanket agreement** = agreement which covers many items; **blanket insurance policy** = policy covering several items; **blanket refusal** = refusal to accept many different items

blaspheme [blæs'fiːm] *verb* to ridicule or deny God or the Christian religion

blasphemy ['blæsfəmi] *noun* formerly the crime of ridiculing or denying God or the Christian religion in a scandalous way

bloc [blɒk] *noun* group of countries linked together by having similar regimes or ideals; *the Western bloc*; *the pro-Communist bloc*

block [blɒk] **1** *noun* **(a)** series of items grouped together; *he bought a block of 6,000 shares*; **block booking** = booking of several seats or rooms at the same time; *the company has a block booking for twenty seats on the plane or for ten rooms at the hotel*; **block vote** = casting of a large number of votes at the same time (such as of trade union members) by a person who has been delegated by the holders of the votes to vote for them in this way **(b)** series of buildings forming a square with streets on all sides; **a block of offices** *or* **an office block** = a large building which contains only offices **(c)** building in a prison; **H-block** = building in a prison built with a central section and two end wings, forming the shape of the letter H; **hospital block** = section of a prison which contains the hospital **(d)** **block capitals** *or* **block letters** = capital letters (A, B, C, as opposed to a, b, c); *write your name and address in block letters* **2** *verb* to stop something taking place; *he used his casting vote to block the motion*; *the planning committee blocked the plan to build a motorway through the middle of the town*; **blocked currency** = currency which cannot be taken out of a country because of exchange controls

blockade [blɒ'keɪd] **1** *noun* act of preventing goods or people going into or out of a place; *the government brought in goods by air to beat the blockade*; *the enemy lifted the blockade of the port for two months to let emergency supplies in* **2** *verb* to prevent goods, food or people going into or coming out of a place; *the town was blockaded by the enemy navy*

blood [blʌd] *noun* **blood relationship** = relationship between people who have a common ancestor; **blood sample** = small amount of blood taken from someone for a blood test (such as to establish the alcohol level in the blood); **blood test** *or* **blood grouping test** = test to establish the paternity of a child

blotter ['blɒtə] *noun US* book in which arrests are recorded at a police station

blue bag ['blu: 'bæg] *noun* blue bag in which a junior barrister carries his gown; *see also* RED BAG

Blue Book ['blu: 'buk] *noun* official report of a Royal Commission

blue laws ['blu: 'lɔ:z] *plural noun US* laws relating to what can or cannot be done on a Sunday

blue sky laws ['blu: 'skaɪ 'lɔ:z] *plural noun US* state laws to protect investors against fraudulent traders in securities

board [bɔ:d] *noun* **(a) board of directors** = group of directors elected by the shareholders to run a company; *the bank has two representatives on the board*; *he sits on the board as a representative of the bank*; *two directors were removed from the board at the AGM*; **board meeting** = meeting of the directors of a company **(b)** group of people who run a trust or a society; **advisory board** = group of advisors; **editorial board** = group of editors; **parole board** = group of people who advise the Home Secretary if a prisoner should be released on parole before the end of his sentence; **board of visitors** = group of people appointed by the Home Secretary to visit and inspect the conditions in prisons

bobby ['bɒbi] *noun (informal) GB* policeman

bodily ['bɒdɪli] *adverb* to the body; **actual bodily harm (ABH)** = really hitting and hurting someone; **grievous bodily harm (GBH)** = crime of causing serious injury to someone

body ['bɒdi] *noun* **(a)** organization or group of people who work together; *Parliament is an elected body*; *the governing body of the university has to approve the plan to give the President a honorary degree* **(b)** large group or amount; **body of opinion** = group of people who have a certain idea; *there is a considerable body of opinion which believes that capital punishment should be reintroduced*

bodyguard ['bɒdigɑ:d] *noun* person who protects someone; *the minister was followed by his three bodyguards*

the body politic ['bɒdi 'pɒlɪtɪk] *noun* the people of a state

boilerplate ['bɔɪləpleɪt] *noun US* standard form of agreement or contract (with blank spaces to be filled in)

bona fides *or* **bona fide** ['bəʊnə 'faɪdi:z] *Latin phrase meaning* 'good faith' or 'in good faith'; *he acted bona fide*; *the respondent was not acting bona fides*; a **bona fide offer** = an offer which is made honestly, which can be trusted; **bona fide purchaser** = purchaser who buys something in good faith

bona vacantia ['bəʊnə və'kæntiə] *noun* property with no owner, or which does not have an obvious owner, and which usually passes to the Crown, as in the case of the estate of a person dying intestate and with no living relatives

bond [bɒnd] *noun* **(a)** contract document promising to repay money borrowed by a company or by the government; *government bonds or treasury bonds*; *see also* PREMIUM BONDS **(b)** contract document promising to repay money borrowed by a person; **bearer bond** = bond which is payable to the bearer and does not have a name written on it; **debenture bond** = certificate showing that a debenture has been issued; **mortgage bond** = certificate showing that a mortgage exists and that the property is security for it **(c)** signed legal document which binds one or more parties to do or not to do something; **bail bond** = signed document which is given to the court as security for payment of a judgment; **goods (held) in bond** = goods held by the customs until duty has been paid; **entry of goods under bond** = bringing goods into a country in bond; **to take goods out of bond** = to pay duty on goods so that they can be released by the customs

bonded ['bɒndɪd] *adjective* held in bond; **bonded goods** = goods which are held by the customs under a bond until duty has been paid; **bonded warehouse** = warehouse where goods are stored in bond until duty is paid

bondholder [ˈbɒndhəʊldə] *noun* person who holds government bonds

bondsman [ˈbɒndzmən] *noun* person who has stood surety for another person

book [bʊk] **1** *noun* **(a)** set of sheets of paper attached together; **a company's books** = the financial records of a company; **book value** = value of a company's assets as shown in the company accounts **(b) phone book** *or* **telephone book** = book which lists names of people or companies with their addresses and telephone numbers **(c) to bring someone to book** = to find a suspect and charge him with a crime; *(informal)* **to throw the book at someone** = to charge someone with every possible crime; *if ever we get the gang in the police station, we'll throw the book at them* **2** *verb* **(a)** to order or to reserve something; *to book a room in a hotel or a table at a restaurant or a ticket on a plane; I booked a table for 7.45; he booked a ticket through to Cairo;* **to book someone into a hotel** *or* **onto a flight** = to order a room or a plane ticket for someone **(b)** *(informal)* to charge someone with a crime; *he was booked for driving on the wrong side of the road*

booking [ˈbʊkɪŋ] *noun* act of ordering a room or a seat

boot camp [ˈbuːt ˈkæmp] *noun* US camp providing a form of treatment for young offenders where they are subjected to harsh discipline for a short period

booth [buːð] *noun* small cabin, usually with three sides, where one person can stand or sit; **polling booth** *or* **voting booth** = small enclosed space in a polling station, where the voter goes to mark his ballot paper in private

bootleg [ˈbuːtleg] *adjective* illicit (alcohol)

bootlegger [ˈbuːtlegə] *noun* person who makes or supplies illicit alcohol

bootlegging [ˈbuːtlegɪŋ] *noun* **(a)** making illicit alcohol **(b)** making illegal records or tapes from live concerts

borough [ˈbʌrə] *noun* town which has been incorporated; **borough council** = representatives elected to run a borough; **borough architect** *or* **borough engineer** *or* **borough treasurer** = officials in charge of the new buildings, machinery or finances of a borough

COMMENT: a borough is an officially incorporated town, which has a charter granted by Parliament. A borough is run by an elected council, with a mayor as its official head. Most boroughs are represented in Parliament by at least one MP

borrow [ˈbɒrəʊ] *verb* **(a)** to take money from someone for a time, possibly paying interest for it, and repaying it at the end of the period; *he borrowed £1,000 from the bank; the company had to borrow heavily to repay its debts; they borrowed £25,000 against the security of the factory* **(b)** *(slang)* to steal

borrower [ˈbɒrəʊə] *noun* person who borrows; *borrowers from the bank pay 12% interest*

borrowing [ˈbɒrəʊɪŋ] *noun* **(a)** action of borrowing money; *the new factory was financed by bank borrowing;* **borrowing power** = amount of money which a company can borrow **(b) borrowings** = money borrowed; *the company's borrowings have doubled;* **bank borrowings** = loans made by banks

borstal [ˈbɔːstəl] *noun (formerly)* centre where a young offender was sent for training if he had committed a crime which would normally be punishable by a prison sentence (NOTE: now replaced by **Young Offender Institutions**)

boss [bɒs] *noun* head of a Mafia family or other criminal gang

bottomry [ˈbɒtəmri] *noun* mortgage of a ship or cargo; **bottomry bond** = bond which secures a ship or cargo against a loan

bounce [baʊns] *verb (informal) (of a cheque)* to be returned to the person who has tried to cash it, because there is not enough money in the payer's account to pay it; *he paid for the car with a cheque that bounced*

bound [baʊnd] *see* BIND, DUTY

boundary (line) [ˈbaʊndri] *noun* line marking the edge of a piece of land owned by someone; *the boundary dispute dragged through the courts for years*

Boundary Commission [ˈbaʊndri kəˈmɪʃn] *noun* committee which examines the area and population of constituencies for the House of Commons and recommends changes to ensure that each Member of Parliament represents approximately the same number of people

bounty [ˈbaʊnti] *noun* (i) government subsidy made to help an industry; (ii) payment made by government to someone who has saved lives or found treasure

bourgeois [ˈbʊəʒwɑː] *adjective* **(a)** middle class, referring to the class of businessmen and professional people (as opposed to the aristocracy, the clergy, manual or clerical workers, the Armed Forces, etc.); **petty bourgeois** = referring to the lower middle class, to small shopkeepers, etc. **(b)** *(used as criticism)* traditional and reactionary, not revolutionary; *the Party is trying to reduce its bourgeois image by promoting young activists to the Central Committee*

bourgeoisie [bʊəʒwɑːˈziː] *noun* the middle class (usually the richer upper levels of the middle class, formed of businessmen and professional people); **petty bourgeoisie** = the lower middle class of shopkeepers, minor civil servants, etc.

box [bɒks] *noun* **(a)** container; *the goods were sent in thin cardboard boxes; the drugs were hidden in boxes of office stationery*; **envelopes come in boxes of two hundred** = packed two hundred to a box; **box file** = file (for papers) made like a box; **ballot box** = sealed box into which

ballot papers are put **(b) witness box** = place in a courtroom where the witnesses give evidence (NOTE: American English is **witness stand**) **(c) box number** = reference number used in a post office or an advertisement to avoid giving an address; *please reply to Box No. 209; our address is: P.O. Box 74209, Edinburgh*

boycott [ˈbɔɪkɒt] **1** *noun* refusal to buy or to deal in goods from a certain country, company or person, used as a punishment; *the union organized a boycott against or of imported cars* **2** *verb* to refuse to buy or to deal in goods from a certain country, company or person, as a punishment; *the company's products have been boycotted by the main department stores; we are boycotting all imports from that country*; **the management has boycotted the meeting** = has refused to attend the meeting

bracelets [ˈbreɪsləts] *plural noun (slang)* handcuffs

bracket [ˈbrækɪt] **1** *noun* group of items or people of a certain type taken together; **income bracket** *or* **tax bracket** = level of income where a certain percentage tax applies **2** *verb* **to bracket together** = to treat several items together in the same way

branch [brɑːnʃ] *noun* **(a)** local office of a bank or large business; local shop of a large chain of shops; *the bank or the store has branches in most towns in the south of the country; the insurance company has closed its branches in South America; he is the manager of our local branch of Lloyds bank; we have decided to open a branch office in Chicago; the manager of our branch in Lagos or of our Lagos branch*; **branch manager** = manager of a branch **(b)** part or separate section (of the law); *the Law of Contract and the Law of Tort are branches of civil law* **(c)** *see also* SPECIAL BRANCH

brand [brænd] **1** *noun* make of product, which can be recognized by a name or by a design **2** *verb* to mark with a special mark

branded [ˈbrændɪd] *adjective* **branded goods** = goods sold under brand names

breach [briːtʃ] *noun* **(a)** failure to carry out the terms of an agreement; *they alleged that a breach of international obligations had been committed*; **in breach of** = failing to do something which was agreed, not acting according to; *we are in breach of Community law*; *the defendant is in breach of his statutory duty*; **breach of confidence** = betraying a secret which someone has told you; **breach of contract** = failing to do something which is in a contract; **the company is in breach of contract** = the company has failed to carry out what was agreed in the contract; **breach of promise** = formerly, complaint in court that someone had promised to marry the plaintiff and then had not done so; **breach of trust** = failure to act properly on the part of a trustee in regard to a trust; **breach of warranty** = supplying goods which do not meet the standards of the warranty applied to them **(b)** failure to obey the law; *the soldier was charged with a serious breach of discipline*; **breach of the peace** = creating a disturbance which is likely to annoy or frighten people

COMMENT: anyone can arrest a person who is committing a breach of peace; a policeman can arrest someone who is committing a breach of the peace without charging him

breach of privilege [briːtʃ əv ˈprɪvəlɪdʒ] *noun* acting in a way which may diminish the reputation or power of Parliament (by speaking in a defamatory way about an MP or about Parliament itself)

COMMENT: breaches of parliamentary privilege can take the form of many types of action; the commonest are threats to MPs, or insulting language about MPs; speaking in a rude way about Parliament in public; wild behaviour in the public galleries; trying to influence witnesses appearing before parliamentary committees

break [breɪk] **1** *noun* short space of time, when you can rest; *the court adjourned for a ten-minute break* **2** *verb* **(a) to break the law** = to do something which is against the law; *if you hit a policeman you will be breaking the law*; *he is breaking the law by parking on the pavement*; *the company broke section 26 of the Companies Act* **(b)** to fail to carry out the duties of a contract; *the company has broken the contract or the agreement*; **to break an engagement to do something** = not to do what has been agreed **(c)** to cancel (a contract); *the company is hoping to be able to break the contract* (NOTE: **breaking - broke - broken**)

breakages [ˈbreɪkɪdʒɪz] *plural noun* breaking of items; *customers are expected to pay for breakages*

break down [ˈbreɪk ˈdaʊn] *verb* **(a)** to stop working because of mechanical failure; *the two-way radio has broken down*; *what do you do when your squad car breaks down?* **(b)** to stop; *negotiations broke down after six hours*; *their marriage broke down and they separated* **(c)** to show all the items in a total list; *we broke the crime figures down into crimes against the person and crimes against property*; *can you break down this invoice into spare parts and labour?*

breakdown [ˈbreɪkdaʊn] *noun* **(a)** stopping work because of mechanical failure; *we cannot communicate with our squad car because of the breakdown of the radio link* **(b)** stopping work, discussion; *a breakdown in wage negotiations* **(c) irretrievable breakdown of a marriage** = situation where the two spouses can no longer live together, where the marriage cannot be saved and therefore divorce proceedings can be started; *she petitioned for divorce on account of the breakdown of their marriage* **(d)** showing details item by item; *give me a breakdown of the latest clear-up figures*

break in [ˈbreɪk ˈɪn] *verb* to go into a building by force in order to steal; *burglars broke in through a window at the back of the house*

break-in [ˈbreɪkɪn] *noun* (*informal*) crime of breaking into a house; *there have been three break-ins in our street in one week*

breaking and entering ['breɪkɪŋ ənd 'entrɪŋ] *noun* crime of going into a building by force and stealing things; *he was charged with breaking and entering*; *see also* HOUSEBREAKING

break into ['breɪk 'ɪntu] *verb* to go into (a building) by force to steal things; *their house was broken into while they were on holiday*; *looters broke into the supermarket*

break off ['breɪk 'ɒf] *verb* to stop; *we broke off the discussion at midnight*; *management broke off negotiations with the union*

break up ['breɪk 'ʌp] *verb* **(a)** to split something large into small sections; *the company was broken up and separate divisions sold off* **(b)** to come to an end, to make something come to an end; *the meeting broke up at 12.30*; *the police broke up the protest meeting*

breathalyse ['breθəlaɪz] *verb* to test someone's breath using a breathalyser

breathalyser ['breθəlaɪzə] *noun* device for testing the amount of alcohol a person has drunk by testing his breath

breath test ['breθ 'test] *noun* test where a person's breath is sampled to establish the amount of alcohol he has drunk

bribe [braɪb] **1** *noun* money offered corruptly to someone to get him to do something to help you; *the police sergeant was dismissed for taking bribes* **2** *verb* to give someone a bribe; *he bribed the police sergeant to get the charges dropped*

bribery ['braɪbri] *noun* crime of giving someone a bribe; *bribery in the security warehouse is impossible to stamp out*

bridewell ['braɪdwel] *noun (slang)* cells in a police station

bridging loan ['brɪdʒɪŋ 'ləʊn] *noun* short term loan to help someone buy a new house when he has not yet sold his old one

bridleway ['braɪdlweɪ] *noun* path used by people on horseback

brief [briːf] **1** *noun* **(a)** details of a client's case, prepared by his solicitor and given to the barrister who is going to argue the case in court **(b)** *(slang)* lawyer or barrister **2** *verb* to explain something to someone in detail; *the superintendent briefed the press on the progress of the investigation*; *to brief a barrister* = to give a barrister all the details of the case which he will argue in court

briefcase ['briːfkeɪs] *noun* case with a handle for carrying papers and documents; *he put all the files into his briefcase*

briefing ['briːfɪŋ] *noun* telling someone details; *all the detectives on the case attended a briefing given by the commander*

bring forward ['brɪŋ 'fɔːwəd] *verb* to make earlier; *to bring forward the date of repayment*; *the date of the hearing has been brought forward to March*

bring in ['brɪŋ 'ɪn] *verb* to decide a verdict; *the jury brought in a verdict of not guilty*

bring up ['brɪŋ 'ʌp] *verb* to refer to something for the first time; *the chairman brought up the question of corruption in the police force*

broker ['brəʊkə] *noun* person who buys or sells on behalf of others; **insurance broker** = person who sells insurance to clients

brothel ['brɒθl] *noun* house where sexual intercourse is offered for money

budget ['bʌdʒɪt] *noun* **(a)** plan of expected spending and income (usually for one year); *to draw up a budget*; *we have agreed the budgets for next year* **(b)** the **Budget** = the annual plan of taxes and government spending proposed by a finance minister; *the minister put forward a budget aimed at slowing down the economy*; *to balance the budget* = to plan income and expenditure so that they balance; *the president is planning for a balanced budget*

budgetary [ˈbʌdʒɪtri] *adjective* referring to a budget; **budgetary policy** = policy of planning income and expenditure; **budgetary control** = keeping check on spending; **budgetary requirements** = spending or income required to meet the expected budget

budgeting [ˈbʌdʒɪtɪŋ] *noun* preparing of budgets to help plan expenditure and income

bug [bʌg] **1** *noun* small device which can record conversations secretly and send them to a secret radio receiver; *the cleaners planted a bug under the lawyer's desk* **2** *verb* to place a secret device in a place so that conversations can be heard and recorded secretly; *the agents bugged the President's office*; **bugging device** = bug; *police found a bugging device under the lawyer's desk*

buggery [ˈbʌgri] *noun* notifiable offence of sexual intercourse with animals, rectal intercourse with man or woman

building society [ˈbɪldɪŋ səˈsaɪəti] *noun* *GB* financial institution which accepts and pays interest on deposits and lends money to people who are buying property

bumping [ˈbʌmpɪŋ] *noun* *US* situation where a senior employee takes the place of a junior (in a restaurant or in a job)

bunco [ˈbʌŋkəʊ] *noun* *(slang)* swindle, cheating someone out of money (usually at cards)

bundle [ˈbʌndl] *noun* **trial bundle** = all the documents brought together by the claimant for a trial, indexed and in a ring binder

burden of proof [ˈbɜːdən əv ˈpruːf] *noun* duty to prove that something which has been alleged in court is true; **to discharge a burden of proof** = to prove something which has been alleged in court; **the burden of proof is on the prosecution** = the prosecution must prove that what it alleges is true

bureau [ˈbjʊərəʊ] *noun* office which specializes; **computer bureau** = office which offers to do work on its computers for companies which do not own their own computers; **employment bureau** = office which finds jobs for people; **information bureau** = office which gives information; *US* **Federal Bureau of Investigation (FBI)** = American government office, a section of the Department of Justice, which investigates crimes against federal law and subversive acts in the USA (NOTE: the plural is **bureaux**)

burgh [ˈbʌrə] *noun* Scottish borough

burglar [ˈbɜːglə] *noun* person who steals (or tries to steal) goods from property, or who enters property intending to commit a crime; **burglar alarm** = bell which is set to ring when someone tries to break into a house or shop; *as he put his hand through the window he set off the burglar alarm*

burglarize [ˈbɜːglaraɪz] *verb* *US* *(informal)* to steal things from (a building or a household)

burglary [ˈbɜːgləri] *noun* crime of going into a building at night (usually by force) and stealing things; *he was charged with burglary*; *there has been a series of burglaries in our street*; **aggravated burglary** = burglary where guns or other offensive weapons are carried or used

burgle [ˈbɜːgl] *verb* to steal things from (a building or a household); *the school was burgled when the caretaker was on holiday*

burn [bɜːn] *verb* to destroy by fire; *the chief accountant burned the documents before the police arrived* (NOTE: **burning - burned** or **burnt**)

burn down [ˈbɜːn ˈdaʊn] *verb* to destroy completely in a fire

business [ˈbɪznəs] *noun* **(a)** work of buying or selling; **on business** = on commercial work; **(b)** commercial company; *he owns a small car repair business*; *she runs a business from her home*; *he set up in business as an insurance broker*; *(in civil cases)* **business**

day = any day except Saturdays, Sundays or bank holidays; **business hours** = time (usually 9 a.m. to 5 p.m.) when a business is open; **business name** = name under which a firm or company trades; **business premises** = building used for business purposes, and therefore charged with a business rate; **business rate** = local tax levied on businesses, usually at a higher rate than for householders **(c)** affairs discussed; *the main business of the meeting was finished by 3 p.m.*; **move the business forward** = go on to the next item on the agenda; **any other business (AOB)** = item at the end of an agenda, where any matter can be raised; **the business of the House** *or* **business of the day** = matters for discussion in the House of Commons on a certain day; **business committee** = committee set up by the House of Commons to work out the agenda of business, especially the length of time allocated to discussion of each Bill; **order of business** = agenda of the House of Commons for a certain day, order in which items are discussed or dealt with in the House

COMMENT: the normal order of business of the House of Commons begins with prayers, followed by messages from the Queen or official messages from foreign governments; then motions for writs to hold by-elections; private business; Question Time, when ministers answer questions about the work of their departments. Following this, various matters can be discussed, including debate on motions and public Bills

buy [baɪ] **1** *verb* to get something by paying money; *he bought 10,000 shares*;

the company has been bought by its leading supplier; *to buy wholesale and sell retail*; **to buy forward** = to buy foreign currency before you need it, in order to be sure of the exchange rate (NOTE: **buying - bought**) **2** *noun* **good buy** *or* **bad buy** = thing bought which is or is not worth the money paid for it; *that watch was a good buy*; *this car was a bad buy*

buy back [baɪ ˈbæk] *verb* to buy something which you have sold; *he sold the shop last year and is now trying to buy it back*

buyer [ˈbaɪə] *noun* **(a)** person who buys **(b)** person who buys a certain type of goods wholesale, which are then stocked by a large store; **head buyer** = most important buyer in a store

by-election [ˈbaɪɪˈlekʃn] *noun* election for Parliament or for a council during a term of office (because of the death or retirement of the person first elected)

bylaw *or* **byelaw** *or* **by-law** *or* **bye-law** [ˈbaɪlɔː] *noun* **(a)** rules governing the internal running of a club or association, etc. **(b)** *US* rules governing the internal running of a corporation (the number of meetings, the appointment of officers, etc.) (NOTE: in the UK, called **Articles of Association**) **(c)** rule or law made by a local authority or public body and not by central government; *the bylaws forbid playing ball in the public gardens*; *according to the local bylaws, noise must be limited in the town centre*

COMMENT: bylaws must be made by bodies which have been authorized by Parliament, before they can become legally effective

Cc

C [si:] *third letter of the alphabet;* **category 'C' prisoners** = prisoners who are not likely to try to escape, but who cannot be kept in open prisons; **Class 'C' drugs:** = drugs which are related to the amphetamines, such as benzphetamine; **Schedule C** = schedule to the Finance Acts under which tax is charged on profits from government stock; **Table C** = model memorandum and articles of association set out in the Companies Act, 1985 for a company limited by guarantee having no share capital

© the copyright symbol

COMMENT: the symbol adopted by the Universal Copyright Convention in Geneva in 1952. Publications bearing the symbol are automatically covered by the convention. The copyright line in a book should give the © followed by the name of the copyright holder and the date

CAB ['si: 'eɪ 'bi:] = CITIZENS' ADVICE BUREAU

cabal [kə'bæl] *noun* small group of politicians who plan action in secret (either to overthrow a government or to do something illegal)

cabinet ['kæbɪnət] *noun* **(a)** piece of furniture for storing records or for display; *last year's correspondence is in the bottom drawer of the filing cabinet* **(b)** committee formed of the most important members of the government, chosen by the Prime Minister or President to be in charge of the main government departments; *Cabinet meetings are held in the Cabinet room; the Cabinet meets on Thursday mornings; the Prime Minister held a meeting of the Cabinet yesterday;* **inner cabinet** = group of the most important members of the Cabinet, who meet with the Prime Minister and decide policy; **kitchen cabinet** = private unofficial committee of ministers, advisers and friends who advise the Prime Minister; **Cabinet Committees** = committees which are formed from Cabinet ministers, junior ministers or civil servants, who advise the Cabinet and Prime Minister on certain matters; **Cabinet government** = form of government where a Prime Minister or President forms a cabinet of ministers to run various ministries; **Cabinet Minister** = minister who is a member of the Cabinet; **Cabinet Office** = section of the British Civil Service which works for the Prime Minister and the Cabinet; **Cabinet Secretary** *or* **Secretary to the Cabinet** = head of the Cabinet Office (and also of the British Civil Service), who attends Cabinet meetings (NOTE: the word **Cabinet** is used both for the group of people and for a meeting of the group: **the Prime Minister held a Cabinet yesterday; the decision was taken at Thursday's Cabinet**) **(c)** *(in the EU)* the private office of one of the Commissioners, headed by a Chef de Cabinet

COMMENT: in most forms of Cabinet government (as in the UK), the Prime Minister or President chooses the members of his Cabinet and can dismiss them if necessary. In some countries, MPs of the ruling party elect the members of the Cabinet, with the result that the Prime Minister has less overall power over the decisions of the Cabinet, and cannot dismiss ministers easily

cadaver [kə'dævə] *noun US* dead body (NOTE: British English is **corpse**)

cadet [kə'det] *noun* trainee police officer; *he has entered the police cadet college*; *she joined the police force as a cadet*

cadre ['kɑːdə] *noun* active member or group of key members of a party (especially a Marxist party)

calendar ['kæləndə] *noun* (a) book, set of sheets of paper showing the days and months in a year, often attached to pictures; **calendar month** = a whole month as on a calendar, from the 1st to the 28th, 30th or 31st; **calendar year** = year from the 1st January to 31st December (b) **Parliamentary calendar** = timetable of events in Parliament, with dates for discussion of each Bill (c) *US* list of Bills for consideration by committees of the House of Representatives or the Senate; **calendar Wednesday** = Wednesday when the House of Representatives can consider bills from committees during a short debate

COMMENT: the Senate has only one calendar, but the House of Representatives has several: the Consent Calendar for uncontroversial bills; the Discharge Calendar for motions to discharge a committee of its responsibility for a bill; the House Calendar for bills which do not involve raising revenue or spending money; and the Union Calendar for bills which raise revenue or appropriate money for expenditure

call [kɔːl] **1** *noun* (a) conversation on the telephone; **local call** = call to a number on the same exchange; **trunk call** *or* **long-distance call** = call to a number in a different zone or area; **overseas call** *or* **international call** = call to another country; **person-to-person call** = call where you ask the operator to connect you with a named person (b) (i) demand for repayment of a loan by a lender; (ii) demand by a company to pay for shares; **money at call** *or* **money on call** *or* **call money** = money loaned for which repayment can be demanded without

notice; **call option** = option to buy shares at a certain price (c) (i) admission of a barrister to the bar; (ii) number of years a barrister has practised at the bar; **he is ten years' call** = he has been practising for ten years (d) visit; *the salesmen make six calls a day*; **business call** = visit to talk to someone on business **2** *verb* (a) to telephone to someone; *I shall call you at your office tomorrow* (b) to admit someone to the bar to practise as a barrister; *he was called (to the bar) in 1989*

call in ['kɔːl 'ɪn] *verb* (a) to ask someone to come to help; *the local police decided to call in the CID to help in the murder hunt* (b) to ask for plans to be sent to the ministry for examination; *the minister has called in the plans for the new supermarket*

camera ['kæmrə] *see* BICAMERALISM, IN CAMERA

campaign [kæm'peɪn] **1** *noun* (a) planned method of working; *the government has launched a campaign against drunken drivers* (b) **election campaign** = period immediately before an election, when candidates canvass for support; **campaign trail** = series of meetings or visits which form part of an election campaign; *she is out on the campaign trail again this week* **2** *verb* (a) to try to change something by writing about it, by organizing protest meetings or by lobbying Members of Parliament; *they are campaigning for the abolition of the death penalty or they are campaigning against the death penalty*; *she is campaigning for the reintroduction of the death penalty*; *he is campaigning for a revision of the Official Secrets Act* (b) to try to get the voters to vote for you in an election; *she is campaigning on the issue of more money for the school system*; *he had been campaigning all day from the top of a bus*

campaigner [kæm'peɪnə] *noun* person who is campaigning for a party, for a candidate or for a cause; *he is an experienced political campaigner*; *she is a campaigner for women's rights*

cancel ['kænsəl] *verb* **(a)** to stop something which has been agreed or planned; *to cancel an appointment or a meeting*; *to cancel a contract* **(b)** to cancel a cheque = to stop payment of a cheque which you have signed (NOTE: British English is **cancelling - cancelled** but American English **canceling - canceled**)

cancellandi [kænsə'lændi:] *see* ANIMUS

cancellation [kænsə'leɪʃn] *noun* stopping something which has been agreed or planned; *cancellation of an appointment*; *cancellation of an agreement*; **cancellation clause** = clause in a contract which states the terms on which the contract may be cancelled

candidacy *or* candidature

['kændɪdəsi or 'kændɪdətʃə] *noun* state of being a candidate; *the Senator has announced his candidacy for the Presidential election*

candidate ['kændɪdət] *noun* **(a)** person who applies for a job; *there are six candidates for the post of security guard*; *we interviewed ten candidates for the job* **(b)** person who puts himself forward for election; *all the candidates in the election appeared on television*; *which candidate are you voting for?*

canon law ['kænən 'lɔː] *noun* law applied by the church to priests; also, formerly to other members of the church in cases of marriage, legitimacy and personal property

canvass ['kænvəs] *verb* to visit people to ask them to vote or to say what they think; *party workers are out canvassing voters*; **to canvass support** = to ask people to support you; *he is canvassing support for his Bill among members of the Opposition*

canvasser ['kænvəsə] *noun* person who canvasses

canvassing ['kænvəsɪŋ] *noun* action of asking people to vote or to say what they think

capacity [kə'pæsəti] *noun* **(a)** amount which can be produced, amount of work which can be done **(b)** amount of space; **storage capacity** = space available for storing goods or information **(c)** ability; *he has a particular capacity for business* **(d)** ability to enter into a legal contract, one of the essential elements of a contract; **person of full age and capacity** = person who is over eighteen years of age and of sound mind, and therefore able to enter into a contract **(e)** in his capacity as chairman = acting as chairman; **speaking in an official capacity** = speaking officially

capax ['kæpæks] *see* DOLI

capias ['kæpiæs] *Latin word meaning* 'that you take': used in phrases to indicate that several writs have been issued together; **capias ad respondendum** = writ for the arrest of a defendant, as well as summoning him to attend court

capita ['kæpɪtə] *see* PER CAPITA

capital ['kæpɪtl] **1** *noun* **(a)** money, property and assets used in a business; **capital gains** = money made by selling a fixed asset or by selling shares at a profit; **capital gains tax (CGT)** = tax paid on capital gains; **capital transfer tax (CTT)** = tax paid on the transfer of capital or assets from one person to another; **to make political capital out of something** = to use something to give you an advantage in politics; *the Opposition made a lot of capital out of the Minister's mistake on TV*; *see also* EXPENDITURE **(b)** main town in a country or province, where the government is; *London is the capital of the UK and Washington is the capital of the USA*; **state capital** *or* **provincial capital** = main town in a state or province **(c)** **capital letters** *or* **block capitals** = letters written as A, B, C, D, etc., and not a, b, c, d; *write your name in block capitals at the top of the form* **2** *adjective* **capital crime** *or* **offence** = crime for which the punishment is death; **capital punishment** = punishment of a criminal by execution

COMMENT: in the UK the only capital crime is now treason

capitalism ['kæpɪtəlɪzm] *noun* **(a)** belief in private ownership of money, property and other assets, used to create profits **(b)** economic system, where money, property and other assets are owned by individuals and where the economy is led by demand, with supply and prices being determined by market forces

capitalist ['kæpɪtəlɪst] **1** *noun* (*sometimes used as criticism*) person who owns money, property, and other assets which he uses to make profits **2** *adjective* based on capitalism as a system of economy; **capitalist countries** = countries (mainly in the West) whose economies are run on capitalist principles; **the capitalist system** = all capitalist countries working together

capitalization [kæpɪtəlaɪ'zeɪʃn] *noun* **market capitalization** = value of a company calculated by multiplying the price of its shares on the Stock Exchange by the number of shares issued

Capitol ['kæpɪtəl] *noun* **(a)** building in Washington, D.C., where the US Senate and House of Representatives meet; **Capitol Hill** = hill on which the Capitol building stands, together with other important government buildings; **on Capitol Hill** = in the US Senate or House of Representatives; *the feeling on Capitol Hill is that the President will veto the proposal* **(b)** State Capitol = building in the main city of a State, housing the State legislature

caption ['kæpʃn] *noun* formal heading of an indictment, affidavit or other court document (giving details of the names of the parties, the court which is hearing the case, relevant reference numbers, etc.)

card [kɑːd] *noun* piece of stiff paper; **party card** = card which proves that the person whose name is on it is a member of the political party which issues it; **card vote** = vote taken at meetings where delegates vote on behalf of their membership by holding up a card showing the total number of votes which they are casting

care [keə] *noun* **(a)** act of looking after someone; *the children were put in the care of the social services department*; **care and control** = responsibility for day-to-day decisions relating to the welfare of a child; *compare* CUSTODY; **child in care** = child who has been put into the care of the local social services department; **care order** = order from a juvenile court, putting a child into the care of a local authority; **care proceedings** = action in court to put a child into the care of someone **(b)** making sure that someone is not harmed; **duty of care** = duty which everyone has not to act negligently; **driving without due care and attention** = driving a car in a careless way, so that other people are in danger

careless ['keələs] *adjective* without paying attention to other people; **careless driving** = driving without due care and attention

caretaker ['keəteɪkə] *noun* person whose job is to look after property; **caretaker Prime Minister** *or* **caretaker chairman** = Prime Minister or chairman who occupies the office temporarily until a newly elected or appointed official arrives

carriage ['kærɪdʒ] *noun* act of carrying goods from one place to another; *carriage charges*; *carriage by air*

carriageway ['kærɪdʒweɪ] *noun* way where the public have a right to go in vehicles

carrier ['kæriə] *noun* person or company which takes goods from one place to another; **common carrier** = firm which carries goods or passengers, which cannot normally refuse to do so, and which can be used by anyone; **private carrier** = firm which carries goods or passengers, but which is not contractually bound to offer the service to anyone; **carrier's lien** = right of a carrier to hold goods until he has been paid for carrying them

carry ['kæri] *verb* **(a)** to take from one place to another; *the train was carrying a consignment of cars*; **carrying offensive weapons** = offence of holding a weapon or something (such as a bottle) which could be used as a weapon **(b)** to vote to approve; **the motion was carried** = the motion was accepted after a vote **(c)** to be punishable by; *the offence carries a maximum sentence of two years' imprisonment*

carte blanche ['ka:t 'blɒnʃ] *French phrase meaning* 'white card': permission given by someone to another person, allowing him to do anything or to act in any way; *he has carte blanche to act on behalf of the company or the company has given him carte blanche to act on its behalf*

case [keɪs] **1** *noun* **(a)** possible crime and its investigation by the police; *we have three detectives working on the case*; *the police are treating the case as murder or are treating it as a murder case*; *we had six cases of looting during the night* **(b)** court case = legal action or trial; **the case is being heard next week** = the case is coming to court; **case law** = law as established by precedents, that is by the decisions of courts in earlier cases; **case management conference** = court hearing fixed when a case is allocated to the fast track, when the parties to the case are asked about their preparations for the case, and the court decides on the disclosure of documents, expert evidence, etc.; the legal representatives of the parties are also present; **case summary** = short document (not more than 500 words) prepared by the claimant to help the court understand what the case is about **(c)** arguments or facts put forward by one side in legal proceedings; *defence counsel put his case*; *there is a strong case against the accused*; **case stated** = statement of the facts of a case which has been heard in a lower court, drawn up so that a higher court can decide on an appeal (such as a case stated by a Magistrates' Court for opinion by the High Court); *he appealed by way of case stated*; *the Appeal Court dismissed the appeal by way of case stated*; **the case rests** = all the

arguments for one side have been put forward; **no case to answer** = submission by the defence (after the prosecution has put its case) that the case should be dismissed **2** *verb (slang)* **to case a joint** = to look at a building carefully before deciding how to break into it

COMMENT: a case is referred to by the names of the parties, the date and the reference source where details of it can be found: *Smith v. Jones [1985] 2 W.L.R. 250*. This shows that the case involved Smith as plaintiff and Jones as defendant, it was heard in 1985, and is reported in the second volume of the Weekly Law Reports for that year on page 250

cast [ka:st] *verb* **to cast a vote** = to vote; *the number of votes cast in the election was 125,458*; **under proportional representation, the number of seats occupied by each party is related to the number of votes cast for that party**; **casting vote** = vote used by the chairman in a case where the votes for and against a proposal are equal; *the chairman has a casting vote*; *he used his casting vote to block the motion* (NOTE: **casting - cast - has cast**)

casual ['kæʒuəl] *adjective* **(a)** not permanent or not regular; **casual labour** = workers who are hired for a short period; **casual work** = work where the workers are hired for a short period; **casual labourer** *or* **casual worker** = worker who can be hired for a short period **(b)** not formal; *he appeared in court wearing casual clothes*

casus belli ['ka:zus 'beli:] *Latin phrase meaning* 'case for war': reason which is used to justify a declaration of war

catch [kætʃ] *verb (of an MP)* **to catch the Speaker's eye** = to stand up and ask the Speaker to be allowed to speak in a debate

category ['kætəgəri] *noun* type, sort of item; *the theft comes into the category of petty crime*; **category 'A' prisoners** = prisoners who are dangerous, and would be a danger to the public if they escaped from prison; **category 'B' prisoners** = less dangerous prisoners, who still have to be guarded carefully to prevent them from escaping; **category 'C' prisoners** = prisoners who are not likely to try to escape, but who cannot be kept in open prisons; **category 'D' prisoners** = reliable prisoners who can be kept in open prisons

caucus ['kɔːkəs] *noun* **(a)** group of people in a political party who are strong enough to influence policy **(b)** *US* private meeting of powerful members of a political party to make a decision (such as to decide how they will vote in a presidential election); meeting of local party members to chose a candidate for nomination (NOTE: plural is **caucuses**)

causa ['kauzə] *see* DONATIO

cause [kɔːz] **1** *noun* **(a)** thing which makes something happen; **cause of action** = reason why a case is brought to court; **challenge for cause** = objection to a proposed juror, stating the reasons for the objection; **challenge without cause** = objection to a proposed juror, not stating the reasons for the objection; **contributory causes** = causes which help something to take place; *the report listed bad community relations as one of the contributory causes to the riot*; **to show cause** = to give a reason for something; *the judgment debtor was given fourteen days in which to show cause why the charging order should not be made absolute* **(b)** legal proceedings; **cause list** = list of cases which are to be heard by a court; **matrimonial causes** = cases referring to the rights of partners in a marriage **2** *verb* to make something happen; *the recession caused hundreds of bankruptcies*

caution ['kɔːʃn] **1** *noun* **(a)** warning from a policeman, telling someone not to repeat a minor crime; *the boys were let off with a caution* **(b)** warning by a police officer, that someone will be charged with a crime, and that what he says may be used in evidence; *he typed his confession under caution* **(c)** document lodged at the Land Registry to prevent land or property being

sold without notice to the cautioner (NOTE: in meaning (b) and (c) can be used without **the** or **a: to lodge caution**) **2** *verb* **(a)** to warn (someone) that what he has done is wrong and should not be repeated; *the policeman cautioned the boys after he caught them stealing fruit* **(b)** to warn (someone) that he will be charged with a crime, and that what he says may be used as evidence in his trial; *the accused was arrested by the detectives and cautioned*

> COMMENT: the person who is cautioned has the right not to answer any question put to him or her

cautioner ['kɔːʃənə] *noun* person who lodges caution at the Land Registry

caveat ['kæviæt] *noun* warning; **to enter a caveat** = to warn legally that you have an interest in a case, and that no steps can be taken without notice to you (especially warning to a probate court not to grant probate)

caveat emptor ['kæviæt 'emptɔː] *Latin phrase meaning* 'let the buyer beware': phrase meaning that the buyer is himself responsible for checking that what he buys is in good order

caveator ['kæviætə] *noun* person who warns the court not to give probate without asking his consent

CB ['siː 'biː] *(in the armed forces)* = CONFINED TO BARRACKS

CC ['siː 'siː] = CHIEF CONSTABLE

CCR = COUNTY COURT RULES

CD ['siː 'diː] = CERTIFICATE OF DEPOSIT

CDS = CRIMINAL DEFENCE SERVICE

cease and desist order ['siːs ən dɪ'zɪst 'ɔːdə] *noun US* court order telling someone to stop doing something

cede ['siːd] *verb* to pass possession of a territory to another country; *the Philippines were ceded to the USA by Spain in 1898*; *see also* CESSION

cell [sel] *noun* small room in a prison or police station where a criminal can be kept locked up; *she was put in a small cell for the night*; *he shares a cell with two other prisoners*; **condemned cell** = cell where a prisoner is kept who has been condemned to death (NOTE: often used in the plural, meaning the cells in a police station: **he spent the night in the cells**)

cellmate ['selmeɪt] *noun* person who shares a prison cell with someone else

censor ['sensə] **1** *noun* official whose job is to say whether books, films or TV programmes, etc., are acceptable and can be published or shown to the public; *the film was cut or was banned or was passed by the censor* **2** *verb* to say that a book, film or TV programme, etc., cannot be shown or published because it is not considered right to do so; *all press reports are censored by the government*; *the news of the riots was censored*; *the TV report has been censored and only parts of it can be shown*

censorship ['sensəʃɪp] *noun* act of censoring; *TV reporters complained of government censorship*; *the government has imposed strict press censorship or censorship of the press*

censure ['senʃə] **1** *noun* criticism; **motion of censure** *or* **censure motion** = proposal from the Opposition to pass a vote to criticize the government; **vote of censure** *or* **censure vote** = vote which criticizes someone, especially a vote in parliament which criticizes the Government; *the meeting passed a vote of censure on the minister* **2** *verb* to criticize; *the Opposition put forward a motion to censure the Government*; *the Borough Architect was censured for failing to consult the engineers*

central ['sentrəl] *adjective* organized at one main point; **central office** = main office which controls all smaller offices; **Central Criminal Court** = the Crown Court sitting in London (= THE OLD BAILEY)

centre *US* **center** ['sentə] *noun* **(a)** group or parties whose political position is between right and left, such as the Liberals or Democrats; **left of centre** = tending towards socialism; **right of centre** = tending towards conservatism; *a left-of-centre political group*; *the Cabinet is formed mainly of right-of-centre supporters of the Prime Minister* (NOTE: usually used with **the: the centre combined with the right to defeat the motion**) **(b)** **business centre** = part of a town where the main banks, shops and offices are **(c)** important town; *an industrial centre*; *the centre for the shoe industry* **(d)** office; **Job Centre** = government office which lists and helps to fill jobs which are vacant; **Law Centre** = local office with a staff of full-time lawyers who advise and represent clients free of charge; **Legal Aid Centre** = local office giving advice to clients with legal problems, giving advice on obtaining Legal Aid and recommending clients to solicitors

centrist ['sentrɪst] **1** *adjective* in favour of the centre in politics; *the group advocates a return to centrist politics* **2** *noun* person who is in favour of the centre in politics

ceremonial [serɪ'məʊnɪəl] **1** *adjective* referring to a ceremony; *the mayor wore his ceremonial robes for the opening ceremony*; *the President rode in a ceremonial procession* **2** *noun* ceremonies; *the book lays out the rules for court ceremonial*; *there is a lot of ceremonial attached to the job of Lord Mayor*

ceremony ['serəmənɪ] *noun* official occasion (such as the State Opening of Parliament); *the mayor presided at the ceremony to open the new council offices*; *special police were present at ceremonies to mark the National Day*

certificate [sɜ:'tɪfɪkət] *noun* official document which shows that something is true; **clearance certificate** = document showing that goods have been passed by customs; **fire certificate** = document from the municipal fire department to say that a building is properly protected against fire; **land certificate** = document which shows who owns a piece of land, and whether there are any charges on it; **practising certificate** = certificate from the Law Society allowing someone to work as a solicitor; **share certificate** = document proving that you own shares; **certificate of approval** = document showing that an item has been officially approved; **certificate of deposit (CD)** = document from a bank showing that money has been deposited; **certificate of incorporation** = document showing that a company has been officially registered; **certificate of judgment** = official document showing a decision of a court; **certificate of origin** = document showing where goods were made or produced; **certificate of registration** = document showing that an item has been registered; **certificate of registry** = document showing that a ship has been officially registered; **certificate of service** = certificate by which a court proves that a document was sent and is deemed to have been served

certificated [sə'tɪfɪkeɪtɪd] *adjective* **certificated bankrupt** = bankrupt who has been discharged from bankruptcy with a certificate to show that he was not at fault

certify ['sɜːtɪfaɪ] *verb* to make an official declaration in writing; *I certify that this is a true copy*; *the document is certified as a true copy*; **certified accountant** = accountant who has passed the professional examinations and is a member of the Chartered Association of Certified Accountants; **certified cheque, US certified check** = cheque which a bank says is good and will be paid out of money put aside from the bank account; **certified copy** = copy which is certified as being the same as the original

certiorari [sɜːtiə'rɑːri] *Latin word meaning* 'to be informed'; **order of certiorari** = order which transfers a case from a lower court to the High Court for investigation into its legality; *he applied for judicial review by way of certiorari*; *the court ordered certiorari following*

judicial review, quashing the order made by the juvenile court

cessate grant ['seseɪt 'grɑːnt] *noun* special grant of probate made because of the incapacity of an executor; grant made to renew a grant which has expired

cesser ['sesə] *noun* ending (of a mortgage, charter, etc.)

cession ['seʃn] *noun* giving up property to someone (especially a creditor)

CFI *(in the EU)* = COURT OF FIRST INSTANCE

CGT ['siː 'dʒiː 'tiː] = CAPITAL GAINS TAX

chair [tʃeə] **1** *noun* **(a)** piece of furniture for sitting on; **electric chair** *or* **the chair** = chair attached to a powerful electric current, used in the USA for executing criminals **(b)** position of the chairman, presiding over a meeting; *to be in the chair*; *she was voted into the chair*; *she is Chair of the Finance Committee*; *this can be done by Chair's action and confirmed later*; **Mr Jones took the chair** = Mr Jones presided over the meeting; **to address the chair** = in a meeting, to speak to the chairman and not directly to the rest of the people at the meeting; **to ask a question through the chair** = to ask someone a question directly, by speaking to him through the chairman; *may I ask the councillor through the chair why he did not declare his interest in the matter?* (NOTE: the word **chair** is now often used to mean the person, as it avoids making a distinction between men and women) **2** *verb* to preside over a meeting; *the meeting was chaired by Mrs Smith*

chairman ['tʃeəmən] *noun* **(a)** person who is in charge of a meeting; person who presides over meetings of a Committee of the House of Commons or of a local council; *chairman of the magistrates or of the bench*; *Mr Howard was chairman or acted as chairman*; **Mr Chairman** *or* **Madam Chairman** = way of speaking to the chairman; **Chairman of Ways and Means** = person elected at the beginning of

Parliament to be the chairman of the Committee of the Whole House, also acting as Deputy Speaker **(b)** person who presides over the board meetings of a company; *the chairman of the board or the company chairman*

chairmanship ['tʃeəmənʃɪp] *noun* being a chairman; **the committee met under the chairmanship of Mr Jones =** Mr Jones chaired the meeting of the committee

chairperson ['tʃeəpɜːsən] *noun* person who is in charge of a meeting

chairwoman ['tʃeəwʊmən] *noun* woman who is in charge of a meeting

challenge ['tʃælɪnʒ] **1** *noun* act of objecting to a decision, and asking it to be set aside; **challenge for cause =** objecting to a juror, stating the reason for the objection; **challenge without cause =** objecting to a juror, not stating the reason for the objection; **peremptory challenge =** challenge without cause **2** *verb* to object to, to refuse to accept (a juror or evidence); *to challenge a sentence passed by magistrates by appeal to the Crown Court*

chamber ['tʃeɪmbə] *noun* **(a)** room where a committee or legislature meets; *the meeting will be held in the council chamber* **(b)** part of a parliament where a group of representatives meet; *the British Parliament is formed of two chambers - the House of Commons and the House of Lords*; **the Upper Chamber =** the House of Lords or the Senate

Chamber of Commerce *or* **Chamber of Trade** ['tʃeɪmbə əv 'kɒmɜːs *or* treɪd] *noun* group of local businessmen who meet to discuss problems which they have in common, and to promote business in the town

chambers ['tʃeɪmbəz] *plural noun* **(a)** offices of a group of barristers who work together and share the same staff (NOTE: actually called 'a set of chambers') **(b)** office of a judge; **the judge heard the case in chambers =** in his private rooms, without the public being present and not in open

court (NOTE: the phrase **hear the case in private** is preferred to **hear the case in chambers**)

champerty ['tʃæmpəti] *noun (formerly)* financial help given to a person starting a proceedings against a party, where the person giving help has a share in the damages to be recovered

Chancellor ['tʃɑːnsələ] *noun* **(a)** *(in the United Kingdom)* **Chancellor of the Duchy of Lancaster =** member of the British government with no specific responsibilities; **Chancellor of the Exchequer =** chief finance minister in the British government; **the Lord Chancellor =** chief minister of justice in the UK **(b)** head of a government (in Germany and Austria) (NOTE: can be used as a title with names: **Chancellor Kohl**) **(c)** *US* judge who presides over a court of equity

Chancery ['tʃɑːnsri] *noun* **the Chancery Bar =** barristers who specialize in the Chancery Division; **Chancery business =** legal cases relating to the sale of land, mortgages, trusts, estates, bankruptcies, partnerships, patents and copyrights, probate, and cases involving companies; **Chancery Court =** formerly the court presided over by the Lord Chancellor, which established case law or equity; **Chancery Division =** one of the three divisions of the High Court, dealing with wills, partnerships and companies, taxation, bankruptcies, etc.

channel ['tʃænəl] *noun* way in which information or goods are passed from one place to another; **to go through the official channels =** to deal with government officials (especially when making a request); **to open up new channels of communication =** new ways of communicating with someone

chaplain ['tʃæplɪn] *noun* priest employed by someone or attached to a group; **prison chaplain =** priest attached to a prison, who looks after the welfare of prisoners; **the Speaker's Chaplain =** priest who reads prayers at the beginning of each sitting of the House of Commons

chapter ['tʃæptə] *noun* **(a)** official term for an Act of Parliament **(b)** *US* section of an Act of Congress; **Chapter 7** = section of the US Bankruptcy Reform Act 1978, which sets out the rules for the liquidation of an incorporated company; **Chapter 11** = section of the US Bankruptcy Reform Act 1978, which allows a corporation to be protected from demands made by its creditors for a period of time, while it is reorganized with a view to paying its debts; the officers of the corporation will negotiate with its creditors as to the best way of reorganizing the business; **Chapter 13** = section of the Bankruptcy Reform Act 1978, which allows a business to continue trading and to pay off its creditors by regular monthly payments over a period of time

character ['kærəktə] *noun* general qualities of a person which make him different from others; **he is a man of good character** = he is an honest, hard-working or decent man; **to give someone a character reference** = to say that someone has good qualities; **to introduce character evidence** = to produce witnesses to say that a person is of good or bad character

charge [tʃɑːdʒ] **1** *noun* **(a)** money which must be paid, price of a service; *to make no charge for delivery*; *to make a small charge for rental*; *there is no charge for service or no charge is made for service*; **admission charge** *or* **entry charge** = price to be paid before going into an exhibition, etc.; **scale of charges** = list showing various prices; **free of charge** = free, with no payment to be made; **solicitors' charges** = payments to be made to solicitors for work done on behalf of clients **(b)** **charge on land** *or* **charge over property** = mortgage or liability on a property which has been used as security for a loan; **fixed charge** = charge over a particular asset or property; **floating charge** = charge over changing assets of a business; **charge by way of legal mortgage** = way of borrowing money on the security of a property, where the mortgagor signs a deed which gives the mortgagee an interest in the property **(c)**

official statement in a court accusing someone of having committed a crime; *he appeared in court on a charge of embezzling or on an embezzlement charge*; *the clerk of the court read out the charges*; **charge sheet** = document listing the charges which a magistrate will hear, listing the charges against the accused together with details of the crime committed; **to answer charges** = to appear in court to plead guilty or not guilty to a charge; *the charges against him were withdrawn or dropped* = the prosecution decided not to continue with the trial; **to press charges against someone** = to say formally that someone has committed a crime; *he was very angry when his neighbour's son set fire to his car, but decided not to press charges*; **holding charge** = minor charge brought against someone so that he can be held in custody while more serious charges are being prepared **(d)** instructions given by the judge to the jury, summing up the evidence and giving advice on the points of law which have to be considered **2** *verb* **(a)** to ask someone to pay for services; to ask for money to be paid; *to charge £5 for delivery*; *how much does he charge?*; *he charges £6 an hour* = he asks to be paid £6 for an hour's work **(b)** *(in a court)* to accuse someone formally of having committed a crime; *he was charged with embezzling his clients' money*; *they were charged with murder* (NOTE: you charge someone **with** a crime)

chargeable ['tʃɑːdʒəbl] *adjective* which can be charged

chargee [tʃɑːˈdʒiː] *noun* person who holds a charge over a property

charging order ['tʃɑːdʒɪŋ 'ɔːdə] *noun* court order made in favour of a judgment creditor granting him a charge over a debtor's property

charity ['tʃærəti] *noun* body which aims not to make money, but to benefit the general public by helping the poor, by promoting education or religion or by doing other useful work; **the Charity Commissioners** = body which governs charities and sees that they follow the law and use their funds for the purposes intended

charitable trust *US* **charitable corporation** ['tʃærɪtəbl trʌst or kɔːpə'reɪʃn] *noun* trust which benefits the public as a whole, which promotes education or religion, which helps the poor or which does other useful work

charter ['tʃɑːtə] **1** *noun* **(a)** document from the Crown establishing a town, a corporation, a university or a company; **bank charter** = official government document allowing the establishment of a bank **(b)** hiring transport for a special purpose; **charter flight** = flight in an aircraft which has been hired for that purpose; **charter plane** = plane which has been chartered; **boat on charter to Mr Smith** = boat which Mr Smith has hired for a voyage; **bareboat charter** = charter of a ship where the owner provides only the ship, not the crew, the fuel or the insurance **2** *verb* to hire for a special purpose; *to charter a plane or a boat or a bus*

chartered ['tʃɑːtəd] *adjective* **(a) chartered accountant** = accountant who has passed the professional examinations and is a member of the Institute of Chartered Accountants **(b)** (company) which has been set up by royal charter, and not registered as a company **(c) chartered ship** *or* **bus** *or* **plane** = ship or bus or plane which has been hired for a special purpose

charterer ['tʃɑːtrə] *noun* person who hires a ship, etc., for a special purpose

chartering ['tʃɑːtrɪŋ] *noun* act of hiring for a special purpose

charterparty ['tʃɑːtəpɑːti] *noun* contract where the owner of a ship charters his ship to someone for carrying goods

chattel mortgage ['tʃætəl 'mɔːgɪdʒ] *noun US* mortgage using personal property as security

chattels ['tʃætəlz] *plural noun* **goods and chattels** = movable property (but not freehold real estate); **chattels real** = leaseholds; **chattels personal** = any

property that is not real property; **incorporeal chattels** = intangible properties (such as patents or copyrights)

check [tʃek] **1** *noun* **(a)** sudden stop; **to put a check on the sale of firearms** = to stop some firearms being sold **(b) check sample** = sample to be used to see if a consignment is acceptable **(c)** investigation or examination; *the auditors carried out checks on the petty cash book*; *a routine check of the fire equipment*; **baggage check** = examination of passengers' baggage to see if it contains bombs **(d)** *US* = CHEQUE **2** *verb* **(a)** to stop or to delay; *to check the entry of contraband into the country* **(b)** to examine or to investigate; *to check that an invoice is correct*; *to check and sign for goods*; **he checked the computer printout against the invoices** = he examined the printout and the invoices to see if the figures were the same **(c)** *US* to mark with a sign to show that something is correct

Chef de Cabinet ['ʃef də 'kæbɪneɪ] *French phrase (in the EU)* person who runs the private office, or Cabinet, of one of the European Commissioners

cheque *US* **check** [tʃek] *noun* order to a bank to pay money from your account to the person whose name is written on it; **cheque account** = bank account which allows the customer to write cheques; **cheque (guarantee) card** = plastic card from a bank which guarantees payment of a cheque up to a certain amount, even if there is no money in the account; **crossed cheque** = cheque with two lines across it showing that it can only be deposited at a bank and not exchanged for cash; **open** *or* **uncrossed cheque** = cheque which can be exchanged for cash anywhere; **blank cheque** = cheque with the amount of money and the payee left blank, but signed by the drawer; **traveller's cheques**, *US* **traveler's checks** = cheques used by a traveller which can be exchanged for cash in a foreign country **(b) to endorse a cheque** = to sign a cheque on the back to make it payable to someone else; **to make out a cheque to someone** = to write out a cheque to someone; **to pay by cheque** = to pay by writing a cheque, and not by using cash or a credit card; **to pay a cheque into your account** = to deposit a cheque; **to dishonour a cheque** *(informal)* **to bounce a cheque** = to refuse to pay a cheque because there is not enough money in the account to pay it; **the bank referred the cheque to drawer** = returned the cheque to the person who wrote it because there was not enough money in the account to pay it; **to sign a cheque** = to sign on the front of a cheque to show that you authorize the bank to pay the money from your account; **to stop a cheque** = to ask a bank not to pay a cheque which you have written

chief [tʃiːf] *adjective* **(a)** most important; *he is the chief accountant of an industrial group GB*; **Lord Chief Justice** = chief judge of the Queen's Bench Division of the High Court who is also a member of the Court of Appeal; *US* **Chief Justice** = main judge in a court, including the main judge in the Supreme Court; **Chief Constable** = person in charge of a police force; **Assistant Chief Constable** *or* **Deputy Chief Constable** = ranks in the police force below Chief Constable; **Chief Inspector** *or* **Chief Superintendent** = ranks in the police force above Inspector or Superintendent; **Chief Executive** = official permanent administrator of a town, who works under the instructions of the council; **Chief Minister** = head of government in a semi-autonomous region (as in an Indian state), equivalent to a Premier; **Chief Secretary to the Treasury** = British government minister, working under the Chancellor of the Exchequer, dealing especially with budgets and planning; **Chief Officer** = local civil servant who is head of a department in a local authority **(b) in chief** = in person; **examination in chief,** *US* **direct examination** = asking a witness questions (by counsel for his side) to give oral evidence in court

COMMENT: a local authority will have several Chief Officers: Chief Education Officer, Chief Housing Officer, Chief Planning Officer, and so on, all of whom are responsible to the Chief Executive. In some authorities they are called Director: Director of Education, Director of Finance, etc.

child [tʃaɪld] *noun* person under the age of majority (ie. under the age of 18); **child benefit** = money paid by the state to the person who is responsible for a child under 16 years of age (or 19, if the child is in full-time education); **child destruction** = notifiable offence of killing an unborn child capable of being born alive; **child stealing** = notifiable offence of taking away a child from its parents or guardian; *US* **child support** = money paid as part of a divorce settlement, to help maintain a child of divorced parents

COMMENT: In Great Britain a child does not have full legal status until the age of eighteen. A contract is not binding on a child, and a child cannot own land, cannot make a will, cannot vote, cannot drive a car (under the age of seventeen). A child cannot marry before the age of sixteen, and can only marry between the ages of 16 and 18 with written permission of his or her parents. A child who is less than ten years old is not considered capable of committing a crime; a child between ten and fourteen years of age may be considered capable of committing a crime if there is evidence of malice or knowledge, and so children of these ages can in certain circumstances be convicted. In criminal law the term 'child' is used for children between the ages of 10 and 14; for children between 14 and 17, the term 'young person' is used; all children are termed 'juveniles'

Chiltern Hundreds

[ˈtʃɪltən ˈhʌndrədz] *noun* former administrative division of the country, west of London, in Buckinghamshire; **Stewardship of the Chiltern Hundreds** = nominal government position, which disqualifies a person from being a Member of Parliament; *(formal)* **to apply for the Stewardship of the Chiltern Hundreds,** *(informal)* **to apply for the Chiltern Hundreds** = to apply to resign from Parliament

COMMENT: as MPs are not allowed to resign from Parliament, the only way in which they can do so is to apply for an office of profit under the crown, such as this or the Stewardship of the Manor of Northstead

chose [ʃəuz] *French word meaning* 'item' *or* 'thing'; **chose in action** = personal right which can be enforced or claimed as if it were property (such as a patent, copyright, debt or cheque); **chose in possession** = physical thing which can be owned (such as a piece of furniture)

Christmas Day [ˈkrɪsməs ˈdeɪ] *noun* 25th December, one of the four quarter days when rent is payable on land

CID = CRIMINAL INVESTIGATION DEPARTMENT

c.i.f. [ˈsiː ˈaɪ ˈef] = COST, INSURANCE, FREIGHT contract for the sale of goods where the seller arranges the export licence, loading, carriage, and insurance and provides a bill of lading, and the purchaser pays on delivery of documents and pays duties and the unloading

circuit [ˈsɜːkɪt] *noun* one of six divisions of England and Wales for legal purposes; *he is a judge on the Welsh Circuit*; **circuit judge** = judge in the Crown Court or a County Court

COMMENT: the six circuits are: Northern, North-Eastern, Midland and Oxford, Wales and Chester, South-Eastern, and Western

circulation [sɜːkjuˈleɪʃn] *noun* **(a)** movement; *the company is trying to improve the circulation of information between departments*; **circulation of capital** = movement of capital from one investment to another; **free circulation of goods** = movement of goods from one country to another without import quotas or other restrictions **(b) to put money into circulation** = to issue new notes to business and the public; *the amount of money in circulation increased more than had been expected* **(c)** *(of newspapers)*

number of copies sold; **a circulation battle** = competition between two newspapers to try to sell more copies in the same market

circumstances [ˈsɜːkəmstænsɪz] *plural noun* situation as it is when something happens; *the police inspector described the circumstances leading to the riot*; *see also* EXTENUATING

circumstantial [sɜːkəmˈstænʃl] *adjective* which allows someone to infer facts; **circumstantial evidence** = evidence which suggests that something happened, but does not give firm proof of it

citation [saɪˈteɪʃn] *noun* **(a)** official request asking someone to appear in court (NOTE: used mainly in the Scottish and American courts); **(b)** quotation of a legal case, authority or precedent; **citation clause** = clause in a Bill which gives the short title by which it should be known when it becomes an Act **(c)** words used in giving someone an award or honour, explaining why the award is being made

cite [saɪt] *verb* **(a)** to summon someone to appear in court **(b)** to quote, to refer to something; *the judge cited several previous cases in his summing up* **(c)** to refer to an Act of Parliament using the short title; *this Act may be cited as the Electronic Communications Act 1999*

citizen [ˈsɪtɪzən] *noun* **(a)** person who lives in a city **(b)** person who has the nationality of a certain country; *he is a French citizen by birth*; **Citizens' Advice Bureau (CAB)** = office where people can go to get free advice on legal and administrative problems; **citizen's arrest** = arrest of a suspected criminal by an ordinary citizen without a warrant; **Citizen's Charter** = promise by the government that the ordinary citizen must be fairly dealt with, in particular by government departments and state-controlled bodies

citizenship [ˈsɪtɪzənʃɪp] *noun* state of being a citizen of a country; *the Treaty has established European citizenship for everyone who is a citizen of the Member State of the EU*

COMMENT: a person has British citizenship if he is born in the UK and his father or mother is a British citizen, or if his father or mother has settled in the UK, or if he is adopted in the UK by a British citizen; British citizenship can also be granted to wives of British citizens

city ['sɪti] *noun* **(a)** large town; *the largest cities in Europe are linked by hourly flights*; **capital city** = main town in a country, where the government and parliament are situated **(b) the City** = old centre of London, where banks and large companies have their main offices; the London financial centre

COMMENT: in Britain a city is a large town (usually with a cathedral) which has been given the status of a city by the Crown

civic ['sɪvɪk] *adjective* referring to a city or the official business of running a city; *their civic pride showed in the beautiful gardens to be found everywhere in the city*; **civic centre** = town hall, the main offices of a city council; **civic dignitaries** = the mayor and other senior officials of a city or town

civil ['sɪvl] *adjective* **(a)** referring to the rights and duties of private persons or corporate bodies (as opposed to criminal, military or ecclesiastical); **civil action** = court case brought by a person or a company (the claimant) against someone who is alleged to have done them wrong (the defendant); **civil court** = court where civil actions are heard; **civil law** = laws relating to people's rights and agreements between individuals (as opposed to criminal law); **civil liberties** = freedom to act within the law (liberty of the press, liberty of the individual, etc.); **Civil Procedure Rules (CPR)** = rules laying out how civil cases are to be brought to court and heard; **civil rights** = rights and privileges of each individual person according to the law; **Civil Trial Centre** = court (but not the Royal Courts of Justice in London) which deals with multi-track claims **(b)** referring to the public in

general; **civil disorder** = riots or fighting in public places; **civil strife** = trouble where gangs of people fight each other, usually over matters of principle; **civil war** = situation in a country where the nation is divided into two or more sections which fight each other **(c) Civil List** = money appropriated from the Consolidated Fund for paying the Royal Family and their expenses

civilian [sɪ'vɪliən] **1** *adjective* referring to the ordinary citizen (as opposed to the armed forces); *civilian rule was restored after several years of military dictatorship*; *the military leaders called general elections and gave way to a democratically elected civilian government* **2** *noun* ordinary citizen who is not a member of the armed forces; *the head of the military junta has appointed several civilians to the Cabinet*

civil servant ['sɪvl 'sɜːvənt] *noun* person who works in the civil service

civil service ['sɪvl 'sɜːvɪs] *noun* organization which administers a country; *he has a job in the civil service*; *you have to pass an examination to get a job in the civil service or to get a civil service job*

COMMENT: members of the armed forces, magistrates and judges are not part of the British civil service

CJ ['siː 'dʒeɪ] = CHIEF JUSTICE

claim ['kleɪm] **1** *noun* **(a)** (i) assertion of a legal right; (ii) document used in the County Court to start a legal action; **particulars of claim** = pleading containing details of a claimant's case and the relief sought against the defendant, forming part of the claim form (NOTE: since the introduction of the new Civil Procedure Rules in April 1999, this term has replaced statement of claim); **claim for personal injuries** = claim where the claimant claims damages for disease or physical or mental disablement **(b)** statement that someone has a right to property held by another person; **legal claim to something** = statement that you think you own something legally; *he has no legal claim to the property or to the car*

(c) asking for money; **wage claim** = asking for an increase in wages; **the union put in a 6% wage claim** = the union asked for a 6% increase in wages for its members; *she put in a claim for £250,000 damages against the driver of the other car* **(d) insurance claim** = asking an insurance company to pay for damages or for loss; **no claims bonus** = reduction of premiums to be paid because no claims have been made against the insurance policy; **to put in a claim** = to ask the insurance company officially to pay for damage or loss; *she put in a claim for repairs to the car*; **to settle a claim** = to agree to pay what is asked for **(e) small claim** = claim for less than £5000 in the County Court; **small claims court** = court which deals with disputes over small amounts of money; *see also* SMALL CLAIMS TRACK **2** *verb* **(a)** to state a grievance in court **(b)** to ask for money; *he claimed £100,000 damages against the cleaning firm*; *she claimed for repairs to the car against her insurance* **(c)** to say that you have a right to property held by someone else; *he is claiming possession of the house*; *no one claimed the umbrella found in my office* **(d)** to state that something is a fact; *he claims he never received the goods*; *she claims that the shares are her property* **(e)** *(slang)* (i) to attack someone in prison; (ii) to arrest someone

claimant ['kleɪmənt] *noun* **(a)** person who claims; **rightful claimant** = person who has a legal claim to something **(b)** person who makes a claim against someone in the civil courts; *compare* DEFENDANT (NOTE: since the introduction of the new Civil Procedure Rules in April 1999, this term has replaced **plaintiff**)

claim back ['kleɪm 'bæk] *verb* to ask for money to be paid back

claim form ['kleɪm 'fɔːm] *noun* **(a)** form which has to be completed when making an insurance claim; *he filled in the claim form and sent it to the insurance company* **(b)** form issued by a court when requested by a claimant; it contains the particulars of claim and a statement of value; *see also* PRODUCTION CENTRE (NOTE: since

the introduction of the new Civil Procedure Rules in April 1999, this term has replaced the **writ of summons**)

> COMMENT: the claim form must be served on the defendant within four months of being issued. If a claim form has been issued but not served, the defendant can ask for it to be served, and if the claimant does not do so, the claim may be dismissed

class [klɑːs] **1** *noun* **(a)** category or group into which things are classified; **first-class** = top quality, most expensive; **Class F charge** = charge on a property registered by a spouse who is not an owner, claiming the right to live in the property; **class gift** = gift to a defined group of people; *US* **class action** *or* **class suit** = legal action brought on behalf of a group of people **(b)** **social class** = group of people who have a certain position in society; **upper class** = aristocracy and the richest and most influential business and professional people; **upper middle class** = wealthy professional people and businessmen; **middle class** = professional people and businessmen; **lower middle class** = small businessmen, shopkeepers, minor civil servants, etc.; **working class** = manual workers and people in low-paid jobs **2** *verb* to put into a category, to classify; *the magazine was classed as an obscene publication*

> COMMENT: in the UK the population is classified into social classes for statistical purposes. These are: **Class A:** higher managers, administrators and professionals; **Class B:** intermediate managers, administrators and professionals; **Class C1:** supervisors, clerical workers and junior managers; **Class C2:** skilled manual workers; **Class D:** semi-skilled or unskilled manual workers; **Class E:** pensioners, casual workers, long-term unemployed

classify ['klæsɪfaɪ] *verb* **(a)** to put into classes or categories; **classified directory** = book which lists businesses grouped under various headings (such as computer shops, newsagents, hairdressers) **(b)**

classified information = information which is secret and can be told only to certain people

clause [klɔːz] *noun* section of a contract or of a constitution; *there are ten clauses in the contract*; *according to clause six, payment will not be due until next year*; **exclusion clause** = clause in an insurance policy or contract which says which items are not covered by the policy, gives details of circumstances where the insurance company will refuse to pay; **forfeit clause** = clause in a contract which says that goods or a deposit will be forfeited if the contract is not obeyed; **liability clause** = clause in the articles of association of a company which states that the liability of its members is limited; **penalty clause** = clause which lists the penalties which will be imposed if the terms of the contract are not fulfilled; **termination clause** = clause which explains how and when a contract can be terminated

claw back [klɔː 'bæk] *verb* (i) to take back money which has been allocated; (ii) *(of the Inland Revenue)* to take back tax relief which was previously granted; *income tax claws back 25% of pensions paid out by the government*; *of the £1m allocated to the development of the system, the government clawed back £100,000 in taxes*

clawback ['klɔːbæk] *noun* (i) money taken back; (ii) loss of tax relief previously granted

clean bill ['kliːn 'bɪl] *noun US* bill made up of the original text, with deletions made and amendments added during Committee, which is presented to the House of Representatives or Senate again as one whole new bill, so as to avoid having to discuss each amendment separately

clean hands ['kliːn 'hændz] *plural noun* the plaintiff or claimant must have clean hands = the claimant cannot claim successfully if his motives or actions are dishonest or if he has not discharged his own obligations to the defendant

COMMENT: from the maxim: 'he who comes to equity must come with clean hands'

clear ['klɪə] **1** *adjective* **(a)** easily understood; *he made it clear that he wanted the manager to resign*; *there was no clear evidence or clear proof that he was in the house at the time of the murder* **(b) clear profit** = profit after all expenses have been paid; *we made $6,000 clear profit on the sale*; **to have a clear title to something** = to have a right to something with no limitations or charges **(c) clear days** = total period of time, calculated without including the first day when the period starts and the last day when it finishes; **three clear days** = three whole working days; *allow three clear days for the cheque to be paid into your account* **2** *verb* **(a)** to sell cheaply in order to get rid of stock **(b) to clear goods through the customs** = to have all documentation passed by the customs so that goods can leave the country **(c) to clear 10%** *or* **$5,000 on the deal** = to make 10% *or* $5,000 clear profit; **we cleared only our expenses** = the sales revenue paid only for the costs and expenses without making any profit **(d) to clear a cheque** = to pass a cheque through the banking system, so that the money is transferred from the payer's account to another account; *the cheque took ten days to clear or the bank took ten days to clear the cheque* **(e) to clear someone of charges** = to find that someone is not guilty of the charges against him; *he was cleared of all charges or he was cleared on all counts*

clearance ['klɪrəns] *noun* **customs clearance** = act of clearing goods through the customs; **clearance certificate** = document which shows that goods have been passed by customs

clearing ['klɪərɪŋ] *noun* **(a) clearing of goods through the customs** = passing of goods through the customs **(b) clearing of a debt** = paying all of a debt **(c) clearing bank** = bank which clears cheques, one of the major British High Street banks;

clearing house = central office where clearing banks exchange cheques

clear up ['klɪə 'ʌp] *verb* to solve a crime, to discover who has committed a crime and arrest them; *half the crimes committed are never cleared up*; **clear-up rate** = number of crimes solved, as a percentage of all crimes committed

> COMMENT: clear up can be divided into two categories: **primary clear up**, when a crime is solved by arresting the suspect, and **secondary clear up**, where a person charged with one crime then confesses to another which had not previously been solved

clemency ['klemənsi] *noun* pardon or mercy; *as an act of clemency, the president granted an amnesty to all political prisoners*; *US* **executive clemency** = pardon granted by the President

clerical ['klerɪkl] *adjective* **(a)** (work) done in an office, done by a clerk; **clerical error** = mistake made in an office; **clerical staff** = staff of an office; **clerical work** = paperwork done in an office; **clerical worker** = person who works in an office **(b)** referring to the church

clerk [klɑːk] *noun* person who works in an office; *accounts clerk*; *sales clerk*; *wages clerk*; **articled clerk** = trainee who is bound by a contract to work in a solicitor's office for some years to learn the law; **chief clerk** *or* **head clerk** = most important clerk; **Town Clerk** = former term for the most important permanent official of the administration of a town, working under the instructions of the town council (the official is now usually referred to as the Chief Executive); **Clerk of the House (of Commons)** = head of the administrative staff which runs the House of Commons and advises the Speaker on points of procedure; **Clerk of the Parliaments** = head of the administrative staff in the House of Lords; *US* **Clerk of the House** = head of the administrative staff which runs the House of Representatives; *see also* SECRETARY OF THE SENATE; **clerk to the justices** =

official of a magistrates' court (a qualified lawyer) who advises the magistrates on legal questions; *the functions of a justices' clerk include giving advice about law, practice and procedure*; *the Clerk of the House advised the Speaker that the speech could be considered breach of Parliamentary privilege*

clerkess ['klɑːkes] *noun (in Scotland)* woman clerk

clerkship ['klɜːkʃɪp] *noun US* time when a student lawyer is working in the office of a lawyer before being admitted to the bar

click-wrap agreement ['klɪk'ræp ə'griːmənt] *noun* contract entered into using only the Internet (as when purchasing an item over the net, where no paper documentation exists, and the agreement to purchase is made by clicking on the appropriate button)

client ['klaɪənt] *noun* **(a)** person who pays for a service carried out by a professional person (such as an accountant or a solicitor) **(b)** person who is represented by a lawyer; *the solicitor paid the fine on behalf of his client*

clientele [kliːɒn'tel] *noun* all the clients of a business; all the customers of a shop

close 1 [kləuz] *noun* end; *at the close of the day's trading the shares had fallen 20%* **2** [kləus] *adjective* **close to** = very near, almost; *the company was close to bankruptcy*; *we are close to solving the crime* **3** [kləuz] *verb* **(a)** to stop doing business for the day; *the office closes at 5.30*; *we close early on Saturdays* **(b)** to **close the accounts** = to come to the end of an accounting period and make up the profit and loss account **(c)** to **close an account** = (i) to stop supplying a customer on credit; (ii) to take all the money out of a bank account and stop the account **(d)** the **shares closed at $15** = at the end of the day's trading the price of the shares was $15

close company *US* **close(d) corporation** ['kləus 'kʌmpni or 'kləuzd kɔːpə'reɪʃn] *noun* privately owned company where the public may own a small number of shares

closed [kləuzd] *adjective* **(a)** shut, not open or not doing business; *the office is closed on Mondays; all the banks are closed on the National Day* **(b)** restricted to a few people; **closed shop,** *US* **union shop** = system where a company agrees to employ only union members in certain jobs; *a closed shop agreement; the union is asking the management to agree to a closed shop;* **closed market** = market where a supplier deals only with one agent and does not supply any others direct; *they signed a closed market agreement with an American company;* **closed session** = meeting which is not open to the public or to journalists; *the town council met in closed session to discuss staff problems in the Education Department; the public gallery was cleared when the meeting went into closed session*

close down ['kləuz 'daun] *verb* to shut a shop or factory for a long period or for ever; *the company is closing down its London office; the strike closed down the railway system*

closing ['kləuzɪŋ] **1** *adjective* **(a)** final, coming at the end; **closing speeches** = final speeches for and against a motion in a debate, for prosecution and defence at the end of a trial **(b)** at the end of an accounting period such as a financial year; **closing stock** = value of stock at the end of an accounting period **2** *noun* **(a)** shutting of a shop, being shut; **Sunday closing** = not opening a shop on Sundays; **closing time** = time when a shop or office stops work; **early closing day** = weekday (usually Wednesday or Thursday) when many shops close in the afternoon **(b)** **closing of an account** = act of stopping supply to a customer on credit

closure ['kləuʒə] *noun* **(a)** act of closing **(b)** *(in the House of Commons)* ending of the debate (such as on a clause in a Bill); **closure motion** = proposal to end a debate

COMMENT: when an MP wishes to end the debate on a motion, he says 'I move that the question be now put' and the Speaker immediately puts the motion to the vote

cloture ['kləutʃə] *noun US* motion to end a filibuster in the Senate, requiring sixteen senators to introduce it and a two-thirds majority to pass

CLS = COMMUNITY LEGAL SERVICE

clue [kluː] *noun* thing which helps someone solve a crime; *the police have searched the room for clues; the police have several clues to the identity of the murdered*

Cmnd = COMMAND PAPERS

c/o ['siː 'əu] = CARE OF

Co = COMPANY; *J. Smith & Co Ltd*

co- [kəu] *prefix* working or acting together; **co-creditor** = person who is a creditor of the same company as you are; **co-defendant** = person who appears in a case with another defendant; **co-director** = person who is a director of the same company as you; **co-insurance** = insurance policy where the risk is shared among several insurers

coalition [kəuə'lɪʃn] *noun* group of two or more political parties who come together to form a government, when no single party has a majority; *the coalition government fell when one of the parties withdrew support*

c.o.d. ['siː 'əu 'diː] = CASH ON DELIVERY, *US* COLLECT ON DELIVERY

code [kəud] **1** *noun* **(a)** official set of laws or regulations; **the Highway Code** = rules which govern the behaviour of people and vehicles using roads; **the penal code** = set of laws governing crime and its punishment; *failure to observe the code does not render anyone liable to proceedings* **(b)** set of laws of a country; *US* **the Louisiana Code** = laws of the state of Louisiana; **Code Napoleon** = civil laws of France (introduced by Napoleon) **(c)** set of semi-official rules; **code of conduct** = informal (sometimes written) rules by which a group of people work; **code of practice** = (i) rules to be followed when applying a law; (ii) rules drawn up by an association which the members must follow when doing business; *the Code of Practice on Picketing has been issued by the Secretary of State* **(d)** system of signs, numbers or letters which mean something; *the spy sent his message in code*; **area code** = numbers which indicate an area for telephoning; **machine-readable codes** = sets of signs or letters (such as bar codes or post codes) which can be read by computers; **post code,** *US* **zip code** = letters and numbers used to indicate a town or street in an address on an envelope **2** *verb* to write (a message) using secret signs; *we received coded instructions from our agent in New York*

co-decision procedure [ˈkəʊdɪˈsɪʒn prəˈsiːdjə] *noun (in the EU)* procedure by which the Commission sends proposed legislation to both the Council of the European Union and the European Parliament for approval

coding [ˈkəʊdɪŋ] *noun* act of putting a code on something; *the coding of invoices*

codicil [ˈkəʊdɪsɪl] *noun* document executed in the same way as a will, making additions or changes to an existing will

codification [kəʊdɪfɪˈkeɪʃn] *noun* **(a)** putting all laws together into a formal legal code **(b)** bringing together all statutes and case law relating to a certain issue, to make a single Act of Parliament; *see also* CONSOLIDATION

codify [ˈkəʊdɪfaɪ] *verb* to put (laws) together to form a code

coercion [kəʊˈɜːʃn] *noun* forcing someone by pressure to commit a crime or do some act

coexist [kəʊɪgˈzɪst] *verb* to exist together

coexistence [kəʊɪgˈzɪstəns] *noun* act of existing together; **peaceful coexistence** = situation where governments may be in complete disagreement, but exist together without threatening war

cohabit [kəʊˈhæbɪt] *verb (of a man and a woman)* to live together as man and wife

cohabitant [kəʊˈhæbɪtənt] *noun* = COHABITEE

cohabitation [kəʊhæbɪˈteɪʃn] *noun* living together as man and wife (whether married or not)

cohabiter *or* **cohabitee** [kəʊˈhæbɪtə or kəʊhæbɪˈtiː] *noun* person who lives with another as husband or wife, but is not married

co-heir [ˈkəʊˈeə] *noun* person who is an heir with others

collateral [kəˈlætərəl] *adjective & noun* **(a)** (security) used to provide a guarantee for a loan; **collateral contract** = contract which induces a person to enter into a more important contract **(b) collateral issue** = issue which arises from a plea in a criminal court

collation [kəˈleɪʃn] *noun* comparing a copy with the original to see if it is perfect

collect [kəˈlekt] **1** *verb* **(a)** to make someone pay money which is owed; **to collect a debt** = to go and make someone pay a debt **(b)** to take goods away from a place; *we have to collect the stock from the warehouse*; *can you collect my letters from the typing pool?*; **letters are collected twice a day** = the post office workers take them from the letter box to the post office so that they can be sent off **2** *adverb & adjective US* (phone call) where the person receiving the call agrees to pay for it; *to make a collect call*; *he called his office collect*

collecting [kəˈlektɪŋ] *noun* **collecting agency** = agency which collects money owed to other companies for a commission

collection [kəˈlekʃn] *noun* **(a)** getting money together, making someone pay money which is owed; **debt collection** = collecting money which is owed; **debt collection agency** = company which collects debts for other companies for a commission; **bills for collection** = bills where payment is due **(b)** fetching of goods; *the stock is in the warehouse awaiting collection*; **collection charges** *or* **collection rates** = charge for collecting something; **to hand something in for collection** = to leave something for someone to come and collect **(c) collections** = money which has been collected **(d)** taking of letters from a letter box or mail room to the post office to be sent off; *there are six collections a day from the letter box*

collective [kə'lektɪv] *adjective* working together; **(free) collective bargaining** = negotiations about wages and working conditions between management and workers' representatives; **collective ownership** = ownership of a business by the workers who work in it; **collective responsibility** = doctrine that all members of a group (such as the British cabinet) are responsible together for the actions of the group; **they signed a collective wage agreement** = an agreement was signed between management and the trade union about wages; **collective security** = security of a group of states together (such as the general security of member states of the UN, under the protection of the Security Council)

collectivism [kə'lektɪvɪzm] *noun* any economic theory where the country's economy is centrally planned and the employers, trade unions and government all work together for the improvement of the economy

collector [kə'lektə] *noun* person who makes people pay money which is owed; *collector of taxes* or *tax collector*; *debt collector*

college ['kɒlɪdʒ] *noun* **(a)** place where people can study after they have left school; **business college** *or* **commercial college** = college which teaches general business methods; **correspondence**

college = college where the teaching is done by mail (sending work to the students who then return it to be marked); **secretarial college** = college which teaches shorthand, typing and word-processing **(b) electoral college** = group of people elected by larger groups to vote on their behalf in an election

collusion [kə'luːʒn] *noun* illicit co-operation between people, agreement between parties in order to cheat another party, or in order to defraud another party of a right; *he was suspected of (acting in) collusion with the owner of the property*

collusive action [kə'luːsɪv 'ækʃən] *noun* action which is taken in collusion with another party

colonial [kə'ləʊnɪəl] **1** *adjective* referring to a colony or colonies; *granting of independence ended a period of a hundred years of colonial rule*; *the colonial government was overthrown by a coup led by the local police force*; **colonial dependency** = colony or territory ruled and settled by another country **2** *noun* person living in a colony; person who was born in a colony

colonialism [kə'ləʊnɪəlɪzm] *noun* theory or practice of establishing colonies; *the meeting denounced colonialism, and demanded independence*

colonist ['kɒlənɪst] *noun* person who goes abroad (or is sent abroad) to settle in a colony

colonization [kɒlənaɪ'zeɪʃn] *noun* act of taking a country and turning it into a colony

colonize ['kɒlənaɪz] *verb* to take possession of an area or country and rule it as a colony; *the government was accused of trying to colonize the Antarctic Region*

colony ['kɒləni] *noun* country or area ruled and settled by another country (usually one which is overseas); *Australia was originally a group of British colonies*; *the Romans established colonies in North Africa*

column ['kɒləm] *noun* list of figures one written underneath the other; **debit column** *or* **credit column** = lists of figures in accounts, showing money paid to others or owed by others

comfort ['kʌmfət] *noun* **letter of comfort** *or* **comfort letter** = letter supporting someone who is trying to get a loan, letter which reassures someone on a particular point

comity ['kɒmɪti] *noun* **(a) comity of nations** = custom whereby the courts of one country acknowledge and apply the laws of another country in certain cases **(b)** *US* custom by which courts in one state defer to the jurisdiction of courts in other states or to federal courts

command [kə'mɑːnd] *noun* order; **by Royal Command** = by order of the Queen or King; **Command papers** = papers (such as White papers, Green Papers or reports of Royal Commissions) which are presented to Parliament by the government

commander [kə'mɑːndə] *noun* high rank in the Metropolitan Police force (equivalent to Assistant Chief Constable)

commencement [kə'mensmənt] *noun* beginning; **commencement of proceedings** = the start of proceedings in the County Court; **date of commencement** = date when an Act of Parliament takes effect

comment ['kɒment] **1** *noun* remark, spoken or written opinion; *the judge made a comment on the evidence presented by the defence*; *the newspaper has some short comments about the trial*; **fair comment** = remark which is honestly made on a matter of public interest and so is not defamatory **2** *verb* to remark or to express an opinion; *the judge commented on the lack of evidence*; *the newspapers commented on the result of the trial*

commentary ['kɒməntri] *noun* (i) textbook which comments on the law; (ii) brief notes which comment on the main points of a judgment

commerce ['kɒmɜːs] *noun* business, buying and selling of goods and services; **Chamber of Commerce** = group of local businessmen who meet to discuss problems which they have in common and to promote business in their town

commercial [kə'mɜːʃl] *adjective* **(a)** referring to business; **commercial college** = college which teaches business studies; **commercial course** = course where business skills are studied; **Commercial Court** = court in the Queen's Bench Division which hears cases relating to business disputes; **commercial directory** = book which lists all the businesses and business people in a town; **commercial law** = laws regarding business **(b)** profitable; **not a commercial proposition** = not likely to make a profit

commission [kə'mɪʃn] *noun* **(a)** official order to someone, giving him authority and explaining what his duties are; **he has a commission in the armed forces** = he is an officer in the armed forces **(b)** payment (usually a percentage of turnover) made to an agent; *he has an agent's commission of 15% of sales* **(c)** group of people officially appointed to examine some problem; *the government has appointed a commission of inquiry to look into the problems of prison overcrowding*; *he is the chairman of the government commission on football violence*; **Law Commission** = permanent committee which reviews English law and recommends changes to it; **Royal Commission** = group of people specially appointed by a minister to examine and report on a major problem **(d) Commission of the European Community** = main executive body of the EC, one of the four bodies which form the basis of the European Community, made up of members from each state

COMMENT: the Commission is formed of 20 members or Commissioners who are appointed by the governments of the Member States. The larger Member States (France, Germany, Italy, Spain and the UK) have two Commissioners each and the other smaller countries appoint one each. Each Commissioner is appointed for a five-year renewable term, and all the appointments end together, so the Commission is either changed or renewed every five years. Member States cannot dismiss the Commission, but can refuse to renew the term of appointment. The European Parliament can force the entire Commission to resign, but cannot dismiss an individual Commissioner. The European Court of Justice can force a Commissioner to retire on grounds of misconduct. The Commission is headed by the President of the European Commission, with two Vice-Presidents. The Commissioners are not supposed to be the representatives of their respective governments but must take the interests of the Community as a whole into account. Each commissioner has his or her own private office or Cabinet, headed by a Chef de Cabinet. The Commission has 23 departments called Directorates General, each headed by a Director-General; the Directorates General are subdivided into Directorates, and these are subdivided into Divisions. Each Directorate General is responsible to one of the Commissioners. The Commission represents all the Member States in negotiations with other parties, for example in trade negotiations with the USA. The Commission proposes laws for the European Community, and the Council of Ministers makes decisions accordingly. The Commission can make proposals regarding some legal matters and some matters concerning the internal security of Member States, but its main role is that of a watchdog, seeing that treaty obligations are carried out by Member States

commissioner [kəˈmɪʃənə] *noun* **(a)** member of an official commission; person who has an official commission; **the Commissioners of Inland Revenue** = the Board of Inland Revenue; **commissioner for oaths** = solicitor appointed by the Lord Chancellor to administer affidavits which may be used in court; **commissioner of police** *or* **police commissioner** = highest rank in a police force; **Metropolitan Police Commissioner** = head of the Metropolitan Police in London **(b)** member of the Commission of the European Community

commit [kəˈmɪt] *verb* **(a)** to send (someone) to prison or to a court; *he was committed for trial in the Central Criminal Court; the magistrates committed her for trial at the Crown Court* **(b)** to carry out (a crime); *the gang committed six robberies before they were caught* (NOTE: **committing - committed**)

commitment [kəˈmɪtmənt] *noun* **(a)** order for sending someone to prison **(b)** **commitments** = obligations, things which have to be done; **to honour one's commitments** = to do what one is obliged to do; **financial commitments** = money which is owed, debts which have to be paid

committal [kəˈmɪtəl] *noun* sending someone to a court or to prison; **committal order** = order sending someone to prison for contempt of court; **committal proceedings** = preliminary hearing of a case before the magistrates' court, to decide if it is serious enough to be tried before a jury in a higher court; **committal for trial** = sending someone to be tried in a higher court following committal proceedings in a magistrates' court; **committal for sentence** = sending someone who has been convicted in a magistrates' court to be sentenced in a higher court; **committal warrant** = order sending someone to serve a prison sentence

committee [kəˈmɪti] *noun* **(a)** official group of people who organize or plan for a larger group; *to be a member of a committee or to sit on a committee; he was elected to the Finance Committee; the new plans have to be approved by the committee members; she is attending a committee meeting; he is the chairman of the Planning Committee; she is the secretary of the Housing Committee;* **to**

chair a committee = to be the chairman of a committee; **steering committee** = committee which works out the agenda for discussion by a main committee or conference (and so can influence the way the main committee or conference works) **(b)** section of a legislature which considers bills passed to it by the main chamber; *(in the House of Commons)* **Committee Stage** = one of the stages in the discussion of a Bill, where each clause is examined in detail; *the Bill is at Committee Stage and will not become law for several months*; **joint committee** = committee formed of equal numbers of members of the House of Commons and House of Lords; **select committee** = special committee of the House of Commons (with members representing various political parties) which examines the work of a ministry or which deals with a particular problem; *see note at* SELECT; **standing committee** = permanent committee which deals with matters not given to other committees, parliamentary committee which examines Bills not sent to other committees; **Committee of the Whole House,** *US* **Committee of the Whole** = the House of Commons or House of Representatives acting as a committee to examine the clauses of a Bill; **the House went into Committee** = the House of Commons became a Committee of the Whole House; **Committee of the Parliamentary Commission** = committee which examines reports by the Ombudsman; **Committee of Privileges** = special committee of the House of Commons which examines cases of breach of privilege; **Committee of Selection** = committee which chooses the members of the other committees in the House of Commons; **Public Accounts Committee** = committee of the House of Commons which examines the spending of each ministry and department, and of the government as a whole

commodity [kəˈmɒdəti] *noun* thing sold in very large quantities, especially raw materials and food such as metals or corn; **primary** *or* **basic commodities** = farm produce grown in large quantities, such as corn, rice, cotton; **commodity market** *or*

commodity exchange = place where people buy and sell commodities; **commodity futures** = trading in commodities for delivery at a later date; *silver rose 5% on the commodity futures market yesterday*; **commodity trader** = person whose business is buying and selling commodities

common [ˈkɒmən] **1** *noun* area of land on which anyone can walk, and may have the right to keep animals, pick wood, etc. (NOTE: now usually used in place names such as **Clapham Common) 2** *adjective* **(a)** which happens very often; *putting the carbon paper in the wrong way round is a common mistake*; *being caught by the customs is very common these days* **(b)** referring to or belonging to several different people or to everyone; **common assault** = crime or tort of acting in such a way that another person is afraid he will be attacked and hurt; **common carrier** = firm which carries goods or passengers, which cannot normally refuse to do so and which can be used by anyone; **common land** = land on which anyone can walk and may have the right to keep animals, pick wood, etc.; **common nuisance** = criminal act which causes harm or danger to members of the public in general or to their rights; **common ownership** = ownership of a company or a property by a group of people who each own a part; **common pricing** = illegal fixing of prices by several businesses so that they all charge the same price; **common seal** = seal which a corporation must possess, and which is used to seal official papers; *US* **common stock** = ordinary shares in a corporation **(c) in common** = together; **ownership in common** = COMMON OWNERSHIP; **tenancy in common** = situation where two or more persons jointly lease a property and each can leave his interest to his heirs when he dies; *compare* JOINT TENANCY

common law [ˈkɒmən ˈlɔː] *noun* **(a)** law as laid down in decisions of courts, rather than by statute **(b)** general system of laws which formerly were the only laws existing in England, and which in some cases have been superseded by statute (NOTE: you say **at common law** when referring to something happening according to the principles of common law)

common-law ['kɒmənlɔ:] *adjective* according to the old unwritten system of law; **common-law marriage** = situation where two people live together as husband and wife without being married; **common-law spouse** *or* **wife** = person who has lived or is living with another as man or wife, although they have not been legally married (NOTE: not quite the same as **cohabitee** where the implication is that they are currently living together)

Common Market ['kɒmən 'mɑːkɪt] *noun* former name for the European Community

common position ['kɒmən pə'sɪʃn] *noun (in the EU)* position taken by the Council of the European Union on proposed legislation; this position is then passed to the European Parliament for approval. It can be adopted or rejected by the Parliament, and the Parliament may propose changes to the proposed 'common position'

Commons ['kɒmənz] *plural noun* = HOUSE OF COMMONS; *the Commons voted against the Bill; the majority of the Commons are in favour of law reform*

Common Serjeant ['kɒmən 'sɑːdʒənt] *noun* senior barrister who sits as a judge in the City of London and acts as adviser to the City of London Corporation

Commonwealth ['kɒmənwelθ] *noun* **(a) the Commonwealth** = association of independent sovereign states which were once ruled by Britain; **the Old Commonwealth** = the oldest members of the Commonwealth (such as Canada, Australia and New Zealand); **the Commonwealth Secretariat** = office and officials based in London, organizing the links between the member states of the Commonwealth (the office is headed by the Commonwealth Secretary-General) **(b)** *(used in titles)* state where all people are

equal; *the Commonwealth of Australia*; *the Commonwealth of Massachusetts*

commorientes [kɒmɒri'enti:z] *plural noun* people who die at the same time (as a husband and wife who die in an accident)

> COMMENT: in such cases, the law assumes that the younger person has died after the older one; this rule also applies to testators and beneficiaries who die at the same time

commune ['kɒmjuːn] *noun* **(a)** group of people who live and work together, and share their possessions **(b)** small administrative area in some countries (such as Switzerland or France)

communicate [kə'mjuːnɪkeɪt] *verb* to pass information to someone; *the members of the jury must not communicate with the witnesses*

communication [kəmjuːnɪ'keɪʃn] *noun* **(a)** passing of information; **to enter into communication with someone** = to start discussing something with someone, usually in writing; *we have entered into communication with the relevant government department* **(b)** official message; *we have had a communication from the local tax inspector*; **privileged communication** = letter which could be libellous, but which is protected by privilege (such as a letter from a client to his lawyer) **(c) communications** = being able to contact people, to pass messages; *after the flood all communications with the outside world were broken*

community [kə'mjuːnəti] *noun* **(a)** group of people living or working in the same place; **the local business community** = the business people living and working in the area; **community charge** = local tax levied on each eligible taxpayer; **community home** = house which belongs to a local authority, where children in care can be kept; **community policing** = way of policing a section of a town, whereby the people in the area and the local police force act together to prevent crime and disorder; **community service** = working on behalf of the local community; **community**

service order = punishment where a criminal is sentenced to do unpaid work in the local community **(b) the European Community** = a group of European countries linked together by the Treaty of Rome in such a way that trade is more free, people can move from one country to another more freely, and people can work more freely in other countries of the group; **the Community finance ministers** = the finance ministers of all the countries of the European Community, meeting as a group; **Community legislation** *or* **Community law** = (i) regulations or directives issued by the EC Council of Ministers or the EC Commission; (ii) laws created by the European Community which are binding on Member States and their citizens **(c)** *(in the USA, Canada, France and many other countries)* **community property** = situation where the husband and wife jointly own any property which they acquire during the course of their marriage (as opposed to 'separate property', which they each owned before their marriage)

Community Legal Service (CLS)

[kə'mju:nəti 'li:gl 'sɜ:vɪs] *noun* British government service which provides legal advice and assistance in each community to people with very little money

COMMENT: the service replaces the Legal Aid scheme in civil and family cases, and is run through a series of Community Legal Service Partnerships, one in each local authority

commutation [kɒmju'teɪʃn] *noun* reducing a harsh sentence to a lesser one

commute [kə'mju:t] *verb* **(a)** to travel to work from home each day; *he commutes from the country to his office in the centre of town* **(b)** to change a right into cash **(c)** to reduce a harsh sentence to a lesser one; *the death sentence was commuted to life imprisonment*

compact ['kɒmpækt] *noun* agreement

company ['kʌmpni] *noun* **(a)** business, group of people organized to buy, sell or provide a service **(b)** group of people organized to buy or sell or provide a service which has been legally incorporated, and so is a legal entity separate from its individual members; **to put a company into liquidation** = to close a company by selling its assets to pay its creditors; **to set up a company** = to start a company legally; **associate company** = company which is partly owned by another company; **close company** = privately owned company where the public may own a small number of shares; **family company** = company where most of the shares are owned by members of the same family; **holding company** = company which exists only to own shares in subsidiary companies; **joint-stock company** = company whose shares are held by many people; **limited (liability) company** = company where a shareholder is responsible for repaying the company's debts only to the face value of the shares he owns; **listed company** = company whose shares can be bought or sold on the Stock Exchange; **parent company** = company which owns more than half of another company's shares; **private (limited) company** = company with a small number of shareholders, whose shares are not traded on the Stock Exchange; **public limited company (plc)** = company whose shares can be bought on the Stock Exchange; **subsidiary company** = company which is owned by a parent company **(c) finance company** = company which provides money for hire-purchase; **insurance company** = company whose business is insurance; **shipping company** = company whose business is in carrying goods by sea; **a tractor** *or* **aircraft** *or* **chocolate company** = company which makes tractors or aircraft or chocolate **(d) company director** = person appointed by the shareholders to run a company; **company law** = laws which refer to the way companies may work; **company member** = shareholder in a company; **company secretary** = person responsible for the company's legal and financial affairs; **the Companies Act** = Act of the British parliament which states the legal limits within which a company may do business; **Registrar of Companies** =

official who keeps a record of all incorporated companies, the details of their directors and financial state; **register of companies** *or* **companies' register** = list of companies showing details of their directors and registered addresses; **Companies House** = office which keeps details of incorporated companies **(e)** organization in the City of London which does mainly charitable work, and is derived from one of the former trade associations; *the Drapers' Company*; *the Grocers' Company*

comparative law [kɒmˈpærətɪv ˈlɔ:] *noun* study which compares the legal systems of different countries

compel [kʌmˈpel] *verb* to force (someone) to do something; *the Act compels all drivers to have adequate insurance* (NOTE: **compelling - compelled**)

compellability *noun* being compellable

compellable [kɒmˈpeləbl] *adjective* (person) who can be forced to do something; *a compellable witness*

compensate [ˈkɒmpənseɪt] *verb* to pay for damage done; *to compensate a manager for loss of commission*

compensation [kɒmpənˈseɪʃn] *noun* **(a)** payment made by someone to cover the cost of damage or hardship which he has caused; *unlimited compensation may be awarded in the Crown Court*; **compensation for damage** = payment for damage done; **compensation for loss of office** = payment to a director who is asked to leave a company before his contract ends; **compensation for loss of earnings** = payment to someone who has stopped earning money or who is not able to earn money; **compensation fund** = special fund set up by the Law Society to compensate clients for loss suffered because of the actions of solicitors; **compensation order** = order made by a criminal court to compel a criminal to pay money to his victim **(b)** *US* salary, payment made to someone for work which he has done; **compensation**

package = salary, pension and other benefits offered with a job

compensatory [kɒmpənˈseɪtəri] *adjective* **compensatory damages** = damages which compensate for loss or harm suffered

compete [kʌmˈpi:t] *verb* to compete **with someone** *or* **with a company** = to try to do better than another person or another company; *the gangs were competing for control of the drugs market*

competence *or* **competency** [ˈkɒmpɪtəns] *noun* **(a)** *(of a witness)* being able to give evidence (anyone is able to give evidence, except the sovereign, persons who are mentally ill, and spouses, in the case where the other spouse is being prosecuted) **(b)** the case falls within the competence of the court = the court is legally able to deal with the case

competent [ˈkɒmpɪtənt] *adjective* **(a)** able to do something; efficient; *she is a competent secretary* or *a competent manager* **(b)** legally able to do something; *most people are competent to give evidence*; **the court is not competent to deal with this case** = the court is not legally able to deal with the case

competition [kɒmpəˈtɪʃn] *noun* competing with another company, trying to do better than another company; **free competition** = being free to compete without government interference; **unfair competition** = trying to do better than another company by using methods such as importing foreign products at very low prices or by wrongly criticizing a competitor's products

competitor [kəmˈpetɪtə] *noun* person or company which competes; *two German firms are our main competitors*; *the contract of employment forbids members of staff from leaving to go to work for competitors*

complain [kəmˈpleɪn] *verb* to say that something is no good or does not work properly; *the office is so cold the staff have started complaining*; *she complained* *about the service; they are complaining that our prices are too high; if you want to complain, write to the manager*

complainant [kəm'pleɪnənt] *noun* person who makes a complaint or who starts proceedings against someone

complaint [kəm'pleɪnt] *noun* **(a)** statement that you feel something is wrong; *when making a complaint, always quote the reference number; she sent her letter of complaint to the managing director;* **to make** *or* **lodge a complaint against someone** = to write and send an official complaint to someone's superior; **complaints procedure** = agreed way for workers to make complaints to the management about working conditions; **Police Complaints Committee** = group of people who investigate complaints made by members of the public against the police **(b)** document signed to start proceedings in a Magistrates' Court **(c)** statement of the case made by the claimant at the beginning of a civil action

complete [kəm'pliːt] **1** *adjective* whole, with nothing missing; *the order is complete and ready for sending; the order should be delivered only if it is complete* **2** *verb* **(a)** to finish; *the factory completed the order in two weeks; how long will it take you to complete the job?* **(b)** to **complete a conveyance** = to convey a property to a purchaser, when the purchaser pays the purchase price and the vendor hands over the signed conveyance and the deeds of the property

completion [kəm'pliːʃn] *noun* act of finishing something; **completion date** = date when something will be finished; **completion of a conveyance** = last stage in the sale of a property when the solicitors for the two parties meet, when the purchaser pays and the vendor passes the conveyance and the deeds to the purchaser; **completion statement** = statement of account from a solicitor to a client showing all the costs of the sale or purchase of a property

complex ['kɒmpleks] **1** *noun* series of large buildings; *a large industrial complex* **2** *adjective* with many different parts; *a complex system of import controls; the regulations governing immigration are very complex*

compliance [kəm'plaɪəns] *noun* agreement to do what is ordered; *the documents have been drawn up in compliance with the provisions of the Act;* **declaration of compliance** = declaration made by a person forming a limited company, that the requirements of the Companies' Act have been met

compliant [kəm'plaɪənt] *adjective* which agrees with something; **not compliant with** = not in agreement with; *the settlement is not compliant with the earlier order of the court*

comply [kəm'plaɪ] *verb* **to comply with** = to obey; *the company has complied with the court order; she refused to comply with the injunction*

composition [kɒmpə'zɪʃn] *noun* agreement between a debtor and creditors to settle a debt immediately by repaying only part of it

compos mentis ['kɒmpɒs 'mentɪs] *Latin phrase meaning* 'of sound mind' or 'sane'

compound 1 ['kɒmpaʊnd] *adjective* **compound interest** = interest which is added to the capital and then itself earns interest **2** [kəm'paʊnd] *verb* **(a)** to agree with creditors to settle a debt by paying part of what is owed **(b) to compound an offence** = to agree (in return for payment) not to prosecute someone who has committed an offence (NOTE: formerly 'to compound a felony', which is still used in the USA)

comprehensive [kɒmprɪ'hensɪv] *adjective* which includes everything; **comprehensive insurance** = insurance policy which covers you against a large number of possible risks

compromise ['kɒmprəmaɪz] **1** *noun* agreement between two sides, where each side gives way a little in order to reach a settlement; *management offered £5 an hour, the union asked for £9, and a compromise of £7.50 was reached; after some discussion a compromise solution was reached* **2** *verb* **(a)** to reach an agreement by giving way a little; *he asked £15 for it, I offered £7 and we compromised on £10* **(b)** to involve someone in something which makes his reputation less good; *the minister was compromised in the bribery case*

comptroller [kən'trəʊlə] *noun* person in charge, especially referring to accounts; **Comptroller and Auditor General** = official whose duty is to examine the accounts of ministries and government departments

compulsory [kəm'pʌlsəri] *adjective* which is forced or ordered; **compulsory liquidation** *or* **compulsory winding up** = liquidation which is ordered by a court; **compulsory purchase** = buying of a property by the local council or the government even if the owner does not want to sell; **compulsory purchase order** = official order from the local council or from the government ordering an owner to sell his property (NOTE: in the USA, this is **expropriation**); **compulsory winding up order** = order from a court saying that a company must be wound up

computer [kəm'pjuːtə] *noun* electronic machine which calculates, stores information and processes it automatically; **computer bureau** = office which offers to do work on its computers for companies which do not have their own computers; **computer error** = mistake made by a computer; **computer file** = section of information on a computer (such as a list of addresses or customer accounts); **computer fraud** = fraud committed by using computer files (such as in a bank); **computer language** = system of signs, letters and words used to instruct a computer; **computer program** = instructions to a computer, telling it to do a particular piece of work

computerize [kəm'pjuːtəraɪz] *verb* to change from a manual system to one using computers; *the police criminal records have been completely computerized*

con [kɒn] **1** *noun* **(a)** *(informal)* trick done to try to get money from someone; *trying to get us to pay him for ten hours' overtime was just a con* **(b)** *(slang)* (i) convict, prisoner; (ii) conviction **2** *verb* *(informal)* to trick someone to try to get money; *they conned the bank into lending them £25,000 with no security; he conned the finance company out of £100,000* (NOTE: **con - conning - conned.** Note also you con someone **into** doing something)

conceal [kən'siːl] *verb* to hide; *he was accused of concealing information; the accused had a gun concealed under his coat*

concealment [kən'siːlmənt] *noun* hiding for criminal purposes; **concealment of assets** = hiding assets so that creditors do not know they exist; **concealment of birth** = notifiable offence of hiding the fact that a child has been born

concede [kən'siːd] *verb* to admit (that the opposing party is right); *counsel conceded that his client owed the money; the witness conceded under questioning that he had never been near the house;* **to concede defeat** = to admit that you have lost

concern [kən'sɜːn] **1** *noun* business, company; **his business is a going concern** = the company is working (and making a profit); **sold as a going concern** = sold as an actively trading company **2** *verb* to deal with, to be connected with; *the court is not concerned with the value of the items stolen; the report does not concern itself with the impartiality of the judge; he has been asked to give evidence to the commission of inquiry concerning the breakdown of law and order; the contract was drawn up with the agreement of all parties concerned*

concert party ['kɒnsət 'pɑːti] *noun* arrangement where several people or companies act together in secret to take over a company

concession [kən'seʃn] *noun* **(a)** right to use someone else's property for business purposes; **mining concession** = right to dig a mine on a piece of land which you do not own **(b)** right to be the only seller of a product in a place; *she runs a jewellery concession in a department store* **(c)** allowance; **tax concession** = allowing less tax to be paid **(d)** admission of defeat; **concession speech** = speech made by a loser in an election, admitting that he has lost

concessionaire [kənseʃə'neə] *noun* person who has the right to be the only seller of a product in a place

concessionary [kə'seʃnənri] *adjective* **concessionary fare** = reduced fare for certain types of passenger (such as employees of the transport company)

conciliation [kənsɪlɪ'eɪʃn] *noun* bringing together the parties in a dispute so that the dispute can be settled; **the Conciliation Service** = ADVISORY, CONCILIATION AND ARBITRATION SERVICE

conclude [kən'kluːd] *verb* **(a)** to complete successfully; *to conclude an agreement with someone* **(b)** to believe from evidence; *the police concluded that the thief had got into the building through the main entrance*

conclusion [kən'kluːʒn] *noun* **(a)** believing, deciding from evidence; *the police have come to the conclusion or have reached the conclusion that the bomb was set off by radio control* **(b)** US **conclusion of fact** = statement of a decision by a judge, based on facts; **conclusion of law** = statement of a decision by a judge, based on rules of law **(c)** final completion; *the conclusion of the defence counsel's address*; **in conclusion** = finally, at the end; *in conclusion, the judge thanked the jury for their long and patient service*

conclusive [kən'kluːsɪv] *adjective* which proves something; *the fingerprints on the gun were conclusive evidence that the accused was guilty*

conclusively [kən'kluːsɪvli] *adverb* in a way which proves a fact; *the evidence of the eye witness proved conclusively that the accused was in the town at the time the robbery was committed*

concordat [kɒn'kɔːdæt] *noun* agreement between the Roman Catholic Church and a government, which allows the Church certain rights and privileges

concur [kən'kɜː] *verb* to agree; *Smith LJ dismissed the appeal, Jones and White LJJ concurring*

concurrence [kən'kʌrəns] *noun* agreement; *in concurrence with the other judges, Smith LJ dismissed the appeal*

concurrent [kən'kʌrənt] *adjective* taking place at the same time; **concurrent sentence** = sentence which takes place at the same time as another; *he was given two concurrent jail sentences of six months*; *(in the EU)* **concurrent power** = power which is held concurrently by a Member State and by the community, where the Member State can exercise the power up to the point at which the community exercises its rights (if the community acts, the power becomes exclusive to the community and the Member State can no longer act)

concurrently [kən'kʌrəntli] *adverb* taking place at the same time; *he was sentenced to two periods of two years in prison, the sentences to run concurrently*; *see also* CONSECUTIVE, CONSECUTIVELY

condemn [kən'dem] *verb* **(a)** to sentence someone to suffer punishment; *the prisoners were condemned to death*; **condemned cell** = cell where a prisoner is kept who has been sentenced to death **(b)** to say that a dwelling is not fit for people to live in

condemnation [kɒndem'neɪʃn] *noun* **(a)** sentencing of someone to a certain punishment **(b)** forfeiting a piece of property when it has been legally seized

condition [kən'dıʃn] *noun* **(a)** term of a contract or duty which has to be carried out as part of a contract, something which has to be agreed before a contract becomes valid; **conditions of employment** *or* **conditions of service** = terms of a contract of employment; **conditions of sale** = agreed ways in which a sale takes place (such as discounts or credit terms); **on condition that** = provided that; *they were granted the lease on condition that they paid the legal costs*; **condition precedent** = condition which says that a right will not be granted until something is done; **condition subsequent** = condition which says that a contract will be modified or annulled if something is not done **(b)** general state; *item sold in good condition*; *what was the condition of the car when it was sold?*

conditional [kən'dıʃənl] *adjective* provided that certain things take place, (agreement) which is dependent on something; **to give a conditional acceptance** = to accept, provided that certain things happen or certain terms apply; **the offer is conditional on the board's acceptance** = the offer will only go through if the board accepts it; **he made a conditional offer** = he offered to buy, provided that certain terms applied; **conditional discharge** = allowing a prisoner to be set free, with no punishment, provided that he does not commit a crime for a period of time; **conditional will** = will which takes effect when the person dies, but only if certain conditions apply

conditional fee [kən'dıʃənl 'fi:] *noun* fee which is paid only if the case is won (NOTE: also called a **contingent fee** *or* **success fee**); **conditional fee agreement** = agreement between a client and a lawyer that the lawyer will only receive a fee if the case is successful

COMMENT: conditional fee agreements originally covered a limited range of cases, but are now applied to insolvency, defamation, civil liberties, intellectual property, employment and many other areas of action. These agreements allow clients to agree with their lawyers that the lawyers will not receive all or part of the usual fees or expenses if the case is lost; if the case is won, on the other hand, the client agrees to pay an extra fee in addition to the normal fee. Insurance policies are available to people contemplating legal action to cover the costs of the other party and the client's own fees if the case is lost

conditionally [kən'dıʃənli] *adverb* provided certain things take place; **to accept an offer conditionally** = to accept provided certain conditions are fulfilled

condominium [kɒndə'mınıəm] *noun* **(a)** rule of a colony or protected territory by two or more countries together **(b)** *US* system of ownership, where a person owns an individual apartment in a building, together with a share of the land and common parts (stairs, roof, etc.)

condonation [kɒndə'neıʃn] *noun* the forgiving by one spouse of the acts of the other (especially forgiving adultery)

condone [kən'dəun] *verb* to forgive (criminal behaviour); *the court cannot condone your treatment of your children*

conducive [kən'dju:sıv] *adjective* which is likely to produce; *the threat of strike action is not conducive to an easy solution to the dispute*

conduct 1 ['kɒndʌkt] *noun* **(a)** way of behaving; *he was arrested for disorderly conduct in the street*; **code of conduct** = informal (sometimes written) rules by which a group of people work **(b)** bad way of behaving; *she divorced her husband because of his conduct*; **conduct conducive to a breach of the peace** = way of behaving (using rude or threatening language in speech or writing) which seems likely to cause a breach of the peace **2** [kən'dʌkt] *verb* to carry on; *to conduct discussions or negotiations*; *the chairman conducted the proceedings very efficiently*

Confederacy or **Confederate States** [kən'fedərəsi or kən'fedərət 'steɪts]; *(American History)* group of Southern states which seceded from the Union and fought the North in the American Civil War (1861 - 1865)

confederation or **confederacy** [kənfedə'reɪʃn or kən'fedərəsi] *noun* group of independent states or organizations working together for common aims; *a loose confederation of states in the area*; **the Confederation of British Industry (CBI)** = organization representing employers in the UK; **Confédération Helvétique** = official name for Switzerland

COMMENT: a confederation (as in Switzerland) is a less centralized form of government than a federation (such as Germany)

confer [kən'fɜ:] *verb* **(a)** to give power or responsibility to someone; *the discretionary powers conferred on the tribunal by statute* **(b)** to discuss; *the Chief Constable conferred with the Superintendent in charge of the case*

conference ['kɒnfərəns] *noun* **(a)** meeting of a group of people to discuss something; *the Police Federation is holding its annual conference this week*; *the Labour Party Annual Conference was held in Brighton this year*; *he presented a motion to the conference*; *the conference passed a motion in favour of unilateral nuclear disarmament*; **conference agenda** = business which is to be discussed at a conference; **conference papers** = copies of lectures given at a conference, printed and published after the conference has ended; **conference proceedings** = written report of what has been discussed at a conference; **press conference** = meeting where reporters from newspapers and TV are invited to ask a minister questions, to hear the result of a court case, etc. (NOTE: in some political parties (such as the British Labour Party), the word **Conference** is used without **the** to indicate that it is not simply a meeting, but a decision-making body: **decisions of Conference are binding on the Executive; Conference passed a motion in support of**

trade unions) **(b)** *US* meeting between representatives of the Senate and House of Representatives (called managers) to discuss differences of opinion over a bill

confess [kən'fes] *verb* to admit that you have committed a crime; *after six hours' questioning by the police the accused man confessed*

confession [kən'feʃn] *noun* (i) admitting that you have committed a crime; (ii) document in which you admit that you have committed a crime; *the police sergeant asked him to sign his confession*; *the accused typed his own confession statement*; *the confession was not admitted in court, because the accused claimed it had been extorted*; **confession and avoidance** = admission by a party of the allegations made against him, but at the same time bringing forward new pleadings which make the allegations void

confidence ['kɒnfɪdəns] *noun* **(a)** feeling sure, being certain or having trust in (someone); *the sales teams do not have much confidence in their manager*; *the board has total confidence in the managing director*; **confidence vote** or **vote of no confidence** = vote to show that a person or group is or is not trusted; *he proposed a vote of confidence in the government*; *the chairman resigned after the motion of no confidence was passed at the AGM* **(b)** trusting someone with a secret; **breach of confidence** = betraying a secret which someone has told you; **in confidence** = in secret; *I will show you the report in confidence*

confidence trick *US* **confidence game** ['kɒnfɪdəns 'trɪk or 'geɪm] *noun* business deal where someone gains another person's confidence and then tricks him

confidence trickster *US* **confidence man** ['kɒnfɪdəns 'trɪkstə] *noun* person who carries out confidence tricks on people

confidential [kɒnfɪ'denʃl] *adjective* secret between two persons or a small group of people; *the letter was marked 'Private and Confidential'*; **confidential**

information = information which is secret, and which must not be passed on to other people; *he was accused of passing on confidential information*; *the knowledge which an employee has of the working of the firm for which he works can be seen to be confidential information which he must not pass on to another firm*

confidentiality [kɒnfɪdenʃiˈælətɪ] *noun* state of being confidential

confine [kənˈfaɪn] *verb* to keep (a criminal) in a room or area; **confined to barracks (CB)** = (soldier) who is sentenced to stay in the barracks for a set period of time and not to go outside

confinement [kənˈfaɪnmənt] *noun* being kept in a place as a punishment; **solitary confinement** = being kept alone in a cell, without being able to speak to other prisoners; *he was kept in solitary confinement for a week*

confirm [kənˈfɜːm] *verb* to say that something is certain or is correct; *the Court of Appeal has confirmed the judge's decision*; *his secretary phoned to confirm the hotel room* or *the ticket* or *the agreement* or *the booking*; **to confirm someone in a job** = to say that someone is now permanently in the job

confiscation [kɒnfɪsˈkeɪʃn] *noun* act of confiscating

confiscate [ˈkɒnfɪskeɪt] *verb* to take away private property into the possession of the state; *the court ordered the drugs to be confiscated*

conflict 1 [ˈkɒnflɪkt] *noun* **conflict of interest(s)** = situation where a person may profit personally from decisions which he takes in his official capacity, may not be able to act properly because of some other person or matter with which he is connected; **Conflict of Laws** = section in a country's legal statutes which deals with disputes between that country's laws and those of another country **2** [kənˈflɪkt] *verb* not to agree; *the evidence of the wife conflicts with that of her husband*; *the UK legislation conflicts with the directives of the EC*

conflicting evidence [kənˈflɪktɪŋ ˈevɪdəns] *noun* evidence from different witnesses which does not agree; *the jury has to decide who to believe among a mass of conflicting evidence*

conform [kənˈfɔːm] *verb* to act in accordance with something; *the proposed Bill conforms to the recommendations of the Royal Commission*

conformance [kənˈfɔːməns] *noun* acting in accordance with a rule; *in conformance with the directives of the Commission*; *he was criticized for non-conformance with the regulations*

conformity [kənˈfɔːmətɪ] *noun* **in conformity with** = agreeing with; *he has acted in conformity with the regulations*

Congress [ˈkɒŋgres] *noun* elected federal legislative body in many countries, especially in the USA (formed of the House of Representatives and the Senate); *the President is counting on a Democrat majority in Congress*; *he was first elected to Congress in 1988*; *at a joint session of Congress, the President called for support for his plan* (NOTE: often used without **the** except when referring to a particular legislature: **the US Congress met in emergency session; the Republicans had a majority in both houses of the 1974 Congress**); **Congress Party** = one of the largest political parties in India

Congressional [kənˈgreʃənl] *adjective* referring to Congress; *a Congressional subcommittee*; **the Congressional Record** = printed record of proceedings in the House of Representatives and Senate, with verbatim text of the speeches made

Congressman *or* **Congresswoman** [ˈkɒŋgresmən *or* ˈkɒŋgreswʊmən] *noun* member of the US Congress (NOTE: when used with a name, **Congressman Smith**, it refers to a member of the House of Representatives)

conjugal [ˈkɒndʒəgəl] *adjective* referring to marriage; **conjugal rights** =

rights of a husband and wife in relation to each other

conman ['kɒnmæn] *noun (informal)* = CONFIDENCE TRICKSTER

connected persons [kə'nektɪd 'pɜːsənz] *noun* people who are closely related to, or have a close business association with, a certain company director

connection [kə'nekʃn] *noun* link, something which joins; *is there a connection between the loss of the documents and the death of the lawyer?*; **in connection with** = referring to; *the police want to interview the man in connection with burglaries committed last November*

connivance [kə'naɪvəns] *noun* shutting one's eyes to wrongdoing, knowing that a crime is being committed, but not reporting it; *with the connivance of the customs officers, he managed to bring the goods into the country*

connive [kə'naɪv] *verb* **to connive at something** = to shut one's eyes to wrongdoing, to know that a crime is being committed, but not to report it

consecutive *adjective* which follows; **consecutive sentences** = two or more sentences which follow one after the other

consecutively [kən'sekjʊtɪvli] *adverb* which follows; *he was sentenced to two periods of two years in jail, the sentences to run consecutively*; *see also* CONCURRENT, CONCURRENTLY

consensual [kən'sensjuəl] *adjective* which happens by agreement; **consensual acts** = sexual acts which both parties agree should take place

consensus [kə'sensəs] *noun* general agreement; *there was a consensus between all parties as to the next steps to be taken*; *in the absence of a consensus, no decisions could be reached*; **consensus politics** = way of ruling a country, where the main political parties agree in general on policy

consensus ad idem [kɒn'sensəs 'æd 'ɪdem] *Latin phrase meaning* 'agreement to this same thing': real agreement to a contract by both parties

consent [kən'sent] **1** *noun* agreeing that something should happen; *he borrowed the car without the owner's consent*; **the age of consent** = sixteen years old (when a girl can agree to have sexual intercourse); **informed consent** = agreement given by a patient or the guardians of a patient after they have been given all the necessary information, that an operation can be carried out; **consent judgment,** *US* **consent decree** = agreement of the parties in a lawsuit to a judgment which then becomes the settlement; **consent order** = court order that someone must not do something without the agreement of another party; *US* **Consent Calendar** *see comment at* CALENDAR **2** *verb* to agree that something should be done; *the judge consented to the request of the prosecution counsel*

consequent on *or* **upon** ['kɒnsɪkwənt 'ɒn] *adjective* which follows as a result of; *the manufacturer is not liable for injuries consequent on the use of this apparatus*

consequential [kɒnsɪ'kwenʃl] *adjective* which follows as a result of; **consequential damages** = damages suffered as a consequence of using a piece of equipment, software, etc. (for example, the stoppage of business activities because of computer or software failure)

consider [kən'sɪdə] *verb* **(a)** to think seriously about something; **to consider the terms of a contract** = to examine and discuss if the terms are acceptable; **the judge asked the jury to consider their verdict** = he asked the jury to discuss the evidence they had heard and decide if the accused was guilty or not **(b)** to believe; *he is considered to be one of the leading divorce lawyers*; *the law on libel is considered too lenient*

consideration [kənsɪdə'reɪʃn] *noun* **(a)** serious thought; *we are giving* *consideration to moving the head office to Scotland*; **to take something into consideration** = to think about something when deciding what to do; *having taken the age of the accused into consideration, the court has decided to give him a suspended sentence*; **to ask for other offences to be taken into consideration** = to confess to other offences after being accused or convicted of one offence, so that the sentence can cover all of them; *the accused admitted six other offences, and asked for them to be taken into consideration* **(b)** the price (but not necessarily money, it could be a free holiday, for example) paid by one person in exchange for another person promising to do something, an essential element in the formation of a contract; **for a small consideration** = for a small fee or payment; **executed consideration** = consideration where one party has made a promise in exchange for which the other party has done something for him; **executory consideration** = consideration where one party makes a promise in exchange for a counter-promise from the other party

consign [kənˈsaɪn] *verb* **to consign goods to someone** = to send goods to someone for him to use or to sell for you

consignation [kɒnsaɪˈneɪʃn] *noun* act of consigning

consignee [kɒnsaɪˈniː] *noun* person who receives goods from someone for his own use or to sell for the person who sends them

consignment [kənˈsaɪnmənt] *noun* **(a)** sending of goods to someone who will hold them for you and sell them on your behalf; **consignment note** = note saying that goods have been sent; **goods on consignment** = goods kept for another company to be sold on their behalf for a commission **(b)** certain quantity of goods sent for sale; *a consignment of goods has arrived*; *we are expecting a consignment of cars from Japan*

consignor [kənˈsaɪnə] *noun* person who consigns goods to someone

COMMENT: the goods remain the property of the consignor until the consignee sells them

consistent [kənˈsɪstənt] *adjective* which does not contradict, which agrees with; *the sentence is consistent with government policy on the treatment of young offenders*

consolidate [kənˈsɒlɪdeɪt] *verb* to bring several Acts of Parliament together into one act; to hear several sets of proceedings together; *the judge ordered the actions to be consolidated*

Consolidated Fund [kənˈsɒlɪdeɪtɪd ˈfʌnd] *noun* fund of money formed of all taxes and other government revenues; *see also* EXCHEQUER

Consolidating Act [kənˈsɒlɪdeɪtɪŋ ˈækt] *noun* Act of Parliament which brings together several previous Acts which relate to the same subject; *see also* CODIFICATION

consolidation [kənsɒlɪˈdeɪʃn] *noun* (i) bringing together various Acts of Parliament which deal with one subject into one single Act; (ii) procedure whereby several sets of proceedings are heard together by the court

consortium [kənˈsɔːtɪəm] *noun* **(a)** group of different companies which work together on one project **(b)** right of a husband and wife to the love and support of the other

conspiracy [kənˈspɪrəsi] *noun* agreeing with another person or other people to commit a crime or tort

COMMENT: conspiracy to commit a crime is itself a crime

conspire [kənˈspaɪə] *verb* to agree with another person or other people to commit a crime or tort

constable [ˈkʌnstəbl] *noun* **police constable** *or* **woman police constable** = lowest rank of police officer; *the sergeant* *and six constables searched the premises* (NOTE: constable can be used to address a policeman; also used with a name: **Constable Smith;** it is usually abbreviated to PC or WPC)

constituency [kən'stɪtjuənsi] *noun* **(a)** area of a country which is represented by a Member of Parliament; *he represents one of the northern constituencies*; *the UK is divided into 650 single-member constituencies*; **a good constituency MP** = an MP who looks after the interests of his constituents well; **constituency party** = branch of a national political party in a constituency **(b)** area of support; *the leader's natural constituency is the working class*

constituent [kən'stɪtjuənt] *noun* person who lives in a constituency; *the MP had a mass of letters from his constituents complaining about aircraft noise*

constitute ['kɒnstɪtjuːt] *verb* to make or to form; *the documents constitute primary evidence*; *this Act constitutes a major change in government policy*; *conduct tending to interfere with the course of justice constitutes contempt of court*

constitution [kɒnstɪ'tjuːʃn] *noun* **(a)** (usually written) laws under which a country is ruled; *the freedom of the individual is guaranteed by the country's constitution*; *the new president asked the assembly to draft a new constitution* **(b)** written rules or regulations of a society, association or club; *under the society's constitution, the chairman is elected for a two-year period*; *payments to officers of the association are not allowed by the constitution*

COMMENT: most countries have written constitutions, usually drafted by lawyers, which can be amended by an Act of the country's legislative body. The United States constitution was drawn up by Thomas Jefferson after the country became independent, and has numerous amendments (the first ten amendments being the Bill of Rights). Great Britain is unusual in that it has no written constitution, and relies on precedent and the body of laws passed over the years to act as a safeguard of the rights of the citizens and the legality of government

constitutional [kɒnstɪ'tjuːʃnl] *adjective* **(a)** referring to a country's constitution; *censorship of the press is not constitutional*; **constitutional law** = laws under which a country is ruled, laws relating to government and its function; **constitutional lawyer** = lawyer who specializes in constitutional law, in drafting or interpreting constitutions; **constitutional right** = right which is guaranteed by a constitution **(b)** according to an organisation's constitution; *the re-election of the chairman for a second term is not constitutional*; *see also* MONARCHY, UNCONSTITUTIONAL

construction [kən'strʌkʃn] *noun* **(a)** building; **construction company** = company which specializes in building; **under construction** = being built; *the airport is under construction* **(b)** interpreting the meaning of words; **to put a construction on words** = to suggest a meaning for words which is not immediately obvious

constructive [kən'strʌktɪv] *adjective* which helps in the making of something; *she made some constructive suggestions for improving management-worker relations*; *we had a constructive proposal from a shipping company in Italy*; **constructive dismissal** = situation when a worker leaves his job voluntarily, but because of pressure from the management; **constructive knowledge** = knowledge of a fact or matter which the law says a person has, whether or not that person actually has it; **constructive notice** = knowledge which the law says a person has of something (whether or not the person actually has it) because certain information is available to him if he makes reasonable inquiry; *(insurance)* **constructive total loss** = loss where the item insured has been thrown away as it is likely to be irreplaceable;

constructive trust = trust arising by reason of a person's behaviour

construe [kən'struː] *verb* to interpret the meaning of words or of a document; *the court construed the words to mean that there was a contract between the parties*; *written opinion is not admissible as evidence for the purposes of construing a deed of settlement*

consul ['kɒnsl] *noun* **(a)** person who represents a country in a foreign city, and helps his country's citizens and business interests there; *the British Consul in Seville*; *the French Consul in Manchester*; **honorary consul** = person who represents a country in a foreign city, but is not an employee of the country's government **(b)** *(in Roman government)* one of two magistrates, elected every year; **First Consul** = title originally taken by Napoleon, before he became Emperor

consular ['kɒnsjʊlə] *adjective* referring to a consul; *the consular offices are open every weekday*; *he spends most of his time on consular duties*; **consular agent** = person with the duties of a consul in a small foreign town

consulate ['kɒnsjʊlət] *noun* house or office of a consul; *there will be a party at the consulate on National Day*

consul-general ['kɒnsl'dʒenrəl] *noun* consul based in a large foreign city, who is responsible for other consuls in the area (NOTE: plural is **consuls-general** or **consul-generals**)

consult [kən'sʌlt] *verb* to ask an expert for advice; *he consulted his solicitor about the letter*

consultancy [kən'sʌltənsi] *noun* act of giving specialist advice; *a consultancy firm*; *he offers a consultancy service*

consultant [kən'sʌltənt] *noun* specialist who gives advice; *engineering consultant*; *management consultant*; *tax consultant*

consultation [kɒnsʌl'teɪʃn] *noun* **(a)** asking for specialist advice; **consultation paper** = paper which is issued by a

government department to people who are asked to comment and make suggestions for improvement **(b)** meeting between a client and his professional adviser, such as between a QC (and often a junior barrister) and a solicitor and clients

consultative [kən'sʌltətɪv] *adjective* being asked to give advice; *the report of a consultative body*; *he is acting in a consultative capacity*; **consultative document** = paper which is issued by a government department to people who are asked to comment and make suggestions for improvement

consulting [kən'sʌltɪŋ] *adjective* person who gives specialist advice; *consulting engineer*

consumer [kən'sjuːmə] *noun* person or company which buys and uses goods and services; *gas consumers are protesting at the increase in prices*; *the factory is a heavy consumer of water*; **consumer council** = group representing the interests of consumers; **consumer credit** = provision of loans by finance companies to help people buy goods; **consumer goods** = goods bought by the general public and not by businesses; **consumer legislation** = laws which give rights to people who buy goods or who pay for services; **consumer protection** = protecting consumers from unfair or illegal business practices

consummation [kɒnsə'meɪʃn] *noun* having sexual intercourse for the first time after the marriage ceremony

contact 1 ['kɒntækt] *noun* **(a)** person you know, person you can ask for help or advice; *he has many contacts in the city*; *who is your contact in the Ministry?* **(b)** act of getting in touch with someone; **I have lost contact with them** = I do not communicate with them any longer; **he put me in contact with a good lawyer** = he told me how to get in touch with a good lawyer **2** [kən'tækt] *verb* to get in touch with someone, to communicate with someone; *he tried to contact his office by phone*; *can you contact the solicitors representing the vendors?*

contemnor [kənˈtemnə] *noun* person who commits a contempt of court

contempt [kənˈtempt] *noun* being rude, showing lack of respect to a court or Parliament; **to be in contempt** = to have shown disrespect to a court, especially by disobeying a court order; **contempt of court** = being rude to a court, as by bad behaviour in court, or by refusing to carry out a court order; *at common law, conduct tending to interfere with the course of justice in particular legal proceedings constitutes criminal contempt*; **contempt of Parliament** *or* **contempt of the House** = conduct which may bring the authority of Parliament into disrepute; **to purge one's contempt** = to apologize, to do something to show that you are sorry for the lack of respect shown

content [ˈkɒntent] *noun* the ideas inside a letter, etc.; **the content of the letter** = the real meaning of the letter

contents [ˈkɒntents] *plural noun* things contained, what is inside something; *the contents of the bottle poured out onto the floor*; *the customs officials inspected the contents of the box*; **the contents of the letter** = the words written in the letter

contentious [kənˈtenʃəs] *adjective & noun* (legal business) where there is a dispute

contest 1 [ˈkɒntest] *noun* competition, especially in an election **2** [kənˈtest] *verb* **(a)** to argue that a decision or a ruling is wrong; *I wish to contest the statement made by the witness* **(b)** to fight (an election); *the seat is being contested by five candidates* **(c)** **contested takeover** = takeover where the directors of the company being bought do not recommend the bid and try to fight it

context [ˈkɒntekst] *noun* other words which surround a word or phrase; general situation in which something happens; *the words can only be understood in the context of the phrase in which they occur*; *the action of the police has to be seen in the context of the riots against the government*; **the words were quoted out of context** = the words were quoted without the rest of the surrounding text, so as to give them a different meaning (NOTE: an example of words being quoted out of context might be: 'the Minister has said that the government might review the case', when what the Minister actually said was: 'it is true that under certain circumstances the government might review such a case, but the present situation is quite different')

contingency [kənˈtɪnʒənsi] *noun* possible state of emergency when decisions will have to be taken quickly; **contingency fund** *or* **contingency reserve** = money set aside in case it is needed urgently; **contingency plan** = plan which will be put into action if something happens which is expected to happen

contingent [kənˈtɪnʒənt] *adjective* **contingent expenses** = expenses which will be incurred only if something happens; **contingent fee** = fee paid to a lawyer which is a proportion of the damages recovered in the case; *US* **contingent interest** = interest in property which may or may not exist in the future; **contingent policy** = policy which pays out only if something happens (as if the person named in the policy dies before the person due to benefit)

contra [ˈkɒntrə] **1** *preposition* against, differing **2** *noun* **contra account** = account which offsets another account; **contra entry** = entry made in the opposite side of an account to make an earlier entry worthless (i.e. a debit against a credit); **per contra** *or* **as per contra** = words showing that a contra entry has been made **3** *verb* **to contra an entry** = to enter a similar amount in the opposite side of an account

contraband [ˈkɒntrəbænd] *noun* **contraband (goods)** = goods brought into or taken out of a country illegally, without paying customs duty

contract [ˈkɒntrækt] **1** *noun* **(a)** legal agreement between two or more parties; *to draw up a contract*; *to draft a contract*; *to sign a contract*; **the contract is binding on both parties** = both parties signing the contract must do what is agreed; **by private contract** = by private legal agreement; **under contract** = bound by the terms of a contract; *the firm is under contract to deliver the goods by November*; **to void a contract** = to make a contract invalid; **contract of service** *or* **of employment** = contract between management and employee showing all conditions of work; **service contract** = contract between a company and a director or employee showing all conditions of work; **exchange of contracts** = point in the conveyance of a property when the solicitors for the buyer and seller hand over the contract of sale which then becomes binding; **contract note** = note showing that shares have been bought or sold but not yet paid for **(b) contract law** *or* **law of contract** = laws relating to agreements **(c) contract for services** = agreement for supply of a service or goods; *contract for the supply of spare parts*; *to enter into a contract to supply spare parts*; *to sign a contract for £10,000 worth of spare parts*; **to put work out to contract** = to decide that work should be done by another company on a contract, rather than employing members of staff to do it; **to award a contract to a company** *or* **to place a contract with a company** = to decide that a company shall have the contract to do work for you; **to tender for a contract** = to put forward an estimate of cost for work to be carried out under contract; **breach of contract** = breaking the terms of a contract; **the company is in breach of contract** = the company has failed to do what was agreed in the contract; **contract work** = work done according to a written agreement **(d)** *(slang)* agreement to kill someone for a payment; **there is a contract out for him** = someone has offered money for him to be killed; **contract killer** = person who will kill someone if paid to do so **2** *verb* to agree to do some work by contract; *to contract to supply spare parts* *or* *to contract for the supply of spare parts*; **the supply of spare parts was contracted out to Smith Ltd** = Smith Ltd was given the contract for supplying spare parts; **to contract out of an agreement** = to

withdraw from an agreement with written permission of the other party

COMMENT: a contract is an agreement between two or more parties to create legal obligations between them. Some contracts are made 'under seal', i.e. they are signed and sealed by the parties; most contracts are made orally or in writing. The essential elements of a contract are: (a) that an offer made by one party should be accepted by the other; (b) consideration; (c) the intention to create legal relations. The terms of a contract may be express or implied. A breach of contract by one party entitles the other party to sue for damages or in some cases to seek specific performance

contracting ['kɒntræktɪŋ] *adjective* **contracting party** = person or company which signs a contract

contractor [kən'træktə] *noun* person who enters into a contract, especially a person or company which does work according to a written agreement

contractual [kən'træktʃuəl] *adjective* according to a contract; **contractual liability** = legal responsibility for something as stated in a contract; **to fulfil your contractual obligations** = to do what you have agreed to do in a contract; **he is under no contractual obligation to buy** = he has signed no agreement to buy

contractually [kən'træktʃuəli] *adverb* according to a contract; *the company is contractually bound to pay his expenses*

contradict [kɒntrə'dɪkt] *verb* not to agree with, to say exactly the opposite; *the statement contradicts the report in the newspapers*; *the witness contradicted himself several times*

contradiction [kɒntrə'dɪkʃn] *noun* statement which contradicts; *the witness' evidence was a mass of contradictions*; *there is a contradiction between the Minister's statement in the House of Commons and the reports published in the newspapers*

contradictory [kɒntrə'dɪktri] *adjective* which does not agree; *a mass of contradictory evidence*

contra proferentem ['kɒntræ prɒfə'rentem] *Latin phrase meaning* 'against the one making the point': rule that an ambiguity in a document is construed against the party who drafted it

contrary ['kɒntrəri] *noun* opposite instructions; **failing instructions to the contrary** = unless different instructions are given; **on the contrary** = quite the opposite; *counsel was not annoyed with the witness - on the contrary, he praised her*

contravene [kɒntrə'viːn] *verb* to break or to go against (rules, regulations); *the workshop has contravened the employment regulations; the fire department can close a restaurant if it contravenes the safety regulations*

contravention [kɒntrə'venʃn] *noun* act of breaking a regulation; **in contravention of** = which contravenes; *the restaurant is in contravention of the safety regulations; the management of the cinema locked the fire exits in contravention of the fire regulations*

contribute [kən'trɪbjuːt] *verb* (a) to give money, to add to money; *to contribute 10% of the profits; he contributed to the pension fund for ten years* (b) **to contribute to** = to help something; *the public response to the request for information contributed to the capture of the gang*

contribution [kɒntrɪ'bjuːʃn] *noun* (a) money paid to add to a sum; **employer's contribution** = money paid by an employer towards a worker's pension; **National Insurance contributions** = money paid each month by a worker and the company to the National Insurance; **pension contributions** = money paid by a company or worker into a pension fund (b) *(in civil cases)* the right of someone to get money from a third party to cover the amount which he himself has to pay

contributor [kən'trɪbjutə] *noun* **contributor of capital** = person who contributes capital to a company

contributory [kən'trɪbjutəri] **1** *adjective* **contributory pension plan** *or* **scheme** = pension plan where the employee has to contribute a percentage of salary; **contributory causes** = causes which help something to take place; **contributory factor** = something which contributes to a result; **contributory negligence** = negligence partly caused by the claimant and partly by the defendant, which results in harm done to the claimant and for which part of the blame can be apportioned to the claimant **2** *noun* shareholder who is liable in respect of partly paid shares to a company being wound up

con trick ['kɒn 'trɪk] *noun (informal)* = CONFIDENCE TRICK

control [kən'trəʊl] **1** *noun* **(a)** power, being able to direct something; *the company is under the control of three shareholders; the family lost control of its business*; **to gain control of a business** = to buy more than 50% of the shares so that you can direct the business; **to lose control of a business** = to find that you have less than 50% of the shares in a company, and so are not longer able to direct it; **control test** = test to decide if someone is an employee or is self-employed (used for purposes of tax assessment) **(b)** restricting or checking something, making sure that something is kept in check; **under control** = kept in check; **out of control** = not kept in check **(c)** **exchange controls** = government restrictions on changing the local currency into foreign currency; *the government imposed exchange controls to stop the rush to buy dollars*; **price controls** = legal measures to prevent prices rising too fast; **rent controls** = government regulation of rents charged by landlords **(d)** **control systems** = systems used to check that a computer system is working correctly **2** *verb* **(a) to control a business** = to direct a business; *the business is controlled by a company based in Luxembourg; the company is controlled* *by the majority shareholder* **(b)** to make sure that something is kept in check or is not allowed to develop; *the government is fighting to control inflation* or *to control the rise in the cost of living*

controlled [kənˈtrəʊld] *adjective* **(a)** ruled, kept in check; **government-controlled** = ruled by a government; **controlled economy** = economy where most business activity is directed by orders from the government **(b) controlled drugs,** *US* **controlled substances** = drugs which are not freely available, which are restricted by law, and which are classified (Class A, B, C), and of which possession may be an offence; *see comment at* DRUG

controller [kənˈtrəʊlə] *noun* **(a)** person who controls (especially the finances of a company) **(b)** *US* chief accountant in a company

controlling [kənˈtrəʊlɪŋ] *adjective* **to have a controlling interest in a company** = to own more than 50% of the shares so that you can direct how the company is run

convene [kənˈviːn] *verb* to ask people to come together; *to convene a meeting of shareholders*

convenience [kənˈviːnɪəns] *noun* **at your earliest convenience** = as soon as you find it possible; **ship sailing under a flag of convenience** = ship flying the flag of a country which may have no ships of its own but allows ships of other countries to be registered in its ports

convenient [kənˈviːnɪənt] *adjective* suitable, handy; *a bank draft is a convenient way of sending money abroad*; *is 9.30 a.m. a convenient time for the meeting?*

convenor [kənˈviːnə] *noun* person who convenes a meeting, especially a trade unionist who organizes union meetings

convention [kənˈvenʃn] *noun* **(a)** general way in which something is usually done, though not enforced by law; *it is the convention for American lawyers to designate themselves 'Esquire'* **(b)**

meeting or series of meetings held to discuss and decide important matters; *the Democratic Party Convention to select the presidential candidate was held in Washington* **(c)** international treaty; *the Geneva Convention on Human Rights*; *the three countries are all signatories of the convention*

conversion [kənˈvɜːʃn] *noun* tort of dealing with a person's property in a way which is not consistent with that person's rights over it; **conversion of funds** = using money which does not belong to you for a purpose for which it is not supposed to be used

convert [kənˈvɜːt] *verb* **(a)** to change property into another form (as into cash) **(b)** to change money of one country for money of another; *we converted our pounds into Swiss francs* **(c) to convert funds to one's own use** = to use someone else's money for yourself

convertible [kənˈvɜːtəbl] *adjective* which can be changed into something else (such as cash); **convertible loan stock** = money which can be exchanged for shares at a later date

convey [kənˈveɪ] *verb* **(a)** to carry goods from one place to another **(b) to convey a property to a purchaser** = to pass the ownership of the property to the purchaser

conveyance [kənˈveɪəns] *noun* legal document which transfers the ownership of land from the seller to the buyer; **fraudulent conveyance** = putting a property into someone else's possession to avoid it being seized to pay creditors

conveyancer [kənˈveɪənsə] *noun* person who draws up a conveyance

conveyancing [kənˈveɪənsɪŋ] *noun* (i) drawing up the document which legally transfers a property from a seller to a buyer; (ii) law and procedure relating to the purchase and sale of property; **do-it-yourself conveyancing** = drawing up a legal conveyance without the help of a lawyer

convict 1 [ˈkɒnvɪkt] *noun* person who is kept in prison as a punishment for a crime; **convict settlement** = prison camp where convicts are sent **2** [kənˈvɪkt] *verb* **to convict someone of a crime** = to find that someone is guilty of a crime; *he was convicted of manslaughter and sent to prison*; **convicted criminal** = criminal who has been found guilty and sentenced

conviction [kənˈvɪkʃn] *noun* **(a)** being sure that something is true; *it is his conviction that the claimant has brought the case maliciously* **(b)** finding that a person accused of a crime is guilty; *he has had ten convictions for burglary*; *see also* SPENT; *compare* SENTENCE

cooling off period *US* cooling time [ˈkuːlɪŋ ˈɒf ˈpiːriəd] *noun* (i) during an industrial dispute, a period when negotiations have to be carried on and no action can be taken by either side; (ii) period when a person is allowed to think about something which he has agreed to buy on hire-purchase and possibly change his mind

co-operation procedure [kəʊɒpəˈreɪʃn prəˈsiːdʒə] *noun* *(in the EU)* procedure introduced by the Single European Act which gives the European Parliament a more important role in considering European legislation

COMMENT: originally the co-operation procedure was restricted to measures concerning the internal market (free movement of people within the union, no discrimination on grounds of nationality, harmonization of health and safety in the workplace, etc.). It is now used also in connection with European transport policy, training, environmental issues, etc. The co-operation procedure implies that at the end of a discussion period the Council will adopt a 'common position' which must then be approved by the European Parliament. See also COMMON POSITION

co-operative [kəʊˈɒpərətɪv] *noun* business run by a group of workers who are the owners and who share the profits; *industrial co-operative*; *to set up a workers' co-operative*

co-opt [kəʊˈɒpt] *verb* **to co-opt someone onto a committee** = to ask someone to join a committee without being elected

co-owner [kəʊˈəʊnə] *noun* person who owns something jointly with another person or persons; *the two sisters are co-owners of the property*

co-ownership [kəʊˈəʊnəʃɪp] *noun* **(a)** arrangement where two or more persons own a property **(b)** arrangement where partners or workers have shares in a company

cop [kɒp] **1** *noun* *(informal)* **(a)** policeman **(b)** arrest; **it's a fair cop** = you have caught me **2** *verb* *(slang)* to get or to receive; **to cop a plea** = to plead guilty to a lesser charge and so hope the court will give a shorter sentence to save the time of a full trial

co-partner [kəʊˈpɑːtnə] *noun* person who is a partner in a business with another person

co-partnership [kəʊˈpɑːtnəʃɪp] *noun* arrangement where partners or workers have shares in the company

copper [ˈkɒpə] *noun* *GB* *(informal)* policeman

copper-bottomed [ˈkɒpəˈbɒtəmd] *adjective* (guarantee) which cannot possibly be broken

co-property [ˈkəʊˈprɒpəti] *noun* ownership of property by two or more people together

co-proprietor [ˈkəʊprəˈpraɪətə] *noun* person who owns a property with another person or several other people

copy [ˈkɒpi] **1** *noun* **(a)** document which looks the same as another; **carbon copy** = copy made with carbon paper; **certified copy** = document which is certified as being exactly the same in content as the original; **file copy** = copy of a document which is filed in an office for reference **(b)** anything which copies information in a document, by whatever means, including electronic copies, recordings, etc. (**c**) any document; **fair copy** *or* **final copy** = document which is written or typed with no changes or mistakes; **hard copy** = printout of a text which is on a computer, printed copy of something which is on microfilm; **rough copy** = draft of a document which, it is expected, will have changes made to it before it is complete; **top copy** = first or top sheet of a document which is typed with carbon copies **2** *verb* (**a**) to make a second document which is like the first; *he copied the company report at night and took it home* (**b**) to make something which is similar to something else; *she simply copied the design from another fashion designer; he is successful because he copies good ideas from other businesses*

copyright ['kɒpiraɪt] **1** *noun* an author's legal right to publish his or her own work and not to have it copied (lasting fifty years after the author's death under the Berne Convention); similar right of an artist, film maker or musician; **Copyright Act** = an Act of Parliament (such as the Copyright Acts 1911, 1956, 1988, etc.) making copyright legal, and controlling the copying of copyright material; **copyright deposit** = depositing a copy of a published work in a copyright library (usually the main national library), which is part of the formal copyrighting of copyright material; **copyright holder** *or* **copyright owner** = person who owns the copyright in a work; **copyright law** = laws concerning the protection of copyright; **copyright line** = COPYRIGHT NOTICE; **work which is out of copyright** = work by a writer, etc., who has been dead for fifty years, and which anyone can publish; **work still in copyright** = work by a living writer, or by a writer who has not been dead for fifty years; **infringement of copyright** *or* **copyright infringement** = act of illegally copying a work which is in copyright; **copyright notice** = note in a book showing who owns the copyright and the date of ownership; *see also* MORAL RIGHT, PATERNITY **2** *verb* to confirm the copyright of a written work by printing a copyright notice and publishing the work **3** *adjective* covered by the laws of copyright; *it is illegal to take copies of a copyright work*

COMMENT: Copyright exists in original written works, in works of art and works of music; it covers films, broadcasts, recordings, etc.; it also covers the layout of books, newspapers and magazines. Copyright only exists if the work is created by a person who is qualified to hold a copyright, and is published in a country which is qualified to hold a copyright. There is no copyright in ideas, items of news, historical events, items of information, or in titles of artistic works. When a copyright is established, the owner of the copyright can copy his work himself, sell copies of it to the public, perform his work or exhibit it in public, broadcast his work, or adapt it in some way. No other person has the right to do any of these things. Copyright lasts for 50 years after the author's death according to the Berne Convention, and for 25 years according to the Universal Copyright Convention. In the USA, copyright is for 50 years after the death of an author for books published after January 1st, 1978. For books published before that date, the original copyright was for 28 years after the death of the author, and this can be extended for a further 28 year period up to a maximum of 75 years. In 1995, the European Union adopted a copyright term of 70 years after the death of the author. The copyright holder has the right to refuse or to grant permission to copy copyright material, though under the Paris agreement of 1971, the original publishers (representing the author or copyright holder) must, under certain circumstances, grant licences to reprint copyright material. The copyright notice has to include the symbol © the name of the copyright holder and the date of the copyright (which is usually the date of first publication). The notice must be printed in the book and usually appears on the reverse of the title page. A copyright notice is also printed on other forms of printed material such as posters

copyrighted ['kɒpiraɪtɪd] *adjective* in copyright

cordon ['kɔːdən] **1** *noun* **a police cordon** = barriers and policemen put round an area to prevent anyone getting near it **2** *verb* **to cordon off** = to put barriers and policemen round (an area) so that no one can get near it; *the street was cordoned off after the bomb was discovered*

COREPER (= COMMITTEE OF PERMANENT REPRESENTATIVES) *(in the EU)* committee formed of the ambassadors (or permanent representatives) of each Member State to the European Union, set up to make sure that matters are dealt with on a continuing basis when ministers themselves are not taking part in Council meetings. The permanent representatives act as representatives of their national governments, but also form a cohesive body as members of COREPER

co-respondent ['kəʊrɪs'pɒndənt] *noun* party to divorce proceedings who has committed adultery with another person (NOTE: do not confuse with **correspondent**)

coroner ['kɒrənə] *noun* public official (either a doctor or a lawyer) who investigates sudden violent deaths; **coroner's court** = court presided over by a coroner; **coroner's inquest** = inquest carried out by a coroner into a death

COMMENT: coroners investigate deaths which are violent or unexpected, deaths which may be murder or manslaughter, deaths of prisoners and deaths involving the police. A coroner must also be notified when someone finds treasure; see TRESAURE TROVER

corporal punishment ['kɔːprəl 'pʌnɪʃmənt] *noun* punishing a criminal by beating him

corporate ['kɔːprət] *adjective* referring to a company; **corporate personality** = legal status of a company, so that it can be treated as a person; **corporate planning** = planning the future work of a whole company; **corporate profits** = profits of a corporation

corporation [kɔːpə'reɪʃn] *noun* **(a)** legal body (such as a limited company or town council) which has been incorporated **(b)** *US* company which is incorporated in the United States **(c)** generally, any large company; **finance corporation** = company which provides money for hire purchase

corporatism ['kɔːpərətɪzm] *noun* system of government where large powerful pressure groups (such as trade unions or institutions) influence the policies of the government

corporatist ['kɔːpərətɪst] *adjective* referring to corporatism; *he holds corporatist views*

corporeal hereditaments [kɔː'pɔːriəl herɪ'dɪtəmənts] *plural noun* rights of property which physically exist, such as houses and furniture

corpse [kɔːps] *noun GB* body of a dead person (NOTE: American English is **cadaver**)

corpus ['kɔːpəs] *noun* body (of laws) (NOTE: plural is **corpora**); *see also* HABEAS CORPUS

corpus delicti ['kɔːpəs dɪ'lɪktaɪ] *Latin phrase meaning* 'the body of the crime': the real proof that a crime has been committed

corpus legis ['kɔːpəs 'ledʒɪs] *Latin phrase meaning* 'body of laws': books containing Roman civil law

correctional institution ['kə'rekʃnl ɪnstɪ'tjuːʃn] *noun US* prison

corrective [kə'rektɪv] *adjective* which punishes (a criminal) in such a way that he becomes a better person; *he was sent to the detention centre for corrective training*

correspondent [kɒrə'spɒndənt] *noun* **(a)** person who writes letters **(b)** journalist who writes articles for a newspaper on specialist subjects; *The Times' legal correspondent*; *he is the Paris correspondent of the Telegraph*; **a court correspondent** = journalist who reports on the activities of a king or queen and the royal family; **a lobby correspondent** = journalist from a newspaper who is part of the lobby which gets private briefings from government ministers (NOTE: do not confuse with **co-respondent**)

corrigendum [kɒrɪˈdʒendəm] *noun* correction, word which has been corrected (NOTE: plural is **corrigenda**)

corroborate [kəˈrɒbəreɪt] *verb* to prove evidence which has already been given; *the witness corroborated the accused's alibi, saying that at the time of the murder he had seen him in Brighton*

corroboration [kərɒbəˈreɪʃn] *noun* evidence which confirms and supports other evidence; *the witness was unable to provide corroboration of what he had told the police*

corroborative [kəˈrɒbərətɪv] *adjective* which corroborates; *the letter provides corroborative evidence, showing that the accused did know that the victim lived alone*

corrupt [kəˈrʌpt] **1** *adjective* (person, especially an official) who takes bribes **2** *verb* **to corrupt someone's morals** = to make someone willing to commit a crime or to act against normal standards of behaviour

corruption [kəˈrʌpʃn] *noun* paying money or giving a favour to someone (usually an official) so that he does what you want; *the government is keen to stamp out corruption in the police force; bribery and corruption are difficult to control*

corruptly [kəˈrʌptli] *adverb* in a corrupt way; *he corruptly offered the officer money to get the charges dropped*

Cosa Nostra [ˈkəʊzə ˈnɒstrə] = MAFIA

cosponsor [ˈkəʊˈspɒnsə] *noun* person who sponsors something with someone else; *the three cosponsors of the bill*

cost [kɒst] **1** *noun* **(a)** amount of money which has to be paid for something; *computer costs are falling each year; we*

cannot afford the cost of two telephone lines*; **to cover costs** = to produce enough money in sales to pay for the costs of production **(b) costs** = expenses involved in a court case, including the fees, expenses and charges levied by the court itself, which can be awarded by the judge to the party which wins (so that the losing side pays the expenses of both sides); *the judge awarded costs to the defendant*; *costs of the case will be borne by the prosecution*; *the court awarded the claimant £2,000 in damages, with costs*; **to pay costs** = to pay the expenses of a court case; **costs order** = court order requiring someone to pay costs; **fixed costs** = set amount of money to which a claimant is entitled in legal proceedings; **taxed costs** = varying amount of costs which can be awarded in legal proceedings; **costs judge** = official of the Supreme Court who assesses the costs of a court action (NOTE: since the introduction of the new Civil Procedure Rules in April 1999, this term has in some cases replaced **Taxing Master**) **2** *verb* **(a)** to have a price; *how much does the machine cost?; rent of the room will cost £50 a day* **(b)** to cost a **product** = to calculate how much money will be needed to make a product, and so work out its selling price

cost of living [ˈkɒst əv ˈlɪvɪŋ] *noun* money which has to be paid for food, heating, rent etc.; *to allow for the cost of living in salaries*; **cost-of-living allowance** = addition to normal salary to cover increases in the cost of living; **cost-of-living increase** = increase in salary to allow it to keep up with the increased cost of living; **cost-of-living index** = way of measuring the cost of living which is shown as a percentage increase on the figure for the previous year

coterminous [ˈkəʊˈtɜːmɪnəs] *adjective* (two things) which terminate at the same time; *the leases are coterminous*

council [ˈkaʊnsəl] *noun* **(a)** official group chosen to run something or to advise on a problem; **consumer council** = group representing the interests of consumers; **borough council** *or* **town council** = representatives elected to run a town;

Security Council = permanent ruling body of the United Nations **(b)** = PRIVY COUNCIL; **Order in Council** = legislation made by the Queen in Council, which is allowed by an Act of Parliament and does not have to be ratified by Parliament

councillor ['kaʊnsələ] *noun* member of a council, especially member of a town council; *see also* PRIVY COUNCILLOR

Council of the European Union

['kaʊnsl əv ðə juːrə'piːən 'juːniən] *noun* one of the four bodies which form the basis of the European Community (NOTE: not to be confused with the **European Council;** formerly the Council of the European Union was called the **Council of Ministers** and it is still sometimes called this)

COMMENT: the Council does not have fixed members, but the Member States are each represented by the relevant government minister. The Council is headed by a President, and the Presidency rotates among the Member States in alphabetical order, each serving for a six-month period. In practice this means that each Member State can control the agenda of the Council, and therefore that of the European Union, for a period of six months, and can try to get as many of its proposals put into legislation as it can during that period. When meeting to discuss general matters the Council is formed of the foreign ministers of the Member States, but when it discusses specialized problems it is formed of the relevant government minister: when discussing agriculture, for example, it is formed of the Agriculture Ministers of the Member States

Council of Ministers ['kaʊnsəl əv 'mɪnɪstəz] *noun see* COUNCIL OF THE EUROPEAN UNION

counsel ['kaʊnsəl] *noun* barrister (or barristers) acting for one of the parties in a legal action; *defence counsel*; *prosecution counsel*; *the claimant appeared in court with his solicitor and two counsel*; **counsel's advice** *or* **opinion** = written

opinion of a barrister about a case; **leading counsel** = main barrister (usually a QC) in a team appearing for one side in a case; **King's Counsel (KC)** *or* **Queen's Counsel (QC)** = senior British lawyer appointed to the rank by the Lord Chancellor (NOTE: there is no plural for **counsel** which is always used in the singular whether it refers to one barrister or several, and it is never used with the article **the** or **a.** On the other hand, the abbreviation QC can have a plural: **two QCs represented the defendant)**

counsellor ['kaʊnsələ] *noun* **(a)** one of the ranks in the diplomatic corps, below Minister **(b)** trained person who gives advice or help; *they went to see a marriage guidance counsellor* **(c)** *US* lawyer who advises a person in a case

count [kaʊnt] **1** *noun* separate charge against an accused person read out in court in the indictment; *he was found guilty on all four counts* **2** *verb* **(a)** to add figures together to make a total; *he counted up the sales for the six months to December* **(b)** to include; *did the defence count the accused's theft of money from the till as part of the total theft?*

counter ['kaʊntə] **1** *noun* long flat surface in a shop for displaying and selling goods; **over the counter** = legally; **goods sold over the counter** = retail sales of goods in shops; **under the counter** = illegally; **under-the-counter sales** = black market sales **2** *adverb* **counter to** = against, opposite; *the decision of the court runs counter to the advice of the clerk to the justices*

counter- ['kaʊntə] *prefix* against

counterclaim ['kaʊntəkleɪm] **1** *noun* **(a)** claim in a court by a defendant against the claimant who is bringing a claim against him (the counterclaim is included in the same proceedings and statement of case as the claim) (NOTE: also called a **Part 20 claim) (b)** claim for damages made in reply to a previous claim; *Jones claimed £25,000 in damages against Smith, and Smith entered a counterclaim of £50,000 for loss of office* **2** *verb* to put in a counterclaim; *Jones claimed £25,000 in damages and Smith counterclaimed £50,000 for loss of office*

counterfeit ['kauntəfit] **1** *adjective* false or imitation (money, or other objects of value); *he was charged with passing counterfeit notes in shops*; *she was selling counterfeit Rolex watches* **2** *verb* to make imitation money or other objects of value

counterfeiting ['kauntəfitiŋ] *noun* crime of making imitation money or other objects of value

counter-intelligence ['kauntəin'telidʒəns] *noun* organization of secret agents whose job is to work against the secret agents of another country; *the offices were bugged by counter-intelligence agents*

countermand ['kauntəmɑ:nd] *verb* to **countermand an order** = to say that an order must not be carried out

counteroffer ['kauntərɒfə] *noun* offer made in reply to another offer

counterpart ['kauntəpɑ:t] *noun* **(a)** copy of a lease **(b)** person who has a similar job in another company; **John is my counterpart in Smith's** = he has a similar post at Smith's as I have here

counter-promise ['kauntəprɒmis] *noun* promise made in reply to a promise

countersign ['kauntəsain] *verb* to sign a document which has already been signed by someone else; *the payment has to be countersigned by the mortgagor*

country ['kʌntri] *noun* land which is an entity and governs itself; *the contract covers sales in the countries of the European Union*; *some African countries export oil*; **country of origin** = country where the goods have been produced or made

county ['kaunti] *noun* one of the administrative divisions of a country; **county council** = group of people elected to run a county; **county town** = town which

is the administrative centre of a county in Britain

COMMENT: rural areas in many countries (such as Britain, New Zealand) and sections of federal states (such as the Provinces of Canada and the States in the USA) are divided into counties. Most counties in Britain are shires (Berkshire, Staffordshire, etc.). Otherwise, the word is used as a title, before the name in Britain (the County of Durham) and after the name in the USA (Marlboro County)

County Court ['kaunti 'kɔ:t] *noun* one of the types of court in England and Wales which hears local civil cases; **County Court Rules (CCR)** = book of procedural rules for County Courts; *see also* GREEN BOOK

COMMENT: there are about 270 County Courts in England and Wales. County Courts are presided over by either district judges or circuit judges. They deal mainly with claims regarding money, but also deal with family matters, bankruptcies and claims concerning land. A district judge will hear most civil cases up to a value of £5,000, and a circuit judge will deal with more serious cases

coup (d'état) ['ku: dei'tæ] *noun* rapid change of government which removes one government by force and replaces it by another; *after the coup, groups of students attacked the police stations*

COMMENT: a coup is usually carried out by a small number of people, who already have some power (such as army officers), while a revolution is a general uprising of a large number of ordinary people. A coup changes the members of a government, but a revolution changes the whole social system

court [kɔ:t] *noun* **(a)** **court of law** *or* **law court** = place where a trial is held; *the law courts are in the centre of the town*; *she works in the law courts as an usher*; **court action** *or* **court case** = legal action or trial; **to take someone to court** = to start legal proceedings against someone; **in court** = present during a trial; *the defendant was in court for three hours*; **in open court** = in a courtroom with members of the public present; **a settlement was reached out of court** *or* **the two parties reached an out-of-court settlement** = the dispute was settled between the two parties privately without continuing the court case; **contempt of court** = being rude to a court, as by bad behaviour in the courtroom or by refusing to carry out a court order; **court officer** = member of the staff of a court, especially a County Court; **court order** = legal order made by a court, telling someone to do or not to do something; *the court made an order for maintenance or made a maintenance order; he refused to obey the court order and was sent to prison for contempt* (b) **Criminal Court** *or* **Civil Court** = court where criminal or civil cases are heard; **Court of Appeal** *or* **Appeal Court** = civil or criminal court to which a person may go to ask for an award or a sentence to be changed; **home court** = the County Court for the district in which a defendant lives or has his address for service (NOTE: American English is **domestic court**); **High Court (of Justice)** = main civil court in England and Wales, based on the six circuits; **International Court of Justice** = the court of the United Nations, which sits in the Hague, Netherlands; **magistrates' court** = court presided over by magistrates; **Supreme Court (of Judicature)** = (i) highest court in England and Wales (except for the House of Lords), formed of the High Court and the Court of Appeal; (ii) highest federal court in the USA; *(in Scotland)* **Court of Session** = highest civil court in Scotland; *see also* COUNTY COURT (c) the judges or magistrates in a court; *the court will retire for thirty minutes* (d) *(in the EU)* **court or tribunal** = any body which has official status and which has the power to give binding rulings on legal rights and obligations, although it may not have the actual title of 'court' (the Deputy High Bailiff's Court in the Isle of Man and the Dutch Appeals Committee for General Medicine have each been held to be a 'court or tribunal' according to Community law)

> COMMENT: in England and Wales the main courts are: **the Magistrates' Court:** trying minor criminal offences such as petty crime; adoption; affiliation; maintenance and domestic violence; licensing; **the County Court:** most civil actions up to a value of £5,000; **the High Court:** most civil claims where the value exceeds £5,000; **the Crown Court:** major crime; **the Court of Appeal:** appeals from lower courts, such as the High Court; **the House of Lords:** the highest court of appeal in the country; **the Privy Council:** appeals on certain matters from England and Wales, and appeals from certain Commonwealth countries; **the European Court of Justice:** appeals where EC legislation is involved. Other courts include **Industrial tribunals:** employment disputes; **courts-martial:** military matters

courthouse [ˈkɔːthaʊs] *noun especially US* building in which trials take place; *there was police cordon round the courthouse*

court-martial [ˈkɔːtˈmɑːʃl] **1** *noun* (a) court which tries someone serving in the armed forces for offences against military discipline; *he was found guilty by the court-martial and sentenced to imprisonment* (b) trial of someone serving in the armed forces by the armed forces authorities; *the court-martial was held in the army headquarters* (NOTE: plural is **courts-martial**) **2** *verb* to try someone who is serving in the armed forces (NOTE: **court-martialled**)

Court of Auditors [ˈkɔːt əv ˈɔːdɪtəz]; *see* AUDITOR

court of first instance [ˈkɔːt əv ˈfɜːst ˈɪnstəns] *noun* (a) court where a case is heard first (b) *(in the EU)* **Court of First Instance (CFI)** = court set up under the Single European Act, to hear certain types of cases before they go on to the ECJ

COMMENT: the CFI hears cases concerning the staff of the EU, cases concerning the coal and steel industries and cases regarding competition. The court is formed of 15 judges, and its judgements can be appealed to the ECJ

Court of Protection ['kɔːt əv prə'tekʃn] *noun* court appointed to protect the interests of people who are incapable of dealing with their own affairs, such as patients (the mentally ill)

courtroom ['kɔːtruːm] *noun* room where a judge presides over a trial

covenant ['kʌvnənt] **1** *noun* agreement or undertaking to do something or not to do something, contained in a deed or contract; *he signed a covenant against underletting the premises*; **deed of covenant** = official signed agreement to do something (such as to pay someone a sum of money each year); **covenant to repair** = agreement by a landlord or tenant to keep a rented property in good repair; **restrictive covenant** = clause in a contract which prevents someone from doing something **2** *verb* to agree to pay a sum of money each year by contract; *to covenant to pay £10 per annum to a charity*

COMMENT: examples of restrictive covenants could be a clause in a contract of employment which prevents the employee from going to work for a competitor, or a clause in a contract for the sale of a property which prevents the purchaser from altering the building. There is a tax advantage to the recipient of covenanted money; a charity pays no tax, so it can reclaim tax at the standard rate on the money covenanted to it

cover ['kʌvə] **1** *noun* **(a)** insurance **cover** = protection guaranteed by an insurance policy; *do you have cover against theft?*; **to operate without adequate cover** = without being protected by insurance; **to ask for additional cover** = to ask the insurance company to increase the amount for which you are insured; **full**

cover = insurance against all types of risk; **cover note** = letter from an insurance company giving basic details of an insurance policy and confirming that the policy exists **(b)** security to guarantee a loan; *do you have sufficient cover for this loan?* **(c) to send something under separate cover** = in a separate envelope; **to send a document under plain cover** = in an ordinary envelope with no company name printed on it **2** *verb* **(a)** to deal with, to refer to something completely; *the agreement covers all agencies*; *the newspapers have covered the murder trial*; *the fraud case has been covered by the consumer protection legislation* **(b) to cover a risk** = to be protected by insurance against a risk; **to be fully covered** = to have insurance against all risks; *the insurance covers fire, theft and loss of work* **(c)** *US* to purchase goods from another supplier to replace those which have not been delivered according to contract **(d)** to have enough money to pay; to ask for security against a loan which you are making; **the damage was covered by the insurance** = the insurance company paid for the damage; **to cover a position** = to have enough money to be able to pay for a forward purchase **(e)** to earn enough money to pay for costs, expenses, etc.; *we do not make enough sales to cover the expense of running the shop*; *we hope to reach the point soon when sales will cover all costs*; **the dividend is covered four times** = profits are four times the dividend paid out

coverage ['kʌvrɪdʒ] *noun* **(a)** press coverage *or* media coverage = reports about something in the newspapers, on TV, etc.; *the company had good media coverage for the launch of its new model* **(b)** *US* protection guaranteed by insurance; *do you have coverage against fire damage?*

covering ['kʌvrɪŋ] *adjective* **covering letter** *or* **covering note** = letter or note sent with documents to say why you are sending them

covert ['kəʊvɜːt] *adjective* hidden, secret; **covert action** = action which is secret (such as spying); *see also* FEME COVERT

coverture ['kʌvətʃuə] *noun* state of being married (of a woman)

CPR = CIVIL PROCEDURE RULES

CPS ['siː 'piː 'es] = CROWN PROSECUTION SERVICE

cracksman ['kræksmən] *noun (slang)* criminal who specializes in breaking safes

credentials *or* **letters of credence** [krɪ'denʃlz *or* 'letəz əv 'kriːdəns] *noun* official documents, proving that an ambassador has really been appointed legally; *(of an ambassador)* **to present his credentials** *or* **to present his letters of credence** = to visit for the first time the head of the state of the country where he is ambassador, to hand over documents showing that he has been legally appointed

credere ['kreɪdəri] *see* DEL CREDERE

credit ['kredɪt] **1** *noun* **(a)** time given to a debtor before he has to pay; *to give someone six months' credit; to sell on good credit terms;* **credit account** = account which a customer has with a shop which allows him to buy goods and pay for them later; **credit agency** *US* **credit bureau** = company which reports on the ability of customers to pay their debts and shows whether they should be allowed credit; **credit bank** = bank which lends money; **credit card** = plastic card which allows the owner to borrow money, and to buy goods without paying for them immediately; **credit facilities** = arrangement with a bank or supplier to have credit so as to buy goods; **letter of credit** = letter from a bank authorizing payment of a certain sum to a person or company (usually in another country); **irrevocable letter of credit** = letter of credit which cannot be cancelled or changed; **credit limit** = fixed amount which is the most a customer can owe; **credit rating** = amount which a credit agency feels a customer should be allowed

to borrow; **to buy on credit** = without paying immediately **(b)** money received by a person or company and recorded in the accounts; *to enter £100 to someone's credit; to pay in £100 to the credit of Mr Smith;* **debit and credit** = money which a company owes and which it is entitled to receive; **credit side** = right side of accounts which records money received **2** *verb* to put money into someone's account; to note money received in an account; *to credit an account with £100 or to credit £100 to an account*

creditor ['kredɪtə] *noun* person who is owed money; **creditors' meeting** = meeting of all persons to whom a company in receivership owes money; **judgment creditor** = person who has been given a court order making a debtor pay a debt; **preferential creditor** = creditor who must be paid first if a company is in liquidation; **secured** *or* **unsecured creditor** = creditor who holds *or* does not hold a mortgage or charge against the debtor's property as security for the loan

crime [kraɪm] *noun* **(a)** act which is against the law and which is punishable by law; *there has been a 50% increase in crimes of violence* **(b)** illegal acts in general; *crime is on the increase; there has been an increase in violent crime;* **crime rate** = number of crimes committed, shown as a percentage of the total population; **crime wave** = sudden increase in crime

COMMENT: a crime is an illegal act which may result in prosecution and punishment by the state if the accused is convicted. Generally, in order to be convicted of a crime, the accused must be shown to have committed an unlawful act **(actus reus)** with a criminal state of mind **(mens rea)**. The main types of crime are: **1. crimes against the person:** murder; manslaughter; assault, battery, wounding; grievous bodily harm; abduction; **2. crimes against property:** theft; robbery; burglary;

obtaining property or services or pecuniary advantage by deception; blackmail; handling stolen goods; going equipped to steal; criminal damage; possessing something with intent to damage or destroy property; forgery; **3. sexual offences:** rape; buggery; bigamy; indecency; **4. political offences:** treason; terrorism; sedition; breach of the Official Secrets Act; **5. offences against justice:** assisting an offender; conspiracy; perjury; contempt of court; perverting the course of justice; **6. public order offences:** obstruction of the police; unlawful assembly; obscenity; possessing weapons; misuse of drugs; breach of the peace; **7. road traffic offences:** careless or reckless driving; drunken driving; driving without a licence or insurance. Most minor crime is tried before the Magistrates' Courts; more serious crime is tried at the Crown Court which has greater powers to sentence offenders. Most crimes are prosecuted by the police or the Crown Prosecutors, though private prosecutions brought by individuals are possible

criminal ['krɪmɪnəl] **1** *adjective* **(a)** illegal; *misappropriation of funds is a criminal act*; **criminal offence** = action which is against the law **(b)** referring to crime; **criminal action** = court case brought by the state against someone who is charged with a crime; **criminal bankruptcy** = bankruptcy of a criminal in the Crown Court as a result of crimes of which he has been convicted; **criminal court** = court (such as a Crown Court) which hears criminal cases; **criminal damage** = notifiable offence of causing serious damage; **criminal law** = laws relating to acts committed against the laws of the land, and which are punished by the state; **criminal libel** = serious libel which might cause a breach of the peace; **criminal negligence** = acting recklessly with the result that harm is done to other people; **the criminal population** = all people who have committed crimes; **criminal record** = note of previous crimes

for which someone has been convicted; *the accused had no criminal record*; *he has a criminal record going back to the time when he was still at school* **2** *noun* person who has committed a crime, person who often commits crimes; *the police have contacted known criminals to get leads on the gangland murder*; **a hardened criminal** = a person who has committed many crimes

Criminal Defence Service (CDS)

['krɪmɪnl dɪ'fens 'sɜːvɪs] *noun* British government service which provides legal advice and assistance in each community to people with very little money who are suspected of criminal offences or are facing criminal proceedings

> COMMENT: the service replaces part of the Legal Aid scheme (the Community Legal Service deals with civil and family cases)

Criminal Injuries Compensation Board

['krɪmɪnəl 'ɪndʒəriz kɒmpən'seɪʃn 'bɔːd] *noun* committee which administers the awarding of compensation to victims of crime

Criminal Investigation department (CID)

['krɪmɪnəl ɪnvestɪ'geɪʃn dɪ'pɑːtmənt] *noun* section of the British police which investigates serious crimes

criminal responsibility

['krɪmɪnəl rɪspɒnsɪ'bɪləti] *noun* being responsible for a crime; **age of criminal responsibility** = age at which a person is considered to be capable of committing a crime

> COMMENT: the age of criminal responsibility is ten years. Children under ten years old cannot be charged with a crime

criminology [krɪmɪ'nɒlədʒi] *noun* academic study of crime

criterion [kraɪ'tɪəriən] *noun* standard by which something can be judged; *using the criterion of the ratio of cases solved to cases reported, the police force is becoming more efficient* (NOTE: plural is **criteria**)

crook [krʊk] *noun (slang)* criminal, a person who has committed a crime, especially involving deceit

cross [krɒs] *verb* **(a) crossed cheque** = cheque with two lines across it to show that it can only be deposited at a bank and not exchanged for cash **(b)** *(of a sitting MP)* **to cross the floor (of the House)** = to change political party

cross benches ['krɒs 'bentʃɪz] *noun* seats in the House of Commons or House of Lords (some of them running across the chamber) where Lords or MPs sit if they are not members of a political party

crossbencher ['krɒs'bentʃə] *noun* MP who is a not a member of one the main political parties, who is sitting as an independent or who has resigned the party whip

cross-examination ['krɒsɪgzæmɪ'neɪʃn] *noun* questioning of a witness called by the other side in a case (NOTE: the opposite is **evidence in chief**)

cross-examine ['krɒsɪg'zæmɪn] *verb* to question witnesses called by the other side in a case, in the hope that you can destroy their evidence

cross off ['krɒs 'ɒf] *verb* to remove something from a list; *he crossed my name off his list*; *you can cross him off our mailing list*

cross out ['krɒs 'aʊt] *verb* to put a line through something which has been written; *she crossed out £250 and put in £500*

Crown [kraʊn] *noun GB* **(a) the Crown** = the King or Queen as representing the State; *Mr Smith is appearing for the Crown*; *the Crown submitted that the maximum sentence should be applied in this case*; *the Crown case or the case for the Crown was that the defendants were guilty of espionage* (NOTE: in legal reports, the Crown is referred to as **Rex** *or* **Regina** (abbreviated to **R.**) depending on whether there is a King or Queen reigning at the time: **the case of** *R. v. Smith Limited*) **(b) associate of the Crown Office** = official who is responsible for the clerical and administrative work of

a court; **Crown Lands** *or* **Crown property** = land or property belonging to the King or Queen; **Crown copyright** = copyright in government publications

Crown Court ['kraʊn 'kɔːt] *noun* court, above the level of the magistrates' courts, which is based on the six circuits in England and Wales

COMMENT: a Crown Court is formed of a circuit judge and jury, and hears major criminal cases

Crown privilege ['kraʊn 'prɪvɪlɪdʒ] *noun* right of the Crown or the government not to have to produce documents to a court by reason of the interest of the state

Crown Prosecution Service (CPS) ['kraʊn prɒsɪ'kjuːʃn 'sɜːvɪs] *noun* government department, headed by the Director of Public Prosecutions, which is responsible for the conduct of all criminal cases instituted by the police in England and Wales, except for those prosecuted by the Serious Fraud Office

Crown prosecutor ['kraʊn 'prɒsɪkjuːtə] *noun* official of the Crown Prosecution Service who is responsible for prosecuting criminals in one of 13 areas in England Wales

cruelty ['kruːəltɪ] *noun* **(a)** hurting a person or animal **(b)** acting harshly to a spouse

cryptographic [krɪptə'græfɪk] *adjective* referring to cryptography

cryptography [krɪp'tɒɡrəfɪ] *noun* science of codes which allow ordinary text to be encrypted so that it cannot be read without a key; **public key cryptography** = coding system where the sender of the message encrypts it using a publicly available key, and the receiver decrypts it using a secret decryption key; **cryptography support service** = service which helps senders or receivers of encrypted electronic messages to read those messages

CS gas ['siː 'es 'gæs] *noun* gas given off by solid crystals of $C_6H_4(Cl)CH$, used by police as a method of crowd control

CTT ['siː 'tiː 'tiː] = CAPITAL TRANSFER TAX

culpability [kʌlpə'bɪləti] *noun* being culpable

culpable ['kʌlpəbl] *adjective* which is likely to attract blame; **culpable homicide** = murder, manslaughter; **culpable negligence** = negligence which is so bad that it amounts to an offence

culprit ['kʌlprɪt] *noun* person who is responsible for a crime or for something which has gone wrong

curiam ['kjʊriəm] *see* PER CURIAM

currency ['kʌrənsi] *noun* money in coins and notes which is used in a particular country; **blocked currency** = money which cannot be taken out of a country because of exchange controls; **foreign currency** = currency of another country; **free currency** = currency which a government allows to be bought or sold without restriction; **hard currency** = currency of a country which has a strong economy and which can be changed into other currencies easily; **legal currency** = money which is legally used in a country; **soft currency** = currency of a country with a weak economy, which is cheap to buy and difficult to exchange for other currencies

current ['kʌrənt] *adjective* referring to the present time; **current account** = ordinary account in a bank into which money can be deposited and on which cheques can be drawn; **current liabilities** = debts which a company has to pay within the next accounting period

curriculum vitae (CV) [kə'rɪkjʊləm 'viːtaɪ] *noun* summary of a person's life story showing details of education and work experience; *candidates should send a letter of application with a curriculum vitae to the administrative office* (NOTE: the American English is **résumé**)

curtilage ['kɜːtɪlɪdʒ] *noun* land round a house

custodial [kʌs'təʊdiəl] *adjective* **custodial establishment** *or* **institution** = prison or other institution where criminals are kept; **custodial sentence** = sentence which involves sending someone to prison

custodian [kʌs'təʊdiən] *noun* person who guards a museum or public building

custody ['kʌstədi] *noun* **(a)** being kept in prison, in a cell; **in police custody** = held by the police, but not actually arrested, while helping the police with their inquiries; *the young men were kept in police custody overnight*; **remanded in custody** = remanded to be kept in prison until the trial starts **(b)** control of a thing under the law **(c)** control of a person, such as the right and duty of a parent to keep and bring up a child after a divorce; *custody of the children was awarded to the mother*; *the court granted the mother custody of both children*

custom ['kʌstəm] *noun* **(a)** unwritten law which lays down how things are usually done and have been done since time immemorial; *it is the custom that everyone stands up when the magistrates enter the courtroom*; **local custom** = way in which things are usually done in a particular place; **the customs of the trade** = general way of working in a trade **(b)** use of a shop by regular shoppers; **to lose someone's custom** = to do something which makes a regular customer go to another shop

customs *or* **Customs and Excise** ['kʌstəmz] *plural noun* the government department which deals with VAT and with the collection of taxes on imports and on taxable products, such as alcohol, which are produced in the country; office of this department at a port or airport; **to go through customs** = to pass through the area of a port or airport where customs officials examine goods; *he was stopped by customs*; *her car was searched by customs*; **customs barrier** = customs duty intended to prevent imports; **customs**

clearance = act of clearing goods through customs; **customs declaration** = statement showing goods being imported on which duty will have to be paid; **customs union** = agreement between several countries that goods can travel between them without paying duty, while goods from other countries have to pay special duties

cut [kʌt] **1** *noun* **(a)** sudden lowering of a price, salary or numbers of jobs; *price cuts or cuts in prices*; *salary cuts or cuts in salaries* **(b)** share in a payment; *he introduces new customers and gets a cut of the salesman's commission* **2** *verb* **(a)** to lower suddenly; *we are cutting prices on all our models*; **to cut (back) production** = to reduce the quantity of products made **(b)** to stop, to reduce the number of something; **to cut jobs** = to reduce the number of jobs by making people redundant

cut in on [ˈkʌt ˈɪn ˈɒn] *verb* **to cut someone in on a deal** = to offer someone part of the profits of a deal

CV [ˈsiː ˈviː] *noun* = CURRICULUM VITAE; *please apply in writing, enclosing a current CV*

cyberlaw [ˈsaɪbəlɔː] *noun* laws in relation to the Internet, especially commercial law relating to commercial transactions carried out over the Internet, copyright law as regards information available on the net, or defamation law regarding statements made public on the net

cycle [ˈsaɪkl] *noun* period of time when something leaves its original position and then returns to it

cyclical [ˈsɪklɪkl] *adjective* which happens in cycles; **cyclical factors** = way in which a trade cycle affects businesses

cy-près [ˈsiː ˈpreɪ] *adjective & adverb* as near as possible; **cy-près doctrine** = rule that if a charity cannot apply its funds to the purposes for which they were intended, a court can apply the funds to a purpose which is as close as possible to the original intention

Dd

D [diː] *fourth letter of the alphabet;* **category 'D' prisoners** = reliable prisoners who can be kept in open prisons; **Schedule D** = schedule to the Finance Acts under which tax is charged on income from trades, professions, interest and other earnings which do not come from employment; **Table D** = model memorandum and articles of association of a public company with share capital limited by guarantee, set out in the Companies Act, 1985

DA [ˈdiː ˈeɪ] *US* = DISTRICT ATTORNEY

dabs [dæbz] *plural noun (slang)* fingerprints

Dail (Éireann) [ˈdɔɪl ˈeərən] *noun* lower house of the parliament in the Republic of Ireland; *the Foreign Minister reported on the meeting to the Dail* (NOTE: the members of the Dail are called **Teachta Dala (TD)**)

damage [ˈdæmɪdʒ] **1** *noun* harm done to things; **fire damage** = damage caused by a fire; **storm damage** = damage caused by a storm; **to suffer damage** = to be harmed; **to cause damage** = to harm something; **causing criminal damage** = notifiable offence where serious damage is caused; **malicious damage** = deliberate and intentional harming of property; **damage feasant** = situation where the animals of one person damage the property of another person (NOTE: no plural in this sense) **2** *verb* to harm; *the storm damaged the cargo; stock which has been damaged by water; he alleged that the newspaper article was damaging to the company's reputation*

damaged [ˈdæmɪdʒd] *adjective* which has suffered damage or which has been harmed; **fire-damaged goods** = goods harmed in a fire

damages [ˈdæmɪdʒɪz] *noun* (i) money claimed by a claimant from a defendant as compensation for harm done; (ii) money awarded by a court as compensation to a claimant; *to claim £1,000 in damages; to be liable for or in damages; to pay £25,000 in damages;* **to bring an action for damages against someone** = to take someone to court and claim damages; **aggravated damages** = damages awarded by a court against a defendant who has behaved maliciously or wilfully; **compensatory damages** = damages which compensate for the loss or harm suffered; **exemplary damages** *or* **punitive damages** = heavy damages which punish the defendant for the loss or harm caused to the claimant, awarded to show that the court feels the defendant has behaved badly towards the claimant; **general damages** = damages awarded by court to compensate for a loss which cannot be calculated (such as an injury); **liquidated damages** = the specific amount which has been calculated as the loss suffered; **measure of damages** = calculation of how much money a court should order one party to pay another to compensate for a tort or breach; **mitigation of damages** = reduction in the extent of damages awarded; **nominal damages** = very small amount of damages, awarded to show that the loss or harm suffered was technical rather than actual; **provisional damages** = damages claimed by a claimant while the case is still being heard; **special damages** = damages awarded by a court to compensate for a loss which can be calculated (such as the expense of repairing something) (NOTE: damages are noted at the end of a report on a case as: *Special damages: £100; General damages: £2,500)*

danger ['deɪnʒə] *noun* **(a)** possibility of being harmed or killed; *there is danger to the workers in using old machinery* **(b)** likelihood or possibility; **there is no danger of the case being heard early** = it is not likely that the case will be heard early; **in danger of** = which may easily happen; *he is in danger to being in contempt of court*

danger money ['deɪnʒə 'mʌni] *noun* extra money paid to workers in dangerous jobs; *the workers have stopped work and asked for danger money*

dangerous ['deɪnʒrəs] *adjective* which can be harmful; **dangerous animals** = animals, such as certain breeds of dog and certain wild animals, which may attack people and have to be kept under strict conditions, or for which a licence has to be held; **dangerous driving** = offence of driving dangerously (now called 'reckless driving'); **dangerous drugs** = drugs which may be harmful to people who take them, and so can be prohibited from import and general sales; **dangerous job** = job where the workers may be killed or hurt; **dangerous weapon** = device or weapon which can hurt someone

data ['deɪtə] *noun* information (letters or figures) which is available on computer; **data bank** *or* **bank of data** = store of information in a computer; **data processing** = selecting and examining data in a computer to produce special information; **data protection** = protecting information (such as records about private people) in a computer from being copied or used wrongly (NOTE: data is usually singular: **the data is easily available**)

database ['deɪtəbeɪs] *noun* store of information in a large computer; *the police maintain a database of fingerprints*

date of commencement ['deɪt əv kə'mensmənt] *noun* date when an Act of Parliament takes effect

day [deɪ] *noun* **(a)** period of 24 hours; *there are thirty days in June; the first day of the month is a public holiday;* **three clear days** = three whole working days; *to give ten clear days' notice; allow four clear days for the cheque to be paid into the account;* **early day motion** = motion proposed in the House of Commons for discussion at an early date (usually used to introduce the particular point of view of the MP proposing the motion, without necessarily going to a full debate) **(b)** period of work during a 24 hour day; *the trial lasted ten days*

day-to-day ['deɪtə'deɪ] *adjective* ordinary, which goes on all the time; *the clerk organizes the day-to-day running of the courts*

day training centre ['deɪ 'treɪnɪŋ 'sentə] *noun* centre where young offenders attend courses as a condition of being on probation

D.C. ['di: 'si:] = DISTRICT OF COLUMBIA

DC ['di: 'si:] = DETECTIVE CONSTABLE; DISTRICT COUNCIL

DCC ['di: 'si: 'si:] = DEPUTY CHIEF CONSTABLE

dead [ded] *adjective* **(a)** not alive; *six people were dead as a result of the accident; we inherited the house from my dead grandfather* **(b)** not working; **dead account** = account which is no longer used; **dead letter** = regulation which is no longer valid; *this law has become a dead letter;* **dead loss** = total loss; *the car was written off as a dead loss*

dealing ['di:lɪŋ] *noun* **(a)** buying and selling on the Stock Exchange; **fair dealing** = (i) legal trade, legal buying and selling of shares; (ii) legal quoting of small sections of a copyright work; **foreign exchange dealing** = buying and selling foreign currencies; **forward dealings** = buying or selling commodities forward;

insider dealing = illegal buying or selling of shares, such as by staff of a company who have secret information about the company's plans **(b)** buying and selling goods; **to have dealings with someone** = to do business with someone

death [deθ] *noun* act of dying; **death benefit** = insurance benefit paid to the family of someone who dies in an accident at wórk; **death certificate** = official certificate signed by a doctor, stating that a person has died and giving details of the cause of death; **death grant** = state grant to the family of a person who has died, which is supposed to contribute to the funeral expenses; **death in service** = insurance benefit or pension paid when someone dies while employed by a company; **death penalty** = sentence of a criminal to be executed; *US* **death duty** *or* **death tax** = tax paid on the property left by a dead person; **presumption of death** = situation where a person has not been seen for seven years and is presumed to be legally dead

debate [dɪ'beɪt] **1** *noun* discussion leading to a vote, especially the discussion of a motion in Parliament; *several MPs criticized the government in or during the debate on the Finance Bill; the Bill passed its Second Reading after a short debate; the debate continued until 3 a.m.* **2** *verb* to discuss a proposal, especially in Parliament; *the MPs are still debating the Data Protection Bill*

debenture [dɪ'bentʃə] *noun* document whereby a company acknowledges it owes a debt, and gives the company's assets as security; **mortgage debenture** = debenture where the lender can be repaid by selling the company's property; **debenture issue** *or* **issue of debentures** = borrowing money against the security of the company's assets; **debenture bond** = certificate showing that a debenture has been issued; **debenture capital** *or* **debenture stock** = capital borrowed by a company, using its fixed assets as security; **debenture holder** = person who holds a debenture for money lent; **debenture register** *or* **register of debentures** = list of debenture holders of a company

debit ['debɪt] **1** *noun* money which a company owes; **debit and credit** = money which a company owes and money it is entitled to receive; **debit column** = left-hand column in accounts showing the money paid or owed to others; **debit entry** = entry on the debit side of an account; **debit note** = note showing that a customer owes money; **debit side** = left-hand side of an account showing the money paid or owed to others; **direct debit** = system where a customer allows a company to charge costs to his bank account automatically and where the amount charged can be increased or decreased automatically, the customer being informed of the change by letter; *compare* STANDING ORDER **2** *verb* **to debit an account** = to charge an account with a cost; *his account was debited with the sum of £25*

debt [det] *noun* money owed for goods or services; *the company stopped trading with debts of over $1 million;* **to be in debt** = to owe money; **to get into debt** = to start to borrow more money than you can pay back; **to be out of debt** = not to owe money any more; **to pay back a debt** = to pay all the money owed; **to pay off a debt** = to finish paying money owed; **to service a debt** = to pay interest on a debt; **bad debt** = money owed which will never be paid back; **debt collection** *or* **collecting** = collecting money which is owed; **debt collection agency** *or* **collecting agency** = company which collects debts for other companies for a commission; **debt collector** = person who collects debts; **debt factor** = person who buys debts at a discount and enforces them for himself, person who enforces debts for a commission

debtor ['detə] *noun* person who owes money; **judgment debtor** = person who has been ordered by a court to pay a debt; **debtor side** = debit side of an account; **debtor nation** = country whose foreign debts are larger than money owed to it by other countries

decease [dɪ'siːs] *noun (formal)* death; *on his decease all his property will go to his widow*

deceased [dɪ'siːst] *adjective & noun* (person) who has died; *the deceased left all his property to his widow*; *she inherited the estate of a deceased aunt*

deceit *or* **deception** [dɪ'siːt or dɪ'sepʃn] *noun* making a wrong statement to someone in order to trick him into paying money or in order to make him do something which will harm him; *she obtained £10,000 by deception*; **obtaining a pecuniary advantage by deception** = crime of tricking someone into handing over money; **obtaining property by deception** = tricking someone into handing over possession of property

decide [dɪ'saɪd] *verb* **(a)** to give a judgment in a civil case; *the judge decided in favour of the claimant* **(b)** to make up your mind to do something; *we have decided to take our neighbours to court*; *the tribunal decided against awarding any damages*

decided case [dɪ'saɪdɪd 'keɪs] *noun* case where a court has decided, and where that decision then becomes a precedent

decidendi [desɪ'dendaɪ] *see* RATIO

deciding factor [dɪ'saɪdɪŋ 'fæktə] *noun* most important factor which influences a decision

decision [dɪ'sɪʒn] *noun* **(a)** judgment in a civil court; **the decision of the House of Lords is final** = there is no appeal against a decision of the House of Lords **(b)** making up one's mind to do something; *to come to a decision or to reach a decision*; **decision making** = act of coming to a decision; **the decision-making processes** = ways in which decisions are reached; **decision maker** = person who has to decide **(c)** *(in the EU)* **decisions** = legally binding acts of the European Community which apply to individual Member States of the EU or to groups of people or individual citizens of those states

decisis [dɪ'saɪsɪs] *see* STARE DECISIS

declaration [deklə'reɪʃn] *noun* official statement; **declaration of association** = statement in the articles of association of a company, saying that the members have agreed to form the company and buy shares in it; **declaration of bankruptcy** = official statement that someone is bankrupt; **declaration of income** = statement declaring income to the tax office; **customs declaration** = statement declaring goods brought into a country on which customs duty may be paid; **statutory declaration** = (i) statement made to the Registrar of Companies that a company has complied with certain legal conditions; (ii) statement made, signed and witnessed for official purposes; **VAT declaration** = statement declaring VAT income to the VAT office; *see also* INDEPENDENCE

declaratory judgment [dɪ'klærətri 'dʒʌdʒmənt] *noun* judgment where a court states what the legal position of the various parties is

declare [dɪ'kleə] *verb* to make an official statement, to announce to the public; *to declare someone bankrupt*; *to declare a dividend of 10%*; **to declare goods to customs** = to state that you are importing goods which are liable to duty; **to declare an interest** = to state in public that you own shares in a company being investigated, that you are related to someone who can benefit from your contacts, etc.

declared [dɪ'kleəd] *adjective* which has been made public or officially stated; **declared value** = value of goods entered on a customs declaration

declassification [diːklæsɪfɪ'keɪʃn] *noun* making something no longer secret

declassify [diː'klæsɪfaɪ] *verb* to make a document or piece of information no longer secret, so that it can be made public; *the government papers relating to the war have recently been declassified*

decontrol [diːkən'trəʊl] *verb* to stop or remove controls from something; **to decontrol the price of petrol** = to stop controlling the price of petrol so that a free market price can be reached (NOTE: decontrolled - decontrolling)

decree [dɪ'kriː] **1** *noun* **(a)** order made by a head of state, but which is not passed by a parliament; **to govern by decree** = to rule a country by issuing orders without having them debated and voted in a parliament **(b)** **decree nisi** = order from a court which ends a marriage for the time being, and becomes final when decree absolute is pronounced; **decree absolute** = order from a court which ends a marriage finally **2** *verb* to make an order; *the President decreed that June 1st (his birthday) should be a National Holiday*

decriminalize [dɪ'krɪmɪnəlaɪz] *verb* to make the possession or use of something no longer a crime; *there are plans to decriminalize certain soft drugs*

decrypt [diː'krɪpt] *verb* to read an encrypted text by using a special key

decryption [diː'krɪpʃn] *noun* action of reading encrypted text using a special key

deducing title [dɪ'djuːsɪŋ 'taɪtl] *noun* proving (by the vendor) of his title to the property being sold

deduct [dɪ'dʌkt] *verb* to remove money from a total; *to deduct £3 from the price*; *to deduct a sum for expenses*; *to deduct 5% from salaries*; **tax deducted at source** = tax which is removed from a salary, interest payment or dividend payment on shares before the money is paid

deductible [dɪ'dʌktəbl] *adjective* which can be deducted; **tax-deductible** = which can be deducted from an income before tax is paid; **these expenses are not tax-deductible** = tax has to be paid on these expenses

deduction [dɪ'dʌkʃn] *noun* **(a)** conclusion which is reached by observing something; *by deduction, the detective came to the conclusion that the dead person had not been murdered* **(b)** removing of money from a total, money removed from a total; *net salary is salary after deduction of tax and social security contributions*; **deductions from salary** *or*

salary deductions *or* **deductions at source** = money which a company removes from salaries to give to the government as tax, national insurance contributions, etc.; **tax deductions** = (i) money removed from a salary to pay tax; (ii) *US* expenses which can be claimed against tax

deed [diːd] *noun* legal document which has been signed, sealed and delivered by the person making it; **deed of arrangement** = agreement made between a debtor and his creditors whereby the creditors accept an agreed sum in settlement of their claim rather than make the debtor bankrupt; **deed of assignment** = agreement which legally transfers a property from a debtor to a creditor; **deed of covenant** = signed legal agreement to do something (such as to pay someone a sum of money every year); **deed of partnership** = agreement which sets up a partnership; **deed of transfer** = agreement which transfers the ownership of shares; **title deeds** = document showing who owns a property; *we have deposited the deeds of the house in the bank*

deed poll ['diːd 'pəʊl] *noun* document made under seal, to which there is only one party; **to change one's name by deed poll** = to sign a legal document by which you change your name

deem [diːm] *verb* to believe or to consider; *the judge deemed it necessary to order the court to be cleared*; *if no payment is made, the party shall be deemed to have defaulted*; **deeming provision** *or* **deemed service** = service which is assumed to have taken place (if using first class post, service is deemed to have taken place on the second day after the documents were posted)

de facto ['deɪ 'fæktəʊ] *Latin phrase meaning* 'in fact': as a matter of fact, even though the legal title may not be certain; *he is the de facto owner of the property*; *the de facto government has been recognized*; **de facto authority** *or* **de facto rule** = authority or rule of a country by a group because it is actually ruling; **de facto**

recognition = recognition of a new government because it is in power, whether it is ruling legally or not; *see also* DE JURE

defalcation [di:fæl'keɪʃn] *noun* illegal use of money by someone who is not the owner but who has been trusted to look after it

defamation [defə'meɪʃn] *noun* **defamation of character** = act of injuring someone's reputation by maliciously saying or writing things about him

COMMENT: defamation is a tort and may be libel (if it is in a permanent form, such as printed matter) or slander (if it is spoken)

defamatory [dɪ'fæmətri] *adjective* **defamatory statement** = statement which is made to defame someone's character

defame [dɪ'feɪm] *verb* to say or write things about the character of someone so as to damage his or her reputation

default [dɪ'fɔ:lt] **1** *noun* failure to do something which is required by law, such as failure to carry out the terms of a contract, especially failure to pay back a debt; **in default of payment** = if no payment is made; **to be in default** = not to do or not to have done something which is required by law; **the company is in default** = the company has failed to carry out the terms of the contract; **by default** = because no one else will act; **he was elected by default** = he was elected because all the other candidates withdrew, because there were no other candidates; **judgment by default** *or* **default judgment** = judgment without trial against a defendant who fails to respond to a claim; *see also* PECUNIARY; **default action** = County Court action to get back money owed; **default summons** = County Court summons to someone to pay what is owed **2** *verb* to fail to carry out the terms of a contract, especially to fail to pay back a debt; **to default on payments** = not to make payments which are due under the terms of a contract

defaulter [dɪ'fɔ:ltə] *noun* person who defaults

defeasance [dɪ'fi:zəns] *noun* clause (in a collateral deed) which says that a contract, bond or recognizance will be revoked if something happens or if some act is performed

defeat [dɪ'fi:t] **1** *noun* failure to get a majority in a vote; *the minister offered to resign after the defeat of the motion in the House of Commons* **2** *verb* **(a)** to beat someone or something in a vote; *the bill was defeated in the Lords by 52 to 64*; *the government was defeated in a vote on law and order* **(b)** to revoke or to render invalid (an agreement, a contract or a bond)

defect **1** ['di:fekt] *noun* something which is wrong, which stops a machine from working properly **2** [dɪ'fekt] *verb (of a spy, agent or government employee)* to leave your country and go to work for an enemy country

defective [dɪ'fektɪv] *adjective* **(a)** faulty, not working properly; *the machine broke down because of a defective cooling system* **(b)** not legally valid; *his title to the property is defective*

defence *US* **defense** [dɪ'fens] *noun* **(a)** (i) party in a legal case which is sued by the claimant; (ii) party in a criminal case which is being prosecuted; (iii) lawyers representing a party being sued or prosecuted; **defence counsel** = lawyer who represents the defendant or the accused; *compare* PROSECUTION **(b)** arguments used when fighting a case; *his defence was that he did not know the property was stolen*; **defence before claim** = defence that the defendant offered the claimant the amount of money claimed before the claimant started proceedings against him (NOTE: also called **tender before claim**) **(c)** document, a pleading setting out the defendant's case; *a defence must say which parts of a claim are denied or admitted, and which must be proved by the claimant*; **to file a defence** = to state that you wish to defend a case, and outline the reasons for doing so **(d)** protecting someone or something against attack; **Ministry of Defence,** US **Defense Department** = government department in charge of the armed forces; **Secretary of State for Defence** or **Defence Secretary,** US **Secretary for Defense** or **Defense Secretary** = government minister in charge of the armed forces

defend [dɪ'fend] verb **(a)** to fight to protect someone or something which is being attacked; *the company is defending itself against the takeover bid* **(b)** to speak on behalf of someone who has been charged with a crime; *he hired the best lawyers to defend him against the tax authorities*; **to defend an action** = to appear in court to state your case when accused of something

defendant [dɪ'fendənt] noun **(a)** person who is sued in a civil case; *compare* CLAIMANT, PLAINTIFF **(b)** person who is accused of a crime in a criminal case (NOTE: usually called the **accused**)

defer [dɪ'fɜː] verb to put back to a later date, to postpone; *to defer judgment*; *the decision has been deferred until the next meeting* (NOTE: deferring - deferred)

deferment [dɪ'fɜːmənt] noun postponement, putting back to a later date; *deferment of payment*; *deferment of a decision*; **deferment of sentence** = putting back the sentencing of a convicted criminal until a later date to see how he behaves

deferred [dɪ'fɜːd] adjective put back to a later date; **deferred creditor** = person who is owed money by a bankrupt but who is paid only after all other creditors; **deferred payment** = payment for goods by instalments over a long period; **deferred stock** or **shares** = shares which receive a dividend after all other dividends have been paid

deficiency [dɪ'fɪʃənsi] noun US amount of tax owing by a taxpayer after he has submitted a tax return which is too low; **deficiencies** = SUPPLEMENTAL APPROPRIATIONS

deficit ['defɪsɪt] noun amount by which spending is higher than income; *the council is trying to agree on how to reduce its current deficit*; *the President has promised to reduce the budget deficit*; **trade deficit** = situation where a country imports more goods than it exports

deforce [diː'fɔːs] verb to take wrongfully and hold land which belongs to someone else

deforcement [diː'fɔːsmənt] noun wrongful taking and holding of another person's land

defraud [dɪ'frɔːd] verb to trick someone so as to obtain money illegally; *he defrauded the Inland Revenue of thousands of pounds* (NOTE: you defraud someone **of** something)

defray [dɪ'freɪ] verb to provide money to pay (costs); *the company agreed to defray the costs of the prosecution*

degree [dɪ'griː] noun **(a)** level or measure of a relationship; **prohibited degrees** = relationships which make it illegal for a man and woman to marry (such as father and daughter) **(b)** US system for classifying murders; **first degree murder** = premeditated and deliberate murder; **second degree murder** = murder without premeditation

COMMENT: in the US, the penalty for first degree murder can be death

de jure ['deɪ 'dʒuəreɪ] Latin phrase meaning 'by law': as a matter of law, where the legal title is clear; *he is the de jure owner of the property*; see also DE FACTO

delay [dɪ'leɪ] **1** noun time when someone or something is later than planned; *there was a delay of thirty minutes before the hearing started* or *the hearing started after a thirty minute delay* **2** verb to be late; to make someone late; *judgment was delayed while the magistrates asked for advice*

del credere agent ['del 'kreɪdəri 'eɪdʒənt] noun agent who receives a high commission because he guarantees payment by customers to his principal

delegate 1 [ˈdelɪgət] *noun* person who is elected by others to put their case at a meeting; *the management refused to meet the trade union delegates* 2 [ˈdelɪgeɪt] *verb* to pass authority or responsibility to someone else; **delegated legislation** = orders, which have the power of Acts of Parliament, but which are passed by a minister to whom Parliament has delegated its authority; *(in the EU)* legislation which is proposed by the Commission and implemented by the Council of Ministers

delegation [delɪˈgeɪʃn] *noun* **(a)** group of delegates; *a Chinese trade delegation*; *the management met a union delegation* **(b)** act of passing authority or responsibility to someone else

delegatus non potest delegare [delɪˈgɑːtʌs nɒn pɒˈtest delɪˈgɑːreɪ] *Latin phrase meaning* 'the delegate cannot delegate to someone else'

deliberate 1 [dɪˈlɪbrət] *adjective* done on purpose; *the police suggest that the letter was a deliberate attempt to encourage disorder* 2 [dɪˈlɪbəreɪt] *verb* to consider or to discuss a problem; *the committee deliberated for several hours before reaching a decision*

deliberations [dɪlɪbəˈreɪʃnz] *plural noun* discussions; *the result of the committee's deliberations was passed to the newspapers*

delicti [dɪˈlɪktaɪ] *see* CORPUS

delicto [dɪˈlɪktəʊ] *see* IN FLAGRANTE DELICTO

delinquency [dɪˈlɪŋkwənsi] *noun* the act of committing crime, usually minor crime

delinquent [dɪˈlɪŋkwənt] 1 *adjective* US overdue (debt) 2 *noun* **a juvenile delinquent,** US **a delinquent** = young criminal who commits minor crimes, especially crimes against property

deliver [dɪˈlɪvə] *verb* to transport goods to a customer; **goods delivered free** *or* **free delivered goods** = goods carried to the customer's address at a price which includes transport costs; **goods delivered on board** = goods carried free to the ship or plane but not to the customer's warehouse

delivery [dɪˈlɪvri] *noun* **(a)** **delivery of goods** = transport of goods to a customer's address; **delivery note** = list of goods being delivered, given to the customer with the goods; **delivery order** = instructions given by the customer to the person holding his goods, to tell him to deliver them; **recorded delivery** = mail service where the letters are signed for by the person receiving them; **cash on delivery** = payment in cash when the goods are delivered; **to take delivery of goods** = to accept goods when they are delivered; *(infringement of copyright)* **delivery up** = the action of delivering goods which have been made in infringement of a copyright or patent to the claimant, so that they can be destroyed **(b)** goods being delivered; *we take in three deliveries a day*; *there were four items missing in the last delivery* **(c)** transfer of a bill of exchange **(d)** formal act whereby a deed becomes effective; *deeds take effect only from the time of delivery*

demagogue [ˈdeməgɒg] *noun* *(usually as criticism)* leader who is able to get the support of the people by exciting their lowest feelings and prejudices

demagogy *or* **demagoguery** [ˈdeməgɒgi *or* ˈdeməgɒgri] *noun* acting as a demagogue, by appealing to the lowest feelings (usually fear, greed or hatred) of the mass of the people

demand [dɪˈmɑːnd] 1 *noun* **(a)** asking for payment; **payable on demand** = which must be paid when payment is asked for; **demand bill** = bill of exchange which must be paid when payment is asked for; **final demand** = last reminder from a supplier, after which he will sue for payment; **letter of demand** = letter issued by a party or lawyer demanding payment before taking legal action **(b)** need for goods at a certain price; **supply and demand** = amount of a product which is available at a certain price and the amount which is wanted by customers at that price; **law of supply and demand** = general rule that the amount of a product which is available is related to the needs of possible customers **2** *verb* to ask for something and expect to get it; *they were accused of demanding payment with threats*

demanding with menaces

[dɪˈmɑːndɪŋ wɪθ ˈmenəsɪz] *noun* crime of demanding money by threatening someone

démarche [ˈdeɪmɑːʃ] *noun* official diplomatic move (such as a visit to the Foreign Office, passing a letter from a head of government)

de minimis non curat lex [deɪ ˈmɪnɪmɪs nɒn ˈkjʊəræt ˈleks] *Latin phrase* meaning 'the law does not deal with trivial things'

demise [dɪˈmaɪz] *noun* **(a)** death; *on his demise the estate passed to his daughter*; **demise of the Crown** = death of a king or queen **(b)** granting of property on a lease; **demise charter** = charter of a ship without the crew

democracy [dɪˈmɒkrəsi] *noun* **(a)** theory or system of government by freely elected representatives of the people; the right to fair government, free election of representatives and equality in voting; *after the coup, democracy was replaced by a military dictatorship* **(b)** country ruled in this way; *the pact was welcomed by western democracies*

democrat [ˈdeməkræt] *noun* person who believes in democracy

democratic [deməˈkrætɪk] *adjective* **(a)** referring to a democracy; *after the coup the democratic processes of government were replaced by government by decree* **(b)** free and fair, reflecting the views of the majority; *the resolution was passed by a democratic vote of the council*; *the action of the leader is against the wishes of the party as expressed in a democratic vote at the party conference*

demonstrative legacy

[dɪˈmɒnstrətɪv ˈlegəsi] *noun* gift in a will which is ordered to be paid out of a special account

demur [dɪˈmɜː] **1** *noun* objection; *counsel made no demur to the proposal* **2** *verb* **(a)** not to agree; *counsel stated that there was no case to answer, but the judge demurred* **(b)** to make a formal objection that the facts as alleged are not sufficient to warrant the civil action (NOTE: **demurring - demurred**)

demurrage [dɪˈmʌrɪdʒ] *noun* money paid to the owner of a cargo when a ship is delayed in a port

demurrer [dɪˈmɜːrə] *noun* in a civil action, a plea that although the facts of the case are correct, they are not sufficient to warrant the action

denomination [dɪnɒmɪˈneɪʃn] *noun* unit of money (on a coin, stamp or banknote); *small denomination banknotes*; *coins of all denominations*

de novo [ˈdeɪ ˈnəuvəu] *Latin phrase* meaning 'starting again'

denial [dɪˈnaɪəl] *noun* **(a)** act of not allowing something; **denial of human rights** = refusing someone a right which is generally accepted as fair; **denial of justice** = situation where justice appears not to have been done **(b)** act of stating that you have not done something; *in spite of his denials he was found guilty*

deny [dɪˈnaɪ] *verb* **(a)** not to allow something; *he was denied the right to see his lawyer* **(b)** to say that you have not done something; *he denied being in the house at the time of the murder* (NOTE: you deny someone something or deny doing *or* having done something)

depart [dɪˈpɑːt] *verb* **to depart from normal practice** = to act in a different way from the normal practice

department [dɪˈpɑːtmənt] *noun* **(a)** specialized section of a large company; **accounts department** = section which deals with money paid or received; **legal**

department = section of a company dealing with legal matters; **head of department** *or* **department head** *or* **department manager** = person in charge of a department **(b)** section of a large store selling one type of product; **furniture department** = department in a large store which sells furniture **(c) Department of State** = (i) major section of the British government headed by a Secretary of State; (ii) major section of the US government headed by a Secretary; *the Department of Trade and Industry*; *the Lord Chancellor's Department*; **State Department** = department in the US government dealing with relations with other countries; *compare* MINISTRY **(d)** one of the administrative divisions of a country, such as France

departmental [diːpɑːˈtmentl] *adjective* referring to a department; *if you want to complain, you should first talk to your departmental head*

departure from [dɪˈpɑːtʃə ˈfrɒm] *phrase* thing which is different from what happened before; *this forms a departure from established practice*; *any departure from the terms and conditions of the contract must be advised in writing*

dependant [dɪˈpendənt] *noun* **(a)** person who is supported financially by someone else; *he has to provide for his family and dependants out of a very small salary* **(b)** *(in the EU)* person who is a member of an EU worker's family, even if not a EU citizen

COMMENT: for the purposes of EU law, dependants are classified as the spouse of a EU citizen, the children and parents of a EU citizen, the grandchildren and grandparents of a EU citizen (in the case of children and grandchildren, they count as dependants up to the age of 21)

dependent [dɪˈpendənt] *adjective* **(a)** (person) who is supported financially by someone else; *tax relief is allowed for dependent relatives* **(b)** referring to a dependant; *(in the EU)* **dependent rights** = the rights of a dependant to enter a EU

country along with a parent or other close relative; *compare* INDEPENDENT RIGHTS

deponent [dɪˈpəʊnənt] *noun* person who makes a statement under oath, by affirmation or by affidavit

deport [dɪˈpɔːt] *verb* to send (someone) away from a country; *the illegal immigrants were deported*

deportation [diːpɔːˈteɪʃn] *noun* sending of someone away from a country; *the convicts were sentenced to deportation*; **deportation order** = official order to send someone away from a country; *the minister signed the deportation order*

depose [dɪˈpəʊz] *verb* **(a)** to state under oath **(b)** to remove (a king) from the throne

deposit [dɪˈpɒzɪt] **1** *noun* **(a)** money placed in a bank for safe keeping or to earn interest; **certificate of deposit** = certificate from a bank to show that money has been deposited; **deposit account** = bank account which pays interest but on which notice has to be given to withdraw money; **licensed deposit-taker** = business (such as a bank) which takes deposits from individuals and lends the money to others **(b) safe deposit** = bank safe where you can leave jewellery or documents; **safe deposit box** = small box which you can rent, in which you can keep jewellery or documents in a bank's safe **(c)** money given in advance so that the thing which you want to buy will not be sold to someone else; *to leave £10 as deposit*; **to forfeit a deposit** = to lose a deposit because you have decided not to buy the item **(d)** money paid by a candidate when nominated for an election, which is forfeited if the candidate does not win enough votes; *he polled only 25 votes and lost his deposit* **2** *verb* **(a)** to put documents somewhere for safe keeping; *we have deposited the deeds of the house with the bank*; *he deposited his will with his solicitor* **(b)** to put money into a bank account; *to deposit £100 in a current account*

depositary [dɪˈpɒzɪtri] *noun US* person or corporation which can place money or documents for safekeeping with a depository (NOTE: do not confuse with **depository**)

deposition [depə'zıʃn] *noun* written statement of evidence from a witness

depositor [dɪ'pɒzɪtə] *noun* person who deposits money in a bank

depository [dɪ'pɒzɪtri] *noun* **(a)** **furniture depository** = warehouse where you can store household furniture **(b)** person or company with whom money or documents can be deposited (NOTE: do not confuse with **depositary**)

deprave [dɪ'preɪv] *verb* to make someone's character bad; *TV programmes which may deprave the minds of children who watch them*

dept [dɪ'pɑːtmənt] = DEPARTMENT

deputize ['depjutaɪz] *verb* **to deputize for someone** = to take the place of someone who is absent; **to deputize someone** = to appoint someone as a deputy

deputy ["depjuti] *noun* **(a)** person who takes the place of a higher official, who assists a higher official; *he acted as deputy for the chairman* or *he acted as the chairman's deputy*; **Deputy Mayor** = member of a town council who stands in for a mayor if the latter is absent; **Deputy Prime Minister** = title given to a senior cabinet minister who stands in for the Prime Minister when the latter is unable to act; **Deputy Speaker** = Chairman of Ways and Means, who stands in for the Speaker when the latter is absent **(b)** *US* person who acts for or assists a sheriff **(c)** *(in Canada)* **Deputy Minister** = chief civil servant in charge of a ministry (NOTE: in the UK, this is the **Permanent Secretary**) **(d)** *(in some countries)* member of parliament, member of a legislative body; *after the Prime Minister resigned, the deputies of his party started to discuss the election of a successor*; **Chamber of Deputies** = lower house of the legislature in some countries (as opposed to the Senate)

deregulation [diːregjʊ'leɪʃn] *noun* reducing government control over an industry; *the deregulation of the airlines*

derelict ['derɪlɪkt] *noun* abandoned floating boat

dereliction of duty [derɪ'lɪkʃn əv 'djuːti] *noun* failure to do what you ought to do; *he was found guilty of gross dereliction of duty*

derivative action [dɪ'rɪvətɪv 'ækʃn] *noun* action started by a shareholder (or a group of shareholders) which is derived from the company's rights but which the company itself does not want to proceed with

derive [dɪ'raɪv] *verb* **(a)** to come from; *this law derives from* or *is derived from the former Roman law of property* **(b)** to obtain; *he derived financial benefit from the transaction*

derogate ['derəgeɪt] *verb* **to derogate from something which has been agreed** = to act to prevent something which has been agreed from being fully implemented

derogation [derə'geɪʃn] *noun* **(a)** act of avoiding or destroying something; **derogation of responsibility** = avoiding doing a duty **(b)** *(in the EU)* action by which an EC directive is not applied

COMMENT: derogations from the principle of equality of access to employment may be where the job can only be done by someone of one particular sex (such as a person modelling men's clothes)

descendant [dɪ'sendənt] *noun (in the EU)* child or grandchild of a person (NOTE: the opposite, the parents or grandparents of a person are **ascendants**)

descent [dɪ'sent] *noun* **(a)** family ties of inheritance between parents and children; **he is British by descent** or **he is of British descent** = one (or both) of his parents is British; **lineal descent** = direct descent from parent to child **(b)** **by descent** = way of inheriting property by an heir, where there is no will

description [dɪ'skrɪpʃn] *noun* words which show what something is like; *the police circulated a description of the missing boy or of the wanted man*; **false description of contents** = wrongly stating the contents of a packet to trick customers into buying it; **trade description** = description of a product to attract customers; *GB* **Trade Descriptions Act** = Act of Parliament which limits the way in which products can be described so as to protect consumers from wrong descriptions made by the makers

desegregate [diː'segrəgeɪt] *verb* to end segregation, to stop (schools, buses, etc.) being segregated

desegregation [diːsegrə'geɪʃn] *noun* ending of segregation

deselect [diːsə'lekt] *verb* to decide that a person who had been selected by a political party as a candidate for a constituency is no longer the candidate

deselection [diːsə'lekʃn] *noun* act of deselecting; *some factions in the local party have proposed the deselection of the candidate*

desert [dɪ'zɜːt] *verb* **(a)** to leave the armed forces without permission; *he deserted and went to live in South America* **(b)** to leave a family or spouse; *the two children have been deserted by their father*

deserter [dɪ'zɜːtə] *noun* person who has left the armed forces without permission

desertion [dɪ'zɜːʃn] *noun* **(a)** leaving the armed forces without permission **(b)** leaving one's spouse; *he divorced his wife because of her desertion*

desist [dɪ'zɪst] *verb see* CEASE AND DESIST

despatch [dɪ'spætʃ] *verb* to send; *the letters about the rates were despatched yesterday*; *the Defence Minister was despatched to take charge of the operation*

despatch box [dɪ'spætʃ 'bɒks] *noun* **(a)** red box in which government papers are sent to ministers **(b)** one of two boxes on the centre table in the House of Commons at which a Minister or member of the Opposition Front Bench stands to speak; *(of a minister)* **to be at the despatch box** = to be speaking in parliament

destruction [dɪ'strʌkʃn] *noun* action of killing someone, or of ending the existence of something completely; *the destruction of the evidence in the fire at the police station made it difficult to prosecute*; **child destruction** = notifiable offence of killing an unborn child capable of being born alive

detain [dɪ'teɪn] *verb* to hold a person so that he cannot leave; *the suspects were detained by the police for questioning*

detainee [diːteɪ'niː] *noun* person who has been detained

detainer [dɪ'teɪnə] *noun* act of holding a person

detect [dɪ'tekt] *verb* to notice or to discover (something which is hidden or difficult to see); *the machine can detect explosives*

detection [dɪ'tekʃn] *noun* discovering something, especially discovering who has committed a crime or how a crime has been committed; **detection rate** = number of crimes which are solved, as a percentage of all crimes

detective [dɪ'tektɪv] *noun* person, usually a policeman, who tries to solve a crime; **private detective** = person who for a fee will try to solve mysteries, to find missing people or will keep watch on someone; **detective agency** = office which hires out the services of private detectives

COMMENT: the ranks of detectives in the British Police Force are Detective Constable, Detective Sergeant, Detective Inspector, Detective Chief Inspector, Detective Superintendent, and Detective Chief Superintendent

détente [deɪtɒnt] *noun* relaxation of tension between two countries

detention [dɪ'tenʃn] *noun* **(a)** keeping someone so that he cannot escape; *the* suspects were placed in detention; **detention centre** = place where young offenders (aged between 14 and 21) can be kept for corrective training, instead of being sent to prison, if they are convicted of crimes which would normally carry a sentence of three months' imprisonment or more; **detention order** = court order asking for someone to be kept in detention; *US* **pretrial detention** = being kept in prison until the trial starts (NOTE: the British equivalent is **remanded in custody**) **(b)** wrongfully holding goods which belong to someone else

determine [dɪ'tɜːmɪn] *verb* **(a)** to fix, to arrange or to decide; *to determine prices or quantities*; *the conditions of the contract are still to be determined* **(b)** to bring to an end; *the tenancy was determined by a notice to quit*

deterrence [dɪ'terəns] *noun* idea that the harsh punishment of one criminal will deter other people from committing crimes

deterrent [dɪ'terənt] **1** *noun* punishment which will deter people from committing crimes; *a long prison sentence will act as a deterrent to other possible criminals* **2** *adjective* **deterrent sentence** = harsh sentence which the judge hopes will deter other people from committing crimes

detinue ['detɪnjuː] *noun* tort of wrongfully holding goods which belong to someone else; **action in detinue** = action formerly brought to regain possession of goods which were wrongfully held by someone

detriment ['detrɪmənt] *noun* damage or harm; **without detriment to his claim** = without harming his claim; **his action was to the detriment of the claimant** = his action harmed the claimant

detrimental [detrɪ'mentəl] *adjective* which may harm; *action detrimental to the maintenance of public order*

develop [dɪ'veləp] *verb* **(a)** to plan and produce; *to develop a new product* **(b)** to plan and build an area; *to develop an industrial estate*

developer [dɪ'veləpə] *noun* **a property developer** = person who plans and builds a group of new houses or new factories

development [dɪ'veləpmənt] *noun* **(a)** planning the production of a new product or new town; **industrial development** = planning and building of new industries in special areas; **development area** *or* **development zone** = area which has been given special help from a government to encourage businesses and factories to be set up there **(b)** change which has taken place; *the case represents a new development in the law of libel*

devil ['devəl] **1** *noun* barrister to whom another barrister passes work because he is too busy **2** *verb* to pass instruction to another barrister because you are too busy to deal with the case yourself; **to devil for someone** = to do unpleasant or boring work for someone

devise [dɪ'vaɪz] **1** *noun* giving freehold land to someone in a will; **residuary devise** = devise to someone of what is left of the testator's property after other devises have been made and taxes have been paid; **specific devise** = devise of a certain specified property to someone **2** *verb* to give freehold property to someone in a will

COMMENT: giving of other types of property is a **bequest**

devisee [diːvaɪ'ziː] *noun* person who receives freehold property in a will

devolution [devə'luːʃn] *noun* passing of power to govern or to make decisions from a central authority to a local authority

COMMENT: devolution involves passing more power than decentralization. In a devolved state, the regional authorities are almost autonomous

devolve [dɪ'vɒlv] *verb* **(a)** to pass power to another authority; *power is devolved to regional assemblies* **(b)** to pass to someone under the terms of a will

dictator [dɪk'teɪtə] *noun* ruler who has complete personal power; *the country has* *been ruled by a military dictator for six years*; *the MPs accused the party leader of behaving like a dictator*

dictatorial [dɪktə'tɔːrɪəl] *adjective* **(a)** referring to a dictator; *a dictatorial form of government* **(b)** behaving like a dictator; *officials dislike the Minister's dictatorial way of working*

dictatorship [dɪk'teɪtəʃɪp] *noun* **(a)** rule by a dictator; *under the dictatorship of Mussolini, personal freedom was restricted*; **the dictatorship of the proletariat** = in Marxist theory, the period after a revolution when the Communist Party takes control until a true classless society develops **(b)** country ruled by a dictator; **a military dictatorship** = country ruled by an army officer as a dictator

dictum ['dɪktəm] *noun* saying or statement made by a judge; **obiter dicta** = part of a judgment which does not form an essential part of it; *see also* RATIO DECIDENDI (NOTE: plural is **dicta**)

digest ['daɪdʒest] *noun* book which collects summaries of court decisions together, used for reference purposes by lawyers

dilatory ['dɪlətrɪ] *adjective* too slow; **dilatory motion** = motion in the House of Commons to delay the debate on a proposal; **dilatory plea** = plea by a defendant relating to the jurisdiction of the court, which has the effect of delaying the action

diminish [dɪ'mɪnɪʃ] *verb* to get, to make smaller; **diminished responsibility,** *US* **diminished capacity** = mental state of a criminal (inherited or caused by illness or injury) which means that he cannot be held responsible for a crime which he has committed

DInsp = DETECTIVE INSPECTOR

dip [dɪp] *noun (slang)* pickpocket

diplomacy [dɪ'pləʊməsɪ] *noun* **(a)** management of a country's interest in another country, by its diplomats; *the art of diplomacy is to anticipate the next move by the other government*; **gunboat**

diplomacy = trying to solve international problems by force, or by threatening to use force; **quiet diplomacy** = discussing problems with officials of another country in a calm way, without telling the press about it; **secret diplomacy** = discussing problems with another country in secret **(b)** quiet and tactful way of persuading people to do what you want, of settling problems; **he is a master of diplomacy** = he is very good at negotiating

diplomat *or* **diplomatist** ['dɪpləmæt or dɪ'pləʊmətɪst] *noun* person (such as an ambassador) who is an official representative of his country in another country

diplomatic [dɪplə'mætɪk] *adjective* **(a)** referring to diplomats; *his car had a diplomatic number plate*; *she was using a diplomatic passport*; **diplomatic agent** = person officially employed by the embassy of a foreign country; **the diplomatic bag** = bag or box containing official government documents which is carried from one country to another by diplomats and cannot be opened by officials of another country; *he was accused of shipping arms into the country in the diplomatic bag*; **diplomatic channels** = communicating between countries through their diplomats; *the message was delivered by diplomatic channels*; *they are working to restore diplomatic channels between the two countries*; **diplomatic corps** = all foreign diplomats in a city or country; **diplomatic immunity** = not being subject to the laws of the country in which you are living, because you are a diplomat; *he claimed diplomatic immunity to avoid being arrested*; **to grant someone diplomatic status** = to give someone the rights of a diplomat **(b)** quiet and tactful, when dealing with other people

direct [daɪ'rekt] **1** *verb* to order, to give an order to (someone); *the judge directed the jury to acquit all the defendants*; *the Crown Court directed the justices to rehear the case* **2** *adjective* straight, with no interference; **direct evidence** = first-hand evidence, such as the testimony of an eye witness or the production of original documents; **direct examination** = asking a witness questions (by lawyers for his side) so that he gives oral evidence in court; **direct mail** = selling a product by sending advertising material by post to possible buyers; **direct selling** = selling a product direct to the customer without going through a shop; **direct taxation** = tax, such as income tax, which is paid direct to the government; *see also* DEBIT **3** *adverb* straight, with no third party involved; *we pay income tax direct to the government; the fine is paid direct to the court*

direct effect [daɪ'rekt ɪ'fekt] *noun (in the EU)* one of the twin pillars of EC law (the other is supremacy), the effect of a legal decision of the European Community which creates rights for citizens

> COMMENT: direct effect applies vertically, from the state giving a right to the citizen, and from the citizen who has an obligation to the state. It can also apply horizontally between individual citizens who have rights and obligations to each other

direction [dɪ'rekʃn] *noun* **(a)** way in which something is going; *the new evidence changed the direction of the hearing* **(b)** organizing or managing; *he took over the direction of a large bank* **(c)** **practice direction** = rules laid down in the Civil Procedure Rules for the management of cases under a particular track **(d)** **directions** = (i) order which explains how something should be done; (ii) instructions from a judge to a jury; (iii) orders given by a judge concerning the general way of proceeding with a case; *the court is not able to give directions to the local authority*; **special directions** = directions given by a court in a particular case, which are additional to the normal standard directions; **standard directions** = directions as laid out in the practice direction for a particular track

directive [daɪ'rektɪv] *noun* **(a)** order or command to someone to do something **(b)** *(in the EU)* legally binding act of the European Community which is binding on the Member States of the EU but not on individuals until it has been made part of national law; *the Commission issued a directive on food prices*

> COMMENT: a directive is binding in the result which is to be achieved. Directives do not have a direct effect before any time limit for their implementation has expired, and they do not have any horizontal direct effect (ie an effect between citizens); *compare* REGULATIONS

director [dɪ'rektə] *noun* **(a)** person appointed by the shareholders to manage a company; **managing director** = the most senior executive director in a company; **chairman and managing director** = managing director who is also chairman of the board of directors; **board of directors** = all the directors of a company; **directors' report** = annual report from the board of directors to the shareholders; **executive director** = director who actually works full-time in the company; **non-executive director** = director who attends board meetings and gives advice, but does not work full-time for the company; **outside director** = director who is not employed by the company **(b)** person who is in charge of a programme of work, an official institute, etc.; *he is the director of a government institute*; *she was appointed director of the charity* **(c)** *(in the EU)* person who heads one of the Directorates in the Commission

Directorate [daɪ'rektərət] *noun (in the EU)* one of the subdivisions of the main departments of the Commission, headed by a Director

Directorate General [daɪ'rektərət 'dʒenərl] *noun (in the EU)* one of the 23 main departments of the Commission, responsible directly to one of the Commissioners; it is headed by a Director-General (NOTE: the plural is **Directorates General**)

Director-General [daɪ'rektə'dʒenərl] *noun* **(a)** person in charge of a large public office; **Director-General of Fair Trading** = official in charge of the Office of Fair Trading, dealing with consumers and the law **(b)** *(in the EU)* person who heads one of the Directorates General in the Commission (NOTE: the plural is **Directors-General)**

Director of Public Prosecutions (DPP) [dɪ'rektə əv 'pʌblɪk prɒsɪ'kjuːʃnz]

noun government official in charge of the Crown Prosecution Service (working under the Attorney-General), who can prosecute in important cases and advises other government departments if prosecutions should be started; *the papers in the fraud case have been sent to the Director of Public Prosecutions*

directory [daɪ'rektri] *noun* list of people or businesses with information about their addresses and telephone numbers; **classified directory** = list of businesses grouped under various headings, such as computer shops or newsagents; **commercial directory** *or* **trade directory** = book which lists all the businesses and business people in a town; **street directory** = (i) list of people living in a street; (ii) map of a town which lists all the streets in alphabetical order in an index; **telephone directory** = book which lists all people and businesses who have telephones, in alphabetical order with their phone numbers

disability [dɪsə'bɪləti] *noun* **(a)** being unable to use one's body properly (as because you are blind, cannot walk, etc.) **(b)** lack of legal capacity to act in one's own right (such as because of one's age or mental state); **person under a disability** = person who is not capable to taking legal action for himself

disabled person [dɪs'eɪbld 'pɜːsən] *noun* person who is physically handicapped in some way (such as being blind or not capable of walking)

disabling statute [dɪs'eɪblɪŋ 'stætjuːt] *noun* statute which removes a right from someone (the opposite of an 'enabling statute')

disallow [dɪsə'laʊ] *verb* to reject, not to accept; *the judge disallowed the defence evidence*; *he claimed £2000 for fire damage, but the claim was disallowed*

disapproval [dɪsə'pruːvl] *noun* act of disapproving a decision made by a lower court

disapprove [dɪsə'pruːv] *verb* **(a)** to show doubt about (a decision made by a lower court), but not to reverse or overrule it; *the Appeal Court disapproved the County Court decision* **(b) to disapprove of something** = to show that you do not approve of something, that you do not think something is good; *the judge openly disapproves of juries*

disbar [dɪs'bɑː] *verb* to stop a barrister from practising (NOTE: **disbarring - disbarred**)

disburse [dɪs'bɜːs] *verb* to pay money

disbursement [dɪs'bɜːsmənt] *noun* payment of money

discharge 1 ['dɪstʃɑːdʒ] *noun* **(a)** ending of a contract by performing all the conditions of the contract, by releasing a party from the terms of the contract or by being in breach of contract; **discharge by agreement** = situation where both parties agree to end a contract; **discharge by performance** = situation where the terms of a contract have been fulfilled; **discharge in** *or* **of bankruptcy** = order of a court to release someone from bankruptcy **(b)** payment of debt; **in full discharge of a debt** = paying a debt completely, paying less than the total amount owed, by agreement; **final discharge** = final payment of what is left of a debt **(c)** release from prison or from military service; **absolute discharge** = letting an offender go free without any punishment; **conditional discharge** = allowing an offender to be set free without any immediate punishment on condition that he does not commit an offence during the following period **(d) in discharge of his duties as director** = carrying out his duties as director **(e)** *US* **Discharge Calendar;** *see comment at* CALENDAR **2** [dɪs'tʃɑːdʒ] *verb* **(a)** to let (someone) go free; *the prisoners were discharged by the judge*;

the judge discharged the jury = the judge told the jury that they were no longer needed **(b) to discharge a bankrupt** = to release someone from bankruptcy (as when a person has paid his debts) **(c) to discharge a debt** *or* **to discharge one's liabilities** = to pay a debt or one's liabilities in full **(d)** to dismiss, to sack; *to discharge an employee*

discipline ['dɪsɪplɪn] *verb* to punish (an official); *the clerk was disciplined for leaking the report to the newspapers*

disciplinary [dɪsɪ'plɪnəri] *adjective* **disciplinary procedure** = way of warning a worker officially that he is breaking rules or that he is working badly; **to take disciplinary action against someone** = to punish someone

disclaim [dɪs'kleɪm] *verb* **(a)** to refuse to admit; *he disclaimed all knowledge of the bomb*; *the management disclaims all responsibility for customers' property* **(b)** to refuse to accept a legacy or devise made to you under someone's will

disclaimer [dɪs'keɪmə] *noun* **(a)** legal refusal to accept responsibility or to accept a right **(b)** clause in a contract where a party disclaims responsibility for something **(c)** refusing to accept property bequeathed to you under someone's will

disclose [dɪs'kləʊz] *verb* **(a)** to tell details; *the bank has no right to disclose details of my account to the tax office* **(b)** *(in civil cases)* to say that a document exists; *parties to a case are required to disclose relevant documents*

disclosure [dɪs'kləʊʒə] *noun* **(a)** act of telling details or of publishing a secret; *the disclosure of the takeover bid raised the price of the shares*; *the defendant's case was made stronger by the disclosure that the claimant was an undischarged bankrupt*; *see also* NON-DISCLOSURE **(b)** stating that documents exist or have existed before a hearing starts in the civil courts (usually done by preparing a list of documents: parties to whom documents have been disclosed have the right to inspect them) (NOTE: since the introduction of

the new Civil Procedure Rules in April 1999, this term has in some contexts replaced **discovery**); **specific disclosure** = order by a court for a party to disclose certain documents or to search for them and disclose them if they are found to exist; **standard disclosure** = statement by a party that certain documents exist (these are documents which will support his case, documents which do not support his case, and documents which will support the case of the other party); *see also* FISHING EXPEDITION

discontinuance [dɪskən'tɪnjuəns] *noun* action of discontinuing a claim or action; *the claimant has served notice of discontinuance*

discontinue [dɪskən'tɪnjuː] *verb* to stop a claim which has been issued or an action which has started; *a claimant may need to seek permission of the court to discontinue a claim*

discovery [dɪs'kʌvri] *noun* **discovery of documents** = disclosure of each party's documents to the other before a hearing starts in the civil courts (NOTE: since the introduction of the new Civil Procedure Rules in April 1999, this term has in some contexts been replaced by **disclosure**)

discredit [dɪs'kredɪt] *verb* to show that a person is not reliable; *the prosecution counsel tried to discredit the defence witnesses*

discrepancy [dɪs'krepənsi] *noun* difference between two sets of figures; *there is a discrepancy between the crime figures released by the Home Office and those of the Metropolitan Police Force*

discretion [dɪs'kreʃn] *noun* being able to decide correctly what should be done; *magistrates have a discretion to allow an accused person to change his election from a summary trial to a jury trial*; *the judge refused the application, on the ground that he had a judicial discretion to examine inadmissible evidence*; **to exercise one's discretion** = to decide which of several possible ways to act; **the court exercised its discretion** = the court decided what should be done; **I leave it to**

your discretion = I leave it for you to decide what to do; **at the discretion of someone** = if someone decides; *membership is at the discretion of the committee*; *sentencing is at the discretion of the judge*; *the granting of an injunction is at the discretion of the court*

discretionary [dɪs'kreʃənri] *adjective* which can be done if someone wants; **the minister's discretionary powers** = powers which the minister could use if he thought he should do so; **the tribunal has wide discretionary power** = the tribunal can decide on many different courses of action; **discretionary trust** = trust where the trustees decide how to invest the income and when and how much income should be paid to the beneficiaries

discriminate [dɪs'krɪmɪneɪt] *verb* to note differences between things and act accordingly; *the planning committee finds it difficult to discriminate between applications which improve the community, and those which are purely commercial*; **to discriminate against someone** = to treat someone unequally; *the council was accused of discriminating against women in its recruitment policy*; *he claimed he had been discriminated against because of his colour*

discrimination [dɪskrɪmɪ'neɪʃn] *noun* (a) noting the differences between things; *the arts committee showed discrimination in selecting the design for the new civic centre* (b) treating people in different ways because of class, religion, race, language, colour or sex; *racial discrimination is against the law*; *she accused the council of sexual discrimination in their recruitment policy*; **age discrimination** = treating people differently because of age (an offence in the USA); *(in the EU)* **direct discrimination** = illegal discrimination where similar cases are treated differently or where different cases are treated in the same way; *(in the EU)* **indirect discrimination** = discrimination by applying an abstract principle, so that the result is that people of different sexes are treated differently; **positive discrimination** = discriminating in favour

of one category of workers, such as women, to enable them to be more equal; *the council's policy of positive discrimination has ensured that more women are appointed to senior posts*; **sexual discrimination** *or* **sex discrimination** *or* **discrimination on grounds of sex** = treating men and women in different ways, implying that one is less important than the other

disenfranchise *or* **disfranchise** [dɪsɪn'fræntʃaɪz] *verb* to take away someone's right to vote; *the company has tried to disenfranchise the ordinary shareholders*

dishonour [dɪs'ɒnə] **1** *verb* to refuse to pay a cheque or bill of exchange because there is not enough money in the account to pay it; *the bank dishonoured his cheque* **2** *noun* act of dishonouring a cheque; *the dishonour of the cheque brought her business to a stop*; **notice of dishonour** = letter or document warning a person to pay a cheque or risk being sued

disinherit [dɪsɪn'herɪt] *verb* to make a will which prevents someone from inheriting; *he was disinherited by his father*

disk [dɪsk] *noun* round flat object, used to store information in computers; **floppy disk** = small disk for storing information for a computer; **hard disk** = solid disk which will store a large amount of computer information in a sealed case; **disk drive** = part of a computer which makes a disk turn round in order to read it or store information on it

diskette [dɪ'sket] *noun* very small floppy disk

dismiss [dɪs'mɪs] *verb* **(a) to dismiss an employee** = to remove an employee from a job; *he was dismissed for being late* **(b)** to refuse to accept; *the court dismissed the appeal or the application or the action*; *the justices dismissed the witness' evidence out of hand*

dismissal [dɪs'mɪsl] *noun* **(a)** cancelling (an action) **(b)** removal of an employee from a job; **dismissal procedure** = correct way of dismissing an employee, following the rules in the contract of employment; **constructive dismissal** = situation where an employee leaves his job voluntarily but because of pressure from the management; **unfair dismissal** = removing someone from a job by an employer who appears not to be acting in a reasonable way (i.e., as by dismissing someone who wants to join a union); **wrongful dismissal** = removing someone from a job for a reason which does not justify dismissal and which is in breach of the contract of employment

COMMENT: an employee can complain of unfair dismissal to an industrial tribunal, or of wrongful dismissal to the County Court

disobedience [dɪsə'biːdiəns] *noun* not obeying; *the prisoners were put in solitary confinement as punishment for their disobedience of the governor's orders*; **civil disobedience** = disobeying orders by civil authorities (such as the police) as an act of protest; *the group planned a campaign of civil disobedience as a protest against restrictions on immigrants*

disorder [dɪs'ɔːdə] *noun* lack of order or of control; **civil disorder** *or* **public disorder(s)** *or* **public disorders** = riots, disturbances or fighting in the streets; **mental disorder** = sickness of the mind

disorderly [dɪs'ɔːdəli] *adjective* badly behaved, wild; *he was charged with disorderly conduct or with being drunk and disorderly*; **keeping a disorderly house** = being the proprietor or manager of a brothel

dispensation [dɪspən'seɪʃn] *noun* **(a)** act of giving out justice **(b)** special permission to do something which is normally not allowed or is against the law

dispense [dɪ'spens] *verb* **(a)** to give out (justice) **(b) to dispense with something** = not to use something, to do without something; *the chairman of the tribunal dispensed with the formality of taking minutes*; *the accused decided to dispense with the services of a lawyer*

disposable [dɪ'spəʊzəbl] *adjective* **(a)** which can be used and then thrown away **(b) disposable income** = income left after tax and national insurance have been deducted

disposal [dɪ'spəʊzl] *noun* sale; *disposal of securities or of property*; **lease** *or* **business for disposal** = lease *or* business for sale

dispose [dɪ'spəʊz] *verb* **to dispose of** = to get rid of, to sell cheaply; *to dispose of excess stock*; *to dispose of one's business*

disposition [dɪspə'zɪʃn] *noun* act of passing property (land or goods) to another person, especially in a will; *to make testamentary dispositions*

dispossess [dɪspə'zes] *verb* to deprive someone wrongfully of his possession of land

dispossession [dɪspə'zeʃn] *noun* act of wrongfully depriving someone of possession of land

dispute [dɪ'spjuːt] **1** *noun* disagreement or argument between parties; **industrial disputes** *or* **labour disputes** = arguments between management and workers; **to adjudicate** *or* **to mediate in a dispute** = to try to settle a dispute between other parties; *(in the EU)* **genuine dispute** = real conflict between parties; *the ECJ refused to hear the reference because it considered there was no genuine dispute between the parties*; **trade dispute** = (i) international dispute over trade matters; (ii) dispute between management and workers over conditions of employment or union membership **2** *verb* to argue against something; **the defendant disputed the claim** = the defendant argued that the claim was not correct; **she disputed the policeman's version of events** = she said that the policeman's story of what had happened was wrong; **to dispute the jurisdiction of a court** = to argue that a court has no jurisdiction over a case

disqualification [dɪskwɒlɪfɪ'keɪʃn] *noun* **(a)** being disqualified from doing something; **Parliamentary**

disqualification = being disqualified from being a Member of Parliament, as when someone is a paid member of a commission or tribunal **(b)** being disqualified from driving a car **(c) disqualification from office** = rule which forces a director to be removed from a directorship if he does not fulfil certain conditions

disqualify [dɪsˈkwɒlɪfaɪ] *verb* to make (someone) not able to do something; *being a judge disqualifies him from being a Member of Parliament*; *after the accident he was fined £1000 and disqualified from driving for two years*; *he was convicted of driving a motor vehicle while disqualified*

disrepute [dɪsrɪˈpjuːt] *noun* bad reputation; **to bring something into disrepute** = to give something a bad reputation; *he was accused of bringing the club into disrepute by his bad behaviour*

disrespect [dɪsrɪsˈpekt] *noun* lack of respect; *he was accused of showing disrespect to the judge*

disseisin [dɪsˈsiːzɪn] *noun* dispossession, wrongfully depriving someone of possession of land

dissemination [dɪsemɪˈneɪʃn] *noun* act of passing information, slanderous or libellous statements to other members of the public

dissent [dɪˈsent] **1** *noun* not agreeing; *the opposition showed its dissent by voting against the Bill* **2** *verb* not to agree with someone; *one of the appeal judges dissented*; **dissenting judgment** = judgment of a judge, showing that he disagrees with other judges in a case which has been heard by several judges

dissolution [dɪsəˈluːʃn] *noun* ending (of a partnership or a marriage); **dissolution of Parliament** = ending of a Parliament, so forcing a general election; *the government lost the vote of no confidence, and so the Prime Minister asked for a dissolution of parliament*

COMMENT: the British Parliament can only be dissolved by the Queen, acting on the advice of the Prime Minister

dissolve [dɪˈzɒlv] *verb* to bring to an end; *to dissolve a marriage or a partnership or a company*; **to dissolve Parliament** = to end a session of Parliament, and so force a general election

distinguish [dɪˈstɪŋgwɪʃ] *verb* to state the difference between two things; **to distinguish a case** = to point to differences between a case and a previously decided case so as not to be bound by the precedent (NOTE: you distinguish one thing **from** another, or you distinguish **between** two things)

distrain [dɪˈstreɪn] *verb* to seize (goods) to pay for debts

distress [dɪˈstres] *noun* taking someone's goods to pay for debts; **distress sale** = selling of someone's goods to pay his debts

distribute [dɪˈstrɪbjuːt] *verb* to share out or to give out (to various people); *the money in the estate is to be distributed among the members of the deceased's family*

distribution [dɪstrɪˈbjuːʃn] *noun* sharing out property in an estate; **distribution of assets** = sharing the assets of a company among the shareholders

district [ˈdɪstrɪkt] *noun* section of a town or of a country

district attorney (DA) [ˈdɪstrɪkt əˈtɜːni] *noun US* (i) prosecuting attorney in a federal district; (ii) state prosecuting attorney

district council [ˈdɪstrɪkt ˈkaʊnsəl] *noun* elected body which runs a local area

COMMENT: there are two kinds of district council: those covering large urban areas or metropolitan districts, which are responsible for all local matters; and non-metropolitan districts which deal with some local matters, but leaving other matters to be dealt with by the county council

district court ['dɪstrɪkt 'kɔːt] *noun US* court in a federal district

District of Columbia (D.C.)
['dɪstrɪkt əv kə'lʌmbɪə] *noun* district of which Washington is the centre, which is not part of any state of the USA and is administered directly by Congress

disturb [dɪ'stɜːb] *verb* **to disturb the peace** = to make a noise which annoys people in the area

disturbance [dɪ'stɜːbəns] *noun* noise or movement of people which annoys other people; *street disturbances forced the government to resign*; *he was accused of making a disturbance in the public library*

divide [dɪ'vaɪd] *verb* **(a)** to cut into separate sections; *England and Wales are divided into six court circuits*; *the two companies agreed to divide the market between them* **(b)** *(in the House of Commons)* to vote; *the House divided at 10.30*

dividend ['dɪvɪdend] *noun* payment to shareholders of a proportion of a company's profits; **final dividend** = dividend paid at the end of a year; **interim dividend** = dividend paid at the end of a half-year

division [dɪ'vɪʒn] *noun* **(a)** section of something which is divided into several sections; *Smith's is now a division of the Brown group of companies* **(b)** separate section of the High Court (the Queen's Bench Division, the Family Division and the Chancery Division) or a separate section of the Appeal Court (Civil Division and Criminal Division) **(c)** vote in the House of Commons; *in the division on the Law and Order Bill, the government had a comfortable majority*; **division bell** = bell which is rung to warn MPs that a vote is going to be taken; **division bell area** = area round the House of Commons which is near enough for MPs to hear the division bell and run to vote (eight minutes is allowed between the bell and the vote); *he has a flat in the division bell area*; **division lobby** = one of the two corridors beside the House of Commons where MPs

pass to vote (the Ayes lobby and the Noes lobby); *US* **division vote** *or* **standing vote** = vote in the House of Representatives, where members stand up to be counted and the vote is not recorded in the record **(d)** act of dividing or of being divided; **to have a division of opinion** = to disagree; **division of responsibility** = act of splitting the responsibility for something between several people **(e)** *(in the EU)* one of the subdivisions of a Directorate in the Commission, with a Head of Division at its head

COMMENT: when a division is called in the House of Commons, the Speaker names four MPs as tellers, bells are rung and the doors out of the division lobbies are closed. MPs file through the lobbies and are counted as they pass through the doors and go back into the chamber. At the end of the division, the tellers report the numbers of Ayes and Noes, and the Speaker declares the result by saying 'the Ayes have it' or 'the Noes have it'

divisional [dɪ'vɪʒnəl] *adjective* referring to a division; **divisional court** = one of courts of the High Court; **divisional judge** = judge in a division of the High Court

divorce [dɪ'vɔːs] **1** *noun* legal ending of a marriage; **divorce petition** = official request to a court to end a marriage; *she was granted a divorce on the grounds of unreasonable behaviour by her husband*; *see also* GETT **2** *verb* to stop being married (to someone); *he divorced his wife and married his secretary*

COMMENT: under English law, the only basis of divorce is the irretrievable breakdown of marriage. This is proved by one of five grounds: (a) adultery; (b) unreasonable behaviour; (c) one of the parties has deserted the other for a period of two years; (d) the parties have lived apart for two years and agree to a divorce; (e) the parties have lived apart for five years. In the context of divorce proceedings the court has wide powers to make orders regarding custody and care and control of children, and ancillary relief. Divorce proceedings are normally dealt with by the County Court, or in London at the Divorce Registry. Where divorce proceedings are defended, they are transferred to the High Court, but this is rare and most divorce cases are now conducted by what is called the 'special procedure'

Divorce Registry [dɪ'vɔːs 'redʒɪstri] noun court which deals with divorce cases in London

DMC = DONTATIO MORTIS CAUSA

dock [dɒk] noun part of a court where an accused prisoner stands; **the prisoner in the dock** = the prisoner who is being tried for a crime; **dock brief** = former system where an accused person could choose a barrister from those present in court to represent him for a small fee

docket ['dɒkɪt] noun **(a)** list of contents of a package which is being sent **(b)** US list of cases for trial

doctrine ['dɒktrɪn] noun general principle of law; US **the Monroe Doctrine** = the principle that the USA has an interest in preventing outside interference in the internal affairs of other American states

document 1 ['dɒkjumənt] noun **(a)** any paper, which is printed, typed or handwritten; **deeds, contracts and wills are all legal documents**; **document exchange (DX)** = bureau which receives documents for clients and holds them securely in numbered boxes (service can be effected through a document exchange in cases where this is given as the address for service) **(b)** anything in which information is recorded, such as maps, designs, computer files, databases, etc.; see also COPY **(c) list of documents** = list prepared by parties in a civil action giving disclosure of documents relevant to the action **(d)** official paper from a government department; **consultation document** or **consultative document** = paper which is issued by a government department to people who are asked to comment and make suggestions for improvement **2** verb ['dɒkjument] to put in

a published paper; **the cases of unparliamentary language are well documented in Hansard**

documentary [dɒkju'mentri] adjective in the form of documents; **documentary evidence**; **documentary proof**

documentation [dɒkjumen'teɪʃn] noun all documents referring to something; **please send me the complete documentation concerning the sale**

Dod's Parliamentary Companion ['dɒdz pɑːlə'mentri kəm'pænjən] noun small reference book, containing details of all MPs, their constituencies, government posts, etc.

Doe [dəʊ]; **John Doe** = name used as an example in fictitious cases

doli capax or **doli incapax** ['dəʊli 'kæpæks or 'ɪnkæpæks] Latin phrases meaning 'capable of crime' or 'incapable of crime'

COMMENT: children under ten years of age are doli incapax and cannot be prosecuted for criminal offences; children aged between 10 and 14 are presumed to be doli incapax but the presumption can be reversed if there is evidence of malice or knowledge

domain [də'meɪn] noun area of responsibility; **public domain** = land, property or information which belongs to and is available to the public; **work which is in the public domain** = work which is no longer in copyright; **if a document is disclosed in court it may be considered to have passed into the public domain**; **he downloaded some public domain software**

Domesday Book ['duːmzdeɪ 'bʊk] noun record made for King William I in 1086, which recorded lands in England and their owners and inhabitants for tax purposes

domestic [də'mestɪk] adjective **(a)** referring to a family; **domestic premises** = house, flat, etc., used for private accommodation; **domestic proceedings** = court case which involves a man and his wife, or parents and children **(b)** referring to the market of the country where a business is situated; **domestic consumption** = consumption on the home market; **domestic market** = market in the country where a company is based; **domestic production** = production of goods in the home country **(c)** _US_ **domestic court** = court which covers the district in which a defendant lives or has his address for service (NOTE: British English is **home court**)

domicile ['dɒmɪsaɪl] **1** _noun_ country where someone is deemed to live permanently, where a company's office is registered (especially for tax purposes); **domicile of origin** = domicile which a person has from birth (usually the domicile of the father); **domicile of choice** = country where someone has chosen to live, which is not the domicile of origin **2** _verb_ to live in a place officially; _the defendant is domiciled in Scotland_; **bills domiciled in France** = bills of exchange which have to be paid in France

dominant ['dɒmɪnənt] _adjective_ which is more important; **dominant owner** = someone who has the right to use someone else's property; **dominant tenement** = land which has been granted an easement over another property (NOTE: also called 'dominant estate' in the USA)

COMMENT: the grantor of the easement is the **servient tenement**

dominion [də'mɪnjən] _noun_ **(a)** power of control; _to exercise dominion over a country_ **(b)** **a Dominion** = an independent state, part of the British Commonwealth; _the Dominion of Canada_; **Dominion Day** = Canadian National Day (1st July)

donatio mortis causa [də'nɑːtɪəʊ 'mɔːtɪs 'kaʊzə] _Latin phrase meaning_ 'gift because of death': transfer of property made when death is imminent

donation [də'neɪʃn] _noun_ gift (especially to a charity)

donee [dəʊ'niː] _noun_ person who receives a gift from a donor

donor ['dəʊnə] _noun_ person who gives property to another

dormant ['dɔːmənt] _adjective_ not active; **dormant account** = bank account which is not used; **dormant partner** = SLEEPING PARTNER

double [dʌbl] **1** _adjective_ **(a)** twice as large, two times the size; **in double figures** = with two figures (i.e. from 10 to 99); _inflation is in double figures_; _we have had double-figure inflation for some years_ **(b)** which happens twice; **double taxation** = taxing the same income twice; **double taxation agreement** _or_ **treaty** = agreement between two countries that a person living in one country shall not be taxed in both countries on the income earned in the other country; **double jeopardy** = the possibility that a citizen may be tried twice for the same crime (usually prohibited in most legal systems) **2** _verb_ to become twice as big; to make something twice as big

doubt [daʊt] _noun_ not being sure that something is correct; **beyond reasonable doubt,** _US_ **beyond a reasonable doubt** = proof needed to convict a person in a criminal case

dove [dʌv] _noun_ person who prefers diplomacy and tries to achieve peace (as opposed to a hawk)

doveish ['dʌvɪʃ] _adjective_ like a dove; _he was accused of having doveish tendencies_

Downing Street ['daʊnɪŋ 'striːt] _noun_ street in London where the Prime Minister and Chancellor of the Exchequer have their official houses; **10 Downing Street** = house of the Prime Minister, where the cabinet meets and which is the centre of the executive branch of the British government; _see also_ NUMBER TEN; **No. 11 Downing Street** = official house of the Chancellor of the Exchequer (NOTE: the words 'Downing Street' are often used to mean 'the Prime Minister' or even 'the British government': a Downing Street spokesman revealed that the plan had still to be approved by the Treasury; Downing Street sources indicate that the Prime Minister has given the go-ahead for the change; Downing Street is angry at suggestions that the treaty will not be ratified)

dowry ['dauri] *noun* money or property brought by a wife to her husband when she marries him

doyen of the diplomatic corps

['dɔɪən əv ðə dɪplə'mætɪk 'kɔː] *noun* senior ambassador in a country (that is, the ambassador who has been in that country the longest)

DPP ['diː 'piː 'piː] = DIRECTOR OF PUBLIC PROSECUTIONS

draft [drɑːft] **1** *noun* **(a)** order for money to be paid by a bank; **to make a draft on a bank** = to ask a bank to pay money for you; **bank draft** *or* **banker's draft** = cheque payable by a bank; **sight draft** = bill of exchange which is payable when it is presented **(b)** first rough plan, document which has not been finished; *he drew up the draft agreement on the back of an envelope*; *the first draft of the contract was corrected by the managing director*; *the draft Bill is with the House of Commons lawyers*; **rough draft** = plan of a document which may have changes made to it before it is complete **2** *verb* to make a first rough plan of a document; *to draft a contract or a document or a bill*; *the contract is still being drafted or is still in the drafting stage*

drafter ['drɑːftə] *noun* person who makes a draft

drafting ['drɑːftɪŋ] *noun* act of preparing the draft of a document; *the drafting of the contract took six weeks*; *the drafting stage of a parliamentary Bill*

draftsman ['drɑːftsmən] *noun* person who drafts documents; **costs draftsman** = person who draws up a bill of costs for assessment by the costs judge; **parliamentary draftsman** = lawyer who drafts Bills going before Parliament

draw [drɔː] *verb* **(a)** to take money away; *to draw money out of an account*; **to draw a salary** = to have a salary paid by a company **(b)** to write a cheque; *to draw a*

cheque on a bank; *he paid the invoice with a cheque drawn on an Egyptian bank*

drawee [drɔː'iː] *noun* person or bank asked to make a payment by a drawer

drawer ['drɔːə] *noun* person who writes a cheque or a bill asking a drawee to pay money to a payee; **the bank returned the cheque to drawer** = the bank could not pay the cheque because the person who wrote it did not have enough money in his account to pay it; *see also* RD

drawings ['drɔːɪŋz] *plural noun* money taken out of a partnership by a partner as his salary

draw up ['drɔː 'ʌp] *verb* to write a legal document; *to draw up a contract or an agreement*; *to draw up a company's articles of association*

drive [draɪv] *verb* **(a)** to make a car, lorry, etc., go in a certain direction; *he was driving to work when he heard the news on the car radio*; *she drives a company car*; **careless driving** *or* **driving without due care and attention** = offence of driving in such a way that other people and property may be harmed; **drunken driving,** *US* **driving while intoxicated (DWI)** = offence of driving a car when under the influence of alcohol (also called 'driving with alcohol concentrations above a certain limit'); **reckless driving** = offence of driving a car in a wild way where the driver does not think that he is causing a risk to other people **(b)** **he drives a hard bargain** = he is a difficult negotiator (NOTE: **driving - drove - driven**)

drop [drɒp] **1** *noun* **(a)** fall; *drop in sales*; *sales show a drop of 10%*; *a drop in prices* **(b)** **drop shipment** = delivery of a large order from the factory direct to a customer's shop or warehouse without going through an agent or wholesaler **2** *verb* **(a)** to fall; *sales have dropped by 10% or have dropped 10%*; *the pound dropped three points against the dollar* **(b)** to stop a case; *the prosecution dropped all charges against the accused*; *the claimant decided to drop the case against his neighbour* (NOTE: **dropping - dropped**)

drop ship ['drɒp 'ʃɪp] *verb* to deliver a large order direct to a customer

drug [drʌg] *noun* medicine, especially substances which can be harmful if taken regularly; **controlled drugs,** *US* **controlled substances** = drugs which are not freely available, which are restricted by law, and which are classified (Class A, B, C), and of which possession may be an offence; **dangerous drugs** = drugs which may be harmful to people who take them, and so can be prohibited from import and general sale; **drug addiction** = being mentally and physically dependent on taking a drug regularly; **the Drug Squad** = section of the police force which investigates crime related to drugs; **drug trafficking** = buying and selling drugs illegally

COMMENT: there are three classes of controlled drugs: **Class 'A' drugs:** (cocaine, heroin, crack, LSD, etc.); **Class 'B' drugs:** (amphetamines, cannabis, codeine, etc.); and **Class 'C' drugs:** (drugs which are related to the amphetamines, such as benzphetamine). The drugs are covered by five schedules under the Misuse of Drugs Regulations: **Schedule 1:** drugs which are not used medicinally, such as cannabis and LSD, for which possession and supply are prohibited; **Schedule 2:** drugs which can be used medicinally, such as heroin, morphine, cocaine, and amphetamines: these are fully controlled as regards prescriptions by doctors, safe custody in pharmacies, registering of sales, etc. **Schedule 3:** barbiturates, which are controlled as regards prescriptions, but need not be kept in safe custody; **Schedule 4:** benzodiazepines, which are controlled as regards registers of purchasers; **Schedule 5:** other substances for which invoices showing purchase must be kept

drunk [drʌŋk] *adjective* incapable because of having drunk too much alcohol; **drunk and disorderly** = incapable and behaving in a wild way because of having drunk too much alcohol

drunkard ['drʌŋkəd] *noun* person who is frequently drunk; *see also* HABITUAL

DSgt = DETECTIVE SERGEANT

dual [dju:əl] *adjective* referring to two things; **person of dual nationality** *or* **person who has dual nationality** = person who is a citizen of two countries

duchess ['dʌtʃɪs] *noun* wife of a duke

duchy ['dʌtʃi] *noun* territory ruled by a duke; *see also* CHANCELLOR

dud [dʌd] *adjective & noun (informal)* false, not good (coin or banknote); *the £50 note was a dud*; **dud cheque** = cheque which the bank refuses to pay because the person writing it has not enough money in his account to pay it

due [dju:] *adjective* **(a)** owed; **to fall due** *or* **to become due** = to be ready for payment; **bill due on May 1st** = bill which has to be paid on May 1st; **balance due to us** = amount owed to us which should be paid; **due date** = date on which a debt has to be paid **(b)** expected to arrive; *the plane is due to arrive at 10.30 or is due at 10.30* **(c)** proper, as is right; **in due form** = written in the correct legal form; *receipt in due form*; *contract drawn up in due form*; **driving without due care and attention** = offence of driving in such a way that other people and property may be harmed; **after due consideration of the problem** = after thinking seriously about the problem; **due diligence** = carrying out of your duty as efficiently as is necessary; *the executor acted with due diligence to pay the liabilities of the estate*; **due execution of a will** = making a will in the correct way: a will must be written (handwritten, typed, written on a standard form, etc.), it must be signed by the testator and witnessed by two witnesses in the presence of the testator; *(in the EU)* **due process** = rule that the forms of law must be followed correctly; **the due process of the law** = the formal work of a fair legal action

dues [dju:z] *plural noun* **(a)** **dock dues** *or* **port dues** *or* **harbour dues** = payment which a ship makes to the harbour authorities for the right to use the harbour **(b)** orders taken but not supplied until new stock arrives

duke [dju:k] *noun* nobleman of the highest rank; *see also* DUCHY

duly ['dju:li] *adverb* **(a)** properly; *duly authorized representative* **(b)** as was expected; *we duly received his letter of 21st October*

dummy ['dʌmi] *noun* paper with the titles of a Bill, presented in the House of Commons for the First Reading when the short title is read out by the clerk

dungeon ['dʌnʒən] *noun* underground prison (often in a castle)

duress [dju'res] *noun* force, illegal threat to use force on someone to make him do something; *duress provides no defence to a charge of murder*; *under duress =* being forced to do something; *they alleged they had committed the crime under duress from another defendant*; *he signed the confession under duress* = he signed the confession because he was threatened

dutiable ['dju:tiəbl] *adjective* **dutiable goods** *or* **dutiable items** = goods on which a customs or excise duty has to be paid

duty ['dju:ti] *noun* **(a)** work which a person has to do; *it is the duty of every citizen to serve on a jury if called*; *the government has a duty to protect the citizens from criminals*; **duty of care** = duty which every citizen has not to act negligently **(b)** official work which you have to do in a job; **to be on duty** = to be doing official work at a special time; **night duty** = work done at night; *PC Smith is on night duty this week*; **point duty** = work of a policeman or traffic warden to direct the traffic at crossroads; **duty sergeant** = police sergeant who is on duty at a particular time; **duty solicitor** = solicitor who is on duty at a magistrates' court and can be contacted at any time by a party who

is appearing in that court or by a party who has been taken to a police station under arrest or for questioning **(c)** tax which has to be paid; *to take the duty off alcohol*; *to put a duty on cigarettes*; **ad valorem duty** = duty calculated on the sales value of the goods; **customs duty** *or* **import duty** = tax on goods imported into a country; **estate duty,** *US* **death duty** = tax paid on the property left by a dead person; **excise duty** = tax on the sale of goods (such as alcohol and petrol) which are produced in the country, tax on imports where the duty was not paid on entry into the country; **goods which are liable to duty** = goods on which customs or excise tax has to be paid; **duty-paid goods** = goods where the duty has been paid; **stamp duty** = tax on legal documents (such as the conveyance of a property to a new owner)

duty bound ['dju:ti 'baʊnd] *adjective* bound to do something because it is your duty; *witnesses under oath are duty bound to tell the truth*

duty-free ['dju:ti 'fri:] *adjective & adverb* sold with no duty to be paid; *he bought a duty-free watch at the airport or he bought the watch duty-free*; **duty-free shop** = shop at an airport or on a ship where goods can be bought without paying duty

dwelling ['dwelɪŋ] *noun* place where someone lives (such as a house or flat); *the tax on dwellings has been raised*

DWI ['di: 'dʌblju: 'aɪ] *US* = DRIVING WHILE INTOXICATED

DX = DOCUMENT EXCHANGE

dynastic [dɪ'næstɪk] *adjective* referring to a dynasty; *the rules of dynastic succession*

dynasty ['dɪnəsti] *noun* **(a)** family of rulers, following one after the other; *the Ming dynasty ruled China from 1368 to 1644* **(b)** period of rule by members of the same family

Ee

E [iː] *fifth letter of the alphabet;* **Schedule E** = schedule to the Finance Acts under which tax is charged on wages, salaries and pensions; **E list** = list of the names of prisoners who frequently try to escape from prison; **Table E** = model memorandum and articles of association of an unlimited company with share capital set out in the Companies Act, 1985

e. & o.e. [iː ənd 'əʊ 'iː] = ERRORS AND OMISSIONS EXCEPTED

early ['ɜːli] *adjective & adverb* **(a)** before the usual time; **early closing day** = weekday, usually Wednesday or Thursday, when most shops in a town close in the afternoon; **at your earliest convenience** = as soon as you find it possible; **at an early date** = very soon; **early day motion** = motion proposed in the House of Commons for discussion at an early date (usually used to introduce a particular point of view without necessarily going to a full debate) **(b)** at the beginning of a period of time; *he took an early flight to Paris*; *we hope for an early resumption of negotiations* = we hope negotiations will start again soon

earmark ['ɪəmɑːk] *verb* to reserve for a special purpose; *to earmark funds for a project*; *the grant is earmarked for computer systems development*

earn [ɜːn] *verb* **(a)** to be paid money for working; *to earn £150 a week*; *our agent in Paris certainly does not earn his commission* **(b)** to produce interest or dividends; *what level of dividend do these shares earn?*; *account which earns interest at 10%*

earnest ['ɜːnɪst] *noun* money paid as a down payment to show one's serious intention to proceed with a contract; *he deposited £1,000 with the solicitor as earnest of his intention to purchase*

earnings ['ɜːnɪŋz] *plural noun* **(a)** salary or wages, profits and dividends or interest received by an individual; **attachment of earnings** = legal power to take money from a person's salary to pay money which is owed to the courts or to a judgment creditor; *see also* GARNISHEE ORDER **(b)** profits of a business; **earnings per share** = money earned in profit per share

easement ['iːzmənt] *noun* right which someone (the dominant owner) has to use land belonging to someone else (the servient owner), such as for a path; **affirmative easement** = easement where the servient owner allows the dominant owner to do something; **negative easement** = easement where the servient owner stops the dominant owner from doing something; *see also* DOMINANT, SERVIENT, TENEMENT

Easter ['iːstə] *noun* one of the four sittings of the Law Courts; one of the four law terms

EC ['iː 'siː] = EUROPEAN COMMUNITY; *EC ministers met today in Brussels*; *the USA is increasing its trade with the EC*

ECB = EUROPEAN CENTRAL BANK

ecclesiastical [ɪkliːzi'æstɪkl] *adjective* referring to the church; **ecclesiastical court** = court which hears matters referring to the church

ECJ = EUROPEAN COURT OF JUSTICE

e-commerce ['iː'kɒmɜːs] *noun (= ELECTRONIC COMMERCE)* general term used to refer to the buying and selling of goods and services on the internet

economic [iːkə'nɒmɪk] *adjective* referring to economy; *(in the EU)* **economic activity** = work; **economic sanctions** = restrictions on trade with a country in order to influence its political situation or in order to make its government change its policy

economically [iːkə'nɒmɪkli] *adverb (in the EU)* **economically active** = being an active worker; *economically active persons have the right to move freely from one EU country to another with their families*

economy [ɪ'kɒnəmi] *noun* **(a)** being careful not to waste money or materials; **an economy measure** = action to try to save money or materials; **economies of scale** = making a product more cheaply by producing it or buying it in large quantities **(b)** financial state of a country, the way in which a country makes and uses its money; **black economy** = work which is paid for in cash, goods but not declared to the tax authorities; **free market economy** = system where the government does not interfere in business activity in any way

ecoterrorist [iːkəʊ'terərɪst] *noun* person who destroys things for ecological reasons; *ecoterrorists attacked several fields of crops*

edict ['iːdɪkt] *noun* public announcement of a law

editor ['edɪtə] *noun* (i) person in charge of a newspaper or a section of a newspaper; (ii) person who is responsible for a reference book; (iii) person who checks the work of a writer; **the city editor** = business or finance editor of a British newspaper

editorial [edɪ'tɔːriəl] **1** *adjective* referring to an editor; **editorial board** = group of editors (on a newspaper, etc.) **2** *noun* main article in a newspaper, written by the editor

EEC = EUROPEAN ECONOMIC COMMUNITY

effect [ɪ'fekt] **1** *noun* **(a)** result; **terms of a contract which take effect** *or* **come into effect from January 1st** = terms which start to operate on January 1st; **prices are increased 10% with effect from January 1st** = new prices will apply from January 1st; **to remain in effect** = to continue to be applied **(b)** meaning; **clause to the effect that** = clause which means that; **we have made provision to this effect** = we have put into the contract terms which will make this work **(c)** **personal effects** = personal belongings **2** *verb* to carry out; **to effect a payment** = to make a payment; **to effect customs clearance** = to clear something through customs; **to effect a settlement between two parties** = to bring two parties together and make them agree to a settlement

effective [ɪ'fektɪv] *adjective* which works well, which gives the correct result; *the police are trying to find an effective means of dealing with young offenders*; **effective date** = date on which a rule or a contract starts to be applied; **clause effective as from January 1st** = clause which starts to be applied on January 1st

effectiveness [ɪ'fektɪvnəs] *noun* being effective; *(in the EU)* **test of effectiveness** = test to show if an action is more effective when taken by a Member State (one of the tests to decide on subsidiarity); *compare* SCALE

e.g. ['iː 'dʒiː] for example, such as; *the contract is valid in some countries (e.g. France and Belgium) but not in others*

egalitarian [ɪgælɪ'teəriən] **1** *adjective* referring to egalitarianism; *he holds egalitarian views* **2** *noun* person who supports egalitarianism

egalitarianism [ɪgælɪ'teəriənɪzm] *noun* political theory that all members of society have equal rights and should have equal treatment

EGM = EXTRAORDINARY GENERAL MEETING

eject [ɪ'dʒekt] *verb* to make (someone) leave a property which he is occupying illegally

ejection [ɪ'dʒekʃn] *noun* action of making someone leave a property which he is occupying illegally

COMMENT: the ejection of someone who is legally occupying a property is an **ouster,** while removing a tenant is **eviction**

ejectment [ɪ'dʒekmənt] *noun* **action of ejectment** = court action to force someone to leave a property which he is occupying illegally

ejusdem generis *or* **eiusdem generis** [iː'dʒusdem or eɪ'juːsdem 'dʒenərɪs] *Latin phrase meaning* 'of the same kind': a rule of legal interpretation, that when a word or phrase follows two or more other words or phrases, it is construed to be of the same type as the words or phrases which precede it

COMMENT: in the phrase **houses, flats and other buildings** / other buildings can mean only other dwellings, and would not include, for example, a church

elapse [ɪ'læps] *verb (of time)* to pass; *six weeks elapsed before the court order was put into effect*; *we must allow sufficient time to elapse before making a complaint*

elect [ɪ'lekt] *verb* **(a)** to choose someone by a vote; *a vote to elect the officers of an association*; *she was elected chair of the committee*; *he was first elected for this constituency in 1992* **(b)** to choose to do something; *he elected to stand trial by jury*

-elect [ɪ'lekt] *suffix* person who has been elected but has not yet started the term of office; *she is the president-elect* (NOTE: the plural is **presidents-elect)**

election [ɪ'lekʃn] *noun* **(a)** act of electing; *his election as president of the society* **(b)** act of electing a representative or representatives; **general election** = choosing of a parliament by all the voters in a country; **local elections** *or* **municipal elections** = elections to choose representatives for local government, for a town or county council; **election agent** = agent appointed by a party to organize its campaign in a constituency during an election; *the ruling party lost votes in the general election* **or** *in the elections for local councils*; *the election results are shown on television*; *see also* BY-ELECTION **(c)** act of choosing a course of action; *the accused made his election for jury trial* **(d)** choice by a legatee to take a benefit under a will, and to relinquish a claim to the estate at the same time

COMMENT: in Britain, a Parliament can only last for a maximum of five years, and a dissolution is usually called by the Prime Minister before the end of that period. The Lord Chancellor then issues a writ for the election of MPs. All British subjects (including Commonwealth and Irish citizens), are eligible to vote in British elections provided they are on the electoral register, are over 18 years of age, are sane, are not members of the House of Lords and are not serving prison sentences for serious crime. In the USA, members of the House of Representatives are elected for a two-year period. Senators are elected for six-year terms, one third of the Senate being elected every two years. The President of the USA is elected by an electoral college made up of people elected by voters in each of the states of the USA. Each state elects the same number of electors to the electoral college as it has Congressmen, plus two. This guarantees that the college is broadly representative of voters across the country. The presidential candidate with an overall majority in the college is elected president. A presidential term of office is four years, and a president can stand for re-election once

electioneer [ɪlekʃə'nɪə] *verb (often as criticism)* to try to attract votes in an election; *cutting taxes just before the election is pure electioneering*

elector [ɪ'lektə] *noun* person who votes, or who is eligible to vote in an election; **register of electors** = official list of names and addresses of people living in a certain area who are eligible to vote in local or national elections

electoral [ɪ'lektərəl] *adjective* referring to an election; **electoral roll** *or* **electoral register** = REGISTER OF ELECTORS; **electoral college** = group of people elected by a larger group to vote on their behalf in an election

electorate [ɪ'lektərət] *noun* all electors taken as a group

electric chair [ɪ'lektrɪk 'tʃeə] *noun* chair attached to a powerful electric current, used in some states of the USA for executing criminals

electronic [ɪlek'trɒnɪk] *adjective* using devices such as silicon chips which affect the electric current which passes through them; **electronic communication** = message which is sent from one person to another by telephone or by other electronic means; **electronic mail** = e-mail, the system of sending messages from one computer to another, via telephone lines; **electronic signature** = electronic text or symbols attached to a document which act in a similar way to a handwritten signature, in that they prove the authenticity of the document

eleemosynary [eliː'mɒzɪnəri] *adjective* referring to charity

element ['elɪmənt] *noun* basic part; *the elements of a settlement*

eligibility [elɪdʒɪ'bɪləti] *noun* being eligible; *the chairman questioned her eligibility to stand for re-election*

eligible ['elɪdʒɪbl] *adjective* person who can be chosen; *she is eligible for re-election*

e-mail *or* **email** ['iːmeɪl] **1** *noun* **(a)** electronic mail, a system of sending messages from one computer to another, using telephone lines; *his lawyer contacted me by e-mail*; *let me give you my e-mail address* **(b)** message sent by e-mail; *I had two e-mails from him this morning* **2** *verb* to send a message using electronic mail; *we e-mailed him about the meeting*

emancipation [ɪmænsɪ'peɪʃn] *noun* making free, especially making a slave free or giving someone the right to vote

embargo [ɪm'bɑːgəʊ] **1** *noun* government order which stops a type of trade; **to lay** *or* **put an embargo on trade with a country** = to say that trade with a country must not take place; **to lift an embargo** = to allow trade to start again; **to be under an embargo** = to be forbidden (NOTE: plural is **embargoes**) **2** *verb* to stop something, not to allow something to take place; *the government has embargoed trade with the Eastern countries*; **the press release was embargoed until 1st January** = the information in the release could not be published until 1st January

embassy ['embəsi] *noun* building where an ambassador and other diplomats work in a foreign country; *each embassy is guarded by special police*; *the embassy cleaners planted bugs in the ambassador's office*; *the American Embassy is in Grosvenor Square*

COMMENT: an embassy is the territory of the country which it represents. The police and armed forces of the country where the embassy is situated are not allowed to enter the embassy without official permission. People seeking asylum can take refuge in embassies, but it is not easy for them to leave, as to do so they have to step back into the country against which they are seeking protection

embezzle [ɪm'bezl] *verb* to use illegally or steal money which is not yours, or which you are looking after for someone; *he was sent to prison for six months for embezzling his clients' money*

embezzlement [ɪm'bezlmənt] *noun* act of embezzling; *he was sent to prison for six months for embezzlement*

embezzler [ɪm'bezlə] *noun* person who embezzles

emblements ['embləmənts] *plural noun* vegetable products which come from farming

embracery [ɪm'breɪsrɪ] *noun* offence of corruptly seeking to influence jurors

emergency [ɪ'mɜːdʒənsɪ] *noun* dangerous situation where decisions have to be taken quickly; **the government declared a state of emergency** = the government decided that the situation was so dangerous that the police or army had to run the country; **to call for an emergency debate** = to ask for a special debate on a certain subject which is very important; **to take emergency measures** = to take action rapidly to stop a serious state of affairs developing; **emergency planning department** = department in a local council which plans for action to be taken in case of major accidents, etc.; **emergency planning officer** = council official who plans and supervises action to deal with crises, such as major accidents, etc.; **emergency powers** = special powers granted by law to a government or to a minister to deal with an emergency, usually without going through the normal democratic processes; **emergency reserves** = ready cash held in case it is needed suddenly; **emergency services** = police, fire and ambulance services, which are ready for action if an emergency arises

emigrate ['emɪgreɪt] *verb* to go to another country to live permanently; *compare* IMMIGRATE

emigration [emɪ'greɪʃn] *noun* leaving a country to go to live permanently in another country; *compare* IMMIGRATION

emigrant ['emɪgrənt] *noun* person who emigrates; *compare* IMMIGRANT

eminent domain ['emɪnənt də'meɪn] *noun* right of the state to appropriate private property for public use

emoluments [ɪ'mɒljumənts] *plural noun* wages, salaries, fees or any monetary benefit from an employment

empanel [ɪm'pænəl] *verb* **to empanel a jury** = to choose and swear in jurors (NOTE: **empanelling - empanelled**)

employ [ɪm'plɔɪ] *verb* to give someone regular paid work; **employed advocate** = person employed to plead in court (as, for example, a Crown Prosecutor)

employee [ɪmplɔɪ'iː] *noun* worker, person employed by someone; *employees of the firm are eligible to join a profit-sharing scheme*; *relations between management and employees have improved*; *the company has decided to take on new employees*; **employee share ownership** = scheme which allows employees to obtain shares in the company for which they work (sometimes at a price lower than the current market price)

employer [ɪm'plɔɪə] *noun* person or company which has employees and pays them; **employers' organization** *or* **association** = group of employers with similar interests; **employer's contribution** = money paid by an employer towards an employee's pension; **employer's liability** = legal responsibility of an employer when employees suffer accidents due to negligence on the part of the employer

employment [ɪm'plɔɪmənt] *noun* contractual relationship between an employer and his employees; **conditions of employment** = terms of a contract whereby someone is employed; **contract of employment** *or* **employment contract** = contract between an employer and an employee showing all the conditions of work; **security of employment** = feeling by a worker that he has the right to keep his job until he retires; **employment office** *or* **bureau** *or* **agency** = office which finds jobs for people; **Employment Appeal Tribunal** = court which hears appeals from industrial tribunals

empower [ɪmˈpauə] *verb* to give someone the power to do something; *the agent is empowered to sell the property*; *she was empowered by the company to sign the contract*; *a constable is empowered to arrest a person whom he suspects of having committed an offence*

emptor [ˈemptə] *see* CAVEAT

enable [ɪˈneɪbl] *verb* to make it possible for something to happen; **enabling legislation** *or* **statute** = Act of Parliament which gives a minister the power to put other legislation into effect (the opposite is 'disabling statute')

enact [ɪˈnækt] *verb* to make (a law); **enacting clause** *or* **enacting words** = first clause in a bill or act (starting with the words 'be it enacted that') which makes the act lawful

enactment [ɪˈnæktmənt] *noun* (i) action of making a law; (ii) an Act of Parliament

enclosure [ɪnˈkləuʒə] *noun* **(a)** document enclosed with a letter **(b)** removing land from common use, by putting fences round it

encroachment [ɪnˈkrəutʃmənt] *noun* illegally taking over someone's property little by little

encrypt [ɪnˈkrɪpt] *verb* to take ordinary text and convert it to a series of figures or letters which make it unreadable without a special key

encryption [ɪnˈkrɪpʃn] *noun* action of encrypting text

encumbrance [ɪnˈkʌmbrəns] *noun* liability (such as a mortgage or charge) which is attached usually to a property or land

endanger [ɪnˈdeɪnʒə] *verb* to put someone in danger of being killed or hurt; **endangering railway passengers** *or* **endangering life at sea** *or* **criminal damage endangering life** = notifiable offences where human life is put at risk

endorse [ɪnˈdɔːs] *verb* **(a)** to agree with; *the court endorsed counsel's view* **(b)** to

endorse a bill *or* **a cheque** = to sign a bill or a cheque on the back to make it payable to someone else **(c)** to make a note on a driving licence that the holder has been convicted of a traffic offence **(d)** to write a summary of the contents of a legal document on the outside of the folded document

endorsee [endɔːˈsiː] *noun* person in whose favour a bill or a cheque is endorsed

endorsement [ɪnˈdɔːsmənt] *noun* **(a)** act of endorsing; signature on a document which endorses it; summary of a legal document noted on the outside of the folded document **(b)** note on an insurance policy which adds conditions to the policy **(c)** note on a driving licence to show that the holder has been convicted of a traffic offence; *see also* TOTTING UP

endorser [ɪnˈdɔːsə] *noun* person who endorses a bill or cheque

endowment [ɪnˈdaumənt] *noun* giving money to provide a regular income; **endowment assurance** *or* **endowment policy** = assurance policy where a sum of money is paid to the insured person on a certain date, or to his heirs if he dies; **endowment mortgage** = mortgage backed by an endowment policy

enforce [ɪnˈfɔːs] *verb* to make sure something is done or is obeyed; *to enforce the terms of a contract*; **to enforce a debt** = to make sure a debt is paid

enforceable [ɪnˈfɔːsəbl] *adjective* which can be enforced

enforcement [ɪnˈfɔːsmənt] *noun* **(a)** making sure that something is obeyed; *enforcement of the terms of a contract*; **law enforcement** = making sure that a law is obeyed; **law enforcement officers** = members of the police force, the Drug Squad, etc. **(b)** *(in the EU)* power of forcing someone to comply with the law; **enforcement proceedings** = legal proceedings used by the Commission to ensure that Member States fulfil their treaty obligations

enfranchise [ɪnˈfræntʃaɪz] *verb* to give (someone) the right to vote

enfranchisement [ɪnˈfræntʃaɪzmənt] *noun* action of giving someone a vote; **leasehold enfranchisement** = right of a leaseholder to buy the freehold of the property which he is leasing

engage [ɪnˈgeɪdʒ] *verb* (a) to **engage someone to do something** = to bind someone contractually to do something; *the contract engages the company to purchase minimum annual quantities of goods* (b) to employ; *we have engaged the best commercial lawyer to represent us* (c) **to be engaged in** = to be busy with; *he is engaged in work on computers; the company is engaged in trade with Africa*

engagement [ɪnˈgeɪdʒmənt] *noun* agreement to do something; **to break an engagement to do something** = not to do what you have legally agreed to do

engross [ɪnˈgrəʊs] *verb* to draw up a legal document in its final form ready for signature; *US* **engrossed Bill** = Bill which has been passed by either the House of Representatives or the Senate, which is written out in its final form with all its amendments to be sent to the other chamber for discussion

engrossment [ɪnˈgrəʊsmənt] *noun* (i) drawing up of a legal document in its final form; (ii) legal document in its final form; **engrossment paper** = thick heavy paper on which court documents are engrossed

enjoin [ɪnˈdʒɔɪn] *verb* to order someone to do something

enjoyment [ɪnˈdʒɔɪmənt] *noun* **quiet enjoyment of land** = right of an occupier to occupy a property under a tenancy without anyone interfering with that right

enquire, enquiry [ɪnˈkwæɪə or ɪnˈkwæɪri] = INQUIRE, INQUIRY

enrolled bill [ɪnˈrəʊld ˈbɪl] *noun US* final copy of a bill which has been passed by both House and Senate, and is written out with all its amendments for signature by the Speaker of the House of

Representatives, the President of the Senate and the President of the USA

entail [ɪnˈteɪl] *noun* interest in land where the land is given to another person and the heirs of his body, but reverts to the donor when the donee and his heirs have all died; *see also* FEE TAIL

entente [ɒnˈtɒnt] *noun* agreement between two countries (used especially of the 'Entente Cordiale' between Britain and France in 1904)

enter [ˈentə] *verb* (a) to go in; *they all stood up when the judges entered the courtroom; the company has spent millions trying to enter the do-it-yourself market; (in the EU)* **right to enter** = right of a EU citizen to go into another EU country to look for work (b) to write in; *to enter a name on a list; the clerk entered the objection in the records; the defendant entered defence of justification;* **to enter appearance** = to register with a court that a defendant intends to defend an action; **to enter a bid for something** = to offer (usually in writing) to buy something; **to enter a caveat** = to warn legally that you have an interest in a case or a grant of probate, and that no steps can be taken without notice to you; **to enter judgment for someone** = to make a legal judgment on someone's behalf; *judgment was entered for the claimant;* **the claimant entered judgment** = the claimant took judgment (usually because the defendant failed to defend an action) (c) **to enter into** = (i) to begin to do something; (ii) to agree to do something; *to enter into relations with someone; to enter into negotiations with a foreign government; to enter into a partnership with a friend; to enter into an agreement or a contract*

entering [ˈentrɪŋ] *noun* act of writing items in a record

enterprise [ˈentəpraɪz] *noun* (a) system of carrying on a business; **free enterprise** = system of business free from government interference; **enterprise zone** = area of a country, where the government offers special subsidies to firms to encourage them to set up businesses **(b)** business which is carried on; *she runs a mail order enterprise*

entertain [entə'teɪn] *verb* to be ready to consider a proposal; *the judge will not entertain any proposal from the prosecution to delay the start of the hearing*

entice [ɪn'taɪs] *verb* to try to persuade someone to do something (by offering money); *they tried to entice the managers to join the new company*

enticement [ɪn'taɪsmənt] *noun* trying to persuade someone to do something (especially trying to persuade a worker to leave his job, or a wife to leave her husband)

entitle [ɪn'taɪtl] *verb* to give (someone) the right to something; **he is entitled to four weeks' holiday** = he has the right to take four weeks' holiday

entitlement [ɪn'taɪtlmənt] *noun* right, thing to which you are entitled; **holiday entitlement** = number of days' paid holiday which a worker has the right to take; **pension entitlement** = amount of pension which someone has the right to receive when he retires

entity ['entɪti] *noun* thing which exists in law; *his private company is a separate entity*

entrapment [ɪn'træpmənt] *noun (done by someone in authority, such as a police officer)* enticing someone to commit a crime, so as to be able to arrest him (not a defence in British law, but it exists in US law)

entrenched [ɪn'trenʃt] *adjective* fixed, which cannot be moved; *the government's entrenched position on employees' rights*; **entrenched clause** = clause in a constitution which stipulates that it cannot be amended except by an extraordinary process

entry ['entri] *noun* **(a)** going into; **forcible entry** = formerly, the criminal offence of entering a building or land and

taking possession of it by force; *(in the EU)* **right of entry** = RIGHT TO ENTER **(b)** **entry of appearance** = lodging by the defendant of a document in court to confirm his intention to defend an action; **entry of judgment** = recording the judgment of a court in the official records

entryism ['entriɪzm] *noun* way of taking control of a political party or elected body, where extremists join or are elected in a normal way, and are able to take over because of their numbers or because they are more active than other members

entryist ['entriɪst] *adjective* referring to entryism; *the party leader condemned entryist techniques*

environment [ɪn'vaɪrənmənt] *noun* area or surroundings in which people live or work; **Department of the Environment** = British government department concerned with the conditions in which people live, and which also is responsible for contacts between central government and certain aspects of local government

environmental [ɪnvaɪrən'mentəl] *adjective* referring to the environment; *the Opposition spokesman on environmental issues*; **environmental health** = the health of the public as a whole; **Environmental Health Officer** = official of a local council who deals with matters of public health such as air pollution, bad sanitation, noise pollution, etc.

envoy ['envɔɪ] *noun* **(a)** person who is sent with a message from one government or organization to another; *the President's special envoy to the Middle East* **(b)** senior diplomat with a rank below that of ambassador

equal ['iːkwəl] *adjective* exactly the same; *male and female workers have equal pay*; **Equal Opportunities Commission** = official committee set up to make sure that men and women have equal chances of employment and to remove discrimination between the sexes (NOTE: the American equivalent is **Equal Employment Opportunity Commission**); **equal opportunities programme** = programme to avoid discrimination in employment (NOTE: in American English this is **affirmative action program**); **equal pay** = paying the same salary for the same type of work (as, for example, for men and women employed in the same or similar jobs)

equality [ɪ'kwɒləti] *noun* **(a)** condition where all citizens are equal, have equal rights and are treated equally by the state **(b)** *(in the EU)* **equality of access** = situation where men and women must be given the same opportunities to apply for and take up work; **equality of opportunity** = situation where each citizen has the same opportunity to get a job, be elected, etc.

equality of treatment [ɪ'kwɒləti əv 'triːtmənt] *noun* **(a)** treatment of men and women must be the same as regards opportunities of employment, promotion, training, etc. **(b)** *(in the EU)* treatment of workers who are nationals of other Member States of the EU must be equal to that of nationals of the country where they work

equalize [iːkwəlaɪz] *verb* to make equal; *to equalize dividends*

equally ['iːkwəli] *adverb* in the same way; *costs will be shared equally between the two parties*

equitable ['ekwɪtəbl] *adjective* fair and just; referring to equity; **equitable jurisdiction** = power of a court to enforce a person's rights; **equitable lien** = right of someone to hold property (which legally he does not own) until the owner pays money due; **equitable mortgage** = mortgage which does not give the mortgagee a legal estate in the land mortgaged

equity ['ekwɪti] *noun* **(a)** fair system of laws, system of British law which developed in parallel with the common law to make the common law fairer, summarized in the maxim 'equity does not suffer a wrong to be without a remedy'; **equity of redemption** = right of a mortgagor to redeem the estate by paying off the principal and interest **(b)** right to receive dividends as part of the profit of a company in which you own shares **(c)**

shareholders' equity *or* **equity capital** = amount of a company's capital which is owned by shareholders

equities ['ekwɪtiːz] *plural noun* ordinary shares

equivocal [ɪ'kwɪvəkl] *adjective* not certain, ambiguous; *the court took the view that the defendant's plea was equivocal*

error ['erə] *noun* mistake; *he made an error in calculating the total*; *the secretary must have made a typing error*; **clerical error** = mistake made in an office; **computer error** = mistake made by a computer; **errors and omissions excepted** (**e. & o.e.**) = words written on an invoice to show that the company has no responsibility for mistakes in the invoice

Erskine May ['ɜːskɪn 'meɪ] *noun* book on the procedure and privileges of Parliament

COMMENT: Erskine May's 'Treatise on the Law, Privileges, Proceedings and Usage of Parliament' was originally published in 1844. The author, Sir Thomas Erskine May, was Clerk of the House of Commons. The book is updated frequently, and is the authority on questions of parliamentary procedure

escalate ['eskəleɪt] *verb* to increase at a constant rate

escalation [eskə'leɪʃn] *noun* **escalation of prices** = constant increase in prices; **escalation clause** = ESCALATOR CLAUSE

escalator clause ['eskəleɪtə 'klɔːz] *noun* clause in a contract allowing for regular price increases because of increased costs

escape [ɪ'skeɪp] **1** *noun* getting away from a difficult situation; **escape clause** = clause in a contract which allows one of the parties to avoid carrying out the terms of the contract under certain conditions without penalty **2** *verb* to get away from (a prison); *three prisoners escaped by climbing over the wall*

escrow ['eskrəʊ] *noun* deed which the parties to it deliver to an independent person who hands it over only when certain conditions have been fulfilled; **in escrow =** held in safe keeping by a third party; **document held in escrow =** document given to a third party to keep and to pass on to someone when, for example, money has been paid; *US* **escrow account =** account where money is held in escrow until a contract is signed, until goods are delivered, etc.

espionage ['espɪɒnɑːʒ] *noun* spying; **industrial espionage =** trying to find out the secrets of a competitor's work or products, usually by illegal means

esquire [ɪ'skwaɪə] *noun* (a) *GB* title written after the name of a man, in an address; *letter addressed to J. Smith, Esq.* (NOTE: you can use **Mr** before a name, or **Esq.** after it; both are titles, but **Esq.** is more formal and suggests that the man is more important. **Esq.** is used by lawyers, bank managers, etc., when writing to clients) (b) *US* title given to an American lawyer (male or female)

establish [ɪ'stæblɪʃ] *verb* (a) to set up, to make or to open; *the company has established a branch in Australia*; *the business was established in Scotland in 1823*; **established post =** permanent post in the civil service or similar organization; **to establish oneself in business =** to become successful in a new business (b) **established use =** use of land for a certain purpose which is recognised by a local authority because the land has been used for this purpose for some time (c) to decide what is correct, what is fact; *the police are trying to establish his movements on the night of the murder*; *it is an established fact that the car could not have been used because it was out of petrol*

establishment [ɪ'stæblɪʃmənt] *noun* (a) commercial business; *he runs an important printing establishment* (b) *(in the EU)* **right of establishment =** right of an EC citizen to live and work in any EC country (c) number of people working in a company; **establishment charges =** cost of people and property, in a company's accounts; **establishment officer =** civil servant in charge of personnel in a government department; **to be on the establishment =** to be a full-time employee; **office with an establishment of fifteen =** office with a permanent staff of fifteen (d) **the Establishment =** powerful and important people who run the country and its government

estate [ɪ'steɪt] *noun* (a) interest in or right to hold and occupy land (b) **real estate =** property (land or buildings); **estate agency =** office which arranges for the sale of property; **estate agent =** person in charge of an estate agency (c) **industrial estate** *or* **trading estate =** area of land near a town specially for factories and warehouses (d) property left by a dead person; *his estate was valued at £100,000* *or* *he left estate valued at £100,000*; **estate duty,** *US* **estate tax =** tax on property left by a person now dead

estop [ə'stɒp] *verb* to stop someone doing something, such as exercising a right; *(in the EU)* to prevent something from happening

estoppel [ɪ'stɒpəl] *noun* rule of evidence whereby someone is prevented from denying or asserting a fact in legal proceedings; **estoppel of** *or* **by record =** rule that a person cannot reopen a matter which has already been decided by a court; **estoppel by deed =** rule that a person cannot deny having done something which is recorded in a deed; **estoppel by conduct** *or* **in pais =** rule that no one can deny things which he has done or failed to do which have had an effect on other persons' actions if that person has acted in a way which relied on the others' behaviour; *see also* PROMISSORY

estovers [ɪ'stəʊvəz] *plural noun* right of a tenant to take wood and timber from land which he rents

estreat [ɪ'striːt] *verb* to get a copy of a record of bail or a fine awarded by a court; **estreated recognizance =** recognizance which is forfeited because the person making it has not come to court

et al. *or* **et alia** [ˈet ˈæl or ˈet ˈeɪliə] *Latin phrase meaning* 'and others' or 'and other things'

ethnic [ˈeθnɪk] *adjective* referring to a certain nation or race; **ethnic group =** people of a certain nation or race; **ethnic minority =** group of people of one race in a country where most people are of another race

etiquette [etɪˈket] *noun* rules governing the way people should behave, such as the way in which a solicitor or barrister behaves towards clients in court

et seq. *or* **et sequentes** [ˈet ˈsek] *Latin phrase meaning* 'and the following'

EU [ˈiː ˈjuː] = EUROPEAN UNION

Euro- [ˈjuərəu] *prefix* referring to Europe or the European Community; **Euro-constituency** *or* **Euro-seat =** constituency which elects an MEP to the European Parliament; **Euro-MP =** MEP, Member of the European Parliament

Eurocrat [ˈjuərəukræt] *noun (informal)* bureaucrat working in the European Community or the European Parliament

European [juərəuˈpiːən] *adjective* referring to Europe; **the European Community (EC)** or **European Union (EU) =** a group of European countries linked together by the Treaty of Rome in such a way that trade is more free, people can move from one country to another more freely, and people can work more freely in other countries of the group; **European Atomic Energy Community Treaty (EURATOM) =** treaty established in 1957 to develop nuclear energy within the Common Market; **European Coal and Steel Community Treaty (ECSC) =** treaty set up in 1951 to create a common market for coal and steel within the signing members; **European Community Law =** law created by the European Community and enforceable in EC states; **European Commission** *or* **Commission of the European Community =** main executive body of the EC, made up of members nominated by each Member State;

European Court of Human Rights = court considering the rights of citizens of states which are parties to the European Convention for the Protection of Human Rights (NOTE: its formal name is the **European Court for the Protection of Human Rights**)

European Convention on Human Rights [juərəuˈpiːən kənˈvenʃn ɒn ˈhjuːmən ˈraɪts] *noun* convention signed by all members of the Council of Europe covering the rights of all its citizens

COMMENT: the convention recognises property rights, religious rights, the right of citizens to privacy, the due process of law, the principle of legal review. Note that the European Convention on Human Rights does not form part of English law

European Council [juərəuˈpiːən kaunsl] *noun* group formed by the heads of government of the Member States of the European Union; the president of the European Council is the head of the state which is currently president of the council of ministers (NOTE: do not confuse with the **Council of the European Union**)

European Court of Justice

(ECJ) [juərəuˈpiːən kɔːt əv ˈdʒʌstɪs] *noun* court set up to see that the principles of law within the EU as laid out in the Treaty are observed and applied correctly; the court is responsible for settling disputes relating to European Community Law, and also acting as a last Court of Appeal against judgments in individual countries

COMMENT: the ECJ has 15 judges and 8 Advocates General; these are appointed by the governments of Member States for a period of six years. The judges come from all the Member States, and bring with them the legal traditions of each state. The court can either meet as a full court, or in chambers where only two or three judges are present. The court normally conducts its business in French, though if an action is brought before the court by or against a Member State, that Member State can choose the language in which the case will be heard. The Court can hear actions against institutions, actions brought either by the Commission or by a Member State against another Member State. The Court also acts as Court of Appeal for appeals from the Court of First Instance. The court also interprets legislation and as such acts in a semi-legislative capacity

European Parliament [juərəu'piːən 'pɑːləmən't] *noun* parliament of members (MEPs) elected in each member country of the EU, representing the peoples of the Member States of the EU

COMMENT: the members of the European Parliaments (MEPs) are elected by constituencies in their countries; there are 610 MEPs, elected according to the size of the state they come from (the largest member state, Germany, has 99 MEPs, and the smallest, Luxembourg, has only 6). The European Parliament has the duty to supervise the working of the European Commission, and can if necessary, decide to demand the resignation of the entire Commission, although it cannot demand the resignation of one single commissioner. The Parliament takes part in making the legislation of the EU, especially by advising on new legislation being proposed by the Commission.

euthanasia [juːθə'neɪziə] *noun* mercy killing, the killing of a sick person to put an end to his or her suffering

evade [ɪ'veɪd] *verb* to try to avoid something; **to evade tax** = to try illegally to avoid paying tax

evaluate [ɪ'væljueɪt] *verb* to calculate a value; *to evaluate costs*

evaluation [ɪvælju'eɪʃn] *noun* calculation of value; **job evaluation** = examining different jobs within an organization to see what skills and qualifications are needed to carry them out

with a view to establishing appropriate salaries

evasion [ɪ'veɪʒn] *noun* avoiding; **tax evasion** = illegally trying not to pay tax; *see also* AVOIDANCE

evasive [ɪ'veɪzɪv] *adjective* which tries to avoid; **to give evasive answers** = to try to avoid answering questions directly

evict [ɪ'vɪkt] *verb* to force (someone, especially a tenant) to leave a property; *all the tenants were evicted by the new landlords*

eviction [ɪ'vɪkʃn] *noun* forcing someone (especially a tenant) to leave a property

evidence [evɪdəns] **1** *noun* written or spoken statement of facts which helps to prove something at a trial; *all the evidence points to arson*; **circumstantial evidence** = evidence which suggests that something must have happened, but does not give firm proof of it; **direct evidence** = first-hand evidence, such as the testimony of an eye witness or the production of original documents; **documentary evidence** = evidence in the form of documents; **evidence in chief** = questioning of a witness by the party who called him or her (NOTE: the opposite is **cross-examination**); **the secretary gave evidence against her former employer** = the secretary was a witness, and her statement suggested that her former employer was guilty; **to plant evidence** = to put items at the scene of a crime after the crime has taken place, so that a person is incriminated and can be arrested; **rule of evidence** = rule established by law which determines the type of evidence which a court will consider and how such evidence must be given; **to turn Queen's evidence,** *US* **to turn state's evidence** = to confess to a crime and then act as witness against the other criminals involved, in the hope of getting a lighter sentence (NOTE: no plural; to refer to a single item say **a piece of evidence**) **2** *verb* to show; *the lack of good will, as evidenced by the defendant's behaviour in the witness stand*

ex [eks] *preposition & prefix* **(a)** out of, from; **price ex warehouse** = price for a product which is to be collected from the factory or from an agent's warehouse and so does not include delivery; **price ex works** *or* **ex factory** = price not including transport from the maker's factory **(b)** **share quoted ex dividend** = share price not including the right to receive the next dividend **(c)** former *or* formerly; *Mr Smith, the ex-chairman of the company; she claimed maintenance from her ex-husband* **(d)** **ex-directory number** = telephone number which is not printed in the list of people having telephone numbers

examine [ɪgˈzæmɪn] *verb* to look at someone or something very carefully to see if it can be accepted; *the customs officials asked to examine the inside of the car; the police are examining the papers from the managing director's safe;* **examining justice** *or* **magistrate** = magistrate who hears a case when it is presented for the first time, and decides if there should be a prosecution; *see also* CROSS-EXAMINE

examination [ɪgzæmɪˈneɪʃn] *noun* **(a)** asking someone questions to find out facts, such as the questioning of a prisoner by a magistrate **(b)** **examination in chief,** *US* **direct examination** = asking a witness questions (by counsel for his side) to give oral evidence in court **(c)** looking at something very carefully to see if it is acceptable; **customs examination** = looking at goods or baggage by customs officials; *see also* CROSS-EXAMINATION

exceed [ɪkˈsiːd] *verb* to be more than; **to exceed one's powers** = to act in a way which one is not legally entitled to do; *the judge exceeded his powers in criticizing the court of appeal;* **he was arrested for exceeding the speed limit** = he was arrested for driving faster than was permitted; **he has exceeded his credit limit** = he has borrowed more money than he is allowed to do

excepted [ɪkˈseptɪd] *adverb* not including; **errors and omissions excepted** = note on an invoice to show that the company has no responsibility for mistakes in the invoice; **excepted persons** = types of workers listed in an insurance policy as not being covered by the insurance

exception [ɪkˈsepʃn] *noun* **(a)** thing which is not included with others; *all the accused were acquitted with the exception of Jones who was sent to prison for three months* **(b)** objection raised to the ruling of a judge; **to take exception to something** = to object to something, to protest against something; *counsel for the defence took exception to the witness' remarks; he has taken exception to the reports of the trial in the newspapers*

exceptional [ɪkˈsepʃənəl] *adjective* not usual, different; **exceptional items** = items in a balance sheet which do not appear there each year; **exceptional needs payment** = payment made by the social services to a claimant who has a particular urgent need (such as for clothes)

excess [ɪkˈses] *noun* **(a)** amount which is more than what is allowed; **excess alcohol in the blood** = more alcohol in the blood than a driver is permitted to have; **excess fare** = extra fare to be paid (such as for travelling first class with a second class ticket); **excess of jurisdiction** = case where a judge or magistrate has exceeded his powers; **excess profits** = profits which are more than is considered to be normal; **in excess of** = above, more than; *quantities in excess of twenty-five kilos* **(b)** amount to be paid by the insured as part of any claim made under the terms of an insurance policy; *he has to pay a £50 excess, and the damage amounted to over £1,000*

excessive [ɪkˈsesɪv] *adjective* too large; *we found the bill for costs excessive and applied to have it reduced; the driver had an excessive amount of alcohol in his blood*

exchange [ɪksˈtʃeɪnʒ] **1** *noun* **(a)** giving of one thing for another; **part exchange** = giving an old product as part of the payment for a new one; **exchange of contracts** = point in the conveyance of a property when the solicitors for the buyer and the seller hand over the contract which then becomes binding **(b) foreign exchange** = (i) exchanging the money of one country for that of another; (ii) money of another country; **foreign exchange broker** = person who buys and sells foreign currency on behalf of other people; **foreign exchange market** = dealings in foreign currencies; **rate of exchange** *or* **exchange rate** = price at which one currency is exchanged for another; **exchange controls** = government instructions on changing the local currency for foreign currency; *the government had to impose exchange controls to stop the rush to buy dollars;* *GB* **Exchange Equalization Account** = account with the Bank of England used by the government when buying or selling foreign currency to influence the exchange rate for the pound **(c) bill of exchange** = document ordering the person to whom it is directed to pay a person money on demand or at a certain date **(d) Stock Exchange** = place where stocks and shares are bought and sold; **commodity exchange** = place where commodities are bought and sold **2** *verb* **(a) to exchange an article for another** = to give one thing in place of something else **(b) to exchange contracts** = to hand over a contract when buying or selling a property (done by both buyer and seller at the same time) **(c)** to change money of one country for money of another

exchanger [ɪksˈtʃeɪnʒə] *noun* person who buys and sells foreign currency

Exchequer [ɪksˈtʃekə] *noun* fund of all money received by the government of the UK from taxes and other revenues; *see also* CHANCELLOR

excise 1 [ˈeksaɪz] *noun* **(a) excise duty** *or* **tax** = tax on certain goods produced in a country (such as alcohol) **(b) Customs and Excise** *or* **Excise Department** = government department which deals with VAT and with taxes on imports and on taxable products, such as alcohol, produced in the country **2** [ɪkˈsaɪz] *verb* to cut out; *the chairman ordered the remarks to be excised from the official record*

exciseman [ˈeksaɪzmən] *noun* person who works in the Excise Department

exclude *verb* [ɪksˈkluːd] to keep out, not to include; to remove someone from a group; *the right to enter can be excluded to a EU citizen on the grounds of danger to public health or safety*

excluding [ɪksˈkluːdɪŋ] *preposition* not including; *the regulations apply to members of the public, excluding those serving in the emergency services;* **not excluding** = including; *government servants, not excluding judges, are covered by the Bill*

exclusion [ɪksˈkluːʒn] *noun* act of excluding, of not including; **exclusion clause** = clause in a contract which limits the liability of a party, for example a clause in an insurance policy which says which items are not covered; **to the exclusion of** = not including, without including; **exclusion order** = court order in matrimonial proceedings which stops a wife or husband from going into the matrimonial home; **exclusion zone** = area (usually an area of sea) near a country, which is forbidden to military forces of other countries

exclusive [ɪksˈkluːzɪv] *adjective* **(a) exclusive agreement** = agreement where a person or firm is made sole agent for a product in a market; **exclusive licence** = licence where the licensee is the only person to be able to enjoy the licence; **exclusive right to market a product** = right to be the only person to market the product **(b) exclusive of** = not including

exclusivity [ekskluːˈzɪvəti] *noun* exclusive right to market a product

execute [ˈeksɪkjuːt] *verb* **(a)** to carry out (an order); to carry out (the terms of a contract); to seal (a deed); **executed consideration** = consideration where one party has made a promise in exchange for which the other party has done something for him **(b)** to kill someone who has been sentenced to death by a court; *he was executed by firing squad*

execution [eksɪˈkjuːʃn] *noun* **(a)** carrying out of a court order or of the terms of a contract; **stay of execution** = temporary stopping of a legal order; *the court granted the company a two-week stay of execution* **(b)** seizure and sale of goods belonging to a debtor; **warrant of execution** = warrant issued by a court which gives the bailiffs or sheriffs the power to seize goods from a debtor in order to pay his debts **(c) due execution of a will** = making a will in the correct way: a will must be written (handwritten, typed, written on a standard form, etc.), it must be signed by the testator and witnessed by two witnesses in the presence of the testator **(d)** killing of someone who has been sentenced to death by a court

executioner [eksɪˈkjuːʃnə] *noun* person who executes people who have been sentenced to death

executive [ɪgˈzekjʊtɪv] **1** *adjective* **(a)** which puts decisions into action; **executive committee** = committee which runs a society or a club; **executive director** = director who works full-time in the company; **executive powers** = right to put decisions into actions; *US* **executive session** = meeting of a congressional committee where only committee members, witnesses and other members of Congress may attend, and the public is excluded **(b)** referring to the branch of government which puts laws into effect; **executive detention** = detention of suspected terrorists, illegal immigrants, etc., for a limited period **(c)** referring to the President of the USA as head of government; **executive clemency** = pardon granted by the President; **executive document** = document (such as a treaty) sent by the President of the USA to the Senate for ratification; **executive order** = order by the president of the USA or of a state governor; **executive privilege** = privilege of the President of the USA not to reveal matters which he considers secret **2** *noun* **(a)** person in an organization who takes decisions, a manager or director; **Chief Executive** = (i) official permanent administrator of a town or county council;

(ii) executive director in charge of a company; **legal executive** = clerk in a solicitor's office who is not a solicitor and is not articled to become one, but has passed the examinations of the Institute of Legal Executives **(b) the Executive** = (i) section of a government which puts into effect the laws passed by Parliament (ii) *US* the president

executor [ɪgˈzekjʊtə] *noun* someone who is appointed by a person making his will who will see that the terms of the will are carried out; *he was named executor of his brother's will*

executorship [ɪgˈzekjʊtəʃɪp] *noun* position of being an executor or executrix

executory [ɪgˈzekjʊtrɪ] *adjective* which is still being carried out; **executory consideration** = consideration where one party makes a promise in exchange for a counter-promise from the other party (NOTE: after they have been carried out, executory contracts and trusts are said to have been **executed**)

executrix [ɪgˈzekjʊtrɪks] *noun* female executor

exemplary [ɪgˈzemplərɪ] *adjective* which is so good that it serves as an example to others; *her conduct in the case was exemplary*; **exemplary damages** = heavy damages which punish the defendant for the loss or harm caused to the claimant, awarded to show that the court feels the defendant has behaved badly towards the claimant; **exemplary sentence** = particularly harsh sentence which aims at deterring others from committing the same type of crime

exempt [ɪgˈzempt] **1** *adjective* **(a)** not covered by a law; not forced to obey a law; **exempt from tax** *or* **tax-exempt** = not required to pay tax; **exempt supplies** = sales of goods or services on which VAT does not have to be paid **(b) exempt information** = information which may be kept secret from the public (because if it were disclosed it might be unfair to an individual or harmful to the council); *the council resolved that the press and public* *be excluded for item 10 (applications for headships) as it involved the likely disclosure of exempt information* **2** *verb* to free something from having tax paid on it, from having to pay tax; *non profit-making organizations are exempt(ed) from tax; food is exempt(ed) from sales tax; the government exempted trusts from tax;* **exempted business** = certain types of business in the House of Commons, which cannot be interrupted if started late in the sitting (i.e. after 10 p.m. on weekdays, or after 4 p.m. on Fridays)

exemption [ɪgˈzempʃn] *noun* act of exempting something from a contract or from a tax; *the Commission is the only body which can grant exemptions from Community competition law; (in the EU)* **block exemption** = exemption granted to a large business or group of businesses exempting them from certain obligations under competition law; **individual exemption** = exemption granted to a person or small business, exempting them from certain obligations; **exemption clause** = clause in a contract exempting a party from certain liabilities; **exemption from tax** *or* **tax exemption** = being free from having to pay tax; *as a non profit-making organization you can claim tax exemption*

exercise [ˈeksəsaɪz] **1** *noun* use (of a power); *a court can give directions to a local authority as to the exercise of its powers in relation to children in care;* **exercise of an option** = using an option, putting an option into action **2** *verb* to use or to put into practice; **to exercise one's discretion** = to decide which of several courses to take; *the magistrates exercised their discretion and let the accused off with a suspended sentence;* **to exercise an option** = to put an option into action; *he exercised his option to acquire sole marketing rights for the product; not many shareholders exercised their option to buy the new issue of shares*

ex gratia [ˈeks ˈgreɪʃə] *Latin phrase meaning* 'as a favour'; **an ex gratia payment** = payment made as a gift, with no obligations

exhibit [ɪgˈzɪbɪt] *noun* object (such as a gun, coat or document) which is shown as evidence to a court

exile [ˈegzaɪl] **1** *noun* **(a)** being sent to live in another country as a punishment; *the ten members of the opposition party were sent into exile* **(b)** person who has been sent to live in another country as a punishment **2** *verb* to send someone to live in another country as a punishment; *he was exiled for life; she was exiled to an island in the North Sea*

exist [ɪgˈzɪst] *verb* to be; *the right of way has existed since the early nineteenth century*

existence [ɪgˈzɪstəns] *noun* being; **to come into existence** = to start to be; *the custom came into existence during the eighteenth century;* **immemorial existence** = before 1189, the date from which events are supposed to be remembered

ex officio [eks əˈfɪʃiəʊ] *Latin phrase meaning* 'because of an office held'; *the treasurer is ex officio a member or an ex officio member of the finance committee*

exonerate [ɪgˈzɒnəreɪt] *verb* to say that someone who has been blamed, should not be blamed; *the judge exonerated the driver from all responsibility for the accident*

exoneration [ɪgzɒnəˈreɪʃn] *noun* act of exonerating

ex parte [ˈeks ˈpɑːteɪ] *Latin phrase meaning* 'on behalf of', 'on the part of one side only'; **an ex parte application** = application made to a court where only one side is represented and no notice is given to the other side (often where the application is for an injunction); *the wife applied ex parte for an ouster order against her husband; see also* INTER PARTES (NOTE: in legal reports, abbreviated to **ex p** as in: *Williams v. Smith, ex p White* showing that White was the party which applied for the hearing to take place; note also that the phrase **application made without notice to the other party** is now preferred to **ex parte application**)

expatriate 1 [eks'pætriət] *noun* person who lives abroad; *there is a large expatriate community or a large community of expatriates in Geneva* **2** [eks'pætrieɪt] *verb* to force someone to leave the country where he is living

expatriation [ekspætri'eɪʃn] *noun* forcing someone to leave the country where he is living

expectancy *or* **expectation** [ɪks'pektənsi or ekspel'teɪʃn] *noun* hope that you will succeed to a property; **expectation of life** *or* **life expectancy** = number of years a person is likely to live

expectations [ekspek'teɪʃnz] *see* LEGITIMATE EXPECTATIONS

expenditure [ek'spendɪtʃə] *noun* amounts of money spent; **capital expenditure** = (i) money spent on assets (such as property or machinery); (ii) major costs of a council or central government (such as schools, roads, hospitals, etc.); **revenue expenditure** = day-to-day costs of a council (such as salaries and wages, maintenance of buildings, etc.) (NOTE: no plural in British English; American English uses **expenditures**)

expense [ɪk'spens] *noun* **(a)** money spent; **at great expense** = having spent a lot of money **(b)** **expense account** = money which a businessman is allowed by his company to spend on travelling and entertaining clients in connection with his business

expenses [ɪk'spensɪz] *plural noun* money paid for doing something; **all expenses paid** = with all costs paid by the company; **allowable expenses** = business expenses which are allowed against tax; **business expenses** = money spent on running a business, not on stock or assets; **entertainment expenses** = money spent on giving meals to business visitors; **fixed expenses** = money which is spent regularly (such as rent, electricity, telephone); **incidental expenses** = small amounts of money spent at various times, in addition to larger amounts; **legal expenses** = money spent on fees to lawyers; **overhead**

expenses *or* **general expenses** *or* **running expenses** = money spent on the day-to-day costs of a business; **travelling expenses** = money spent on travelling and hotels for business purposes; **election expenses** = money spent by a candidate or political party during an election campaign

COMMENT: in the UK, there is a limit to the amount of money each individual candidate can spend, so as not to favour rich candidates against poor ones. After the election the candidates and their agents have to make a return of expenses to show that they have not overspent. There is no limit to the spending of the political parties on a national level, and most of the campaign expenditure is made in this way, with national TV advertising, advertisements in the national press, etc. In the USA, the government subsidizes election expenses by paying an equivalent sum to that raised by each candidate. The candidates for the main elected positions (especially that of President) have to be rich, or at any rate to have rich supporters

expert ['ekspɜːt] *noun* person who knows a lot about something; *an expert in the field of fingerprints or a fingerprints expert; the company asked a financial expert for advice or asked for expert financial advice;* **expert evidence** = evidence given by an expert witness; **expert's report** = report written by an expert (usually for a court case); **expert witness** = witness who is a specialist in a subject and is asked to give his opinion on technical matters

expiration [ekspɪ'reɪʃn] *noun* coming to an end; *expiration of an insurance policy; to repay before the expiration of the stated period;* **on expiration of the lease** = when the lease comes to an end

expire [ek'spaɪə] *verb* to come to an end; *the lease expires in 2010; his passport has expired* = his passport is no longer valid

expiry [ek'spaɪri] *noun* coming to an end; *expiry of an insurance policy;* **expiry date** = (i) date when something will end, such as the last date for exercising an option; (ii) the last date on which a credit card can be used

explicit [ık'splısıt] *adjective* which is clearly stated; *his explicit intention was to leave his house to his wife*

explicitly [ık'splısıtli] *adverb* in a clear way; *the contract explicitly prohibits sale of the goods in Europe*

export 1 ['ekspɔːt] *noun* sending of goods to a foreign country to be sold; **export licence** = permit which allows a company to send a certain type of product abroad to be sold **2** [ık'spɔːt] *verb* to send goods abroad to be sold; *most of the company's products are exported to the USA*

exposure [ık'spəʊʒə] *noun* act of showing something which was hidden; *the report's exposure of corruption in the police force*; **indecent exposure** = offence where a male person shows his sexual organs to a woman

ex post facto ['eks 'pəʊst 'fæktəʊ] *Latin phrase meaning* 'after the event'

express [ık'spres] **1** *adjective* **(a)** rapid, very fast; *express letter*; *express delivery* **(b)** clearly shown in words; *the contract has an express condition forbidding sale in Africa*; **express term** = term in a contract which is clearly stated (as opposed to an implied term) **2** *verb* **(a)** to put into words or diagrams; *this chart shows crime in London expressed as a percentage of total crime in the UK* **(b)** to send very fast; *we expressed the order to the customer's warehouse*

expressly [ık'spresli] *adverb* clearly in words; *the contract expressly forbids sales to the United States*; *the franchisee is expressly forbidden to sell goods other than those supplied by the franchiser*

expressio unius est exclusio alterius [ık'spresiəʊ 'uːniəs est ıks'kluːziəʊ ɔːl'teriəs] *Latin phrase meaning* 'the mention that one thing is included implies that another thing is excluded'

expropriation [ıksprəʊpri'eıʃn] *noun* **(a)** action of the state in taking private property for public use (without paying compensation) **(b)** *US* action of the state in taking private property for public use (and paying compensation to the former owner) (NOTE: the equivalent in the UK is **compulsory purchase**)

expunge [ık'spʌnʒ] *verb* to remove (from a record); *inadmissible hearsay evidence was expunged from the report*

extend [ık'stend] *verb* **(a)** to make available, to give; *to extend credit to a customer* **(b)** to make longer; *to extend a contract for two years*; *the court extended the defendant's time for serving his defence by fourteen days*; **extended credit** = credit allowing the borrower a longer time to pay; **extended family** = group of related people, including distant relatives and close friends; **extended sentence** = sentence which is made longer than usual because the criminal is likely to repeat the offence; *he was sentenced to five years imprisonment, extended*

extension [ık'stenʃn] *noun* allowing longer time; **to get an extension of credit** = to get more time to pay back; **extension of a contract** = continuing the contract for a further period; **extension of time** = allowance by court to a party of more time in which to do something; *the defendant applied for an extension of time in which to serve her defence*

extenuating circumstances
[ık'stenjueıtıŋ 'sɜːkəmstænsız] *plural noun* factors which excuse a crime in some way

extenuation [ıkstenju'eıʃn] *noun* **in extenuation of something** = in order to excuse something; *counsel pleaded the accused's age in extenuation of his actions*

extinction [ık'stıŋkʃn] *noun* coming to an end; *the extinction of a legal right*

extinguishment [ıks'tıŋgwıʃmənt] *noun* act of cancelling a right or a power (especially the right to sue for non-payment once payment has been made)

extort [ɪkˈstɔːt] *verb* to get money, promises or a confession from someone, by using threats; *he extorted £20,000 from local shopkeepers*

extortion [ɪkˈstɔːʃn] *noun* getting money by threats; **extortion racket** = racket to make money by threatening people

extortionate [ɪkˈstɔːʃənət] at very high cost, too much; **extortionate credit bargain** = transaction whereby money is lent at a very high rate of interest, thereby rendering the transaction illegal

extortionist [ɪkˈstɔːʃənɪst] person who extorts money from people

extra- [ˈekstrə] *prefix* outside; **extra-authority** *or* **extra-borough** *or* **extra-district payments** = payments made to another authority for services provided by that authority; **extra-territorial waters** = international waters, outside the jurisdiction of a country

extract 1 [ˈekstrækt] *noun* printed document which is part of a larger document; *the solicitor sent an extract of the deeds* **2** [ɪkˈstrækt] *verb* to get something, such as information, from someone by force; *the confession was extracted under torture; the magistrate extracted an admission from the witness that he had not seen the accident*

extradite [ˈekstrədaɪt] *verb* to bring an arrested person from another country to your country because he is wanted for trial for a crime which he committed in your country; *he was arrested in France and extradited to stand trial in Germany*

extradition [ekstrəˈdɪʃn] *noun* act of extraditing; *the USA is seeking the extradition of the leader of the drug gang*; **extradition treaty** = agreement between two countries that a person arrested in one country can be sent to the other to stand trial for a crime committed there

extraordinary [ekˈstrɔːdnəri] *adjective* different from normal; **Extraordinary General Meeting (EGM)** = special meeting of shareholders or members of a club, etc., to discuss an important matter

which cannot wait until the next Annual General Meeting; **extraordinary items** = items in accounts which do not appear each year; *the auditors noted several extraordinary items in the accounts*; **extraordinary resolution** = resolution which needs 75% of the votes before it can be carried

COMMENT: notice that an extraordinary resolution will be put to a meeting must be given, but no minimum period is specified by law, as opposed to a 'special resolution' for which 21 days' notice must be given. An extraordinary resolution could be a proposal to wind up a company voluntarily, but changes to the articles of association, such as a change of name, or of the objects of the company, need a special resolution

extra-territoriality [ˈekstrəterɪtɔːriˈælɪti] *noun* being outside the territory of the country where you are living, and so not subject to its laws (used of diplomats)

extremist [ɪkˈstriːmɪst] **1** *noun (as criticism)* person in favour of very strong, sometimes violent methods; *the party has been taken over by left-wing extremists*; *the meeting was broken up by extremists from the right of the party* **2** *adjective* in favour of strong methods; *the electorate decisively rejected the extremist parties*

extremism [ɪkˈstriːmɪzm] *noun (as criticism)* ideas and practices that favour very strong action, even the use of violence

extrinsic evidence [eksˈtrɪnsɪk ˈevɪdəns] *noun* evidence used in the interpretation of a document which is not found in the document itself; *compare* INTRINSIC

ex turpi causa non oritur actio [ˈeks ˈtuəpiː ˈkauzə nɒn ˈɒrɪtə ˈæktiəu] *Latin phrase meaning* 'from a base cause no action can proceed': it is not legally possible to enforce an illegal contract

eye witness [ˈaɪ ˈwɪtnəs] *noun* person who saw something happen (such as an accident or a crime); *he gave an eye witness account of the bank hold-up*

Ff

F [ef] *sixth letter of the alphabet;* **Class F charge** = charge on a property registered by a spouse who is not the owner, claiming a right to live in the property; **Schedule F** = schedule to the Finance Acts under which tax is charged on income from dividends

face [feɪs] **1** *noun* front part of something; **face value** = value written on a coin, share certificate or banknote **2** *verb* **to face a charge** = to appear in court and be charged with a crime; *he faces three charges relating to firearms*

facie [ˈfeɪʃi] *see* PRIMA FACIE

facsimile (copy) [fəkˈsɪməli] *noun* exact copy of a document; *see also* FAX

fact [fækt] *noun* something which is true and real, especially something which has been proved by evidence in court; *the chairman of the tribunal asked to see all the facts on the income tax claim*; **in fact** *or* **in point of fact** = really; **witness of fact** = person who gives evidence to say that facts in a claim are true; **matters of fact** = facts relevant to a case which is being tried at court; *see also* ACCESSORY

faction [ˈfækʃn] *noun (sometimes as criticism)* group of people within a larger organization such as a political party, who have different views or have special aims; *arguments broke out between different factions at the party conference*; *the Prime Minister has the support of most factions in the party*

factional [ˈfækʃənl] *adjective* referring to factions; *factional infighting has weakened the party structure*

facto [ˈfæktəʊ] *see* DE FACTO, IPSO FACTO

factor [ˈfæktə] *noun* **(a)** thing which is important, which influences; *the rise in unemployment is an important factor in the increased crime rate*; **cyclical factors** = way in which a trade cycle affects businesses; **contributory factor** = something which contributes to a result; **deciding factor** = most important factor which influences a decision; **factors of production** = things needed to produce a product (land, labour and capital) **(b)** agent or person who buys or sells as an agent for another in exchange for a commission; **debt factor** = person who buys debts at a discount, and enforces them for himself or enforces them for a commission

factoring [ˈfæktrɪŋ] *noun* selling debts to a debt factor

faculty [ˈfækʌlti] *noun* special permission to do something, granted by a church (such as permission to get married without publishing banns)

Faculty of Advocates [ˈfækʌlti əv ˈædvəkəts] *noun* legal body to which Scottish barristers belong

fair [feə] **1** *noun* **trade fair** = large exhibition and meeting for advertising and selling a certain type of product **2** *adjective* **(a)** honest or correct; **fair comment** = remark which is honestly made on a matter of public interest and so is not defamatory; **fair dealing** = (i) legal buying and selling of shares; (ii) quoting small sections of a copyright work; (iii) = FAIR TRADING; **fair price** = good price for both buyer and seller; **fair rent** = reasonable rent for a property, bearing in mind the size and type of property and its situation; **fair trade** = international business system where countries agree not to charge import duties on certain items imported from their trading partners; **fair trading** = way of doing business which is reasonable and does not harm the consumer; **Office of Fair Trading** = British government department which protects consumers against unfair or illegal business; **fair use** = use which can be legally made of a quotation from a copyright text without the permission of the copyright owner; **fair value**, *US* **fair market value** = price paid by a buyer who knows the value of what he is buying to a seller who also knows the value of what he is selling (i.e. neither is cheating the other); **fair wear and tear** = acceptable damage caused by normal use; *the insurance policy covers most damage, but not fair wear and tear to the machine* **(b) fair copy** = document which is written or typed with no corrections or mistakes

faith [feɪθ] *noun* **to have faith in something** *or* **someone** = to believe that something or a person is good or will work well; **in good faith** = in an honest way; **he acted in good faith** = he acted honestly; **he acted in bad faith** = he acted dishonestly; **to buy something in good faith** = to buy something honestly, in the course of an honest transaction; *he bought the car in good faith, not knowing it had been stolen*

fake [feɪk] **1** *noun* forgery, copy made for criminal purposes; *the shipment came with fake documentation* **2** *verb* to make an imitation for criminal purposes; *they faked a break-in to make the police believe the documents had been stolen*

fall [fɔːl] *verb* **(a)** to happen, to take place; *the national holiday falls on a Monday*; **the bill fell due** = the bill was due to be paid; **to fall outside** = not to be part of a list, not to be covered by a rule; *the case falls outside the jurisdiction of the court*; **to fall within** = to become part of a list, to be covered by a rule; *the newspaper report falls within the category of defamation*; *the case falls within the competence of the*

court (b) *(of a motion)* not to succeed; *the Bill was talked out and so fell*

false [fɒls] *adjective* not true or not correct; *to make a false entry in the record*; **false accounting** = notifiable offence of changing, destroying or hiding records for money; **false imprisonment** = (i) tort of keeping someone imprisoned wrongfully; (ii) sending someone to prison for a wrong reason; **false pretence(s)**, *US* **false pretense** = doing or saying something to cheat someone; *he was sent to prison for obtaining money by false pretences*; **false representation** = offence of making a wrong statement; **false weight** = weight on shop scales which is wrong and so cheats customers

falsehood [ˈfɒlshʊd] *noun* lie, incorrect statement; **injurious falsehood** *or* **malicious falsehood** = tort of making a wrong statement about someone so as to harm his reputation (usually in relation to his business or property)

falsification [fɒlsɪfɪˈkeɪʃn] *noun* **falsification of accounts** = action of making false entries in a record or of destroying a record

falsify [ˈfɒlsɪfaɪ] *verb* to change something to make it wrong; **to falsify accounts** = to change or destroy a record

family [ˈfæmli] *noun* **(a)** group of people who are related (including husband, wife, mother, father, children); **extended family** = group of related people including distant relatives and close friends; **family company** = company where most of the shares are owned by members of the same family; **Family Division** = one of the three divisions of the High Court which deals with divorce cases and cases involving parents and children; **family law** = laws relating to families or to the rights and duties of the members of a family **(b)** *(slang)* group of organized Mafia gangsters, ruled by a boss or godfather

fast track [ˈfɑːst ˈtræk] *noun* case management system normally applied to civil cases involving sums between £5000 and £15,000

COMMENT: the timetable for the fast track is given in the directions for the case. A typical timetable starts from the date of the notice of allocation, and gives four weeks to disclosure, 10 weeks for the exchange of experts' reports, 20 weeks for the court to send out listing questionnaires and 30 weeks to the hearing; the trial must not last more than one day, and such issues as liability and quantum may be decided separately

fast-track ['fɑːst'træk] *adjective* which goes forward at a faster rate; *there is a new fast-track procedure for hearing claims*

fatal ['feɪtl] *adjective* which causes a death; *he took a fatal dose of drugs*; *there were six fatal accidents in the first week of the year*

Father of the House ['fɑːðə əv ðə 'haʊs] *noun* the MP who has been an MP for the longest time without a break

fax [fæks] **1** *noun* (i) system for sending facsimile copies of documents via the telephone lines; (ii) document sent by this method; *we received a fax of the report this morning*; *are you willing to accept service by fax?* **2** *verb* to send a message by fax; *the details of the case were faxed to the parties this morning*

COMMENT: fax can be used for service of documents, if the parties concerned have said that they are willing to accept service in this way. On the other hand, banks will not accept fax messages as binding instructions (as for example, a faxed order for money to be transferred from one account to another)

FBI ['ef 'biː 'eɪ] = FEDERAL BUREAU OF INVESTIGATION

feasant ['fiːzənt] *see* DAMAGE FEASANT

feasibility [fiːzə'bɪləti] *noun* ability to be done; **feasibility study** *or* **feasibility report** = work done to see if something which has been planned is a good idea; *the council asked the Planning Department to comment on the feasibility of the project;*

the department has produced a feasibility report on the development project

feasible ['fiːzəbl] *adjective* which can be done; *the Planning Department says it is not feasible to produce draft plans at this stage*

federal ['fedrl] *adjective* **(a)** referring to a system of government in which a group of states are linked together in a federation; **a federal constitution** = constitution (such as that in Germany) which provides for a series of semi-autonomous states joined together in a national federation **(b)** referring especially to the central government of the United States; **federal court** *or* **federal laws** = court or laws of the USA, as opposed to state courts or state laws

Federal Bureau of Investigation (FBI) ['fedrl 'bjʊərəʊ əv ɪnvestɪ'geɪʃn] *noun* section of the US Department of Justice, which investigates crimes against federal law and subversive acts in the USA

federalism ['fedrəlɪzm] *noun* type of government, in which the state is a federation of semi-autonomous provinces or states, with a central federal government

Federal Reserve Bank ['fedrl rɪ'sɜːv 'bæŋk] *noun US* one of the twelve central banks in the USA which are owned by the state and directed by the Federal Reserve Board

Federal Reserve Board ['fedrl rɪ'sɜːv 'bɔːd] *noun US* government organization which runs the central banks in the USA

federation [fedə'reɪʃn] *noun* group of states or organizations which have a central government, a body which represents them and looks after their common interests; *see also* CONFEDERATION

COMMENT: many federations exist, though they are not always called such: the USA, Canada, Australia, and Germany are all federations

fee [fiː] *noun* **(a)** money paid for work carried out by a professional person (such as an accountant, a doctor or a lawyer); *we charge a small fee for our services*; *a barrister's fees*; **contingent fee** = fee paid to a lawyer which is a proportion of the damages recovered in a case **(b)** money paid for something; *entrance fee* or *admission fee*; *registration fee* **(c)** ownership of land which may be inherited; **fee simple** = freehold ownership of land with no restrictions to it; *to hold an estate in fee simple*; **fee tail** = interest in land which is passed on to the owner's direct descendants, and which cannot be passed to anyone else; *see also* ENTAIL

felonious [fəˈləʊniəs] *adjective* criminal; *he carried out a felonious act*

felony [ˈfeləni] *noun* old term for a serious crime; *to commit a felony* (NOTE: still used in the expression **treason felony**)

feme covert [ˈfæm ˈkəʊvət] *French phrase meaning* 'married woman'

feme sole [ˈfæm ˈsəʊl] *French phrase meaning* 'unmarried woman'

fence [fens] **1** *noun (informal)* person who receives and sells stolen goods **2** *verb* to receive stolen goods to sell

feudalism [ˈfjuːdəlɪzm] *noun* medieval system, where land was granted by a king to his aristocracy, and by the aristocrats to the peasants, on condition that each paid a service (or feudal duty) to his superior

feudal society [ˈfjuːdl səˈsaɪəti] *noun* society where each class or level has a duty to serve the class above it

fiat [ˈfiːæt] *noun* **(a)** agreement (as of the Attorney-General) to bring a prosecution **(b)** **fiat money** = coins or notes which are not worth much as paper or metal, but are said by the government to have a value

fiat justitia [ˈfiːæt dʒʌsˈtɪsiə] *Latin phrase meaning* 'let justice be done'

fiction [ˈfɪkʃn] *noun* **fiction of law** or **legal fiction** = assuming something to be true, even if it is not proved to be so (a procedural device by courts to get round problems caused by statute)

fictitious [fɪkˈtɪʃəs] *adjective* false, which does not exist; **fictitious assets** = assets which do not really exist, but are entered as assets to balance the accounts

fide [ˈfaɪdiː] *see* BONA FIDE

fiduciary [fɪˈdjuːʃiəri] *adjective & noun* (person) acting as trustee for someone else, being in a position of trust; *a company director owes a fiduciary duty to the company*; **he was acting in a fiduciary capacity** = he was acting as a trustee

fieri facias [ˈfaɪraɪ ˈfeɪʃiæs] *Latin phrase meaning* 'make it happen'; **writ of fieri facias** = court order to a sheriff telling him to seize the goods of a debtor against whom judgment has been made (NOTE: often abbreviated to **fi. fa.**)

fi. fa. *see* FIERI FACIAS

FIFO = FIRST IN FIRST OUT

Fifth Amendment [ˈfɪfθ əˈmendmənt] *noun* amendment to the constitution of the USA, which says that no person can be forced to give evidence which might incriminate himself; **to plead the Fifth Amendment** *or* **to take the Fifth Amendment** = to refuse to give evidence to a court, tribunal or committee, because the evidence might incriminate you

file [faɪl] **1** *noun* **(a)** cardboard holder for documents, which can fit in the drawer of a filing cabinet; *put these letters in the unsolved cases file*; *look in the file marked 'Scottish police forces'*; **box file** = cardboard box for holding documents **(b)** documents kept for reference, either on paper or as data on a computer, like staff salaries, address list, customer accounts; *the police keep a file of missing vehicles*; *look up her description in the missing persons' file*; **to place something on file** = to keep a record of something; **to keep someone's name on file** = to keep someone's name on a list for reference; **file copy** = copy of a document which is kept for reference in an office; **card file** = information kept on filing cards; **computer file** = section of information on a computer (such as a list of addresses or of unsolved cases); *how can we protect our computer files?* **2** *verb* **(a) to file documents** = to put documents in order so that they can be found easily; *the correspondence is filed under 'complaints'* **(b)** to make an official request; **to file a petition in bankruptcy** = to ask officially to be made bankrupt, to ask officially for someone else to be made bankrupt **(c)** to send a document to court; *when a defendant is served with particulars of claim he can file a defence*; **the defence must be filed and served in seven days** = the defence must be sent to court and to the other party within seven days **(d)** to register something officially; *to file an application for a patent*; *to file a return to the tax office*

filibuster ['fɪlɪbʌstə] *noun* continuing to talk for a long time in a debate, so that the debate cannot be closed and a vote taken; *the Democrats organized a filibuster in the Senate*

filibustering ['fɪlɪbʌstrɪŋ] *noun* organizing or carrying out of a filibuster

COMMENT: filibusters are possible in the US Senate, because the rules of the Senate allow unlimited debate. A filibuster may be ended by a cloture motion; the technique is also used in the UK (see also TALK OUT)

filing ['faɪlɪŋ] *noun* **(a)** delivering a legal document to the court office (by post, special delivery, fax, etc.) **(b)** documents which have to be put in order; *there is a lot of filing to do at the end of the week*; *the manager looked through the week's filing to see what letters had been sent*; **filing basket** *or* **filing tray** = container kept on a desk for documents which have to be filed; **filing cabinet** = metal box with several drawers for keeping files; **filing card** = card with information written on it, used to classify information into the correct order; **filing clerk** = clerk who files documents; **filing system** = way of putting documents in order for reference

final ['faɪnl] *adjective* last, coming at the end of a period; *to pay the final instalment*; *to make the final payment*; *to put the final details on a document*; **final**

date for payment = last date by which payment should be made; **final demand** = last reminder from a supplier, after which he will sue for payment; **final discharge** = last payment of what is left of a debt; **final dividend** = dividend paid at the end of the year; **final hearing** = the actual hearing of a case in the small claims track, which aims at being informal and rapid; **final judgment** = judgment which is awarded at the end of an action after trial, as opposed to an interlocutory judgment

finance 1 ['faɪnæns] *noun* **(a)** money used by a company, provided by its shareholders or by loans; **finance charge** = (i) the cost of borrowing money; (ii) additional charge made to a customer who asks for extended credit **(b)** public money used by a government or local authority; *where will the authority find the finance to pay the higher salaries?*; *he is the secretary of the local authority finance committee*; **Finance Bill and Finance Act** = annual Bill and Act of Parliament which gives the Government the power to raise taxes to produce money for the Exchequer, and which then can be spent as proposed in the Budget; **Finance Minister** *or* **Minister of Finance** = government minister responsible for finance (both taxation and expenditure) **2** [faɪ'næns] *verb* to pay for something; *the new building must be financed by the local authority*; *a government-financed programme of prison construction*

financial [faɪ'nænʃl] *adjective* referring to money or finance; *he has a financial interest in the company*; **financial assistance** = help in the form of money; *she receives financial assistance from the local authority*; **financial intermediary** = institution which takes deposits or loans from individuals and lends money to clients (banks, building societies, hire-purchase companies are all financial intermediaries); **financial institution** = bank or other company which provides finance; **to make financial provision for someone** = to arrange for someone to receive money to live on (by attachment of earnings, etc.); **Financial Secretary to the**

Treasury = minister of state in charge of the Treasury, under the Chancellor of the Exchequer; *see also* CHIEF SECRETARY; **financial statement** = document which shows the financial situation of a company at the end of an accounting period and the transactions which have taken place during that period (it includes the balance sheet, the profit and loss account, etc.)

COMMENT: in most countries, the government department dealing with finance is called the Finance Ministry, with a Finance Minister in charge. Both in the UK and the USA, the department is called the Treasury, and the minister in charge is the Chancellor of the Exchequer in the UK, and the Treasury Secretary in the USA

find [faɪnd] *verb* **(a)** to get something which was not there before; *to find backing for a project* **(b)** to make a legal decision in court; *the tribunal found that both parties were at fault*; *the court found the accused guilty on all charges*; **the judge found for the defendant** = the judge decided that the defendant was right (NOTE: **finding - found**)

finder's fee [ˈfaɪndəz ˈfiː] *noun* fee paid to a person who finds a client for another

findings [ˈfaɪndɪŋz] *noun* decision reached by a court; **the findings of a commission of enquiry** = the conclusions of the commission

fine [faɪn] **1** *noun* money paid as a punishment because something wrong has been done; *the court sentenced him to pay a £25,000 fine*; *we had to pay a £10 parking fine*; *the sentence for dangerous driving is a £1,000 fine or two months in prison* **2** *verb* to punish someone by making him pay money; *to fine someone £2,500 for obtaining money by false pretences*

fingerprint [ˈfɪŋgəprɪnt] **1** *noun* mark left on a surface by fingers, from which a person may be identified; *they found his fingerprints on the murder weapon*; *the*

court heard evidence from a fingerprint expert; **to take someone's fingerprints** = to take a copy of a person's fingerprints (by printing them with ink on film or a filing card) so that he can be identified in future **2** *verb* to take someone's fingerprints; *the police fingerprinted the suspect after charging him*

fire [ˈfaɪə] **1** *noun* **(a)** burning; *the shipment was damaged in the fire on board the cargo boat*; *half the stock was destroyed in the warehouse fire*; **to catch fire** = to start to burn; *the papers in the waste paper basket caught fire*; **fire certificate** = certificate from the municipal fire department to say that a building is properly protected against fire; **fire damage** = damage caused by fire; *he claimed £2500 for fire damage*; **fire-damaged goods** = goods which have been damaged in a fire; **fire door** = special door to prevent fire going from one part of a building to another; **fire escape** = door or stairs which allow staff to get out of a building which is on fire; **fire hazard** *or* **fire risk** = situation or materials which could start a fire; *that warehouse full of paper is a fire hazard*; **fire insurance** = insurance against damage by fire; **fire regulations** = local or national regulations which owners of buildings used by the public have to obey in order to be granted a fire certificate **(b)** act of shooting; **the police opened fire on the crowd** = the police started to shoot at the crowd **2** *verb* **(a)** to shoot (with a gun); *he fired two shots at the crowd* **(b)** **to fire someone** = to dismiss someone from a job; *the new managing director fired half the sales force*

firearm [ˈfaɪəɑːm] *noun* gun or other weapon used to shoot; **firearms certificate** = official document saying that someone has permission to own a gun

fireproof [ˈfaɪəpruːf] *adjective* which cannot be damaged by fire; *we packed the papers in a fireproof safe*; *it is impossible to make the office completely fireproof*

fire-raiser [ˈfaɪəˈreɪzə] *noun* person who sets fire to property; *see also* ARSONIST

fire-raising ['faɪə'reɪzɪŋ] *noun* setting fire to property on purpose; *see also* ARSON

firing squad ['faɪrɪŋ 'skwɒd] *noun* group of soldiers who execute someone by shooting

firm [fɜːm] **1** *noun* partnership or any other business which is not a company; *he is a partner in a law firm*; *a firm of accountants*; *an important publishing firm* (NOTE: firm is often used when referring to incorporated companies, but this is not correct) **2** *adjective* **(a)** which cannot be changed; *to make a firm offer for something*; *to place a firm offer for two aircraft*; *they are quoting a firm price of £1.22 per case* **(b)** not dropping in price, and possibly going to rise; *the pound was firmer on the foreign exchange markets*; *shares remained firm* **3** *verb* to remain at a price and seem likely to go up; *the shares firmed at £1.50*

firmness ['fɜːmnəs] *noun* remaining at a price, being likely to rise; *the firmness of the pound*

first [fɜːst] *noun & adjective* person or thing which is there at the beginning, earlier than others; *our company was one of the first to sell into the European market*; **the First Amendment** = first amendment to the Constitution of the USA, guaranteeing freedom of speech and religion; **First Lord of the Treasury** = British government post, now combined with that of Prime Minister; **first quarter** = three months' period from January to the end of March; **first half** *or* **first half-year** = six months' period from January to the end of June; **first in first out (FIFO)** = (i) redundancy policy, where the people who have been working longest are the first to be made redundant; (ii) accounting policy where stock is valued at the price of the oldest purchases; **case of first impression** = case which raises points of law for which there are no precedents; **first offence** = committing an offence for the first time; **first offender** = person who has committed an offence for the first time; **first-past-the-post** = electoral system (as in the UK), where the candidate with most votes wins the election (even if he does not have more than half of all votes cast); *see also* PROPORTIONAL REPRESENTATION; **First Reading** = formal introduction of a Bill into the House of Commons, after which it is printed

first degree murder ['fɜːst dɪ'griː 'mɜːdə] *noun US* premeditated and deliberate murder

first instance ['fɜːst 'ɪnstəns] *noun* **court of first instance** = court in which a case is tried first

fiscal ['fɪskl] *adjective* **(a)** referring to tax or to government revenue; *the government's fiscal policies*; **fiscal measures** = tax changes made by a government to improve the working of the economy; **fiscal year** = twelve-month period on which taxes are calculated (in the UK, April 6th to April 5th) **(b) Procurator Fiscal** = Scottish law officer who decides whether an alleged criminal should be prosecuted

fishing expedition ['fɪʃɪŋ ekspə'dɪʃn] *noun (informal)* using the pre-hearing disclosure of documents to try to find other documents belonging to the defendant which the claimant does not know about and which might help him with his claim

fit [fɪt] *adjective* physically or mentally able to do something; *the solicitor stated that his client was not fit to plead*

fitness ['fɪtnəs] *noun* state of being of the necessary standard; **fitness for purpose** = implied contractual term that goods sold will be of the necessary standard to be used for the purpose for which they were bought

fittings ['fɪtɪŋz] *see* FIXTURE

fixed [fɪkst] *adjective* permanent, which cannot be removed; **fixed assets** = property or machinery which a company owns and uses; **fixed capital** = capital in the form of buildings and machinery; **fixed charge** = charge over a particular asset or property *(see also* FLOATING CHARGE) **fixed costs** = (i) set amount of money to which a claimant is entitled in legal proceedings (as opposed to taxed costs); (ii) cost of producing a product, which does not increase with the amount of product made (such as rent); **fixed deposit** = deposit which pays a stated interest over a set period; **fixed expenses** = money which is spent regularly (such as rent, electricity, telephone); **fixed income** = income which does not change (such as from an annuity); **fixed-interest investments** = investments producing an interest which does not change; **fixed-price agreement** = agreement where a company provides a service or a product at a price which stays the same for the whole period of the agreement; **fixed scale of charges** = rate of charging which cannot be altered; **fixed term** = period which is fixed when a contract is signed and which cannot be changed afterwards

fixing ['fɪksɪŋ] *noun* **(a)** arranging; *fixing of charges*; *fixing of a mortgage rate* **(b) price fixing** = illegal agreement between companies to charge the same price for competing products **(c) the London gold fixing** = system where the world price for gold is set each day in London

fixture ['fɪkstʃə] *noun* item in a property which is permanently attached to it (such as a sink or lavatory) and which passes to a new owner with the property itself; **fixtures and fittings** = objects in a property which are sold with the property (both those which cannot be removed and those which can); *see also* TRADE FIXTURES

flag [flæg] **1** *noun* **(a)** piece of coloured cloth which is used to represent a country; **flag of convenience** = flag of a country which may have no ships of its own but allows ships of other countries to be registered in its ports; **to fly a flag** = (i) to attach the flag in an obvious position to show that your ship belongs to a certain country; (ii) to act in a certain way to show that you are proud of belonging to a certain country or working for a certain company; *ship flying the British flag*; *ship flying a flag of convenience*; *the Trade Minister has gone to the World Fair to fly the flag*; *he is only attending the conference to fly the flag for the company* **(b)** *(in computer*

programming or on documents) marker, way of indicating something special in a text or database **2** *verb* **(a) to flag a ship** = to give a ship the right to fly a flag, by registering it; *see also* REFLAG **(b)** *(in computing or on documents)* to set markers, to indicate something special in a text or database; *the committee clerk flagged all the references to building repairs*; *will members please note the flagged items which we will consider separately?*

flagrant ['fleɪgrənt] *adjective* clear and obvious; *a flagrant case of contempt of court*; *a flagrant violation of human rights*

flagrante [flə'grænti] *see* IN FLAGRANTE DELICTO

flat [flæt] **1** *adjective* **(a)** falling because of low demand; *the market was flat today* **(b)** fixed, not changing; **flat rate** = charge which always stays the same; *we pay a flat rate for electricity each quarter*; *he is paid a flat rate of £2 per thousand* **2** *noun* set of rooms for one family in a building with other sets of similar rooms; *he has a flat in the centre of town*; *she is buying a flat close to her office*; **company flat** = flat owned by a company and used by members of staff from time to time (NOTE: American English is **apartment**)

floating charge ['fləʊtɪŋ 'tʃɑːdʒ] *noun* a charge over the changing assets (such as debts or stock) of a business, as opposed to a fixed charge

floating voter ['fləʊtɪŋ 'vəʊtə] *noun* (i) voter who has not decided how to vote; (ii) voter who does not always vote for the same party, but changes from election to election; **the floating vote** = votes of floating voters; *the Opposition is trying to capture the bulk of the floating vote*

floor [flɔː] *noun* in a building, the part on which people stand; **the floor of the House** = the main part of the House of Commons or Congress; *debates on the floor of the House are often lively*; *the Senate majority leader is the floor spokesman for his party in the Senate*; **floor manager** =

member (usually the chairman of the reporting committee) who is responsible for getting a bill through the House (NOTE: in the UK, 'floor' is usually taken to refer to the backbenchers: **the feeling on the floor of the House was that the Minister should resign**)

flotsam ['flɒtsəm] *noun* **flotsam and jetsam** = rubbish floating in the water after a ship has been wrecked and rubbish washed on to the land

flout [flaʊt] *verb* to break, to go against (a rule or the law); *by selling alcohol to minors, the shop is deliberately flouting the law*

FO ['ef 'əʊ] = FOREIGN OFFICE

f.o.b. ['ef 'əʊ 'biː] = FREE ON BOARD

fodder ['fɒdə] *see* LOBBY

Foggy Bottom ['fɒgi 'bɒtəm] *noun US (informal)* the State Department

follow ['fɒləʊ] *verb* to act in accordance with (a rule); *the court has followed the precedent set in the 1972 case*

foolscap ['fuːlzkæp] *noun* large size of writing paper; *the letter was on six sheets of foolscap*; **a foolscap envelope** = large envelope which takes foolscap paper

forbear [fɔːˈbeə] *verb* **to forbear from doing something** = not to do something which you intended to do; *he forbore from taking any further action* (NOTE: **forbearing - forbore - has forborne**)

forbearance [fɔːˈbeərəns] *noun* not doing something which could have been done, such as not enforcing payment of a debt

force [fɔːs] *noun* strength; **to be in force** = to be operating or working; *the rules have been in force since 1946*; **to come into force** = to start to operate or work; *the new regulations will come into force on January 1st*; **the new regulations have the force of law** = they are the same as if they had been voted into law by parliament

forced [fɔːst] *adjective* **forced sale** = sale which takes place because a court orders it

or because it is the only way to avoid insolvency

force majeure ['fɔːs mæ'ʒɜː] something which happens which is out of the control of the parties who have signed a contract (such as strike, war, storm) and which prevents the contract being fulfilled

forcible ['fɔːsɪbl] *adjective* by force, using force; **forcible entry** = formerly, the criminal offence of entering a building or land and taking possession of it by force; **forcible feeding** = giving food by force to a prisoner on hunger strike

foreclose [fɔːˈkləʊz] *verb* to take possession of a property because the owner cannot repay money which he has borrowed (using the property as security); *to foreclose on a mortgaged property*

foreclosure [fɔːˈkləʊʒə] *noun* act of foreclosing; **foreclosure order nisi** = court order which makes a mortgagor pay outstanding debts to a mortgagee within a certain period of time; **foreclosure order absolute** = court order giving the mortgagee full rights to the property

foreign ['fɒrən] *adjective* not belonging to one's own country; *foreign cars have flooded our market*; *we are increasing our trade with foreign countries*; **foreign currency** = money of another country; **foreign goods** = goods produced in other countries; **foreign investments** = money invested in other countries; **foreign policy** = policy followed by a country when dealing with other countries; **the Foreign Service** = government department responsible for a country's representation in other countries; **foreign trade** = trade with other countries

foreigner ['fɒrənə] *noun* person from another country

foreign exchange ['fɒrən ɪksˈtʃeɪndʒ] *noun* exchanging the money of one country for that of another; **foreign exchange broker** *or* **dealer** = person who deals on the foreign exchange market; **foreign exchange dealing** = buying and selling foreign currencies; **the foreign exchange**

markets = market where people buy and sell foreign currencies; **foreign exchange reserves** = foreign money held by a government to support its own currency and pay its debts; **foreign exchange transfer** = sending of money from one country to another

Foreign (and Commonwealth) Office ['fɒrən ənd 'kɒmənwelθ 'ɒfɪs]
noun British government department dealing with relations with other countries

Foreign Secretary ['fɒrən 'sekrtri]
noun British government minister in charge of relations with other countries

> COMMENT: in most countries, the government department dealing with other countries is called the Foreign Ministry, with the Foreign Minister in charge. In the UK, these are the Foreign Office and Foreign Secretary; in the USA, they are the State Department and the Secretary of State

foreman of the jury ['fɔːmən əv ðə 'dʒʊəri] *noun* person elected by the other jurors, who chairs the meetings of a jury, and pronounces the verdict in court afterwards

forensic [fə'renzɪk] *adjective* referring to courts, the law, pleading a case or punishing crime; **forensic medicine** = medical science concerned with solving crimes against people (such as autopsies of murdered people, taking blood samples from clothes); **forensic science** = science used in solving legal problems and criminal cases

foresee [fɔː'siː] *verb* to imagine (correctly) what is going to happen in the future (NOTE: **foreseeing - foresaw - has foreseen**)

foreseeability [fɔːsiːə'bɪləti] *noun* ability of something to be foreseen; **foreseeability test** = test for calculating liability on the part of a person who should have foreseen the consequences of his action, especially in cases of negligence

forfeit ['fɔːfɪt] **1** *noun* taking something away as a punishment; **forfeit clause** = clause in a contract which says that goods or a deposit will be taken away if the contract is not obeyed; **the goods were declared forfeit** = the court said that the goods had to be taken away from their owner **2** *verb* to have something taken away as a punishment; **to forfeit a deposit** = to lose a deposit which was left for an item because you have decided not to buy that item

forfeiture ['fɔːfɪtʃə] *noun* act of forfeiting a property or a right; **forfeiture of shares** = losing the right to shares which a shareholder has not claimed; **forfeiture rule** = unwritten rule that someone who has unlawfully killed another person should not benefit from the dead person's will

forge [fɔːdʒ] *verb* to copy money or a signature illegally, to make a document which looks like a real one; *he tried to enter the country with forged documents; she wanted to pay the bill with a forged £10 note*

forgery ['fɔːdʒri] *noun* **(a)** crime of making an illegal copy of a document, recording, or banknote to use as if it were a real one; *he was sent to prison for forgery* **(b)** illegal copy; *the signature was proved to be a forgery*

fori ['fɔːri] *see* LEX FORI

form [fɔːm] **1** *noun* **(a) form of words** = words correctly laid out for a legal document; **receipt in due form** = correctly written receipt **(b)** official printed paper with blank spaces which have to be filled in with information; *you have to fill in form A20; customs declaration form; a pad of order forms*; **application form** = form which has to be filled in to apply for something; **claim form** = form which has to be filled in when making an insurance claim **2** *verb* to start, to organize; *the brothers have formed a new company*

forma ['fɔːmə] *see* PRO FORMA

formal ['fɔːməl] *adjective* clearly and legally written; *to make a formal application*; *to send a formal order*

formality [fɔː'mælǝti] *noun* formal procedure, thing which has to be done to obey the law or because it is the custom; *the chairman dispensed with the formality of reading the minutes*; **customs formalities** = declaration of goods by the shipper and examination of them by the customs

formally ['fɔːmǝli] *adverb* in a formal way; *we have formally applied for planning permission for the new shopping precinct*

forthwith [fɔː'θwıθ] *adverb* immediately

fortiori [fɔːti'ɔːraı] *see* A FORTIORI

forum ['fɔːrǝm] *noun* court, place where matters are discussed; *the magistrates' court is not the appropriate forum for this application*

forward ['fɔːwǝd] **1** *adjective* in advance, to be paid at a later date; **forward buying** *or* **buying forward** = buying shares, currency or commodities at today's price for delivery at a later date; **forward contract** = agreement to buy foreign currency, shares or commodities at a later date at a certain price; **forward market** = market for purchasing foreign currency, oil or commodities for delivery at a later date; **forward (exchange) rate** = rate for purchase of foreign currency at a fixed price for delivery at a later date; **forward sales** = sales for delivery at a later date **2** *adverb* **(a) to date an invoice forward** = to put a later date than the present one on an invoice; **carriage forward** *or* **freight forward** = deal where the customer pays for shipping the goods; **charges forward** = charges which will be paid by the customer **(b) to buy forward** = to buy foreign currency, gold or commodities before you need them, in order to be certain of the exchange rate; **to sell forward** = to sell foreign currency, gold or commodities for delivery at a later date **(c) balance brought forward** *or* **carried forward** = balance which is entered in an account at

the end of a period or page and is then taken to be the starting point of the next period or page **3** *verb* **to forward something to someone** = to send something to someone; **please forward** *or* **to be forwarded** = words written on an envelope, asking the person receiving it to send it on to the person whose name is written on it

foster ['fɒstǝ] *verb* to look after and bring up (a child who is not your own); **foster child** = child brought up by people who are not its own parents; **foster home** = home where a foster child is brought up; **foster mother** *or* **foster father** *or* **fosterparent** = woman or man who looks after a child and brings it up

foul [faʊl] *adjective* **foul bill of lading** = bill of lading which says that the goods were in bad condition when received by the shipper

founder ['faʊndǝ] *noun* person who starts a company; **founder's shares** = shares issued to the founder of a company, which carry special rights

fours [fɔːz] *see* ALL

frais [freı] *see* SANS FRAIS

frame [freım] *verb (informal)* to arrange for someone to appear to be guilty; **he has been framed** = he is innocent, but the situation has been arranged in such a way that he appears guilty

franchise ['fræntʃaız] **1** *noun* **(a)** right granted to someone to do something, especially the right to vote in local or general elections; **universal franchise** = right to vote which is given to all adult members of the population **(b)** licence to trade using a brand name and paying a royalty for it; *he has bought a printing franchise or a hot dog franchise* **2** *verb* to sell licences for people to trade using a brand name and paying a royalty; *his sandwich bar was so successful that he decided to franchise it*

franchisee [fræntʃaı'ziː] *noun* person who runs a franchise

franchiser ['fræntʃaɪzə] *noun* person who licenses a franchise

franchising ['fræntʃaɪzɪŋ] *noun* act of selling a licence to trade as a franchise; *he runs his sandwich chain as a franchising operation*

franchisor [fræntʃaɪ'zɔː] *noun* = FRANCHISER

franco ['fræŋkəʊ] *adverb* free

frank [fræŋk] **1** *noun* privilege of sending official mail free of charge, using the signature of a member of Parliament or Congress on the envelope instead of a stamp **2** *verb* to stamp the date and postage on a letter; **franking machine** = machine which marks the date and postage on letters so that the person sending them does not need to use stamps

fraud [frɔːd] *noun* **(a)** harming someone (by obtaining property or money from him) after making him believe something which is not true; *he got possession of the property by fraud*; *he was accused of frauds relating to foreign currency*; **to obtain money by fraud** = to obtain money by saying or doing something to cheat someone; **Fraud Squad** = special police department which investigates frauds **(b)** act of deceiving someone in order to make money; *he was convicted of a series of frauds against insurance companies*; **computer fraud** = fraud committed by using computer files (as in a bank)

COMMENT: frauds are divided into **fraud by a director** and other fraud

fraudulent ['frɔːdjʊlənt] *adjective* not honest, aiming to cheat people; **fraudulent conveyance** = putting a property into someone else's possession to avoid it being seized to pay creditors; **fraudulent misrepresentation** = false statement made to trick someone, to persuade someone to enter into a contract; **fraudulent preference** = payment made by an insolvent company to a particular creditor in preference to other creditors; **fraudulent trading** = carrying on the business of a

company, knowing that the company is insolvent

fraudulently ['frɔːdjʊləntli] *adverb* not honestly; *goods imported fraudulently*

free [friː] **1** *adjective & adverb* **(a)** not costing any money; *he was given a free ticket to the exhibition*; *the price includes free delivery*; *goods are delivered free*; *price list sent free on request*; **free gift** = present given by a shop to a customer who buys a certain amount of goods; **free sample** = sample given free to advertise a product; **free trial** = testing of a machine with no payment involved; *to send a piece of equipment for two weeks' free trial*; **free of charge** = with no payment to be made; **free on board (f.o.b.)** = (i) international contract whereby the seller promises to deliver goods on board ship and notify the buyer of delivery, and the buyer arranges freight, pays the shipping cost and takes the risk once the goods have passed onto the ship; (ii) *US* contract for sale whereby the price includes all the seller's costs until the goods are delivered to a certain place **(b)** not in prison; **to set someone free** = to let someone leave prison; *the crowd attacked the police station and set the three prisoners free* **(c)** with no restrictions; **free circulation of goods** = movement of goods from one country to another without import quotas or other restrictions; **free collective bargaining** = negotiations over wages and working conditions between the management and the workers' representatives without government interference; **free competition** = being free to compete without government interference; **free currency** = currency which is allowed by the government to be bought and sold without restriction; **free enterprise** = system of business with no interference from the government; **free market economy** = system where the government does not interfere in business activity in any way; **free movement of capital** = ability to transfer capital from one EC country to another; **free port** *or* **free trade zone** = port or area where there are no customs duties; **free of tax** *or*

tax-free = with no tax having to be paid; **interest-free credit** *or* **loan** = credit or loan where no interest is paid by the borrower; **free of duty** *or* **duty-free** = with no duty to be paid; **free trade** = system where goods can go from one country to another without any restrictions; **free trade area** = group of countries practising free trade **(d)** not busy, not occupied; *are there any tables free in the restaurant?*; *the solicitor will be free in a few minutes*; *the hearing was delayed because there was no courtroom free* **2** *verb* to release someone from a responsibility or from prison; *will the new law free owners from responsibility to their tenants?*; *the new president freed all political prisoners*

freedom ['fri:dəm] *noun* **(a)** being free, not being held in custody; *the president gave the accused man his freedom* **(b)** being free to do something without restriction; **freedom of association** = being able to join together in a group with other people without being afraid of prosecution, provided that you do not break the law; **freedom of assembly** *or* **of meeting** = being able to meet as a group without being afraid of prosecution, provided that you do not break the law; **freedom of information** = allowing citizens access to information which is held by government departments and other bodies; **freedom of the press** = being able to write and publish in a newspaper what you wish without being afraid of prosecution, provided that you do not break the law; **freedom of speech** = being able to say what you want without being afraid of prosecution, provided that you do not break the law; **testamentary freedom** = freedom to dispose of your property in a will as you want

freedom of movement ['fri:dəm əv 'mu:vmənt] *noun (in the EU)* fundamental right of workers within the EU to be able to move to other EU countries to seek work

COMMENT: freedom of movement has been extended to three types of people who are not economically active: students, retired people and people with sufficient private income

freehold ['fri:həʊld] *noun* absolute right to hold land or property for an unlimited time without paying rent; **freehold property** = property which the owner holds in freehold

freeholder ['fri:həʊldə] *noun* person who holds a freehold property

freely ['fri:li] *adverb* with no restrictions; *money should circulate freely within the Common Market*

free movement ['fri: 'mu:vmənt] *noun* right for workers from any EU country to enter other EU countries to work, and to stay in other countries as workers with the same rights as the nationals of those countries

free pardon ['fri: 'pɑ:dən] *noun* pardon given to a convicted person where both the sentence and conviction are recorded as void

freeze [fri:z] *verb* to order a person not to move money, not to sell assets; *the court ordered the company's bank account to be frozen*; **frozen assets** = assets of a company which cannot be sold because a person has a claim against them

freezing injunction ['fri:zɪŋ ɪn'dʒʌŋkʃn] *noun* court order to freeze the assets of a defendant or of a person who has gone overseas or of a company based overseas to prevent them being taken out of the country (the injunction can apply to assets within the jurisdiction of the court, or on a worldwide basis) (NOTE: since the introduction of the new Civil Procedure Rules in April 1999, this term has replaced **Mareva injunction)**

freight [freɪt] *noun* cargo or goods which are carried by land, sea or air; **freight charges** *or* **freight rates** = money charged for carrying goods

French [frentʃ] *noun* language spoken in France

COMMENT: French was used in England together with Latin as the language of the law courts for some centuries after the conquest by King William I. It still survives in some legal words and phrases, such as **chose, tort, oyez, puisne, autrefois convict, feme covert**

fresh pursuit ['freʃ pə'sjuːt] *noun* chasing a thief, etc., to get back what he has stolen

friend [frend] *see* LITIGATION FRIEND, NEXT FRIEND

friendly society ['frendli sə'saɪəti] *noun* group of people who pay regular contributions which are used to help members of the group when they retire, are ill or in financial difficulty

frisk [frɪsk] *verb* to search someone by passing your hands over his clothes to see if he is carrying a weapon, or a package

frivolous ['frɪvələs] *adjective* frivolous complaint *or* frivolous action = complaint or action which is not brought for a serious reason

frolic ['frɒlɪk] *noun* frolic of his own = situation where an employee does damage outside the normal course of his employment, and for which his employer cannot be held responsible

front [frʌnt] *noun* (a) political group (usually formed of several smaller groups); to form a common front = to join into a unified group; *the parties of the left have formed a common front to fight the forces of reaction* (b) organization or company which serves to hide criminal activity; *his ice-cream shop was just a front for an extortion racket*

front benches ['frʌnt 'bentʃɪz] *noun* two rows of seats in the House of Commons, facing each other with the table between them, where Government ministers or members of the Opposition Shadow Cabinet sit; **the Opposition front bench** = (i) the seat for the Opposition Shadow Cabinet; (ii) the Shadow Cabinet; **the Government front bench** *or* **the**

Treasury bench = the seats where the members of the Government sit; *an Opposition front bench spokesman asked why the Government had been so slow in investigating the affair*

front organization ['frʌnt ɔːɡənaɪ'zeɪʃn] *noun* organization which appears to be neutral, but is in fact an active supporter of a political party or is actively engaged in illegal trade

frozen ['frəʊzn] *see* FREEZE

frustrate [frʌ'streɪt] *verb* to prevent something (especially the terms of a contract) being fulfilled

frustration [frʌ'streɪʃn] *noun* situation where the terms of a contract cannot possibly be fulfilled (as where the contract requires the use of something which then is destroyed)

fugitive ['fjuːdʒətɪv] *adjective & noun* (person) who is running away from justice; **fugitive offender,** *US* **fugitive from justice** = person running away from the police who, if he is caught, is sent back to the place where the offence was committed

fulfil *US* **fulfill** [fʊl'fɪl] *verb* to do everything which is promised in a contract; *the company has fulfilled all the terms of the agreement*

full [fʊl] *adjective* complete, including everything; **we are working at full capacity** = we are doing as much work as possible; **full costs** = all the costs of manufacturing a product, including both fixed and variable costs; **full cover** = insurance cover against all types of risk; **in full discharge of a debt** = paying a debt completely, paying less than the total amount owed by agreement; *the claimant accepted £500 in full and final settlement of his claim for £600, to avoid going to court*; **full title** = complete title of an Act of Parliament; **full trial** = properly organized trial according to the correct procedure

fully ['fʊli] *adverb* completely; **fully paid-up shares** = shares where the full face value has been paid; **fully paid-up**

capital = all money paid for the issued capital shares

functus officio ['fʌŋktəs ɒ'fɪʃiəʊ] *Latin phrase meaning* 'no longer having power or jurisdiction' (because the power has been exercised); *the justices' clerk asserted that the justices were functi officio* (NOTE: plural is **functi officio**)

fund [fʌnd] *noun* (a) amount of money collected for a special purpose; **pension fund** = money which provides pensions for retired members of staff (b) **funds** = money available for a purpose; **conversion of funds** = using money which does not belong to you for a purpose for which it is not supposed to be used; **to convert funds to one's own use** = to use someone else's money for yourself

fundamental [fʌndə'mentl] *adjective* basic or essential; **fundamental breach** = breach of an essential or basic term of a contract by one party, entitling the other party to treat the contract as terminated

fungible goods *or* **fungibles** ['fʌndʒɪbl 'gʊdz] *plural noun* goods (such as seeds or coins) which are measured by weight or counted

furandi [fʊ'rændi] *see* ANIMUS

further information ['fɜːðə ɪnfə'meɪʃn] *noun* request made by a party through the court for another party to provide more details which will help clarify the case (the second party may refuse to respond for various reasons) (NOTE: since the introduction of the new Civil Procedure Rules in April 1999, this term has replaced **interrogatories**)

future ['fjuːtʃə] 1 *adjective* referring to time to come, to something which has not yet happened; **future delivery** = delivery at a later date; **future estate** = old term for the possession and enjoyment of an estate at some time in the future; **future interest** = interest in property which will be enjoyed in the future 2 *noun* time which has not yet happened; *try to be more careful in future*; *in future all reports must be sent to Australia by air*

futures ['fjuːtʃəz] *plural noun* trading in shares, currencies or commodities for delivery at a later date

fuzz [fʌz] *noun* (*slang*) the police

Gg

gag [gæg] *verb* to try to stop someone talking or writing; *the government was accused of using the Official Secrets Act as a means of gagging the press*; **gag rule** = rule in the House of Representatives which limits the time for debate

gain [geɪn] **1** *noun* **(a)** increase, becoming larger; **gain in experience** = act of getting more experience **(b)** increase in profit, price or value; **to deal in stolen goods for gain** = to buy and sell stolen goods to make a profit; **capital gains** = money made by selling a fixed asset or by selling shares at a profit; **capital gains tax** = tax paid on capital gains **(c)** (i) increase in a share of the vote; (ii) winning a seat in an election; *the latest poll shows a socialist gain of 2%*; *the Conservatives had 20 gains and 10 losses in the local elections* **2** *verb* **(a)** to get, to obtain; *he gained some useful experience working in a bank*; **to gain control of a business** = to buy more than 50% of the shares so that you can direct the business; **to gain control of a council** = to win a majority of the seats **(b)** to win (a seat); *the Socialists gained six seats on the council at the expense of the Tories*

gainful [ˈgeɪnfʊl] *adjective* **gainful employment** = employment which pays money

gainfully [ˈgeɪnfli] *adverb* **he is not gainfully employed** = he has no regular paid work

gallery [ˈgæləri] *noun* seats above and around the benches in the House of Commons and House of Lords, where the public and journalists sit; **the Speaker ordered the galleries to be cleared** = the Speaker asked for all visitors to leave the Chamber; **Members' Gallery** = seats for visitors invited by Members of Parliament; **public gallery** = area where members of the public can sit to listen to cases in the Law Courts, debates in a council chamber or the House of Commons, etc.; **Strangers' Gallery** = public gallery in the House of Commons or House of Lords

gallows [ˈgæləuz] *plural noun* wooden support from which criminals are executed by hanging

game [geɪm] *noun* **(a)** birds and animals which are hunted, especially for food; **game licence** = official permit which allows someone to sell game **(b) game of chance** = game (such as roulette) where the result depends on luck

gaming [ˈgeɪmɪŋ] *noun* playing games of chance for money; **gaming licence** = official permit which allows someone or a club to organize games of chance

gang [gæŋ] *noun* group of criminals working together; *a drugs gang*; *a gang of jewel thieves*

gangland [ˈgæŋlænd] *noun* all gangs considered as a group; **a gangland murder** = murder of a gangster by another gangster

gangster [ˈgæŋstə] *noun* person who is a member of a gang of criminals; *the police shot three gangsters in the bank raid*

gangway [ˈgæŋweɪ] *noun* space running across the Chamber, dividing the benches on either side of the House of Commons

COMMENT: members sitting below the gangway (i.e. further away from the Speaker) are more independent and less party-minded than those who sit near the Speaker

gaol [dʒeɪl] **1** *noun GB* prison **2** *verb GB* to put someone in prison; *for examples see* JAIL

gaoler [ˈdʒeɪlə] *noun GB* person who works in a prison or who is in charge of a prison; *for examples see* JAILER

garnish [ˈgɑːnɪʃ] *verb* to tell a debtor to pay his debts, not to the creditor, but to a creditor of the creditor who has a judgment

garnishee [gɑːnɪˈʃiː] *noun* person who owes money to a creditor and is ordered by a court to pay that money to a creditor of the creditor, and not to the creditor himself; **garnishee order** = court order, making a garnishee pay money to a judgment creditor; **garnishee proceedings** = court proceedings against a debtor leading to a garnishee order

gas chamber [ˈgæs ˈtʃeɪmbə] *noun* room in which a convicted prisoner is executed by poisonous gas

COMMENT: used in some states in the USA

gavel [ˈgævl] *noun* small wooden hammer used by a chairman of a meeting to call the meeting to order; *the chairman banged his gavel on the table and shouted to the councillors to be quiet*

COMMENT: there is no mace in the American Senate. Instead, a ceremonial gavel is placed on the Vice-President's desk when the Senate is in session

gazump [gəˈzʌmp] *verb* **he was gazumped** = his agreement to buy the house was cancelled because someone offered more money before exchange of contracts

gazumping [gəˈzʌmpɪŋ] *noun* (*of a buyer*) offering more money for a house than another buyer has done, so as to be

sure of buying it; (*of a seller*) removing the house from a sale which has been agreed, so as to accept a higher offer

GBH [ˈdʒiː ˈbiː ˈeɪtʃ] = GRIEVOUS BODILY HARM

GDP [ˈdʒiː ˈdiː ˈpiː] = GROSS DOMESTIC PRODUCT

general [ˈdʒenrl] *adjective* (**a**) ordinary, not special; **general expenses** = all kinds of minor expenses, money spent on the day-to-day costs of running a business; **general manager** = manager in charge of the administration of a company; **general office** = main administrative office of a company (**b**) dealing with everything or with everybody; **general audit** = examining all the books and accounts of a company; **general average** = sharing of the cost of lost goods between all parties to an insurance; **general damages** = damages awarded by a court to compensate for an unquantifiable loss (such as an injury); **general election** = election of a parliament by all the voters in a country; **general lien** = holding goods or property until a debt has been paid; *compare also* PARTICULAR AVERAGE, PARTICULAR LIEN; **general meeting** = meeting of all the shareholders of a company; **general strike** = strike of all the workers in a country; **Annual General Meeting (AGM),** *US* **Annual Meeting** = meeting of all the shareholders or all the members of a club, which takes place once a year to approve the accounts; **Extraordinary General Meeting (EGM)** = special meeting of shareholders or members of a club to discuss an important matter which cannot wait until the next Annual General Meeting

General Assembly [ˈdʒenrl əˈsembli] *noun* meeting of all the members of the United Nations, where each country is represented and each has a vote

General Purposes Committee

[ˈdʒenrl ˈpɜːpəsiz kəˈmiti] *noun* council committee which deals with matters which do not come under any other committee

Geneva Convention(s)
[dʒəˈniːvə kənˈvenʃnz] *noun* international treaties

signed in Geneva, governing behaviour of countries at war; *the attacking army was accused of violating the Geneva Convention*; **Geneva Conventions for the Protection of Victims of War (1949)** = international treaty relating to the treatment of civilians and other non-combatants; **Geneva Conventions on Negotiable Instruments (1930)** = international treaty relating to international bills of exchange, cheques, letters of credit, etc.; *see also* HAGUE

genocide ['dʒenəsaɪd] *noun* killing of a whole race, ethnic group or religious group

gentleman's agreement *US* **gentlemen's agreement** ['dʒentlmənz ə'griːmənt] *noun* verbal agreement between two parties who trust each other (not usually enforceable by law)

genuine ['dʒenjuɪn] *adjective* true or real; *a genuine Picasso*; *a genuine leather purse*; **the genuine article** = real article, not an imitation; **genuine purchaser** = someone who is really interested in buying

genuineness ['dʒenjuɪnnəs] *noun* being real, not being an imitation

germane [dʒɜː'meɪn] *adjective* which refers to a question; *the argument is not germane to the motion*

gerrymandering ['dʒerimændrɪŋ] *noun* reorganizing parliamentary constituencies or electoral districts to get an advantage in the next election

get *or* **gett** [get] *noun* divorce according to Jewish religious custom, where the husband agrees to a divorce which his wife has requested

get-up ['getʌp] *noun* general appearance of an article, or trade name, which is part of the goodwill attached to the article (get-up can be a combination of colours, distinctive shape, etc.)

gift [gɪft] **1** *noun* thing given to someone; **gift inter vivos** = present given by a living person to another living person; **free gift** = present given by a shop to a customer who buys a certain amount of goods **2** *verb* to give

COMMENT: a gift is irrevocable

Gillette defence [dʒɪ'let dɪ'fens] *noun* defence against a claim for infringement of patent, by which the defendant claims that he was using the process before it was patented

COMMENT: called after the case of *Gillette v. Anglo American Trading*

gilt-edged securities *or* **gilts** ['gɪlt'edʒd sɪ'kjʊərɪtɪz] *plural noun* British government securities (assumed to be a safe investment)

gloss [glɒs] **1** *noun* (i) note which explains or gives a meaning to a word or phrase; (ii) interpretation, meaning given to a word or phrase **2** *verb* **to gloss over** = to cover up a mistake or fault; *the report glosses over the errors made by the officials in the department*

GNP ['dʒiː 'en 'piː] = GROSS NATIONAL PRODUCT

godfather ['gɒdfɑːðə] *noun (slang)* Mafia boss

going concern ['gəʊɪŋ kən'sɜːn] *noun* business which is actively trading

going equipped for stealing ['gəʊɪŋ ɪ'kwɪpt fə 'stiːlɪŋ] *noun* notifiable offence of carrying tools which could be used for burglary

golden rule ['gəʊldən 'ruːl] *noun* rule that when interpreting a statute, the court should interpret the wording of the statute to give the best effect to what Parliament intended when passing the law

good behaviour ['gʊd bɪ'heɪvjə] *noun* behaving well, acting in a peaceful and lawful way; *the magistrates bound him over to be of good behaviour*; *she was sentenced to four years in prison, but was released early for good behaviour*

good cause ['gʊd 'kɔːz] *noun* reason which is accepted in law; *the court asked the accused to show good cause why he* should not be sent to prison (NOTE: not used with **'the'**)

good consideration [ˈgʊd kənsɪdəˈreɪʃn] *noun* proper consideration

good faith [ˈgʊd ˈfeɪθ] *noun* general honesty; **in good faith** = in an honest way; **he acted in good faith** = he did it honestly; **to buy something in good faith** = to buy something honestly, in the course of an honest transaction; *he bought the car in good faith, not knowing that it had been stolen*

goods [gʊdz] *plural noun* **(a) goods and chattels** = movable personal possessions; **household goods** = items which are used in the home **(b)** items which can be moved and are for sale; **goods (held) in bond** = imported goods held by customs until duty is paid; **capital goods** = machinery, buildings and raw materials which are used to make other goods; **consumer goods** = goods bought by the general public and not by businesses; **goods train** = train for carrying freight

good title [ˈgʊd ˈtaɪtl] *noun* title to a property which gives the owner full rights of ownership

goodwill [gʊdˈwɪl] *noun* good reputation of a business and its contacts with its customers (such as the name of the product which it sells or its popular appeal to customers); *he paid £10,000 for the goodwill of the shop and £4,000 for the stock*

COMMENT: goodwill can include the trading reputation, the patents, the trade names used, the value of a 'good site', etc., and is very difficult to establish accurately. It is an intangible asset, and so is not shown as an asset in a company's accounts, unless it figures as part of the purchase price paid when acquiring another company

---

go to law [ˈgəʊ tə ˈlɔː] *verb* to start legal proceedings about something; *we went to law to try to regain our property*

govern [ˈgʌvən] *verb* **(a)** to rule a country; *the country is governed by a group of military leaders* **(b)** to rule, to be in authority; *the amount of damages is governed by the seriousness of the injuries suffered*

government [ˈgʌvənmənt] *noun* **(a)** way of ruling or controlling a country; *people want democratic government; the leader of the Opposition is promising to provide effective government* **(b)** organization which administers a country; *the government has decided to introduce new immigration laws*; **central government** = main organization dealing with the affairs of the whole country; **local government** = organizations dealing with the affairs of small areas of the country **(c)** coming from the government, referring to the government; *government intervention or intervention by the government*; *a government ban on the import of arms*; *a government investigation into organized crime*; *government officials prevented him leaving the country*; *government policy is outlined in the Green Paper*; *government regulations state that import duty has to be paid on expensive items*; **government contractor** = company which supplies goods or services to the government on contract (NOTE: **government** can take a singular or plural verb: **the government have decided to repeal the Act; the government feels it is not time to make a statement.** Note also that the word **government** is used, especially by officials, without the article 'the': **Government has decided that the plan will be turned down; the plan is funded by central government**)

governmental [gʌvənˈmentl] *adjective* referring to a government

governor [ˈgʌvnə] *noun* **(a)** person who governs a state or province; *Ronald Reagan was Governor of California before becoming President* **(b)** person representing the Crown, such as the official in charge of a colony **(c)** person in charge of a prison; *a prison governor; the prisoners applied to the governor for parole* **(d)** member of a group responsible for controlling a public institution, such as a hospital or school

Governor-General [ˈgʌvnəˈdʒenrəl] *noun* person representing the British Crown in a Commonwealth country (such as Canada or Australia) which is still a monarchy with the British Queen as head of state; *see also* LIEUTENANT-GOVERNOR

gown [gaʊn] *noun* long black item of clothing worn by a lawyer, judge, etc., over normal clothes when appearing in court; *see also* SILK

grace [greɪs] *noun* favour shown by granting a delay; **to give a debtor a period of grace** *or* **two weeks' grace** = to allow a debtor time to pay *or* two weeks to pay

graft [ˈgrɑːft] *noun (informal)* corruption of officials

grand jury [ˈgrænd ˈdʒʊəri] *noun* US group of jurors (between twelve and twenty-four) who assemble as a preliminary to a trial to decide if an indictment should be issued to start criminal proceedings

grand larceny [ˈgrænd ˈlɑːsni] *noun* US theft of goods valued at more than a certain price

grant [grɑːnt] **1** *noun* **(a)** act of giving something to someone (permanently or temporarily) by a written document, where the object itself cannot be transferred; *the government made a grant of land to settlers*; **grant of letters of administration** = giving of documents to administrators to enable them to administer the estate of a dead person who has not made a will; **grant of probate** = official document proving that a will is genuine, given to the executors so that they can act on the terms of the will **(b)** money given by the government, local authority or other organization to help pay for something; *the institute has a government grant to cover the cost of the development programme*; *the local authority has allocated grants towards the costs of the scheme*; *many charities give grants for educational*

projects; **grant-aided scheme** = scheme which is backed by funds from the government; **grant-in-aid** = money given by central government to local government to help pay for a project; **death grant** = state grant to the family of a person who has died, which is supposed to contribute to the funeral expenses **2** *verb* to agree to give someone something, to agree to allow someone to do something; *to grant someone permission to build a house or to leave the country*; *the local authority granted the company an interest-free loan to start up the new factory*; *he was granted parole*; *the government granted an amnesty to all political prisoners*

grantee [grɑːnˈtiː] *noun* person who is assigned an interest in a property or who receives a grant

grantor [grɑːnˈtɔː] *noun* person who assigns an interest in a property (especially to a lender) or who makes a grant

grass [grɑːs]; *(slang)* **1** *noun* criminal who gives information to the police about other criminals; *see also* SUPERGRASS **2** *verb* **to grass on someone** = to give information to the police about someone

grass roots [ˈgrɑːs ˈruts] *noun* basic ordinary members of a political party or of society in general; *what is the grass-roots reaction to the constitutional changes?*; *the party has considerable support at grass-roots level*; *the Chairman has no grass-root support*

grata [ˈgrɑːtə] *see* PERSONA

gratia [ˈgreɪʃə] *see* EX GRATIA

gratis [ˈgrɑːtɪs] *adverb* free, not costing anything or without paying anything; *we got into the exhibition gratis*

gratuitous [grəˈtjuːɪtəs] *adjective* free, with no money being offered; **gratuitous promise** = promise to do something, without asking for consideration (it cannot be enforced because no money has been involved)

gratuity [grə'tjuːɪti] *noun* tip, money given to someone who has helped you; *the staff are instructed not to accept gratuities*

Gray's Inn ['greɪz 'ɪn] *noun* one of the four Inns of Court in London

Great Seal ['greɪt 'siːl] *noun* seal, kept by the Lord Chancellor, used for sealing important public documents on behalf of the Queen

Green Book ['griːn 'bʊk] *noun* the County Court Rules (book of procedural rules of county courts)

green card ['griːn 'kɑːd] *noun* **(a)** special British insurance certificate to prove that a car is insured for travel abroad **(b)** registration card for a non-US citizen going to live permanently in the USA

green form ['griːn 'fɔːm] *noun* form for giving free or subsidized legal advice to clients who are eligible for Legal Aid; **the green form scheme** = scheme where a solicitor will give advice to someone free of charge or at a subsidized rate, if the client has filled in the green form

Green Paper ['griːn 'peɪpə] *noun* report from the British government on proposals for a new law to be discussed in Parliament

grievance ['griːvəns] *noun* complaint made by a trade union or an employee to the management; **grievance procedure** = agreed way of presenting complaints from a trade union or an employee to the management of a company

grievous bodily harm (GBH) ['griːvəs 'bɒdɪli 'hɑːm] *noun* crime of causing serious physical injury to someone

gross [grəʊs] *adjective* **(a)** total, with no deductions; **gross domestic product (GDP)** = annual value of goods sold and services paid for inside a country; **gross earnings** *or* **gross income** *or* **gross salary** = total earnings before tax and other deductions; **gross margin** = percentage difference between sales income and the cost of sales; **gross national product (GNP)** = annual value of goods and services in a country including income from other countries; **gross profit** = profit calculated as sales income less the cost of the goods sold; **gross receipts** = total amount of money received before expenses are deducted; **gross weight** = weight of both the container and its contents **(b)** serious; **gross indecency** = crime entailing unlawful sexual contact between men or with a child; **gross negligence** = act showing very serious neglect of duty towards other people

ground [graʊnd] *noun* **(a)** soil or earth; **ground landlord** = person or company which owns the freehold of a property which is then leased and subleased; **ground lease** = first lease on a freehold building; **ground rent** = rent paid by a lessee to the ground landlord **(b)** **grounds** = basic reasons; *does he have good grounds for complaint?*; *there are no grounds on which we can be sued*; *what are the grounds for the claim for damages?* (NOTE: can be used in the singular if only one reason exists: **the judge refused the application on the ground that he had discretion to remove the hearsay evidence from the report**)

guarantee [gærən'tiː] **1** *noun* **(a)** legal document which promises that goods purchased will work properly, that an item is of good quality; *certificate of guarantee or guarantee certificate*; *the guarantee lasts for two years*; *the dishwasher is sold with a two-year guarantee*; **the car is still under guarantee** = the car is still covered by the maker's certificate of guarantee **(b)** promise made by a person that he will do what someone else is obliged to do if that other person fails to do it (for example, to pay another person's debts if the latter is unable to pay them) **(c)** thing given as a security; *to leave share certificates as a guarantee* **2** *verb* to give a promise that something will happen; **to guarantee a debt** = to promise that you will pay a debt incurred by someone else if that person fails to pay it; **to guarantee an associated company** = to promise that an associate company will pay its debts; **to guarantee a bill of exchange** = to promise to pay a bill;

the product is guaranteed for twelve months = the maker states that the product will work well for twelve months, and promises to mend it free of charge if it breaks down within that period

> COMMENT: in English law, a guarantee must usually be in writing; the person making a guarantee is secondarily liable if the person who is primarily liable defaults. Compare INDEMNITY

guarantor [gærən'tɔ:] *noun* person who gives a guarantee; **to stand guarantor for someone** = to promise to pay someone's debts

guaranty ['gærənti:] *US* = GUARANTEE

guard [gɑ:d] **1** *noun* **(a)** person whose job is to protect people or property; *there were three guards on duty at the door of the bank* or *three bank guards were on duty*; *the prisoner was shot by the guards as he tried to escape*; **security guard** = person whose job is to protect money, valuables or buildings against theft **(b)** state of being protected by a guard; *the prisoners were brought into the courtroom under armed guard* **2** *verb* to protect someone, to prevent someone being harmed, to prevent someone escaping; *the building is guarded by a fence and ten guard dogs*; *the prisoners are guarded night and day*

guardian ['gɑ:diən] *noun* person (an adult) or an authority (such as the High Court) appointed by law to act on behalf of someone (such as a child) who cannot act on his or her own behalf; **guardian ad litem** = person who acts on behalf of a minor who is a defendant in a court case; *see also* NEXT FRIEND

guardianship ['gɑ:diənʃip] *noun* state of being a guardian; **guardianship order** = court order appointing a local authority to be the guardian of a child

guerilla [gə'rilə] *noun* armed person (not a regular soldier) who engages in unofficial war; *the train was attacked by guerillas*; *the appeal was made by a guerilla radio station*

guidelines ['gaidlainz] *plural noun* unofficial suggestions from the government or some other body as to how something should be done; *the government has issued guidelines on increases in wages and prices*; *the Law Society has issued guidelines to its members on dealing with rape cases*; *the Secretary of State can issue guidelines for expenditure*; *the Lord Justice said he was not laying down guidelines for sentencing*

guillotine ['giləti:n] **1** *noun* **(a)** machine used in France for executing criminals by cutting off their heads **(b)** motion in the House of Commons to end a debate at a certain time **2** *verb* **(a)** to execute someone by cutting his head off with a guillotine **(b)** to end (a debate) at a certain time

guilt [gilt] *noun* being guilty, state of having committed a crime or done some other legal wrong; **guilt by association** = presumption that a person is guilty because of his connection with another guilty person; *he admitted his guilt* = he admitted that he had committed the crime

guilty ['gilti] *adjective* **(a)** finding after a trial that a person has done something which is against the law; *he was found guilty of libel*; *the company was guilty of evading the VAT regulations*; *(of a judge or jury)* **to find someone guilty** or **to return a verdict of guilty** or **to return a guilty verdict** = to say at the end of the trial that the accused is guilty **(b)** *(of an accused person)* **to plead guilty** = to say at the beginning of a trial that you did commit the crime of which you are accused; **to plead not guilty** = to say at the beginning of a trial that you did not commit the crime of which you are accused; *the accused pleaded not guilty to the charge of murder, but pleaded guilty to the lesser charge of manslaughter*; **guilty knowledge** = MENS REA

gun [gʌn] *noun* weapon used for shooting; *the police are not allowed to* *carry guns; they shouted to the robbers to drop their guns*

gunboat ['gʌnbəʊt] *see* DIPLOMACY

gun down ['gʌn 'daʊn] *verb* to kill someone with a gun; *he was gunned down in the street outside his office* (NOTE: gunned - gunning)

gunman ['gʌnmən] *noun* man who carries and uses a gun; *the security van was held up by three gunmen*

gunpoint ['gʌnpɔɪnt] *noun* **at gunpoint** = with a gun pointing at you; *he was forced at gunpoint to open the safe*

gunshot ['gʌnʃɒt] *noun* result of shooting with a gun; *he died of gunshot wounds*

Hh

habeas corpus ['heɪbiəs 'kɔːpəs] *Latin phrase meaning* 'may you have the body': legal remedy against being wrongly imprisoned; **writ of habeas corpus** = writ to obtain the release of someone who has been unlawfully held in prison or in police custody, or to make the person holding him bring him to court to explain why he is being held

habendum [hə'bendəm] *noun* section of a conveyance which gives details of how the property is to be assigned to the purchaser, using the words 'to hold'

habitual [hə'bɪtjuəl] *adjective* (person) who does something frequently; **habitual criminal** *or* **habitual offender** = person who has been convicted of a similar crime at least twice before; **habitual drunkard** = person who drinks alcohol so frequently that he is almost always dangerous or incapable; **habitual residence** = (i) fact of living normally in a place; (ii) the place where someone normally lives

Hague conventions ['heɪg kən'venʃnz] *plural noun* international agreements regarding the definition of war, and the barring of the use of chemical and biological weapons; *see also* GENEVA

hallmark ['hɔːlmɑːk] **1** *noun* mark put on gold or silver items to show that the metal is of the correct quality **2** *verb* to put a hallmark on a piece of gold or silver; *a hallmarked spoon*

hand [hænd] *noun* (a) **by hand** = using the hands, not a machine; **to send a letter by hand** = to ask someone to carry and deliver a letter personally, not sending it through the post (b) **in hand**, *US* **on hand**

= kept in reserve; **balance in hand** *or* **cash in hand** = cash held to pay small debts and running costs; **work in hand** = work which is in progress but not finished (c) **goods left on hand** = goods which have not been sold and are left with the retailer or producer (d) **out of hand** = immediately, without taking time to think; *the justices dismissed his evidence out of hand* (e) **to hand** = here, present; **I have the invoice to hand** = I have the invoice in front of me (f) **show of hands** = way of casting votes where people show how they vote by raising their hands; *the motion was carried on a show of hands* (g) **to change hands** = to be sold to a new owner; *the shop changed hands for £100,000* (h) signature; **note of hand** = signed document where someone promises to pay money at a stated time without conditions; **in witness whereof, I set my hand** = I sign as a witness

handcuffed ['hændkʌft] *adjective* secured by handcuffs; *the accused appeared in court handcuffed to two policemen*

handcuffs ['hændkʌfs] *plural noun* two metal rings chained together which are locked round the wrists of someone who is being arrested

hand down ['hænd 'daʊn] *verb* (a) to pass (property) from one generation to another; *the house has been handed down from father to son since the nineteenth century* (b) **to hand down a verdict** = to announce a verdict

handgun ['hændgʌn] *noun* small gun which is carried in the hand; *the police* *found six handguns when they searched the car*

handling [ˈhændlɪŋ] *noun* moving something by hand, dealing with something; **handling charge** *or* **handling fee** = money to be paid for packing and making invoices, for dealing with something in general, for moving goods from one place to another; **handling stolen goods** = notifiable offence of dealing with goods (receiving them or selling them) which you know to have been stolen

COMMENT: handling stolen goods is a more serious crime than theft, and the penalty can be higher

hand over [ˈhænd ˈəʊvə] *verb* to pass something to someone; *she handed over the documents to the lawyer*; **he handed over to his deputy** = he passed his responsibilities to his deputy

hand up [ˈhænd ˈʌp] *verb* to pass to someone who is in a higher place; *the exhibit was handed up to the judge*

handwriting [ˈhændraɪtɪŋ] *noun* **(a)** writing done by hand; **send a letter of application in your own handwriting** = written by you with a pen, and not typed; **handwriting expert** = person who is able to identify a person by examining his handwriting **(b)** *(slang)* particular way of committing a crime which identifies a criminal

handwritten [ˈhændrɪtən] *adjective* written by hand, not typed; *it is more professional to send in a typed rather than a handwritten letter of application*

hang [hæŋ] *verb* to execute someone by hanging him by a rope round his neck (NOTE: **hanging - hanged**; note: not **hung**)

hanging [ˈhæŋɪŋ] *noun* act of executing someone by hanging; *the hangings took place in front of the prison*

hangman [ˈhæŋmən] *noun* man who executes criminals by hanging them

Hansard [ˈhænsɑːd] *noun* official verbatim report of what is said and done in the House of Commons and the House of Lords; **Hansard reporters** = people who take shorthand notes of the debates in Parliament for printing in Hansard; *compare* JOURNAL

COMMENT: these reports were originally published by a Mr Hansard in the 19th century, and are now published by the Stationery Office. Hansard is published daily. Each page is divided into two numbered columns, so a reference to a particular speech in Hansard could read: Vol.120, No.24, 22 July 1987, Col. 370

harass [ˈhærəs or həˈræs] *verb* to worry or to bother someone, especially by continually checking on them or taking them into custody

harassment [ˈhærəsmənt or həˈræsmənt] *noun* action of harassing someone; *he complained of police harassment or of harassment by the police*

harbour [ˈhɑːbə] *verb* to give shelter and protection to (a criminal)

hard [hɑːd] *adjective* **(a)** strong, not weak; **to take a hard line in trade union negotiations** = to refuse to accept any proposal from the other side **(b)** difficult; **a hard case** = a criminal or an addict who cannot be reformed **(c)** solid, real; **hard cash** = money in notes and coins which is ready at hand; *he paid out £100 in hard cash for the chair*; **hard copy** = printout of a text which is on computer, printed copy of a document which is on microfilm; **hard disk** = computer disk which has a sealed case and can store large quantities of information **(d)** hard bargain = bargain with difficult terms; **to drive a hard bargain** = to be a difficult negotiator; **to strike a hard bargain** = to agree a deal where the terms are favourable to you **(e)** **hard currency** = currency of a country which has a strong economy and which can be changed into other currencies easily

hardened criminal [ˈhɑːdənd ˈkrɪmɪnəl] *noun* criminal who has committed many crimes and who will never go straight

hard labour ['hɑːd 'leɪbə] *noun* formerly, the punishment of sending someone to prison to do hard manual labour there

harmonization [hɑːmənaɪ'zeɪʃn] *noun (in the EU)* trying to make broadly similar the legislation, rates of VAT, etc., in all Member States

harmonize ['hɑːmənaɪz] *verb (in the EU)* to try to make things such as tax rates or VAT rates the same in all Member States

hat [hæt] *noun* piece of clothing worn on the head

COMMENT: formerly, if an MP wished to speak while a division was taking place, he had to wear a hat, and an old top hat was kept in the House of Commons for this purpose

hatred ['heɪtrəd] *noun* violent dislike of someone or something; **racial hatred** = violent dislike of someone because of his race

hawk [hɔːk] *noun* person who believes in threatening the use of armed force as a means of settling problems between countries (NOTE: the opposite is **dove**)

hawkish ['hɔːkɪʃ] *adjective* acting like a hawk; *the agreement will not satisfy the more hawkish members of the Cabinet*

hazard ['hæzəd] *noun* danger; **fire hazard** = situation or materials which could start a fire

H-block ['eɪtʃ'blɒk] *noun* building in a prison built with a central section and two end wings, forming the shape of the letter H

head [hed] **1** *noun* **(a)** most important person; **head of department** *or* **departmental head** = person in charge of a department **(b) head of government** = leader of a country's government; *compare* HEAD OF STATE; *see also* PRIME MINISTER **(c)** most important, main; *head clerk*; *head porter*; *head salesman*; *head waiter*; **head office** = main office, where the board of directors works and

meets **(d)** top part, first part; *write the name of the company at the head of the list* **(e)** person; *allow £10 per head for expenses*; *factory inspectors cost on average £25,000 per head per annum* **(f) heads of agreement** = draft agreement containing the most important points but not all the details; **head of damage** = item of damage in a pleading or claim **2** *verb* **(a)** to be the manager, to be the most important person; *to head a department*; *he is heading a government delegation to China* **(b)** to be first; *the list of Bills to be considered is headed by the Bill on the adoption services*; *the two largest oil companies head the list of stock market results*

head lease ['hed 'liːs] *noun* first lease given by a freeholder to a tenant

head licence ['hed 'laɪsəns] *noun* first licence given by the owner of a patent or copyright to someone who will use it

headnote ['hednəʊt] *noun* note at the beginning of a law report, giving a summary of the case

head of state ['hed əv 'steɪt] *noun* official leader of a country

COMMENT: a head of state may not have much political power, and may be restricted to ceremonial duties (meeting ambassadors, laying wreaths at national memorials, opening parliament, etc.) The head of government is usually the effective ruler of the country, except in countries where the President is the executive ruler, and the head of government is in charge of the administration. In the United Kingdom, the Queen is head of state, and the Prime Minister is head of government. In the United States, the President is both head of state and head of government

headquarters [hed'kwɔːtəz] *plural noun* main office; **police headquarters** = central office of a police force

hear [hɪə] *verb* **(a)** to sense a sound with the ears; *you can hear the printer in the* *next office*; *the traffic makes so much noise that I cannot hear my phone ringing* **(b)** to have a letter or a phone call from someone; *we have not heard from them for some time*; *we hope to hear from the lawyers within a few days* **(c)** to listen to the arguments in a court case; *the judge heard the case in chambers*; *the case will be heard next month*; *the court has heard the evidence for the defence* **(d)** **hear! hear!** = words used in a meeting to show that you agree with the person speaking (NOTE: **hearing - heard**)

hearing ['hɪərɪŋ] *noun* **(a)** case which is being heard by a committee, tribunal or court of law; *the hearing about the planning application lasted ten days*; **final hearing** = the actual hearing of a case in the small claims track, which aims at being informal and rapid; **hearing in private** = court case which is heard with no member of the public present; **open hearing** = case where the public and journalists may attend; **preliminary hearing** = (i) court proceedings where the witnesses and the defendant are examined to see if there are sufficient grounds for the case to proceed; (ii) in the small claims track, a hearing to decide if special directions should be issued, or if the statement of case should be struck out; (iii) court proceedings to try a specific issue rather than the whole case **(b)** being heard by an official body; *he asked to be given a hearing by the full council so that he could state his case*

hearsay evidence ['hɪəseɪ 'evɪdəns] *noun* evidence by a witness who has heard it from another source, but did not witness the acts himself

> COMMENT: hearsay evidence may not be given as much weight by the court as direct witness evidence. If a party intends to rely on hearsay evidence, they must serve notice to that effect

heavily ['hevɪli] *adverb* **he had to borrow heavily to pay the fine** = he had to borrow a lot of money

heavy ['hevi] **1** *adjective* harsh, not treating someone in a kind way; *the looters*

were given heavy jail sentences; *he was sentenced to pay a heavy fine* **2** *noun* (slang) strong man employed to frighten people

hegemony [hɪ'geməni] *noun* leadership by one strong state over a group of neighbouring states

heir [eə] *noun* person who receives or will receive property when someone dies; *his heirs split the estate between them*; **heirs, successors and assigns** = people who have inherited property and had it transferred to them; **heir apparent** = heir who will certainly inherit if a person dies before him; **heir presumptive** = heir who will inherit if a person dies at this moment, but whose inheritance may be altered in the future

heiress ['eəres] *noun* female heir

heirloom ['eəluːm] *noun* piece of family property (such as silver, a painting or a jewel) which has been handed down for several generations; *the burglars stole some family heirlooms*

heist [heist] *noun* (slang) holdup

help [help] *verb* to make it easy for something to be done; *his evidence did not help the case for the defendant*; *his case was not helped by the evidence of the expert witness*; *see also* INQUIRY

henceforth [hens'fɔːθ] *adverb* from this time on; *henceforth it will be more difficult to avoid customs examinations*

here- [hɪə] *prefix* this time, this point

hereafter [hɪər'ɑːftə] *adverb* from this time or point on

hereby [hɪə'baɪ] *adverb* in this way, by this letter; *we hereby revoke the agreement of January 1st 1982*

hereditament [herɪ'dɪtəmənt] *noun* property, including land and buildings, which can be inherited; **corporeal hereditaments** = rights of property which physically exist, such as houses, furniture; **incorporeal hereditaments** = rights (such as patents or copyrights) which can form part of an estate and be inherited; **mixed hereditaments** = properties which are used for both domestic and business purposes

hereditary [hɪˈredɪtri] *adjective* which is inherited, which is passed from one member of a family to another; **hereditary office** = official position which is inherited; **hereditary peer** = peer who has inherited his title

herein [hɪərˈɪn] *adverb* in this document; *the conditions stated herein; see the reference herein above*

hereinafter [hɪərɪnˈɑːftə] *adverb* stated later in this document; *the conditions hereinafter listed*

hereof [hɪəˈrɒv] *adverb* of this; **in confirmation hereof we attach a bank statement** = to confirm this we attach a bank statement

hereto [hɪəˈtuː] *adverb* to this; *according to the schedule of payments attached hereto*; **as witness hereto** = as a witness of this fact; **the parties hereto** = the parties to this agreement

heretofore [hɪətuˈfɔː] *adverb* previously or earlier; *the parties heretofore acting as trustees*

hereunder [hɪəˈrʌndə] *adverb* under this heading, below this phrase; *see the documents listed hereunder*

herewith [hɪəˈwɪð] *adverb* together with this letter; *please find the cheque enclosed herewith*

Her Majesty's pleasure [ˈhɜː ˈmædʒəstɪz ˈpleʒə] *noun* **detention at** *or* **during Her Majesty's pleasure** = detention for an indefinite period, until the Home Secretary decides that a prisoner can be released

COMMENT: used as a punishment for people under a disability and children who commit murder

hidden [ˈhɪdn] *adjective* which cannot be seen; **hidden asset** = asset which is valued in the company's accounts at much less than its true market value; **hidden reserves** = illegal reserves which are not declared in the company's balance sheet; **hidden defect in the program** = defect which was not noticed when a computer program was tested

High Commission [ˈhaɪ kəˈmɪʃn] *noun* building where a High Commissioner lives and works; organization of the office of a High Commissioner; *the British High Commission in Ottawa*; *the High Commission staff were told not to speak to journalists*; *she is joining the High Commission as an interpreter*

High Commissioner [ˈhaɪ kəˈmɪʃnə] *noun* person who represents a Commonwealth country in another Commonwealth country, having the same rank and the same duties as an ambassador

High Court (of Justice) [ˈhaɪ ˈkɔːt] *noun* main civil court in England and Wales, based on the six circuits

COMMENT: in England and Wales, the High Court is divided into three divisions: the Queen's Bench, the Chancery and the Family Divisions; the Court hears most civil claims with a high value

High Court of Justiciary [ˈhaɪ ˈkɔːt əv dʒʌˈstɪʃɪəri] *noun* the supreme criminal court of Scotland

high seas [ˈhaɪ ˈsiːz] *plural noun* part of the sea which is further than three miles or five kilometres from a coast, and so is under international jurisdiction (NOTE: usually used with 'the': **an accident on the high seas**)

High Sheriff [ˈhaɪ ˈʃerɪf] *noun* senior representative appointed by the government in a county

highway [ˈhaɪweɪ] *noun* road or path with a right of way which anyone may use; **the Highway Code** = rules which govern the behaviour of people and vehicles using roads

COMMENT: the Highway Code is not itself part of English law

hijack ['haɪdʒæk] **1** *noun* act of taking control of a plane, ship, train, bus or lorry which is moving; *the hijack was organized by a group of opponents to the government* **2** *verb* to take control of a moving plane, ship, train, bus or lorry, with passengers on board, by threatening the crew; *the plane was hijacked by six armed terrorists*; *the bandits hijacked the lorry and killed the driver*

hijacker ['haɪdʒækə] *noun* person who hijacks a vehicle

hijacking ['haɪdʒækɪŋ] *noun* act of taking control of a moving plane, ship, train, bus or lorry by force; *the hijacking took place just after the plane took off*; *there have been six hijackings so far this year*

Hilary ['hɪləri] *noun* one of the four sittings of the law courts; one of the four law terms

hire purchase ['haɪə 'pɜːtʃəs] *noun* system of buying something by paying a sum regularly each month until you own it completely; *to buy a refrigerator on hire purchase*; **to sign a hire-purchase agreement** = to sign a contract to pay for something by instalments; **hire-purchase company** = company which provides money for hire purchase (NOTE: American English is the **installment plan**)

hirer ['haɪərə] *noun* person who hires something

hit [hɪt] *verb (slang)* to kill

hit and run ['hɪt ən 'rʌn] *noun* situation where a vehicle hits someone and continues without stopping

hit man ['hɪt 'mæn] *noun (slang)* hired killer, person who will kill for a fee

hoax [həʊks] *noun* action which is liable to make someone believe something, such as that a dangerous situation exists; **bomb hoax** = placing an imitation bomb in a public place, making a phone call to report a bomb which does not exist; **hoax phone call** = call to inform the police or fire service of a dangerous situation which does not exist

hoc [hɒk] *see* AD HOC

hold [həʊld] *verb* **(a)** to make something happen; *to hold a meeting or a discussion*; *the hearings were held in private*; *the receiver will hold an auction of the company's assets*; *the inquiry will be held in London in June* **(b)** to keep (someone) in custody; *the prisoners are being held in the police station*; *twenty people were held in the police raid*; *she was held for six days without being able to see her lawyer* **(c)** to decide, to make a judgment; *the court held that there was no case to answer*; *the appeal judge held that the defendant was not in breach of his statutory duty* (NOTE: **holding - held**)

holder ['həʊldə] *noun* **(a)** person who owns or keeps something; *the holder of an insurance policy or a policy holder*; *she is a British passport holder or she is the holder of a British passport*; **credit card holder** = person who has a credit card; **debenture holder** = person who holds a debenture for money lent; *see also* SHAREHOLDER **(b)** person to whom a cheque is made payable and who has possession of it **(c)** person who is holding a bill of exchange or promissory note; **holder in due course** = person who takes a bill, promissory note or cheque before it becomes overdue or is dishonoured **(d)** thing which keeps something, which protects something; **card holder** *or* **message holder** = frame which protects a card or a message; **credit card holder** = plastic wallet for keeping credit cards

holding ['həʊldɪŋ] *noun* group of shares owned; *he has sold all his holdings in the Far East*; *the company has holdings in German manufacturing companies*; **cross holdings** = situation where two companies own shares in each other in order to stop each from being taken over; *the two companies have protected themselves from takeover by a system of cross holdings*; *see also* SHAREHOLDING

holding charge ['həʊldɪŋ 'tʃɑːdʒ] *noun* minor charge brought against someone so that he can be held in custody while more serious charges are being prepared

holding company ['həʊldɪŋ 'kʌmpni] *noun* company which exists only to own shares in subsidiary companies

holding over *US* **holdover** ['həʊldɪŋ 'əʊvə or 'həʊldəʊvə] *noun* situation where a person who had a lease for a certain period continues to occupy the property after the end of the lease

hold out ['həʊld 'aʊt] *verb* **(a)** to behave in a way which misleads others; **he held himself out as a director of the company** = he behaved as if he were a director of the company **(b) to hold out for** = to ask for something and refuse to act until you get what you asked for; *he held out for a 50% discount*; *the union is holding out for a 10% wage increase*

hold to ['həʊld 'tʊ] *verb* not to allow something to change; **we will try to hold him to the contract** = we will try to make sure that he follows the terms of the contract; **the government hopes to hold wage increases to 5%** = the government hopes that wage increases will not be more than 5%

hold up ['həʊld 'ʌp] *verb* **(a)** to go into a bank, to stop a lorry, etc., in order to steal money; *six gunmen held up the bank or the security van* **(b)** to stay at a high level; *share prices have held up well*; *sales held up during the tourist season* **(c)** to delay; *the shipment has been held up at the customs*; *payment will be held up until the contract has been signed*; *the strike will hold up delivery for some weeks*

hold-up ['həʊldʌp] *noun* **(a)** act of holding up a bank, etc.; *the gang committed three armed hold-ups on the same day* **(b)** delay; *the strike caused hold-ups in the shipment of goods*

holiday ['hɒlɪdeɪ] *noun* **(a) bank holiday** = a weekday which is a public holiday when the banks are closed (in legal cases, this includes Good Friday); *Easter Monday is a bank holiday*; **public holiday** = day when all workers rest and enjoy themselves instead of working; **statutory holiday** = holiday which is fixed by law **(b)** period when a worker does not work, but rests, goes away and enjoys himself; *to take a holiday or to go on holiday*; *when is the manager taking his holidays?*; *my secretary is off on holiday tomorrow*; *he is away on holiday for two weeks*; **the job carries five weeks' holiday** = one of the conditions of the job is that you have five weeks' holiday; **holiday entitlement** = number of days' paid holiday which a worker has the right to take; **holiday pay** = salary which is still paid during the holiday **(c) tax holiday** = period when a new business is exempted from paying tax

holograph ['hɒləɡrɑːf] *noun* document written by hand; **holograph will** = handwritten will

holographic ['hɒlə'ɡræfɪk] *adjective US* **holographic will** = HOLOGRAPH WILL

home court ['həʊm 'kɔːt] *noun* the County Court for the district in which a defendant lives or has his address for service (NOTE: American English is **domestic court**)

homeless person ['həʊmləs 'pɜːsən] *noun* person with no fixed accommodation, who is therefore eligible for the provision of accommodation by his local council

Home Office ['həʊm 'ɒfɪs] *noun* British government ministry dealing with internal affairs, including the police and prisons

Home Secretary ['həʊm 'sekrətri] *noun* member of the British government, the minister in charge of the Home Office, dealing with law and order, the police and prisons

COMMENT: in most countries the government department dealing with the internal order of the country is called the Ministry of the Interior, with a Minister of the Interior in charge

homestead ['həʊmsted] *noun US* house and land where a family lives

> COMMENT: a homestead cannot be the subject of a sale by court order to satisfy creditors

homicidal [hɒmɪ'saɪdl] *adjective* (person) who is likely to commit murder

homicide ['hɒmɪsaɪd] *noun* **(a)** killing of a person (either accidental or illegal); *he was found guilty of homicide*; *the homicide rate has doubled in the last ten years*; **culpable homicide** = murder or manslaughter; **justifiable homicide** = killing of a person for an acceptable reason (such as in self-defence) **(b)** murder; **the Homicide Squad** = special section of the police force which investigates murders

> COMMENT: homicide covers the crimes of murder, manslaughter and infanticide

honest ['ɒnɪst] *adjective* truthful, saying what is right; **to play the honest broker** = to act for the parties in a negotiation to try to help them agree to a solution

honestly ['ɒnəstli] *adverb* saying what is right, not cheating

honesty ['ɒnəsti] *noun* being honest, telling the truth; *the court praised the witness for her honesty in informing the police of the crime*

honorarium [ɒnə'reərɪəm] *noun* money paid to a professional person, such as an accountant or a lawyer, which is less than a full fee

honorary ['ɒnəri] *adjective* person who is not paid a salary; *the honorary secretary of the cricket club*; **honorary consul** = person who represents a country but is not paid a salary, and is not a member of the diplomatic corps, although he is may be granted diplomatic status; **honorary member** = member of a club or group who does not have to pay a subscription

honour *US* **honor** ['ɒnə] *verb* to accept and pay a cheque or bill of exchange; **to honour a debt** = to pay a debt because it is owed and is correct; **to honour a signature** = to pay something because the signature is correct

honourable ['ɒnərəbl] *adjective* title used when one MP addresses another; *the hon. Member for London East would do well to remember the conditions in his constituency*; *will my hon. Friend give way?*; *the hon. Gentleman is perfectly entitled to ask that question*; **Right Honourable** = title given to members of the Privy Council (NOTE: usually written **Hon.: the Hon. Member; the Rt. Hon. William Smith, M.P.**)

> COMMENT: various conventions are attached to the use of the word in Parliament. In general, MPs can refer to each other as 'the hon. Member for...'; the Speaker will refer to all MPs as 'hon. Members'. To distinguish MPs of one's own party from those on the other side of the House, an MP will say 'my hon. Friend'. To distinguish between women and men MPs, you can say 'the hon. Lady' or 'the hon. Gentleman'. Lawyers may be addressed as 'hon. and learned'

hoodlum ['hu:dləm] *noun US* gangster

hooligan ['hu:lɪgən] *noun* person who behaves violently in public; *the police put up barriers to prevent the football hooligans from damaging property*

hooliganism ['hu:lɪgənɪzm] *noun* violent behaviour; **football hooliganism** = violent behaviour by football supporters in connection with football matches

hopper ['hɒpə] *noun US* box where bills are put after being introduced in the House of Representatives

horse-trading ['hɔːs'treɪdɪŋ] *noun* bargaining between political parties, politicians or members of a committee to obtain a general agreement for something; *after a period of horse-trading, the committee agreed on the election of a member of one of the smaller parties as Chairman*

hospital ['hɒspɪtəl] *noun* place where sick people can be kept and treated; **hospital order** = court order putting an insane offender in hospital instead of in prison

hostage ['hɒstɪdʒ] *noun* person captured by an enemy or by criminals and kept until a ransom is paid; *he was taken hostage by the guerillas*; *the bandits took away the bank manager and kept him hostage*; *the terrorists released three hostages*

hostage taker ['hɒstɪdʒ 'teɪkə] *noun* person who takes someone hostage; *two of the hostage takers were killed in a shootout with the security forces*

hostile ['hɒstaɪl] *adjective* not friendly; **hostile witness** = witness called by a party, whose evidence goes unexpectedly against that party, and who can then be cross-examined by his own side as if he were giving evidence for the other side; *she was ruled a hostile witness by the judge*

hot [hɒt] *adjective* **(a) hot money** = money which is moved from country to country to get the best interest rates **(b)** *(informal)* stolen or illegal; *hot jewels*; *a hot car*

hot pursuit [hɒt pɜː'sjuːt] *noun* right in international law to chase a ship into international waters, or to chase suspected criminals across an international border into another country

hotchpot ['hɒtʃpɒt] *noun* bringing together into one fund money to be distributed under a will; **hotchpot rule** = rule that money passed to one child during his lifetime by a deceased person should be counted as part of the total estate to be distributed to all the children in the case where the person died intestate

house [haʊs] *noun* **(a)** whole building in which someone lives; **house property** = private houses, not shops, offices or factories; **house agent** = estate agent who deals in buying or selling houses **(b)** one of the two parts of the British Parliament (the House of Commons and the House of Lords); *the minister brought a matter to*

the attention of the House; **the Houses of Parliament** = (i) the building where the British Parliament meets, containing the chambers of the House of Commons and the House of Lords; (ii) the British Parliament **(c)** one of the two chambers of Congress; *the bill was passed by both houses and sent to the President for signature; US* **the House** = the House of Representatives; **House Calendar** = list of bills which do not appropriate money or raise revenue

house arrest ['haʊs ə'rest] *noun* being ordered by a court to stay in your house and not to leave it; *the opposition leader has been under house arrest for six years*

housebreaker ['haʊsbreɪkə] *noun* burglar, person who breaks into houses and steals things

housebreaking ['haʊsbreɪkɪŋ] *noun* burglary, entering a house and stealing things

household ['haʊshəʊld] *noun* people living in a house; **household effects** = furniture and other items used in a house, and moved with the owner when he moves house

householder ['haʊshəʊldə] *noun* person who occupies a private house

House leader ['haʊs 'liːdə] *noun* **(a)** *(in Britain)* Leader of the House, a main government minister and member of the cabinet, who is responsible for the administration of legislation in the House of Commons or House of Lords, and is the main government spokesman in the House **(b)** *(in the USA)* chief of one of the political parties in the House of Representatives; **the House Republican Leader** = head of the Republican Party in the House of Representatives

House of Commons ['haʊs əv 'kɒmənz] *noun* (i) lower house of the British Parliament, made up of 659 elected members; (ii) lower house of a legislature (as in Canada)

COMMENT: members of the House of Commons (called MPs) are elected for five years, which is the maximum length of a Parliament. Bills can be presented in either the House of Commons or House of Lords, and sent to the other chamber for discussion and amendment. All bills relating to revenue must be introduced in the House of Commons, and most other bills are introduced there also

House of Lords ['haʊs əv 'lɔːdz] *noun* upper house of the British Parliament; **Judicial Committee of the House of Lords** = highest court of appeal in both civil and criminal cases in England and Wales

COMMENT: the House of Lords was made up of hereditary lords, life peers, leading judges and bishops, but its composition is being changed and hereditary peers no longer sit there by right. As a court, the decisions of the House of Lords are binding on all other courts, and the only appeal from the House of Lords is to the European Court of Justice

House of Representatives ['haʊs əv reprɪ'zentətɪvz] *noun* (i) lower house of the Congress of the United States, made up of 435 elected members; (ii) lower house of a legislature (as in Australia)

COMMENT: the members of the House of Representatives (called Congressmen) are elected for two years. All bills relating to revenue must originate in the House of Representatives; otherwise bills can be proposed in either the House or the Senate and sent to the other chamber for discussion and amendment.

human ['hjuːmən] *adjective* referring to men and women; **human error** = mistake made by a person, not by a machine; **human rights** = rights of individual men and women to basic freedoms, such as freedom of association, freedom of speech

hung [hʌŋ] *adjective* with no majority; **hung jury** = jury which cannot arrive at a unanimous or majority verdict; **hung**

parliament = parliament where no single party has enough votes to form a government; *see also* HANG

hunger strike ['hʌŋgə 'straɪk] *noun* protest (often by a prisoner), where the person refuses to eat until his demands have been met; *he went on hunger strike until the prison authorities allowed him to receive mail*

hurdle ['hɜːdl] *noun* thing which prevents something happening; *the defendant will have to overcome two hurdles if his appeal is to be successful*

husband ['hʌzbənd] *noun* male spouse

hush money ['hʌʃ 'mʌni] *noun* (*informal*) money paid to someone to stop him talking

hustings ['hʌstɪŋz] *noun* **at the hustings** = at a parliamentary election

COMMENT: the hustings were formerly the booths where votes were taken, or the platform on which candidates stood to speak, but now the word is used simply to mean 'an election'

Hybrid Bill ['haɪbrɪd 'bɪl] *noun* term used to refer to a Public Bill which affects the private interests of a particular person or organization

hybrid offence ['haɪbrɪd ə'fens] *noun* offence which can be tried either by magistrates or by a judge and jury

hypothecation [haɪpɒθə'keɪʃn] *noun* (a) using property such as securities as collateral for a loan, but not transferring legal ownership to the lender (as opposed to a mortgage, where the lender holds the title to the property) (b) action of earmarking money derived from certain sources for certain related expenditure, as when investing taxes from private cars or petrol sales solely on public transport

hypothetical question [haɪpə'θetɪkl 'kwestʃn] *noun* question which is posed as an academic exercise in decision-making, but which does not actually exist in real life

Ii

ibid *or* **ibidem** ['ɪbɪd] *adverb* just the same, in the same place in a book

ID ['aɪ 'diː] = IDENTITY; **ID card** = IDENTITY CARD

id *or* **idem** ['ɪd or 'ɪdem] *pronoun* the same thing, the same person; **ad idem** = in agreement

identification [aɪdentɪfɪ'keɪʃn] *noun* act of identifying someone or something; **proof of identification** = (i) proving that something is what the evidence says it is; (ii) proving that someone is who he says he is; *the policeman asked him for proof of identification*; **identification parade** = arranging for a group of people (including a suspect) to stand in line at a police station so that a witness can point out the criminal

identify [aɪ'dentɪfaɪ] *verb* to say who someone is or what something is; *she was able to identify her attacker*; *passengers were asked to identify their suitcases*; *the dead man was identified by his fingerprints*

identikit [aɪ'dentɪkɪt] *noun* method of making a picture of a criminal from descriptions given by witnesses, using pieces of photographs and drawings of different types of faces; *the police issued an identikit picture of the mugger* (NOTE: now replaced by **Photofit pictures**)

identity [aɪ'dentəti] *noun* **(a)** who someone is; **he changed his identity** = he assumed a different name, changed his appearance, etc., (usually done to avoid being recognized); **he was asked for proof of identity** = he was asked to prove he really was the person he said he was; **identity card** *or* **ID card** *or* **identity disk** = card or disk carried to show who the holder is; **identity parade** = IDENTIFICATION PARADE; **case of mistaken identity** = situation where a person is wrongly thought to be someone else **(b)** being the same; **identity of parties** = situation where the parties in different actions are the same

ignorance ['ɪgnərəns] *noun* not knowing; **ignorance of the law is no excuse** = the fact that someone does not know that he has committed an offence does not make the offence any the less

ignorantia legis non *or* **neminem** *or* **haud excusat** [ɪgnə'ræntiə 'ledʒɪs nɒn eks'kjuːzæt] *Latin phrase meaning* 'ignorance of the law is not an excuse for anyone'

ILEX = INSTITUTE OF LEGAL EXECUTIVES

illegal [ɪ'liːgəl] *adjective* not legal, against criminal law; *the illegal carrying of arms*; *illegal immigrants are deported*; **illegal contract** = contract which cannot be enforced in law (such as a contract to commit a crime)

illegality [ɪlɪ'gæləti] *noun* being illegal

illegitimacy [ɪlɪ'dʒɪtɪməsi] *noun* being illegitimate

illegitimate [ɪlɪ'dʒɪtɪmət] *adjective* **(a)** against the law **(b)** (person) born to parents who are not married to each other

COMMENT: children who are illegitimate can nevertheless inherit from their parents

illicit [ɪˈlɪsɪt] *adjective* not legal, not permitted; *illicit sale of alcohol*; *trade in illicit alcohol*

ILO [ˈaɪ ˈel ˈəʊ] = INTERNATIONAL LABOUR ORGANIZATION

IMF [ˈaɪ ˈem ˈef] = INTERNATIONAL MONETARY FUND

imitation [ɪmɪˈteɪʃn] *noun* thing which copies another; **beware of imitations** = be careful not to buy low quality goods which are made to look like other more expensive items

immaterial [ɪməˈtɪərɪəl] *adjective* (evidence) which is not relevant to the case

immemorial [ɪməˈmɔːrɪəl] *adjective* so old it cannot be remembered; **immemorial existence** *or* **time immemorial** = before 1189, the date from which events are supposed to be remembered; **from time immemorial** = for so long that no one can remember when it started; *villagers said that there had been a footpath across the field from time immemorial*

immigrate [ˈɪmɪgreɪt] *verb* to move to this country to live permanently; *compare* EMIGRATE

immigration [ɪmɪˈgreɪʃn] *noun* moving to this country to live permanently; **Immigration Laws** = legislation regarding immigration into a country; **immigration officers** = staff at airports and harbours, whose duty is to check passports and visas; *compare* EMIGRATION

immigrant [ˈɪmɪgrənt] *noun* person who moves to this country to live permanently; **illegal immigrant** = person who enters a country to live permanently without having the permission of the government to do so; *compare* EMIGRANT

immoral earnings [ɪˈmɒrəl ˈɜːnɪŋz] *plural noun* money earned from prostitution; **living off immoral earnings**

= offence of making a living from money obtained from prostitutes

immovable [ɪˈmuːvəbl] *adjective* & *noun* which cannot be moved; **immovable property** *or* **immovables** = land, and houses and other buildings on land

immunity [ɪˈmjuːnəti] *noun* protection against arrest or prosecution; **diplomatic immunity** = not being subject to the laws of the country in which you are living because of being a diplomat; **when he offered to give information to the police, he was granted immunity from prosecution** = he was told he would not be prosecuted; **judicial immunity** = safety from prosecution granted to judges when acting in a judicial capacity; **sovereign immunity** = immunity of a foreign head of state or former head of state from prosecution outside his country for crimes committed inside his country in the course of exercising his public function

COMMENT: immunity from prosecution is also granted to magistrates, counsel and witnesses as regards their statements in judicial proceedings. Families and servants of diplomats may be covered by diplomatic immunity. In the USA, immunity is the protection of members of Congress against being sued for libel or slander for statements made on the floor of the House (in the UK this is called **privilege**)

impanel [ɪmˈpænəl] = EMPANEL

impartial [ɪmˈpɑːʃl] *adjective* not partial, not biased, not prejudiced; *a judgment must be impartial*; *to give someone a fair and impartial hearing*

impartiality [ɪmpɑːʃiˈæləti] *noun* state of being impartial; *the newspapers doubted the impartiality of the judge*

impartially [ɪmˈpɑːʃəli] *adverb* not showing any bias or favour towards someone; *the adjudicator has to decide impartially between the two parties*

impeach [ɪmˈpiːtʃ] *verb* **(a)** (formerly) to charge a person with treason before

Parliament **(b)** to charge a head of state with treason **(c)** *US* to charge any government official with misconduct **(d)** *US* to discredit (a witness)

impeachment [ɪmˈpiːtʃmənt] *noun* charge of treason brought against a head of state (in the USA, also a charge of misconduct against any public official); *US* **articles of impeachment** = statement of the grounds on which a public official is to be impeached

imperfect [ɪmˈpɜːfɪkt] *adjective* not perfect; *sale of imperfect items*; *to check a shipment for imperfect products*

imperfection [ɪmpəˈfekʃn] *noun* part of an item which is not perfect; *to check a shipment for imperfections*

imperial [ɪmˈpɪəriəl] *adjective* referring to an empire

imperialism [ɪmˈpɪəriəlɪzm] *noun* *(often as criticism)* (i) idea or practice of having an empire formed of colonies; (ii) controlling other countries as if they were part of an empire

imperialist [ɪmˈpɪəriəlɪst] **1** *adjective* referring to imperialism **2** *noun* person who is in favour of empires and imperialism

COMMENT: although imperialism is used to refer to states which have or had colonies (such as Britain, France, Belgium, the Netherlands, etc.,) it is now widely used to refer to states which exert strong influence over other states. This influence can be political, military or commercial

impersonate [ɪmˈpɜːsəneɪt] *verb* to pretend to be someone else; *he gained entrance to the house by impersonating a local authority inspector*

impersonation [ɪmpɜːsəˈneɪʃn] *noun* pretending to be someone else; *he was charged with impersonation of a police officer*

impleader [ɪmˈpliːdə] *noun* *US* procedure to join a third party to an original action, undertaken either by the plaintiff or the defendant (NOTE: the British equivalent is third party proceedings)

implicit [ɪmˈplɪsɪt] *adjective* implied, not clearly stated

implied [ɪmˈplaɪd] *adjective* which is presumed to exist or which can be established by circumstantial evidence; **implied contract** = agreement which is considered to be a contract, because the parties intended it to be a contract or because the law considers it to be a contract; **implied malice** = intention to commit grievous bodily harm on someone; **implied term** = term in a contract which is not clearly set out in the contract (as opposed to an express term); **implied terms and conditions** = terms and conditions which are not written in a contract, but which are legally taken to be present in the contract; **implied trust** = trust which is implied by the intentions and actions of the parties

imply [ɪmˈplaɪ] *verb* to suggest (that something may be true); *counsel implied that the witness had not in fact seen the accident take place*; *do you wish to imply that the police acted improperly?*

import 1 [ˈɪmpɔːt] *noun* bringing foreign goods into a country to be sold; *the import of firearms is forbidden*; **import levy** = tax on imports, especially in the EC a tax on imports of farm produce from outside the EC; **import licence** = permit which allows a company to bring a certain type of product into a country **2** [ɪmˈpɔːt] *verb* to bring foreign goods into a country

imports [ˈɪmpɔːts] *plural noun* goods brought into a country; *all imports must be declared to customs*

importune [ɪmpəˈtjuːn] *verb* to ask someone to have sexual relations (used both of prostitutes looking for clients, or of men looking for prostitutes)

importuning [ɪmpəˈtjuːnɪŋ] *noun* crime of asking someone to have sexual relations with you (usually for money)

impose [ɪmˈpəʊz] *verb* to ask someone to pay a fine; to put a tax or a duty on goods; *the court imposed a fine of £100; to impose a tax on bicycles; they tried to impose a ban on smoking; the government imposed a special duty on oil; the authorities have imposed a 10% tax increase on electrical items; the unions have asked the government to impose trade barriers on foreign cars*

imposition [ɪmpə'zɪʃn] *noun* putting a tax on goods or services

impossibility of performance [ɪmpɒsɪ'bɪlɪti əv pə'fɔːməns] *noun* situation where a party to a contract is unable to perform his part of the contract

impound [ɪm'paʊnd] *verb* to take something away and keep it until a tax is paid or until documents are checked to see if they are correct; *the customs impounded the whole cargo*

impounding [ɪm'paʊndɪŋ] *noun* act of taking something and keeping it

impression [ɪm'preʃn] *noun* effect which something or someone makes on a person; **case of first impression** = case which raises points of law for which there are no precedents

imprison [ɪm'prɪzən] *verb* to put (someone) in prison; *he was imprisoned by the secret police for six months*

imprisonment [ɪm'prɪzənmənt] *noun* being put in prison; *the penalty for the first offence is a fine of £200 or six weeks' imprisonment*; **a term of imprisonment** = time which a prisoner has to spend in prison; *he was sentenced to the maximum term of imprisonment*; **false imprisonment** = (i) tort of keeping someone wrongly imprisoned; (ii) sending someone to prison for a wrong reason; **life imprisonment** = being put in prison for a long time (the penalty for murder)

COMMENT: life imprisonment is a term of many years, but in the UK not necessarily for the rest of the prisoner's life

improper [ɪm'prɒpə] *adjective* not correct, not as it should be

improperly [ɪm'prɒpəli] *adverb* not correctly; *the police constable's report was improperly made out; he was accused of acting improperly in going to see the prisoner's father*

impulse [ˈɪmpʌls] *noun* strong wish to do something; **irresistible impulse** = strong wish to do something which you cannot resist because of insanity

impunity [ɪm'pjuːnəti] *noun* **with impunity** = without punishment; *no one can flout the law with impunity*

imputation [ɪmpjuˈteɪʃn] *noun* suggestion (that someone has done something wrong); **imputation of malice** = suggestion that someone acted out of malice

impute [ɪm'pjuːt] *verb* to suggest; **to impute a motive to someone** = to suggest that someone had a certain motive in acting as he did

in absentia [ɪn əb'sentiə] *adverb* in someone's absence; *she was tried and sentenced to death in absentia*

inadmissible [ɪnəd'mɪsəbl] *adjective* (evidence) which a court cannot admit

inalienable [ɪn'eɪliənəbl] *adjective* (right) which cannot be taken away or transferred

inapplicable [ɪnə'plɪkəbl] *adjective* which cannot be applied; *the government argued that the national legislation had not been applied and was inapplicable in this case*

Inc = INCORPORATED

in camera [ˈɪn ˈkæmərə] *adverb* with no members of the public permitted to be present; *the case was heard in camera* (NOTE: since the introduction of the new Civil Procedure Rules in April 1999, this term has been replaced by **in private**)

incapable [ɪn'keɪpəbl] *adjective* not able; *he was incapable of fulfilling the terms of the contract; a child is considered legally incapable of committing a crime*; **drunk and incapable** = offence of having drunk so much alcohol that you are not able to act normally

incapacity [ɪnkə'pæsɪti] *noun* not being legally able to do something; *the court had to act because of the incapacity of the trustees*

incapax ['ɪnkæpæks] *see* DOLI INCAPAX

incarcerate [ɪn'kɑːsəreɪt] *verb* to put in prison; *he was incarcerated in a stone tower*

incarceration [ɪnkɑːsə'reɪʃn] *noun* imprisonment, act of putting a criminal in prison

inception [ɪn'sepʃn] *noun* beginning; *some people believe that subsidiarity has existed in the Community ever since its inception*

incest ['ɪnsest] *noun* notifiable offence of having sexual intercourse with a close relative (daughter, son, mother, father)

in chambers ['ɪn 'tʃeɪmbəz] *adverb* in the office of a judge, and not in court; *the judge heard the application in chambers*

inchoate [ɪn'kəʊeɪt] *adjective* started, but not complete; **inchoate instrument** = document which is not complete; **inchoate offences** = offences (such as incitement, attempt or conspiracy to commit a crime) which are offences even though the substantive offence may not have been committed

incidence ['ɪnsɪdəns] *noun* how often something happens; *the incidence of cases of rape has increased over the last years; a high incidence of accidents relating to drunken drivers*

incident ['ɪnsɪdənt] *noun* **1** thing which has happened (especially a crime or accident); *three incidents were reported when police vehicles were attacked by a crowd*; **incident room** = special room in a police station to deal with a particular crime or accident **2** *adjective* **incident to something** = which depends on something else

incidental [ɪnsɪ'dentl] *adjective* not important; **incidental expenses** = small amounts of money spent at various times, in addition to larger amounts

incite [ɪn'saɪt] *verb* to encourage, persuade or advise (someone) to commit a crime

incitement [ɪn'saɪtmənt] *noun* crime of encouraging, persuading or advising someone to commit a crime; **incitement to racial hatred** = offence of encouraging (by words, actions or writing) people to attack others because of their race

COMMENT: it is not necessary for a crime to have been committed for incitement to be proved

inciter [ɪn'saɪtə] *noun* person who incites someone to commit a crime

income ['ɪnkʌm] *noun* money which a person receives as salary, dividend or interest; **income support** = financial help given by the state to families with low incomes; **income tax** = tax on a person's income

incoming [ɪn'kʌmɪŋ] *adjective* **(a)** **incoming mail** = mail which comes into an office **(b)** which has recently been elected or appointed; **the incoming government** *or* **Minister** = the new government, the Minister who has just been appointed and is about to start working; *the chairman welcomed the incoming committee; the incoming cabinet was sworn in at the Presidential palace*

incompetent [ɪn'kɒmpɪtənt] *adjective* **(a)** who cannot work well, who is not able to do something; *the sales manager is quite incompetent; the company has an incompetent sales director* **(b)** not legally able to do something; *he is incompetent to sign the contract*

incompetency [ɪn'kɒmpɪtənsi] *noun* state of not being legally competent to do something

incorporate [ɪn'kɔːpəreɪt] *verb* **(a)** to bring something in to form part of a main group, to make a document part of another document; *income from the 1998 acquisition is incorporated into the accounts*; *the list of markets is incorporated into the main contract* **(b)** to form a registered company; *a company incorporated in the USA*; *an incorporated company*; *J. Doe Inc*

incorporation [ɪnkɔːpəˈreɪʃn] *noun* act of incorporating a company; **articles of incorporation** = document which regulates the way in which a company's affairs are managed; **certificate of incorporation** = certificate issued by the Registrar of Companies showing that a company has been officially incorporated and the date at which it came into existence

incorporeal [ɪnkɔːˈpɔːriəl] *adjective* which is not physical, which cannot be touched; **incorporeal chattels** = properties like patents or copyrights; **incorporeal hereditaments** = rights (such as patents or copyrights) which can form part of an estate and be inherited

incorrect [ɪnkəˈrekt] *adjective* wrong, not correct; *the minutes of the meeting were incorrect and had to be changed*

incorrectly [ɪnkəˈrektli] *adverb* wrongly, not correctly; *the extradition papers were incorrectly worded*

incorrigible [ɪnˈkɒrɪdʒəbl] *adjective* (criminal) whose behaviour cannot be corrected

incriminate [ɪnˈkrɪmɪneɪt] *verb* to show that a person has committed a criminal act; *he was incriminated by the recorded message he sent to the victim*

incriminating [ɪnˈkrɪmɪneɪtɪŋ] *adjective* which shows that someone has committed a crime; *incriminating evidence was found in his car*

incumbent [ɪnˈkʌmbənt] **1** *adjective* **it is incumbent upon him** = he has to do this, because it is his duty; *it is incumbent on us to check our facts before making an accusation*; *it is incumbent upon justices to give some warning of their doubts about a case* **2** *noun* person who holds an official position; *there will be no changes*

in the governor's staff while the present incumbent is still in office

incumbrance [ɪnˈkʌmbrəns] = ENCUMBRANCE

incur [ɪnˈkɜː] *verb* to make yourself liable to; **to incur the risk of a penalty** = to make it possible that you risk paying a penalty; **to incur debts** *or* **costs** = to do something which means that you owe money, that you will have to pay costs; **the company has incurred heavy costs to implement the development programme** = the company has had to pay large sums of money (NOTE: **incurring - incurred**)

incuriam [ɪnˈkjuːriæm] *see* PER INCURIAM

indebted [ɪnˈdetɪd] *adjective* owing money to someone; *to be indebted to a property company*

indebtedness [ɪnˈdetɪdnəs] *noun* amount of money owed by someone; **state of indebtedness** = being in debt, owing money

indecent [ɪnˈdiːsənt] *adjective* rude, not decent, which an ordinary person would find shocking; **indecent assault** = crime of assaulting a person together with an indecent act or proposal; **indecent exposure** = offence where a male person shows his sexual organs to a woman

indecency [ɪnˈdiːsənsi] *noun* being indecent; *(of a man)* **to commit an act of gross indecency** = to have unlawful sexual contact with another man or with a child

indefeasible right [ɪndɪˈfiːzəbl ˈraɪt] *noun* right which cannot be made void

indemnification [ɪndemnɪfɪˈkeɪʃn] *noun* payment for damage

indemnify [ɪnˈdemnɪfaɪ] *verb* to pay for damage suffered; *to indemnify someone for a loss*

indemnity [ɪnˈdemnəti] *noun* (i) statement of liability to pay compensation for a loss or for a wrong in a transaction to which you are a party; (ii) *(in general)* compensation for a loss or a wrong (iii) *(in* *civil cases)* right of someone to recover from a third party the amount which he himself is liable to pay; *he had to pay an indemnity of £100*; **letter of indemnity** = letter promising payment of compensation for a loss

> COMMENT: the person making an indemnity is primarily liable and can be sued by the person with whom he makes the transaction. Compare GUARANTEE

indenture [ɪnˈdentʃə] **1** *noun* deed made between two or more parties; **indentures** *or* **articles of indenture** = contract by which a trainee craftsman works for a master for some years to learn a trade **2** *verb* to contract with a trainee who will work for some years to learn a trade; *he was indentured to a builder*

independence [ɪndɪˈpendəns] *noun* **(a)** freedom from rule, control or influence of others; *the colony struggled to achieve independence*; *Britain granted her colonies independence in the years after the Second World War*; *an independence movement grew in the colony*; the **American War of Independence** = war by the American colonies against Britain (1775-1786) by which the colonies became independent; **Declaration of Independence** = document written by Thomas Jefferson (1776) by which the former American colonies declared their independence from Britain; **Unilateral Declaration of Independence (UDI)** = act whereby a colony declares itself independent without the agreement of the colonial power **(b)** time when a country became independent; *the ten years since independence have seen many changes*; **Independence Day** = day when a country celebrates its independence (July 4th in the USA)

independent [ɪndɪˈpendənt] *adjective* free, not controlled by anyone; **independent company** = company which is not controlled by another company; **independent contractor** = person or company working independently, which is told what to do by a person or company

giving a contract, but not how to do the work; *(in the EU)* **independent rights** = rights of employed people, students, retired people and people with private incomes, to enter, live and work in a EU country; *compare* DEPENDENT RIGHTS; **independent trader** *or* **independent shop** = shop which is owned by an individual proprietor, not by a chain

indicator [ˈɪndɪkeɪtə] *noun* thing which indicates; **government economic indicators** = figures which show how the country's economy is going to perform in the short or long term

indict [ɪnˈdaɪt] *verb* to charge (someone) with a crime; *he was indicted for murder*

indictable offence [ɪnˈdaɪtəbl əˈfens] *noun* formerly, a serious offence which could be tried in the Crown Court (NOTE: now called **notifiable offence**)

indictment [ɪnˈdaɪtmənt] *noun* written statement of the details of the crime with which someone is charged in the Crown Court; *the clerk to the justices read out the indictment*; **bill of indictment** = (i) draft of an indictment which is examined by the court and, when signed, becomes an indictment; (ii) *US* list of charges given to a grand jury, asking them to indict the accused

indorse [ɪnˈdɔːs] *verb* to write something on the back of a document, especially to note details of a claimant's claim on a writ; *the writ was indorsed with details of the claimant's claim*; *he indorsed the cheque over to his solicitor* = he signed the cheque on the back so as to make it payable to his solicitor; *see also* ENDORSE

indorsement [ɪnˈdɔːsmənt] *noun* writing notes on a document, especially writing the details of a claimant's claim on a writ; **special indorsement** = full details of a claim involving money, land or goods which a claimant is trying to recover; *see also* ENDORSEMENT

induce [ɪnˈdjuːs] *verb* to help persuade someone to do something; *he was induced* *to steal the plans by an offer of a large amount of money*

inducement [ɪnˈdjuːsmənt] *noun* thing which helps to persuade someone to do something; *they offered him a company car as an inducement to stay*; **inducement to break contract** = tort of persuading someone to break a contract he has entered into

industrial [ɪnˈdʌstriəl] *adjective* relating to work; **industrial dispute** = argument between management and workers; **industrial property** = intangible property owned by a company such as patents, trademarks, company names, etc.; **industrial tribunal** = court which decides in disputes between employers and employees or trade unions

in esse [ˈɪn ˈeseɪ] *Latin phrase meaning* 'in being'

infant [ˈɪnfənt] *noun* person aged less than eighteen years (NOTE: this is an old term, now replaced by **minor**)

infanticide [ɪnˈfæntisaɪd] *noun* notifiable offence of killing a child, especially the killing of a child by its mother before it is twelve months old

infer [ɪnˈfɜː] *verb* to reach an opinion about something; *he inferred from the letter that the accused knew the murder victim*; *counsel inferred that the witness had not been present at the time of the accident*

inferior [ɪnˈfɪəriə] *adjective* not as good as others; *inferior products or products of inferior quality*; **inferior court** = lower court (such as a magistrates' court or County Court)

in flagrante delicto [ɪn fləˈɡrænti dɪˈlɪktəʊ] *Latin phrase meaning* '(caught) in the act of committing a crime'

inflation [ɪnˈfleɪʃn] *noun* situation where prices rise to keep up with production costs; **rate of inflation** *or* **inflation rate** = percentage increase in prices over the period of one year

influence [ˈɪnfluəns] **1** *noun* effect which is had on someone or something; *he was charged with driving under the influence of alcohol*; *we are suffering from the influence of a high exchange rate*; **undue influence** = pressure put on someone which prevents that person from acting independently **2** *verb* to have an effect on someone or something; *the court was influenced in its decision by the youth of the accused*; *the price of oil has influenced the price of industrial goods*; *he was accused of trying to influence the magistrates*

influence peddling [ˈɪnfluəns ˈpedlɪŋ] *noun* offering to use one's influence, especially political power, for payment, to help a person or group achieve something

inform [ɪnˈfɔːm] *verb* **(a)** to tell someone officially; *I regret to inform you that your tender was not acceptable*; *we are pleased to inform you that your offer has been accepted*; *we have been informed by the Department of Trade that new tariffs are coming into force* **(b)** to inform on someone = to tell the police that someone has committed a crime

informant [ɪnˈfɔːmənt] *noun* person who informs, who gives information to someone; *is your informant reliable?*

in forma pauperis [ˈɪn ˈfɔːmə ˈpɔːpərɪs] *Latin phrase meaning* 'as a poor person'

COMMENT: a term formerly used to allow a person who could prove that he had little money to bring an action even if he could not pay the costs of the case; now replaced by Legal Aid

information [ɪnfəˈmeɪʃn] *noun* **(a)** details which explain something; *have you any information on or about deposit accounts?*; *I enclose this leaflet for your information*; *to disclose a piece of information*; *to answer a request for information*; *for further information, please write to Department 27*; **disclosure of confidential information** = telling someone information which should be secret; **freedom of information** = making government information available to ordinary people, making official records about private people available to each person concerned **(b)** details of a crime drawn up by the clerk and given to a magistrate; **laying (an) information** = starting criminal proceedings in a magistrates' court by informing the magistrate of the offence; *the justices were ordered to rehear the information* **(c)** **further information** = request made by a party through the court for another party to provide more details which will help clarify the case (the second party may refuse to respond for various reasons) (NOTE: since the introduction of the new Civil Procedure Rules in April 1999, this term has replaced **interrogatories**) **(d)** **information technology** = working with computer data; **information retrieval** = storing and then finding data in a computer **(e)** **information bureau** *or* **information office** = office which gives information to tourists or visitors; **information officer** = person whose job is to give information about a company, an organization or a government department to the public; person whose job is to give information to other departments in the same organization (NOTE: no plural: to indicate one item use **a piece of information**)

informed [ɪnˈfɔːmd] *adjective* having the latest information; *informed opinion thinks that he will lose the appeal*; **informed consent** = agreement given by a patient or the guardians of a patient after they have been given all the necessary information, that an operation can be carried out

informer [ɪnˈfɔːmə] *noun* person who gives information to the police about a crime or about criminals

infringe [ɪnˈfrɪndʒ] *verb* to break a law or a right; **to infringe a copyright** = to copy a copyright text illegally; **to infringe a patent** = to make a product which works in the same way as a patented product and not pay a royalty to the patent holder; **infringing goods** = goods which are made in infringement of a copyright or patent

infringement [ɪnˈfrɪndʒmənt] *noun* breaking a law or a right; **infringement of copyright** *or* **copyright infringement** = act of illegally copying a work which is in copyright; **infringement of patent** *or* **patent infringement** = act of illegally using, making or selling an invention which is patented without the permission of the patent holder

infringer [ɪnˈfrɪndʒə] *noun* person who infringes a right, such as a copyright; *a copyright infringer*

inherit [ɪnˈherɪt] *verb* to succeed to an estate in realty; to acquire something from a person who has died; *when her father died she inherited the shop*; *he inherited £10,000 from his grandfather*

inheritance [ɪnˈherɪtəns] *noun* property which is received from a dead person

inheritor [ɪnˈherɪtə] *noun* person who receives something from a person who has died

iniquity [ɪˈnɪkwəti] *noun* doing wrong

initial [ɪˈnɪʃəl] **1** *adjective* first, starting; **initial capital** = capital which is used to start a business; *he started the business with an initial expenditure or initial investment of £500* **2** *noun* **initials** = first letters of the words in a name; *what do the initials QC stand for?*; *the chairman wrote his initials by each alteration in the contract he was signing* **3** *verb* to write your initials on a document to show you have read it and approved; *to initial an amendment to a contract*; *please initial the agreement at the place marked with an X*

initiative [ɪˈnɪʃətɪv] *noun* **(a)** decision to start doing something; *the president took the initiative in asking the rebel leader to come for a meeting*; *the minister has proposed several initiatives to try to restart the deadlocked negotiations*; *(in the EU)* **legislative initiative** = the power to propose legislation; *Member States of the EU have the right of initiative in all legal and internal matters* **(b)** *(in Switzerland and the USA)* move by a group of citizens to propose that something should be decided by a referendum

initio [ı'nıʃiəʊ] *see* AB INITIO

injunction [ın'dʒʌŋkʃn] *noun* court order compelling someone to stop doing something, or not to do something; *he got an injunction preventing the company from selling his car*; *the company applied for an injunction to stop their competitor from marketing a similar product*; **interim injunction** = injunction which prevents someone from doing something until a certain date; **interlocutory** *or* **temporary injunction** = injunction which is granted until a case comes to court; **prohibitory injunction** = injunction which prevents someone from doing an illegal act; *see also* FREEZING INJUNCTION

injure ['ındʒə] *verb* to hurt (someone); *two workers were injured in the fire*

injured party ['ındʒəd 'pɑːti] *noun* party in a court case which has been harmed by another party

injurious [ın'dʒʊəriəs] *adjective* which can cause an injury; **injurious falsehood** = tort of making a wrong statement about someone so as to affect his reputation

injury ['ındʒəri] *noun* **(a)** violation of a person's rights **(b)** hurt caused to a person; **injury benefit** = money paid to a worker who has been hurt at work; **industrial injuries** = injuries caused to workers at work; **personal injury** = injury to the body suffered by the victim of an accident

injustice [ın'dʒʌstıs] *noun* lack of justice

inland ['ınlænd] *adjective* **(a)** inside a country; **inland postage** = postage for a letter to another part of the country; **inland freight charges** = charges for carrying goods from one part of the country to another **(b)** **the Inland Revenue** = British government department dealing with income tax

in loco parentis ['ın 'ləʊkəʊ pə'rentıs] *Latin phrase meaning* 'in the place of a parent'; *the court is acting in loco parentis*

Inn [ın] *noun* **the Inns of Court** = four societies in London, of which the members are lawyers and are called to the bar as barristers

COMMENT: the four societies are **Gray's Inn, Lincoln's Inn, Inner Temple and Middle Temple**

Inner Temple ['ınə 'templ] *see* INN

innocence ['ınəsəns] *noun* being innocent, not being guilty; *he tried to establish his innocence*

innocent ['ınəsənt] *adjective* not guilty of a crime; *the accused was found to be innocent*; *in English law, the accused is presumed to be innocent until he is proved to be guilty*

innuendo [ınjʊ'endəʊ] *noun* spoken words which are defamatory because they have a double meaning; *an apparently innocent statement may be defamatory if it contains an innuendo*

in personam ['ın pɜː'səʊnæm] *Latin phrase meaning* 'against a person'; **action in personam** = action against an individual person; *compare* IN REM

in private ['ın 'praıvət] *adverb* with no members of the public permitted to be present; *the case was heard in private* (NOTE: since the introduction of the new Civil Procedure Rules in April 1999, this term has replaced **in camera**)

input ['ınpʊt] **1** *noun* material or information put into something; **input tax** = VAT paid on goods or services bought **2** *verb* to put information into a computer (NOTE: **inputting - inputted**)

inquest ['ıŋkwest] *noun* inquiry (by a coroner) into a death

COMMENT: an inquest has to take place where death is violent or unexpected, where death could be murder or manslaughter, where a prisoner dies and when police are involved

inquire [ıŋ'kwaıə] *verb* to ask questions about something; to conduct an official investigation into something; *the police are inquiring into his background* (NOTE: also spelled **enquire**)

inquiry [ɪŋˈkaaɪəri] *noun* question about something; *the police are making inquiries into the whereabouts of the stolen car*; **preliminary inquiries =** investigation by the solicitor for the purchaser addressed to the vendor's solicitor concerning the vendor's title to the property for which the purchaser has made an offer; **to help police with their inquiries =** to be taken to the police station for questioning (NOTE: also spelled **enquiry**)

> COMMENT: if the police want someone to help them with their inquiries and he refuses, they can arrest him and force him to go to the police station. Anyone who helps the police with their inquiries voluntarily has the right to leave the police station when he wants (unless the police arrest him)

inquisitorial procedure

[ɪnkwɪzəˈtɔːriəl prəˈsiːdʒə] *noun* procedure in countries where Roman law is applied, where an examining magistrate has the duty to investigate the case and produce the evidence; *compare* ACCUSATORIAL

inquorate [ɪnˈkwɔːreɪt] *adjective* without a quorum; *the meeting was declared inquorate and had to be abandoned*

in re [ˈɪn ˈreɪ] *Latin phrase meaning* 'concerning' or 'in the case of'

in rem [ˈɪn ˈrem] *Latin phrase meaning* 'against a thing'; **action in rem =** action against a property, or all persons, as opposed to a single person; *see* IN PERSONAM

insane [ɪnˈseɪn] *adjective* mad, suffering from a state of mind which makes it impossible for you to know that you are doing wrong, and so you cannot be held responsible for your actions

insanity [ɪnˈsænəti] *noun* being mad, not being sane

> COMMENT: where an accused is found to be insane, a verdict of 'not guilty by reason of insanity' is returned and the accused is ordered to be detained at Her Majesty's pleasure

inside [ɪnˈsaɪd] *adjective & adverb* **(a)** in, especially in a company's office or building; **inside job =** crime which has been committed on a company's property by one of the employees of the company; **inside worker =** worker who works in the office or factory (not in the open air, not a salesman) **(b)** *(slang)* in prison; *he spent six months inside in 1996*

insider [ɪnˈsaɪdə] *noun* person who works in an organization and therefore knows its secrets; **insider dealing** *or* **insider trading =** illegal buying or selling of shares by staff of a company or other persons who have secret information about the company's plans

insolvency [ɪnˈsɒlvənsi] *noun* not being able to pay debts; **the company was in a state of insolvency =** it could not pay its debts

insolvent [ɪnˈsɒlvənt] *adjective* not able to pay debts; *the company was declared insolvent* (NOTE: **insolvent** and **insolvency** are general terms, but are usually applied to companies; individuals or partners are usually described as **bankrupt** once they have been declared so by a court)

inspect [ɪnˈspekt] *verb* to examine in detail; *to inspect a machine or a prison*; *to inspect the accounts of a company*; **to inspect products for defects =** to look at products in detail to see if they have any defects

inspection [ɪnˈspekʃn] *noun* **(a)** close examination of something, especially the examination of the site of a crime by the judge and jury; *to make an inspection or to carry out an inspection of a machine or a new prison*; *inspection of a product for defects*; **to carry out a tour of inspection =** to visit various places, offices or factories to inspect them; **inspection stamp =** stamp placed on something to show it has been inspected **(b)** the examination of documents after disclosure; *inspection was ordered to take place seven days after disclosure;* to issue an inspection order = to order a defendant to allow a claimant to inspect documents, where the claimant thinks the defendant has not disclosed all relevant documents

inspector [ɪnˈspektə] *noun* **(a)** official who inspects; **inspector of factories** *or* **factory inspector** = government official who inspects factories to see if they are safely run; **the Chief Inspector of Prisons** = government official who is the head of the Inspectorate of Prisons, and whose job is to inspect prisons to see that they are being run correctly and efficiently; **inspector of taxes** *or* **tax inspector** = official of the Inland Revenue who examines tax returns and decides how much tax people should pay; **inspector of weights and measures** = government official who inspects weighing machines and goods sold in shops to see if the quantities and weights are correct **(b)** rank in the police force above a sergeant and below chief inspector; **chief inspector** = rank in the police force above inspector

inspectorate [ɪnˈspektərət] *noun* all inspectors; **the factory inspectorate** = all inspectors of factories; **the Inspectorate of Prisons** *or* **the Prisons Inspectorate** = section of the Prison Service which deals with the inspection of prisons to see that they are being run correctly and efficiently

inst [ɪnst] = INSTANT

instalment *US* installment

[ɪnˈstɔːlmənt] *noun* payment of part of the total purchase price, of part of the sum due; *he paid off his creditors in twelve instalments*; *you pay £25 down and twelve monthly instalments of £20*

installment plan [ɪnˈstɔːlmənt ˈplæn] *noun US* system of buying something by paying a sum regularly each month until the purchase is completed (NOTE: British English is **hire purchase**)

instance [ˈɪnstəns] *noun* **(a)** particular example or case; *in this instance we will*

overlook the delay **(b)** *see also* COURT OF FIRST INSTANCE

instant [ˈɪnstənt] *adjective* **(a)** at this point; **our letter of the 6th instant** *or* **of the 6th inst.** = our letter of the 6th of this current month; **the instant case** = the case now being considered by the court **(b)** immediately available; *instant credit*

in statu quo [ɪn ˈstætuː ˈkwəʊ] *Latin phrase meaning* 'in the present state'

institute [ˈɪnstɪtjuːt] **1** *noun* official organization; **research institute** = organization set up to do research **2** *verb* to start; *to institute proceedings against someone*

institution [ɪnstɪˈtjuːʃn] *noun* **(a)** organization or society set up for a particular purpose; **financial institution** = bank, investment trust or insurance company whose work involves lending or investing large sums of money; *(in the EU)* **the Community institutions** = the four bodies which legally form the European Community - the Commission, the Council, the European Parliament and the European Court of Justice **(b)** building for a special purpose; **mental institution** = special hospital for patients suffering from mental disorders; **penal institution** = place (such as a prison) where convicted criminals are kept; **Young Offender Institution** = centre where young offenders are sent for training if they have committed crimes which would normally be punishable by a prison sentence

institutional [ɪnstɪˈtjuːʃnl] *adjective* referring to a financial institution; **institutional buying** *or* **selling** = buying or selling shares by financial institutions; **institutional investors** = financial institutions who invest money in securities

institutionalized [ɪnstɪˈtjuːʃnlaɪzd] *noun* **(a)** *(person)* who has been put in a mental institution **(b)** *(position)* which has become an institution; *the office of US President has become institutionalized*

instruct [ɪnˈstrʌkt] *verb* **(a)** to give an order to someone; **to instruct someone to**

do something = to tell someone officially to do something; *he instructed the credit controller to take action* **(b) to instruct a solicitor** = to give information to a solicitor and to ask him to start legal proceedings on your behalf; *(of a solicitor)* **to instruct a barrister** = to give a barrister all the details of a case which he will plead in court

instructions [ɪnˈstrʌkʃnz] *plural noun* **(a)** order which tells what should be done or how something is to be used; *he gave instructions to his stockbroker to sell the shares immediately*; **to await instructions** = to wait for someone to tell you what to do; **to issue instructions** = to tell everyone what to do; **in accordance with** *or* **according to instructions** = as the instructions show; **failing instructions to the contrary** = unless someone tells you to do the opposite; **forwarding instructions** *or* **shipping instructions** = details of how goods are to be shipped and delivered **(b)** details of a case given by a client to a solicitor, or by a solicitor to a barrister **(c)** *US* **instructions to the jury** = speech by a judge at the end of a trial where he reviews all the evidence and arguments and notes important points of law for the benefit of the jury (NOTE: British English is **summing up**)

instructor [ɪnˈstrʌktə] *noun* person who shows how something is to be done

instrument [ˈɪnstrəmənt] *noun* **(a)** tool, piece of equipment; *the technical staff have instruments to measure the output of electricity* **(b)** legal document; **inchoate instrument** = document which is not complete; **negotiable instrument** = document (such as a bill of exchange or a cheque) which can be exchanged for cash; **statutory instrument (SI)** = order (which has the force of law) made under authority granted to a minister by an Act of Parliament

insult [ɪnˈsʌlt] *verb* to say rude things about someone; **insulting behaviour** = offence of acting (shouting or making rude signs) in a way which shows that you are insulting someone

insurable [ɪnˈʃʊərəbl] *adjective* which can be insured; **insurable interest** = interest which a person taking out an insurance policy must have in what is being insured

insurance [ɪnˈʃʊərəns] *noun* **(a)** agreement that in return for regular small payments, a company will pay compensation for loss, damage, injury or death; **to take out an insurance against fire** = to pay a premium, so that if a fire happens, compensation will be paid **(b)** **accident insurance** = insurance which will pay if an accident takes place; **car insurance** *or* **motor insurance** = insuring a car, the driver and passengers in case of accident; **legal expenses insurance** = insurance which will pay the costs of a court case; **life insurance** = situation which pays a sum of money when someone dies; **medical insurance** = insurance which pays the cost of medical treatment, especially when travelling abroad; **National Insurance** = state insurance which pays for medical care, hospitals, unemployment benefits, etc.; **term insurance** = life assurance which covers a person's life for a fixed period of time; **third-party insurance** = insurance which pays compensation if someone who is not the insured person incurs loss or injury; **whole-life insurance** = insurance where the insured person pays premiums for all his life and the insurance company pays a sum when he dies (NOTE: for life insurance, British English prefers to use **assurance**)

insure [ɪnˈʃʊə] *verb* to have a contract with a company where, if regular small payments are made, the company will pay compensation for loss, damage, injury or death; *to insure a house against fire*; *he was insured for £100,000*; *to insure baggage against loss*; *to insure against bad weather*; *to insure against loss of earnings*; **the life insured** = the person whose life is covered by a life assurance; **the sum insured** = the largest amount of money that an insurer will pay under an insurance (NOTE: for life insurance, British English prefers to use **assure**)

insurer [ɪnˈʃʊərə] *noun* company which insures (NOTE: for life insurance, British English prefers to use **assurer)**

intangible [ɪnˈtændʒəbl] *adjective* which cannot be touched; **intangible assets** = assets which have a value, but which cannot be seen (such as goodwill, a patent or a trademark)

integration [ɪntɪˈɡreɪʃn] *noun (in the EU)* **negative integration** = the removal of trade barriers within the EU, according to the interpretation of legislation by the ECJ

integrity [ɪnˈtegrəti] *noun* original state, not being adapted or changed in any way; *the electronic signature confirms the integrity of the document*

intellectual [ɪntəˈlektʃuəl] *adjective* belonging to the mind; **intellectual property** = ownership of something (a copyright, patent or design) which is intangible

intelligible [ɪnˈtelɪdʒəbl] *adjective* which can be understood; *a key is required to make an encrypted message intelligible*

intend [ɪnˈtend] *verb* to plan, to want to do something; *the company intends to sue for damages*; *we intend to offer jobs to 250 unemployed young people*; **intended murder** = murder which was planned in advance

intent [ɪnˈtent] *noun* what is planned; **letter of intent** = letter which states what someone intends to do if a certain thing takes place; *see also* LOITERING, WOUND

intention [ɪnˈtenʃn] *noun* **(a)** wanting or planning to do something; *he was accused of perjury with the intention of incriminating his employer* **(b)** knowing that something will happen as the result of an action **(c)** meaning of the words in a document such as a will (which may not be the same as what the maker of the document had actually written)

COMMENT: intention to create a legal relationship is one of the essential elements of a contract

intentional [ɪnˈtenʃnl] *adjective* which is intended; *an act of intentional cruelty*

intentionally [ɪnˈtenʃnəli] *adverb* on purpose, as intended; *he intentionally altered the date on the contract*

inter- [ˈɪntə] *prefix* between; **inter-bank loan** = loan from one bank to another; **the inter-city rail services are good** = train services between cities are good; **inter-company dealings** = dealings between two companies in the same group; **inter-company comparisons** = comparing the results of one company with those of another in the same product area

inter alia [ˈɪntə ˈeɪliə] *Latin phrase* meaning 'among other things'

intercept [ɪntəˈsept] *verb* to stop something as it is passing; *we have intercepted a message from one of the enemy agents in London*

interception [ɪntəˈsepʃn] *noun* action of intercepting a message

intercourse [ˈɪntəkɔːs] *noun* **sexual intercourse** = sexual act between man and woman; *sexual intercourse with a girl under sixteen is an offence*

interdict [ˈɪntədɪkt] *noun (in Scotland)* ban, written court order, telling someone not to do something

interest [ˈɪntrəst] **1** *noun* **(a)** special attention; *the managing director takes no interest in the staff club*; *the police showed a lot of interest in the abandoned car*; *see also* PUBLIC INTEREST **(b)** payment made by a borrower for the use of money, calculated as a percentage of the capital borrowed; **simple interest** = interest calculated on the capital only, and not added to it; **compound interest** = interest which is added to the capital and then itself earns interest; **accrued interest** = interest which is accumulating and is due for payment at a later date; **back interest** = interest which has not yet been paid; **fixed interest** = interest which is paid at a set rate **(c)** money paid as income on investments or loans; *the bank pays 10% interest on deposits*; *to receive interest at 5%*; *deposit* *which yields or gives or produces or bears 5% interest*; *account which earns interest at 10% or which earns 10% interest*; **interest-bearing deposits** = deposits which produce interest **(d)** percentage to be paid for borrowing; **interest charges** = cost of paying interest; **interest rate** *or* **rate of interest** = percentage charge for borrowing money; **interest-free credit** *or* **loan** = credit or loan where no interest is paid by the borrower; *the company gives its staff interest-free loans* **(e)** right or title to a property, money invested in a company or financial share in, and part control over, a company; **beneficial interest** = (i) interest of the beneficiary of a property or trust, which allows someone to occupy or receive rent from a property, while the property is owned by a trustee; (ii) situation where someone has an interest in shares even though the shares may be held in the name of another person; **conflict of interest(s)** = situation where a person may profit personally from decisions which he takes in his official capacity, may not be able to act properly because of some other person or matter with which he is connected; **he has a controlling interest in the company** = he owns more than 50% of the shares and so can direct how the company is run; **life interest** = situation where someone benefits from a property as long as he or she is alive; **majority interest** *or* **minority interest** = situation where someone owns a majority *or* a minority of shares in a company; *he has a majority interest in a supermarket chain*; **to acquire a substantial interest in the company** = to buy a large number of shares in a company; **to declare** *or* **disclose an interest** = to state in public that you own shares in a company which is being investigated, or that you are connected with someone who may benefit from your contacts **2** *verb* **(a)** to attract someone's attention; *he tried to interest several companies in his new invention*; **interested in** = paying attention to; *the managing director is interested only in increasing profitability* **(b)** **interested party** = person or company with a financial interest in a company

interfere [ɪntə'fɪə] *verb* to get involved, to try to change something which is not your concern; **to interfere with witnesses** = to try to get in touch with witnesses to influence their evidence

interference with vehicles

[ɪntə'fɪərəns wɪð 'viːɪklz] *noun* offence, where someone interferes with a vehicle with the intention of stealing it, or part of it, or of stealing its contents

interim ['ɪntrɪm] *adjective* temporary, not final; **interim dividend** = dividend paid at the end of a half-year; **interim injunction** = injunction which prevents someone from doing something until a certain date; **interim order** = order given which has effect while a case is still being heard; **interim payment** = part payment of a dividend or of money owed; **interim relief** = INTERIM REMEDY; **interim report** = (i) report (from a commission) which is not final; (ii) financial report given at the end of a half-year; **in the interim** = meanwhile, for the time being

interim remedy ['ɪntrɪm 'remədi] *noun* action by a court to grant relief to a party while a claim is being processed, and even after judgment has been given

COMMENT: interim remedies include interim injunctions, freezing injunctions, search orders, inspection of property, interim payments, etc.

interior [ɪn'tɪərɪə] *noun* what is inside; **Ministry of the Interior** *or* **Interior Ministry** = government department dealing with law and order, usually including the police

COMMENT: in the UK, this ministry is called the Home Office

interlocutory [ɪntə'lɒkjʊtri] *adjective* temporary, provisional; happening at a court hearing which takes place before full trial; **interlocutory injunction** = injunction which is granted for the period until a case comes to court; **interlocutory judgment** = judgment given during the course of an action before full trial (as opposed to a final judgment);

interlocutory matter = subsidiary dispute which is dealt with before full trial; **interlocutory proceedings** = court hearings that take place before the full trial

intermeddle [ɪntəˈmedl] *verb* to deal in someone's affairs; *if an executor pays the debts of an estate, this can be considered intermeddling, and thus is acceptance of the office of executor*

intermediary [ɪntəˈmiːdiəri] *noun* person who is the link between parties who do not agree or who are negotiating; *he refused to act as an intermediary between the two directors*

intern [ɪnˈtɜːn] *verb* to put (someone) in prison or in a camp without trial (usually for political reasons)

internal [ɪnˈtɜːnəl] *adjective* referring to the inside; **an internal call** = telephone call from one office to another in a building; **an internal memo** = memo from one department in an organization to another; **internal affairs of a country** = way in which a country deals with its own citizens; *it is not usual for one country to criticize the internal affairs of another; US* **Internal Revenue Service (IRS)** = American government department dealing with income tax (NOTE: the British equivalent is the **Inland Revenue**)

international [ɪntəˈnæʃnl] *adjective* working between countries; **International Bar Association** = international lawyers' organization formed to promote international law; **international call** = telephone call to another country; **international law** = laws governing relations between countries

International Court of Justice

[ɪntəˈnæʃnl ˈkɔːt əv ˈdʒʌstɪs] the court of the United Nations, which sits in the Hague, Netherlands

International Labour Organization (ILO)

[ɪntəˈnæʃnl ˈleɪbə ɔːgənaɪˈzeɪʃn] section of the United Nations, an organization which tries to improve working conditions and workers' pay in member countries

internee [ɪntɜːˈniː] *noun* person who is interned

Internet [ˈɪntənet] *noun* international electronic network that provides a vast library of information that is easy to access using the world-wide web, as well as file and data transfer, and electronic mail functions for millions of users round the world; anyone can use the Internet; *see also* CLICK-WRAP, CYBERLAW

internment [ɪnˈtɜːnmənt] *noun* being put in prison or into a camp without trial

inter partes [ˈɪntə ˈpɑːtɪz] *Latin phrase meaning* 'between the parties': case heard where both parties are represented; *the court's opinion was that the case should be heard inter partes as soon as possible*; *see also* EX PARTE

interpleader [ɪntəˈpliːdə] *noun* court action started by a person who has property which is not his, but which is claimed by two or more people, or by a person who may be sued by two different parties (NOTE: do not confuse with the American term **impleader**)

Interpol [ˈɪntəpɒl] *noun* international police organization whereby the member countries co-operate in solving crimes; *they warned Interpol that the criminals might be disguised as women* (NOTE: used without **the**)

interpret [ɪnˈtɜːprət] *verb* **(a)** to say what you think a law or precedent means; *the role of the ECJ is to interpret a law, while the role of the national court is to apply it*; *courts in Member States cannot give authoritative rulings on how community law should be interpreted* **(b)** to translate what someone has said into another language; *my assistant knows Greek, so he will interpret for us*

interpretation [ɪntɜːprəˈteɪʃn] *noun* what someone thinks is the meaning of a law or precedent; *interpretation of the Treaty has been entrusted to the European Court of Justice*; **to put an interpretation on something** = to make something have a different meaning; *his* *ruling puts quite a different interpretation on the responsibility of trustees*; **Interpretation Act** = Act of Parliament which rules how words used in other Acts of Parliament are to be understood; **interpretation clause** = clause in a contract stating the meaning to be given to terms in the contract

interpreter [ɪnˈtɜːprətə] *noun* person who translates what someone has said into another language; *my secretary will act as interpreter*; *the witness could not speak English and the court had to appoint an interpreter*

interpretive [ɪnˈtɜːprətɪv] *adjective (in the EU)* referring to interpretation; *there is an interpretive obligation on Member States to interpret national laws in a way which accords with the aims and objectives of the directives of the EU*

interregnum [ɪntəˈregnəm] *noun* period between the death (or deposition) of one king and accession of the next

interrogate [ɪnˈterəgeɪt] *verb* to ask questions in a severe manner; *the prisoners were interrogated for three hours*

interrogation [ɪnterəˈgeɪʃn] *noun* severe questioning; *he confessed to the crime during his interrogation*; *under interrogation, she gave the names of her accomplices*

interrogator [ɪnˈterəgeɪtə] *noun* person who interrogates

interrogatories [ɪntəˈrɒgətriz] *plural noun* questions put in writing during a civil action by one side to the other, and which have to be answered on oath (NOTE: since the introduction of the new Civil Procedure Rules in April 1999, this term has been replaced by **further information**)

in terrorem [ˈɪn teˈrɔːrəm] *Latin phrase* meaning 'in order to cause terror': used when a threat is implied in a contract (in which case the contract is invalid)

interrupt [ɪntəˈrʌpt] *verb* to try to speak or to shout when someone else is talking

COMMENT: in the House of Commons, an MP is allowed to interrupt another MP only if he wants to ask the member who is speaking to explain something or to raise a point of order

intervene [ɪntəˈviːn] *verb* **(a)** to come between people or things so as to make a change; **to intervene in a dispute** = to try to settle a dispute **(b)** to become a party to an action

intervener [ɪntəˈviːnə] *noun* person who intervenes in an action to which he or she was not originally a party

intervention [ɪntəˈvenʃn] *noun* **(a)** acting to make a change; *the government's intervention in the foreign exchange markets*; *the central bank's intervention in the banking crisis*; *the Association's intervention in the labour dispute*; *(in the EU)* **intervention price** = price at which the EC will buy farm produce which farmers cannot sell, in order to store it **(b)** acting to interfere in another country's affairs; *the Minister of Foreign Affairs said the President's remarks were an intervention in the domestic affairs of his country*

interview [ˈɪntəvjuː] *noun* meeting between a suspect and one or more police officers, who ask him or her questions

COMMENT: suspects must be cautioned before an interview takes place. The interview should be recorded and the record must be shown to the suspect at the end of the interview. If there is any possibility that the police have threatened the suspect so as to get a confession, that confession will not be admitted in court

interview room [ˈɪntəvjuː ˈruːm] *noun* room where a person is asked questions or is interviewed

inter vivos [ˈɪntə ˈvaɪvəʊs] *Latin phrase* meaning 'among living people'; **gift inter vivos** = gift given by a living person to another living person

COMMENT: an inter vivos transfer of property can be used as a way of passing property to someone without using a will; it does not necessarily take effect when someone dies, but can be put into effect as soon as it is signed

intestacy [ɪn'testəsi] *noun* dying without having made a will; **total intestacy** = state where a person has not made a will, or where a previous will has been revoked; **partial intestacy** = state where a person dies leaving a will which does not cover all his estate

intestate [ɪn'testeɪt] *adjective* **to die intestate** = to die without having made a will; **intestate succession** = rules which apply when someone dies without having made a will

COMMENT: when someone dies intestate, the property automatically goes to the surviving partner, unless there are children

intimidate [ɪn'tɪmɪdeɪt] *verb* to frighten someone to make him do something or to prevent him from doing something; *the accused was said to have intimidated the witnesses*

intimidation [ɪntɪmɪ'deɪʃn] *noun* act of frightening someone to make him do something or to prevent him from doing something

intoxicated [ɪn'tɒksɪkeɪtɪd] *adjective* drunk, under the effects of alcohol

intoxication [ɪntɒksɪ'keɪʃn] *noun* state of being drunk

in transit ['ɪn 'trænzɪt] *adverb* **goods in transit** = goods being carried from one place to another

intra vires ['ɪntrə 'vaɪriːz] *Latin phrase meaning* 'within the permitted powers'; *the minister's action was ruled to be intra vires*; *see* ULTRA VIRES

intrinsic evidence [ɪn'trɪnzɪk 'evɪdəns] *noun* evidence used to interpret a document which can be found in the document itself; *see also* EXTRINSIC

introduce [ɪntrə'djuːs] *verb* to present, to put forward; *he is introducing a Bill in Parliament to prevent the sale of drugs*; *the prosecution has introduced some new evidence*

introduction [ɪntrə'dʌkʃn] *noun* presenting, putting forward; *the introduction of new evidence into the case*; **introduction of a Bill** = putting forward a Bill for discussion in Parliament

invalid [ɪn'vælɪd] *adjective* not valid, not legal; *permit that is invalid*; *claim which has been declared invalid*; *national courts cannot find Community legislation to be invalid*

invalidate [ɪn'vælɪdeɪt] *verb* to make something invalid; *because the company has been taken over, the contract has been invalidated*

invalidation [ɪnvælɪ'deɪʃn] *noun* making invalid

invalidity [ɪnvə'lɪdəti] *noun* being invalid; *the invalidity of the contract*

invasion of privacy [ɪn'veɪʒn əv 'prɪvəsi] *noun* action (such as being followed by newspaper reporters) which does not allow someone to live a normal private life

inventory ['ɪnvəntri] **1** *noun* **(a)** list of the contents of a house for sale, of an office for rent, or the estate of a deceased person, etc. **(b)** *US* quantity of goods for sale; **inventory control** = making sure that enough inventory is kept in a warehouse, and noting quantities and movements of goods **2** *verb* to make a list of the contents of a property

invest [ɪn'vest] *verb* to put money somewhere (in a bank or by buying shares) where it should increase in value; *he invested all his money in a shop*; *she was advised to invest in real estate*

investigate [ɪn'vestɪgeɪt] *verb* to examine something which may be wrong

investigation [ɪnvestɪˈgeɪʃn] *noun* examination to find out what is wrong; *to conduct an investigation into irregularities in share dealings*; **preliminary investigation** = examining of the details of a case by a magistrate who then has to decide if the case should be committed to a higher court for trial

investigator [ɪnˈvestɪgeɪtə] *noun* person who investigates; *a government investigator*

investment [ɪnˈvesmənt] *noun* **(a)** money which has been invested; *he lost all his money in risky investments on the Stock Exchange* **(b)** placing of money so that it will increase in value and produce an income (either in an asset, such as a building, or by purchasing shares, placing money on deposit, etc.); *US* **investment bank** = bank which deals with the underwriting of new issues, and advises corporations on their financial affairs (the British equivalent is an 'issuing house'); **investment company** *or* **investment trust** = company whose shares can be bought on the Stock Exchange, and whose business is to make money by buying and selling stocks and shares

investor [ɪnˈvestə] *noun* person or company which invests money

invitation [ɪnvɪˈteɪʃn] *noun* asking someone to do something; *to issue an invitation to someone to join the board* or *an invitation to tender for a contract* or *an invitation to subscribe to a new issue*; **invitation to treat** = asking someone to make an offer to buy (as by putting items for sale in a shop window)

invite [ɪnˈvaɪt] *verb* to ask someone to do something; *to invite someone to a meeting*; *to invite someone to join the board*; *to invite shareholders to subscribe to a new issue*; *to invite tenders for a contract*

invitee [ɪnvaɪˈtiː] *noun* person who has accepted an invitation to go into a property

invoice [ˈɪnvɔɪs] *noun* note asking for payment of goods or services supplied

involuntary [ɪnˈvɒləntri] *adjective* **(a)** not done willingly; **involuntary conduct** = conduct beyond a person's control (a defence to a criminal charge); **involuntary manslaughter** = killing someone without having intended to do so **(b)** without wanting to; **involuntary unemployment** = situation where someone is made redundant and loses his job without wanting this to happen; *compare* VOLUNTARY

involuntarily [ɪnˈvɒləntrəli] *adverb* not willingly; *the accused's defence was that he acted involuntarily*

IOU [ˈaɪ ˈəʊ ˈjuː] *noun* (= I OWE YOU) signed document promising that you will pay back money borrowed; *to pay a pile of IOUs*

ipso facto [ˈɪpsəʊ ˈfæktəʊ] *Latin phrase meaning* 'by this very fact' or 'the fact itself shows'; *the writing of the letter was ipso facto an admission of guilt*; *he was found in the vehicle at the time of the accident and ipso facto was deemed to be in charge of it*

ipso jure [ˈɪpsəʊ ˈdʒʊəreɪ] *Latin phrase meaning* 'by the operation of the law itself'

irreconcilable [ɪrekənˈsaɪləbl] *adjective* (differences between husband and wife) which cannot be reconciled, usually leading to a divorce

irrecoverable [ɪrɪˈkʌvrəbl] *adjective* which cannot be recovered; **irrecoverable debt** = debt which will never be paid

irredeemable [ɪrɪˈdiːməbl] *adjective* which cannot be redeemed; **irredeemable bond** = bond which has no date of maturity and which therefore provides interest but can never be redeemed at full value

irredentism [ɪrɪˈdentɪzm] *noun* trying to get back a colony or territory which has been lost to another country or which is felt to belong to the country (because of similar language, culture, etc.)

irredentist [ɪrɪˈdentɪst] *noun* person who wants a territory returned; *the meeting was disrupted by Albanian irredentists*

irregular [ɪ'regjʊlə] *adjective* not correct, not done in the correct way; *irregular documentation*; *this procedure is highly irregular*

irregularity [ɪregjʊ'lærəti] *noun* (a) not being regular, not being on time; *the irregularity of the postal deliveries* (b) **irregularities** = things which are not done in the correct way and which are possibly illegal; *to investigate irregularities in the share dealings*

irrelevant [ɪ'reləvənt] *adjective* (evidence) which is not relevant to a case

irreparable [ɪ'repərəbl] *adjective* which cannot be repaired; *the infringement of the copyright has caused irreparable harm to my client*

irresistible [ɪrɪ'zɪstəbl] *adjective* which cannot be resisted; **irresistible impulse** = impulse to do something which you cannot resist due to insanity; *his irresistible impulse to set fire to shoe shops*

irretrievable [ɪrɪ'triːvəbl] *adjective* which cannot be brought back to its former state; **irretrievable breakdown of a marriage** = situation where the two spouses can no longer live together, where the marriage cannot be saved and therefore divorce proceedings can be started

irrevocable [ɪ'revəkəbl] *adjective* which cannot be changed; which cannot be revoked; **irrevocable acceptance** = acceptance which cannot be withdrawn; **irrevocable letter of credit** = letter of credit which cannot be cancelled or changed (NOTE: the opposite is **revocable**)

IRS ['aɪ 'ɑː 'es] *US* = INTERNAL REVENUE SERVICE

Islam ['ɪzlɑːm] *noun* the religion of the Muslims, based on the teachings of the prophet Muhammad

Islamic [ɪz'læmɪk] *adjective* referring to Islam; **Islamic Law** = law of Muslim countries set out in the Koran and the teachings of the prophet Muhammad; the law itself cannot be changed, but it can be interpreted in different ways

isolation [aɪsə'leɪʃn] *noun* (a) being alone, not being linked by treaties with other countries; **splendid isolation** = policy where a country refuses to link with other countries in treaties (b) **in isolation** = all alone; *the plans for the new bus station should not be seen in isolation - they are part of a major redevelopment scheme for the town centre*

isolationism [aɪsə'leɪʃnɪzm] *noun* political policy where a country refuses to get involved in the affairs of other countries and refuses to sign treaties with them

isolationist [aɪsə'leɪʃnɪst] *noun* person who believes that his country should not get involved in the affairs of other countries, especially should not fight wars to protect other countries

issuance ['ɪʃʊəns] *noun* act of issuing; *upon issuance of the order, the bailiffs seized the property*

issue ['ɪʃuː] **1** *noun* (a) child or children of a parent; *he had issue two sons and one daughter*; *she died without issue*; *they have no issue* (NOTE: in this meaning issue is either singular or plural and is not used with **the**) (b) subject of a dispute; **collateral issue** = issue which arises from a plea in a criminal court; **point at issue** = the point which is being disputed; *the point at issue is the ownership of the property* (c) giving out new shares; **bonus issue** *or* **scrip issue** = new shares given free to shareholders; **issue of new shares** *or* **share issue** = selling new shares in a company to the public; **rights issue** = giving shareholders the right to buy more shares **2** *verb* to put out, to give out; *to issue a letter of credit*; *to issue shares in a new company*; *to issue a writ against someone*; *the government issued a report on London's traffic*; *the Secretary of State issued guidelines for expenditure*; *he issued writs for libel in connection with allegations made in a Sunday newspaper*

issued ['ɪʃuːd] *adjective* **issued capital** = amount of capital which is given out as shares to shareholders; **issued price** = price of shares in a new company when they are offered for sale for the first time

issuing ['ɪʃuːɪŋ] *noun* which organizes an issue of shares; **issuing bank** *or* **issuing house** = bank which organizes the selling of shares in a new company

item ['aɪtəm] *noun* **(a)** thing for sale; **cash items** = goods sold for cash **(b)** piece of information; **extraordinary items** = items in accounts which do not appear each year

and need to be noted; **item of expenditure** = goods or services which have been paid for and appear in the accounts **(c)** point on a list; **we will now take item four on the agenda** = we will now discuss the fourth point on the agenda

itemize ['aɪtəmaɪz] *verb* to make a detailed list of things; *itemizing the sales figures will take about two days*; **itemized account** = detailed record of money paid or owed

Jj

J [dʒeɪ] *abbreviation* Justice; *Smith J said he was not laying down guidelines for sentencing* (NOTE: often put after the name of a High Court judge: **Smith J** is spoken as 'Mr Justice Smith')

jactitation [dʒæktɪ'teɪʃn] *noun* boasting, saying proudly that something is true when it is not; **jactitation of marriage** = boasting that you are married to someone when you are not

jail [dʒeɪl] **1** *noun* prison, place where criminals are kept; *he spent ten years in jail* **2** *verb* to put someone in prison; *the judge jailed her for three years*; *he was jailed for manslaughter* (NOTE: also spelled **gaol** in British English)

jailbird ['dʒeɪlbɜːd] *noun* person who is in prison or who has often been sent to prison

jailbreak ['dʒeɪlbreɪk] *noun* escape from prison; **mass jailbreak** = escape from prison of several prisoners at the same time

jailer ['dʒeɪlə] *noun* person who works in a jail or who is in charge of a jail

jaywalker ['dʒeɪwɔːkə] *noun* person who walks across a street at a place which is not a proper crossing place

jaywalking ['dʒeɪwɔːkɪŋ] *noun* offence of walking across a street at a place which is not a proper crossing point for pedestrians

jeopardize ['dʒepədaɪz] *verb* to be likely to harm; *her arrest for drunken driving may jeopardize her work as a doctor specializing in child care*

jeopardy ['dʒepədi] *noun* **to be in jeopardy** = to be in danger of punishment or of harm; *his driving licence is in jeopardy* = he may lose his driving licence; *see also* **DOUBLE JEOPARDY**

jetsam ['dʒetsəm] *noun* cargo which is thrown off a sinking ship; **flotsam and jetsam** = rubbish floating in the water after a ship has been wrecked and rubbish washed on to the land

jettison ['dʒetɪzən] *verb* to throw cargo from a ship into the sea to make the ship lighter

join [dʒɔɪn] *verb* **to join someone to an action** = to attach someone's name as one of the parties to an action

joinder ['dʒɔɪndə] *noun* bringing together several actions or several parties in one action; *see also* **MISJOINDER**, **NONJOINDER**

joint [dʒɔɪnt] **1** *adjective* **(a)** with two or more organizations or people linked together; **joint account** = bank account for two people; **joint commission of inquiry** *or* **joint committee** = commission or committee with representatives of various organizations on it; **joint discussions** = discussions between management and workers before something is done; **joint liability** = situation where two or more parties share a single liability; **joint management** = management done by two or more people; **joint ownership** = situation where two or more persons own the same property; *US* **joint resolution** = Bill which has been passed by both House and Senate, and is sent to the President for signature; **joint-stock bank** = bank which is a public company quoted on the Stock Exchange; **joint-stock company** = public company whose shares are owned by many people; **joint venture,** *US also* **joint adventure** = very large business partnership where two or more companies join together as partners for a limited period **(b)** one of two or more people who work together or who are linked; *joint beneficiary; joint managing director; joint owner; joint signatory;* **joint heir** = person who is an heir with someone else; **joint tortfeasors** = two or more people who are responsible and liable for a tort **2** *noun (slang)* place or building; **to case a joint** = to look at a building carefully before deciding how to break into it

joint and several ['dʒɔɪnt ənd 'sevrəl] *adjective* as a group together and also separately; **joint and several liability** = situation where two or more parties share a single liability, and each party is also liable for the whole claim

jointly ['dʒɔɪntli] *adverb* together with one or more other people; *to own a property jointly; to manage a company jointly; they are jointly liable for damages;* **jointly and severally liable** = liable both as a group and as individuals; *executors exercise their duties jointly and severally*

joint tenancy ['dʒɔɪnt 'tenənsi] *noun* situation where two or more persons acquire an interest in a property together, where if one of the joint tenants dies, his share goes to the others who survive him; *see also* TENANCY IN COMMON

jointure ['dʒɔɪntʃə] *noun* estate settled on a wife as part of the marriage settlement

journal ['dʒɜːnəl] *noun* **(a)** diary, record of something which happens each day; *the chairman kept a journal during the negotiations* **(b)** official record of the proceedings of the legislature (House of Commons, House of Lords, House of Representatives or Senate), but not including verbatim speeches which are recorded in Hansard or in the Congressional Record

joy riding ['dʒɔɪ 'raɪdɪŋ] *noun* offence of taking a car without the permission of the owner and using it to drive about

JP ['dʒeɪ 'piː] *noun* = *JUSTICE OF THE PEACE* (NOTE: the plural is **JPs**)

judge [dʒʌdʒ] **1** *noun* **(a)** official who presides over a court and in civil cases decides which party is in the right; *a County Court judge; a judge in the Divorce Court; the judge sent him to prison for embezzlement;* **judge in chambers** = judge who hears a case in his private room without the public being present and not in open court; **Judges' Rules** = informal set of rules governing how the police may question a suspect **(b)** *(in the EU)* one of the fifteen members of the European Court of Justice, appointed by the Member States **2** *verb* to decide; *he judged it was time to call an end to the discussions*

COMMENT: In England, judges are appointed by the Lord Chancellor. The minimum requirement is that one should be a barrister or solicitor of ten years' standing. The majority of judges are barristers, but they cannot practise as barristers. Recorders are practising barristers who act as judges on a part-time basis. The appointment of judges is not a political appointment, and judges remain in office unless they are found guilty of gross misconduct. Judges cannot be Members of Parliament. In the USA, state judges can be appointed by the state governor or can be elected; in the federal courts and the Supreme Court, judges are appointed by the President, but the appointment has to be approved by Congress

Judge Advocate-General of the Forces

['dʒʌdʒ 'ædvəkət 'dʒenrəl əv ðə 'fɔːsɪz] *noun* lawyer appointed by the state to advise on all legal matters concerning the Army and Air Force

Judge Advocate of the Fleet

['dʒʌdʒ 'ædvəkət əv ðə 'fliːt] *noun* lawyer appointed by the state to advise on all legal matters concerning the Royal Navy

judgment *or* judgement

['dʒʌdʒmənt] *noun* legal decision, official decision of a court; **certificate of judgment** = official document showing the decision of a court; **judgment by default** *or* **default judgment** = judgment without trial against a defendant who fails to respond to a claim; **final judgment** = judgment which is given at the end of an action after trial; **interlocutory judgment** = judgment given during the course of an action before full trial; **to pronounce judgment** *or* **to give one's judgment on something** = to give an official or legal decision about something; **to enter judgement** *or* **to take judgment** = to record an official judgment on a case; **to enter judgment for the claimant** = to make a legal judgment that the claimant's claim is accepted; **to enter judgment against the claimant** = to make a legal judgment that the claimant's claim is not accepted; **the claimant entered judgment in default** = the claimant took judgment (because the defendant failed to defend the case); **entry of judgment** = recording the judgment of the court in the official records; **judgment creditor** = person who has been given a court order making a debtor pay him a debt; **judgment debtor** = debtor who has been ordered by a court to pay a debt; **judgment summons** = summons by a court to enforce a court order, such as ordering a judgment debtor to pay or to go to prison (NOTE: the spelling **judgment** is used by lawyers)

judicata [dʒuːdɪ'kɑːtə] *see* RES

judicature ['dʒuːdɪkətʃə] *noun* administration of justice; **judicature paper** = thick heavy paper on which court documents are engrossed; *see also* SUPREME COURT

judice ['dʒuːdəsi] *see* SUB JUDICE

judicial [dʒuː'dɪʃəl] *adjective* referring to a judge or the law; done in a court or by a judge; **the Judicial Committee of the House of Lords** = the highest appeal court in England and Wales; **the Judicial Committee of the Privy Council** = the appeal court for appeals from courts outside the UK, such as the courts of some Commonwealth countries; **judicial immunity** = safety from prosecution granted to a judge when acting in a judicial capacity; **judicial notice** = facts and matters which a judge is presumed to know, so that evidence does not have to be produced to prove them (such as that New Year's Day is January 1st, that a small baby is not capable of walking); **high judicial office** = important position in the legal system, such as Lord Chancellor, high court judge, etc.; **judicial precedent** = precedent set by a court decision, which can be reversed only by a higher court; **judicial processes** = the ways in which the law works; **judicial review** = (i) examination of a case a second time by a higher court because a lower court has acted wrongly; (ii) examination of administrative decisions by a court; **judicial separation** = legal separation of man and wife, ordered by the court, where each becomes separated, but neither is allowed to marry again

judiciary [dʒuː'dɪʃəri] *noun* **the judiciary** = all judges, the court system, the judicial power in general

jump [dʒʌmp] *see* BAIL

junior ['dʒuːniə] **1** *adjective* younger or lower in rank; **junior clerk** = clerk, usually young, who has lower status than a senior clerk; **junior executive** *or* **junior manager** = less important manager in a company; **junior partner** = person who has a small part of the shares in a partnership; **John Smith, Junior** = the younger John Smith (i.e. the son of John Smith, Senior) **2** *noun* **(a)** (i) barrister who is not a Queen's Counsel; (ii) barrister appearing with a leader (NOTE: also called a 'junior barrister') **(b) office junior** = young man or woman who does all types of work in an office

jurat ['dʒuəræt] *noun* words at the end of an affidavit, showing the details of when and by whom it was sworn

juridical [dʒuː'rɪdɪkl] *adjective* referring to the law or to judges

jurisdiction [dʒʊərɪsˈdɪkʃn] *noun* legal power over someone or something; **within the jurisdiction of the court** = in the legal power of a court; **outside the jurisdiction of the court** = not covered by the legal power of the court; **the prisoner refused to recognize the jurisdiction of the court** = the prisoner said that he did not believe that the court had the legal right to try him; **equitable jurisdiction** = power of a court to enforce a person's rights

jurisdictional [dʒʊərɪsˈdɪkʃnl] *adjective* referring to court's jurisdiction

jurisprudence [dʒʊərɪsˈpruːdəns] *noun* study of the law and the legal system

jurist [ˈdʒʊərɪst] *noun* person who has specialized in the study and practice of law

juristic [dʒʊəˈrɪstɪk] *adjective* according to the practice of law; **juristic person** = ARTIFICIAL PERSON

juror [ˈdʒʊərə] *noun* member of a jury

COMMENT: jurors can be selected from registered electors who are between eighteen and sixty-five years old and who have been resident in the UK for five years. Barristers, solicitors, judges, priests, doctors, Members of Parliament, people who are insane are among the categories of people disqualified from being jurors

jury [ˈdʒʊəri] *noun* group of twelve citizens who are sworn to decide whether someone is guilty or not guilty on the basis of the evidence they hear in court; **trial by jury** *or* **jury trial** = proceedings where an accused is tried by a jury and judge; **he has been called for jury service;** *US* **for jury duty** = he has been asked to do his duty as a citizen and serve on a jury; **'Members of the jury'** = way of speaking to a jury in court; **the foreman of the jury** = the chief juror, elected by the other jurors, who chairs the discussions of the jury and pronounces the verdict in court afterwards; **jury vetting** = examination of each of the proposed members of a jury to see if he or she is qualified to be a juror; *US* **grand jury** = group of between twelve and twenty-four jurors who meet as a

preliminary to a trial to decide if an indictment should be issued to start criminal proceedings *(mainly US)* **petty jury** = ordinary jury of twelve jurors (NOTE: the word jury can take a plural verb)

COMMENT: juries are used in criminal cases, and in some civil actions, notably actions for libel. They are also used in some coroner's inquests. The role of the jury is use their common sense to decide if the verdict should be for or against the accused. Jurors have no knowledge of the law and follow the explanations given to them by the judge. Anyone whose name appears on the electoral register and who is between the ages of 18 and 70 is eligible for jury service. Judges, magistrates, barristers and solicitors are not eligible for jury service, nor are priests, people who are on bail, and people suffering from mental illness. People who are excused jury service include members of the armed forces, Members of Parliament and doctors. Potential jurors can be challenged if one of the parties to the case thinks they are or may be biased

jury box [ˈdʒʊəri bɒks] *noun* place where the jury sit in the courtroom

juryman [ˈdʒʊərimæn] *noun* member of a jury (NOTE: plural is **jurymen**)

jury room [ˈdʒʊəri ˈruːm] *noun* room where the jury meet to discuss the trial and reach a verdict

jus [dʒʌs] *Latin word meaning* 'law' or 'right'

jus accrescendi [ˈdʒʌs ækreˈsendi] *see* SURVIVORSHIP

just [dʒʌst] *adjective* fair or right; **to show just cause** = to show a reason which is fair and acceptable in law; **just war** = war which is considered to be morally right

justice [ˈdʒʌstɪs] *noun* **(a)** fair treatment (in law); **to administer justice** = to make sure that the laws are correctly and fairly applied; **to bring a criminal to justice** = to find a criminal and charge him with an offence; **natural justice** = the general principles of justice; *US* **Department of Justice** *or* **Justice Department** = department of the US government responsible for federal legal cases, headed by the Attorney-General; *see also note at* MINISTRY **(b)** magistrate; **chairman of the justices** = chief magistrate in a magistrates' court; **justices' chief executive** = senior administrator appointed by a Magistrates' Courts Committee to run the courts in an area, but not to give legal advice; **justices' clerk** *or* **clerk to the justices** = official of a Magistrates' Court who gives advice to the justices on law, practice or procedure; he or she reports to the justices' chief executive of their area **(c)** judge; **Lord Chief Justice** = chief judge of the Queen's Bench Division of the High Court, and second most senior judge after the Lord Chancellor; *US* **Chief Justice** = senior judge in a court **(d)** title given to a High Court judge; *Mr Justice Adams*; **Lord Justice** = title given to a judge who is a member of the House of Lords (NOTE: usually written as **J** or **LJ** after the name: **Adams J; Smith LJ**)

justice of the peace (JP) ['dʒʌstɪs əv ðə 'piːs] *noun* magistrate or local judge

justiciable [dʒʌs'tɪʃəbl] *adjective (in the EU)* (legal principle) which can be subject to laws; *some people question whether subsidiarity is justiciable*

justiciary [dʒʌ'stɪʃəri] *noun* all judges; **High Court of Justiciary** = supreme criminal court in Scotland

justifiable [dʒʌstɪ'faɪəbl] *adjective* which can be excused; **justifiable homicide** = killing of a person for an acceptable reason (such as in self-defence)

justification [dʒʌstɪfɪ'keɪʃn] *noun* showing an acceptable reason for an act; **in justification** = as an acceptable excuse; *in justification, the accused claimed that the burglar had attacked him with an axe*; *the defendant entered defence of justification*

justify ['dʒʌstɪfaɪ] *verb* to give an excuse for; **the end justifies the means** = if the result is right, the means used to reach it are acceptable

justitia [dʒʌs'tɪsɪə] *see* FIAT

juvenile ['dʒuːvənaɪl] *noun & adjective* young person under seventeen years of age; **Juvenile Court** = court which tries young offenders; *the appeal court quashed the care order made by the juvenile court* (NOTE: the **Juvenile Court** is now called the **Youth Court**); **juvenile delinquent** = young criminal who commits minor crimes, especially against property; **juvenile offender** = former term for a young person tried in a Juvenile Court (NOTE: now replaced by **young offender**)

Kk

kangaroo [kæŋgə'ruː] *noun* system used when discussing a Bill, where some clauses are not discussed at all, but simply voted on, with the discussion then moving on to the next item

kangaroo court [kæŋgə'ruː 'kɔːt] *noun* unofficial and illegal court set up by a group of people

KC ['keɪ 'siː] = KING'S COUNSEL

keep [kiːp] *verb* to do what is necessary; **to keep an appointment** = to be there when you said you would be; **to keep the books of a company** *or* **to keep a company's books** = to note the accounts of a company; **to keep the law** = to make sure the law is obeyed; **to keep the peace** = to obey the law, to behave well and not to create a disturbance; *he was bound over to keep the peace* (NOTE: **keeping - kept**)

keeper ['kiːpə] *noun* person who keeps something; **Keeper of the Great Seal** = the Lord Chancellor

keeping ['kiːpɪŋ] *noun* **safe keeping** = being looked after carefully; *we put the documents into the bank for safe keeping*; **keeping a disorderly house** = offence of being the proprietor or manager of a brothel

Keogh plan ['kiːəʊ 'plæn] *noun US* private pension programme which allows self-employed businessmen and professionals to set up pension plans for themselves

kerb crawling ['kɜːb 'krɑːlɪŋ] *noun* driving slowly in order to importune women standing on the pavement

key [kiː] *noun* code, password, etc., which allows someone to read encrypted text; *see also* PUBLIC KEY CRYPTOGRAPHY

key money ['kiː 'mʌni] *noun* premium paid when taking over the keys of a flat or office which you are renting

kickback ['kɪkbæk] *noun* illegal commission paid to someone (especially a government official) who helps in a business deal

kidnap ['kɪdnæp] *verb* to take away (a child or a person) and keep him alone by force (usually asking for money to be paid before he is released)

kidnapper ['kɪdnæpə] *noun* person who kidnaps someone

kidnapping ['kɪdnæpɪŋ] *noun* notifiable offence of taking away a person by force

kill [kɪl] *verb* to make someone die; *he was accused of killing his girl friend with a knife*

killer ['kɪlə] *noun* person who kills; *the police are searching for the girl's killer*

kin [kɪn] *plural noun* relatives or close members of the family; *see also* NEXT OF KIN

king [kɪŋ] *noun* man who rules a monarchy; *Juan Carlos is the King of Spain*; *see also* QUEEN (NOTE: often used with a name as a title: **King Juan Carlos**)

kingdom ['kıŋdəm] *noun* country ruled by a king or queen; *the United Kingdom of Great Britain and Northern Ireland*; *the kingdom of Saudi Arabia*

kitchen cabinet ['kıtʃən 'kæbınət] *noun* private, unofficial committee of ministers, advisers and friends who advise the Prime Minister

kitemark ['kaıtmɑːk] *noun* mark put on British goods to show that they meet official standards

kleptomania [kleptə'meıniə] *noun* mental illness which makes someone steal things

kleptomaniac [kleptə'meıniæk] *noun* person who steals things because he suffers from kleptomania

knock-for-knock agreement ['nɒkfə'nɒk ə'griːmənt] *noun* agreement between two insurance companies that they will not take legal action against each other, and that each will pay the claims of their own clients

knowingly ['nəʊıŋli] *adverb* deliberately, on purpose; *it was charged that he knowingly broke the Official Secrets Act by publishing the document in his newspaper*

knowledge ['nɒlıdʒ] *noun* what is known to be true; **he had no knowledge of the contract** = he did not know that the contract existed; **to the best of my knowledge** = I am reasonable certain of the fact; *the witness said that to the best of his knowledge the accused had never left the room*; **constructive knowledge** = knowledge of a fact or matter which the law says a person has whether or not that person actually has such knowledge

LI

labour *US* **labor** ['leɪbə] *noun* **(a)** heavy work; **manual labour** = work done by hand; **to charge for materials and labour** = to charge for both the materials used in a job and also the hours of work involved; **hard labour** = punishment of sending someone to prison to do hard manual work **(b)** workers in general; **casual labour** = workers who are hired for a short period; **cheap labour** = workers who do not earn much money; **local labour** = workers recruited near a factory, not brought in from somewhere else; **organized labour** = workers who are members of trade unions; **skilled labour** = workers who have special knowledge or qualifications; **labour-intensive industry** = industry which needs large numbers of workers or where labour costs are high in relation to turnover **(c) labour disputes** = arguments between management and workers; **labour law** *or* **labour laws** *or* **labour legislation** = laws relating to the employment of workers; **labour relations** = relations between management and workers; *US* **labor union** = organization which represents workers who are its members in discussions about wages and conditions of work with management **(d) International Labour Organization (ILO)** = section of the United Nations which tries to improve working conditions and workers' pay in member countries

Labor Day ['leɪbə 'deɪ] *noun US* annual holiday to honour workers (similar to May 1st in Europe) celebrated on the first Monday in September

labourer *US* **laborer** ['leɪbərə] *noun* person who does unskilled work; **casual labourer** = worker who can be hired for a

short period; **manual labourer** = person who does work with his hands

laches ['lætʃɪz] *noun* long delay or neglect in asserting a legal right; *see also* STATUTE OF LIMITATIONS

lading ['leɪdɪŋ] *see* BILL

Lady Day ['leɪdi 'deɪ] *noun* 25th March, one of the quarter days when rent is paid for land

lag [læg] *noun* **old lag** = criminal who has served many (short) prison sentences, one who will never go straight

laissez-faire *or* laisser-faire

['leseɪ'feə] *noun* political theory where a government does nothing to control the economy; *laissez-faire policies resulted in increased economic activity, but contributed to a rise in imports*

lame duck president ['leɪm 'dʌk 'prezidənt] *noun* president in the last part of his term of office, who cannot stand for re-election, and so lacks political force; *no foreign policy decisions can be made because of the lame duck presidency*

land [lænd] *noun* **(a)** area of earth; **land agent** = person who manages a farm or a large area of land for someone; **land certificate** = document which shows who owns a piece of land, and whether there are any charges on it; **land charges** = covenants, mortgages, etc., which are attached to a piece of land; **land register** = register of land, showing who owns it and what buildings are on it; **land registration** = system of registering land and its owners; **Land Registry** = British government office where land is registered; **land taxes** = taxes on the amount of land owned by someone **(b) lands** = estate, large area of land owned by one owner; **Crown Lands** = estates belonging to the King or Queen

COMMENT: under English law, the ownership of all land is vested in the Crown; individuals or other legal persons may however hold estates in land, the most important of which are freehold estates (which amount to absolute ownership) and leasehold estates (which last for a fixed period of time). Ownership of land usually confers ownership of everything above and below the land. The process of buying and selling land is 'conveyancing'. Any contract transferring land or any interest in land must be in writing. Interests in land can be disposed of by a will

landing ['lændɪŋ] *noun* **landing card** = card given to passengers who have passed customs and can land from a ship or an aircraft; **landing charges** = payment for putting goods on land and for customs duties; **landing order** = permit which allows goods to be unloaded into a bonded warehouse without paying customs duty

landlady ['lænleɪdɪ] *noun* woman who owns a property which she lets

landlord ['lænlɔːd] *noun* person or company that owns a property which is let; **ground landlord** = person or company that owns the freehold of a property which is then let and sublet; *our ground landlord is an insurance company*; **the Landlord and Tenant Act** = Act of Parliament which regulates the letting of property

landmark decision ['lænmɑːk dɪ'sɪʒn] *noun* legal or legislative decision which creates an important legal precedent

landowner ['lændəʊnə] *noun* person who owns large areas of land

Lands Tribunal ['lænz traɪ'bjuːnəl] *noun* court which deals with compensation claims relating to land

language ['læŋgwɪdʒ] *noun* words spoken or written by people in a certain country; *he was accused of using offensive language to a policeman* = he was accused of saying rude words; **computer language** *or* **programming language** = system of signs, letters and words used to instruct a computer

lapse [læps] **1** *noun* **(a) a lapse of time** = a period of time which has passed **(b)** ending of a right, a privilege or an offer (such as the termination of an insurance policy because the premiums have not been paid) **(c)** failure of a legacy because the beneficiary has died before the testator **2** *verb* to stop being valid, to stop being active; **to let an offer lapse** = to allow time to pass so that an offer is no longer valid; **lapsed legacy** = legacy which cannot be put into effect because the person who should have received it died before the person who made the will; **lapsed passport** = passport which is out of date; **lapsed (insurance) policy** = insurance which is no longer valid because the premiums have not been paid

larceny ['lɑːsnɪ] *noun* crime of stealing goods which belong to another person; *he was convicted of larceny*; **grand larceny** = very large thefts; **petty larceny** = minor thefts

COMMENT: larceny no longer exists in English law, having been replaced by the crime of theft

at large [ət 'lɑːdʒ] *phrase* not in prison; *three prisoners escaped - two were recaptured, but one is still at large*

last [lɑːst] *adjective & adverb* coming at the end of a series; *out of a queue of twenty people, I was served last*; *this is our last board meeting before we move to our new offices*; *this is the last case which the magistrates will hear before lunch*; **last quarter** = period of three months to the end of the financial year; **court of last resort** = highest court from which no appeals can be made; **lender of the last resort** = central bank which lends money to commercial banks; **last will and testament** = *see* WILL

last in first out (LIFO) ['lɑːst 'ɪn 'fɜːst 'aʊt] *phrase* **(a)** redundancy policy, where the people who have been most recently appointed are the first to be made redundant **(b)** accounting method where stock is valued at the price of the latest purchases

late [leɪt] *adjective* **(a)** after the time stated or agreed; *we apologize for the late arrival of the plane from Amsterdam*; **there is a penalty for late delivery** = if delivery is later than the agreed date, the supplier has to pay a fine **(b)** at the end of a period of time; **latest date for signature of the contract** = the last acceptable date for signing the contract **(c)** dead; *he inherited a fortune from his late uncle*

latent ['leɪtənt] *adjective* hidden, which cannot immediately be seen; **latent ambiguity** = words in a contract which can mean two or more things, but which do not at first sight seem to be misleading; **latent defect** = fault which cannot be seen immediately

Latin ['lætɪn] *noun* language used by the Romans

COMMENT: Latin was used as the language of the law courts for centuries, and its use still exists in many common legal phrases, such as **habeas corpus, in flagrante delicto, de jure, sine die** and **de facto.** Although Latin was first abolished in legal proceedings in 1730, it was rapidly reintroduced as some phrases (such as habeas corpus) proved to be difficult to translate briefly into English. Recent changes to the civil procedures have removed some Latin terms, but many still remain in use

launder ['lɔːndə] *verb (slang)* to transfer illegal or stolen money into an ordinary bank account, usually by a complex process to avoid detection; *the proceeds of the robbery were laundered through a bank in the Caribbean*

law [lɔː] *noun* **(a)** rule (which may be written or unwritten) by which a country is governed and the activities of people and organizations controlled; in particular, an Act of Parliament which has received the Royal Assent, or an Act of Congress which has been signed by the President of the USA, or which has been passed by Congress over the President's veto; *a law has to be passed by Parliament*; *the government has proposed a new law to regulate the sale of goods on Sundays*; **conflict of laws** = section in a country's statutes which deals with disputes between that country's laws and those of another country; **labour laws** = laws concerning the employment of workers **(b)** **law** = all the statutes of a country taken together; **case law** = law as established by precedents, that is by decisions of courts in earlier cases; **civil law** = laws relating to people's rights, and to agreements between individuals; **commercial law** = laws regarding business; **company law** = laws which refer to the way companies work; **constitutional law** = laws under which a country is ruled, laws relating to government and its function; **contract law** *or* **the law of contract** = laws relating to agreements; **copyright law** = laws concerning the protection of copyright; **criminal law** = laws relating to acts committed against the laws of the land and which are punishable by the state; **international law** = laws referring to the way countries deal with each other; **maritime law** *or* **the law of the sea** = laws referring to ships, ports, etc.; **mercantile law** *or* **law merchant** = law relating to commerce; **private law** = law relating to relations between individual persons (such as the law of contract); **public law** = laws which refer to people in general (such as administrative and constitutional law); **law and order** = situation where the laws of a country are being obeyed by most people; *there was a breakdown of law and order following the assassination of the president*; **law reform** = continuing process of revising laws to make them better suited to the needs of society; **to take someone to law** = to sue someone; **inside the law** *or* **within the law** = obeying the laws of a country; **against the law** *or* **outside the law** = not according to the laws of a country; *dismissing a worker without reason is against the law*; *the company is* *operating outside the law*; in law = according to the law; *what are the duties in law of a guardian?*; to break the law = to do something which is not allowed by law; *he is breaking the law by selling goods on Sunday*; *you will be breaking the law if you try to take that computer out of the country without an export licence* (c) general rule; law of supply and demand = general rule that the amount of a product which is available is related to the needs of the possible customers (d) *(informal)* the law = the police and the courts; *the law will catch up with him in the end*; *if you don't stop making that noise I'll have the law on you*; the strong *or* long arm of the law = ability of the police to catch criminals and deal with crime

lawbreaker ['lɔːbreɪkə] *noun* person who breaks the law

law-breaking ['lɔːbreɪkɪŋ] *noun* act of doing something which is against the law

Law Centre ['lɔː 'sentə] *noun* local office (mainly in London) with full-time staff who advise and represent clients free of charge

Law Commission ['lɔː kə'mɪʃn] *noun* permanent committee which reviews English law and recommends changes to it

law court ['lɔː 'kɔːt] *noun* place where a trial is held, place where a judge listens to cases

COMMENT: in civil cases he decides which party is right legally; in criminal cases the decision is made by a jury, and the judge passes sentence

lawful ['lɔːfl] *adjective* acting within the law; lawful practice = action which is permitted by the law; lawful trade = trade which is allowed by law

lawfully ['lɔːfli] *adverb* acting within the law

lawless ['lɔːləs] *adjective* not controlled by the law or by the police; *the magistrates criticized the lawless behaviour of the football crowd*

lawlessness ['lɔːləsnəs] *noun* being lawless; *the government is trying to fight lawlessness in large cities*

Law List ['lɔː 'lɪst] *noun* annual published list of barristers and solicitors

Law Lords ['lɔː 'lɔːdz] *plural noun* members of the House of Lords who are or were judges (including the Lord Chancellor, the Lords of Appeal in Ordinary and other peers)

law-making ['lɔːmeɪkɪŋ] *noun* making of laws; *Parliament is the law-making body in Great Britain*

lawman ['lɔːmən] *noun US* policeman (NOTE: plural is **lawmen**)

Law Officers ['lɔː 'ɒfɪsəz] *plural noun* (a) legal members of the British government (but not members of the Cabinet): the Attorney-General and Solicitor-General in England and Wales, and the Lord Advocate and Solicitor-General in Scotland (b) law enforcement officers = see ENFORCEMENT

COMMENT: the Law Officers advise the government and individual ministries on legal matters. The Attorney-General will prosecute in trials for serious crimes

Law Reports ['lɔː rɪ'pɔːts] *plural noun* regular reports of new cases and legislation

law school ['lɔː 'skuːl] *noun* school where lawyers are trained

Law Society ['lɔː sə'saɪəti] *noun* organization of solicitors in England and Wales, which represents and regulates the profession

Laws of Oleron ['lɔːz əv 'ɒlərɒn] *plural noun* the first maritime laws, drawn up in 1216 and used as a base for subsequent international laws

lawsuit ['lɔːsuːt] *noun* case brought to a court by a private person; to bring a lawsuit against someone = to tell someone to appear in court to settle an argument; to defend a lawsuit = to appear in court to state your case

lawyer ['lɔːjə] *noun* person who has studied law and can act for people on legal business; **commercial lawyer** *or* **company lawyer** = person who specializes in company law or who advises companies on legal problems; **constitutional lawyer** = lawyer who specializes in constitutional law or in interpreting constitutions; **international lawyer** = person who specializes in international law; **maritime lawyer** = person who specializes in laws concerning ships

lay [leɪ] **1** *verb* **(a)** to put or to place; **to lay an embargo on trade with a country** = to forbid trade with a country; **to lay (an) information** = to start criminal proceedings in a magistrates' court by giving the magistrate details of the offence; **to lay a proposal before the House** = to introduce a new Bill before Parliament for discussion **(b) to lay down** = to state clearly; *the conditions are laid down in the document*; *the guidelines lay down rules for dealing with traffic offences* (NOTE: **laying - laid - has laid**) **2** *adjective* not belonging to a certain profession; **lay assessor** = person (not a lawyer) with technical knowledge who advises a court on specialized matters; **lay magistrate** = magistrate who is not usually a qualified lawyer (as opposed to a stipendiary magistrate); **lay representative** = any person representing someone in a case in the small claims track who is not a solicitor, barrister or legal executive

layman ['leɪmən] *noun* person who does not belong to the legal profession (NOTE: plural is **laymen**)

LC ['el 'siː] = LORD CHANCELLOR

L/C ['el 'siː] = LETTER OF CREDIT

LCJ ['el 'siː 'dʒeɪ] = LORD CHIEF JUSTICE

lead [liːd] **1** *noun* clue, piece of information which may help solve a crime; *the police are following up several leads in the murder investigation* **2** *verb* **(a)** to be the first, to be in front; *the company leads the market in cheap computers* **(b)** to be the main person in a group (especially in a team of barristers appearing for one side in a case); *the prosecution is led by J.M. Jones, QC; Mr Smith is leading for the Crown* **(c)** to start to do something (especially to start to present a case in court); *Mr Jones led for the prosecution; the Home Secretary will lead for the Government in the emergency debate* **(d)** to bring evidence before a court **(e)** to try to make a witness answer a question in court in a certain way; *counsel must not lead the witness* (NOTE: **leading - led - has led**)

leader ['liːdə] *noun* **(a)** person who manages or directs others; *the leader of the construction workers' union or the construction workers' leader; she is the leader of the trade delegation to Nigeria; the minister was the leader of the party of lawyers on a tour of American courts* **(b)** main barrister (usually a QC) in a team appearing for one side in a case **(c)** product which sells best; **a market leader** = product which sells most in a market or company which has the largest share of a market; **loss-leader** = article which is sold very cheaply to attract customers **(d)** important share, share which is often bought or sold on the Stock Exchange **(e)** **council leader** *or* **leader of a council** = head of the majority party in a local council; *the matter will be referred to the Leader; Councillor Jenkins, Leader of the Council, stated that the report would be examined at the next meeting; see also* MAYOR; **party leader** = head of a political party, who usually becomes head of government if the party wins power; US **majority leader** *or* **minority leader** = spokesmen for the majority or minority party in the House or Senate, elected by other members of the party

COMMENT: normally a party leader has a great deal of power when it comes to making appointments and deciding party policy. In Britain, the leader of a party may feel bound to follow policy decisions laid down by the party conference. This may restrict the leader's room for manoeuvre

Leader of the House ['liːdə əv ðə 'haus] *noun* senior government minister and member of the cabinet, who is responsible for the administration of legislation in the House of Commons or House of Lords, and is the main government spokesman in the House

> COMMENT: both can be referred to as Leader of the House: to be more specific, say Leader of the Commons and Leader of the Lords

Leader of the Opposition ['liːdə əv ðə ɒpə'zɪʃn] *noun* head of the largest party opposing the government

leading ['liːdɪŋ] *adjective* (a) most important; *leading businessmen feel the end of the recession is near*; *leading shares rose on the Stock Exchange*; *leading shareholders in the company forced a change in management policy*; *they are the leading company in the field*; **leading cases** = important cases which have set precedents; **leading counsel** = main barrister (usually a QC) in a team appearing for one side in a case (b) **leading question** = question put by a barrister to a witness which suggests to the witness what his answer ought to be, question which can only be answered 'Yes' or 'No'

> COMMENT: leading questions may be asked during cross-examination or during examination in chief

leak [liːk] **1** *noun* (i) passing secret information (to newspapers, TV stations, etc.); (ii) unofficial passing of information which has not yet been published, by officials, MPs or councillors (to newspapers or TV stations, etc.); *the government is investigating the latest leak of documents relating to the spy trial* **2** *verb* (i) to pass secret information (to the newspapers or TV stations, etc.); (ii) to pass information unofficially (to newspapers or TV stations, etc.); *information about the government plans has been leaked to the Sunday papers*; *the details of the plan have been leaked to the press to test public reaction*

lease ['liːs] **1** *noun* (a) written contract for letting or renting of a building, a piece of land or a piece of equipment for a period of time, against payment of a fee; **long**

lease = lease which runs for fifty years or more; *to take an office building on a long lease*; **short lease** = lease which runs for up to two or three years; *we have a short lease on our current premises*; *to rent office space on a twenty-year lease*; **full repairing lease** = lease where the tenant has to pay for all repairs to the property; **head lease** = lease from the freeholder to a tenant; **sublease** *or* **underlease** = lease from a tenant to another tenant; **the lease expires** *or* **runs out in 2010** = the lease comes to an end in 2010; **on expiration of the lease** = when the lease comes to an end; *see also* DEMISE (b) **to hold an oil lease in the North Sea** = to have a lease on a section of the North Sea to explore for oil **2** *verb* (a) to let or rent offices, land or machinery for a period; *to lease offices to small firms*; *to lease equipment* (b) to use an office, land or machinery for a time and pay a fee to the landlord or lessor; *to lease an office from an insurance company*; *all our company cars are leased*

lease back ['liːs 'bæk] *verb* to sell a property or machinery to a company and then take it back on a lease; *they sold the office building to raise cash, and then leased it back for twenty-five years*

lease-back ['liːsbæk] *noun* arrangement where property is sold and then taken back on a lease; *they sold the office building and then took it back under a lease-back arrangement*

leasehold ['liːshəʊld] *noun & adjective & adverb* possessing property on a lease, for a fixed time; *the company has some valuable leaseholds*; *to purchase a property leasehold*; **leasehold enfranchisement** = right of a leaseholder to buy the freehold of the property he is leasing

leaseholder ['liːshəʊldə] *noun* person who holds a property on a lease

leasing ['liːsɪŋ] *noun & adjective* which leases, which is working under a lease; *the company has branched out into car leasing*; *a computer-leasing company*; *to run a copier under a leasing arrangement*

leave [liːv] **1** *noun* **(a)** permission to do something; *counsel asked leave of the court to show a film taken of the accident*; **'by your leave'** = with your permission; **leave to defend** = permission from a court allowing someone to defend himself against an accusation **(b)** to be away from work; **leave of absence** = being allowed to be away from work; **maternity leave** = period when a woman is away from work to have a baby; **sick leave** = period when a worker is away from work because of illness; **to go on leave** *or* **to be on leave** = to be away from work; *she is away on sick leave or on maternity leave* **2** *verb* **(a)** to go away from; *he left his office early to go to the meeting*; *the next plane leaves at 10.20* **(b)** to give property to someone when you die; *he left his house to his wife*; *I was left £5,000 by my grandmother in her will* **(c)** to resign; *he left his job and bought a farm* (NOTE: **leaving - left - has left**)

left [ˈleft] *noun* **(a)** **the left** = socialists and communists, their ideals and beliefs; *the left have demanded political reform*; *many members of the left have been arrested*; **swing to the left** = movement of support towards socialist principles **(b)** **the left** = section of a party which is more socialist or more radical than the main party; *he is on the left of the Conservative Party*; *the activists on the Labour left* (NOTE: usually used with the article **the,** and takes a singular or plural verb)

legacy [ˈlegəsi] *noun* money or personal property (but not land) given by someone to someone else in his will; *she received a small legacy in her uncle's will*; **demonstrative legacy** = legacy which is made out of a certain part of the estate (ie, a certain bank account, for example); **residuary legacy** = legacy of what remains of an estate after debts, taxes, and other legacies have been paid; **specific legacy** = legacy of a certain specific item to someone in a will; **statutory legacy** = amount of money which is distributed to a surviving spouse of a person who dies intestate and has other surviving relatives, but no surviving children (currently £200,000)

COMMENT: freehold land left to someone in a will is a **devise**

legal [ˈliːgəl] *adjective* **(a)** according to the law, allowed by the law; *the company's action was completely legal* **(b)** referring to the law; **to take legal action** *or* **to start legal proceedings** = to sue someone, to take someone to court; **to take legal advice** = to ask a lawyer to advise about a problem in law; **legal adviser** = person who advises clients about problems in law; *US* **legal age** = age at which a person can sue or can be sued or can undertake business; **Legal Aid scheme** = British government scheme where a person with very little money can have legal representation and advice paid for by the state (NOTE: the scheme has now been replaced by the **Community Legal Service (CLS)** and the **Criminal Defence Service (CDS)**; the US equivalent is the **Legal Aid Society**); **Legal Aid Centre** = local office giving advice to clients about applications for Legal Aid and recommending clients to solicitors; **legal charge** = charge created over property by a legal mortgage (as opposed to an equitable charge); **legal claim** = statement that someone owns something legally; *he has no legal claim to the property*; **legal costs** *or* **legal charges** *or* **legal expenses** = money spent on fees to lawyers; **legal currency** = money which is legally used in a country; **legal department** *or* **legal section** = section of a company dealing with legal matters; **legal expert** = person who has a wide knowledge of the law; **legal fiction** = assuming something to be true, even if it is not proved to be so (a procedural device used by courts to get round problems caused by statute); **legal holiday** = day when banks and other businesses are closed; **legal personality** = existence as a body and so ability to be affected by the law; **legal representative** = barrister, solicitor, or legal executive, who acts on behalf of a party in a case; **legal right** = right which exists under law; **legal separation** = legal separation of man and wife, ordered by the court, where each becomes separated, but neither is allowed to marry; **legal tender** = coins or notes which can be legally used to pay a debt (small denominations cannot be used to pay large debts); **legal writer** = person who writes and publishes commentaries on legal problems

legal certainty ['li:gl 'sɜ:tənti] *noun (in the EU)* principle of European law which states that vested rights are not retroactive, that legislation shall not have retrospective effect, that the legitimate expectations of a claimant must be respected

legal executive ['li:gl ɪg'zekjʊtɪv] *noun* clerk in a solicitor's office who is not a solicitor and is not articled to become one, but has passed the examinations of the Institute of Legal Executives

> COMMENT: legal executives deal with a lot of the background work in solicitors' offices, including probate, conveyancing, matrimonial disputes, etc. They can speak before a judge on questions which are not contested

legality [lɪ'gæləti] *noun* being allowed by law; *there is doubt about the legality of the company's action in dismissing him*

legalize ['li:gəlaɪz] *verb* to make something legal

legalization [li:gəlaɪ'zeɪʃn] *noun* making something legal; *the campaign for the legalization of cannabis*

legally ['li:gəli] *adverb* according to the law; **the contract is legally binding** = according to the law, the contract has to be obeyed; **the directors are legally responsible** = the law says that the directors are responsible

legal memory ['li:gəl 'memri] *noun* time when things are supposed to be remembered in law, taken to be 1189; *this practice has existed from before the time of legal memory*; *see also* IMMEMORIAL

Legal Services Commission (LSC) ['li:gl 'sɜ:vɪsɪz kə'mɪʃn] *noun* body set up to run the Community Legal Service and the Criminal Defence Service (formerly Legal Aid)

legatee [legə'ti:] *noun* person who receives a legacy from someone who has died

legis ['ledʒɪs] *see* CORPUS

legislate ['ledʒɪsleɪt] *verb* to make a law; *Parliament has legislated against the sale of drugs or to prevent the sale of drugs*

legislation [ledʒɪ'sleɪʃn] *noun* laws, written rules which are passed by Parliament and implemented by the courts; **labour legislation** = laws concerning the employment of workers; *(in the EU)* **primary legislation** = legislation of the Member States of the EU, as opposed to legislation of the EU itself; **secondary legislation** = legislation passed by the EU, as opposed to primary legislation passed by the Member States themselves

legislative ['ledʒɪslətɪv] *adjective* used to make laws; *Parliament has a legislative function; US* **legislative day** = time from the start of a meeting of one of the Houses of Congress to its adjournment (the House of Representatives usually adjourns at the end of each day, but the Senate may not, so that the Senate's legislative day can last several calendar days); **legislative veto** = clause written into legislation relating to government agencies, which states that the agency cannot act in a way that Congress does not approve

legislator ['ledʒɪsleɪtə] *noun* person who makes or passes laws (such as an MP, Congressman, etc.)

legislature ['ledʒɪslətʃə] *noun* (i) body (such as a Parliament) which makes laws; (ii) building where a Parliament meets; *members of the legislature voted against the proposal; the protesters marched towards the State Legislature*

legitimacy [lɪ'dʒɪtɪməsi] *noun* **(a)** state of being legitimate; *the court doubted the legitimacy of his claim* **(b)** court case to make someone legitimate

legitimate 1 [lɪ'dʒɪtɪmət] *adjective* **(a)** allowed by law; *he has a legitimate claim to the property*; *(in the EU)* **legitimate**

expectations = expectations of an employee which are normal and what one might expect employees to have (**b**) born to parents who are married to each other; *he left his property to his legitimate offspring*; *see also* ILLEGITIMATE 2 [lɪˈdʒɪtɪmeɪt] *verb* to make (a child) legitimate

legitimation *or* legitimization

[lɪdʒɪtɪˈmeɪʃn *or* lɪdʒɪtɪmaɪˈzeɪʃn] *noun* making a person legitimate (as by the marriage of the parents)

lend [lend] *verb* to allow someone to use something for a period; *to lend something to someone or to lend someone something*; *he lent the company money or he lent money to the company*; *she lent the company car to her daughter*; *the bank lent him £50,000 to start his business*

lender [ˈlendə] *noun* person who lends money; **lender of the last resort** = central bank which lends money to commercial banks

lending [ˈlendɪŋ] *noun* act of letting someone use money for a time; **lending limit** = limit on the amount of money a bank can lend

lessee [leˈsiː] *noun* person who has a lease, who pays rent for a property he leases from a lessor

lessor [leˈsɔː] *noun* person who grants a lease on a property to a lessee

let [let] **1** *verb* (**a**) to allow someone to do something; *the magistrate let the prisoner speak to his wife* (**b**) to lend a house, an office or a farm to someone for a payment; **to let an office** = to allow someone to use an office for a time in return for payment of rent; **offices to let** = offices which are available to be leased by companies (NOTE: **letting - let - has let**) **2** *noun* (**a**) period of the lease of a property; *they took the office on a short let* (**b**) **without let or hindrance** = without any obstruction

let-out clause [ˈletaʊt ˈklɔːz] *noun* clause which allows someone to avoid doing something in a contract; *he added a let-out clause to the effect that the*

payments would be revised if the exchange rate fell by more than 5%

letter [ˈletə] *noun* (**a**) piece of writing sent from one person or company to another to give information; **business letter** = letter which deals with business matters; **circular letter** = letter sent to many people; **covering letter** = letter sent with documents to say why they are being sent; **follow-up letter** = letter sent to someone after a previous letter or after a visit; **private letter** = letter which deals with personal matters; **standard (form) letter** = letter which is sent without change to various correspondents (**b**) **letter before action** = letter written by a lawyer to give a party the chance to pay his client before he sues; **letter of acknowledgement** = letter which says that something has been received; **letters of administration** = document given by a court to allow someone to deal with the estate of someone who has died without leaving a will or where the executor appointed under the will cannot act; **letter of allotment** *or* **allotment letter** = letter which tells someone how many shares in a new company he has been allotted; **letter of application** = letter in which someone applies for a job or applies for shares in a new company; **letter of appointment** = letter in which someone is appointed to a job; **letter of attorney** = document showing that someone has power of attorney; **letter of comfort** *or* **comfort letter** = letter supporting someone who is trying to get a loan, letter which reassures someone on a certain point; **letter of complaint** = letter in which someone complains; **letter of credit (L/C)** = letter from a bank authorizing payment of a certain sum to a person or company (usually in another country); **letter of demand** = letter issued by a party or by a lawyer demanding payment before taking legal action; **letter of indemnity** = letter promising payment of compensation for a loss; **letter of intent** = letter which states what someone intends to do if something happens; **letters patent** = official document from the Crown, which gives someone the exclusive right to do something (such as becoming a life peer or making and selling an invention); **letter of reference** = letter in which an employer or former employer recommends someone for a new job; **letter of request** *or* **rogatory letter** = letter to a court in another country, asking for evidence to be taken from someone under that court's jurisdiction **(c) air letter** = special thin blue paper which when folded can be sent by air without an envelope; **airmail letter** = letter sent by air; **registered letter** = letter which is noted by the Post Office before it is sent, so that compensation can be claimed if it is lost **(d) to acknowledge receipt by letter** = to write a letter to say that something has been received **(e)** written or printed sign (such as A, B, C); *write your name and address in block letters or in capital letters*

letting ['letɪŋ] *noun* **letting agency** = agency which deals in property to let; **furnished lettings** = furnished property to let; *see also* LET

levy ['levi] **1** *noun* money which is demanded and collected by the government, by an agency or by an official body; **capital levy** = tax on the value of a person's property and possessions; **import levy** = tax on imports, especially in the EC a tax on imports of farm produce from outside the EC; **training levy** = tax to be paid by companies to fund the government's training schemes **2** *verb* to demand payment of a tax or an extra payment and to collect it; *the government has decided to levy a tax on imported cars; to levy a duty on the import of computer parts*

lex [leks] *Latin word meaning* 'law'; **lex fori** = law of the place where the case is being heard; **lex loci actus** = law of the place where the act took place; **lex loci contractus** = law of the place where the contract was made; **lex loci delicti** = law of the place where the crime was committed

liability [laɪə'bɪləti] *noun* **(a)** being legally responsible for paying for damage, loss, etc.; *his insurers have admitted liability but the amount of damages has not yet been agreed*; **to accept** *or* **to admit**

liability for something = to agree that you are responsible for something; **to refuse liability for something** = to refuse to agree that you are responsible for something; **contractual liability** = legal responsibility for something as stated in a contract; **limited liability** = principle that by forming a limited liability company, individual members are liable for that company's debts only to the value of their shares; **limited liability company** = company where a member is responsible for repaying the company's debts only up to the face value of the shares he owns; **liability clause** = clause in the articles of association of a company which states that the liability of its members is limited; **vicarious liability** = liability of one person for torts committed by another, especially the liability of an employer for acts committed by an employee in the course of his work **(b) liabilities** = debts of a business; *the balance sheet shows the company's assets and liabilities*; **current liabilities** = debts which a company should pay within the next accounting period; **long-term liabilities** = debts which are not due to be repaid for some years; **he was not able to meet his liabilities** = he could not pay his debts; **to discharge one's liabilities in full** = to repay all debts

liable ['laɪəbl] *adjective* **(a) liable (for)** = legally responsible (for); *the customer is liable for breakages*; *the chairman was personally liable for the company's debts*; *he was found by the judge to be liable for the accident*; *he will be found liable if he assists a trustee to commit a dishonest breach of trust* **(b) liable to** = which is officially due to be paid; *sales which are liable to stamp duty*; *such an action renders him liable to a fine*

libel ['laɪbəl] **1** *noun* **(a)** written and published or broadcast statement which damages someone's character (in a permanent form); *he claimed that the newspaper report was a libel*; **criminal libel** = serious libel which might cause a breach of the peace; *see also* DEFAMATION, SLANDER **(b)** act of making a libel; **action for libel** *or* **libel**

action = case in a law court where someone says that another person has written a libel about him **2** *verb* to damage someone's character in writing or in a broadcast (NOTE: **libelling - libelled** but American spelling **libeling - libeled**)

libeller ['laɪbələ] *noun* person who has libelled someone

libellous ['laɪbələs] *adjective* which libels someone's character; *he said that the report was libellous*

liberty ['lɪbəti] *noun* being free; **at liberty** = free, not in prison; *they are still at liberty while waiting for charges to be brought*; **civil liberties** = freedom for people to work or write or speak as they want, providing they keep within the law; **liberty of the individual** = freedom for each person to act within the law; **liberty of the press** = freedom of newspapers to publish what they want within the law without censorship; **liberty of the subject** = right of a citizen to be free unless convicted of a crime which is punishable by imprisonment

licence *US* **license** ['laɪsəns] *noun* **(a)** official document which allows someone to do something or to use something; permission given by someone to another person to do something which would otherwise be illegal; *he granted his neighbour a licence to use his field*; **driving licence**, *US* **driver's license** = document which shows that you have passed a driving test and can legally drive a car, truck, etc.; *applicants for the police force should hold a valid driving licence*; **gaming licence** = document which allows someone or a club to organize games of chance, such as roulette; **import licence** *or* **export licence** = document which allows goods to be imported *or* exported; **licence to sell liquor** *or* **liquor licence** = document given by the Magistrates' Court allowing someone to sell alcohol; *GB* **off licence** = (i) licence to sell alcohol to be drunk away from the place where it is bought; (ii) shop which sells alcohol to be taken away for drinking elsewhere; **on licence** = licence to sell alcohol for drinking on the premises

(as in a bar or restaurant); **occasional licence** = licence to sell alcohol at a certain place and time only **(b)** permission for someone to leave prison before the end of his sentence; **release on licence** = being allowed to leave prison on parole; *the appellant will be released on licence after eight months* **(c)** **goods manufactured under licence** = goods made with the permission of the owner of the copyright or patent

license ['laɪsəns] **1** *noun* *US* = LICENCE **2** *verb* to give someone official permission to do something; *licensed to sell beers, wines and spirits*; *to license a company to produce spare parts*; *he is licensed to drive a lorry*; *she is licensed to run an employment agency*; **licensed premises** = inn, restaurant, bar or shop which has a licence to sell alcohol

licensee [laɪsən'siː] *noun* person who has a licence, especially a licence to sell alcohol or to manufacture something

licensing ['laɪsənsɪŋ] *noun* which refers to licences; **licensing agreement** = agreement where a person is granted a licence to manufacture something or to use something, but not an outright sale; *GB* **licensing hours** = hours of the day where alcohol can be bought to be drunk on the premises; **licensing magistrates** = magistrates who grant licences to persons or premises for the sale of alcohol

licit ['lɪsɪt] *adjective* legal

lie [laɪ] *noun* statement which is not true; **lie detector** = machine which detects if a person is telling the truth; *see also* POLYGRAPH

lie upon the table [laɪ ʌ'pɒn ðə 'teɪbl] *verb (of a petition)* to have been put before the House of Commons

> COMMENT: after a petition has been presented by an MP it is said to 'lie upon the table'

lien [liːn] *noun* legal right to hold someone's goods and keep them until a debt has been paid; *the garage had a lien on her car until she paid the repair bill*;

lien on shares = right of a company to sell shares which have not been fully paid up, and where the shareholder refuses to pay for them fully; **carrier's lien** = right of a carrier to hold goods until he has been paid for carrying them; **equitable lien** = right of someone to hold property (which legally he does not own) until the owner pays money due; **general lien** = holding goods or property until a debt has been paid; **maritime lien** = right to seize a ship against an unpaid debt; *US* **mechanic's lien** = lien on buildings or other property which can be enforced by workmen until they have been paid; **particular lien** = right of a person to keep possession of another person's property until debts relating to that property have been paid; **repairer's lien** = right of someone who has been carrying out repairs to keep the goods until the repair bill has been paid (NOTE: you have a lien **on** an item)

lieu [lu:] *noun* **in lieu of** = instead of; **to give someone two months' salary in lieu of notice** = to give an employee money equivalent to the salary for two months' work and ask him to leave immediately

Lieutenant-Governor [lef'tenənt 'gʌvnə] *noun* **(a)** representative of the British Crown in states or provinces of countries which are members of the Commonwealth; *the Lieutenant-Governor of Nova Scotia* **(b)** *US* deputy to the governor of a state

life [laɪf] *noun* **(a)** time when a person is alive; **for life** = for as long as someone is alive; *his pension gives him a comfortable income for life*; **life annuity** *or* **annuity for life** = annual payments made to someone as long as he is alive; **life assurance** *or* **life insurance** = insurance which pays a sum of money when someone dies, or at a certain date if he is still alive then; **the life assured** *or* **the life insured** = the person whose life has been covered by the life assurance; **life expectancy** = number of years a person is likely to live; **life imprisonment** *or* **life sentence** = being sent to prison as a punishment for a serious crime, but not necessarily for the whole of your life (as a penalty for murder, life

imprisonment lasts on average ten years); **life interest** = interest in a property which comes to an end when a person dies; **life peer** = member of the House of Lords who is appointed for life; *(slang)* **life preserver** = heavy club, cosh **(b)** period of time when something is in existence; *the life of a loan*; *during the life of the agreement*; **shelf life of a product** = length of time when a product can stay in the shop and still be good to use

lifer ['laɪfə] *noun (slang)* person serving a life sentence

LIFO ['laɪfəʊ] = LAST IN FIRST OUT

lift [lɪft] *verb* **(a)** to take away or to remove; *the government has lifted the ban on imports of technical equipment*; *the minister has lifted the embargo on export of firearms*; *proceedings will continue when the stay is lifted* **(b)** *(informal)* to steal

light [laɪt] *noun* **ancient lights** = claim by the owner of a property that he has the right to enjoy light in his windows, which must not be blocked by a neighbour's buildings

lightning factor ['laɪtnɪŋ 'fæktə] *noun (informal)* possibility that even a good case may fail for an unexpected reason (one of the factors to be taken into account when preparing a conditional fee agreement)

likelihood ['laɪklihʊd] *noun* being probable, being likely; **likelihood of bias** = being probable that bias will occur

limit ['lɪmɪt] **1** *noun* point at which something ends, point where you can go no further; **to set limits to imports** *or* **to impose limits on imports** = to allow only a certain amount of goods to be imported; **age limit** = top age at which you are permitted to do something; **credit limit** = fixed amount of money which is the most a client can owe; **he has exceeded his credit limit** = he has borrowed more money than is allowed; **lending limit** = restriction on the amount of money a bank can lend; **prescribed limits** = limits which are set down in legislation (such as the limits of alcohol allowed to drivers); **time limit** =

maximum time which can be taken to do something; **weight limit** = maximum permitted weight **2** *verb* to stop something from going beyond a certain point; *the court limited damages to £100*; **the banks have limited their credit** = the banks have allowed their customers only a certain amount of credit

limitation [lɪmɪ'teɪʃn] *noun* **(a)** act of allowing only a certain amount of something; *the contract imposes limitations on the number of cars which can be imported*; **limitation of liability** = (i) making someone liable for only a part of the damage or loss; (ii) making shareholders in a limited company liable for the debts of the company only in proportion to their shareholding; **time limitation** = amount of time which is available **(b) limitation of actions** *or* **statute of limitations** = law which allows only a certain amount of time (usually six years) for someone to start legal proceedings to claim property or compensation for damage, etc.; *(in civil law)* **limitation period** = period during which someone who has a right to claim against another person must start court proceedings (if he does not make the claim in time, this may be used as a defence to the claim)

limited ['lɪmɪtɪd] *adjective* **(a)** restricted, not open; **limited market** = market which can take only a certain quantity of goods; **limited partnership** = partnership where the liability of some of the partners is limited to the amount of capital they have each provided to the business, and where these partners may not take part in the running of the business, while other working partners are fully liable for all the obligations of the partnership; **limited warranty** = warranty over a product which is limited in some way (ie. it is valid only for a certain period of time, or only under certain conditions of use) **(b) limited liability** = principle that by forming a limited liability company, individual members are liable for that company's debts only to the value of their shares;

limited liability company = company where each shareholder is responsible for repaying the company's debts only to the face value of the shares he owns; **private limited company** = company with a small number of shareholders, whose shares are not traded on the Stock Exchange; **Public Limited Company** = company whose shares can be bought on the Stock Exchange (NOTE: a private limited company is called **Ltd** or **Limited**; a Public Limited Company is called **Plc, PLC or plc**)

limiting ['lɪmɪtɪŋ] *adjective* which limits; *a limiting clause in a contract*; *the short holiday season is a limiting factor on the hotel trade*

Lincoln's Inn ['lɪŋkənz 'ɪn] *noun* one of the four Inns of Court in London

lineal descent ['lɪnɪəl dɪ'sent] *noun* direct descent from parent to child

liquid assets ['lɪkwɪd 'æsɪts] *noun* cash, or bills which can be quickly converted into cash

liquidate ['lɪkwɪdeɪt] *verb* **to liquidate a company** = to wind up a company, to close down a company and sell its assets; **to liquidate a debt** = to pay a debt in full; **to liquidate assets** *or* **stock** = to sell assets or stock to raise cash; **liquidated damages** = specific amount which has been calculated as the loss suffered

liquidation [lɪkwɪ'deɪʃn] *noun* **(a) liquidation of a debt** = payment of a debt in full **(b)** winding up, closing of a company and selling of its assets; **the company went into liquidation** = the company was closed and its assets sold; **compulsory liquidation** = liquidation which is ordered by a court; **voluntary liquidation** = situation where a company itself decides to close down

liquidator [lɪkwɪ'deɪtə] *noun* person who administers the assets and supervises the winding up of a company

liquidity [lɪ'kwɪdɪti] *noun* having cash or assets which can easily be sold to raise cash; *the company was going through a liquidity crisis and had to stop payments*

lis [liːs] *Latin word meaning* 'lawsuit'; **lis alibi pendens** = legal action has been started in another place; **lis pendens** = pending suit; *see also* AD LITEM

list [lɪst] **1** *noun* **(a)** several items written one after the other; *list of debtors*; *to add an item to a list*; *to cross someone's name off a list*; *list of cases to be heard*; **list of members** = annual return made by a company listing its shareholders; **address list** *or* **mailing list** = list of names and addresses of people and companies; **black list** = list of goods, companies or countries which are banned for trade; **Law List** = annual published list of barristers and solicitors **(b)** particular court to which cases are allocated according to their subject **(c)** catalogue; **list price** = price as shown in a catalogue **2** *verb* **(a)** to write a series of items one after the other; *the catalogue lists products by category* **(b)** to decide on the date at which a case will be heard; *the case is listed to be heard next week* **(c)** **listed building** = building of special interest (usually because it is old), which the owners cannot alter or demolish; **listed company** = company whose shares can be bought or sold on the Stock Exchange; **listed securities** = shares which can be bought on the Stock Exchange, shares which appear on the official Stock Exchange list

listing ['lɪstɪŋ] *noun* action of scheduling a case to be heard at a certain date; **listing hearing** = hearing which may be held at which a court decides on the date at which a case will be heard; **listing questionnaire** = questionnaire sent by a court to the parties in a case allocated to the fast track, in which they must give details of documents, witnesses, expert evidence, etc.; the questionnaire has to be filed with the court within 14 days and is used by the court to decide on the listing of the case

litem ['laɪtəm] *see* AD LITEM

literal rule ['lɪtərəl 'ruːl] *noun* rule that when interpreting a statute, the court should give the words of the statute their plain obvious meaning

litigate ['lɪtɪgeɪt] *verb* to go to law, to bring a lawsuit against someone to have a dispute settled

litigant ['lɪtɪgənt] *noun* person who brings a lawsuit against someone; **litigant in person** = person bringing a lawsuit who also speaks on his own behalf in court without the help of a lawyer

litigation [lɪtɪ'geɪʃn] *noun* going to law, bringing of a lawsuit against someone to have a dispute settled; *he has got into litigation with the county council*; **litigation friend** = person who represents a child or patient in court, and whose duty is to act in the best interests of the child or patient

litigious [lɪ'tɪdʒəs] *adjective* (person) who likes to bring lawsuits against people

LJ = LORD JUSTICE (NOTE: written after the surname of the judge in legal reports: **Smith LJ said he was not laying down any guidelines for sentencing** but note that **Smith LJ** is spoken as 'Lord Justice Smith')

LJJ = LORD JUSTICES

LL.B. *or* **LL.M.** *or* **LL.D.** ['el 'el 'biː or 'el 'el 'em or 'el 'el 'diː] letters written after someone's name, showing that he has the degree of Bachelor of Laws, Master of Laws or Doctor of Laws

Lloyd's [lɔɪdz] *noun* central London market for underwriting insurances; **Lloyd's Register** = classified list showing details of all the ships in the world; **ship which is A1 at Lloyd's** = ship in very good condition

loan [ləʊn] **1** *noun* money which has been lent; **loan capital** = part of a company's capital which is a loan to be repaid at a later date, and is not equity or preference shares; **loan stock** = money lent to a company at a fixed rate of interest; **convertible loan stock** = money which can be exchanged for shares at a later date; **bank loan** = money lent by a bank; **bridging loan** = short-term loan to help someone buy a new house when he or she has not yet sold the old one; **short-term loan** *or* **long-term loan** = loans which have to be repaid within a few weeks or some years; **soft loan** = loan (from a company to an employee or from one government to another) with no interest payable; **unsecured loan** = loan made with no security **2** *verb* to lend

lobby ['lɒbi] **1** *noun* **(a)** division lobby *or* voting lobby = one of two long rooms at the side of the House of Commons chamber, where MPs go to vote; **lobby fodder** = ordinary MPs who vote as their party tells them, and do not think much about the issues **(b)** group of people or pressure group which tries to influence MPs or the passage of legislation; **the car lobby** = people who try to persuade MPs that cars should be encouraged and not restricted; **the environmentalist lobby** = group who try to persuade MPs that the environment must be protected, pollution stopped, etc. **(c)** group of journalists attached to the House of Commons, who are given 'off-the-record' briefings by senior ministers or their assistants; **lobby correspondent** = journalist who is a member of the Westminster lobby **2** *verb* to ask someone (such as an MP or local official) to do something on your behalf; *a group of local businessmen has gone to London to lobby their MPs on the problems of unemployment in the area*

lobbyist ['lɒbiist] *noun* person who is paid to represent a pressure group

local ['ləʊkəl] *adjective* relating to a certain area or place; **local authority** = section of elected government which runs a certain area (such as a district council); **local court** = court (such as a magistrates' court) which hears cases coming from a certain area; **local government** = system of government of towns and districts by elected councils and their staffs; *a court can give instructions to a local authority as to the exercise of its powers in relation to children in care; a decision of the local authority pursuant to the powers and duties imposed on it by the Act*

COMMENT: local government in England and Wales is a two-tier system: county councils, with non-metropolitan district councils

under them, and metropolitan district councils which are self-governing large urban areas. In Scotland there are nine large Regional Councils instead of county councils

location [lə'keɪʃn] *noun* **trial location** = place where a trial is to be held

loc. cit. ['lɒk 'sɪt] *Latin phrase meaning* 'in the place which has been mentioned' (NOTE: used when referring to a point in a legal text: '**see also Smith J in** *Jones v. Associated Steel Ltd* **loc. cit. line 26'**)

locking up ['lɒkɪŋ 'ʌp] *noun* **the locking up of money in stock** = investing money in stock so that it cannot be used for other, possibly more profitable, investments

lock out ['lɒk 'aʊt] *verb* **to lock out workers** = to shut the factory door so that workers cannot get in and so make them unable to work until the conditions imposed by the management are met

lockout ['lɒkaʊt] *noun* industrial dispute where the management will not let the workers into the factory until they have agreed to the management's conditions

lock up ['lɒk 'ʌp] *verb* **(a)** to put (someone) in prison or in a psychiatric hospital **(b)** **to lock up a shop** *or* **an office** = to close and lock the door at the end of the day's work; **to lock up capital** = to have capital invested in such a way that it cannot be used for other investments

lock-up ['lɒkʌp] **1** *adjective* **lock-up shop** = shop which has no living accommodation which the proprietor locks at night when it is closed **2** *noun* (*informal*) prison

loco ['ləʊkəʊ] *see* IN LOCO PARENTIS

locum (tenens) ['ləʊkəm 'tenenz] *noun* person who takes the place of another person for a time; *locums wanted in South London*

locus ['ləʊkəs] *Latin word meaning* 'place'

locus sigilli ['ləʊkəs sɪ'dʒɪlaɪ] *Latin phrase meaning* 'place of the seal': used to show where to put the seal on a document

locus standi ['ləʊkəs 'stændaɪ] *Latin phrase meaning* 'place to stand': the right to be heard in a court; *the taxpayer does not have locus standi in this court*

lodge [lɒdʒ] *verb* to put or to deposit (officially); **to lodge caution** = to deposit a document with the Land Registry which prevents land or property being sold without notice; **to lodge a complaint against someone** = to make an official complaint about someone; **to lodge money with someone** = to deposit money with someone; **to lodge securities as collateral** = to put securities into a bank to be used as collateral for a loan

lodger ['lɒdʒə] *noun* person who lives in a house or part of a house which is owned by a resident landlord

logrolling ['lɒgrəʊlɪŋ] *noun US* attaching a bill to another more popular bill before Congress in the hope that the two will be passed together

loitering with intent ['lɔɪtrɪŋ wɪθ ɪn'tent] *noun* offence of walking slowly, stopping frequently, especially to solicit sexual relations

long [lɒŋ] **1** *adjective* for a large period of time; **long credit** = credit terms which allow the borrower a long time to pay; **in the long term** = over a long period of time; **to take the long view** = to plan for a long period before current investment becomes profitable **2** *noun* **longs** = government stocks which mature in over fifteen years' time

long-dated ['lɒŋ'deɪtɪd] *adjective* **long-dated bills** *or* **paper** = bills of exchange which are payable in more than three months' time

long-term ['lɒŋ'tɜːm] *adjective* **on a long-term basis** = for a long period of time; **long-term debts** = debts which will be repaid many years later; **long-term forecast** = forecast for a period of over three years; **long-term loan** = loan to be repaid many years later; **long-term objectives** = aims which will take years to fulfil

Long Vacation ['lɒŋ və'keɪʃn] *noun* summer holiday of the law courts and universities

loophole ['luːphəʊl] *noun* **to find a loophole in the law** = to find a means of doing what you want to do, by finding a way of getting round a law which otherwise would prevent you from acting; **to find a tax loophole** = to find a means of legally not paying tax

loot [luːt] **1** *noun* valuables which have been stolen (by gangs of rioters, soldiers, etc.) **2** *verb* to steal valuable goods from shops, warehouses or homes (especially during a riot); *the stores were looted by a mob of hooligans*

looter ['luːtə] *noun* person who steals valuables from shops, warehouses or homes during a riot

looting ['luːtɪŋ] *noun* act of stealing valuable goods; *the police cordoned off the area to prevent looting*

lord [lɔːd] *noun* member of the House of Lords; **Lord of Appeal** = member of the House of Lords who sits when the House is acting as a Court of Appeal; **Lord of Appeal in Ordinary** = one of eleven lords who are paid to sit as members of the House of Lords when it acts as a Court of Appeal; **Lord Justice** = title given to a judge who is a member of the Court of Appeal; **Lord Justice General** = chief judge in the Scottish High Court of Judiciary; **Lord Justice Clerk** = second most important judge in the Scottish High Court of Justiciary (NOTE: Lord Justice is written LJ after the name: **Smith LJ** = Lord Justice Smith)

Lords [lɔːdz] *plural noun* **(a)** the House of Lords; *the Lords voted to amend the Bill* **(b)** members of the House of Lords; **Lords Spiritual** = archbishops and bishops who are members of the House of Lords; **Lords Temporal** = members of the House of Lords who are not bishops; **the Law**

Lords = members of the House of Lords who are or were judges, and are entitled to sit on the Court of Appeal

Lord Advocate ['lɔːd 'ædvəkət] *noun* member of the government who is one of the two Law Officers in Scotland

Lord Chancellor ['lɔːd 'tʃɑːnsələ] *noun* member of the government and cabinet who presides over the debates in the House of Lords and is responsible for the administration of justice and the appointment of judges

---

COMMENT: the Lord Chancellor is a member of the Cabinet appointed by the Prime Minister; he presides over debates in the House of Lords; he is the head of the judicial system and advises on the appointment of judges

---

Lord Chief Justice ['lɔːd 'tʃiːf 'dʒʌstɪs] *noun* chief judge of the Queen's Bench Division of the High Court who is also a member of the Court of Appeal

Lord Lieutenant ['lɔːd lef'tenənt] *noun* representative of the Crown in a county

Lord Ordinary ['lɔːd 'ɔːdɪnri] *noun* judge of first instance in the outer house of the Scottish Court of Session

Lord President ['lɔːd 'prezɪdənt] *noun* judge of the Scottish Court of Session

Lord President of the Council ['lɔːd 'prezɪdənt əv ðə 'kaunsəl] *noun* senior member of the government, a member of the House of Lords who is the head of the Privy Council Office and has other duties allocated by the Prime Minister

Lord Privy Seal ['lɔːd 'prɪvi 'siːl] *noun* senior member of the government, often a member of Cabinet, with duties allocated by the Prime Minister

lose [luːz] *verb* (a) not to win (in legal proceedings); *he lost his appeal to the House of Lords*; *she lost her case for compensation* (b) not to have something any more; **to lose an order** = not to get an order which you were hoping to get;

during the strike, the company lost six orders to American competitors; **to lose control of a company** = to find that you have less than 50% of the shares and so are no longer able to direct the company; **she lost her job when the factory closed** = she was made redundant; **lost profits** = profits which would have been made from a transaction which is the subject of an action for breach of contract (c) to have less money; *he lost £25,000 in his father's computer company*; **the pound has lost value** = the pound is worth less (d) to drop to a lower price; *the dollar lost two cents against the pound*; *gold shares lost 5% on the market yesterday* (NOTE: **losing - lost - has lost**)

loss [lɒs] *noun* (a) not having something which was had before; **compensation for loss of earnings** = payment to someone who has stopped earning money or who is not able to earn money; **compensation for loss of office** = payment to a director who is asked to leave a company before his contract ends (b) having less money than before, not making a profit; **the company suffered a loss** = the company did not make a profit; **to report a loss** = not to show a profit in the accounts at the end of the year; **capital loss** = loss made by selling assets for less than their book value; **trading loss** = situation where the company's receipts are less than its expenditure; **at a loss** = making a loss, not making any profit; *the company is trading at a loss*; *he sold the shop at a loss*; **to cut one's losses** = to stop doing something which was losing money (c) *(insurance)* **partial loss** = loss where the thing insured has not been completely destroyed; **actual total loss** = loss where the thing insured has been destroyed or damaged beyond repair; **constructive total loss** = loss where the thing insured has been thrown away as it is likely to be irreparable; **the car was written off as a dead loss** *or* **a total loss** = the car was so badly damaged that the insurers said it had no value (d) **loss in weight** = goods which weigh less than when they were packed; **loss in transport** = amount of weight which is lost while goods are being shipped

lot [lɒt] *noun* **(a)** group of items sold together at an auction; *he put in a bid for lot 23*; *at the end of the auction half the lots had not been sold* **(b)** group of shares which are sold; *to sell shares in small lots* **(c)** *US* piece of land, especially one to be used for development

lottery ['lɒtri] *noun* game of chance, where numbered tickets are sold and prizes given for certain numbers

lower ['ləʊə] *adjective* less important; **lower chamber** *or* **lower house** = less important of the two houses in a bicameral system of government (NOTE: the opposite is **upper**)

COMMENT: In a bicameral system, the upper chamber is normally a revising chamber, with some limited powers to delay passing of legislation. Bills normally have to passed by both

houses before they can become law. The lower house of the British legislature is the House of Commons, and in many ways it has more power, especially over financial matters, than the House of Lords, which is the upper house.

LSC = LEGAL SERVICES COMMISSION

lump sum ['lʌmp 'sʌm] *noun* money paid in one single payment, not in several small amounts; *he received a lump sum payment of £500*; *the company offer a lump sum of £1,000 as an out-of-court settlement*

lynch [lɪnʃ] *verb* to catch an accused person and kill him (usually by hanging) without a trial

lynch law ['lɪnʃ 'lɔː] *noun* killing of accused persons by a mob without a trial

Mm

mace [meɪs] *noun* large ornamental stick, made of gold or silver, which is the emblem of government and is placed on the table in the House of Commons or House of Lords, or in some local council chambers, to show that business can begin

COMMENT: the significance of the mace in the House of Commons is so great that if it is not on the table, no business can be done. The mace is carried by the Serjeant at Arms in official processions; it is kept under the table in the House of Commons and placed on the table at the beginning of each sitting; it is taken off the table when the House goes into Committee. In the House of Lords, the mace is placed on the Woolsack. Local authorities usually also have maces which are carried in front of the mayor on ceremonial occasions by the mace-bearer, and often placed on the table at full council meetings. In the US House of Representatives, the mace is placed beside the Speaker's chair when the House is in session. There is no mace in the Senate, but a ceremonial gavel is placed on the vice-president's desk when the Senate is in session

mace-bearer   [ˈmeɪsbeərə]   *noun* official who carries a mace in procession

Madam [ˈmædəm] *noun* formal way of addressing a woman, especially one whom you do not know; **Dear Madam** = beginning of a letter to a woman whom you do not know; **Madam Chairman** = way of addressing a woman who is in the chair at the meeting

Mafia [ˈmæfiə] *noun* **(a)** the **Mafia** = Italian secret society, working on criminal activities in Italy and the USA **(b)** any organized group of criminals; *the Russian drugs mafia*

magistrate [ˈmædʒɪstreɪt] *noun* usually unpaid official who tries cases in a police court; **magistrates' clerk** = official of a magistrates' court who gives advice to the magistrates on law, practice or procedure; **magistrates' court** = (i) building where magistrates try cases; (ii) court presided over by magistrates; **magistrates' courts committee** = committee which organizes the administration of the courts in one or more petty sessions areas; **lay magistrate** = unpaid magistrate who is usually not a qualified lawyer; **stipendiary magistrate** = magistrate who is a qualified lawyer and receives a salary (NOTE: unpaid magistrates are also called **Justices of the Peace** or **JPs**; stipendiary magistrates are now called **District Judges**)

COMMENT: the Magistrates' Courts hear cases of petty crime, adoption, affiliation, maintenance and violence in the home; they hear almost all criminal cases. The court can commit someone for trial or for sentence in the Crown Court. A stipendiary magistrate is a qualified lawyer who usually sits alone; lay magistrates usually sit as a bench of three, and can only sit if there is a justices' clerk present to advise them

Magna Carta [ˈmægnə ˈkɑːtə] *noun* the Great Charter, granted by King John in 1215, which gave his subjects certain political and personal freedoms

COMMENT: the Magna Carta is supposed to be the first step taken towards democratic rule, since it gave political power to the aristocracy and reduced the power of the King to override the law. It did not give power to the ordinary people, but confirmed the rights of the individual to own property and receive impartial justice

magnetic tape *(informal)* **mag tape** [mæg'netɪk 'teɪp or 'mæg 'teɪp] *noun* plastic tape for recording information on a large computer

maiden speech ['meɪdən 'spiːtʃ] *noun* first speech by a new MP in the House of Commons

maintain [meɪn'teɪn] *verb* (a) to keep something going or working; *to maintain good relations with one's customers*; *to maintain contact with an overseas market*; *mounted police were brought in to maintain law and order* (b) to keep something working at the same level; *the company has maintained the same volume of business in spite of the recession*; *to maintain an interest rate at 5%*; **to maintain a dividend** = to pay the same dividend as in the previous year (c) to pay for the food and clothing, etc., for a child or a person; *the ex-husband was ordered to maintain his wife and three children*

maintenance ['meɪntnəns] *noun* (a) keeping things going or working; *the maintenance of law and order is in the hands of the local police force* (b) keeping a machine in good working order; **maintenance contract** = contract by which a company keeps a piece of equipment in good working order (c) payment made by a divorced or separated husband or wife to the former spouse, to help pay for living expenses and the cost of bringing up the children; **maintenance agreement** = agreement drawn up between spouses, detailing the financial arrangements which will be set up if they separate; **maintenance order** = court order which orders a divorced or separated husband or wife to pay maintenance to the

former spouse; **maintenance pending suit** = maintenance obtained by a spouse in matrimonial proceedings until there is a full hearing to deal with the couple's financial affairs (NOTE: American English is **alimony**) (d) formerly, the crime or tort of unlawfully providing someone with money to help that person to pay the costs of suing a third party

Majesty ['mædʒəsti] *noun* title given to a King or Queen; *His Majesty, the King*; *Their Majesties, the King and Queen*; *'Your Majesty, the Ambassador has arrived'*; **Her Majesty's government** = the official title of the British government; **on Her Majesty's Service (OHMS)** = words printed on official letters from government departments; *see also* HER MAJESTY'S PLEASURE

majeure [mæ'dʒɜːr] *see* FORCE MAJEURE

major ['meɪdʒə] *adjective* important; **major shareholder** = shareholder with a large number of shares

majority [mə'dʒɒrəti] *noun* (a) larger group than any other; **a majority of the shareholders** = more than 50% of the shareholders; **a majority of members** = more than 50% of MPs or councillors; **the cabinet accepted the proposal by a majority of ten to seven** = ten members of the cabinet voted to accept and seven voted against; **the board accepted the proposal by a majority of three to two** = three members of the board voted to accept and two voted against; **absolute majority** *or* **overall majority** = more than half the votes, the seats in Parliament, etc.; **simple majority** = majority where the winner has more votes than any other single candidate, but not necessarily more than all the other candidates combined; *see also* QUALIFIED; *US* **majority leader** = spokesman for the majority party in the House of Representatives or Senate, elected by the other members of the party; **majority whip** = assistant to the majority leader, whose responsibility is to see that enough members of the party vote; **majority vote** *or* **majority decision** =

decision made after a vote according to the wishes of the larger group; **majority shareholding** *or* **majority interest** = group of shares which is more than 50% of the total; **a majority shareholder** = person who owns more than half the shares in a company; **majority system** = system of voting where half the votes one more must be cast for a proposal for it to be accepted; **majority verdict** = verdict reached by a jury where at least ten jurors vote for the verdict; *compare* PLURALITY (NOTE: in American English **plurality** is used to indicate a majority over another candidate, and **majority** is used to indicate having more votes than all other candidates put together) **(b)** age at which someone becomes responsible for his actions, can sue, can be sued or can undertake business transactions

COMMENT: the age of majority in the UK and USA is eighteen

maladministration

[mæləldmɪnɪˈstreɪʃn] *noun* incompetent or illegal administration

mala in se [ˈmælə ˈɪn ˈseɪ] *Latin phrase meaning* 'wrongs in themselves': acts (such as murder) which are in themselves crimes

mala prohibita [ˈmælə prəʊˈhɪbɪtə] *Latin phrase meaning* 'forbidden wrongs': acts (such as walking on the grass in a park) which are not crimes in themselves, but which are forbidden

malfeasance [mælˈfiːzəns] *noun* unlawful act

malice [ˈmælɪs] *noun* intentionally committing an act from wrong motives, or the intention to commit a crime; **with malice aforethought** = with the intention of committing a crime (especially murder or grievous bodily harm); **express malice** = intention to kill someone; **implied malice** = intention to cause grievous bodily harm to someone

malicious [məˈlɪʃəs] *adjective* without a lawful reason, with an improper motive; **malicious damage** = deliberate and intentional damage to property; **malicious**

falsehood = lie which is said with the intention of harming someone's business interests; **malicious prosecution** = tort of charging someone with a crime out of malice and without proper reason; **malicious wounding** = inflicting grievous bodily harm on someone with the purpose of causing him injury

maliciously [məˈlɪʃəsli] *adverb* in a malicious way, with the intention of causing harm; *he claimed that he had been prosecuted maliciously*

malpractice [mælˈpræktɪs] *noun* acting in an unprofessional or illegal way (by a doctor, lawyer or accountant, etc.)

management [ˈmænɪdʒmənt] *noun* **(a)** directing or running a business; *he studied management at Edinburgh University*; **line management** = organization of a business where each manager is directly responsible for a stage in the operation of the business; **management accountant** = accountant who prepares specialized information (especially budgets) for managers so that they can make decisions; **management accounts** = financial information (on sales, costs, credit, profitability) prepared for a manager or director of a company; **management consultant** = person who gives advice on how to manage a business; **management course** = training course for managers; **management by objectives** = way of managing a business by planning work for the managers and testing to see if it is completed correctly and on time; **management team** = a group of managers working together; **management training** = training managers by making them study problems and work out ways of solving them; **management trainee** = young person being trained to be a manager **(b)** group of managers or directors; **top management** = the main directors of a company; **middle management** = the department managers of a company who carry out the policy set by the directors and organize the work of a group of workers; **junior management** = managers of small departments, deputies to departmental managers

manager ['mænɪdʒə] *noun* **(a)** head of a department in a company; **accounts manager** = head of the accounts department; **area manager** = manager who is responsible for the company's work (usually sales) in an area; **general manager** = manager in charge of the administration in a large company **(b)** person in charge of a branch or shop; **bank manager** = person in charge of a branch of a bank; **branch manager** = person in charge of a branch of a company

manageress [mænɪdʒə'res] *noun* woman who runs a shop, or a department

managerial [mænə'dʒɪəriəl] *adjective* referring to managers or to management; **to be appointed to a managerial position** = to be appointed a manager; **decisions taken at managerial level** = decisions taken by managers

managing ['mænɪdʒɪŋ] *adjective* **managing clerk** = former term for a legal executive; **managing director** = director who is in charge of a whole company; **chairman and managing director** = managing director who is also chairman of the board of directors

mandamus [mæn'deɪməs] *Latin word meaning* 'we command': court order from the Divisional Court of the Queen's Bench Division, ordering a body (such as a lower court or tribunal) to do a certain legal duty; *the Chief Constable applied for an order of mandamus directing the justices to rehear the case*

mandarin ['mændərɪn] *noun (informal)* **Whitehall mandarin** = top British civil servant

mandate 1 ['mændeɪt] *noun* authority given to a person or group authorizing and requiring them to act on behalf of the person giving the authority; *the government has a mandate from the people to carry out the plans put forward in its manifesto*; **bank mandate** = written order allowing someone to sign cheques on behalf of a company; **to seek a new mandate** = to try to be reelected to a position **2** [mæn'deɪt] *verb* (i) to give (a

government) the authority to carry out certain policies; (ii) to give (a person) authority to vote for a group; *the government has been mandated to revise the tax system*; *the delegates were mandated to vote on behalf of their membership*

mandatory ['mændətri] *adjective* which has to be done or to take place; **mandatory injunction** = order from a court which compels someone to do something; **mandatory meeting** = meeting which must be held or which all members have to attend

manendi [mæ'nendaɪ] *see* ANIMUS

manifest ['mænɪfest] **1** *adjective* obvious; *a manifest injustice* **2** *noun* list of goods in a shipment; **passenger manifest** = list of passengers on a ship or plane

manipulate [mə'nɪpjuːleɪt] *verb* **to manipulate the accounts** = to make false accounts so that the company seems profitable; **to manipulate the market** = to work to influence share prices in your favour

manipulation [mənɪpju'leɪʃn] *noun* **stock market manipulation** = trying to influence the price of shares

manipulator [mə'nɪpjuleɪtə] *noun* **stock market manipulator** = person who tries to influence the price of shares in his own favour

manslaughter ['mænslɔːtə] *noun* notifiable offence of killing someone without having intended to do so, or of killing someone intentionally but with mitigating circumstances; *he was accused of manslaughter*; *she was convicted of the manslaughter of her husband*; **involuntary manslaughter** = killing someone through negligence, without having intended to do so; **voluntary manslaughter** = killing someone intentionally, but under mitigating circumstances (such as provocation or diminished responsibility); **corporate manslaughter** = the killing of someone by a limited company, as in a fatal train accident where the railway company is held responsible

manual ['mænjuəl] *noun* **(a)** book which explains how a piece of machinery works; *the computer manual will tell you how to attach a line printer*; *the operating manual is of no help with this error* **(b)** *US* book which explains the organization and procedures of the Houses of Congress

Mareva injunction [mə'reɪvə ɪn'dʒʌŋkʃn] *noun* court order to freeze the assets of a person who has gone overseas or of a company based overseas to prevent them being taken out of the country (NOTE: since the introduction of the new Civil Procedure Rules in April 1999, this term has been replaced by **freezing injunction**)

COMMENT: called after the case of *Mareva Compania Naviera SA v. International Bulk-Carriers SA*

margin ['mɑːdʒɪn] *noun* difference between the money received from selling a product and the money paid for it; **gross margin** = percentage difference between sales income and cost of sales

marginal ['mɑːdʒɪnəl] *adjective & noun* **(a)** slight, not very large; *the rate increases had only a marginal effect on the council's loan repayments* **(b)** **marginal (constituency)** = constituency where the sitting MP has a small majority; *the swing in several crucial marginals showed that the government was going to lose the election*; *MPs representing marginal seats are worried about the government's poor showing in the opinion polls*

Maria [mə'raɪə] *see* BLACK

marine [mə'riːn] **1** *adjective* referring to the sea or ships; **marine insurance** = insurance of ships and their cargoes; **marine underwriter** = person who insures ships and their cargoes **2** *noun* **the merchant marine** = all the commercial ships of a country

marital ['mærɪtl] *adjective* referring to a marriage; **marital privileges** = privilege of a spouse not to give evidence against the

other spouse in certain criminal proceedings

maritime ['mærɪtaɪm] *adjective* referring to the sea or ships; **maritime law** = laws referring to ships, ports, etc.; **maritime lawyer** = lawyer who specializes in legal matters concerning ships and cargoes; **maritime lien** = right to seize a ship against an unpaid debt; **maritime perils** = PERILS OF THE SEA; **maritime trade** = carrying commercial goods by sea

mark [mɑːk] *noun* **(a)** sign put on an item to show something; **assay mark** = hallmark, mark put on gold or silver items to show that the metal is of the correct quality; **kite mark** = mark on British goods to show that they meet official standards **(b)** cross ('X') put on a document in place of a signature by someone who cannot write

marksman ['mɑːksmən] *noun* **(a)** person who can shoot a gun very accurately **(b)** person who cannot write, and who has to put an 'X' in place of a signature

market ['mɑːkɪt] **1** *noun* **(a)** place (often in the open air) where farm produce is sold; **market day** = day when a market is regularly held; **market dues** = rent for a place in a market **(b)** **the Common Market** = former name for the European Community **(c)** place where a product might be sold, group of people who might buy a product; **home** *or* **domestic market** = market in the country where the selling company is based **(d)** possible sales of a certain type of product, demand for a certain type of product; **a growth market** = market where sales are likely to rise rapidly **(e)** **the black market** = buying and selling goods in a way which is not allowed by law; **to pay black market prices** = to pay high prices to obtain items which are not easily available; *there is a lucrative black market in spare parts for cars*; *he bought gold coins on the black market* **(f)** **a buyer's market** = market where goods are sold cheaply because there is little demand; **a seller's market** = market where the seller can ask high prices because there is a large demand for the product **(g)** **closed market** = market where a supplier deals with only one agent and does not supply any others direct; **free market economy** = system where the government does not interfere in business activity in any way; **open market** = market where anyone can buy and sell; **market value** = value of an asset, of a product or of a company, if sold today **(h) capital market** = place where companies can look for investment capital; **the foreign exchange markets** = places where currencies are bought or sold; **forward markets** = places where foreign currency or commodities can be bought or sold for delivery at a later date **(i) stock market** = place where shares are bought and sold; **to buy shares in the open market** = to buy shares on the Stock Exchange, not privately; **market capitalization** = value of a company calculated by multiplying the price of its shares on the Stock Exchange by the number of shares issued; **market price** = price at which a product can be sold **2** *verb* to sell (products); *this product is being marketed in all European countries*

marketable ['mɑːkɪtəbl] *adjective* which can be sold (easily); **marketable title** = title to a property which can be sold (i.e. it is free of major encumbrances)

market overt ['mɑːkɪt 'əʊvɜːt] *noun* market which is open to all, in which a sale gives good title to a buyer, even though the seller's title may be defective

> COMMENT: this was only applied to certain open-air antique markets, and has been abolished

mark up ['mɑːk 'ʌp] *verb US* **to mark up a bill** = to make changes to a bill as it goes through committee

marriage ['mærɪdʒ] *noun* act or state of being joined together as husband and wife; **by marriage** = because of being married; *she became a British citizen by marriage*; **marriage settlement** = agreement which is made before marriage where money or property is given on trust for the benefit of the future spouse; **sham marriage** *or*

marriage of convenience = form of marriage arranged for the purpose of acquiring the nationality of a spouse or for some other financial reason

marshal ['mɑːʃl] *noun* **(a) Marshal of the Admiralty Court** = official in charge of the Admiralty Court **(b)** *US* official who carries out the orders of a court (NOTE: the British equivalent is a **bailiff**) **(c)** *US* federal officer with the same functions as a sheriff at state level

marshalling ['mɑːʃəlɪŋ] *noun* action of a beneficiary of an estate to recover money due to him which was paid to a creditor

martial ['mɑːʃl] *adjective* relating to the armed services; **martial law** = rule of a country or part of a country by the army on the orders of the main government, the ordinary civil law having been suspended; *the president imposed or declared martial law in two provinces*; *the government lifted martial law*; *see also* COURT-MARTIAL

master ['mɑːstə] *noun* **(a)** official in the Queen's Bench Division or Chancery Division of the High Court whose work is to examine and decide on preliminary matters before trial; **Practice Master** = master on duty in the High Court, who will hear solicitors without appointment and give directions in relation to the general conduct of proceedings; *see also* TAXING MASTER **(b) Masters of the Bench** = senior members of one of the Inns of Court **(c) master and servant** = employer and employee; **the law of master and servant** = employment law **(d)** main or original; **master copy of a file** = main copy of a computer file, kept for security purposes

Master of the Rolls ['mɑːstə əv ðə 'rəʊlz] *noun* senior judge who presides over the Civil Division of the Court of Appeal and is responsible for admitting solicitors to the Roll of Solicitors

material [mə'tɪərɪəl] *adjective* important or relevant; **material alteration** = change made to a legal document which alters the rights or duties in it; **material evidence** = evidence which has important relevance to a case; **material witness** = witness whose evidence is important to the case

matricide ['mætrɪsaɪd] *noun* murder of one's mother

matrimonial [mætrɪ'məʊnɪəl] *adjective* referring to marriage; **matrimonial causes** = proceedings concerned with rights of partners in a marriage (such as divorce or separation proceedings); **matrimonial home** = place where a husband and wife live together

matrimony ['mætrɪmʌni] *noun* marriage, state of being joined together as husband and wife

matter ['mætə] **1** *noun* **(a)** problem; **it is a matter of concern to the members of the committee** = the members of the committee are worried about it **(b) printed matter** = printed books, newspapers, advertising material, etc. **(c)** question or problem to be discussed; *the most important matter on the agenda*; *we shall consider first the matter of last month's fall in prices*; **interlocutory matter** = subsidiary dispute which is dealt with before a full trial; **matter of fact** = question of fact which has to be decided; **matters of fact** = facts relevant to a case which is tried at court; **matters of law** = law relevant to a case which is tried at court; *it is a matter of fact whether the parties entered into the contract, but it is a matter of law whether or not the contract is legal* **2** *verb* to be important; *does it matter if one month's sales are down?*

mature [mə'tʃʊə] *verb* to be due for payment; *bill which will mature in three months*

maturity [mə'tʃʊərəti] *noun* time when a bill, government stock or insurance is due for payment

maxim ['mæksɪm] *noun* short phrase which formulates a principle, such as 'let the buyer beware'

May Day ['meɪ 'deɪ] *noun* annual celebration of workers, held in many countries on May 1st; *see also* LABOR DAY

mayhem ['meɪhem] *noun* **(a)** general riot or disturbance; **(b)** violent removal of a person's arm or leg

mayor ['meə] *noun* person who is elected or chosen as the official head of a town *or* city or local council; **Lord Mayor** = Mayor of a very large town (such as London, Liverpool)

COMMENT: previously, a mayor was the head of the elected government of a town, and the head of the majority party. His governmental responsibilities have now been taken over by the Leader of the Council, and the office of mayor is largely ceremonial. It is an honour often given to a long-serving or distinguished councillor. In London, the mayor is elected by popular vote. In Scotland, a mayor is called a Provost. Note also that 'Mayor' is used in English to apply to persons holding similar positions in other countries: the **Mayor of Berlin**

mayoral ['meərəl] *noun* referring to a mayor; *he is carrying out his mayoral duties*; *the mayoress went to the ceremony in the mayoral car*

mayoralty ['meərlti] *noun* the position of a mayor; *the time for which someone is mayor*

mayoress [meə'res] *noun* (i) woman mayor; (ii) wife of a mayor

mayor-making ['meə'meɪkɪŋ] *noun* ceremony which takes place at a council's Annual Meeting, when the new mayor is invested with his chain of office

McNaghten [mək'nɔːtən] *see* M'NAGHTEN

means [miːnz] *plural noun* money which is available; **statement of means** = statement attached to an application for Legal Aid which shows the financial position of the claimant

measure ['meʒə] *noun* **(a)** way of calculating size or quantity; **cubic measure** = volume in cubic feet or metres, calculated by multiplying height, width and length; **square measure** = area in square feet or metres, calculated by multiplying width and length; **inspector of weights and measures** = government inspector who inspects weighing machines and goods sold in shops to see if the quantities and weights are correct; **measure of damages** = calculation of how much money a court should order one party to pay another to compensate for a tort or breach **(b)** type of action, especially a law passed by Parliament or statutory instrument; *a government measure to reduce crime in the inner cities*; **to take measures to prevent something happening** = to act to stop something happening; **to take emergency measures** = to act rapidly to stop a dangerous situation developing; **an economy measure** = an action to save money; **fiscal measures** = tax changes made by the government to improve the working of the economy; **as a precautionary measure** = to prevent something taking place; **safety measures** = actions to make sure that something is or will be safe

mechanical reproduction rights

[mɪˈkænɪkl rɪprəˈdʌkʃn ˈraɪts] *plural noun* right to make a recording of a piece of music, to make a copy of something by photographing it, etc. (usually against payment of a fee)

mechanic's lien [mɪˈkænɪks ˈliːn] *see* LIEN

mediate [ˈmiːdieɪt] *verb* to try to make the two sides in an argument come to an agreement; *to mediate between the manager and his staff*; *the government offered to mediate in the dispute*

mediation [miːdiˈeɪʃn] *noun* attempt by a third party to make the two sides in an argument agree; *the employers refused an offer of government mediation*; *the dispute was ended through the mediation of union officials*

mediator [ˈmiːdieɪtə] *noun* **official mediator** = government official who tries to make the two sides in an industrial dispute agree

medical [ˈmedɪkl] *noun* referring to the study or treatment of illness; **medical certificate** = certificate from a doctor to show that a worker has been ill; **medical inspection** = examining a place of work to see if the conditions are safe; **medical insurance** = insurance which pays the cost of medical treatment especially when travelling abroad; **medical officer of health (MOH)** = person responsible for the health services in a town; **he resigned for medical reasons** = he resigned because he was too ill to work

medicine [ˈmedsɪn] *noun* scientific study of diseases and health; **forensic medicine** = medical science concerned with solving crimes against people (such as autopsies of murdered persons, taking blood samples from clothes, etc.)

meeting [ˈmiːtɪŋ] *noun* **(a)** coming together of a group of people; **board meeting** = meeting of the directors of a company; **general meeting** *or* **meeting of shareholders** *or* **shareholders' meeting** = meeting of all the shareholders of a company, meeting of all the members of a society; **Annual General Meeting, US Annual Meeting** = meeting of all the shareholders of a company which takes place once a year to agree the accounts; **Extraordinary General Meeting** = special meeting of shareholders to discuss an important matter which cannot wait until the next Annual General Meeting **(b) to hold a meeting** = to organize a meeting of a group of people; *the meeting will be held in the committee room*; **to open a meeting** = to start a meeting; **to conduct a meeting** = to be in the chair for a meeting; **to close a meeting** = to end a meeting; **to put a resolution to a meeting** = to ask a meeting to vote on a proposal; **freedom of meeting** = being able to meet as a group without being afraid of prosecution

member [ˈmembə] *noun* **(a)** person who belongs to a group or a society; **ordinary member** = person who pays a subscription to belong to a club or group; **honorary member** = special person who does not have to pay a subscription **(b)** Member of Parliament; *the member for Oxford*; *the* *newly elected member for Windsor*; **members' gallery** = one of the galleries in the House of Commons, where the guests of MPs can sit and listen to the debates **(c)** person elected to a local council; *the members asked for a report from the planning officer*; *officers must carry out the wishes of members* **(d)** shareholder, person who owns shares in a company **(e)** organization which belongs to a society; *the member countries or the Member States of the EU*; *the members of the United Nations*; *the member firms of the Stock Exchange*

Member of Parliament (MP)

['membə əv 'pɑːləmənt] *noun* person elected to represent a constituency in Parliament (NOTE: the plural is **MPs**)

> COMMENT: any British subject over 21 is eligible for election as an MP, but the following are disqualified: peers, ministers of the Church of Scotland, persons holding an office of profit (such as judges and civil servants), bankrupts, people who are insane, and some categories of prisoners

Member of the European Parliament (MEP)

['membə əv ðə juːrə'piːən 'pɑːləmənt] *noun* person elected to represent a Euro-constituency in the European Parliament

membership ['membəʃɪp] *noun* **(a)** belonging to a group; *membership qualifications*; *conditions of membership*; *to pay your membership or your membership fees*; *when did Turkey apply for membership of the European Union?* **(b)** all the members of a group; *the membership was asked to vote for the new president*; **the club's membership secretary** = committee member who deals with the ordinary members of a society; **the club has a membership of five hundred** = the club has five hundred members

Member State ['membə 'steɪt] *noun* *(in the EU)* state which is a member of the European Union

memorandum [memə'rændəm] *noun* short note; **memorandum of association** = legal document setting up a limited company and giving details of its aims, capital structure, and registered office; **memorandum of satisfaction** = document showing that a company has repaid a mortgage or charge (NOTE: plural is **memoranda**)

menace ['menəs] *noun* threat, action which frightens someone; **demanding money with menaces** = crime of getting money by threatening another person

mens rea ['mens 'reɪə] *Latin phrase meaning 'guilty mind':* mental state required to be guilty of committing a crime (intention, recklessness or guilty knowledge); *see note at* CRIME, *and compare* ACTUS REUS

mental ['mentl] *adjective* referring to the mind; **mental cruelty** = cruelty by one spouse to the other, which possibly harms his or her mental state (it is grounds for divorce in the USA); **mental disorder** = sickness of the mind

mentally ['mentli] *adverb* in the mind; *mentally ill criminals are committed to special establishments*

mention ['menʃn] *noun* short hearing at court

mentis ['mentɪs] *see* COMPOS MENTIS

MEP ['em 'iː 'piː] = MEMBER OF THE EUROPEAN PARLIAMENT

mercantile law *or* law merchant

['mɜːkəntaɪl 'lɔː *or* lɔː 'mɜːtʃənt] *noun* law relating to commerce

merchantable quality ['mɜːtʃəntəbl 'kwɒləti] *noun* quality of goods for sale, which are suitable for the purpose for which they are to be used and conform to the description and price of them in the manufacturer's catalogue

mercy ['mɜːsi] *noun* showing that you forgive; **prerogative of mercy** = power (used by the Home Secretary) to commute or remit a sentence

mercy killing ['mɜːsi 'kılıŋ] *noun* euthanasia, the killing of a sick person to put an end to his or her suffering

merge [mɜːdʒ] *verb* to join together; *the two companies have merged*; *the firm merged with its main competitor*

merger ['mɜːdʒə] *noun* (i) joining of a small estate to a large one; (ii) joining together of two or more companies; *as a result of the merger, the company is the largest in the field*

meridiem [mə'rıdiəm] *see* A.M., P.M.

merit ['merıt] *noun* being good or efficient; **merit award** *or* **merit bonus** = extra money given to a worker because he or she has worked well; **merit increase** = increase in pay given to someone because his or her work is good; **merit rating** = judging how well a worker does his work, so that he can be paid according to merit

merits of the case ['merıts əv ðə 'keıs] *plural noun* main question which is at issue in an action

mesne [miːn] *adjective* in the middle; **mesne process** = process in a legal action, which comes after the first writ but before the outcome of the action has been decided; **action for mesne profits** = action to recover money that should be paid to a landowner in place of rent by a person who is in wrongful possession

Messrs ['mesəz] *noun* plural form of Mr, used in names of firms; *Messrs White, White & Smith*

messuage ['meswıdʒ] *noun* house where people live, and the land and buildings attached to it

Met [met] *noun (informal)* the Met = the Metropolitan Police

metropolitan [metrə'pɒlıtən] *adjective* referring to a large city; **Metropolitan District Council** = large administrative area covering an urban area in England or Wales; **the Metropolitan Police** = the police force of Greater London, which is directly responsible to the Home Secretary;

the Metropolitan Police Commissioner = the head of the Metropolitan Police, appointed directly by the Home Secretary; **solicitor for the Metropolitan Police** = solicitor responsible for prosecutions brought by the Metropolitan Police

COMMENT: the higher ranks in the Metropolitan Police are Deputy Assistant Commissioner, Assistant Commissioner, and Commissioner. See also DETECTIVE, POLICE

Michaelmas ['mıklməs] *noun* **(a)** 29th September: one of the quarter days when rent is payable on land **(b)** one of the four sittings of the law courts; one of the four law terms

middle ['mıdl] *adjective* in the centre, between two points; **middle management** = department managers in a company, who carry out the policy set by the directors and organize the work of a group of workers

Middle Temple ['mıdl 'templ] *noun* one of the four Inns of Court in London

Midland and Oxford Circuit ['mıdlənd ənd 'ɒksfəd 'sɜːkıt] *noun* one of the six circuits of the Crown Court, to which barristers belong, with its centre in Birmingham

Midsummer day ['mıdsʌmə 'deı] *noun* 24th June: one of the four quarter days when rent is payable on land

militant ['mılıtənt] *adjective & noun* (person) who very actively supports and works for a cause; *the speaker was shouted down by militant union members*

minder ['maındə] *noun (slang)* bodyguard, a person employed to protect someone

minimis ['mınımiːs] *see* DE MINIMIS

minimum ['mınıməm] **1** *noun* smallest possible quantity, price or number; *to keep expenses to a minimum*; *to reduce the risk of a loss to a minimum* **2** *adjective* smallest possible; **minimum dividend** = smallest dividend which is legal and accepted by the shareholders; **minimum payment** = smallest payment necessary;

minimum sentence = shortest possible sentence allowed in law for a certain offence; **minimum wage** = lowest hourly wage which a company can legally pay its workers

minister ['mɪnɪstə] *noun* **(a)** member of a government who is in charge of a ministry; *a government minister; the Minister of Information or the Information Minister; the Minister of Foreign Affairs or the Foreign Minister; the Minister of Justice or the Justice Minister;* Minister of State = person who is in charge of a section of a government department **(b)** senior diplomat below the rank of ambassador

COMMENT: in the USA, heads of government departments are called **secretary: the Secretary for Commerce;** in the UK, heads of government departments (see below) are called **Secretary of State: the Secretary of State for Defence**

ministerial [ˌmɪnɪ'stɪriəl] *adjective* referring to a minister; **ministerial tribunal** = tribunal set up by a government minister to hear appeals from local tribunals

ministry ['mɪnɪstri] *noun* **(a)** department in the government; *he works in the Ministry of Finance or the Finance Ministry; he is in charge of the Ministry of Information or of the Information Ministry; a ministry official or an official from the ministry* **(b)** government; **during the Wilson ministry** = when the government headed by Prime Minister Wilson was in office

COMMENT: in Britain and the USA, important ministries are called **departments: the Department of Trade and Industry; the Commerce Department.** Note also that the UK does not have a government department called the 'Ministry of Justice', and the duties of supervising the administration of justice fall to the Lord Chancellor's Office and the Home Office

minor ['maɪnə] **1** *adjective* less important; *minor expenditure; minor shareholders;* **a loss of minor importance** = not a very serious loss **2** *noun* person less than eighteen years old

minority [mɪ'nɒrəti] *noun* **(a)** being less than eighteen years old; period when someone is less than eighteen years old; *a person is not liable for debts contracted during his minority* **(b)** number or quantity which is less than half of the total; *a minority of board members opposed the chairman;* **minority shareholding** *or* **minority interest** = group of shares which are less than one half of the shares in a company; **minority shareholder** = person who owns a group of shares but less than half of the shares in a company; **in the minority** = being fewer than half; *the small parties are in the minority on the local council*

minute ['mɪnɪt] **1** *noun* **(a)** one sixtieth part of an hour; *counsel cross-examined the witness for fifty minutes* **(b)** minutes = the record of what happened at a meeting, especially the record of a general meeting of a company; **to take the minutes** = to write notes of what happened at a meeting; **the chairman signed the minutes of the last meeting** = he signed them to show that they were a correct record of what was said and what decisions were taken; **this will not appear in the minutes of the meeting** = this is unofficial and will not be noted as having been said **(c)** minutes of order = a draft order submitted to a court when a party wishes the court to make an order **2** *verb* to put something into the minutes of a meeting; *the chairman's remarks about the auditors were minuted;* **I do not want that to be minuted** *or* **I want that not to be minuted** = do not put that remark into the minutes of the meeting

minutebook ['mɪnɪtbʊk] *noun* book in which the minutes of a meeting are kept

misadventure [mɪsəd'ventʃə] *noun* accident; **death by misadventure** = accidental death; *the coroner's verdict was death by misadventure*

misappropriate [mɪsə'prəuprieɪt] *verb* to steal or to use illegally money which is not yours, but with which you have been trusted

misappropriation [mɪsəprəupri'eɪʃn] *noun* illegal use of money by someone who is not the owner but who has been trusted to look after it

misbehaviour [mɪsbɪ'heɪvjə] *noun* bad behaviour, especially a criminal offence committed by a public official

miscalculate [mɪs'kælkjuleɪt] *verb* to calculate wrongly; *the salesman miscalculated the discount, so we hardly broke even on the deal*

miscalculation [mɪskælkju'leɪʃn] *noun* mistake in calculating

miscarriage of justice ['mɪskærɪdʒ əv 'dʒʌstɪs] *noun* decision wrongly or unjustly reached by a court; decision which goes against the rights of a party in a case, in such a way that the decision may be reversed on appeal

mischief rule ['mɪstʃɪf 'ruːl] *noun* rule that when interpreting a statute, the court should try to see what the wrong was that the statute tried to remedy and what the remedy was that Parliament has enacted

misconduct [mɪs'kɒndʌkt] *noun* illegal action, action which can harm someone; **professional misconduct =** behaviour by a member of a profession (such as a lawyer, accountant or doctor) which the body which regulates that profession considers to be wrong (such as an action by a solicitor which is considered wrong by the Law Society); **wilful misconduct =** doing something which harms someone while knowing it is wrong

misdeed [mɪs'diːd] *noun* crime

misdemeanour *US*
misdemeanor [mɪsdɪ'miːnə] *noun* minor crime; *he was charged with several misdemeanours, including driving without a valid licence and creating a disturbance*

misdescription [mɪsdɪ'skrɪpʃn] *noun* false or misleading description of the subject of a contract

misdirect [mɪsdaɪ'rekt] *verb* to give wrong directions to a jury on a point of law

misdirection [mɪsdɪ'rekʃn] *noun* giving wrong directions to a jury on a point of law

misfeasance [mɪs'fiːzəns] *noun* doing something improperly

misinterpret [mɪsɪn'tɜːprət] *verb* to understand something wrongly; *the fire-fighters misinterpreted the instructions of the police*

misinterpretation [mɪsɪntɜːprɪ'teɪʃn] *noun* wrong interpretation or understanding of something; **clause which is open to misinterpretation =** clause which can be wrongly interpreted

misjoinder [mɪs'dʒɔɪndə] *noun* wrongly joining someone as a party to an action

misprision [mɪs'prɪʒn] *noun* generally, knowing that a crime is being committed, but doing nothing about it; **misprision of treason =** crime of knowing that treason has been committed

misrepresent [mɪsreprɪ'zent] *verb* to report facts wrongly

misrepresentation
[mɪsreprɪzen'teɪʃn] *noun* making a wrong statement with the intention of persuading someone to enter into a contract; **fraudulent misrepresentation =** false statement made wilfully to trick someone or to persuade someone to enter into a contract

mission ['mɪʃn] *noun* **(a)** special purpose for which someone is sent somewhere; *his mission was to try to persuade the rebels to accept the government's terms;* **mission statement =** statement which sets out the aims of an organization **(b)** group of people who go abroad for a special purpose; *a trade mission to Japan; the members of the* *government mission are staying in the embassy* **(c)** embassy, consulate or building where representatives of a foreign country work; *the crowd gathered outside the gates of the British Mission*

mistake in venue [mɪˈsteɪk ɪn ˈvenjuː] *noun* starting legal proceedings in the wrong court

mistaken identity [mɪsˈteɪkn aɪˈdentəti] *noun* situation where someone is wrongly thought to be another person; *he was arrested for burglary, but released after it had been established that it was a case of mistaken identity*

mistrial [mɪsˈtraɪəl] *noun* trial which is not valid

misuse [ˈmɪsˈjuːs] *noun* wrong use; *misuse of funds or of assets*

mitigate [ˈmɪtɪɡeɪt] *verb* to make (a crime) less serious; **mitigating circumstances** *or* **factors** = things which make a crime less serious or which can excuse a crime

mitigation [mɪtɪˈɡeɪʃn] *noun* reduction of a sentence, or of the seriousness of a crime; *in mitigation, counsel submitted evidence of his client's work for charity*; *defence counsel made a speech in mitigation*; **plea in mitigation** = things said in court on behalf of a guilty party to persuade the court to impose a lenient sentence; **mitigation of damages** = reduction in the extent of damages awarded (NOTE: used in the construction **in mitigation of**)

M'Naghten Rules [məkˈnɔːtən ˈruːlz] *noun* rules which a judge applies in deciding if a person charged with a crime is insane

COMMENT: to prove insanity, it has to be shown that because of a diseased mind, the accused did not know what he was doing or did not know that his action was wrong. Based on the case of *R v. M'Naghten*

(1843) in which the House of Lords considered and ruled on the defence of insanity

mob [mɒb] *noun US* the Mafia

mobster [ˈmɒbstə] *noun US* member of an organized crime group

modus operandi [ˈməʊdəs ɒpəˈrændiː] *Latin phrase meaning* 'way of working': especially a particular way of committing crimes which can identify a criminal

modus vivendi [ˈməʊdəs vɪˈvendiː] *Latin phrase meaning* 'way of living'; informal agreement between parties (as between employers and workers, between Church and State) to exist peacefully together; *after years of confrontation, they finally have achieved a modus vivendi*

MOH = MEDICAL OFFICER OF HEALTH

moiety [ˈmɔɪəti] *noun* half

molest [məˈlest] *verb* to threaten violent behaviour against (a child or a woman, especially a spouse) in a sexual way; *he was accused of molesting children in the park*

molestation [məʊleˈsteɪʃn] *noun* act of threatening violent behaviour towards a child or a woman, especially a spouse; **non-molestation order** = order made by a court in matrimonial proceedings to prevent one spouse from molesting the other

molester [məˈlestə] *noun* person who molests; *a convicted child molester*

monarchy [ˈmɒnəki] *noun* **(a)** rule by a king or queen; *the monarchy was overthrown in the revolution, and the king replaced by a president* **(b)** country ruled by a monarch; *Belgium, Sweden and Britain are monarchies*; **constitutional monarchy** = monarchy where the king or queen has limited constitutional powers, and most power is in the hands of an elected legislature and the government is headed by a democratically elected Prime Minister

money ['mʌni] *noun* **(a)** coins and notes used for buying and selling; **cheap money** = money which can be borrowed at a low rate of interest; **danger money** = extra money paid to workers in dangerous jobs; **dear money** = money which has to be borrowed at a high rate of interest; **hot money** = (i) money which is moved from country to country to get the best interest rate; (ii) stolen money, or money which has been obtained illegally; **paper money** = money in notes, not coins; **ready money** = cash, money which is immediately available; **money claim** = claim which involves the payment of money (ie. a claim for repayment of a debt, or a claim for damages); **money had and received** = cause of action where one party has had money which really belongs to someone else **(b) money supply** = amount of money which exists in a country; **money markets** = markets for buying and selling short-term loans; **money rates** = rates of interest for borrowers or lenders **(c) money order** = document which can be bought for sending money through the post; **foreign money order** *or* **international money order** *or* **overseas money order** = money order in a foreign currency which is payable to someone living in a foreign country **(d) monies** = sums of money; *monies owing to the company*; *to collect monies due*

moneylender ['mʌnilendə] *noun* person who lends money at interest

monogamy [mə'nɒgəmi] *noun* system of society where a man is married to one woman at a time; *compare* BIGAMY, POLYGAMY

monopolization [mənɒpəlaɪ'zeɪʃn] *noun* making a monopoly

monopolize [mə'nɒpəlaɪz] *verb* to create a monopoly, to get control of all the supply of a product

monopoly [mə'nɒpəli] *noun* situation where one person or company controls all the market in the supply of a product; the right given to one person or company to control all the market in the supply of a product; *to have the monopoly of alcohol sales or to have the alcohol monopoly*; *the company has the absolute monopoly of imports of French wine*; **public monopoly** *or* **state monopoly** = situation where the state is the only supplier of a product or service (such as the German Post Office, the French tobacco board); **the Monopolies (and Mergers) Commission** = British body which examines takeovers and mergers to make sure that a monopoly is not being created (NOTE: American English uses **trust** more often than **monopoly**)

monopsony [mə'nɒpsəni] *noun* situation where one person or company controls all the purchasing in a certain market

Monroe doctrine [mʌn'rəʊ 'dɒktrɪn] *noun US* principle that the USA has an interest in preventing outside interference in the internal affairs of other American states

COMMENT: so called because it was first proposed by President Monroe in 1823

moonlight ['muːnlaɪt] *verb (informal)* to do a second job for cash (often in the evening) as well as a regular job, and usually not declaring the money earned to the income tax authorities

moonlighter ['muːnlaɪtə] *noun* person who moonlights

moonlighting ['muːnlaɪtɪŋ] *noun* doing a second job; *he makes thousands a year from moonlighting*

mooring ['mʊərɪŋ] *noun* place where boats can be tied up in a harbour

moot case ['muːt 'keɪs] *noun* legal case to be discussed on its own, to establish a precedent

moral ['mɒrəl] *adjective* referring to the difference between what is right and what is wrong; *the high moral standard which should be set by judges*

moral rights ['mɒrəl 'raɪts] *noun* the rights of a copyright holder to be identified as the creator of the work (also called 'paternity'), not to have the work subjected to derogatory treatment, the right to prevent someone else from claiming to be the author of the work

morals ['mɒrəlz] *plural noun* standards of behaviour; **to corrupt someone's morals** = to make someone behave in a way which goes against the normal standard of behaviour

moratorium [mɒrə'tɔːriəm] *noun* temporary stop to repayments of money owed; *the banks called for a moratorium on payments* (NOTE: plural is **moratoria**)

morning hour ['mɔːnɪŋ 'aʊə] *noun* US period at the beginning of each day's sitting of Congress, given up to routine business

mortality [mɔː'tæləti] *noun* **mortality tables** = chart, used by insurers, which shows how long a person of a certain age can be expected to live, on average

mortgage ['mɔːgɪdʒ] **1** *noun* (i) agreement where someone lends money to another person so that he can buy a property, the property being used as the security; (ii) money lent in this way; *to take out a mortgage on a house*; *to buy a house with a £200,000 mortgage*; **mortgage (re)payments** = money paid each month as interest on a mortgage, together with repayment of a small part of the capital borrowed; **endowment mortgage** = mortgage backed by an endowment policy; **equitable mortgage** = mortgage which does not give the mortgagee a legal estate in the land mortgaged; **first mortgage** = main mortgage on a property; **puisne mortgage** = mortgage where the deeds of the property have not been deposited with the lender; **second mortgage** = further mortgage on a property which is already mortgaged, the first mortgage always having a prior claim; **to foreclose on a mortgaged property** = to take possession of a property because the owner cannot pay the interest on the money which he has

borrowed using the property as security; **to pay off a mortgage** = to pay back the principal and all the interest on a loan to buy a property; **mortgage bond** = certificate showing that a mortgage exists and that property is security for it; **mortgage debenture** = debenture where the lender can be repaid by selling the company's property **2** *verb* to accept a loan with a property as security; *the house is mortgaged to the bank*; *he mortgaged his house to set up in business*

mortgagee [mɔːgɪ'dʒiː] *noun* person or company which lends money for someone to buy a property and takes a mortgage of the property as security

mortgagor [mɔːgɪ'dʒɔː] *noun* person who borrows money, giving a property as security

mortem ['mɔːtəm] *see* POST MORTEM

mortis ['mɔːtɪs] *see* DONATIO, RIGOR

most favoured nation ['məʊst 'feɪvəd 'neɪʃn] *noun* country which has the best trade terms; **most-favoured-nation clause** = agreement between two countries that each will offer the best possible terms in commercial contracts

motion ['məʊʃn] *noun* **(a)** moving about; **time and motion study** = study in an office or factory of the time taken to do certain jobs and the movements workers have to make to do them **(b)** proposal which will be put to a meeting for that meeting to vote on; *to propose or to move a motion*; *the meeting voted on the motion*; *to speak against or for a motion*; **the motion was carried** *or* **was defeated by 220 votes to 196** = the motion was approved *or* not approved; **to table a motion** = (i) to put forward a proposal for discussion by putting details of it on the table at a meeting; (ii) US to remove a proposal from discussion by a meeting for an indefinite period; **substantive motion** = motion which is complete in itself; **subsidiary motion** = motion which is related to a substantive motion (such as a motion for adjournment) **(c)** application to a judge in court, asking for an order in favour of the person making the application; **notice of motion** = document telling the other party to a case that an application will be made to the court

movable *or* **moveable** ['muːvəbl] **1** *adjective* which can be moved; **movable property** = chattels and other objects which can be moved (as opposed to land) **2** *plural noun* **movables** = movable property

move ['muːv] *verb* **(a)** to go from one place to another; *the company is moving from London Road to the centre of town*; *we have decided to move our factory to a site near the airport* **(b)** to propose formally that a motion be accepted by a meeting; *he moved that the accounts be agreed*; *I move that the meeting should adjourn for ten minutes* **(c)** to make an application to the court

movement ['muːvmənt] *noun* **(a)** changing position, going up or down; *movements in the money markets*; *cyclical movements of trade*; **movements of capital** = changes of investments from one country to another; **free movement of capital** = ability to transfer capital from one EC country to another without any restrictions; **stock movements** = passing of stock into or out of the warehouse **(b)** group of people working towards the same aim

mover ['muːvə] *noun* person who proposes a motion

MP ['em 'piː] = MEMBER OF PARLIAMENT, MILITARY POLICE

MR = MASTER OF THE ROLLS (NOTE: usually written after the surname: **Lord Smith, MR** but spoken as 'the Master of the Rolls, Lord Smith')

Mr Big ['mɪstə 'bɪg] *noun (informal)* important criminal whose name is not known, but who is supposed to be in control of a large criminal operation

mug [mʌg] **1** *noun (informal)* **(a)** person who is easily cheated **(b)** face; **mug shot** = photograph of a criminal taken after he has been detained, kept in the police records **2**

verb to attack and rob someone; *the tourists were mugged in the station*; *he was accused of mugging an old lady in the street* (NOTE: **mugging - mugged**)

mugger ['mʌgə] *noun* person who attacks and robs someone

mugging ['mʌgɪŋ] *noun* attacking and robbing someone; *the number of muggings has increased sharply over the last few years*

multiple ['mʌltɪpl] *adjective* many; **multiple entry visa** = visa which allows a visitor to enter a country many times; **multiple ownership** = situation where something is owned by several parties

multi-track ['mʌlti'træk] *noun (in civil cases)* case management system which applies to cases involving sums of more than £15,000 or which present particular complications

COMMENT: the multi-track is the track for most High Court actions including claims regarding professional negligence, fatal accidents, fraud, defamation and claims against the police. The timetable for a multi-track action is as follows: the court fixes a date for a case management conference, then one for listing questionnaires to be sent and filed, and finally a date for the trial

municipal [mjuː'nɪsɪpl] *adjective* **(a)** referring to a town; *municipal taxes*; *municipal offices* **(b)** **municipal law** = law which is in operation within a state, as opposed to international law

municipality [mjuːnɪsɪ'pælətɪ] *noun* corporation of a town

muniments ['mjuːnɪmənts] *plural noun* title deeds to property

murder ['mɜːdə] **1** *noun* **(a)** notifiable offence of killing someone illegally and intentionally; *he was charged with murder*; *he was found guilty of murder*; *the murder rate has fallen over the last year* **(b)** an act of killing someone illegally and intentionally; *three murders have* *been committed during the last week*; *see also* FIRST DEGREE, THIRD DEGREE **2** *verb* to kill someone illegally and intentionally; *he was accused of murdering his wife*

murderer ['mɜːdrə] *noun* person who commits a murder

murderess ['mɜːdrəs] *noun* woman who commits a murder

Muslim ['mʌzləm] *adjective* relating to religion and law following the commands of the prophet Muhammad

mutineer [mjuːtɪ'nɪə] *noun* person who takes part in a mutiny

mutiny ['mjuːtɪni] **1** *noun* agreement between two or more members of the armed forces to disobey commands of superior officers and to try to take command themselves **2** *verb* to carry out a mutiny

mutual ['mjuːtʃul] *adjective* belonging to two or more people; **mutual (insurance) company** = company which belongs to insurance policy holders; *US* **mutual funds** = organizations which take money from small investors and invest it in stocks and shares for them, the investment being in the form of shares in the fund; **mutual wills** = wills made by two people, usually each leaving their property to the other (note that mutual wills are less capable of being revoked than normal wills)

mutuality [mjuːtʃu'æləti] *noun* state where two parties are bound contractually to each other

Nn

name [neɪm] **1** *noun* word used to call a thing or a person; **brand name** = name of a particular make of product; **corporate name** = name of a large corporation; **under the name of** = using a particular name; **trading under the name of 'Best Foods'** = using the name 'Best Foods' as a commercial name for selling a product, but not as the name of the company **2** *verb* to give someone a name or to mention someone's name; *the Chief Constable was named in the divorce case*; *(of the Speaker)* **to name a Member of Parliament** = to say that an MP has been guilty of misconduct; *see also* SUSPEND

named [neɪmd] *adjective* **person named in the policy** = person whose name is given on an insurance policy as the person insured

nark [nɑːk] *noun (slang)* informer, a person who gives information to the police

nation [ˈneɪʃn] *noun* country and the people living in it; **nation state** = country which is an independent political unit, usually formed of people with the same language and traditions

national [ˈnæʃnəl] **1** *adjective* referring to a particular country; **National Anthem** = piece of music (sometimes with words which are sung to it) which is used to represent the nation officially, and is played at official ceremonies; *everyone stood up when the National Anthem was played*; *the British National Anthem is 'God Save the Queen'*; **National Audit Office** = independent body, headed by the Comptroller and Auditor-General, which examines the accounts of government departments; **National Crime Squad (NCS)** = section of the national police which deals with crime on a nation-wide basis and is not part of any local police force; **National Criminal Intelligence Service (NCIS)** = central police department which keeps records of criminals from national and international sources and makes them available to police forces all over the country; **National Insurance** = state insurance which pays for medical care, hospitals, unemployment benefits, etc.; **National Insurance contributions (NIC)** = money paid into the National Insurance scheme by the employer and the worker; **National Party** = political party representing the interests of the nation; **gross national product (GNP)** = annual value of goods and services in a country including income from other countries; **National Savings** = savings scheme for small investors run through the Post Office (including a savings bank, savings certificates and premium bonds) **2** *noun* person who is a citizen of a state; *the government ordered the deportation of all foreign nationals*; *any national of a Member State has the right to work in another Member State, under the same conditions as nationals of that state*; *compare* NON-NATIONAL

nationalism [ˈnæʃnlɪzm] *noun* **(a)** wanting independence for one's country **(b)** feeling of great pride in one's country

nationalist [ˈnæʃnlɪst] *noun* **(a)** person who wants his country to be independent; *a Welsh nationalist*; *the Scottish Nationalist Party* **(b)** person who is very proud of his country or feels his country is better than other countries

nationality [næʃəˈnælətɪ] *noun* being the citizen of a state; *the abolition of discrimination based on nationality between workers of Member States*; **he is of United Kingdom nationality** = he is a citizen of the United Kingdom; **he has dual nationality** = he is a citizen of two countries at the same time

nationalization [næʃnəlaɪˈzeɪʃn] *noun* taking over of a private industry by the state; *compare* NATURALIZATION

nationalize [ˈnæʃnəlaɪz] *verb* to put a privately-owned industry under state ownership and control; **nationalized industry** = industry which was once privately owned, but now belongs to the state

natural [ˈnætʃərl] *adjective* **(a)** found in the earth; **natural resources** = raw materials (such as coal, gas, iron) which are found in the earth **(b)** not made by people; **natural fibre** = fibre made from animal hair, plants, etc. **(c)** normal; **natural child** = child (especially an illegitimate child) of a particular parent; **natural justice** = the general principles of justice; **natural law** = general laws of human behaviour, applied in all societies, as distinct from legislation which is applicable to each country; **natural parents** = actual mother and father of a child (as opposed to step-parents, adoptive parents, foster parents, etc.); **natural person** = human being (as opposed to a legal or artificial person such as a company); *in this case, the term 'establishment' is not confined to legal persons, but is extended to natural persons*; **natural right** = general right which people have to live freely, usually stated in a written constitution; **natural wastage** = losing workers because they resign or retire, not through redundancy or dismissals

natural-born subject [ˈnætʃərlˈbɔːn ˈsʌbdʒekt] *noun* term formerly applied to a person born in the UK or a Commonwealth country who was a British citizen by birth

naturalization [nætʃərlaɪˈzeɪʃn] *noun* granting of citizenship of a state to a foreigner; *she has applied for naturalization*; *you must fill in the naturalization papers*; *compare* NATIONALIZATION

naturalized [ˈnætʃərlaɪzd] *adjective* (person) who has become a citizen of another country; *he is a naturalized American citizen*

nature [ˈneɪtʃə] *noun* kind or type; *what is the nature of the contents of the parcel?*; *the nature of his business is not known*

NCIS = NATIONAL CRIMINAL INTELLIGENCE SERVICE

NCS = NATIONAL CRIME SQUAD

neglect [nɪˈglekt] **1** *noun* (i) not doing a duty; (ii) lack of care towards someone or something; *the children were suffering from neglect*; **wilful neglect** = intentionally not doing something which it is your duty to do **2** *verb* **(a)** to fail to take care of someone; *he neglected his three children* **(b)** to neglect to do something = to forget or omit to do something which has to be done; *he neglected to return his income tax form*

neglected [nɪˈglektɪd] *adjective* not well looked after; *the local authority applied for a care order for the family of neglected children*

negligence [ˈneglɪdʒəns] *noun* lack of proper care, not doing a duty (with the result that a person or property is harmed), tort of acting carelessly towards others so as to cause harm entitling the injured party to claim damages; **contributory negligence** = negligence partly caused by the claimant and partly by the defendant, resulting in harm done to the claimant; **criminal negligence** = acting recklessly with the result that harm is done to other people; **culpable negligence** = negligence which is so bad that it amounts to an offence; **gross negligence** = act showing very serious neglect of duty towards other people

negligent ['neglɪdʒənt] *adjective*
showing negligence, not taking proper
care; *the defendant was negligent in
carrying out his duties as a trustee*

negligently ['neglɪdʒəntli] *adverb* in a
way which shows negligence; *the
guardian acted negligently towards his
ward*

negotiability [nɪgəʊʃə'bɪləti] *noun*
ability of a document to be legally
transferred to a person simply by passing it
to him

negotiable [nɪ'gəʊʃəbl] *adjective* **not
negotiable** = which cannot be exchanged
for cash; **'not negotiable'** = words written
on a cheque to show that it can be paid only
to a certain person; **negotiable cheque** =
cheque made payable to bearer (i.e. to
anyone who holds it); **negotiable
instrument** = document (such as a bill of
exchange or cheque) which can be legally
transferred to another owner simply by
passing it to him or by endorsing it, or
which can be exchanged for cash

negotiate [nɪ'gəʊʃieɪt] *verb* **to negotiate
with someone** = to discuss a problem
formally with someone, so as to reach an
agreement; *the management refused to
negotiate with the union*; **to negotiate
terms and conditions** *or* **to negotiate a
contract** = to discuss and agree the terms
of a contract; **negotiating committee** =
group of representatives of management or
unions who negotiate a wage settlement

negotiation [nɪgəʊʃi'eɪʃn] *noun*
discussion of terms and conditions to reach
an agreement; **contract under negotiation**
= contract which is being discussed; **a
matter for negotiation** = something which
must be discussed before a decision is
reached; **to enter into negotiations** *or* **to
start negotiations** = to start discussing a
problem; **to resume negotiations** = to start
discussing a problem again, after talks have
stopped for a time; **to break off
negotiations** = to refuse to go on
discussing a problem; **to conduct
negotiations** = to negotiate

negotiator [nɪ'gəʊʃieɪtə] *noun* person
who discusses with the aim of reaching an
agreement

neighbourhood watch ['neɪbəhʊd
'wɒtʃ] *noun* system where the people living
in an area are encouraged to look out for
criminals or to report any breakdown of
law and order

nemine contradicente *or* **nem
con** ['nemɪneɪ kɒntrædɪ'senteɪ *or* 'nem
'kɒn] *Latin phrase meaning* 'with no one
contradicting': phrase used to show that no
one voted against the proposal; *the motion
was adopted nem con*

nemo dat quod non habet
['neɪməʊ dæt kwɒd nɒn 'hæbet] *Latin
phrase meaning* 'no one can give what he
does not have': rule that no one can pass or
sell to another person something to which
he has no title (such as stolen goods)

neo- ['niːəʊ] *prefix* meaning 'new' or 'in a
new form'; *a neo-fascist movement*; *a
neo-Nazi organization*; **neocolonialism** =
policy of controlling weaker countries as if
they were colonies

net *or* **nett** [net] *adjective & adverb*
(total) left after money has been deducted
for tax, expenses, etc.; *the company's net
profit was £10,000*; **net earnings** *or* **net
income** *or* **net salary** = total earnings after
tax and other deductions; **net estate** =
estate of a deceased person less
administration charges and funeral costs;
net gain = total number of seats gained
after deducting seats lost; *the government
lost twenty seats and gained thirty one,
making a net gain of eleven* (NOTE: the
opposite is **gross**)

neutral ['njuːtrəl] **1** *adjective* **(a)** not
aligned to one or other superpower block;
not taking sides in a dispute; *the
conference agreed to refer the dispute to a
neutral power*; *the UN sent in neutral
observers to observe the elections* **(b)**
(country) which refuses to take part in
wars, which does not join in a war; *during
the Second World War, Switzerland and
Sweden remained neutral*; *the navy was
accused of having attacked neutral*

shipping; *neutral states in the area have tried to bring an end to the war* **2** *noun* country which is neutral

neutralism ['nju:trəlɪzm] *noun* state of affairs where a country does not belong to one or other of the superpower groupings

neutrality [nju:'trælɪti] *noun* being neutral; **armed neutrality** = condition of a country which is neutral during a war, but maintains armed forces to defend itself

new [nju:] *adjective* recent, not old; **under new management** = with a new owner; **new for old policy** = insurance policy which covers the cost of buying a new item to replace an old one which has been stolen or damaged; **new issue** = issue of new shares; **new trial** = trial which can be ordered to take place in civil cases, when the first trial was improper in some way

next friend ['nekst 'frend] *noun* person who brings an action on behalf of a minor

next of kin ['nekst əv 'kɪn] *noun* person or persons who are most closely related to someone; *his only next of kin is an aunt living in Scotland*; *the police have informed the next of kin of the people killed in the accident* (NOTE: can be singular or plural)

NIC = NATIONAL INSURANCE CONTRIBUTIONS

nick [nɪk] *(slang)* **1** *noun* police station **2** *verb* **(a)** to steal **(b)** to arrest

1922 Committee ['naɪntiːn 'twenti'tuː kə'mɪtiː] *noun* committee formed of all backbench Conservative MPs in the British House of Commons

COMMENT: the equivalent in the Labour Party is the Parliamentary Labour Party (PLP)

nisi ['naɪsaɪ] *see* DECREE, FORECLOSURE

no [nəʊ] *noun* vote against a motion; *the proposal received a resounding 'No' vote*; **the Noes have it** = announcement that a motion has been defeated; **the Noes lobby** = lobby in the House of Commons where MPs pass to vote against a motion; *see also* DIVISION

//nobble ['nɒbl] *verb (slang)* to interfere with, to bribe or to influence (a jury); *he tried to nobble one of the jurors*

no-claims bonus ['nəʊ'kleɪmz 'bəʊnəs] *noun* reduction of premiums paid because no claims have been made against an insurance policy

nod [nɒd] *verb* to move the head forwards (to show agreement); *when the chairman asked him if he would head the subcommittee, the treasurer nodded*; **the proposal went through on the nod** = the motion was carried without any discussion and no formal vote; **to nod through** = to agree that an MP's vote is recorded, even if he has not personally gone through the voting lobby (as when an MP is present in the Houses of Parliament, but is too ill to go into the chamber)

nolle prosequi ['nɒli 'prɒsɪkwaɪ] *Latin phrase meaning* 'do not pursue': power used by the Attorney-General to stop a criminal trial

nominal ['nɒmɪnl] *adjective* **(a)** very small (payment); *we make a nominal charge for our services*; *they are paying a nominal rent*; **nominal damages** = very small damages, awarded to show that the loss or harm suffered was technical rather than actual **(b)** **nominal capital** = the total of the face value of all the shares which a company is allowed to issue according to its memorandum and articles of association; **nominal value** = face value, the value written on a share, a coin or a banknote

nominate ['nɒmɪneɪt] *verb* to suggest someone, to name someone for a job; *he was nominated as Labour candidate*; **to nominate someone to a post** = to appoint someone to a post without an election; **to nominate someone as proxy** = to name someone as your proxy

nomination [nɒmɪ'neɪʃn] *noun* **(a)** act of nominating; *he was proposed for* *nomination as Labour candidate*; **nominations close at 10.00 a.m.** = the last time for nominating someone is 10.00; **to lodge** *or* **file nomination papers** = to leave completed papers nominating someone as a candidate with the responsible officer **(b)** person nominated; *there were a number of nominations for the post of Deputy Leader* **(c)** written instruction by a person who is entitled to receive some money (called the nominator) to the person who is in possession of the money, to pay a sum to another person (the nominee) when the nominator dies (this is similar to a will, but is usually used to cover pension scheme contributions)

COMMENT: in the UK, a person who is nominated as a candidate for local or national elections, has to have the signatures of local residents as his sponsors, and (in the case of national elections) has to deposit a sum of money which he forfeits if he does not poll enough votes. In the United States, the executive (i.e. the President) nominates people to federal offices such as members of the Supreme Court or the cabinet, but these nominations are subject to confirmation by the Senate. Most nominations are accepted without discussion, but some are debated, and some are not confirmed. If the executive nominates someone to a federal post in one of the states without consulting the senators for that state, they can object to the nominee by saying that he is 'personally obnoxious' to them

nominator ['nɒmɪneɪtə] *noun* person who is entitled to receive money and writes a nomination

nominee [nɒmɪ'niː] *noun* person who is nominated, especially someone who is appointed to deal with financial matters on behalf of a person; *he is the Party leader's nominee for the post*; **nominee account** = account held on behalf of someone; **nominee shareholder** = person named as the owner of shares, when the shares are in fact owned by another person

non- [nɒn] *prefix* meaning not or without; **non-aggression** = not using force against another country; **a treaty of non-aggression** *or* **a non-aggression treaty** = treaty between two countries who promise not to attack each other; **non-aligned state** = country which is not part of one of the main superpower blocs; **non-member** = person who is not a member of an organization; *non-members may not vote at the AGM*; **non-proliferation treaty** = treaty to prevent the possession and development of nuclear weapons spreading to countries which do not yet possess them

non-acceptance ['nɒnək'septəns] *noun* situation where the person who should pay a bill of exchange does not accept it

non-arrestable offence ['nɒnə'restəbl ə'fens] *noun* crime for which a person cannot be arrested without a warrant

COMMENT: non-arrestable offences are usually crimes which carry a sentence of less than five years imprisonment

non-capital crime *or* **offence** ['nɒn'kæpɪtl 'kraɪm or ə'fens] *noun* crime or offence for which the punishment is not death

non compos mentis ['nɒn 'kɒmpəs 'mentɪs] *Latin phrase meaning* 'mad' or 'not fully sane'

non-conformance ['nɒnkən'fɔːməns] *noun* act of not conforming; *he was criticized for non-conformance with the regulations*

non-consummation ['nɒnkɒnsə'meɪʃn] *noun* **non-consummation of marriage** = not having sexual intercourse (between husband and wife)

non-contributory ['nɒnkən'trɪbjutri] *adjective* **non-contributory pension scheme** = pension scheme where the employee does not make any contributions and the company pays everything

non-direction [ˈnɒndaɪˈrekʃn] *noun (of a judge)* not giving direction to a jury

non-disclosure [ˈnɒndɪsˈkləʊʒə] *noun* failure to disclose information which one has a duty to disclose

non-executive director [ˈnɒnɪgˈzekjʊtɪv daɪˈrektə] *noun* director who attends board meetings and gives advice, but does not work full time for the company

nonfeasance [nɒnˈfiːzəns] *noun* not doing something which should be done by law

nonjoinder [nɒnˈdʒɔɪndə] *noun* plea that a claimant has not joined all the necessary parties to his action

non-molestation order [ˈnɒnməlesˈteɪʃn ˈɔːdə] *noun* order made by a court in matrimonial proceedings to prevent one spouse from molesting the other

non-national [ˈnɒnˈnæʃnl] *noun* person who is not a citizen of a certain state; *non-nationals can be barred from working in an EU country if they do not speak the language*

non-negotiable instrument [ˈnɒnnɪˈgəʊʃəbl ˈɪnstrəmənt] *noun* document (such as a crossed cheque) which is not payable to bearer and so cannot be exchanged for cash

non-payment [ˈnɒnˈpeɪmənt] *noun* **non-payment of a debt** = not paying a debt due

non profit-making organization *US* **non-profit corporation** [ˈnɒnˈprɒfɪtmeɪkɪŋ ɔːgənaɪˈzeɪʃn] *noun* organization (such as a club) which is not allowed by law to make a profit

non-recurring items [ˈnɒnrɪˈkʌrɪŋ ˈaɪtəmz] *noun* special items in a set of accounts which appear only once

non-refundable [ˈnɒnrɪˈfʌndəbl] *adjective* which will not be refunded

non-resident [ˈnɒnˈrezɪdənt] *noun* person who is not considered a resident of a country for tax purposes

non-retroactivity [ˈnɒnretrəʊækˈtɪvəti] *noun (in the EU)* state of not being retroactive

non-returnable [ˈnɒnrɪˈtɜːnəbl] *adjective* which cannot be returned; **non-returnable packing** = packing which is to be thrown away when it has been used and not returned to the person who sent it

nonsufficient funds [ˈnɒnsəfɪʃnt ˈfʌndz] *noun US* not enough money in an account to pay a cheque which has been presented

nonsuit *or* **nonsuited** [ˈnɒnsuːt *or* nɒnˈsuːtɪd] *adjective* **to be nonsuit** *or* **nonsuited** = (i) situation in civil proceedings where a claimant fails to establish a cause of action and is forced to abandon his proceedings; (ii) situation in criminal proceedings where a judge directs a jury to find the defendant not guilty

non-taxable [ˈnɒnˈtæksəbl] *adjective* which is not subject to tax

non-verbal evidence [ˈnɒnˈvɜːbəl ˈevɪdəns] *noun* evidence produced in court in the form of maps, photographs, etc., (as opposed to verbal evidence, which is spoken by a witness)

non-voting shares [ˈnɒnˈvəʊtɪŋ ˈʃeəz] *plural noun* shares which do not allow the shareholder to vote at meetings

North-Eastern Circuit, Northern Circuit [ˈnɔːθˈiːstən *or* ˈnɔːðən ˈsɜːkɪt] *noun* two of the six circuits of the Crown Court to which barristers belong, with centres in Leeds and Manchester

noscitur a sociis [ˈnɒskɪtɜː aː ˈsəʊsɪɪs] *Latin phrase meaning* 'the meaning of the words can be understood from the words around them': ambiguous words or phrases can be clarified by referring to the context in which they are used

notarial [nəʊ'teəriəl] *adjective* referring to notaries; **notarial act** = act which can be carried out only by a notary public

notary public ['nəʊtəri 'pʌblɪk] *noun* lawyer (usually but not necessarily a solicitor) who has the authority to witness and draw up certain documents, and so make them official (NOTE: plural is **notaries public**)

note [nəʊt] **1** *noun* short document or short piece of information; **advice note** = written notice to a customer giving details of goods ordered and shipped but not yet delivered; **contract note** = note showing that shares have been bought or sold but not yet paid for; **cover note** = letter from an insurance company giving details of an insurance policy and confirming that the policy exists; **covering note** = letter sent with documents to explain why you are sending them; **credit note** = note showing that money is owed to a customer; **debit note** = note showing that a customer owes money; **note of costs** = bill or invoice; **note of hand** *or* **promissory note** = document stating that someone promises to pay an amount of money on a certain date **2** *verb* **to note a bill** = to attach a note to a dishonoured bill of exchange, explaining why it has not been honoured

not-for-profit corporation
['nɒtfə'prɒfɪt] *US* = NON-PROFIT CORPORATION

not guilty ['nɒt 'gɪlti] *see* GUILTY

notice ['nəʊtɪs] *noun* **(a)** piece of written information; *the company secretary pinned up a notice about the pension scheme*; **copyright notice** = note in a book showing who owns the copyright and the date of ownership **(b)** official passing of information to someone (such as a warning that a contract is going to end, that terms are going to be changed, that an employee will leave his job at a certain date, or that a tenant must leave the property he is occupying); **to give someone notice** *or* **to serve notice on someone** = to give someone a legal notice; **to give a tenant notice to quit** *or* **to serve a tenant with**

notice to quit = to inform a tenant officially that he has to leave the premises by a certain date; **she has handed in** *or* **given her notice** = she has said she will quit her job at a certain date; **period of notice** = time stated in the contract of employment which the worker or company has to allow between resigning or being fired and the worker actually leaving his job; **until further notice** = until different instructions are given; **at short notice** = with very little warning; **you must give seven days' notice of withdrawal** = you must ask to take money out of the account seven days before you want it **(c)** legal document informing someone of something; **notice of motion** = document telling the other party to a case that an application will be made to the court; **to give notice of appeal** = to start official proceedings for an appeal to be heard; **notice of opposition** = document opposing a patent application; **notice of service** = document issued by a court to show that a claim has been served **(d)** knowledge of a fact; **actual notice** = real knowledge which a person has of something; **constructive notice** = knowledge which the law says a person has of something (whether or not the person actually has it) because the information is available to him if he asks for it; **judicial notice** = facts and matters which a judge is presumed to know, so that evidence does not have to be provided for them

noticeboard ['nəʊtɪsbɔːd] *noun* board fixed to a wall where notices can be put up; *the list of electors is put up on the noticeboard in the local offices*

notifiable [nəʊtɪ'faɪəbl] *adjective* which must be notified; **notifiable offence** = serious offence which can be tried in the Crown Court

not proven ['nɒt 'pruːvn] *adjective (in Scotland)* (verdict) that the prosecution has not produced sufficient evidence to prove the accused to be guilty

notwithstanding [nɒtwɪθ'stændɪŋ] *adverb & preposition* in spite of; *the case proceeded notwithstanding the objections* *of the defendant* or *the defendant's objections notwithstanding* (NOTE: can be used before or after the phrase)

novation [nəʊ'veɪʃn] *noun* transaction in which a new contract is agreed by all parties to replace an existing contract (as where one of the parties to the old contract is released from his liability under the old contract, and this liability is assumed by a third party)

novelty ['nɒvəlti] *noun* state of being new

no win no fee ['nəʊ 'wɪn nəʊ 'fiː] *noun* a basis of calculating a conditional fee agreement

NSF *US* = NONSUFFICIENT FUNDS

nuisance ['njuːsəns] *noun* something which causes harm or inconvenience to someone or to property; **public nuisance** *or* **common nuisance** = criminal act which causes harm or damage to members of the public in general or to their rights; **private nuisance** = a tort, a nuisance which causes harm or damage to a particular person or his rights

null [nʌl] *adjective* with no meaning, which cannot legally be enforced; **the contract was declared null and void** = the contract was said to be no longer valid; **to render a decision null** = to make a decision useless, to cancel a decision

nullification [nʌlɪfɪ'keɪʃn] *noun* act of making something invalid

nullify ['nʌlɪfaɪ] *verb* to make something invalid, to cancel something

nullity ['nʌləti] *noun* **(a)** action which is void or invalid **(b)** situation where a marriage is ruled never to have been in effective existence

Number Ten ['nʌmbə 'ten] *noun* No 10 Downing Street, the official residence of the British Prime Minister; **he is hoping to move into Number Ten after the election** = he is expecting to be elected Prime Minister (NOTE: used to refer to the Prime Minister or to the government in general: **the plan was turned down by Number Ten; sources close to Number Ten say that the cabinet is close to agreement on the draft legislation; it is rumoured that Number Ten was annoyed at the story**)

nuncio ['nʌnsiəʊ] *noun* **Papal Nuncio** = ambassador sent by the Pope to a country

nuncupative will ['nʌnkjupətɪv 'wɪl] *noun* will made orally in the presence of a witness (as by a soldier in time of war)

Oo

oath [əυθ] *noun* solemn legal promise that someone will say or write only what is true; **he was on oath** *or* **under oath** = he had promised in court to say what was true; **to administer an oath to someone** = to make someone swear an oath; **oath of allegiance** = (i) oath which is sworn to put the person under the orders or rules of a country, an army, etc.; (ii) oath sworn by all MPs before they can take their seats in the House of Commons (or alternatively they can affirm); *all officers swore an oath of allegiance to the new president*; **to take the oath** = to swear allegiance to the Queen before taking one's seat as an MP; *after taking the oath, the new MP signs the test roll*; **commissioner for oaths** = solicitor appointed by the Lord Chancellor to administer affidavits which may be used in court; *see also* AFFIRM

obiter dicta ['ɒbıtə 'dıktə] *Latin phrase meaning* 'things which are said in passing': part of a judgment which is not essential to the decision of the judge and does not create a precedent; *see also* RATIO DECIDENDI (NOTE: the singular is **obiter dictum**)

object 1 ['ɒbdʒıkt] *noun* purpose or aim; **objects clause** = section in a company's memorandum of association which says what work the company will do **2** [əb'dʒekt] *verb* to refuse to do something, to say that you do not accept something; *to object to a clause in a contract*; **to object to a juror** = to ask for a juror not to be appointed because he or she may be biased (NOTE: you object **to** something or someone)

objection [əb'dʒekʃn] *noun* **to raise an objection to something** = to object to something; *the union delegates raised an objection to the wording of the agreement*

objective [əb'dʒektıv] **1** *noun* something which you try to do; **long-term objective** *or* **short-term objective** = aim which you hope to achieve within a few years or a few months; **management by objectives** = way of managing a business by planning work for the managers to do and testing if it is completed correctly and on time **2** *adjective* considered from a general point of view and not from that of the person involved; *the judge asked the jury to be objective in considering the evidence put before them*; *you must be objective in assessing the performance of the staff*; *to carry out an objective review of current legislation*

obligate ['ɒblıgeıt] *verb especially US* **to be obligated to do something** = to have a legal duty to do something

obligation [ɒblı'geıʃn] *noun* **(a)** duty to do something; **to be under an obligation to do something** = to feel it is your duty to do something; **he is under no contractual obligation to buy** = he has signed no contract to buy; **to fulfil your contractual obligations** = to do what is stated in a contract; **two weeks' free trial without obligation** = situation where the customer can try the item at home for two weeks without having to buy it at the end of the test **(b)** debt; **to meet your obligations** = to pay your debts

obligatory [ə'blıgətri] *adjective* necessary according to the law or rules; *each new member of staff has to pass an obligatory medical examination*

obligee [ɒblɪˈdʒiː] *noun* person who is owed a duty

obligor [ɒblɪˈgɔː] *noun* person who owes a duty to someone

obscene [əbˈsiːn] *adjective* (play, book, etc.) which is likely to deprave or corrupt someone who sees or reads it, or to offend public morals and decency; *the magazine was classed as an obscene publication; the police seized a number of obscene films*

obscenity [əbˈsenɪti] *noun* being obscene; *the magistrate commented on the obscenity of some parts of the film*; **obscenity laws** = law relating to obscene publications or films

observance [əbˈzɜːvəns] *noun* doing what is required by a law; *the government's observance of international agreements*

observe [əbˈzɜːv] *verb* (a) to obey (a rule or a law); *failure to observe the correct procedure will be punished; all members of the association should observe the code of practice* (b) to watch or to notice what is happening; *officials have been instructed to observe the conduct of the election*

observer [əbˈzɜːvə] *noun* person who observes; *two official observers attended the meeting*

obsolete [ˈɒbsəliːt] *adjective* no longer used, no longer in force; *the law has been made obsolete by new developments in forensic science*

obstruct [əbˈstrʌkt] *verb* (a) to get in the way, to stop something progressing; *several parked cars are obstructing the traffic*; **obstructing the police** = offence of doing something which prevents a policeman carrying out his duty (b) to prevent the business (of the House of Commons) from continuing; *MPs attempted to obstruct the passage of the Bill*

obstruction [əbˈstrʌkʃn] (a) thing which gets in the way; *the car caused an obstruction to the traffic* (b) act of obstructing someone, such as preventing discussion of a Bill in Parliament; **obstruction of the police** = doing anything which prevents a police officer from doing his duty

obstructive [əbˈstrʌktɪv] *adjective* which obstructs; *MPs complained of the obstructive behaviour of some right-wingers*

obtain [əbˈteɪn] *verb* (a) to get; *to obtain supplies from abroad; we find these items very difficult to obtain; to obtain an injunction against a company; he obtained control by buying the family shareholding*; **obtaining by deception** = acquiring money or property by tricking someone into handing it over; **obtaining credit** = offence whereby an undischarged bankrupt obtains credit above a limit of £50; **to obtain a property by fraud** *or* **by deception** = to trick someone into handing over possession of property; **obtaining a pecuniary advantage by deception** = crime of tricking someone into handing over money (b) to be a rule, to have a legal status; *this right does not obtain in judicial proceedings; a rule obtaining in international law*

occasion [əˈkeɪʒn] **1** *noun* time when something takes place; *the opening of the trial was the occasion of protests by the family of the accused* **2** *verb* to make something happen; *he pleaded guilty to assault occasioning actual bodily harm*

occasional [əˈkeɪʒnl] *adjective* which happens from time to time; **occasional licence** = licence to sell alcohol at a certain place and time

occupancy [ˈɒkjʊpənsi] *noun* (a) act of occupying a property (such as a house, an office, a room in a hotel); **with immediate occupancy** = empty and available to be occupied immediately (b) occupying a property which has no owner, and so acquiring title to the property

occupant [ˈɒkjʊpənt] *noun* person or company which occupies a property

occupation [ɒkjuˈpeɪʃn] *noun* **(a)** act of occupying a property which has no owner, and so acquiring title to the property **(b)** work, job

occupational [ɒkjuˈpeɪʃnl] *adjective* referring to a job; **occupational accident** = accident which takes place at work; **occupational disease** = disease which affects people in certain jobs; **occupational hazards** = dangers which apply to certain jobs; **occupational pension scheme** = pension scheme where the worker gets a pension from the company he has worked for

occupier [ˈɒkjupaɪə] *noun* person who lives in a property; **beneficial occupier** = person who occupies a property but does not own it; **occupier's liability** = duty of an occupier to make sure that visitors to a property are not harmed; **owner-occupier** = person who owns the property which he occupies

> COMMENT: the occupier has the right to stay in or on a property, but is not necessarily an owner

occupy [ˈɒkjupaɪ] *verb* to enter and stay in a property illegally; *the rebels occupied the Post Office*; *squatters are occupying the building*

offence US **offense** [əˈfens] *noun* crime, act which is against the law; *he was charged with three serious offences*; *the minister was arrested and charged with offences against the Official Secrets Act*; **offence against the person** = criminal act which harms a person physically (such as murder or manslaughter); **offence against property** = criminal act which damages or destroys property (such as theft, forgery or criminal damage); **offence against public order** = criminal act which disturbs the general calm of society (such as riot or affray); **offence against the state** = act of attacking the lawful government of a country (such as sedition or treason); **first offence** = committing an illegal act for the first time; *as it was a first offence, he was fined and not sent to prison*; **inchoate offences** = offences (such as incitement, attempt or conspiracy to commit a crime) which are offences even though the substantive offence may not have been committed; **substantive offence** = offence which has actually taken place; **notifiable offence** = serious offence which can be tried in the Crown Court; **offence triable either way** = offence which can be tried before the Magistrates' Court or before the Crown Court

offend [əˈfend] *verb* to commit a crime

offender [əˈfendə] *noun* person who commits a crime; **first offender** = person who has been charged with an offence for the first time; **fugitive offender** = criminal running away from the police who, if he is caught, is sent back to the place where the offence was committed; **persistent offender** = person who has been convicted of a crime several times before; *see also* YOUNG OFFENDER

offensive weapon [əˈfensɪv ˈwepn] *noun* object which can be used to harm a person or property; **carrying offensive weapons** = offence of holding a weapon or something (such as a bottle) which could be used as a weapon

> COMMENT: many things can be considered as offensive weapons if they are used as such: a brick, a bottle, a piece of wire, etc.

offer [ˈɒfə] **1** *noun* **(a)** statement by one party to a contract that he proposes to do something (NOTE: the offer (and acceptance by the other party) is one of the essential elements of a contract) **(b) offer to buy** = statement that you are willing to pay a certain amount of money to buy something; *to make an offer for a company*; *he made an offer of £10 a share*; *we made a written offer for the house*; *£1,000 is the best offer I can make*; *to accept an offer of £1,000 for the car*; **the house is under offer** = someone has made an offer to buy the house and the offer has been accepted provisionally; **we are open to offers** = we are ready to discuss the price which we are asking; **cash offer** = being ready to pay in cash; **or near**

offer (o.n.o.) = or an offer of a price which is slightly less than the price asked; *asking price: £200 o.n.o.* **(c) offer to sell** = statement that you are willing to sell something; **offer for sale** = situation where a company advertises new shares for sale; **offer price** = price at which new shares are put on sale; **bargain offer** = sale of a particular type of goods at a cheap price; **special offer** = goods put on sale at a specially low price **(d) he received six offers of jobs** *or* **six job offers** = six companies told him he could have a job with them **2** *verb* **(a)** to propose something to someone, to propose to do something; *he offered to buy the house*; *to offer someone £100,000 for his house*; *the multinational offered £10 a share*; **to offer someone a job** = to tell someone that he can have a job in your company **(b)** to say that you are willing to sell something; *we offered the house for sale*

offeree [ɒfə'riː] *noun* person who receives an offer

offeror [ɒfə'rɔː] *noun* person who makes an offer

office ['ɒfɪs] *noun* **(a)** set of rooms where a company works or where business is done; **branch office** = less important office, usually in a different town or country from the main office; **head office** *or* **main office** = office building where the board of directors works and meets; **registered office** = in Britain, the office address of a company which is officially registered with the Companies' Registrar and to which certain legal documents must normally be sent **(b) office block** *or* a **block of offices** = building which contains only offices; **office hours** = time when an office is open; **office junior** = young man or woman who does all types of work in an office; **office space** *or* **office accommodation** = space available for offices or occupied by offices; **office staff** = people who work in offices **(c)** room where someone works and does business; *come into my office*; *she has a pleasant office which looks out over the park*; *the senior partner's office is on the third floor* **(d) booking office** = office where you can

book seats at a theatre or tickets for the railway; **box office** = office at a theatre where tickets can be bought; **general office** = main administrative office in a company; **information office** *or* **inquiry office** = office where someone can answer questions from members of the public; **ticket office** = office where tickets can be bought **(e)** British government department; **the Foreign Office** = ministry dealing with foreign affairs; **the Home Office** = ministry dealing with the internal affairs of the country, including the police and the prisons; **Office of Fair Trading** = government body which protects consumers against unfair or illegal business **(f)** post or position; *he holds or performs the office of treasurer*; **high office** = important position or job; **office of profit (under the Crown)** = government post which disqualifies someone from being a Member of Parliament; *see also* CHILTERN HUNDREDS; **compensation for loss of office** = payment to a director who is asked to leave a company before his contract ends

officer ['ɒfɪsə] *noun* **(a) police officer** = policeman, policewoman, member of a police force (NOTE: used in American English with a name: **Officers Smith and Jones went to the scene of the accident;** British English is **Constable**) **(b)** person who has an official position; **customs officer** = person working for the Customs and Excise; **fire safety officer** = person responsible for fire safety in a building; **information officer** = person who gives information about a company or about a government department to the public; **training officer** = person who deals with the training of staff; **the company officers** *or* **the officers of a company** = the main executives or directors of a company **(c)** official (usually unpaid) of a club or society, etc.; *the election of officers of an association* **(d)** Law Officers = the posts of Attorney-General and Solicitor-General (in England and Wales) and Lord Advocate and Solicitor-General (in Scotland)

official [ə'fɪʃl] **1** *adjective* **(a)** done because it has been authorized by a government department or organization; *he left official documents in his car*; *she received an official letter of explanation*; **official secret** = piece of information which is classified as important to the state and which it is a crime to reveal; **Official Secrets Act** = Act of Parliament which governs the publication of secret information relating to the state; **speaking in an official capacity** = speaking officially; **to go through official channels** = to deal with officials, especially when making a request **(b)** done or approved by a director or by a person in authority; *this must be an official order - it is written on the company's notepaper*; **the strike was made official** = the local strike was approved by the main trade union office **(c)** **official copy** = copy of an official document which has been sealed by the office which issued it; **Official Journal** = publication which lists the regulations, statutory instruments and directives of the EC; **the Official Receiver** = government official who is appointed to close down a company which is in liquidation, or to deal with the affairs of a bankrupt; **official referee** = expert judge appointed by the High Court to try complicated, usually technical, cases where specialist knowledge is required; **Official Solicitor** = solicitor who acts in the High Court for parties who have no one to act for them, usually because they are under a legal disability **2** *noun* person working in a government department; **customs official** = person working for the Customs and Excise; **high official** = important person in a government department; **minor official** = person in a low position in a government department

officially [ə'fɪʃli] *adverb* in an official way; *officially he knows nothing about the problem, but unofficially he has given us a lot of advice about it*

officio [ə'fɪʃiəu] *see* EX OFFICIO, FUNCTUS OFFICIO

off-licence ['ɒf'laɪsns] *noun* **(a)** licence to sell alcohol for drinking away from the place where you buy it **(b)** shop which sells alcohol for drinking at home

offspring ['ɒfsprɪŋ] *noun* child or children of a parent; *his offspring inherited the estate*; *they had two offspring* (NOTE: offspring is both singular and plural)

OHMS = ON HER MAJESTY'S SERVICE

old age ['əuld 'eɪdʒ] *noun* period when a person is old; **old age pension** = state pension in Britain, given to a man who is 65 or a woman who is 60; **old age pensioner** = person who receives the old age pension

Old Bailey ['əuld 'beɪli] *noun* Central Criminal Court in London

Oleron ['ɒlərɒn] *noun* **Laws of Oleron** = first international maritime laws, drawn up in 1216

oligarchy ['ɒlɪgɑːki] *noun* **(a)** government by a small group of people, who usually have appointed themselves as rulers **(b)** a small ruling group; *the country is ruled by an oligarchy called the 'fifteen families'* **(c)** state ruled by a small group

oligarchical *or* **oligarchic** [ɒlɪ'gɑːkɪk] *adjective* referring to an oligarchy

ombudsman ['ɒmbʌdzmən] *noun* Parliamentary Commissioner, an official who investigates complaints by the public against government departments or other large organizations

COMMENT: there are in fact several ombudsmen: the main one is the Parliamentary Commissioner, but there are also others, such as the Health Service Commissioner, who investigates complaints against the Health Service, and the Local Government Ombudsmen who investigate complaints against local authorities, the Banking Ombudsman, who investigates complaints against banks, etc. The Legal Services Ombudsman investigates complaints against non-legal professional people who supply legal services, such as conveyancing. Although an ombudsman will make his recommendations to the department concerned, and may make his recommendations public, he has no power to enforce them. The Parliamentary Commissioner may only investigate complaints which are addressed to him through an MP; the member of the public first brings his complaint to his MP, and if the MP cannot get satisfaction from the department against which the complaint is made, then the matter is passed to the Ombudsman.

omission [ə'mɪʃn] *noun* failure to do something; **errors and omissions excepted (e. & o.e.)** = words written on an invoice to show that the company has no responsibility for mistakes in the invoice

one minute speech ['wʌn 'mɪnɪt 'spiːtʃ] *noun US* short speech by a member of the House of Representatives on any subject at the beginning of the day's business

one-party state ['wʌn 'pɑːti 'steɪt] *noun* country in which only one party is allowed to exist, although voters generally have a choice of candidates from that party at local level

o.n.o. = OR NEAR OFFER

onus ['əunəs] *noun* responsibility for doing something difficult; **onus of proof** *or* **onus probandi** = duty to prove that what has been alleged in court is correct; *the onus of proof is on the claimant; if there is a prosecution the onus will normally be on the prosecutor to prove the case; see also* BURDEN

op. cit. ['ɒp 'sɪt] *Latin phrase meaning* 'in the work mentioned' (NOTE: used when referring to a legal text: **'see Smith LJ in** *Jones v. Amalgamated Steel Ltd* **op. cit. p. 260'**)

open ['əupn] **1** *adjective* **open account** = unsecured credit, amount owed with no security; **open cheque** = cheque which is not crossed and can be exchanged for cash anywhere; **open court** = court where the hearings are open to the public; **in open court** = in a courtroom with members of the public present (NOTE: the term **in public**

is preferred); **open credit** = bank credit given to good customers without security up to a certain maximum sum; **open market** = market where anyone can buy or sell; **open policy** = marine insurance policy, where the value of what is insured is not stated; **open prison** = prison with minimum security where category 'D' prisoners can be kept; **open ticket** = ticket which can be used on any date; **open verdict** = verdict in a coroner's court which does not decide how the dead person died; *the court recorded an open verdict on the two policemen* **2** *verb* to begin speaking; **counsel for the prosecution** *opened with a description of the accused's family background*; **to open negotiations** = to begin negotiating; *he opened the discussions with a description of the product; the chairman opened the meeting at 10.30*

open-ended *US* open-end

['əupn'endɪd] *adjective* with no fixed limit, with some items not specified; *an open-ended agreement*

opening ['əupnɪŋ] **1** *noun* **(a)** act of starting a new business; *the opening of a new branch or of a new market or of a new office* **(b) opening hours** = hours when a shop or business is open **(c) job openings** = jobs which are empty and need filling; **a market opening** = possibility of starting to do business in a new market **2** *adjective* at the beginning, first; *the judge's opening remarks*; *the opening speech from the defence counsel;* **opening balance** = balance at the beginning of an accounting period; **opening bid** = first bid at an auction; **opening entry** = first entry in an account

operandi [ɒpə'rændiː] *see* MODUS

operating ['ɒpəreɪtɪŋ] *noun* general running of a business or of a machine; **operating budget** = income and expenditure which is expected to be incurred over a period of time; **operating costs** *or* **operating expenses** = costs of the day-to-day organization of a company; **operating profit** *or* **operating loss** = profit or loss made by a company in its usual business; **operating system** = the main program which operates a computer

operation [ɒpəˈreɪʃn] *noun* **(a)** business organization and work; *he heads up the company's operations in Northern Europe*; **operations review** = examining the way in which a company or department works to see how it can be made more efficient and profitable; **a franchising operation** = selling licences to trade as a franchise **(b) Stock Exchange operation** = buying or selling of shares on the Stock Exchange **(c) in operation** = working, being used; *the system will be in operation by June*; *the new system came into operation on June 1st*

operational [ɒpəˈreɪʃnl] *adjective* **(a)** referring to how something works; **operational budget** = expenditure which is expected to be made in running a business, an office or a police force; **operational costs** = costs of running a business or a police force; **operational planning** = planning how something is to be run; **operational research** = study of a method of working to see if it can be made more efficient and cost-effective **(b) the system became operational on June 1st** = the system began working on June 1st

operative [ˈɒprətɪv] *adjective* referring to the working of a system; **to become operative** = to start working; **operative words** = words in a conveyancing document which transfer the land or create an interest in the land

opinion [əˈpɪnjən] *noun* **(a) public opinion** = what people think about something; **opinion poll** *or* **opinion research** = asking a sample group of people what their opinion is, so as to guess the opinion of the whole population; **to be of the opinion** = to believe or to think; *the judge was of the opinion that if the evidence was doubtful the claim should be dismissed* **(b)** piece of expert advice; *the lawyers gave their opinion*; *to ask an adviser for his opinion on a case*; *counsel prepared a written opinion*; **counsel's opinion** = a barrister's written advice about a case **(c)** judgment delivered by a court,

especially the House of Lords **(d)** *(in the EU)* opinion of the European Community which is not legally binding

opponent [əˈpəʊnənt] *noun* person who is against you or who votes against what you propose; *the prosecution tried to discredit their opponents in the case*

oppose [əˈpəʊz] *verb* to try to stop something happening; to vote against something; *a minority of board members opposed the motion*; *we are all opposed to the takeover*; *counsel for the claimant opposed the defendant's application for an adjournment*; **the police opposed bail** *or* **opposed the granting of bail** = the police said that bail should not be granted to the accused

opposition [ɒpəˈzɪʃn] *noun* **(a)** action of trying to stop something, of not agreeing to something; *there was considerable opposition to the plan for reorganizing the divorce courts*; *the voters showed their opposition to the government by voting against the proposal in the referendum*; **notice of opposition** = document opposing a patent application **(b)** (i) the largest political party which opposes the government; (ii) group of parties which oppose the government; *the opposition tried to propose a vote of censure on the Prime Minister*; **Leader of the Opposition** = head of the largest political party opposing the government

option [ˈɒpʃn] *noun* **(a)** offer to someone of the right to enter into a contract at a later date; **option to purchase** *or* **to sell** = giving someone the possibility to buy or sell something within a period of time or when a certain event happens; **first option** = allowing someone to be the first to have the possibility of deciding something; **to grant someone a six-month option on a product** = to allow someone six months to decide if he wants to be the agent for a product, or if he wants to manufacture the product under licence; **to take up an option** *or* **to exercise an option** = to accept the option which has been offered and to put it into action; *he exercised his option or he took up his option to acquire sole* *marketing rights to the product*; **I want to leave my options open** = I want to be able to decide what to do when the time is right; **to take the soft option** = to decide to do something which involves the least risk, effort or problems **(b)** *(Stock Exchange)* **call option** = option to buy shares at a certain price; **put option** = option to sell shares at a certain price; **share option** = right to buy or sell shares at a certain price at a time in the future; **stock option** = right to buy shares at a cheap price given by a company to its employees; **option contract** = right to buy or sell shares at a fixed price; **option dealing** *or* **option trading** = buying and selling share options

oral ['ɔːrl] *adjective* spoken; **oral evidence** = spoken evidence (as opposed to written)

orally ['ɔːrəli] *adverb* in speaking, not writing

order ['ɔːdə] *noun* **(a)** general state of calm, where everything is working as planned and ruled; *there was a serious breakdown of law and order*; **public order** = situation were the general public is calm, where there are no riots; **offence against public order** *or* **public order offence** = riot, street fight, etc. **(b)** **court order** = command (which has no bearing on the final decision in a case) made by a court for someone to do something; *the prisoner was removed by order of the court*; *the factory was sold by order of the receiver*; **committal order** *or* **order of committal** = order sending someone to prison for contempt of court; **compensation order** = order made by a criminal court which forces a criminal to pay compensation to his victim; **delivery order** = instructions given by the customer to the person holding his goods, telling him to deliver them; **order of discharge** = court order releasing a person from bankruptcy; **interim order** = order of a court which has effect while a case is still being heard; **preservation order** = court order which prevents a building from being demolished, a tree from being cut down, etc. **(c)** **orders** = legislation made by ministers, under powers delegated to them

by Act of Parliament, but which still have to be ratified by Parliament before coming into force; **Order in Council** = legislation made by the Queen in Council, which is allowed by an Act of Parliament and which does not have to be ratified by Parliament **(d)** arrangement of business in the House of Commons; **order book** = list showing the House of Commons business for the term of Parliament; **order paper** = agenda of business to be discussed each day in the House of Commons **(e)** **standing orders** = rules or regulations governing the way in which a meeting or a debate in Parliament is conducted; **to call a meeting to order** = to start proceedings officially; **to bring a meeting to order** = to get a meeting back to discussing the agenda again (after an interruption); **order ! order!** = call by the Speaker of the House of Commons to bring the meeting to order; **point of order** = question relating to the way in which a meeting is being conducted; *he raised a point of order*; *on a point of order, Mr Chairman, can this committee approve its own accounts?*; *the meeting was adjourned on a point of order* **(f)** working arrangement; **machine in full working order** = machine which is ready and able to work properly; **the telephone is out of order** = the telephone is not working; **is all the documentation in order?** = are all the documents valid and correct? **(g) pay to Mr Smith or order** = pay money to Mr Smith or as he orders; **pay to the order of Mr Smith** = pay money directly into Mr Smith's account **(h)** official request for goods to be supplied; *to give someone an order or to place an order with someone for twenty filing cabinets*; **to fill** *or* **to fulfil an order** = to supply items which have been ordered; **purchase order** = official paper which places an order for something; **items available to order only** = items which will be made only if someone orders them; **on order** = ordered but not delivered; **back orders** *or* **outstanding orders** = orders received in the past and not yet supplied; **order book** = record of orders; **telephone orders** = orders received over the telephone **(i)** document which allows money to be paid to someone; *he sent us an order on the Chartered Bank*;

banker's order *or* **standing order** = order written by a customer asking a bank to make a regular payment; **money order** = document which can be bought for sending money through the post

ordinance ['ɔːdɪnəns] *noun* **(a)** special decree of a government **(b)** *US* rule made by a municipal authority, and effective only within the jurisdiction of that authority

ordinarily ['ɔːdnrli] *adverb* normally or usually; **ordinarily resident** = usually resident (in a certain country)

ordinary ['ɔːdnri] *adjective* normal or not special; **ordinary member** = person who pays a subscription to belong to a club or group; **ordinary resolution** = resolution which can be passed by a simple majority of shareholders; **ordinary shares** = normal shares in a company, which have no special benefits or restrictions; **ordinary shareholder** = person who owns ordinary shares in a company

organize ['ɔːgənaɪz] *verb* to arrange (a meeting, a business or a demonstration) so that it is run properly and efficiently; **organized crime** = crime which is run as a business, with groups of specialist criminals, assistants, security staff, etc., all run by a group of directors or by a boss; **organized labour** = workers who are members of trade unions

origin ['ɒrɪdʒɪn] *noun* where something comes from; *spare parts of European origin*; **certificate of origin** = document showing where goods were made or produced; **country of origin** = country where certain goods are produced

original [ə'rɪdʒnl] **1** *adjective* which was used or made first; *they sent a copy of the original invoice*; **original evidence** = evidence given by a witness, based on facts which he knows to be true (as opposed to hearsay) **2** *noun* first copy made; *send the original and file two copies*

originate [ə'rɪdʒɪneɪt] *verb* to start, to begin; **originating application** = way of beginning certain types of case in the

County Court; **originating summons** = summons whereby a legal action is commenced (usually in the Chancery Division of the High Court in cases relating to land or the administration of an estate)

orphan ['ɔːfən] *noun* child whose parents have died

ostensible [ɒ'stensəbl] *adjective* appearing to be something, but not really so; **ostensible partner** = person who appears to be a partner (by allowing his name to be used as such) but really has no interest in the partnership

otherwise ['ʌðəwaɪz] *adverb* in another way; *John Smith, otherwise known as 'the Butcher'*; **except as otherwise stated** = except where it is stated in a different way; **unless otherwise agreed** = unless different terms are agreed

ouster ['austə] *noun* removal of an occupier from a property so that he has to sue to regain possession (especially used against a violent spouse in matrimonial proceedings); *he had to apply for an ouster order*; *the judge made an ouster order*; *compare* EJECT

Outer House ['autə 'haus] *noun* part of the Scottish Court of Session, formed of five judges

outlaw ['autlɔː] **1** *noun* old term for a person who was thrown out of society as a punishment **2** *verb* to say that something is unlawful; *the government has proposed a bill to outlaw drinking in public*

outline planning permission ['autlaɪn 'plænɪŋ pə'mɪʃn] *noun* general permission to build a property on a piece of land, but not a final permission because there are no details

out of court ['aut əv 'kɔːt] *adverb & adjective* **a settlement was reached out of court** = a dispute was settled between two parties privately without continuing a court case; *they are hoping to reach an out-of-court settlement*

out of pocket ['aut əv 'pɒkɪt] *adjective & adverb* having paid out money personally; **out-of-pocket expenses** = amount of money to pay a worker back for his own money which he has spent on company business

output ['autput] 1 *noun* **(a)** amount which a company, a person or a machine produces; *output has increased by 10%; 25% of our output is exported;* **output tax** = VAT charged by a company on goods or services sold **(b)** information which is produced by a computer 2 *verb* to produce (by a computer); *the printer will output colour charts; all this information has been outputted from the computer* (NOTE: **outputting - outputted**)

outright ['autrait] *adverb & adjective* completely; **to purchase something outright** *or* **to make an outright purchase** = to buy something completely, including all rights in it

outside [aut'said] *adjective & adverb* not in a company's office or building; **to send work to be done outside** = to send work to be done in other offices; **outside office hours** = when the office is not open; **outside dealer** = person who is not a member of the Stock Exchange but is allowed to trade; **outside director** = director who is not employed by the company; **outside line** = line from an internal office telephone system to the main telephone exchange; **outside worker** = worker who does not work in a company's offices

outstanding [aut'stændiŋ] *adjective* **(a) outstanding offences** = offences for which a person has not yet been convicted, which can be considered at the same time as a similar offence for which he faces sentence **(b)** not yet paid or completed; **outstanding debts** = debts which are waiting to be paid; **outstanding orders** = orders received but not yet supplied; **matters outstanding from the previous meeting** = questions which were not settled at the previous meeting

outvote [aut'vaut] *verb* to defeat in a vote; **the chairman was outvoted** = the majority voted against the chairman

Oval Office ['auvl 'ɒfis] *noun* room in the White House which is the personal office of the President of the United States (NOTE: also used to mean the President himself: **the Oval Office was not pleased by the attitude of the Senate**)

overdue [auvə'dju:] *adjective* which has not been paid on time; **interest payments are three weeks overdue** = interest payments which should have been made three weeks ago; *compare* OUTSTANDING

overreaching [auvə'ri:tʃiŋ] *noun* legal principle where an interest in land is replaced by a direct right to money

override [auvə'raid] *verb* to pay no attention to, to be more important than; *the President vetoed the bill, but Congress overrode his veto; the appeal court overrode the decision of the lower court;* **overriding interest** = interest which comes before that of another party; *his wife established an overriding interest in the property against the bank's charge on it* (NOTE: **overriding - overrode - has overridden**)

> COMMENT: if the President of the USA disapproves of a bill sent to him by Congress for signature, he can send it back with objections within ten days of receiving it. Then if the Congress votes with a two-thirds majority in both Houses to continue with the bill, the bill becomes law and the President's veto is overridden

overrider *or* **overriding commission** [auvə'raidə *or* auvə'raidiŋ kə'miʃn] *noun* special extra commission which is above all other commissions

overrule [auvə'ru:l] *verb* **(a)** *(of a higher court)* to set a new precedent by deciding a case on a different principle from one laid down by a lower court; *the Supreme Court can overrule any other court in the USA* **(b)** *(in a meeting)* not to allow something because you are more powerful than others; *Mr Smith tried to object but his objection was overruled by the chairman;*

Community law must overrule national constitutions of Member States

overt ['əʊvɜːt] *adjective* open or obvious (as opposed to covert); **overt act** = act which is obviously aimed at committing a criminal offence; *see also* MARKET OVERT

overtime ['əʊvətaɪm] **1** *noun* hours worked more than the normal working time; *to work six hours' overtime*; *the overtime rate is one and a half times normal pay*; **overtime ban** = order by a trade union which forbids overtime work by its members; **overtime pay** = pay for extra time worked **2** *adverb* **to work overtime** = to work longer hours than in the contract of employment

overturn [əʊvə'tɜːn] *verb* to cancel a judgment on appeal

own [əʊn] *verb* to have or to possess; **a wholly-owned subsidiary** = a subsidiary which belongs completely to the parent company; **a state-owned industry** = industry which is nationalized

owner ['əʊnə] *noun* person who owns something; **beneficial owner** = true or ultimate owner (whose interest may be concealed by a nominee); **sole owner** = person who owns something alone; **owner-occupier** = person who owns and lives in a house; **goods sent at owner's risk** = situation where it is the owner of the goods who has to insure them while they are being shipped

ownership ['əʊnəʃɪp] *noun* act of owning something; **collective ownership** = situation where a business is owned by the workers who work in it; **common ownership** *or* **ownership in common** = ownership of a company or of a property by a group of people who each own a part; **joint ownership** = situation where two or more persons own the same property; **public ownership** *or* **state ownership** = situation where an industry is nationalized; *the company has been put into state ownership*; **private ownership** = situation where a company is owned by private shareholders; **the ownership of the company has passed to the banks** = the banks have become owners of the company

oyez [əʊ'jez] *French word meaning* 'hear!': used at the beginning of some types of official proceedings

Pp

pack [pæk] *verb* to fill (a committee or a jury) with members who are sympathetic to your views; *the left-wing group packed the general purposes committee with activists*

pact [pækt] *noun* agreement between two parties or countries; *the countries in the region signed a non-aggression pact; the two minority parties signed an electoral pact not to oppose each other in certain constituencies*

paddy wagon ['pædi 'wægən] *noun* (*informal*) van used by the police to take prisoners from one place to another

page [peɪdʒ] *noun* young person employed in the US Congress on junior administrative work

pair [peə] **1** *noun* (**a**) agreement between two MPs from opposite sides of the House of Commons not to vote on a motion, so allowing them both to be away from the House during a vote; *he was not able to find a pair, so had to come back from Paris to attend the debate* (**b**) MP who is paired with another **2** *verb* to arrange for two MPs from opposite sides of the House of Commons to be away from the House at the same time, so that each one's absence cancels out the other's; *he was paired with Mr Smith*

pais [peɪ] *see* ESTOPPEL

palimony ['pælɪmənɪ] *noun* money which a court orders a man to pay regularly to a woman with whom he has been living and from whom he has separated

pan- [pæn] *prefix* meaning 'covering all'; **pan-African** *or* **pan-American** = covering all Africa, all America

panel ['pænl] *see also* EMPANEL

paper ['peɪpə] *noun* (**a**) thin material for writing on or for wrapping; **carbon paper** = sheet of paper with a black coating on one side used in a typewriter to make a copy; **duplicating paper** = special paper to be used in a duplicating machine; **headed paper** = notepaper with the name and address of the company printed on it; **engrossment paper** *or* **judicature paper** = thick heavy paper on which court documents are engrossed; **lined paper** = paper with thin lines printed on it; **typing paper** = thin paper for use in a typewriter; **paper feed** = device which puts paper into a printer or copying machine (**b**) outline report; *the treasurer asked his deputy to write a paper on new funding; the planning department prepared a paper for the committee on the possible uses of the site; see also* GREEN PAPER, WHITE PAPER (**c**) **order paper** = printed agenda of business to be discussed each day in the House of Commons (**d**) **papers** = documents; *the solicitor sent me the relevant papers on the case; the police have sent the papers on the rail accident to the Director of Public Prosecutions; he has lost the customs papers; the office is asking for the VAT papers* (**e**) **on paper** = as explained in writing, but not tested in practice; *on paper the system is ideal, but we have to see it working before we can sign the contract;* **paper loss** = loss made when an asset has fallen in value but has not been sold; **paper profit** = profit made when an asset has increased in value but has not been sold **(f)** documents which can represent money (bills of exchange, promissory notes, etc.); **bankable paper** = document which a bank will accept as security for a loan; **negotiable paper** = document which can be transferred from one owner to another for money **(g) paper money** *or* **paper currency** = banknotes **(h)** newspaper; **trade paper** = newspaper aimed at people working in a certain industry; **free paper** *or* **giveaway paper** = newspaper which is given away free, and which relies for its income on its advertising

parade [pə'reɪd] *noun* **identification** *or* **identity parade** = arrangement where a group of people (including a suspect) stand in line at a police station so that a witness can point out a person whom he recognizes

paralegal [pærə'liːgl] **1** *adjective* connected with, but not part of, the law **2** *noun* person with no legal qualifications who works in a lawyer's office

paramount ['pærəmaʊnt] *adjective* superior (title)

parasitic rights [pærə'sɪtɪk 'raɪts] *noun (in the EU)* rights of persons to live in a EU country if they are dependent for their means of living on persons who have the right to reside and to have employment

parcel ['pɑːsl] *noun* area of land; *for sale: a parcel of land in the Borough of Richmond*

pardon ['pɑːdn] **1** *noun* action of forgiving an offence (by the Sovereign or by Parliament); **free pardon** = pardon given to a convicted person where both the sentence and the conviction are recorded as void **2** *verb* to forgive an offence; *the political prisoners were pardoned by the president*

> COMMENT: not quite the same as 'quashing' a conviction, which means that the conviction has been made void; both 'pardoning' and 'quashing' have the same effect

parens patriae ['pærenz 'pætriː] *Latin phrase meaning* 'parent of the nation',

referring to the king, queen or other head of state as the sovereign and guardian of children or people suffering from a legal disability

parent ['peərənt] *noun* **parents** = father and mother; **parent company** = company which owns more than 50% of the shares of another company

parentis [pə'rentɪs] *see* IN LOCO PARENTIS

pari passu ['pæri 'pæsuː] *Latin phrase meaning* 'equally' *or* 'with no distinction between them'; *the new shares will rank pari passu with the existing ones*

parish ['pærɪʃ] *noun* area which surrounds a church and which is served by that church; **parish council** = smallest unit of local government, representing a group of at least 200 people in a village or small town; **parish meeting** = meeting which must be held once a year in a parish and which all electors in the parish may attend; **parish pump politics** = local politics, concerning only minor local issues and the people in the parish

parity ['pærəti] *noun* being equal; **the female staff want parity with the men** = they want to have the same rates of pay and conditions as the men; **the pound fell to parity with the dollar** = the pound fell to a point where one pound equalled one dollar

parking offences ['pɑːkɪŋ ə'fensɪz] *noun* offences caused when parking a vehicle (parking on yellow lines, too near to street corners or pedestrian crossings, etc.)

parliament ['pɑːləmənt] *noun* elected group of representatives who form the legislative body which votes the laws of a country (in the UK formed of the House of Commons and House of Lords); **Act of Parliament** = decision which has been approved by Parliament and so becomes law; **contempt of Parliament** = conduct which may bring the authority of Parliament into disrepute; **Member of Parliament (MP)** = person elected to represent a constituency in parliament;

Mother of Parliaments = the British Parliament at Westminster; **the European Parliament** = parliament made up of delegates (MEPS or Euro-MPs) elected by each Member State of the EC (NOTE: often used without 'the': Parliament voted to abolish the death penalty; this is one of the Bills which will shortly be coming before Parliament)

parliamentarian [pɑːləmən'teəriən] *noun* **(a)** *GB* member of one of the Houses of Parliament; *a delegation of British parliamentarians was invited to visit Canada* **(b)** *US* one of two officials of Congress (the House Parliamentarian and the Parliamentarian of the Senate) who attend all debates and advise the presiding officers on procedure, precedents and committee jurisdiction

parliamentary [pɑːlə'mentri] *adjective* referring to parliament; **parliamentary agents** = persons (usually solicitors or barristers) who advise private individuals who wish to promote a Bill in Parliament; **Parliamentary Commissioner (for Administration)** = the Ombudsman, the official who investigates complaints by the public against government departments; **parliamentary counsel** *or* **parliamentary draftsman** = lawyer who is responsible for drafting Bills going before Parliament; **Parliamentary Labour Party (PLP)** = group formed of all the Labour backbench MPs (the Conservative equivalent is the 1922 Committee); **Parliamentary privilege** = right of a Member of Parliament or Member of the House of Lords to speak freely to the House without possibility of being sued for slander

Parliamentary Secretary *or* **Parliamentary Under-Secretary** [pɑːlə'mentri 'sekrtri] *noun* government member (an MP or a member of the House of Lords) who works in a department under a Secretary of State or Minister of State (NOTE: to avoid confusion, they are called Parliamentary Under-Secretaries in departments where the head of the department is a Secretary of State)

parol [pə'rəʊl] *adjective* done by speaking; **parol agreement** *or* **contract** = simple contract, informal or oral contract; **parol evidence** = evidence given orally

parole [pə'rəʊl] **1** *noun* (i) allowing a prisoner to leave prison for a short time, on condition that he or she behaves well; (ii) allowing a prisoner who has behaved well to be released from prison early on condition that he or she continues to behave well; *he was given a week's parole to visit his mother in hospital*; *after six month's good conduct in prison she is eligible for parole*; *he was let out on parole and immediately burgled a house*; **parole board** = group of people who advise the Home Secretary if a prisoner should be released on parole before the end of his or her sentence **2** *verb* to let a prisoner out of prison on condition that he or she behaves well; *if you're lucky you will be paroled before Christmas*

parolee [pə'rəʊliː] *noun US* prisoner who is let out on parole

part [pɑːt] *noun* **(a)** piece or section; *part of the shipment was damaged*; *part of the staff is on overtime*; *part of the expenses will be refunded* **(b)** one of the sections of an Act, Bill, or other official document; *see* PART 20 *below* **(c)** **in part** = not completely; *to contribute in part to the costs*; *to pay the costs in part* **(d)** **part-owner** = person who owns something jointly with one or more other persons; **part-ownership** = situation where two or more persons own the same property **(e)** **part exchange** = giving an old product as part of the payment for a new one; **part payment** = paying of part of a whole payment; **part performance** = situation where a party has carried out part of a contract, but not complied with all the terms of it

Part 20 claim ['pɑːt 'twenti 'kleɪm] *noun* any claim other than a claim filed by a claimant against a defendant in the particulars of claim

COMMENT: Part 20 claims include counterclaims by a defendant against a claimant, or against other persons who are not parties to the case, or a claim by another person against any other person. These claims are dealt with under Part 20 of the new Civil Procedure Rules, hence the name

Part 36 offer or Part 36 payment

['pɑːt θɜːti'sɪks 'ɒfə or 'peɪmənt] *noun* offer or payment made by a defendant (the offeror) to a claimant (the offeree) to settle all or part of a claim after proceedings have started (these offers or payments do not apply to small claims)

parte ['pɑːteɪ] *see* EX PARTE, INTER PARTES, AUDI ALTERNAM PARTEM

partial ['pɑːʃl] *adjective* **(a)** not complete; **partial loss** = situation where only part of the insured property has been damaged or lost; **he was awarded partial compensation for the damage to his house** = he was compensated for part of the damage **(b)** biased, showing favour towards one party; *the defendant complained that the judge was partial*

particular [pə'tɪkjʊlə] **1** *adjective* special, different from others; **particular average** = situation where part of a shipment is lost or damaged and the insurance costs are borne by the owner of the lost goods and not shared among all the owners of the shipment; **particular lien** = right of a person to keep possession of another person's property until debts relating to that property have been paid; *compare* GENERAL AVERAGE, GENERAL LIEN **2** *noun* **(a)** particulars = details, especially a statement of the facts of a case made by a party in civil proceedings or a County Court pleading setting out the claimant's claim; *sheet which gives particulars of the items for sale*; *the inspector asked for particulars of the missing car*; **to give full particulars of something** = to list all the known details about something; **request for further and better particulars** = pleading served by one party on another in civil proceedings, asking for information about the other party's claim or defence **(b) in particular** = specially, as a special point; *goods which*

are easily damaged, in particular glasses, need special packing

particulars of claim [pə'tɪkjʊləz ɒv 'kleɪm] *noun* document containing details of a claimant's case and the relief sought against the defendant (NOTE: since the introduction of the new Civil Procedure Rules in April 1999, this term has replaced **statement of claim**)

COMMENT: particulars of claim are usually included in the claim form filed by the claimant. They should give a statement of the facts of the claim, together with details of interest or damages claimed. They must include the following if they are to form part of the claim to be pleaded: details of fraud, illegality, breach of trust, default, or unsoundness of mind on the part of the defendant

partition [pɑː'tɪʃn] *noun* dividing up of land which is held by joint tenants or tenants in common

partly ['pɑːtli] *adverb* not completely; **partly-paid capital** = capital which represents partly-paid shares; **partly-paid up shares** = shares where the shareholders have not paid the full face value; **partly-secured creditors** = creditors whose debts are not fully covered by the value of the security

partner ['pɑːtnə] *noun* person who works in a firm and has a share in it with other partners; *he became a partner in a firm of solicitors*; **active partner** or **working partner** = partner who works in a partnership; **junior partner** = person who has a small part of the shares in a partnership; **senior partner** = person who has a large part of the shares in a partnership; **limited partner** = partner who has only limited liability for the partnership debts; **sleeping partner** or **dormant partner**, *US* **silent partner** = partner who has a share in a business but does not work in it

partnership ['pɑːtnəʃɪp] *noun* **(a)** unregistered business where two or more people share the risks and profits equally;

to go into partnership with someone; *to join with someone to form a partnership*; **articles of partnership** = document which sets up the legal conditions of a partnership; **to offer someone a partnership** *or* **to take someone into partnership with you** = to have a working business and bring someone in to share it with you; **to dissolve a partnership** = to bring a partnership to an end; **partnership at will** = partnership with no fixed time limit stated **(b) limited partnership** = registered business where the liability of some of the partners is limited to the amount of capital they have each provided to the business and where these partners may not take part in the running of the business, while other, working partners, are fully liable for all the obligations of the partnership

party ['pɑːti] *noun* **(a)** company or person involved in a legal dispute, legal agreement or crime; *one of the parties to the suit has died*; *the company is not a party to the agreement*; **to be party to something** = to be involved in a legal action; *how important is this case to those persons who are not party to it?*; **identity of parties** = situation where the parties in different actions are the same; **party and party costs** = normal basis for assessment of costs which includes all costs incurred in the party's case **(b) third party** = any third person, in addition to the two main parties involved in a contract; **third party insurance** *or* **third party policy** = insurance which pays compensation if someone who is not the insured person incurs loss or injury **(c) working party** = group of experts who study a problem; *the government has set up a working party to study the problems of industrial waste*; *Professor Smith is the chairman of the working party on drug abuse* **(d) political party** = organized group of people who believe a country should be run in a certain way; **party politics** = system in which the political life of the country is run by large powerful parties, who make their supporters follow the party line, and where obedience to the party is more important than following its principles; *(in a*

two-party system) **third party** = another, usually smaller, political party, beside the main two; **a third party candidate** = candidate for one of the smaller parties

party list system ['pɑːti 'lɪst 'sɪstəm] *noun* electoral system in some European countries, where each party draws up a list of candidates, and the electors vote for the party, not the candidate; the Parliament is then formed of candidates from each party's list in proportion to the total number of votes which the party has received; *see also* ADDITIONAL MEMBER

party wall ['pɑːti 'wɔːl] *noun* wall which separates two adjoining properties (houses or land) and belongs to both owners equally

pass [pɑːs] **1** *noun* permit to allow someone to go into a building; *you need a pass to enter the ministry offices*; *all members of staff must show their passes* **2** *verb* **(a)** to vote to approve; to vote to make a law; *Parliament passed the Bill which has now become law*; *the finance director has to pass an invoice before it is paid*; *the loan has been passed by the board*; **to pass a resolution** = to vote to agree to a resolution; *the meeting passed a proposal that salaries should be frozen* **(b) to pass sentence on someone** = to give a convicted person the official legal punishment; *the jury returned a verdict of guilty, and the judge will pass sentence next week* **(c) to pass a dividend** = to pay no dividend in a certain year

pass off ['pɑːs 'ɒf] *verb* **to pass something off as something else** = to pretend that it is another thing in order to cheat a customer

passing off ['pɑːsɪŋ 'ɒf] *noun* action of trying to sell goods by giving the impression that they have been made by someone else, using that other person's reputation to make a sale

pass over ['pɑːs 'əʊvə] *verb* to avoid using someone who has been appointed, and use someone else instead

COMMENT: an executor can be passed over in favour of someone else is if he has disappeared, is serving a life sentence in prison, etc.

passport ['pɑːspɔːt] *noun* official document proving that you are a citizen of a country, which you have to show when you travel from one country to another; *we had to show our passports at the customs post*; *his passport is out of date*; *the passport officer stamped my passport*; **passport holder** = person who holds a passport; *she is a British passport holder*

patent ['pætənt or peɪtənt] **1** *noun* **(a)** official document showing that a person has the exclusive right to make and sell an invention; *to take out a patent for a new type of light bulb*; *to apply for a patent for a new invention*; *he has received a grant of patent for his invention*; **patent applied for** *or* **patent pending** = words on a product showing that the inventor has applied for a patent for it; **to forfeit a patent** = to lose a patent because payments have not been made; **to infringe a patent** = to make and sell a product which works in the same way as a patented product and not pay a royalty for it; **patent agent** = person who advises on patents and applies for patents on behalf of clients; **to file a patent application** = to apply for a patent; **patent examiner** = official who checks patent applications to see if the inventions are really new; **patent holder** = person who has been granted a patent; **infringement of patent** *or* **patent infringement** = act of illegally using, making or selling an invention which is patented without the permission of the patentee; **patent number** = reference number given to a patented invention; **patent office** = government office which grants patents and supervises them; **patent proprietor** = a patentee, a person who holds a patent; **patent rights** = rights which an inventor holds under a patent; **patent specification** = full details of an invention which is the subject of a patent application **(b) letters patent** = official document from the Crown, which gives someone the exclusive right to do something (such as becoming a life peer or

granting a patent to make and sell an invention) **2** *verb* **to patent an invention** = to register an invention with the patent office to prevent other people from copying it **3** *adjective* obvious, clear to see; *the prisoner's statement is a patent lie*; **patent defect** = obvious defect

COMMENT: to qualify for a patent an invention must be new and not previously disclosed, it must be an advance on previous inventions, it must be able to be manufactured and it must not involve anything excluded from patent cover. Things excluded from patent cover include scientific theories (because they are confidential information), games and computer programs (which are covered by copyrights), medical treatments, some newly developed plants, animals and other biological processes. When a patent is granted, it gives the patentee a monopoly in his invention for 20 years

patentability [pætəntə'bɪləti] *noun* ability to be the subject of a patent

patentable ['peɪtəntəbl] *adjective* able to be the subject of a patent; *computer programs are not patentable because they are covered by copyright*

patented ['pætntɪd or 'peɪtntɪd] *adjective* which is protected by a patent

patentee [peɪtn'tiː] *noun* person who has been granted a patent

paternity [pə'tɜːnəti] *noun* **(a)** action of being a father **(b)** the moral right of a copyright holder to be identified as the creator of the work

paternity action *or* **suit** [pə'tɜːnəti 'ækʃn or suːt] *noun* lawsuit brought by the mother of an illegitimate child to force the putative father to maintain the child

pathologist [pə'θɒlədʒɪst] *noun* doctor who specializes in pathology, especially a doctor who examines corpses to find out the cause of death; **Home Office pathologist** = official government pathologist employed by the Home Office to examine corpses

pathology [pə'θɒlədʒi] *noun* study of disease

patient ['peɪʃnt] *noun* **(a)** person who is in hospital or who is being treated by a doctor **(b)** *(specific legal meaning)* person who is suffering from a mental disorder and is unable to manage his or her affairs

patrial ['peɪtrɪəl] *noun* person who has the right to live in the UK because he has close family ties with the country (for example, if his grandfather was British)

patricide ['pætrɪsaɪd] *noun* murder of one's father

patrol [pə'trəul] **1** *noun* group of people who walk through an area to see what is happening; **a police patrol** = group of policemen who are patrolling an area; **on patrol** = walking through an area to see what is happening; *we saw six squad cars on patrol in the centre of the town*; **on foot patrol** = patrolling an area on foot, not in a car **2** *verb* to walk regularly through an area to see what is happening; *groups of riot police were patrolling the centre of the town*

patrol car [pə'trəul 'kɑː] *noun* car used by police on patrol

patrolman [pə'trəulmən] *noun* US lowest rank of policeman; *Patrolman Jones was at the scene of the accident*

patronage ['pætrənɪdʒ] *noun* right to give government posts or honours to people; *the Prime Minister has considerable patronage*; **patronage secretary** = official of the Prime Minister's staff who deals with appointments to posts

pauperis ['pɔːpərɪs] *see* IN FORMA PAUPERIS

pawn [pɔːn] **1** *noun* transfer of a piece of property to someone as security for a loan; **to put something in pawn** = to leave a valuable object with someone in exchange for a loan which has to be repaid if you want to take back the object; **to take something out of pawn** = to repay the loan and so get back the object; **pawn ticket** = receipt given by the pawnbroker for the

object left in pawn **2** *verb* **to pawn a watch** = to leave a watch with a pawnbroker who gives a loan against it

pawnbroker ['pɔːnbrəukə] *noun* person who lends money against the security of valuable objects

pawnshop ['pɔːnʃɒp] *noun* pawnbroker's shop

pay [peɪ] **1** *noun* **(a)** salary or wage, money given to someone for regular work; **back pay** = salary which has not been paid; **basic pay** = normal salary without extra payments; **take-home pay** = pay left after tax and insurance have been deducted; **unemployment pay** = money given by the government to someone who is unemployed **(b) pay cheque** = monthly cheque which pays a salary to a worker; **pay day** = day on which wages are paid to workers (usually Friday for workers paid once a week, and during the last week of the month for workers who are paid once a month); **pay negotiations** *or* **pay talks** = discussions between management and workers about pay increases **2** *verb* **(a)** to give money to buy an item or a service; **to pay in advance** = to give money before you receive the item bought or before the service has been completed; **to pay in instalments** = to give money for an item by giving small amounts regularly; **to pay cash** = to pay the complete sum in cash; **to pay costs** = to pay the costs of a court case; **paying party** = the party in a case who is liable to pay costs (NOTE: the other party is the receiving party); **to pay on demand** = to pay money when it is asked for, not after a period of credit; **to pay a dividend** = to give shareholders a part of the profits of a company; **to pay interest** = to give money as interest on money borrowed or invested **(b)** to give a worker money for work done; *the workers have not been paid for three weeks*; *we pay good wages for skilled workers*; *how much do they pay you per hour?*; **to be paid by the hour** = to get money for each hour worked; **to be paid at piece-work rates** = to get money calculated on the number of pieces of work finished (NOTE: **paying - paid - has paid**)

payable ['peɪəbl] *adjective* which is due to be paid; **payable in advance** = which has to be paid before the goods are delivered; **payable on delivery** = which has to be paid when the goods are delivered; **payable on demand** = which must be paid when payment is asked for; **payable at sixty days** = which has to be paid by sixty days after the date of invoice; **cheque made payable to bearer** = cheque which will be paid to the person who has it, not to any particular name written on it; **shares payable on application** = shares which must be paid for when you apply to buy them; **accounts payable** = money owed to creditors; **bills payable** = bills which a debtor will have to pay; **electricity charges are payable by the tenant** = the tenant (and not the landlord) must pay for the electricity

pay as you earn (PAYE) ['peɪ æz juː 'ɜːn] *noun* tax system, where income tax is deducted from the salary before it is paid to the worker (NOTE: the American equivalent is **pay-as-you-go**)

pay-as-you-go ['peɪ æz juː 'gəʊ] *noun* (a) *US* = PAY AS YOU EARN (b) *GB* system of summarily assessing costs in a trial

pay back ['peɪ 'bæk] *verb* to give money back to someone; *I lent him £50 and he promised to pay me back in a month; he has never paid me back the money he borrowed*

payback ['peɪbæk] *noun* paying back money which has been borrowed; **payback clause** = clause in a contract which states the terms for repaying a loan; **payback period** = period of time over which a loan is to be repaid or an investment is to pay for itself

pay cheque *or* **paycheck** ['peɪ 'tʃek] *noun* salary cheque given to an employee

pay down ['peɪ 'daʊn] *verb* **to pay money down** = to make a deposit; *he paid £50 down and the rest in monthly instalments*

PAYE ['piː 'eɪ 'waɪ 'iː] = PAY AS YOU EARN

payee [peɪ'iː] *noun* person who receives money from someone, person whose name is on a cheque or bill of exchange

pay in *or* **into** ['peɪ 'ɪn] *verb (of a defendant)* **to pay in** *or* **to pay money into court** = to deposit money with the court at the beginning of a case, to try to satisfy the claimant's claim

COMMENT: if at trial the claimant fails to recover more than the amount the defendant has paid in, he will have to pay the defendant's costs from the date of the payment in

payment ['peɪmənt] *noun* **(a)** transfer of money from one person to another to satisfy a debt or obligation; *payment in cash or cash payment; payment by cheque*; **payment on account** = paying part of the money owed before a bill is delivered; *the solicitor asked for a payment of £100 on account*; **full payment** *or* **payment in full** = paying all money owed; **payment on invoice** = paying money as soon as an invoice is received; **payment in** *or* **payment into court** = depositing money by the defendant into the court before the case starts, to try to satisfy the claimant's claim **(b)** money paid; **back payment** = paying money which is owed; **deferred payments** = money paid later than the agreed date; **down payment** = part of a total payment made in advance; **interim payment** = payment of part of a sum owed; **part payment** = paying part of a whole payment

pay off ['peɪ 'ɒf] *verb* **(a)** to finish paying money which is owed; *to pay off a mortgage; to pay off a loan* **(b)** to pay all the money owed to someone and terminate his employment; *when the company was taken over the factory was closed and all the workers were paid off*

payoff ['peɪɒf] *noun* money paid to finish paying something which is owed

pay up ['peɪ 'ʌp] *verb* to give money which is owed; *the company paid up only* *when we sent them a letter from our solicitor; he finally paid up six months late*

PC = PERSONAL COMPUTER, POLICE CONSTABLE, PRIVY COUNCIL, PRIVY COUNCILLOR

PDs ['piː 'diːz] = PRACTICE DIRECTIONS

peace [piːs] *noun* (a) being quiet or calm; calm existence; **breach of the peace** = creating a disturbance which is likely to annoy people (b) state of not being at war; *after six years of civil war, the country is now at peace*; *the peace treaty was signed yesterday*; *both sides claimed the other side broke the peace agreement*

pecuniary [pɪˈkjuːniəri] *adjective* referring to money; **obtaining a pecuniary advantage by deception** = crime of deceiving someone so as to derive a financial benefit from the deception; **he gained no pecuniary advantage** = he made no financial gain; **pecuniary default judgment** = judgment without trial against a defendant who fails to respond to a claim, which gives the claimant the money claimed including interest; **pecuniary legacy** = legacy in the form of money

peer ['pɪə] *noun* (a) member of the aristocracy, a person with a title such as Lord, Duke, etc.; **hereditary peer** = peer who has inherited the title and will pass it on to his heir; **life peer** = member of the House of Lords who is appointed for life and whose title does not pass to another member of the family (b) person who is in the same group or rank as another; **peer group** = group of persons of the same level or rank; *the Magna Carta gave every free man the right to be tried by his peers*; *children try to behave like other members of their peer group*

COMMENT: a peer is disqualified from standing for election to the House of Commons, but can renounce the peerage in order to be able to stand for election as an MP

peerage ['pɪərɪdʒ] *noun* (a) all peers, taken as a group (b) position of being a peer; *three new peerages were created in the New Year's Honours List*

peeress [pɪərˈes] *noun* female peer; wife of a peer

penal ['piːnəl] *adjective* referring to punishment; **penal code** = set of laws governing crime and its punishment; **penal colony** = prison camp in a distant place, where prisoners are sent for long periods; **penal institution** = place (such as a prison) where convicted criminals are kept; **penal laws** *or* **the penal system** = system of punishments relating to different crimes; **penal servitude** = former punishment by imprisonment with hard labour

penalize ['piːnəlaɪz] *verb* to punish, to fine; *to penalize a supplier for late deliveries*; *they were penalized for bad service*

penalty ['penəlti] *noun* punishment (such as a fine) which is imposed if something is not done or if a law is not obeyed; *the penalty for carrying an offensive weapon is a fine of £2,000 and three months in prison*; **death penalty** = sentence of a criminal to be executed; *the president has introduced the death penalty for certain crimes against the state*; **penalty clause** = clause which lists the penalties which will be imposed if the terms of the contract are not fulfilled; *the contract contains a penalty clause which fines the company 1% for every week the completion date is late*

COMMENT: penalty clauses in a contract are sometimes unenforceable

pendens ['pendenz] *see* LIS

pendente lite [penˈdenteɪ 'laɪteɪ] *Latin phrase meaning* 'during the lawsuit'; *see also* ALIMONY

pending ['pendɪŋ] *adjective* waiting; **pending action** = action concerned with land which has not been heard; **pending suit** = while a lawsuit is being heard; **maintenance pending suit** = maintenance obtained by a spouse in matrimonial proceedings until there is a full hearing to deal with the couple's financial affairs; **patent pending** = words printed on a product to show that its inventor has applied for a grant of patent but has not yet received it

penitentiary [penɪˈtenʃəri] *noun US* large prison; *the Pennsylvania State Penitentiary*

penology [piːˈnɒlədʒi] *noun* study of sentences in relation to crimes

pension [ˈpenʃn] *noun* (a) money paid regularly to someone who no longer works; **retirement pension** *or* **old age pension** = state pension given to a man who is over 65 or a woman who is over 60; **occupational pension** = pension which is paid by the company by which a worker has been employed (b) **pension contributions** = money paid by a company or worker into a pension fund; **pension entitlement** = amount of pension which someone has the right to receive when he retires; **pension fund** = money which provides pensions for retired members of staff; **pension plan** *or* **pension scheme** = plan worked out by an insurance company which arranges for a worker to pay part of his salary over many years and receive a regular payment when he retires; **contributory pension scheme** = scheme where the worker has to pay a proportion of his salary; **graduated pension scheme** = pension scheme where the benefit is calculated as a percentage of the salary of each person in the scheme; **non-contributory pension scheme** = scheme where the employer pays in all the money on behalf of the worker; **personal pension plan** = pension plan which applies to one worker only, usually a self-employed person, not to a group (NOTE: the American equivalent is **Individual Retirement Account**)

pensionable [ˈpenʃnəbl] *adjective* able to receive a pension; **pensionable age** = age after which someone can take a pension

pensioner [ˈpenʃnə] *noun* person who receives a pension; **old age pensioner** = person who receives the retirement pension

peppercorn rent [ˈpepəkɔːn ˈrent] *noun* very small or nominal rent; *to pay a peppercorn rent; to lease a property for or at a peppercorn rent*

per annum [ˈpə ˈænəm] *adverb* in a year, annually; *the rent is £2,500 per annum; what is their turnover per annum?*

per autre vie [ˈpɜː ˈəutrə ˈviː] *French phrase meaning* 'for the lifetime of another person'

per capita [ˈpə ˈkæpɪtə] *adjective & adverb* (a) divided among beneficiaries individually (as opposed to 'per stirpes') (b) per head, for each person; **average income per capita** *or* **per capita income** = average income of one person; **per capita expenditure** = total money spent divided by the number of people involved

percentage increase [pəˈsentɪdʒ ˈɪŋkriːs] *noun* increase in costs above base costs, which is negotiated as part of a conditional fee agreement

per curiam [ˈpɜː ˈkjuːriəm] *Latin phrase meaning* 'by a court': decision correctly made by a court, which can be used as a precedent; *compare* PER INCURIAM

per diem [ˈpɜː ˈdiːəm] *Latin phrase meaning* 'for each day'

peremptory challenge [pəˈremptri ˈtʃælɪndʒ] *noun* objecting to a juror without stating any reason

perfect right [ˈpɜːfɪkt ˈraɪt] *noun* correct and legally acceptable right

perform [pəˈfɔːm] *verb* to do (a duty), to do what one is obliged to do by a contract

performance [pəˈfɔːməns] *noun* (a) way in which someone or something acts; **the poor performance of the shares on the stock market** = the fall in the share price on the stock market; **as a measure of the company's performance** = as a way of judging if the company's results are good or bad; **performance of personnel against objectives** = how personnel have worked, measured against the objectives set; **performance review** = yearly interview between a manager and each worker to discuss how the worker has worked during the year **(b)** carrying out of something, such as a duty or the terms of a contract; **they were asked to put up a £1m performance bond** = they were asked to deposit £1m as a guarantee that they would carry out the terms of the contract; **discharge by performance** = situation where the terms of a contract have been fulfilled; **impossibility of performance** = situation where a party to a contract is unable to perform his part of the contract; **part performance** = situation where a party has carried out part of a contract, but has not complied with all the terms of it; **specific performance** = court order to a party to carry out his obligations in a contract

performing right [pə'fɔːmɪŋ 'raɪt] *noun* right to allow the playing of a copyright piece of music

peril ['perɪl] *noun* danger (especially possible accident covered by an insurance policy); **perils of the sea** *or* **maritime perils** = accidents which can happen at sea

per incuriam ['pɜː ɪn'kjuːriəm] *Latin phrase meaning* 'because of lack of care': decision wrongly made by a court (which does not therefore set a precedent)

period ['pɪəriəd] *noun* **(a)** length of time; *for a period of time* or *for a period of months* or *for a six-year period; to deposit money for a fixed period* **(b)** accounting **period** = period of time at the end of which the firm's accounts are made up

periodic *or* **periodical** [pɪəri'ɒdɪkl] **1** *adjective* happening regularly from time to time; **periodical payments** = regular payments (such as maintenance paid to a divorced spouse); **periodic tenancy** = tenancy where the tenant rents for several short periods but not for a fixed length of time **2** *noun* **periodical** = magazine which comes out regularly

perjure ['pɜːdʒə] *verb* **to perjure yourself** = to tell lies when you have made an oath to say what is true

perjury ['pɜːdʒəri] *noun* notifiable offence of telling lies when you have made an oath to say what is true in court; *he was sent to prison for perjury; she appeared in court on a charge of perjury* or *on a perjury charge*

Permanent Secretary ['pɜːmənənt 'sekrətri] *noun* chief civil servant in a government department or ministry (NOTE: in Canada, called **Deputy Minister)**

COMMENT: Permanent Secretaries are appointed by the Prime Minister but are responsible to the Secretary of State in charge of the relevant department

permissive waste [pə'mɪsɪv 'weɪst] *noun* damage to a property which is caused by a tenant not carrying out repairs

permit 1 ['pɜːmɪt] *noun* official document which allows someone to do something; **building permit** = official document which allows someone to build on a piece of land; **entry permit** = document allowing someone to enter a country; **export permit** *or* **import permit** = official document which allows goods to be exported or imported; **work permit** = official document which allows someone who is not a citizen to work in a country **2** [pə'mɪt] *verb* to allow someone to do something; *this document permits the export of twenty-five computer systems; the ticket permits three people to go into the exhibition*

per my et per tout ['pɜː miː eɪ pɜː 'tuː] *French phrase meaning* 'by half and by all': used to indicate the relationship between joint tenants

perpetrate ['pɜːpɪtreɪt] *verb* to commit (a crime)

perpetrator ['pɜːpɪtreɪtə] *noun* person who does something (especially person who commits a crime)

perpetuity [pɜːpə'tjuːəti] *noun* **in perpetuity** = for ever; **rule against perpetuities** = rule that an interest can only last for a certain period, no more than 21 years

per pro ['pɜː 'prəʊ] = PER PROCURATIONEM with the authority of; **the secretary signed per pro the manager** = the secretary signed on behalf of, and with the authority of, the manager

per procurationem ['pɜː prɒkjʊræsi'əʊnəm] *Latin phrase meaning* 'with the authority of'

per quod ['pɜː 'kwɒd] *Latin phrase meaning* 'by which' or 'whereby'

per se ['pɜː 'seɪ] *Latin phrase meaning* 'on its own' or 'alone'; **actionable per se** = which is in itself sufficient grounds for bringing an action

persistent offender [pə'sɪstənt ə'fendə] *noun* person who has been convicted of a crime at least three times before, and is likely to commit the crime again

person ['pɜːsən] *noun* **(a)** someone, man or woman; *insurance policy which covers a named person*; **the persons named in the contract** = people whose names are given in the contract; **the document should be witnessed by a third person** = someone who is not named in the document should witness it; **in person** = someone himself or herself; **this important package is to be delivered to the chairman in person** = the package has to be given to the chairman himself (and not to his secretary, assistant, etc.); **he came to see me in person** = he himself came to see me; **litigant in person** = person bringing a lawsuit who also speaks on his own behalf in court without the help of a lawyer **(b) legal person** *or* **artificial person** = company or corporation considered as a legal body; **natural person** = human being (as opposed to a legal or artificial person such as a company); *in this case, the term 'establishment' is not confined to legal persons, but is extended to natural persons* **(c) displaced person** = man or woman who has been forced to leave home and move to another country because of war

persona [pə'səʊnə] *noun* **(a)** thing (such as a company) which has personality **(b) persona non grata** = foreign person who is not acceptable to a government (used especially of diplomats)

personal ['pɜːsnl] *adjective* **(a)** referring to one person; **personal action** = (i) legal action brought by a person himself; (ii) common law term for an action against a person arising out of a contract or tort; (iii) = ACTION IN PERSONAM; **personal allowances** = part of a person's income which is not taxed; **personal assets** = moveable assets which belong to a person; **personal chattels** *or* **chattels personal** = things (furniture, clothes, cars) which belong to a person and which are not land; **personal computer (PC)** = small computer which can be used at home; **personal estate** = things which belong to someone (excluding land) which can be inherited by his heirs; **personal income** = income received by an individual person before tax is paid; **personal injuries** = injuries to a person caused by disease which impair that person's mental or physical condition; *see also* CLAIM; **personal injury** = injury to the body suffered by the victim of an accident; **personal property** = property which belongs to one person (excluding land and buildings, but including money, goods, securities, etc.); **personal service** = act of giving legal documents to someone as part of a legal action (such as serving someone with a writ) **(b)** private; *I want to see the director on a personal matter*; **personal assistant** = secretary who can take on responsibility in various ways when the boss is not there

personal conduct ['pɜːsnl 'kɒndʌkt] *noun (in the EU)* the way in which a person acts in society

COMMENT: personal conduct can be used as a reason for excluding a national of another EU state from entering a country and taking up work

personal representative (pr)

['pɜːsnəl reprɪ'zentətɪv] *noun* person who is the executor of a will or the administrator of the estate of a deceased person; person appointed to deal with the estate of a person who dies intestate

COMMENT: a personal representative can be the executor of the estate, usually appointed by the deceased person in the will, or an administrator who is appointed to deal with the estate of a deceased person who died intestate, or who did not appoint an executor in the will. The personal representative holds the property on trust, pays any liabilities and expenses, and invests money until such time as the estate is distributed

personality [pɜːsə'nælətɪ] *noun* **(a)** **legal personality** = legal existence or status of a person; **corporate personality** = legal existence of an incorporated company which can be treated as a person **(b)** qualities of mind and spirit which make one person different from another; **personality cult** = excessive publicity given to make a political leader into a type of god (found in some, usually autocratic, regimes, where pictures of the leader are everywhere, where the leader's speeches are prominently printed, where the leader is seen to be responsible for everything good which happens in the State)

personalty ['pɜːsnltɪ] *noun* personal property or chattels (as opposed to land)

personam [pə'səʊnəm] *see* ACTION

personation [pɜːsə'neɪʃn] *noun* crime of fraudulently pretending to be someone else

per stirpes ['pɜː 'stɜːpiːz] *Latin phrase meaning* 'by branches': phrase used in wills where the entitlement is divided among branches of a family rather than among individuals (which is 'per capita')

persuasive precedent *or* **authority** [pɜː'sweɪzɪv 'presɪdənt *or* ɔː'θɒrəti] *noun* precedent which a judge is not obliged to follow but is of importance in reaching a judgment, as opposed to a binding precedent

pertain [pɜː'teɪn] *verb* **to pertain to** = to refer to or to relate to; *the law pertaining to public order*

perverse [pə'vɜːs] *adjective* strange or odd; **perverse verdict** = verdict by a jury which goes against what anyone would normally feel to be the right decision, or which goes against the direction of the judge

pervert [pə'vɜːt] *verb* to change or to interfere; **to attempt to pervert the course of justice** = to try to influence the outcome of a trial by tampering with the evidence, bribing the jurors, etc.

COMMENT: perverting the course of justice is a notifiable offence

petition [pə'tɪʃn] **1** *noun* **(a)** written application to a court; **bankruptcy petition** = application to a court asking for an order making someone bankrupt; **to file a petition in bankruptcy** = to apply to the court to be made bankrupt, or to ask for someone else to be made bankrupt; **divorce petition** = application to a court to end a marriage; **winding up petition** = application to a court for an order that a company be put into liquidation **(b)** written request accompanied by a list of signatures of people supporting it; *they presented a petition with a million signatures to Parliament, asking for the law to be repealed* **2** *verb* to make an official request; *he petitioned the government for a special pension*; *the marriage had broken down and the wife petitioned for divorce*

COMMENT: petitions to the House of Commons are written by hand, and have a set form of words. After a petition is presented in the House of Commons at the beginning of the day's business, it is said to 'lie upon the table' and is placed in a bag behind the Speaker's Chair

petitioner [pə'tɪʃnə] *noun* person who puts forward a petition

petty ['peti] *adjective* small, not important; **petty cash** = small amount of money kept in an office to make small purchases; **petty crime,** *US* **petty offenses** = small crimes which are not very serious; **petty sessions** = magistrates' court; **petty theft** = stealing small items or small amounts of money

petty-sessional division *or* **petty sessions area** ['peti'seʃnl dɪ'vɪʒn or 'eəriə] *noun* area of the country covered by a magistrates' courts committee for administration purposes

COMMENT: England and Wales are divided into 45 petty sessions areas

Photofit ['fəʊtəʊfɪt] *noun* method of making a picture of a criminal from descriptions given by witnesses, using pieces of photographs of different types of faces; *the police issued an Photofit picture of the mugger*

picker ['pɪkə] *noun (slang)* one of a group of pickpockets, who actually picks the victim's pocket; *compare* RUNNER

picket ['pɪkɪt] **1** *noun* striking worker who stands at the gate of a factory to try to persuade other workers not to go to work; **picket line** = line of pickets at the gate of a factory **2** *verb* **to picket a factory** = to put pickets at the gate of a factory to try to prevent other workers from going to work

picketing ['pɪkɪtɪŋ] *noun* action of standing at the gates of a factory to prevent workers going to work; **lawful** *or* **peaceful picketing** = picketing which is allowed by law; **mass picketing** = picketing by large numbers of pickets who try to frighten workers who want to work; **secondary picketing** = picketing of another factory or place of work, not directly connected with the strike, to prevent it supplying the striking factory or receiving supplies from it

pickpocket ['pɪkpɒkɪt] *noun* person who steals things from people's pockets

pilfer ['pɪlfə] *verb* to steal small objects or small amounts of money

pilferage *or* **pilfering** ['pɪlfərɪdʒ or 'pɪlfərɪŋ] *noun* stealing small amounts of money or small items

pilferer ['pɪlfərə] *noun* person who steals small objects or small amounts of money

pimp [pɪmp] *noun* man who organizes prostitutes and lives off their earnings

pinch ['pɪntʃ] *verb (informal)* **(a)** to steal **(b)** to arrest

piracy ['paɪrəsi] *noun* **(a)** robbery at sea, by attacking ships **(b)** copying of patented inventions or copyright works; *laws to ban book piracy*

pirate ['paɪrət] **1** *noun* **(a)** person who attacks a ship at sea to steal cargo **(b)** person who copies a patented invention or a copyright work and sells it; *a pirate copy of a book*; **pirate radio station** = radio station which broadcasts without a licence from outside a country's territorial waters **2** *verb* to copy a copyright work; *a pirated book or a pirated design*; *the drawings for the new dress collection were pirated in the Far East*

pith and marrow ['pɪθ ənd 'mærəʊ] *noun* doctrine that a patent can be applied to separate parts of an invention or process as well as to a single invention itself

place [pleɪs] *noun* where something is, where something happens; **meeting place** = room or area where people can meet; **place of performance** = place where a contract is to be performed; **place of work** = office, factory, etc., where people work; **public place** = place (such as a road or park) where the public in general have a right to be; *(in the House of Commons)* **other place** *or* **another place** = the House of Lords (NOTE: the convention is that MPs never refer to the House of Lords in debates, but can only talk of 'the other place': **'following a decision in another place'; 'will my hon. Friend confirm that that opinion was expressed not only in the other place but also in this House?'**)

placement ['pleɪsmənt] *noun* finding work for someone

placing ['pleɪsɪŋ] *noun* **the placing of a line of shares** = finding a buyer for a large number of shares in a new company or a company which is going public

plagiarism ['pleɪdʒərɪzm] *noun* copying the text of a work created by someone else and passing it off as your own

plagiarize ['pleɪdʒəraɪz] *verb* to copy the text of a work created by someone else and pass it off as your own

plainclothes ['pleɪnkləʊðz] *adjective* (person) who is working in ordinary clothes, not in uniform; *a group of plainclothes police went into the house*; *a plainclothes detective travelled on the train*

plaint [pleɪnt] *noun* claim brought by one party (the claimant) against another party (the defendant); **plaint note** = note issued by a County Court at the beginning of a County Court action

plaintiff ['pleɪntɪf] *noun* person who starts an action against someone in the civil courts (NOTE: since the introduction of the new Civil Procedure Rules in April 1999, this term has been replaced by **claimant**)

plan [plæn] **1** *noun* organized way of doing something; **contingency plan** = plan which will be put into action if something happens which is expected to happen; **the government's economic plans** = the government's proposals for running the country's economy; **a Five-Year Plan** = proposals for running a country's economy over a five-year period **2** *verb* to organize carefully how something should be done; *the bank robbery was carefully planned in advance*; *he plans to disguise himself as a policeman*; **to plan for an increase in bank interest charges** = to change a way of doing things because you think there will be an increase in bank interest charges; **to plan investments** = to propose how investments should be made

planned [plænd] *adjective* **planned economy** = system where the government plans all business activity

planning ['plænɪŋ] *noun* **(a)** organizing how something should be done, especially how a company should be run to make increased profits; **economic planning** = planning the future financial state of the country for the government **(b)** organizing how land and buildings are to be used; **planning authority** = local body which gives permission for changes to be made to existing buildings or for new use of land; **planning department** = section of a local government office which deals with requests for planning permission; **planning inquiry** = hearing before a government inspector relating to the decision of a local authority in planning matters; **planning permission** = official document allowing a person or company to plan new buildings on empty land or to alter existing buildings; **outline planning permission** = general permission to build a property on a piece of land, but not the final approval because there are no details given; *he was refused planning permission*; *we are waiting for planning permission before we can start building*; *the land is to be sold with outline planning permission for four houses*

plank ['plæŋk] *noun* one of the items in an electoral platform; *a proposal to raise taxes is the central plank of the party's platform*

plant [plɑːnt] **1** *noun* machinery or goods and chattels needed for a business **2** *verb* **to plant evidence** = to put items at the scene of a crime after the crime has been discovered, so that a person can be incriminated and arrested

plastic bullet ['plæstɪk 'bʊlɪt] *noun* thick bullet made of plastic fired from a special gun, used by the police only in self-defence (NOTE: also called a **baton round**)

platform ['plætfɔːm] *noun* **(a)** raised part in a hall where important people sit; *the central committee was seated on the platform*; *the resolution from the platform was passed unanimously* **(b)** electoral **platform** = proposals set out in a manifesto before an election; *the party is* *campaigning on a platform of lower taxes and less government interference in municipal affairs*

plc *or* **PLC** *or* **Plc** ['pi: 'el 'si:] = PUBLIC LIMITED COMPANY

plea [pli:] *noun* (i) in civil law, answer made by a defendant to the case presented by the claimant; (ii) in criminal law, statement made by a person accused in court in answer to the charge; **to enter a plea of not guilty** = to answer the charge by stating that you are not guilty; **plea in mitigation** = things said in court on behalf of a guilty party to persuade the court to impose a lenient sentence

plea bargaining ['pli: 'bɑ:gnɪŋ] *noun* arrangement where the accused pleads guilty to some charges and the prosecution drops other charges and asks for a lighter sentence; *see also* DILATORY

plead [pli:d] *verb* (a) to make an allegation in legal proceedings; *if fraud is to be pleaded as part of a claim, details of it must be given in the particulars of claim* (b) to answer a charge in a criminal court; **fit to plead** = mentally capable of being tried; **unfit to plead** = mentally not capable of being tried; **to plead guilty** = to say at the beginning of a trial that you did commit the crime of which you are accused; **to plead not guilty** = to say at the beginning of a trial that you did not commit the crime of which you are accused (c) to speak on behalf of a client in court

pleader ['pli:də] *noun* person who pleads a case in court; *the pleader of the defence must deal with each allegation made in the particulars of claim*

pleading ['pli:dɪŋ] *noun* (a) **pleadings** = documents setting out the claim of the claimant or the defence of the defendant, or giving the arguments which the two sides will use in proceedings; *the damage is itemized in the pleading*; *the judge found that the claimant's pleadings disclosed no cause of action*; *pleadings must be submitted to the court when the action is set down for trial* (NOTE: since the introduction of the new Civil Procedure Rules in

April 1999, this term has been replaced by statements of case) **(b)** action of speaking in court on someone's behalf

pleasure ['pleʒə] *see* HER MAJESTY'S PLEASURE

plebiscite ['plebɪsɪt] *noun* type of vote, where the whole population of a town, region or country is asked to vote to decide an important issue; *the province decided by plebiscite to lower the voting age to eighteen*

> COMMENT: a plebiscite may be of a section of a community only; a referendum applies to the whole electorate of a nation

pledge [pledʒ] **1** *noun* **(a)** transfer of objects or documents to someone as security for a loan **(b)** object given by someone (especially to a pawnbroker) as security for a loan; **to redeem a pledge** = to pay back a loan and interest and so get back the security; **unredeemed pledge** = pledge which the borrower has not claimed back by paying back his loan **2** *verb* **to pledge share certificates** = to deposit share certificates with the lender as security for money borrowed

pledgee [ple'dʒi:] *noun* person who receives objects or documents as security for money lent

pledger ['pledʒə] *noun* person who gives objects or documents as security for money borrowed

plenary ['pli:nəri] *adjective* full or complete; **plenary session** = full session (of a congress) with all delegates present

plenipotentiary [plenɪpə'tenʃəri] *noun* official person acting on behalf of a government in international affairs

PLP = PARLIAMENTARY LABOUR PARTY

pluralism ['pluːrəlɪzm] *noun* system allowing different political or religious groups to exist in the same society

pluralist state ['pluːrəlɪst 'steɪt] *noun* state where various political pressure groups can exist and exert influence over the government

plurality [plu:'ræləti] *noun* (i) number of votes which a candidate receives more than those for another candidate; (ii) having more votes than another candidate; *the candidate with a simple plurality wins the seat* (NOTE: **plurality** is more common in American English)

p.m. *or* **post meridiem** ['pi: 'em] *Latin phrase meaning* 'after 12 o'clock midday'; *the train leaves at 6.50 p.m.*; *if you phone New York after 6 p.m. the calls are at a cheaper rate*

PM ['pi: 'em] = PRIME MINISTER

PO = POST OFFICE

poaching ['pəʊtʃɪŋ] *noun* **(a)** crime of killing game which belongs to another person or trespassing on someone's land to kill game **(b)** enticing workers to work for another company, enticing workers to leave one trade union and join another

pocket borough ['pɒkɪt 'bʌrə] *noun* formerly, borough where the votes were controlled by a prominent citizen, so as to ensure the election of the candidate he supported

pocket veto ['pɒkɪt 'vi:təʊ] *noun US* veto by the President over a bill after Congress has adjourned

COMMENT: normally the President has ten days to object to a bill which has been passed to him by Congress; if Congress adjourns during that period, the President's veto kills the bill

point [pɔɪnt] *noun* question relating to a matter; **to take a point** = to agree that the point made by another speaker is correct; **point taken** *or* **I take your point** = I agree that what you say is valid; **point of fact** = question which has to be decided regarding the facts of a case; **in point of fact** = really or actually; **point of law** = question relating to the law as applied to a case; *counsel raised a point of law; the case illustrates an interesting point of legal*

principle; **point of order** = question regarding the way in which a meeting is conducted; *he raised an interesting point of order; on a point of order, Mr Smith asked the chairman to give a ruling on whether the committee could approve its own accounts*

COMMENT: when raising a point of order, a member will say: 'on a point of order, Mr. Chairman', and the Chairman should stop the discussion to hear what the person raising the point wishes to say

poison ['pɔɪzən] **1** *noun* substance which can kill if eaten or drunk; *she killed the old lady by putting poison in her tea*; **poison-pen letter** = anonymous letter containing defamatory allegations about someone **2** *verb* to kill someone, or make them very ill, using poison; *he was not shot, he was poisoned*

police [pə'li:s] *noun* group of people who keep law and order in a country or town; *the police have cordoned off the town centre; the government is relying on the police to keep law and order during the elections; the bank robbers were picked up by the police at the railway station*; **military police** = soldiers who act as policemen to keep order among other soldiers; **secret police** = policemen who work in secret, especially dealing with people working against the state; **police cordon** = barriers and policemen put round an area to prevent anyone moving in or out of the area; **police court** = magistrates' court (NOTE: no plural. The word **police** is usually followed by a plural verb)

COMMENT: under English law, a policeman is primarily an ordinary citizen who has certain powers at common law and by statute. The police are organized by area, each area functioning independently with its own police force. London, and the area round London, is policed by the Metropolitan Police Force under the direct supervision of the Home Secretary. Outside London, each police force is answerable to a local police authority, although day-to-day control of operations is vested entirely in the Chief Constable

police authority [pə'liːs ɔː'θɒrəti] *noun* local committee which supervises a local police force

Police Commissioner [pə'liːs kə'mɪʃənə] *noun* highest rank in certain police forces; **Metropolitan Police Commissioner** = person in charge of the Metropolitan Police in London

Police Complaints Board [pə'liːs kɒm'pleɪnts 'bɔːd] *noun* group which investigates complaints made by members of the public against the police

police constable [pə'liːs 'kʌnstəbl] *noun* ordinary member of the police; *Police Constables Smith and Jones are on patrol; Woman Police Constable MacIntosh was at the scene of the accident* (NOTE: usually abbreviated to **PC** and **WPC**)

police force [pə'liːs 'fɔːs] *noun* group of policemen organized in a certain area; *the members of several local police forces have collaborated in the murder hunt; the London police force is looking for more recruits; see also* DETECTIVE, METROPOLITAN

COMMENT: the ranks in a British police force are: **Police Constable, Police Sergeant, Inspector, Chief Inspector, Superintendent, Chief Superintendent, Assistant Chief Constable, Deputy Chief Constable and Chief Constable**

police headquarters [pə'liːs hed'kwɔːtəz] *noun* main offices of a police force

police inspector [pə'liːs ɪn'spektə] *noun* rank in the police force above a sergeant

policeman [pə'liːsmən] *noun* man who is a member of the police (NOTE: the plural is **policemen**)

police officer [pə'liːs 'ɒfisə] *noun* member of the police

police precinct [pə'liːs 'priːsɪŋkt] *noun US* section of a town with its own police station

police sergeant [pə'liːs 'saːdʒənt] *noun* rank in the police force above constable and below inspector

police station [pə'liːs 'steɪʃn] *noun* local office of a police force

policewoman ['pə'liːswʊmən] *noun* woman member of a police force (NOTE: the plural is **policewomen**)

policing [pə'liːsɪŋ] *noun* keeping law and order in a place, using the police force; **community policing** = way of policing a section of a town, where the members of the local community and the local police force act together to prevent crime and disorder, with policemen on foot patrol, rather than in patrol cars

policy ['pɒlisi] *noun* **(a)** decisions on the general way of doing something; *government policy on wages or government wages policy; our policy is to submit all contracts to the legal department;* the government made a policy statement *or* made a statement of policy = the government declared in public what its plans were; **budgetary policy** = policy of expected income and expenditure; *see also* PUBLIC POLICY **(b) insurance policy** = document which shows the conditions of an insurance contract; **accident policy** = insurance against accidents; **comprehensive** *or* **all-risks policy** = insurance policy which covers risks of any kind, with no exclusions; **contingent policy** = policy which pays out only if something happens (as if the person named in the policy dies before the person due to benefit); **endowment policy** = policy where a sum of money is paid to the insured person on a certain date, or to his estate if he dies earlier; **open policy** = marine insurance policy where the value of what is insured is not stated; **policy holder** = person who is insured by an insurance company

political [pə'lɪtɪkl] *adjective* referring to a certain idea of how a country should be run; **to ask for political asylum** = to ask to be allowed to remain in a foreign country because it would be dangerous to return to the home country for political reasons; **political crime** = crime (such as assassination) committed for a political reason; **political fund** = part of the funds of a trade union which is allocated to subsidize a political party; **political levy** = part of the subscription of a member of a trade union which the union then pays to support a political party; **political officer** = diplomat stationed in a colony, who is concerned mainly with the relations between his government and the colonial administration or the governments of the nearby countries; **political party** = group of people who believe a country should be run in a certain way; **political prisoner** = person kept in prison because he is an opponent of the political party in power

politician [pɒlɪ'tɪʃn] *noun* person involved in politics; **a full-time politician** = person who works full-time in politics, as an elected representative

politics ['pɒlɪtɪks] *noun* the art and practice of running a country, or of governing; **local politics** *or* **national politics** = the practice of governing a local area or a country; **international politics** = relationships between governments of different political parties and systems; **party politics** = system in which the political life of the country is run by large powerful parties, who make their supporters follow the party line, and where obedience to the party is more important than following its principles; **power politics** = the threat to use economic or military force by one country to try to get other countries to do what it wants

poll [pəʊl] **1** *noun* **(a)** voting to choose something; **to go to the polls** = to vote to choose a Member of Parliament or a local councillor; **the polls opened an hour ago** = the voting started officially an hour ago; **the polls close at 10 o'clock** = the voting ends at 10 o'clock **(b) exit poll** = poll taken outside a polling station, asking people

who have just voted how they voted, to get an idea of the result of an election; **straw poll** = rapid poll (especially one taken on voting day), where a few people are asked how they intend to vote or have voted; *a straw poll among members of staff shows the government is in the lead* **(c)** **opinion poll** = asking a sample group of people what they feel about something, so as to guess the opinion of the whole population **(d)** **deed poll** = legal agreement which refers only to one person; **she changed her name by deed poll** = she executed a legal document to change her name **2** *verb* **(a)** to receive a certain number of votes in an election; *he polled only 123 votes in the general election; the centre parties polled 15% of the votes*; **polling booth** = small enclosed place in a polling station, where the elector goes to mark his voting paper in private; **polling day** = day of an election; **polling station** = central public place (such as a library or school) which is set aside for the people of the surrounding area to vote in **(b) to poll a sample of the population** = to ask a sample group of people what they feel about something; **to poll the members of the club on an issue** = to ask the members for their opinion on an issue

pollster ['pəʊlstə] *noun* expert in understanding what polls mean

poll tax ['pəʊl 'tæks] *noun* tax levied equally on each adult member of the population; *see also* COMMUNITY CHARGE

pollutant [pə'luːtənt] *noun* substance or agent which pollutes; *discharge pipes take pollutants away from the coastal area into the sea*; **air pollutant** *or* **atmospheric pollutant** = substance which pollutes the air or the atmosphere, such as gas or smoke

pollute [pə'luːt] *verb* to discharge harmful substances in abnormally high concentrations into the environment, often done by people or companies, but can occur naturally

polluter [pə'luːtə] *noun* person or company which causes pollution; *certain industries are major polluters of the* *environment*; **polluter pays principle** = principle that if pollution occurs, the person or company responsible should be required to pay for the consequences of the pollution and for avoiding it in future

pollution [pə'lu:ʃn] *noun* presence of abnormally high concentrations of harmful substances in the environment, often put there by people; **air pollution** *or* **atmospheric pollution** = polluting of the air by gas, smoke, etc.; **environmental pollution** = polluting of the environment; **noise pollution** = unpleasant sounds which cause discomfort; **water pollution** = polluting of the sea, rivers, lakes, canals; **pollution charges** = cost of repairing or stopping environmental pollution; **pollution control** = means of limiting pollution

COMMENT: pollution is caused by natural sources or by human action. It can be caused by a volcanic eruption or by a nuclear power station. Pollutants are not only chemical substances, but can be a noise from a grinding works or an unpleasant smell from a sewage farm

polygamous [pə'lɪgəməs] *adjective* referring to polygamy; **a polygamous society** = a society where men are allowed to be married to more than one wife at the same time

polygamy [pə'lɪgəmi] *noun* state of having more than one wife; *compare* BIGAMY, MONOGAMY

polygraph ['pɒlɪgrɑ:f] *noun* lie detector, a machine which tells if a person is lying by recording physiological changes which take place while the person is being interviewed

popular ['pɒpjulə] *adjective* referring to the people; **popular vote** = vote of the people; **the president is elected by popular vote** = the president is elected by a majority of all the voters in the country (as opposed to being elected by parliament)

COMMENT: note that the President of the USA is elected by an electoral college, not by popular vote

populist ['pɒpjulɪst] *adjective & noun* (person) who believes ordinary people should have more say in government

pornography [pɔ:'nɒgrəfi] *noun* obscene publications or films

porridge ['pɒrɪdʒ] *noun* (*slang*) imprisonment; **to do porridge** = to serve a term of imprisonment

portfolio ['pɔ:t'fəuliəu] *noun* (a) all the shares owned by someone; *his portfolio contains shares in the major oil companies* (b) office of a minister in the government; **Minister without Portfolio** = minister who does not have responsibility for any particular department

portion ['pɔ:ʃn] *noun* money or property given to a young person to provide money for him or her as income

position [pə'zɪʃn] *noun* (a) situation, state of affairs; **bargaining position** = statement of position by one group during negotiations; **to cover a position** = to have enough money to pay for a forward purchase (b) job, paid work in a company; *to apply for a position as manager*; *we have several positions vacant*; *all the vacant positions have been filled*; *she retired from her position in the accounts department*; **position of trust** = job where the employee is trusted with money or confidential documents, etc.

positive ['pɒzɪtɪv] *adjective* meaning 'yes'; *the board gave a positive reply*; **the breath test was positive** = the breath test showed that he had too much alcohol in his blood; **positive discrimination** = giving more favourable treatment to a minority to help them be more equal; *the council's policy is one of positive discrimination to ensure that more women are appointed to senior posts*; **positive vetting** = thorough examination of a person before that person is allowed to work with classified information

possess [pə'zes] *verb* to own or to be in occupation of or to be in control of; *the company possesses property in the centre of the town*; *he lost all he possessed when his company was put into liquidation*

possession [pə'zeʃn] *noun* (a) control over property; **actual possession** = occupying and controlling land and buildings; **chose in possession** = physical thing which can be owned; **possession in law** = ownership of land or buildings without actually occupying them; **adverse possession** = occupation of property (such as by a squatter) contrary to the rights of the real owner; **vacant possession** = being able to occupy a property immediately after buying it because it is empty; *the property is to be sold with vacant possession* **(b)** physically holding something (which does not necessarily belong to you); **the documents are in his possession** = he is holding the documents; **how did it come into his possession** *or* **how did he get possession of it?** = how did he acquire it?; **unlawful possession of drugs** = offence of having drugs **(c) possessions** = property, things owned; *they lost all their possessions in the fire*

possessive action [pə'zesɪv 'ækʃn] *noun* action to regain possession of land or buildings

possessory [pə'zesəri] *adjective* referring to possession of property; **possessory title** = title to land acquired by occupying it continuously, usually for twelve years

post- [pəust] *prefix* later

posteriori [pɒsteri'ɔːraɪ] *see* A POSTERIORI

posthumous ['pɒstʃuməs] *adjective* (child) born after the death of its father

post mortem ['pəust 'mɔːtəm] *noun* examination of the body of a dead person to see how he died; *the post mortem was carried out or was conducted by the police pathologist*

post obit bond ['pəust 'əubɪt 'bɒnd] *noun* agreement where a borrower will repay a loan when he receives money as a legacy from someone

post scriptum ['pəust 'skrɪptəm] *see* P.S.

power ['pauə] *noun* (a) strength, ability or capacity; **bargaining power** = strength of one person or group when discussing prices, wages or contracts; **borrowing power** = amount of money which a company can borrow; **earning power** = amount of money someone should be able to earn **(b)** authority, legal right; *the powers of a local authority in relation to children in care*; *the powers and duties conferred on the tribunal by the statutory code*; *the president was granted wide powers under the constitution*; **executive power** = right to act as director or to put decisions into action; **power of appointment** = power given to one person (such as a trustee) to dispose of property belonging to another; **power of attorney** = official power which gives someone the right to act on someone's behalf in legal matters; **the full power of the law** = the full force of the law when applied; *we will apply the full power of the law to regain possession of our property*; **power of search** = authority to search premises, which is given to the police and certain other officials, such as Customs and Excise officers **(c)** powerful country or state; *one of the important military powers in the region*

p.p. *verb* **to p.p. a receipt** *or* **a letter** = to sign a receipt or a letter on behalf of someone; *the secretary p.p.'d the letter while the manager was at lunch*; *see also* PER PROCURATIONEM

PR ['piː 'ɑː] = PROPORTIONAL REPRESENTATION, PUBLIC RELATIONS

practice ['præktɪs] *noun* (a) way of doing things; *his practice was to arrive at work at 7.30 and start counting the cash*; **business practices** *or* **industrial practices** *or* **trade practices** = ways of managing or working in business, industry or trade; **restrictive practices** = ways of working which exclude free competition in relation to the supply of goods or labour in order to maintain high prices or wages; **sharp practice** = way of doing business which is not honest, but is not illegal; **code of practice** = rules drawn up by an association which the members must follow when doing business **(b)** way of working in court; **pre-action practice** = the way of working before a case comes to court; **practice directions (PDs)** = notes made by judges as to how certain procedures or formalities should be carried out; **practice form** = form which lays out practice in a certain case **(c)** office and clients (of a professional person); *he has set up in practice as a solicitor or a patent agent*; *he is a partner in a country solicitor's practice* **(d)** carrying on of a profession; *he has been in practice for twenty years*

Practice Master ['præktɪs 'mɑːstə] *noun* Master on duty in the High Court, who will hear solicitors without appointment and give directions in relation to the general conduct of proceedings

practise ['præktɪs] *verb* to work (in a profession); *he is a practising solicitor*; **practising certificate** = certificate from the Law Society allowing someone to work as a solicitor

practitioner [præk'tɪʃənə] *noun* person who does a skilled job; **litigation practitioner** = lawyer who specializes in litigation

praecipe ['priːsɪpi] *noun* written request addressed to a court, asking that court to prepare and issue a document (such as a writ of execution or a witness summons)

pray [preɪ] *verb* to ask; **to pray in aid** = to rely on something in pleading a case; *I pray in aid the Statute of Frauds*

prayer [preə] *noun* **(a)** words at the end of a petition or pleading, which summarize what the litigant is asking the court to do **(b)** request to the House of Commons to do something or not to do something **(c)** **prayers** = address to God, which begins each sitting of the Houses of Parliament **(d)**

motion in the House of Commons asking the Crown to annul a statutory instrument

pre-action ['priː'ækʃn] *adjective* before an action starts; **pre-action practice** = the way of working before a case comes to court; **pre-action protocol** = statements which are agreed before the hearings start between lawyers representing different parties about how a case should proceed, which are then approved by the court in the practice directions (these protocols should try to encourage the parties to try to settle without proceeding to litigation)

preamble [prɪ'æmbl] *noun* first words in an official document (such as a Bill before Parliament, or a contract) introducing the document and setting out the main points in it

precatory ['prekətri] *adjective* which requests; **precatory words** = words (such as in a will) which ask for something to be done

precedent ['presɪdənt] **1** *noun* something (such as a judgment) which has happened earlier than the present, and which can be a guide as to what should be done in the present case; **to set a precedent** = to make a decision in court which will show other courts how to act in future; **to follow a precedent** = to decide in the same way as an earlier decision in the same type of case; *the judge's decision sets a precedent for future cases of contempt of court*; *the tribunal's ruling has established a precedent*; *the court followed the precedent set in 1926*; **binding precedent** = decision of a higher court which has to be followed by a judge in a lower court; **judicial precedent** = precedent set by a court decision which can be reversed only by a higher court; **persuasive precedent** = precedent which a judge does not have to follow but which is of importance in reaching a decision **2** *adjective* **condition precedent** = condition which says that a right will not be granted until something is done

COMMENT: although English law is increasingly governed by statute, the doctrine of precedent still plays a major role. The decisions of higher courts bind lower courts, except in the case of the Court of Appeal, where the court has power to change a previous decision reached per incuriam. Cases can be distinguished by the courts where the facts seem to be sufficiently different

precept ['priːsept] *noun* order asking for local taxes to be paid; **precepting body** = organization which levies a precept

precinct ['priːsɪŋkt] *noun* **(a)** pedestrian **precinct** *or* **shopping precinct** = part of a town which is closed to traffic so that people can walk about and shop **(b)** *US* administrative district in a town; *police precinct*

preclude [prɪ'kluːd] *verb* to forbid or to prevent; *the High Court is precluded by statute from reviewing such a decision; this agreement does not preclude a further agreement between the parties in the future*

predecease [priːdɪ'siːs] *verb* to die before someone; *he predeceased his father; his estate is left to his daughter, but should she predecease him, it will be held in trust for her children*

predecessor ['priːdɪsesə] *noun* person who had a job or position before someone else; *he took over from his predecessor last May; she acquired her predecessor's list of clients*

pre-emption ['priːempʃn] *noun* right of first refusal to purchase something before it is sold to someone else; **pre-emption clause** = clause in a private company's articles of association which requires any shares offered for sale to be offered first to existing shareholders

prefer [prɪ'fɜː] *verb* **(a)** to pay one creditor before any others **(b)** to bring something before a court; **to prefer charges** = to charge someone with an offence (NOTE: **preferring - preferred**)

preference ['prefrəns] *noun* (i) thing which is preferred; (ii) the payment of one creditor before other creditors; **fraudulent preference** = payment made by an insolvent company to a particular creditor before other creditors; **preference shares** = shares (often with no voting rights) which receive their dividend before all other shares and which are repaid first (at face value) if the company is liquidated; **preference shareholders** = owners of preference shares; **cumulative preference shares** = preference shares where the dividend will be paid at a later date even if the company cannot pay a dividend in the current year

preferential [prefə'renʃl] *adjective* showing that something is preferred more than another; **preferential creditor** = creditor who must be paid first if a company is in liquidation; **preferential debt** = debt which is paid before all others; **preferential duty** *or* **preferential tariff** = special low rate of tax; **preferential payment** = payment made to one creditor before others; **preferential terms** *or* **preferential treatment** = terms or way of dealing which is better than usual

COMMENT: in the case of a company liquidation, preferential debts are debts owed to the government or its agencies and include PAYE owed to the Inland Revenue, VAT, social security contributions, contributions to state pensions schemes

preferment [prɪ'fɜːmənt] *noun* **preferment of charges** = act of charging someone with a criminal offence

preferred [prɪ'fɜːd] *adjective* **preferred creditor** = creditor who must be paid first if a company is in liquidation; **preferred shares**, *US* **preferred stock** = shares which receive their dividend before all other shares, and which are repaid first (at face value) if the company is in liquidation; *US* **cumulative preferred stock** = preference shares where the dividend will be paid at a later date even if the company cannot pay a dividend in the current year

prejudge [priː'dʒʌdʒ] *verb* to judge an issue before having heard the evidence; *do* not prejudge the issue - hear what defence counsel has to say

prejudice ['predʒədɪs] **1** *noun* **(a)** bias, unjust feelings against someone; **racial prejudice** = feelings against someone because of his race **(b)** harm done to someone; *forgery is the copying of a real document, so that it is accepted as genuine to someone's prejudice*; **without prejudice** = phrase spoken or written in letters when attempting to negotiate a settlement, meaning that the negotiations cannot be referred to in court or relied upon by the other party if the discussions fail; **to act to the prejudice of a claim** = to do something which may harm a claim **2** *verb* to harm; *to prejudice someone's claim*

preliminary [prɪˈlɪmɪnri] *adjective* early, happening before anything else; **preliminary discussion** *or* **a preliminary meeting** = discussion or meeting which takes place before the main discussion or meeting starts; **preliminary hearing** = (i) court proceedings where the witnesses and the defendant are examined to see if there are sufficient grounds for the case to proceed; (ii) in the small claims track, a hearing to decide if special directions should be issued, or if the statement of case should be struck out; (iii) court proceedings to try a specific issue rather than the whole case; **preliminary inquiries** = investigation by the solicitor for the purchaser addressed to the vendor's solicitor concerning the vendor's title to the property for which the purchaser has made an offer; **preliminary investigation** = first examination of the details of a case by a magistrate who then has to decide if the case should be committed to a higher court for trial; *(in the EU)* **preliminary reference** = reference from a court in a Member State to the ECJ on a question of interpretation of community law, the aim being to ensure that Community laws are interpreted uniformly throughout the Community, and that all national courts are familiar with Community law (the ECJ has used preliminary references as a means of extending the scope of Community law); *(in the EU)* **preliminary ruling** =

provisional decision of the European Court of Justice

premeditated [priːˈmedɪteɪtɪd] *adjective* which has been thought about carefully or which has been planned; *the crime was premeditated*; *a premeditated murder*

premeditation [priːmedɪˈteɪʃn] *noun* thinking about and planning a crime (such as murder)

premier ['premiə] *noun* **(a)** Prime Minister **(b)** *(in a Federal state)* chief minister of a state or province (as opposed to the Prime Minister of the Federal government)

> COMMENT: used in Canada and Australia more than in the UK, especially referring to the provincial or state premiers

premiership ['premiəʃɪp] *noun* period when a prime minister governs; *during the premiership of Harold Wilson*

premises ['premɪsɪz] *plural noun* **(a)** building and the land it stands on; **business premises** *or* **commercial premises** = building used for commercial use; **office premises** *or* **shop premises** = building which houses an office or shop; **lock-up premises** = shop which is locked up at night when the owner goes home; **licensed premises** = shop, restaurant or public house which is licensed to sell alcohol; **on the premises** = in the building; *there is a doctor on the premises at all times* **(b)** things that have been referred to previously (NOTE: used at the end of a pleading: **in the premises the defendant denies that he is indebted to the claimant as alleged or at all**)

premium ['priːmiəm] *noun* **(a)** sum of money paid by one person to another, especially one paid regularly; **insurance premium** = payment made by the insured person or a company to an insurance company; **additional premium** = extra payment made to cover extra items in an existing insurance; *the annual premium is £150*; *you pay either an annual premium of £360 or twelve monthly premiums of*

£32 **(b)** amount to be paid to a landlord or a tenant for the right to take over a lease; *flat to let with a premium of £10,000; annual rent: £8,500 - premium: £25,000* **(c)** extra charge; **exchange premium** = extra cost above the normal rate for buying foreign currency; *the dollar is at a premium*; **shares sold at a premium** = (i) shares whose price is higher than their face value; (ii) new shares whose market price is higher than their issue price **(d) premium bonds** = British government bonds, part of the national savings scheme, which pay no interest, but give the owner the chance to win a monthly prize and which can be redeemed at face value

prerogative [prɪ'rɒgətɪv] *noun* special right which someone has; **royal prerogative** = right of the king or queen to do something; **prerogative order** *or* **writ** = writ from the High Court, which requests a body to do its duty, or not to do some act or to conduct an inquiry into its own actions; **prerogative powers** = special powers used by a government, acting in the name of the King or Queen, to do something (such as declare war, nominate judges or ministers) without needing to ask Parliament to approve the decision

prescribe [prɪ'skraɪb] *verb* **(a)** to claim rights which have been enjoyed for a long time **(b)** to lay down rules; **prescribed limits** = limits which are set down in legislation (such as the limits of alcohol allowed to drivers)

prescription [prɪ'skrɪptʃn] *noun* acquiring a right or exercising a right over a period of time

presence ['prezəns] *noun* being present, being at a place when something happens; *the will was signed in the presence of two witnesses*

present ['preznt] **1** *noun* **these presents** = this document itself; **know all men by these presents** = be informed by this document **2** *verb* to bring or send and show a document; **to present a bill for acceptance** = to send a bill for payment by

the person who has accepted it; **to present a bill for payment** = to send a bill to be paid

presentation [prezən'teɪʃn] *noun* showing a document; *presentation of a bill of exchange*; **cheque payable on presentation** = cheque which will be paid when it is presented; **free admission on presentation of this card** = you do not pay to go in if you show this card

presentment [prɪ'zentmənt] *noun* showing a document; *presentment of a bill of exchange*

preservation order [prezə'veɪʃn 'ɔːdə] *noun* court order which prevents a building from being demolished or a tree from being cut down

preside [prɪ'zaɪd] *verb* to be chairman; *to preside over a meeting*; *the meeting was held in the committee room, Mr Smith presiding*; **presiding judge** = High Court judge who is responsible for a main Crown Court in a circuit

presidency ['prezɪdənsi] *noun* **(a)** position of president; *the presidency of the European Community passes from country to country every six months* **(b)** period when a president is governing; *during Kennedy's presidency* or *during the Kennedy presidency*

president ['prezɪdənt] *noun* **(a)** head of a republic; *the President of the United States* (NOTE: as a title of a head of state, President can be used with a surname: **President Bush, President Wilson**) **(b)** head of a department, company or court; *he was elected president of the sports club*; *A.B.Smith has been appointed president of the company*; **President of the European Commission** = chief executive and civil servant of the EC, elected for a five-year period; **President of the Family Division** = judge who is responsible for the work of the Family Division of the High Court; *US* **President of the Senate** = person who presides over debates in the Senate (usually the Vice-President of the USA, but in his absence a president pro tempore takes the chair)

COMMENT: a president is the head of state of a republic; this may be a ceremonial title, with some executive powers, as in India, while the real power resides in the Prime Minister. In other states (such as the USA), the President is both head of state and head of government. The President of the USA is elected by an electoral college, and holds the executive power under the United States constitution. The legislative power lies with Congress, and the President cannot force Congress to enact legislation, although he can veto legislation which has been passed by Congress

presidential [prezɪ'denʃl] *adjective* referring to a president of a country; *the US presidential elections*; *three presidential candidates have appeared on television*; *the National Guard has surrounded the Presidential Palace*; **presidential government** = type of government where the head of the executive is a president

presidential-style [prezɪ'denʃl'staɪl] *adjective* working in a similar way to the United States presidency; **presidential-style government** = governing in the same way as a President of the USA, who is not a member of the elected legislature; **presidential-style campaign** = election campaign which concentrates on the person of the leader of the party, and not on the party's policies; *the Prime Minister was accused of running a presidential-style government or a presidential-style election campaign*

press [pres] **1** *noun* newspapers and magazines; **the local press** = newspapers which are sold in a small area of the country; **the national press** = newspapers which sell in all parts of the country; **press conference** = meeting where reporters from newspapers are invited to hear news of a new product, of a court case or of a takeover bid, etc.; **Press Complaints Commission** = voluntary body concerned with the self-regulation of the press; **press coverage** = reports about something in the press; **press gallery** = section of the House of Commons, House of Lords or other council chamber, where journalists sit to report on debates; **press release** = sheet giving news about something which is sent to newspapers and TV and radio stations so that they can use the information; **press secretary** = person responsible for contacts with journalists; *the information was communicated by the President's Press Secretary*; **freedom of the press** = being able to write and publish in a newspaper, or on radio or TV, what you wish without being afraid of prosecution, provided that you do not break the law **2** *verb* **to press charges against someone** = to say formally that someone has committed a crime; *he was very angry when his neighbour's son set fire to his car, but decided not to press charges*

pressure ['preʃə] *noun* force, strong influence to make someone change his opinions or his course of action; *the army exerts strong political pressure on the President*; *the Prime Minister gave in to pressure from the backbenchers*; *the Whips applied pressure on the rebel MPs to vote with the government*; **pressure group** = group of people with similar interests, who try to influence government policies; **pressure politics** = attempting to change the government's policies by political pressure

presume [prɪ'zjuːm] *verb* to suppose something is correct; *the court presumes the maintenance payments are being paid on time*; *the company is presumed to be still solvent*; *we presume the shipment has been stolen*; *two sailors are missing, presumed drowned*

COMMENT: in English law, the accused is presumed to be innocent until he is proved to be guilty, and presumed to be sane until he is proved to be insane

presumption [prɪ'zʌmpʃn] *noun* thing which is assumed to be correct, because it is assumed from other facts; **presumption of death** = situation where a person has not been seen for seven years, and is legally presumed to be dead; **presumption of innocence** = assuming that someone is innocent, until he or she has been proved guilty

presumptive [prɪˈzʌmptɪv] *adjective* **presumptive evidence** = circumstantial evidence; **heir presumptive** = heir who will inherit if someone dies at this moment, but whose inheritance may be altered in the future

pretence [prɪˈtens] *noun* **false pretence(s)**, *US* **false pretense** = doing or saying something to cheat someone; *he was sent to prison for obtaining money by false pretences*

pretrial [ˈpriːtraɪəl] *adjective* before a trial starts; *US* **pretrial detention** = being kept in prison until the trial starts (NOTE: the British equivalent is **remanded in custody**) *US* **pretrial release** = release of an accused person pending his return to court to face trial (NOTE: the British equivalent is **bail**); **pretrial review** = meeting of the parties before a civil action, to examine what is likely to arise during the action, so that ways can be found of making it shorter and so reduce costs

prevail [prɪˈveɪl] *verb* **to prevail upon someone to do something** = to persuade someone to do something; *counsel prevailed upon the judge to grant an adjournment*

prevaricate [prɪˈværɪkeɪt] *verb* to be evasive, not to give a straight answer to a question

prevent [prɪˈvent] *verb* to stop something happening; *we must try to prevent the takeover bid*; *the police prevented anyone from leaving the building*; *we have changed the locks on the doors to prevent the former managing director from getting into the building*

prevention [prɪˈvenʃn] *noun* stopping something taking place; **prevention of corruption** = stopping corruption taking place; **the prevention of terrorism** = stopping terrorist acts taking place

preventive [prɪˈventɪv] *adjective* which tries to stop something happening; **to take preventive measures against theft** = to

try to stop things from being stolen; **preventive detention** = formerly, imprisonment of someone who frequently committed a certain type of crime, so as to prevent him from doing it again

COMMENT: now replaced by **extended sentence**

previous [ˈpriːviəs] *adjective* which has happened earlier; **he could not accept the invitation because he had a previous engagement** = because he had earlier accepted another invitation to go somewhere; **to ask for six previous convictions to be taken into consideration** = to ask the court to note that the accused has been convicted earlier of similar crimes; **a person of previous good character** = person with no criminal record

price [praɪs] **1** *noun* **(a)** money which has to be paid to buy something; **agreed price** = price which has been accepted by both the buyer and seller; **all-in price** = price which covers all items in a purchase (goods, insurance, delivery, etc.); **asking price** = price which the seller is hoping to be paid for the item when it is sold; **fair price** = good price for both buyer and seller; **firm price** = price which will not change; **net price** = price which cannot be reduced by a discount; **retail price** = price at which the retailer sells to the final customer; **spot price** = price for immediate delivery of a commodity; **price controls** = legal measures to stop prices rising too fast; **price fixing** = illegal agreement between companies to charge the same price for competing products **(b)** *(on the Stock Exchange)* **asking price** = price which sellers are asking for shares; **closing price** = price at the end of a day's trading; **opening price** = price at the start of a day's trading; **price/earnings ratio** = ratio between the market price of a share and the current earnings it produces **2** *verb* to give a price to a product; *car priced at £5,000*

pricing [ˈpraɪsɪŋ] *noun* giving a price to a product; **pricing policy** = a company's policy in setting prices for its products; **common pricing** = illegal fixing of prices by several businesses so that they all charge the same price

primacy ['praiməsi] *noun (in the EU)* supremacy, one of the twin pillars of EC law; *see* SUPREMACY

prima facie ['praimə 'feiʃi] *Latin phrase meaning* 'on the face of it' or 'as things seem at first'; **there is a prima facie case to answer** = one side in a case has shown that there is a case to answer, and so the action should be proceeded with

primarily ['praimrli] *adverb* in the first place; *he is primarily liable for his debts*; *see also* SECONDARILY

primary ['praimri] *adjective* in the first place; **primary evidence** = best evidence (such as original documents, evidence from eye witnesses); *(in the EU)* **primary legislation** = legislation of the Member States of the EU, as opposed to legislation of the EU itself; *see also* SECONDARY

prime [praim] *adjective* **(a)** most important; **prime time** = most expensive advertising time for TV advertisements **(b)** basic; **prime bills** = bills of exchange which do not involve any risk; **prime cost** = cost involved in producing a product, excluding overheads; **prime rate** = best rate of interest at which a bank lends to its customers

Prime Minister ['praim 'ministə] *noun* head of a government; *the Australian Prime Minister or the Prime Minister of Australia*

COMMENT: the British Prime Minister is not the head of state, but the head of government. The Prime Minister is usually the leader of the party which has the majority of the seats in the House of Commons, and forms a cabinet of executive ministers who are either MPs or members of the House of Lords

primogeniture [praiməu'dʒenitʃə] *noun* former rule that the oldest son inherits all his father's estate

primus inter pares ['praiməs 'intə 'pɑːriːz] *Latin phrase meaning* 'first among equals': used to refer to the office of Prime Minister, implying that all ministers are equal, and the PM is simply the most important of them

principal ['prinsəpl] *noun* **(a)** person who is responsible for something (especially person who is in charge of a company, or a person who commits a crime) **(b)** person or company which is represented by an agent; *the agent has come to London to see his principals* **(c)** money invested or borrowed on which interest is paid; *to repay principal and interest*; *compare* PRINCIPLE

principality [prinsə'pæləti] *noun* country ruled by a prince; *the Principality of Monaco* (NOTE: in Britain, 'the Principality' is the name given to Wales)

principle ['prinsəpl] *noun* basic point, general rule; **in principle** = in agreement with a general rule; **agreement in principle** = agreement with the basic conditions of a proposal; *it is against his principles* = it goes against what he believes to be the correct way to act; *compare* PRINCIPAL

printout ['printaut] *noun* printed copy of information produced by a computer

prior ['praiə] *adjective* earlier; **prior agreement** = agreement which was reached earlier; **prior charge** = charge which ranks before others; **without prior knowledge** = without knowing before

priori [prai'ɔːrai] *see* A PRIORI

priority [prai'ɒrəti] *noun* right to be first (such as the right to be paid first before other creditors); **to have priority** = to have the right to be first; **to have priority over** *or* **to take priority over something** = to be more important than something; *debenture holders have priority over ordinary shareholders*; **to give something top priority** = to make something the most important item; *the government has given the maintenance of law and order top priority*

prison ['prɪzn] *noun* **(a)** safe building where criminals can be kept locked up after they have been convicted or while they await trial; *the government has ordered the construction of six new prisons*; *this prison was built 150 years ago*; **prison governor** = person in charge of a prison; **prison officer** = member of staff in a prison; **open prison** = prison with minimum security where category 'D' prisoners can be kept; **top security prison** = prison with very strict security where category 'A' prisoners are kept **(b)** place where prisoners are kept as a punishment; *he was sent to prison for six years*; *they have spent the last six months in prison*; *he escaped from prison by climbing over the wall* (NOTE: no plural for (b), which is also usually written without the article: **in prison; out of prison; sent to prison**)

prisoner ['prɪznə] *noun* person who is in prison; **prisoner at the bar** = the accused person in the dock, who is being tried in court; **prisoner of war** = member of the armed forces captured and put in prison by the enemy in time of war

prison visitor ['prɪzn 'vɪzɪtə] *noun see* VISITOR

privacy ['prɪvəsi] *noun* private life; **invasion of privacy** = action (such as being followed by newspaper reporters) which prevents someone from living a normal private life

COMMENT: there is no right to privacy in English common law; the European Convention on Human Rights protects individuals' private lives to a certain extent

private ['praɪvət] *adjective* **(a)** belonging to a single person, not a company or the state; **letter marked 'private and confidential'** = letter which must not be opened by anyone other than the person to whom it is addressed; **Private Bill** *or* **Private Act of Parliament** = Bill or Act relating to a particular person, corporation or institution; *see below* PRIVATE MEMBER'S BILL; **private business** = business dealing with the members of a group or matters which cannot be

discussed in public; *the committee held a special meeting to discuss some private business*; **private client** *or* **private customer** = client dealt with by a professional man or by a salesman as a person, not as a company; **private effects** = goods which belong to someone and are used by him; **private detective,** *(informal)* **private eye** = person who for a fee will try to solve mysteries, to find missing persons or to keep watch on someone; **private law** = law as it refers to individuals; **Private Member's Bill** = Bill which is drafted and proposed in the House of Commons by an ordinary Member of Parliament, not by a government minister on behalf of the government; **private nuisance** = act which can harm a particular person or his rights; **private property** = property which belongs to a private person, not to the public; **private prosecution** = prosecution for a criminal act, brought by an ordinary member of the public and not by the police **(b)** **private limited company** = company with a small number of shareholders whose shares are not traded on the Stock Exchange; **private enterprise** = economic system where businesses are owned by private shareholders, not by the state; **the private sector** = all companies which are owned by private shareholders, not by the state

◊ **in private** ['ɪn 'praɪvət] *adverb* **(a)** with no members of the public permitted to be present; *the case was heard in private* (NOTE: since the introduction of the new Civil Procedure Rules in April 1999, this term has replaced **in camera** or **in chambers**) **(b)** *(general meaning)* away from other people; *he asked to see the managing director in private*

privatize ['praɪvətaɪz] *verb* to sell a nationalized industry to private shareholders (usually to members of the public)

privilege ['prɪvlɪdʒ] *noun* **(a)** protection from the law given in certain circumstances; **absolute privilege** = privilege which protects a person from being sued for defamation (such as an MP speaking in the House of Commons, a judge or a lawyer making a statement during judicial proceedings); **breach of parliamentary privilege** = speaking in a defamatory way about Parliament or about a Member of Parliament; **Committee of Privileges** = special committee of the House of Commons which examines cases of breach of privilege; **Crown privilege** = right of the Crown or of the government not to have to produce documents in court; *(in the EU)* **professional privilege** = confidentiality of communications between a client and his lawyer; **qualified privilege** = protection from being sued for defamation which is given to someone only if it can be proved that the statements were made without malice; **question of privilege** = matter which refers to the House or a member of it; *US* **question of personal privilege** = matter referring to a member of Congress (which is usually given priority over other matters) **(b)** *(in civil law)* the right of a party not to disclose a document, or to refuse to answer questions, on the ground of some special interest **(c)** *US* order of priority; **motion of the highest privilege** = motion which will be discussed first, before all other motions

privileged [ˈprɪvlɪdʒd] *adjective* protected by privilege; **privileged communication** = letter which could be libellous but which is protected by privilege (such as a letter from a client to his lawyer); **privileged meeting** *or* **occasion** = meeting where what is said will not be repeated outside; *US* **privileged questions** = order of priority of motions to be discussed

privileged will [ˈprɪvɪlɪdʒd ˈwɪl] *noun* will which is not made in writing and is not signed or witnessed, such as a will made by a soldier on the battlefield or a seaman while at sea

COMMENT: privileged wills are not like ordinary wills, in that they may be oral, or if written, need not be signed or witnessed. It is sufficient that the intention of the testator was made clear at the time

privity of contract [ˈprɪvəti əv ˈkɒntrækt] *noun* relationship between the parties to a contract, which makes the contract enforceable as between them

Privy Council [ˈprɪvi ˈkaʊnsəl] *noun* body of senior advisers who advise the Queen on certain matters; **Judicial Committee of the Privy Council** = appeal court for appeals from courts outside the UK, such as the courts of some Commonwealth countries

COMMENT: the Privy Council is mainly formed of members of the cabinet, and former members of the cabinet. It never meets as a group, but three Privy Councillors need to be present when the Queen signs Orders in Council

Privy Councillor [ˈprɪvi ˈkaʊnslə] *noun* member of the Privy Council (NOTE: Privy Councillors have the title **Rt. Hon,.** say 'Right Honourable')

prize [praɪz] *noun* enemy ship or cargo captured in war; **prize court** = court set up to rule on the ownership of prizes

pro [prəʊ] *preposition & noun* for or on behalf of; **per pro** = with the authority of

probable cause [ˈprɒbəbl ˈkɔːz] *noun* *US* believing that it is likely that a crime has been committed and by a certain person (this is a necessary part of police stop and search procedures)

probate [ˈprəʊbeɪt] *noun* legal acceptance that a document, especially a will, is valid; **grant of probate** = official document proving that a will is genuine, given to the executors so that they can act on the terms of the will; **the executor was granted probate** *or* **obtained a grant of probate** = the executor was told officially that the will was valid; **Probate Registry** = court office which deals with the granting of probate

probation [prəˈbeɪʃn] *noun* **(a)** legal system for dealing with criminals (often young offenders) where they are not sent to prison provided that they continue to behave well under the supervision of a probation officer; *she was sentenced to probation for one year*; **probation officer** = official of the social services who supervises young people on probation; **probation order** = court order putting someone on probation **(b)** period when a new worker is being tested before being confirmed as having a permanent job **(c) on probation** = (i) being tested; (ii) being under a probation order from a court; *he is on three months' probation*; *to take someone on probation*

probationer [prəˈbeɪʃnə] *noun* person who has been put on probation

probative [ˈprəʊbətɪv] *adjective* relating to proof; *US* **probative value** = value of an item as evidence in a trial

problem [ˈprɒbləm] *noun* thing to which it is difficult to find an answer; *the company suffers from cash flow problems or from staff problems*; **to solve a problem** = to find an answer to a problem; **problem area** = area of work which is difficult to manage; *drug-related crime is a problem area in large cities*

procedural [prəˈsiːdʒərl] *adjective* referring to legal procedure; **procedural judge** = judge who deals with the management of a case, its allocation to a particular track, etc.; **procedural law** = rules governing how the civil or criminal law is administered by the courts; **procedural problem** *or* **question** = question concerning procedure; *the hearing was held up while counsel argued over procedural problems*

procedure [prəˈsiːdʒə] *noun* way in which something is done, especially steps taken to bring an action to the court; *to follow the proper procedure*; *this procedure is very irregular* = this is not the set way to do something; **Civil Procedure Rules (CPR)** = rules laying out how civil cases are to be brought to court and heard; **disciplinary procedure** = way of warning a worker that he is breaking the rules of a company or working badly; **complaints procedure** *or* **grievance procedure** = agreed way of presenting

complaints formally from a trade union or from an employee to the management of a company; **dismissal procedures** = correct way of dismissing someone, following the rules in the contract of employment

proceed [prəˈsiːd] *verb* to go on, to continue; *the negotiations are proceeding slowly*; *the hearing proceeded after the protesters were removed from the courtroom*; **to proceed against someone** = to start a legal action against someone; **to proceed with something** = to go on doing something

proceedings [prəˈsiːdɪŋz] *plural noun* **(a) conference proceedings** = written report of what has taken place at a conference **(b) legal proceedings** = legal action, lawsuit; *the court proceedings were adjourned*; **to institute or to start proceedings against someone** = to start a legal action against someone; **committal proceedings** = preliminary hearing of a case before the magistrates' court, to decide if it is serious enough to be tried before a jury in a higher court; **interlocutory proceedings** = court hearings that take place before the full trial

process [ˈprəʊses] **1** *noun* (i) way in which a court acts to assert its jurisdiction; (ii) writs issued by a court to summon the defendant to appear in court; (iii) legal procedure; **the due process of the law** = the formal work of a fair legal action; **abuse of process** = suing someone in bad faith, without proper justification or for malicious reasons **2** *verb* to deal with something in the usual routine way; *to process an insurance claim*; *the incident room is processing information received from the public*

processing [ˈprəʊsesɪŋ] *noun* **the processing of a claim for insurance** = putting a claim for compensation through the usual office routine in the insurance company

process-server [ˈprəʊsesˌsɜːvə] *noun* person who delivers legal documents (such as a writ or summons) to people in person

proctor ['prɒktə] *noun (in a university)* official who is responsible for keeping law and order; **Queen's Proctor** = solicitor acting for the Crown in matrimonial and probate cases

procurationem [prɒkjuræsi'əunəm] *see* PER PROCURATIONEM

Procurator Fiscal ['prɒkjureitə 'fiskl] *noun (in Scotland)* law officer who decides whether an alleged criminal should be prosecuted

procure [prə'kjuə] *verb* to get someone to do something, especially to arrange for a woman to provide sexual intercourse for money

procuring *or* **procurement** [prə'kjuəriŋ *or* prə'kjuəmənt] *noun* notifiable offence of getting a woman to provide sexual intercourse for money

procurer [prə'kjuərə] *noun* person who procures women

product ['prɒdʌkt] *noun* (a) thing which is made; **basic product** = main product made from a raw material; **end product** *or* **final product** *or* **finished product** = product made at the end of a production process; **product liability** = liability of the maker of a product for negligence in the design or production of the product (b) **gross domestic product (GDP)** = annual value of goods sold and services paid for inside a country; **gross national product (GNP)** = annual value of goods and services in a country, including income from other countries

production [prə'dʌkʃn] *noun* (a) showing something; **on production of** = when something is shown; *the goods will be released by customs on production of the relevant documents*; *merchandise can be exchanged only on production of the sales slip* (b) **Production Centre** = central office which issues claim forms

proferentem [prɒfə'rentem] *see* CONTRA

profession [prə'feʃn] *noun* (a) work which needs special learning over a period

of time; **the managing director is a lawyer by profession** = he trained as a lawyer (b) group of specialized workers; **the legal profession** = all lawyers; **the medical profession** = all doctors

professional [prə'feʃnl] *adjective* (a) referring to one of the professions; *the accountant sent in his bill for professional services*; *we had to ask our lawyer for professional advice on the contract*; **a professional man** = man who works in one of the professions (such as a lawyer, doctor, accountant); **professional misconduct** = behaviour by a member of a profession (such as a lawyer, accountant or doctor) which the body which regulates that profession considers to be wrong (such as an action by a solicitor which is considered wrong by the Law Society); **professional qualifications** = documents showing that someone has successfully finished a course of study which allows him or her to work in one of the professions (b) expert; **professional witness** = witness who is a specialist in a subject and is asked to give evidence to a court on technical matters 2 *noun* skilled person, person who does skilled work for money

profit ['prɒfit] *noun* money gained from a sale which is more than the money spent on making the item sold; **clear profit** = profit after all expenses have been paid; **gross profit** = profit calculated as sales income less the cost of the goods sold; **net profit** = result where income from sales is larger than all expenditure; **operating profit** = result where sales from normal business activities are higher than the costs; **trading profit** = result where the company' receipts are higher than its expenditure; **profit and loss account** = statement of a company's expenditure and income over a period of time, almost always one calendar year, showing whether the company has made a profit or loss; **profit before tax** *or* **pretax profit** = profit of a company after expenses have been deducted but before tax has been calculated; **profit after tax** = profit after tax has been deducted

profitability [prɒfitə'bɪləti] *noun* (a) ability to make a profit (b) amount of profit made as a percentage of costs; **measurement of profitability** = way of calculating how profitable something is

profit à prendre ['prɒfi æ 'prɒndrə] *noun* right to take something from land (such as game, or fish from a river passing through the land)

profiteer [prɒfi'tɪə] *noun* person who makes too much profit, especially when goods are rationed or in short supply

pro forma ['prəʊ 'fɔːmə] *Latin phrase meaning* 'for the sake of form'; **pro forma (invoice)** = invoice sent to a buyer before the goods are sent, so that payment can be made or that business documents can be produced; **pro forma letter** = formal letter which informs a court of a decision of another court

prohibit [prə'hɪbɪt] *verb* to forbid, to say that something must not happen; *parking is prohibited in front of the garage*; *the law prohibits the sale of alcohol to minors*; **prohibited degrees** = relationships which make it illegal for a man and woman to marry (such as father and daughter); **prohibited goods** = goods which are not allowed to be imported

prohibition [prəʊhɪ'bɪʃn] *noun* (a) act of forbidding something (b) High Court order forbidding a lower court from doing something which exceeds its jurisdiction

prohibitory injunction [prə'hɪbɪtri ɪn'dʒʌŋkʃn] *noun* order from a court preventing someone from doing an illegal act

promise ['prɒmɪs] *noun* statement that you will do something or not do something; **to keep a promise** = to do what you said you would do; **to go back on a promise** = not to do what you said you would do; **a promise to pay** = a promissory note; **breach of promise** = formerly, a complaint in court that someone had promised to marry the claimant and then had not done so; **gratuitous promise** = promise that cannot be enforced because no money has been involved

promisee [prɒmɪ'siː] *noun* person to whom a promise is made

promisor [prɒmɪ'sɔː] *noun* person who makes a promise

promissory [prə'mɪsri] *adjective* which promises; **promissory estoppel** = promise made by one person to another, so that the second person relies on the promise and acts to his detriment, and the first person is stopped from denying the validity of the promise; **promissory note** = document stating that someone promises to pay an amount of money on a certain date

promote [prə'məʊt] *verb* (a) to introduce a new Bill into Parliament (b) to encourage something to grow; **to promote a new company** = to organize the setting up of a new company

promoter [prə'məʊtə] *noun* (a) person who introduces a new Bill into Parliament (b) **company promoter** = person who organizes the setting up of a new company

prompt [prɒmt] **1** *adjective* rapid, done immediately; *the minister issued a prompt denial of the allegations against him*; **failing prompt payment** = if the payment is not made on time **2** *verb* to tell someone what to say; *the judge warned counsel not to prompt the witness*

proof [pruːf] *noun* (a) thing or evidence which shows that something is true; **documentary proof** = proof in the form of a document; **burden of proof** *or* **onus of proof** = duty to prove that what has been alleged in court is correct; *the onus of proof is on the claimant*; **proof beyond reasonable doubt** = proof that no reasonable person could doubt (proof needed to convict a person in a criminal case) (b) statement or evidence of a creditor to show that he is owed money by a bankrupt or by a company in liquidation; **proof of debt** = proceedings for a creditor to claim payment from a bankrupt's assets; **proof of evidence** = written statement of what a witness intends to say in court; **proof of service** = showing that legal documents have been delivered to someone

proofing ['pruːfɪŋ] *noun* **proofing of witnesses** = action of looking into witnesses' statements

proper ['prɒpə] *adjective* correct or appropriate; **proper law of the contract** = law which the parties signing a contract agree should govern that contract or its formation

property ['prɒpəti] *noun* **(a)** ownership, right to own something; **law of property** = branch of the law dealing with the rights of ownership **(b)** anything which can be owned; *(in the USA, Canada, France and many other countries)* **community property** = situation where the husband and wife jointly own any property which they acquire during the course of their marriage (as opposed to 'separate property', which they each owned before their marriage); **industrial property** = intangible property owned by a company such as patents, trademarks, company names, etc.; **intellectual property** = ownership of something (such as a copyright, patent or trademark) which is intangible; **personal property** = things (but not land) which belong to a person and can be inherited by his heirs; *the storm caused considerable damage to personal property*; *the management is not responsible for personal property left in the hotel rooms*; **separate property** = property owned by a husband and wife before their marriage (as opposed to 'community property') **(c)** **(real) property** = land and buildings; *property tax or tax on property*; *damage to property or property damage*; *the commercial property market is declining*; **property company** = company which buys or constructs buildings to lease them; **property developer** = person who buys old buildings or empty land and builds new buildings for sale or rent; **private property** = land or buildings which belong to a private person and not to the public **(d)** a building; *we have several properties for sale in the centre of the town*

proportion [prə'pɔːʃn] *noun* part (of a total); *a proportion of the pretax profit is set aside for contingencies*; *only a small proportion of our sales comes from retail shops*; **in proportion to** = showing how something is related to something else

proportional [prə'pɔːʃnl] *adjective* directly related; **proportional representation (PR)** = system of electing representatives where each political party is allocated a number of places which is directly related to the number of votes cast for the party

proportionality [prəpɔːʃ'næləti] *noun* **(a)** principle that a government or local authority can only act if the action is in proportion to the aim which is to be achieved, the aim being to protect the rights of ordinary citizens **(b)** principle that a legal action can only take place if the costs are proportionate to the aim to be achieved; *the requirement of proportionality may be a reason for a party to refuse to respond to a request for further information*

proportionate [prə'pɔːʃnət] *adjective* directly related to something, in proportion to something

proposal [prə'pəuzl] *noun* **(a)** suggestion, thing suggested; *to make a proposal or to put forward a proposal*; **to lay a proposal before the House** = to introduce a new Bill before Parliament; **the committee turned down the proposal** = the committee refused to accept what had been suggested **(b)** **proposal form** = official document with details of a property or person to be insured which is sent to the insurance company when asking for an insurance

propose [prə'pəuz] *verb* **(a)** to suggest that something should be done; *the Bill proposes that any party to the proceedings may appeal*; **to propose a motion** = to ask a meeting to vote for a motion and explain the reasons for this; **to propose someone as president** = to ask a group to vote for someone to become president **(b)** **to propose to** = to say that you intend to do something; *I propose to repay the loan at £20 a month*

proprietary [prə'praɪətri] *adjective* **(a)** product (such as a medicine) which is made and owned by a company; **proprietary drug** = drug which is made by a particular company and marketed under a brand name; **proprietary right** = right of someone who owns a property **(b)** *(in South Africa and Australia)* **proprietary company (Pty)** = private limited company

proprietor [prə'praɪətə] *noun* owner of a property

proprietorship [prə'praɪətəʃɪp] *noun* act of being the proprietor of land; **proprietorship register** = land register which shows the details of owners of land

proprietress [prə'praɪətrəs] *noun* woman owner

pro rata ['prəu 'rɑːtə] *adjective & adverb* at a rate which changes according to the importance of something; *a pro rata payment*; *to pay someone pro rata*

prorogation [prəurə'geɪʃn] *noun* end of a session of Parliament

prorogue [prə'rəug] *verb* to end a session of Parliament; *Parliament was prorogued for the summer recess*

proscribe [prəskraɪb] *verb* to ban; a **proscribed organization** *or* **political party** = organization or political party which has been banned

prosecute ['prɒsɪkjuːt] *verb* **(a)** to bring (someone) to court to answer a criminal charge; *he was prosecuted for embezzlement* **(b)** to speak against the accused person on behalf of the party bringing the charge; *Mr Smith is prosecuting, and Mr Jones is appearing for the defence*

prosecution [prɒsɪ'kjuːʃn] *noun* **(a)** act of bringing someone to court to answer a charge; *his prosecution for embezzlement*; *see also* CROWN PROSECUTION SERVICE, DIRECTOR OF PUBLIC PROSECUTIONS **(b)** (i) party who brings a criminal charge against someone; (ii) lawyers representing the party who brings a criminal charge against someone;

the costs of the case will be borne by the prosecution; **prosecution counsel** *or* **counsel for the prosecution** = lawyer acting for the prosecution; *see also* DEFENCE

prosecutor ['prɒsɪkjuːtə] *noun* person who brings criminal charges against someone; **Crown prosecutor** = official of the Crown Prosecution Service who is responsible for prosecuting criminals in one of 13 areas in England Wales; **public prosecutor** = government official who brings charges against alleged criminals (in the UK, the Director of Public Prosecutions)

prosequi ['prɒsɪkwaɪ] *see* NOLLE

prospectus [prə'spektəs] *noun* document which gives information about a company whose shares are being sold to the public for the first time (NOTE: plural is **prospectuses)**

prostitute ['prɒstɪtjuːt] *noun* person who provides sexual intercourse in return for payment

prostitution [prɒstɪ'tjuːʃn] *noun* providing sexual intercourse in return for payment

protect [prə'tekt] *verb* to defend something against harm; *the workers are protected from unfair dismissal by government legislation*; *the computer is protected by a plastic cover*; *the cover protects the machine from dust*; **to protect an industry by imposing tariff barriers** = to stop a local industry from being hit by foreign competition by stopping foreign products from being imported; **protected information** = electronic text which is not intelligible without a decryption key; **protected person** = important person (such as a President or Prime Minister) who has special police protection; **protected tenancy** = tenancy where the tenant is protected from eviction (NOTE: you protect someone **from** something or **from having** something done to him)

protection [prə'tekʃn] *noun* action of protecting; **consumer protection** =

protecting consumers against unfair or illegal traders; **Court of Protection** = court which administers the property of people suffering from a disability; **data protection** = protecting information (such as records about private people) in a computer from being copied or used wrongly; **police protection** = services of the police to protect someone who might be harmed; *the minister was given police protection*; **protection racket** = illegal organization where people demand money from someone (such as a small businessman) to pay for 'protection' against criminal attacks

protective [prə'tektɪv] *adjective* which protects; **to take someone into protective custody** = to put someone in a safe place (such as police station cells) to protect him or her from being harassed or attacked; **protective tariff** = tariff which tries to ban imports to stop them competing with local products

protector [prə'tektə] *noun* person or country which protects; **Lord Protector** = title taken by Oliver Cromwell from 1653 to 1658

protectorate [prə'tektrət] *noun* (a) country which is being protected or governed by another more powerful country; *a British protectorate* (b) the **Protectorate** = period when Oliver Cromwell was Lord Protector

pro tem *or* **pro tempore** ['prəʊ 'tem] *adverb* temporarily, for a time

protest 1 ['prəʊtest] *noun* (a) statement or action to show that you do not approve of something; *to make a protest against high prices*; **sit-down protest** = action by members of the staff who occupy their place of work and refuse to leave; **protest march** = demonstration where protesters march through the streets; **in protest at** = showing that you do not approve of something; *the staff occupied the offices in protest at the low pay offer*; **to do something under protest** = to do something, but say that you do not approve of it (b) official document from a notary

public which notes that a bill of exchange has not been paid **2** [prə'test] *verb* (a) **to protest against something** = to say that you do not approve of something; *the retailers are protesting against the ban on imported goods* (NOTE: in this meaning British English is **protest against something,** but American English is **to protest something**) (b) **to protest a bill** = to draw up a document to prove that a bill of exchange has not been paid

protocol ['prəʊtəkɒl] *noun* (a) (i) draft memorandum; (ii) list of things which have been agreed; *see also* PRE-ACTION PROTOCOL (b) correct diplomatic behaviour

provable ['pruːvəbl] *adjective* which can be proved; **provable debts** = debts which a creditor can prove against a bankrupt estate

prove [pruːv] *verb* to show that something is true; *the tickets proved that he was lying*; *dispatch of the packet was proved by the Post Office receipt*; *the claim was proved to be false*; **to prove a debt** = to show that a bankrupt owes you money; **to prove a will** = to show that a will is valid and obtain a grant of probate

proven ['pruːvn] *adjective (in Scotland)* **not proven** = verdict that the prosecution has not produced sufficient evidence to prove the accused to be guilty

provide [prə'vaɪd] *verb* (a) **to provide for something** = to allow for something which may happen in the future; *the contract provides for an annual increase in charges*; *these expenses have not been provided for*; *payments to be made as provided in schedule 6 attached*; **to provide for someone** = to put aside money to give someone enough to live on; *he provided for his daughter in his will* (b) to put money aside in accounts to cover expenditure or loss in the future; *£25,000 is provided against bad debts* (c) **to provide someone with something** = to supply something to someone; *the defendant provided the court with a detailed account* *of his movements*; *duress provides no defence to a charge of murder*

provided that or **providing**
[prə'vaɪdɪd 'ðæt or prə'vaɪdɪŋ] *conjunction* on condition that; *the judge will sentence the convicted man next week provided (that)* or *providing the psychiatrist's report is received in time* (NOTE: in deeds, the form **provided always that** is often used)

province ['prɒvɪns] *noun* (a) large administrative division of a country; *the ten provinces of Canada*; *the premier of the Province of Alberta* (b) area of a country away from the capital city; **in the provinces** = in the country outside London (c) **the Province** = Northern Ireland

provision [prə'vɪʒn] *noun* (a) **to make provision for** = to see that something is allowed for in the future; **to make financial provision for someone** = to give someone enough money to live on; **there is no provision for** or **no provision has been made for car parking in the plans for the office block** = the plans do not include space for cars to park (b) money put aside in accounts in case it is needed in the future; *the company has made a £2m provision for bad debts* (c) legal condition; **the provisions of a Bill** = conditions listed in a Bill before Parliament; **we have made provision to this effect** = we have put into the contract terms which will make this work

provisional [prə'vɪʒnl] *adjective* temporary, not final or permanent; *they wrote to give their provisional acceptance of the contract*; **provisional liquidator** = official appointed by a court to protect the assets of a company which is the subject of a winding up order; **provisional injunction** = temporary injunction granted until a full court hearing can take place

proviso [prə'vaɪzəʊ] *noun* condition in a contract or deed; *we are signing the contract with the proviso that the terms can be discussed again in six months' time* (NOTE: a proviso usually begins with the phrase **'provided always that'**)

provocation [prɒvə'keɪʃn] *noun* being provoked to commit a crime or to carry out an action which you had not intended; *he acted under provocation*

provoke [prə'vəʊk] *verb* to make someone do something or to make something happen; *the strikers provoked the police into retaliating*; *the murders provoked a campaign to increase police protection for politicians* (NOTE: you provoke someone **into doing** something)

provocateur [prəvɒkə'tɜː] *see* AGENT PROVOCATEUR

provost ['prɒvəst] *noun* official in a Scottish town, with a position similar to that of a mayor in England

proxy ['prɒksi] *noun* (a) document which gives someone the power to act on behalf of someone else; *to sign by proxy*; **proxy vote** = vote made by proxy (b) person who acts on behalf of someone else, especially a person appointed by a shareholder to vote on his behalf at a company meeting; *to act as proxy for someone*

P.S. ['piː 'es] = POST SCRIPTUM additional note at the end of a letter; *did you read the P.S. at the end of the letter?*

PSBR = PUBLIC SECTOR BORROWING REQUIREMENT

psephologist [sɪ'fɒlədʒɪst] *noun* person who makes a study of elections and voting patterns, and analyzes election results

psephology [sɪ'fɒlədʒi] *noun* study of elections, voting patterns, the influence of the media and opinion polls on voting, etc.

Pty = PROPRIETARY COMPANY

public ['pʌblɪk] **1** *adjective* (a) referring to all the people in general; **Public Bill** = Bill referring to a matter applying to the public in general which is introduced in Parliament by a government minister; **public domain** = land, property or information which belongs to and is available to the public; **work in the public domain** = written work which is no longer in copyright; **public holiday** = day when all workers rest and enjoy themselves instead of working; **public house** = building which has been licensed for the sale of alcohol to be drunk on the premises; **public image** = idea which the people have of a company or a person; *the police are trying to improve their public image*; **public key cryptography** = coding system where the sender of the message encrypts it using a publicly available key, and the receiver decrypts it using a secret decryption key; **public law** = law which affects the people or the public as a whole (such as administrative and constitutional law); **public nuisance** = criminal act which can harm members of the public or their rights; **public order** = situation where the general public is calm, where there are no riots; **offence against the public order** *or* **public order offence** = riot, street fight or looting, etc.; **public place** = place (such as a road, park or pavement) where the public in general have a right to be; **public policy** = law that no one can do anything against the general good of all the people; **public transport** = transport (such as buses, trains) which is used by any member of the public; **Public Trustee** = official who is appointed as a trustee of an individual's property **(b)** referring to the government or the state; **Public Accounts Committee** = committee of the House of Commons which examines the spending of each department and ministry; **public administration** = (i) means whereby government policy is carried out; (ii) people responsible for carrying out government policy; **public expenditure** = spending of money by the local or central government; **public finance** = the raising of money by governments (by taxes or borrowing) and the spending of it; **public funds** = government money available for expenditure; **public ownership** = situation where an industry is nationalized **(c)** **public limited company (plc)** = company whose shares can be bought on the Stock Exchange; **the company is going public** = the company is going to place some of its shares for sale on the Stock Exchange so that anyone can buy them **2** *noun* **the public** *or* **the general public** = the people

in general; **in public** = in front of everyone, in a courtroom with members of the public present; *the claimant made serious allegations in public* (NOTE: formerly, the term **in open court** was used)

publication [pʌblɪˈkeɪʃn] *noun* **(a)** making something public (either in speech or writing); *publication of Cabinet papers takes place after thirty years* **(b)** making a libel known to people other than the person libelled **(c)** printed work shown to the public; **obscene publication** = book or magazine which is liable to deprave or corrupt someone who sees or reads it; *the magazine was classed as an obscene publication and seized by customs*

public interest [ˈpʌblɪk ˈɪntrest] *noun* the usefulness of a piece of information to the public, in matters concerning national security, fraud, medical malpractice, etc., used as a defence against accusations of passing on confidential information or of invasion of privacy

> COMMENT: public interest implies that the actions of someone or information held by someone might affect the public in some way: if a newspaper discloses that a group of companies are fixing prices so as not to compete with each other, this disclosure might be held to be in the public interest. If a TV programme reveals that a Member of Parliament regularly took drugs, then this might be held to be in the public interest

public policy [ˈpʌblɪk ˈpɒləsi] *noun (in the EU)* the policy of the government of an EU Member State which protects its nationals, and which can be used to exclude nationals of other EU states from entering the country to take up work, though this excuse cannot be used for economic reasons

public sector [ˈpʌblɪk ˈsektə] *noun* nationalized industries and services; *a report on wage rises in the public sector or on public sector wage settlements*; **public sector borrowing requirement (PSBR)** = amount of money which a government has to borrow to pay for its own spending

public service ['pʌblɪk 'sɜːvɪs] *noun* service in government institutions

COMMENT: free movement of nationals from one EU country to another in order to work does not apply to jobs in public service, and can be used as a reason for refusing public service jobs to nationals of other countries

publish ['pʌblɪʃ] *verb* to have a document (such as a catalogue, book, magazine, newspaper or piece of music) written and printed and then sell or give it to the public; *the society publishes its list of members annually*; *the government has not published the figures on which its proposals are based*; *the company publishes six magazines for the business market*

publisher ['pʌblɪʃə] *noun* person or company which publishes

puisne ['pjuːni] *adjective* lesser, less important; **puisne judge** = High Court judge; **puisne mortgage** = mortgage where the deeds of the property have not been deposited with the lender

punish ['pʌnɪʃ] *verb* to make (someone) suffer for a crime which he or she has committed; *you will be punished for hitting the policeman*

punishable ['pʌnɪʃəbl] *adjective* (crime) which can be punished; *crimes punishable by imprisonment*

punishment ['pʌnɪʃmənt] *noun* **(a)** act of punishing someone; **corporal punishment** = punishing someone by hitting him; **capital punishment** = punishing someone by execution **(b)** treatment of someone as a way of making him suffer for a crime; *the punishment for treason is death*

punitive damages ['pjuːnɪtɪv 'dæmɪdʒɪz] *noun* heavy damages which punish the defendant for the loss or harm caused to the claimant, awarded to show that the court feels the defendant has behaved badly towards the claimant (NOTE: also called **exemplary damages**)

pupil ['pjuːpəl] *noun* trainee barrister, undergoing pupillage

pupillage ['pjuːpɪlɪdʒ] *noun* training period of one year after completing studies at university and passing all examinations, which a person has to serve before he or she can practise independently as a barrister

pur autre vie ['puːə 'əutr 'viː] *see* PER AUTRE VIE

purchase ['pɜːtʃəs] **1** *noun* (i) action of buying something; (ii) thing which has been bought; **purchase order** = official order made out by a purchasing department for goods which a company wants to buy; **purchase price** = price paid for something; **purchase tax** = tax paid on things which are bought; **compulsory purchase** = buying of a property by a local authority or by the government, even if the owner does not wish to sell (NOTE: the American English for this is **expropriation**); **compulsory purchase order** = official order from a local authority or from the government ordering an owner to sell his property; **hire purchase** = system of buying something by paying a sum regularly each month; **hire purchase agreement** = contract to pay for something by instalments **2** *verb* to buy; **to purchase something for cash** = to pay cash for something

purchaser ['pɜːtʃəsə] *noun* person or company which purchases something

purge ['pɜːdʒ] **1** *noun* removing opponents or unacceptable people from a group; *the party has begun a purge of right-wing elements* **2** *verb* **(a)** to remove opponents or unacceptable people from a group; *the activists have purged the party of moderates or have purged the moderates from the party* **(b)** to purge one's contempt *or* to purge a contempt of court = to do something (such as make an apology) to show that you are sorry for the lack of respect you have shown

purpose ['pɜːpəs] *noun* aim, plan or intention; **on purpose** = intentionally; *she hid the knife on purpose*; **we need the invoice for tax purposes** *or* **for the**

purpose of declaration to the tax authorities = in order for it to be declared to the tax authorities; **fitness for purpose =** implied contractual term that goods sold will be of the necessary standard to be used for the purpose for which they were bought

purposive ['pɜːpəsɪv] *adjective* referring to the purpose behind something; *a purposive interpretation of the Treaty on European Union*

pursuant to [pə'sjuːənt 'tʊ] *adverb* relating to or concerning; *matters pursuant to Article 124 of the EC treaty*; *pursuant to the powers conferred on the local authority*

pursue [pə'sjuː] *verb* to continue with (proceedings in court, a debate in Parliament, etc.)

pursuit [pə'sjuːt] *see* FRESH, HOT

purview ['pɜːvjuː] *noun* general scope of an Act of Parliament

put [pʊt] **1** *noun* put option = right to sell shares at a certain price at a certain date **2** *verb* to place or to fix; **to put a proposal to the vote =** to ask a meeting to vote for or against the proposal; **to put a proposal to the board =** to ask the board to consider a suggestion (NOTE: **putting - put - has put**)

putative ['pjuːtətɪv] *adjective* **putative father =** man who is supposed to be or who a court decides must be the father of an illegitimate child

put away ['pʊt ə'weɪ] *verb* to send to prison; *he was put away for ten years*

put down ['pʊt 'daʊn] *verb* **(a)** to make a deposit; *to put down money on a house* **(b)** to write an item in an account book; *to put down a figure for expenses*

put in ['pʊt 'ɪn] *verb* **to put in a bid for something =** to offer (usually in writing) to buy something; **to put in an estimate for something =** to give someone a written calculation of the probable costs of carrying out a job; **to put in a claim for damage** *or* **loss =** to ask an insurance company to pay for damage or loss

put into ['pʊt 'ɪntʊ] *verb* **to put money into a business =** to invest money in a business

put on ['pʊt 'ɒn] *verb* **to put an item on the agenda =** to list an item for discussion at a meeting; **to put an embargo on trade =** to forbid trade

pyramiding ['pɪrəmɪdɪŋ] *noun* illegally using new investors' deposits to pay the interest on the deposits made by existing investors

pyramid selling ['pɪrəmɪd 'selɪŋ] *noun* illegal way of selling goods to the public, where each selling agent pays for the right to sell and sells that right to other agents, so that in the end the commissions earned by the sales of goods will never pay back the agents for the payments they themselves have already made

Qq

QB *or* **QBD** = QUEEN'S BENCH DIVISION

QC ['kjuː 'siː] = QUEEN'S COUNSEL (NOTE: written after the surname of the lawyer: **W. Smith QC**. Note also that the plural is written **QCs**)

qua [kwɑː] *conjunction* as or acting in the capacity of; *a decision of the Lord Chancellor qua head of the judiciary*

qualification [kwɒlɪfɪ'keɪʃn] *noun* **period of qualification** = time which has to pass before something qualifies for something; **qualification shares** = number of shares which a person has to hold to be a director of a company

qualified ['kwɒlɪfaɪd] *adjective* **(a)** having passed special examinations in a subject; *she is a qualified solicitor*; **highly qualified** = with very good results in examinations; *all our staff are highly qualified*; *they employ twenty-six highly qualified legal assistants* **(b)** with some reservations or conditions; *qualified acceptance of a bill of exchange*; *the plan received qualified approval from the board*; **qualified privilege** = protection from being sued for defamation given to someone only if it can be proved that the statements were made without malice; **qualified title** = title to a property which is not absolute because there is some defect **(c) qualified accounts** = accounts which have been commented on by the auditors because they contain something with which the auditors do not agree; **qualified auditors' report** *or* **qualified audit report,** *US* **qualified opinion** = report from a company's auditors which points

out areas in the accounts with which the auditors do not agree or about which they are not prepared to express an opinion, or where the auditors believe the accounts as a whole have not been prepared correctly or where they are unable to decide whether the accounts are correct or not

qualified majority ['kwɒlɪfaɪd mə'dʒɒrəti] *noun (in the EU)* system adopted when voting in the Council of the European Union, where the larger states have more votes than the smaller ones

COMMENT: France, Germany, Italy and the UK have ten votes each, Spain has eight votes, Belgium, Greece, the Netherlands and Portugal have five votes, Sweden and Austria have four votes, Denmark, Ireland and Finland have three votes and Luxembourg has two votes. This makes a total of eighty-seven votes, but a qualified majority needs sixty-two votes

qualify ['kwɒlɪfaɪ] *verb* **(a) to qualify for** = to be in the right position for or to be entitled to; *he does not qualify for Legal Aid*; *she qualifies for unemployment benefit* **(b) to qualify as** = to follow a specialized course and pass examinations so that you can do a certain job; *she has qualified as an accountant*; *he will qualify as a solicitor next year* **(c)** to change, to amend; **the auditors have qualified the accounts** = the auditors have found something in the accounts of the company which they do not agree with, and have noted it

qualifying ['kwɒlɪfaɪɪŋ] *adjective* **(a) qualifying period** = time which has to pass before something qualifies for a grant or subsidy, etc.; *there is a six month qualifying period before you can get a grant from the local authority* **(b) qualifying shares** = number of shares which you need to own to get a free issue, or to be a director of a company

quango ['kwæŋgəʊ] *noun* = *QUASI-AUTONOMOUS NON-GOVERNMENTAL ORGANIZATION GB* group of people appointed by a government with powers to deal with certain problems (such as the Race Relations Board or ACAS) (NOTE: plural is **quangos**)

quantum ['kwɒntəm] *noun* amount (of damages); *liability was admitted by the defendants, but the case went to trial because they could not agree the quantum of damages*

quantum meruit ['kwɒntəm 'meru:ɪt] *Latin phrase meaning* 'as much as he has deserved': rule that, when claiming for breach of contract, a party is entitled to payment for work done

quarantine ['kwɒrənti:n] **1** *noun* period (originally forty days) when a ship, animal or person newly arrived in a country has to be kept away from others in case there is danger of carrying diseases; *the animals were put in quarantine on arrival at the port*; *quarantine restrictions have been lifted on imported animals from that country* (NOTE: used without **the: the dog was put in quarantine** *or* **was held in quarantine** *or* **was released from quarantine**) **2** *verb* to put in quarantine; *the ship was searched and all the passengers and crew were quarantined*

quarter ['kwɔ:tə] *noun* **(a)** period of three months; **first quarter** = period of three months from January to the end of March; **second quarter** = period of three months from April to the end of June; **third quarter** = period of three months from July to the end of September; **fourth quarter** *or* **last quarter** = period of three months from October to the end of the year; *the instalments are payable at the end of each quarter*; *the first quarter's rent is payable in advance*; **quarter day** = day at the end of a quarter, when rents should be paid **(b) Quarter Sessions** = old name for the criminal court (replaced by the Crown Court)

COMMENT: in England the quarter days are 25th March (Lady Day), 24th June (Midsummer Day), 29th September (Michaelmas Day) and 25th December (Christmas Day)

quarterly ['kwɔ:təli] *adjective & adverb* happening every three months, happening four times a year; *there is a quarterly charge for electricity*; *the bank sends us a quarterly statement*; *we agreed to pay the rent quarterly* *or* *on a quarterly basis*

quash [kwɒʃ] *verb* to annul, to make something not exist; *the appeal court quashed the verdict*; *he applied for judicial review to quash the order*; *a conviction obtained by fraud or perjury by a witness will be quashed*

quasi- ['kweɪzaɪ] *prefix* almost, which seems like; *a quasi-official body*; *a quasi-judicial investigation*

quasi-contract ['kweɪzaɪ'kɒntrækt] = IMPLIED CONTRACT

queen [kwi:n] *noun* (i) female ruler of a monarchy; (ii) wife of a king; *the queen of the Netherlands* (NOTE: written with a capital letter when used as a title: **Queen Elizabeth II**)

Queen's Bench Division (QBD) ['kwi:nz 'bentʃ dɪ'vɪʒn] *noun* one of the main divisions of the High Court

Queen's Counsel ['kwi:nz 'kaʊnsl] *noun* senior British barrister, appointed by the Lord Chancellor (NOTE: abbreviated to QC)

Queen's evidence ['kwi:nz 'evɪdəns] *noun* **to turn Queen's evidence** = to confess to a crime and then act as witness against the other criminals involved, in the hope of getting a lighter sentence (NOTE: American English is **to turn state's evidence**)

Queen's Proctor [ˈkwiːnz ˈprɒtə] *noun* solicitor acting for the Crown in matrimonial and probate cases

Queen's Speech [ˈkwiːnz ˈspiːtʃ] *noun* speech made by the Queen at the opening of a session of Parliament, which outlines the government's plans for legislation

> COMMENT: the Queen's Speech is not written by the Queen herself, but by her ministers, and she is not responsible for what is in the speech

question [ˈkwestʃn] **1** *noun* **(a)** words which need an answer; *counsel asked the witness questions about his bank accounts*; *counsel for the prosecution put three questions to the police inspector*; *the managing director refused to answer questions about redundancies*; *the market research team prepared a series of questions to test the public's attitude to problems of law and order*; **Question Time** = period in the House of Commons when Members of Parliament can put questions to ministers about the work of their departments **(b)** problem; *he raised the question of the cost of the lawsuit*; *the main question is that of time*; *the tribunal discussed the question of redundancy payments* **(c)** **question of fact** = fact relevant to a case which is tried at court; **question of law** = law relevant to a case which is tried at court **(d)** matter or motion to be discussed by Parliament; **to put the question** = to ask MPs to say whether they agree with the motion or not **2** *verb* **(a)** to ask questions; *the police questioned the accounts staff for four hours*; *she questioned the chairman about the company's investment policy* **(b)** to query or to suggest that something may be wrong; *counsel questioned the reliability of the witness' evidence*; *the accused questioned the result of the breathalyser test*

> COMMENT: the Speaker puts the question to get the opinion of the House. He reads out the motion, then asks those in favour to say 'Aye' and then those against to say 'No'; he then decides which is the majority and

declares 'the Ayes have it' or 'the Noes have it'. If an MP disagrees with the Speaker's decision, he can challenge it and force a division (i.e. force a vote)

questioning [ˈkwestʃənɪŋ] *noun* action of asking someone questions; *the man was taken to the police station for questioning*; *during questioning by the police, she confessed to the crime*; *the witness became confused during questioning by counsel for the prosecution*

questionnaire [kwestʃəˈneə] *noun* printed list of questions given to people to answer, especially used in market research; **allocation questionnaire** = form to be filled in by each party to a claim, to give the court information to allow it to allocate the case to a particular track; **listing questionnaire** = questionnaire sent by a court to the parties in a case allocated to the fast track, in which they must give details of documents, witnesses, expert evidence, etc.; the questionnaire has to be filed with the court within 14 days and is used by the court to decide on the listing of the case

quickie (divorce) [ˈkwɪki] *noun* divorce which is processed rapidly through the court by use of the special procedure

quid pro quo [ˈkwɪd prəʊ ˈkwəʊ] *Latin phrase meaning* 'one thing for another': action done in return for something done or promised

quiet enjoyment [ˈkwaɪət ɪnˈdʒɔɪmənt] *noun* right of an occupier to occupy property peacefully under a tenancy without the landlord or anyone else interfering with that right

quit [kwɪt] *verb* to leave a job; to leave rented accommodation; *he quit after an argument with the managing director*; *several of the managers are quitting to set up their own company*; **notice to quit** = formal notice served by a landlord on a tenant before proceedings are started for possession; **to serve a tenant with notice to quit** = to inform a tenant that he has to leave premises by a certain date (NOTE: **quitting - quit - has quit**)

quo [kwəʊ] *see* QUID PRO QUO, STATUS QUO

quorate ['kwɔːreɪt] *adjective* having a quorum; *the resolution was invalid because the shareholders' meeting was not quorate*; *see also* INQUORATE

quorum ['kwɔːrəm] *noun* minimum number of people who have to be present at a meeting to make it valid; **to have a quorum** = to have enough people present for a meeting to go ahead; *do we have a quorum?*; *the meeting was adjourned since there was no quorum*

quota ['kwəʊtə] *noun* fixed amount of something which is allowed to be sold, bought or obtained; **import quota** = fixed quantity of a particular type of goods which the government allows to be imported; *the government has imposed a quota on the import of cars*; *the quota on imported cars has been lifted*; **quota system** = system where imports, exports or supplies are regulated by fixing maximum amounts

quotation [kwəʊ'teɪʃn] *noun* **(a)** estimate of how much something will cost; *they sent in their quotation for the job*; *to ask for quotations for building a new courtroom*; *his quotation was much lower than all the others*; *we accepted the lowest quotation* **(b)** quotation on the Stock Exchange *or* Stock Exchange quotation = listing of the price of a share on the Stock Exchange; **the company is going for a quotation on the Stock Exchange** = the company has applied to the Stock Exchange to have its shares listed

quote [kwəʊt] *verb* **(a)** to repeat words used by someone else; to repeat a reference number; *counsel quoted from the statement made by the witness at the police station*; *she quoted figures from the annual report*; *in reply please quote this number: PC 1234* **(b)** to estimate, to say what costs may be; *to quote a price for supplying stationery*; *to quote a price in dollars*; *their prices are always quoted in dollars*; *he quoted me a price of £1,026*; *can you quote for supplying 20,000 envelopes?*; **quoted company** = company whose shares are listed on the Stock Exchange

quo warranto ['kwəʊ 'wærəntəʊ] *Latin phrase meaning* 'by what authority': action which questions the authority of someone

q.v. *or* **quod vide** ['kjuː 'viː] *Latin phrase meaning* 'which see'

Rr

R = REGINA, REX (NOTE: used in reports of cases where the Crown is a party: *R. v. Smith Ltd*)

race [reɪs] *noun* **(a)** test to see who can go fastest or who will win; *the race is on for the Democratic presidential nomination* **(b)** group of people with distinct physical characteristics or culture who are considered to be separate from other groups; **race relations** = relations between different racial groups in a country

racial ['reɪʃl] *adjective* referring to race; **racial hatred** = violent dislike of someone or of a group of people because of race; **incitement to racial hatred** = offence of encouraging (by words, actions or writing) people to attack others because of their race; **racial prejudice** *or* **racial discrimination** = treating people in different ways because of differences in race

racism *or* **racialism** ['reɪsɪzm *or* 'reɪʃəlɪzm] *noun* belief in racist ideas or actions based on racist ideas; *the minority groups have accused the council of racism in their allocation of council houses*

racist *or* **racialist** ['reɪsɪst *or* 'reɪʃəlɪst] *(usually as criticism)* **1** *adjective* (person) believing that people from other racial groups are different and should receive different (and usually inferior) treatment **2** *noun* person with racist ideas

racket ['rækɪt] *noun* illegal deal, business which makes a lot of money by fraud; *he runs a cheap ticket racket*; *see also* PROTECTION

racketeer [rækɪ'tɪə] *noun* person who runs a racket

racketeering [rækɪ'tɪərɪŋ] *noun* running a racket

rack rent ['ræk 'rent] *noun* (i) full yearly rent of a property let on a normal lease; (ii) very high rent

rage [reɪdʒ] *noun* **air rage** = violent attack by a passenger on a member of the crew of an aircraft, caused by drink, tiredness or annoyance at something; **road rage** = violent attack by a driver on another car or its driver, caused by anger at the way the other driver has been driving; *there have been several incidents of road rage lately*; *in the latest road rage attack, the driver leapt out of his car and knocked a cyclist to the ground*

raid [reɪd] **1** *noun* sudden attack or search; *six people were arrested in the police raid on the club* **2** *verb* to make a sudden attack or search; *the police have raided several houses in the town*; *drugs were found when the police raided the club*

raison d'état ['reɪzɒn deɪ'tæ] *noun* reason for a political action, which says that an action is justified because it is for the common good

> COMMENT: raison d'état is open to criticism because it can be used to justify acts such as the abolition of individual rights, if the general good of the people may seem to require it at the time

ransom ['rænsəm] **1** *noun* money paid to abductors to get back someone who has been abducted; *the daughter of the banker was held by kidnappers who asked for a ransom of £1m*; **to hold someone to ransom** = to keep someone secretly until a ransom is paid; **ransom note** = message sent by kidnappers asking for a ransom to be paid **2** *verb* to pay money so that someone is released; *she was ransomed by her family*

rape [reɪp] **1** *noun* notifiable offence of forcing a person to have sexual intercourse without their consent; *he was brought to court and charged with rape*; *the incidence of cases of rape has increased over the last years*; **marital rape** = forcing one's wife to have sexual intercourse without her consent **2** *verb* to force (a person) to have sexual intercourse without their consent

rapporteur [ræpɔːˈtɜː] *noun (in the EU)* one of the judges in the ECJ, who is assigned to a particular case, and whose job it is to examine the written applications and the defence to them, and prepare a report on the case before the court starts oral hearings

rapprochement [ræˈprɒʃmɒn] *French word meaning* 'coming closer', used to mean a situation where two states become friendly after a period of tension; *political commentators have noted the rapprochement which has been taking place since the old president died*

rata [ˈrɑːtə] *see* = PRO RATA

rate [reɪt] **1** *noun* **(a)** money charged for time worked, or for work completed; **all-in rate** = price which covers all items in a purchase (such as delivery, tax and insurance, as well as the goods themselves); **fixed rate** = charge which cannot be changed; **flat rate** = charge which always stays the same; **full rate** = full charge, with no reductions; **reduced rate** = specially cheap charge **(b)** **insurance rates** = amount of premium which has to be paid per £1,000 of insurance; **interest rate** *or* **rate of interest** = percentage charge for borrowing money; **rate of return** = amount of interest or

dividend which comes from an investment, shown as a percentage of the money invested **(c)** **exchange rate** *or* **rate of exchange** = rate at which one currency is exchanged for another; **forward rate** = rate for purchase of foreign currency at a fixed price for delivery at a later date; **freight rates** = charges for carrying goods; **letter rate** *or* **parcel rate** = postage (calculated by weight) for sending a letter or a parcel; **night rate** = cheap telephone calls at night **(d)** amount, number or speed compared with something else; **birth rate** = number of children born per 1,000 of the population; **error rate** = number of mistakes per thousand entries or per page **(e)** *GB* **rates** = local tax on property; **business rates** = tax levied on business property **2** *verb* **to rate someone highly** = to value someone, to think someone is very good

rateable [ˈreɪtəbl] *adjective* **rateable value** = value of a property as a basis for calculating local taxes

ratepayer [ˈreɪtpeɪə] *noun* **business ratepayer** = business which pays business rates on a shop, factory, etc.

ratification [rætɪfɪˈkeɪʃn] *noun* official approval of something which then becomes legally binding

ratify [ˈrætɪfaɪ] *verb* to approve officially (something which has already been agreed); *the treaty was ratified by Congress*; *the agreement has to be ratified by the board*; *although the directors had acted without due authority, the company ratified their actions*

ratio decidendi [ˈrætiəʊ deɪsɪˈdendi] *Latin phrase meaning* 'reason for deciding': main part of a court judgment setting out the legal principles applicable to the case and forming the binding part of the judgment to which other courts must pay regard; *see also* OBITER DICTA

ratio legis [ˈrætiəʊ ˈledʒɪs] *Latin phrase meaning* 'reason of the law': the principle behind a law

RCJ = ROYAL COURTS OF JUSTICE

RD = REFER TO DRAWER

re [ri: or reɪ] *preposition* about, concerning, referring to; *re your inquiry of May 29th*; *re: Smith's memorandum of yesterday*; *re: the agenda for the AGM*; **in re** = concerning, in the case of; *in re Jones & Co. Ltd*; *see also* IN RE, RES

re- [ri:] *prefix* again

rea ['reɪə] *see* MENS REA

reach [ri:tʃ] *verb* to come to or to arrive at; *to reach an agreement*; *the jury was unable to reach a unanimous decision*

reading ['ri:dɪŋ] *noun* (a) First Reading *or* Second Reading *or* Third Reading = the three stages of discussion of a Bill in Parliament (b) *(in the EU)* examination in detail of proposed legislation by the European Parliament

COMMENT: First Reading is the formal presentation of the Bill when the title is read to MPs; Second Reading is the stage when MPs have printed copies of the Bill and it is explained by the Minister proposing it, there is a debate and a vote is taken; the Bill is then discussed in Committee and at the Report Stage; Third Reading is the final discussion of the Bill in the whole House of Commons or House of Lords.
European legislation is placed before the European Parliament for discussion. This is the First Reading, and can be decided by a simple majority in the Parliament. If the Council of the European Union sets out a common position on proposed legislation and communicates this to Parliament, Parliament will consider the proposal and may approve it by an absolute majority of its members

real ['rɪəl] *adjective* (a) true, not an imitation; *his case is made of real leather or he has a real leather case*; *that car is a real bargain at £300*; **real income** *or* **real wages** = income which is available for spending after tax, etc., has been deducted;

in real terms = actually or really; *sales have gone up by 3% but with inflation running at 5% that is a fall in real terms* (b) **real time** = time when a computer is working on the processing of data while the problem to which the data refers is actually taking place; **real-time system** = computer system where data is inputted directly into the computer which automatically processes it to produce information which can be used immediately (c) referring to things as opposed to persons; **chattels real** = leaseholds (d) referring to land (especially freehold land); **real estate** *or* **real property** = land or buildings considered from a legal point of view

realizable [rɪəˈlaɪzəbl] *adjective* **realizable assets** = assets which can be sold for money

realization [rɪəlaɪˈzeɪʃn] *noun* (a) making real; **the realization of a project** = putting a plan into action; *the plan moved a stage nearer realization when the contracts were signed* (b) **realization of assets** = selling of assets for money

realize ['rɪəlaɪz] *verb* (a) to make something become real; **to realize a project** *or* **a plan** = to put a project or a plan into action (b) to sell something to produce money; *to realize property or assets*; *the sale realized £100,000*

realpolitik [reɪˈɑːlpɒlɪtɪk] *German word meaning* 'politics based on real and practical factors and not on moral ideas'

realty ['rɪəlti] *noun* property, real estate or legal rights to land

reasonable ['ri:znəbl] *adjective* sensible, not annoyed; *the magistrates were very reasonable when she explained that the driving licence was necessary for her work*; **beyond reasonable doubt** = so that no reasonable person could doubt it (proof needed to convict a person in a criminal case); *the prosecution in a criminal case has to establish beyond reasonable doubt that the accused committed the crime*; **reasonable financial provision (rfp)** = provision which relatives and dependants of a deceased person may ask a court to provide in cases where the deceased died intestate, or where no provision was made for them under the will; **reasonable force** = force needed (but no more than that) to do something; *the police were instructed to use reasonable force in dealing with the riot*; **reasonable man** = imaginary person, with normal levels of judgment and intelligence, who is used to represent normal standards of social behaviour; **no reasonable offer refused** = we will accept any offer which is not too low

reasoned ['riːznd] *adjective* carefully thought out and explained

rebate ['riːbeɪt] *noun* money returned; **rent rebate** = state subsidy paid to poor people who do not have enough income to pay their rents

rebel 1 ['rebəl] *noun* person who fights against the government or against people in authority; *anti-government rebels have taken six towns*; *rebel ratepayers have occupied the town hall* **2** [rɪ'bel] *verb* to fight against authority (NOTE: **rebelling - rebelled**)

rebellion [rɪ'beljən] *noun* fight against the government or against those in authority; *the army has crushed the rebellion in the southern province*

rebut [rɪ'bʌt] *verb* to contradict or to go against; *he attempted to rebut the assertions made by the prosecution witness* (NOTE: **rebutting - rebutted**)

rebuttable [rɪ'bʌtəbl] *adjective* which can be rebutted

rebuttal [rɪ'bʌtl] *noun* act of rebutting

recall [rɪ'kɔːl] **1** *noun* **(a)** asking someone to come back; *MPs are asking for the recall of Parliament to debate the crisis*; *after his recall, the Ambassador was interviewed at the airport* **(b)** *US* system of ending the term of office of an elected official early, following a popular vote **2** *verb* **(a)** to ask someone to come back; *MPs are asking for Parliament to be recalled to debate the financial crisis*; *the witness was recalled to the witness box*; **to**

recall an ambassador = to ask an ambassador to return to his country (usually as a way of breaking off diplomatic relations) **(b)** to remember; *the witness could not recall having seen the papers*

recd = RECEIVED

receipt [rɪ'siːt] **1** *noun* **(a)** paper showing that money has been paid or that something has been received; *receipt for items purchased*; *please produce your receipt if you want to exchange items*; **receipt book** *or* **book of receipts** = book of blank receipts to be filled in when purchases are made **(b)** act of receiving something; *goods will be supplied within thirty days of receipt of order*; *invoices are payable within thirty days of receipt*; *on receipt of the notification, the company lodged an appeal*; **to acknowledge receipt of a letter** = to write to say that you have received a letter; *we acknowledge receipt of your letter of the 15th*; **in receipt of** = having received; *we are in receipt of a letter of complaint*; *he was accused of being in receipt of stolen cheques* **(c)** **receipts** = money taken in sales; *to itemize receipts and expenditure*; *receipts are down against the same period of last year* **2** *verb* to stamp or to sign a document to show that it has been received, to stamp an invoice to show that it has been paid

receivable [rɪ'siːvəbl] *adjective* which can be received; **accounts receivable** = money owed to a company

receivables [rɪ'siːvəblz] *plural noun* money which is owed to a company

receive [rɪ'siːv] *verb* **to receive stolen goods** = crime of taking in and disposing of property which you know to be stolen

receiver [rɪ'siːvə] *noun* **(a)** person who receives something; **receiver of wrecks** = official of the Department of Trade who deals with legal problems of wrecked ships within his area **(b)** **Official Receiver** = (i) person who is appointed to administer a company for a period until the person who has appointed him has been paid money due; (ii) government official who is appointed to administer the liquidation of a limited company after a winding up by the court or the affairs of a bankrupt after a receiving order has been made; *the court appointed a receiver for the company*; *the company is in the hands of the receiver*; *the Court of Protection appointed a receiver to administer the client's affairs* **(c)** person who receives stolen goods and disposes of them

receivership [rɪ'siːvəʃɪp] *noun* administration by a receiver; **the company went into receivership** = the company was put into the hands of a receiver

receiving [rɪ'siːvɪŋ] *noun* **(a)** act of taking something which has been delivered; **receiving clerk** = official who works in a receiving office; **receiving department** = section of a company which deals with goods or payments which are received by the company; **receiving office** = office where goods or payments are received; **receiving party** = party who is entitled to be paid costs (NOTE: the other party is the **paying party**); **receiving stolen property** = crime of taking in and disposing of goods which are known to be stolen **(b) receiving order** = court order made placing the Official Receiver in charge of a person's assets before a bankruptcy order is made

recess [rɪ'ses] **1** *noun* **(a)** period when Parliament or another body is not sitting; *during August, Parliament is in recess*; *the council's last meeting before the summer recess will be on 23rd July* **(b)** (*in Congress*) period when the chamber does not meet, but is not adjourned **2** *verb* (*of the US Senate*) not to meet, but without adjourning; *the Senate recessed at the end of the afternoon*

recession [rɪ'seʃn] *noun* fall in general trade, of the economy; *the recession has put many people out of work*; *he lost all his money in the recession*

recidivist [rɪ'sɪdəvɪst] *noun* criminal who commits a crime again

reciprocal [rɪ'sɪprəkl] *adjective* given by one country, person or company to

another and vice versa; (arrangement) where each party agrees to benefit the other in the same way; **reciprocal holdings** = situation where two companies own shares in each other to prevent takeover bids; **reciprocal trade** = trade between two countries; **reciprocal wills** = wills where two people (usually man and wife) leave their property to each other

reciprocate [rɪ'sɪprəkeɪt] *verb* to do the same thing to someone as he has just done to you; *they offered us an exclusive agency for their cars and we reciprocated with an offer of the agency for our buses*

reciprocity [resɪ'prɒsəti] *noun* arrangement which applies from one party to another and vice versa

recitals [rɪ'saɪtlz] *plural noun* introduction to a deed or conveyance which sets out the main purpose and the parties to it

reckless ['rekləs] *adjective* (person) who takes a risk even if he knows that what he does may be dangerous; **reckless driving** = offence of driving a vehicle in such a way that it may cause damage to property or injure people, where the driver does not see that he is causing a risk to other people

COMMENT: causing death by reckless driving is a notifiable offence

recklessly ['rekləsli] *adverb* taking risks, and not caring about the effect on other people; *the company recklessly spent millions of pounds on a new factory*; *he was accused of driving recklessly*

recklessness ['rekləsnəs] *noun* (act of) taking risks, without caring if other people may be harmed

reclaim [rɪ'kleɪm] *verb* to claim back money which has been paid earlier

recognition [rekəg'nɪʃn] *noun* act of recognizing; **to grant a government recognition** = to say that a government which has taken power in a foreign country is the legal government of that country; **to**

grant a trade union recognition = to recognize a trade union

recognizance [rɪ'kɒgnɪzns] *noun* obligation undertaken by someone to a court that he or someone else will appear in the court at a later date to answer charges, or if not, he will pay a penalty; *he was bound over on his own recognizance of £4,000*; **estreated recognizance** = recognizance which is forfeited because the person making it has not come to court; *US* **release on recognizance (ROR)** = release of an accused person, provided that he promises to come back to court when asked to do so

recognize ['rekəgnaɪz] *verb* **(a)** to know someone or something because you have seen or heard them before; *she recognized the man who attacked her*; *I recognized his voice before he said who he was*; *do you recognize the handwriting on the letter?* **(b)** to approve something as being legal; **to recognize a government** = to say that a government which has taken power in a foreign country is the legal government of that country; **the prisoner refused to recognize the jurisdiction of the court** = the prisoner said that he did not believe that the court had the legal right to try him; **to recognize a union** = to accept that a union can act on behalf of staff; *although all the staff had joined the union, the management refused to recognize it*; **recognized agent** = agent who is approved by the company for which he acts

recommend [rekə'mend] *verb* to suggest that something should be done; *the legal adviser recommended applying for an injunction against the directors of the company*; *we do not recommend bank shares as a safe investment*; *the Parole Board recommended him for parole*; *he was sentenced to life imprisonment, the judge recommending that he should serve a minimum of twenty years*

recommendation [rekəmen'deɪʃn] *noun* advising that something should be done; *he was sentenced to life imprisonment, with a recommendation that he should serve at least twenty years*;

he was released on the recommendation of the Parole Board or on the Parole Board's recommendation

recommendations [rekəmen'deɪʃnz] *noun* decision of the European Community which is not legally binding

recommit [ri:kə'mɪt] *verb US* to send a bill back to the committee which reported it, for further discussion

recommittal [ri:kə'mɪtl] *noun US* sending a bill back to a committee for further discussion

reconcile ['rekənsaɪl] *verb* to make two accounts or statements agree; *to reconcile one account with another*; *to reconcile the accounts*

reconciliation [rekənsɪli'eɪʃn] *noun* making two accounts, parties or statements agree; **reconciliation statement** = statement which explains why two accounts do or do not agree

reconsider [ri:kən'sɪdə] *verb* to think again; *the applicant asked the committee to reconsider its decision to refuse the application*; *US* **motion to reconsider a vote** = motion at the end of a discussion of any bill, but especially one passed with a close vote, so that a second vote has to be taken to settle the matter

reconstruction [ri:kən'strʌkʃn] *noun* **reconstruction of a crime** = using actors to act a crime again in order to try to get witnesses to remember details of it

reconsultation [ri:kɒnsʌl'teɪʃn] *noun* (*in the EU*) act of consulting again, as when the Council of the European Union looks again at proposed legislation, taking into account objections raised by the European Parliament

reconvict [ri:kən'vɪkt] *verb* to convict someone again who has previously been convicted of a crime

reconviction ['ri:kən'vɪkʃn] *noun* conviction of someone who has been previously convicted of a crime; *the reconviction rate is rising*

record 1 ['rekɔːd] *noun* **(a)** report of something which has happened, especially an official transcript of a court action; *the chairman signed the minutes as a true record of the last meeting*; a **matter of record** = something which has been written down and can be confirmed; **for the record** *or* **to keep the record straight** = to note something which has been done; **on record** = (fact) which has been noted; *the chairman is on record as saying that profits are set to rise*; **off the record** = unofficially or in private; *he made some remarks off the record about the rising crime figures* **(b) records** = documents which give information; *the names of customers are kept in the company's records*; *we find from our records that our invoice number 1234 has not been paid* **(c)** description of what has happened in the past; *the clerk's record of service* or *service record*; *the company's record in industrial relations*; **criminal record** = note of previous crimes for which someone has been convicted; *he has a criminal record stretching back twenty years*; *the court was told she had no previous criminal record*; **track record** = success or failure of someone in the past; *he has a good track record as a detective*; *the company has no track record in the computer market* **(d)** result which is better or higher than anything before; **record crime figures** *or* **record losses** *or* **record profits** = crime figures, losses or profits which are higher than ever before; *1996 was a record year for bankruptcies*; *road accidents in 1998 equalled the record of 1993*; *the figure for muggings has set a new record* or *has broken all previous records* **2** *verb* [rɪ'kɔːd] to note or to report; *the company has recorded another year of increased sales*; *your complaint has been recorded and will be investigated*; *the court recorded a plea of not guilty*; *the coroner recorded a verdict of death by misadventure*; **recorded delivery** = mail service where a receipt for the letter is signed by the person receiving it

recorder [rɪ'kɔːdə] *noun* part-time judge of the Crown Court; **Recorder of London** = chief judge of the Central Criminal Court; *see comment at* JUDGE

recours [rə'kuːəs] *see* SANS

recourse [rɪ'kɔːs] *noun* **to decide to have recourse to the courts** = to decide in the end to start legal proceedings

recover [rɪ'kʌvə] *verb* **(a)** to get back something which has been lost; *the initial investment was never recovered*; *to recover damages from the driver of the car*; *to start a court action to recover property* **(b)** to get better or to rise; *the market has not recovered from the rise in oil prices*; *the stock market fell in the morning, but recovered during the afternoon*

recoverable [rɪ'kʌvrəbl] *adjective* which can be got back

recovery [rɪ'kʌvri] *noun* **(a)** getting back something which has been lost or stolen; *we are aiming for the complete recovery of the money invested*; *to start an action for recovery of property* **(b)** movement upwards of shares or of the economy; *the economy showed signs of a recovery*; *the recovery of the economy after a recession*

rectification [rektɪfɪ'keɪʃn] *noun* making changes to a document or register to make it correct

rectify ['rektɪfaɪ] *verb* to make changes to a document to make it correct; to make something correct; *the court rectified its mistake*

recusal [rɪ'kjuːzl] *noun* disqualification of a judge or jury because of bias

red bag ['red 'bæg] *noun* bag in which a barrister carries his gown, given him by a QC; *see also* BLUE BAG

red box ['red 'bɒks] *noun* large briefcase covered in red leather in which government papers are delivered to ministers

redeem [rɪ'diːm] *verb* **(a)** to pay back all the principal and interest on a loan, a debt or a mortgage **(b) to redeem a bond** = to sell a bond for cash

redeemable [rɪ'diːməbl] *adjective* which can be sold for cash; **redeemable preference shares** = preference shares which the company may buy back from the shareholder for cash

redemption [rɪ'dempʃn] *noun* **(a)** repayment of a loan; **redemption date** = date on which a loan, etc., is due to be repaid; **redemption before due date** = paying back a loan before the date when repayment is due; **redemption value** = value of a security when redeemed **(b)** repayment of a debt or a mortgage; **equity of redemption** = right of a mortgagor to redeem the estate by paying off the principal and interest

red tape ['red 'teɪp] *noun* (i) red ribbon used to tie up a pile of legal documents; (ii) rules which slow down administrative work; *the application has been held up by red tape*

reduce [rɪ'djuːs] *verb* to make smaller or lower; *to reduce expenditure on prisons or on crime detection*; *the Appeal Court reduced the fine imposed by the magistrates or reduced the sentence to seven years' imprisonment*

reduced [rɪ'djuːst] *adjective* lower; *he received a reduced sentence on appeal*

redundancy [rɪ'dʌndənsi] *noun* state where someone is no longer employed, because his job is no longer necessary; **redundancy payment** = payment made to a worker to compensate for losing his job; **voluntary redundancy** = situation where the worker asks to be made redundant, usually in return for a payment

redundant [rɪ'dʌndənt] *adjective* **(a)** more than is needed; useless; something which is no longer needed; *this law is now redundant*; *a redundant clause in a contract*; *the new legislation has made clause 6 redundant* **(b) to make someone redundant** = to decide that a worker is not needed any more; **redundant staff** = staff who have lost their jobs because they are not needed any more

re-entry ['riː'entri] *noun* going back into a property; **right of re-entry** = (i) right of a landlord to take back possession of the property if the tenant breaks his agreement; (ii) right of a person resident in a country to go back into that country after leaving it for a time

re-examine ['riːɪg'zæmɪn] *verb (of counsel)* to ask his own witness more questions after the witness has been cross-examined by counsel for the other party

re-examination ['riːɪgzæmɪ'neɪʃn] *noun* asking a witness more questions after cross-examination by counsel for the other party

refer [rɪ'fɜː] *verb* **(a)** to mention, to deal with or to write about something; *we refer to your letter of May 26th*; *he referred to an article which he had seen in 'The Times'*; *referring to the court order dated June 4th*; **the schedule before referred to** = the schedule which has been mentioned earlier **(b)** to pass a problem on to someone else to decide; *to refer a question to a committee*; *we have referred your complaint to the tribunal* **(c) the bank referred the cheque to drawer** = the bank returned the cheque to person who wrote it because there was not enough money in the account to pay it; **'refer to drawer'** = words written on a cheque which a bank refuses to pay **(d)** *(in the EU)* to pass a case to the ECJ for a ruling (NOTE: **referring - referred**)

referee [refə'riː] *noun* **(a)** person who can give a report on someone's character, ability or speed of work, etc.; *to give someone's name as referee*; *she gave the name of her boss as a referee*; *when applying please give the names of three referees* **(b)** person to whom a problem is passed for a decision; *the question of maintenance payments is with a court-appointed referee*; **official referee** = expert judge appointed by the High Court to try complicated, usually technical, cases where specialist knowledge is required

reference ['refrəns] *noun* **(a)** passing a problem to a referee for his opinion; **terms of reference** = areas which a committee or an inspector can deal with; *under the terms of reference of the committee, it cannot investigate complaints from the public; the tribunal's terms of reference do not cover traffic offences* **(b)** mentioning, dealing with; *with reference to your letter of May 25th* **(c)** numbers or letters which make it possible to find a document which has been filed; *our reference: PC/MS 1234; thank you for your letter (reference ABCD) please quote this reference in all correspondence; when replying please quote reference 1234* **(d)** written report on someone's character, ability, etc.; *to write someone a reference or to give someone a reference; to ask applicants to supply references; to ask a company for trade references or for bank references* = to ask for reports from traders or a bank on the company's financial status and reputation; **letter of reference** = letter in which an employer or former employer recommends someone for a job **(e)** *(in the EU) (of the ECJ)* **to hear a reference** = to discuss a legal point which has been referred to them; *(of a national court)* **to make a reference** = to ask the ECJ to decide on a legal point; *see also* PRELIMINARY REFERENCE **(f)** person who reports on someone's character, ability, etc.; *to give someone's name as reference; please use me as a reference if you wish*

referendum [refə'rendəm] *noun* type of vote, where a whole population is asked to vote on a single question; *the government decided to hold a referendum on the abolition of capital punishment* (NOTE: plural is **referenda**)

referral [rɪ'fɜːrəl] *noun* **(a)** passing a problem on to someone else for a decision; *the referral of the case to the planning committee* **(b)** *(in the EU)* action of referring a case to the ECJ

reflag ['riː'flæg] *verb* to register a ship in a different country, giving it the right to fly a different flag

reform [rɪ'fɔːm] **1** *noun* change made to something to make it better; *they have signed an appeal for the reform of the remand system; the reform in the legislation was intended to make the court procedure more straightforward;* **electoral reform** = changing the electoral system to make it fairer; **law reform** = continuing process of revising laws to make them better suited to the needs of society **2** *verb* to change something to make it better; *the group is pressing for the prison system to be reformed; the prisoner has committed so many crimes of violence that he will never be reformed*

refrain [rɪ'freɪn] *verb* **to refrain from something** = to agree not to do something which you were doing previously; *he was asked to give an undertaking to refrain from political activity*

refresher [rɪ'freʃə] *noun* fee paid to counsel for the second and subsequent days of a hearing; *counsel's brief fee was £1,000 with refreshers of £250*

regard [rɪ'gɑːd] *noun* **having regard to** *or* **as regards** *or* **regarding** = concerning, referring to something; *having regard to the opinion of the European Parliament; as regards or regarding the second of the accused, the jury was unable to reach a majority verdict*

regardless [rɪ'gɑːdləs] *adverb* **regardless of** = without concerning; *such conduct constitutes contempt of court regardless of intent; the court takes a serious view of such crimes, regardless of the age of the accused*

regency ['riːdʒənsi] *noun* period of government by a regent; **the Regency** = period between 1811 and 1820 when Britain was ruled by the Prince of Wales in place of his father, King George III, who was believed to be insane

regent ['riːdʒənt] *noun* person who governs in place of a king or queen (usually when the king or queen is a child)

regime [reɪ'ʒiːm] *noun (sometimes as criticism)* **(a)** type of government; *under a* *military regime, civil liberties may be severely curtailed* **(b)** *period of rule; life was better under the previous regime*

Regina [rɪ'dʒaɪnə] *Latin word meaning* 'the Queen': the Crown or state, as a party in legal proceedings (NOTE: in written reports, usually abbreviated to **R: the case of** *R. v. Smith*)

region ['riːdʒən] *noun* large area of a country

regional [riːdʒnl] *adjective* referring to a region; **Regional Council** = unit of local government in Scotland, covering a very large area of the country; **Regional Development Plan** = government scheme to bring industry, jobs, etc., to a depressed area

register ['redʒɪstə] **1** *noun* official list; *to enter something in a register*; *to keep a register up to date*; **companies' register** *or* **register of companies** = list of companies, showing their directors and registered addresses, and statutory information kept at Companies House for public inspection; **register of charges** = index of charges affecting land; **register of debentures** *or* **debenture register** = list of debentures over a company's assets; **register of directors** = official list of the directors of a company which has to be sent to the Registrar of Companies; **register of electors** = list of names and addresses of all people in an area who are entitled to vote in local or national elections; **land register** = list of land, showing who owns it and what buildings are on it; **Lloyd's register** = classified list showing details of all the ships in the world; **register of members** *or* **of shareholders** *or* **share register** = list of shareholders in a company with their addresses **2** *verb* **(a)** to write something in an official list or record; *to register a company*; *to register a sale*; *to register a property*; *to register a trademark*; *to register a marriage* *or* *a death* **(b)** to send (a letter) by registered post; *I registered the letter, because it contained some money*

registered ['redʒɪstəd] *adjective* **(a)** which has been noted on an official list;

registered company = company which has been properly formed and incorporated; **registered land** = land which has been registered with the land registry; **a company's registered office** = the address of a company which is officially registered with the Registrar of Companies and to which certain legal documents must normally be sent; **registered trademark** = trademark which has been officially recorded; **registered user** = person or company which has been officially given a licence to use a registered trademark **(b)** **registered letter** *or* **registered parcel** = letter or parcel which is noted by the post office before it is sent, so that compensation can be claimed if it is lost; *to send documents by registered mail* *or* *registered post*

Register Office ['redʒɪstə 'ɒfɪs] *noun* office where records of births, marriages and deaths are kept and where civil marriages are performed

registrar [redʒɪ'strɑː] *noun* **(a)** person who keeps official records; **Registrar of Companies** = official who keeps a record of all companies which have been incorporated, with details of directors and turnover; **registrar of trademarks** = official who keeps a record of all trademarks **(b)** official of a court who can hear preliminary arguments in civil cases **(c)** **district registrar** = official who registers births, marriages and deaths in a certain area **(d)** *(in the EU)* head of the registry of the European Court of Justice (he is the manager of the court, and maintains the files of all pleadings)

Registrar-General [redʒɪ'strɑː 'dʒenrl] *noun* official who is responsible for registry offices and the registering of births, marriages and deaths

registration [redʒɪ'streɪʃn] *noun* **(a)** act of having something noted on an official list; *registration of a trademark* *or* *of a share transaction*; **certificate of registration** *or* **registration certificate** = document showing that an item has been registered; **registration fee** = (i) money paid to have something registered, (ii) money paid to attend a conference; **registration number** = official number of something which has been registered (such as the number of a car) **(b) land registration** = system of registering land and its owners

registry ['redʒɪstri] *noun* **(a)** place where official records are kept; **Land Registry** = British government office where details of land and its ownership are kept; **probate registry** = court office which deals with the granting of probate; **district registry** *or* **registry office** = office where records of births, marriages and deaths are kept **(b)** registering of a ship; **certificate of registry** = document showing that a ship has been officially registered; **port of registry** *or* **registry port** = port where a ship is registered **(c)** *(in the EU)* office which administers the ECJ

regulate ['regjuleɪt] *verb* **(a)** to adjust something so that it works well or is correct **(b)** to change or maintain something by law; **prices are regulated by supply and demand** = prices are increased or lowered according to supply and demand; **government-regulated price** = price which is imposed by the government; **regulated tenancy** = PROTECTED TENANCY

regulation [regju'leɪʃn] *noun* act of making sure that something will work well; *the regulation of trading practices*

regulations [regju'leɪʃnz] *plural noun* **(a)** laws, rules made by ministers, which then have to be submitted to Parliament for approval; *the new government regulations on standards for electrical goods*; *safety regulations which apply to places of work*; *regulations concerning imports and exports*; **fire regulations** = local or national regulations which owners of buildings used by the public have to obey in order to be granted a fire certificate **(b)** rules laid down by the Council or Commission of the European Communities, according to the European Union treaties, which are binding on all states that are members of the EU; *compare* DIRECTIVES

COMMENT: regulations are binding on people in general as citizens of Member States of the EU; they have a direct effect on all Member States and on all citizens of Member States

regulatory ['regjələtri] *adjective* which regulates, which makes something work according to law; *the independent radio and television companies are supervised by a regulatory body*; *complaints are referred to several regulatory bodies*

rehabilitate [riːhə'bɪlɪteɪt] *verb* to make (a criminal) fit to become a member of society again

rehabilitation [riːhəbɪlɪ'teɪʃn] *noun* making someone fit to be a member of society again; **rehabilitation of offenders** = principle whereby a person convicted of a crime and being of good character after a period of time is treated as if he had not had a conviction

COMMENT: by the Rehabilitation of Offenders Act, 1974, a person who is convicted of an offence, and then spends a period of time without committing any other offence, is not required to reveal that he has a previous conviction

rehear [riː'hɪə] *verb* to hear a case again (as when the first hearing was in some way invalid)

rehearing [riː'hɪərɪŋ] *noun* hearing of a case again

reign [reɪn] *noun* period of time when someone is King or Queen; *an Act dating back to the reign of Queen Victoria*

reinsurance [riːɪn'ʃuərəns] *noun* insurance where a second insurer (the reinsurer) agrees to cover part of the risk insured by the first insurer

reject [rɪ'dʒekt] *verb* to refuse to accept, to say that something is not satisfactory; *the appeal was rejected by the House of Lords*; *the union rejected the management's proposals*; *the magistrate* *rejected a request from the defendant*; **the company rejected the takeover bid** = the directors recommended that the shareholders should not accept the bid

rejection [rɪ'dʒektʃn] *noun* refusal to accept; *the rejection of the defendant's request*; *the rejection of the appeal by the tribunal*

rejoinder [rɪ'dʒɔɪndə] *noun* formerly, a pleading served in answer to a claimant's reply

related [rɪ'leɪtɪd] *adjective* connected, linked, being of the same family; *offences related to drugs or drug-related offences*; *the law which relates to drunken driving*; **related company** = company which is partly owned by another company; **earnings-related pension** = pension which is linked to the size of the salary

relation [rɪ'leɪʃn] *noun* **(a)** **in relation to** = referring to or connected with; *documents in relation to the case*; *the court's powers in relation to children in care* **(b)** **relation back** = the ability of the administrator of an estate to take action to recover funds which were removed from the estate in the interval between the death and the grant of administration **(c)** **relations** = links (with other people or other companies); **to enter into relations with someone** = to start discussing a business deal with someone; **to break off relations with someone** = to stop dealing with someone; **industrial relations** *or* **labour relations** = relations between management and workers

relator ['rɪ'leɪtə] *noun* private person who suggests to the Attorney-General that proceedings should be brought (usually against a public body)

release [rɪ'li:s] **1** *noun* **(a)** setting (someone) free, allowing someone to leave prison; **release on licence** = allowing a prisoner to leave prison on parole; **day release** = arrangement whereby a company allows a worker to go to college to study for one day each week **(b)** abandoning of rights by someone in favour of someone else **(c)** **press release** = sheet giving news

about something which is sent to newspapers and TV and radio stations so that they can use the information in it; *the company sent out or issued a press release about the launch of the new car* **2** *verb* **(a)** to free (someone or something), to allow (someone) to leave prison; *the president released the opposition leader from prison*; *customs released the goods against payment of a fine*; **to release someone from a debt** *or* **from a contract** = to make someone no longer liable for the debt or for the obligations under the contract **(b)** to make something public; *the company released information about the new mine in Australia*; *the government has refused to release figures for the number of unemployed women*

relevance ['reləvəns] *noun* connection with a subject being discussed; *counsel argued with the judge over the relevance of the documents to the case*

relevant ['reləvənt] *adjective* which has to do with what is being discussed; *the question is not relevant to the case*; *which is the relevant government department?*; *can you give me the relevant papers?*

reliable [rɪ'laɪəbl] *adjective* which can be trusted; *she is a reliable witness*; *the witness is completely reliable*; *the police have reliable information about the gang's movements*

relief [rɪ'li:f] *noun* **(a)** remedy sought by a claimant in a legal action; *the relief the claimant sought was an injunction and damages* **(b)** help; **ancillary relief** = financial provision or adjustment of property rights ordered by a court for a spouse or child in divorce proceedings; **mortgage (interest) relief** = allowing someone to pay no tax on the interest payments on a mortgage up to a certain level; **tax relief** = allowing someone to pay less tax on certain parts of his income

rem [rem] *see* ACTION, IN REM

remainder [rɪ'meɪndə] **1** *noun* **(a)** things left behind; *the remainder of the stock will be sold off at half price*; **remainders** = new books sold cheaply **(b)**

what is left of an estate, or the right to an estate which will return to the owner at the end of a lease; **contingent remainder** = remainder which is contingent upon something happening in the future; **interest in remainder** = interest in land which will come into someone's possession when another person's interest ends; **vested remainder** = remainder which is vested in someone because the identity of that person has been established; *see also* REVERSION 2 *verb* **to remainder books** = to sell new books off cheaply

remainderman [rɪ'meɪndəmæn] *noun* person who receives the remainder of an estate

remand [rɪ'mɑːnd] **1** *noun* sending a prisoner away for a time when a case is adjourned to be heard at a later date; **prisoner on remand** *or* **remand prisoner** = prisoner who has been told to reappear in court at a later date; **remand centre** = special prison for keeping young persons who have been remanded in custody **2** *verb* **(a)** to send (a prisoner) away to reappear later to answer a case which has been adjourned; **he was remanded in custody** *or* **remanded on bail for two weeks** = he was sent to prison *or* allowed to go free on payment of bail while waiting to return to court two weeks later **(b)** *US* to send a case back to a lower court after a higher court has given an opinion on it

remedy ['remədi] **1** *noun* way of repairing harm or damage suffered; *the claimant is seeking remedy through the courts* **2** *verb* to help repair harm or damage

remission [rɪ'mɪʃn] *noun* reduction of a prison sentence; *he was sentenced to five years, but should serve only three with remission; she got six months' remission for good behaviour*

remit 1 ['riːmɪt] *noun* area of responsibility given to someone; *this department can do nothing on the case as it is not part of our remit or it is beyond our remit* **2** [rɪ'mɪt] *verb* **(a)** to reduce (a prison

sentence) **(b)** to send (money); *to remit by cheque* (NOTE: **remitting - remitted**)

remittance [rɪ'mɪtəns] *noun* money which is sent; *please send remittances to the treasurer; the family lives on a weekly remittance from their father in the USA*

remote [rɪ'məut] *adjective* too far to be connected; *the court decided that the damage was too remote to be recoverable by the claimant*

remoteness [rɪ'məutnəs] *noun* being too far to be connected; **remoteness of damage** = legal principle that damage that is insufficiently connected or foreseeable by a defendant should not make the defendant liable to the claimant

render ['rendə] *verb* to make (someone or something) be; *failure to observe the conditions of bail renders the accused liable to arrest; the state of health of the witness renders his appearance in court impossible*

renew [rɪ'njuː] *verb* to grant something again so that it continues for a further period of time; *to renew a bill of exchange or to renew a lease*; **to renew a subscription** = to pay a subscription for another year; **to renew an insurance policy** = to pay the premium for another year's insurance

renewal [rɪ'njuːəl] *noun* act of renewing; *renewal of a lease or of a subscription or of a bill; the lease is up for renewal next month; when is the renewal date of the bill?*; **renewal notice** = note sent by an insurance company asking the insured person to renew the insurance; **renewal premium** = premium to be paid to renew an insurance

renounce [rɪ'nauns] *verb* to give up a right or a planned action; *the government has renounced the use of force in dealing with international terrorists*

rent [rent] *noun* money paid (or occasionally a service provided) for the use of an office, house or factory for a period of time; **high rent** *or* **low rent** = expensive or cheap rent; *to pay three months' rent in* *advance*; **back rent** = rent owed; **ground rent** = rent paid by the lessee to the ground landlord; **nominal rent** = very small rent; **rent action** = proceedings to obtain payment of rent owing; **rent allowance** *or* **rent rebate** = state subsidy paid to people who do not have enough income to pay their rents; **rent controls** = government regulation of rents charged by landlords; **income from rents** *or* **rent income** = income from letting office, houses, etc.; **rent review** = increase in rents which is carried out during the term of a lease (most leases allow for rents to be reviewed every three or five years); **rent tribunal** = court which adjudicates in disputes about rents and awards fair rents

rental ['rentl] *noun* money paid to use an office, house, factory, car or piece of equipment, etc., for a period of time; **rental income** *or* **income from rentals** = income from letting offices, houses, etc.; **rental value** = full value of the rent for a property if it were charged at the current market rate (i.e., calculated between rent reviews)

rentcharge ['rentʃɑːdʒ] *noun* payment of rental on freehold land

> COMMENT: rare except in the case of covenants involving land

renunciation [rɪnʌnsi'eɪʃn] *noun* act of giving up a right, especially the ownership of shares; **letter of renunciation** = form sent with new shares, which allows the person who has been allotted the shares to refuse to accept them and so sell them to someone else

reoffend [riːə'fend] *verb* to commit an offence again; *he came out of prison and immediately reoffended*

reoffender [riːə'fendə] *noun* person who commits an offence again

reopen [riː'əupn] *verb* to start investigating (a case) again; to start (a hearing) again; *after receiving new evidence, the police have reopened the murder inquiry*; *the hearing reopened on Monday afternoon*

reorganization [riːɔːgənaɪ'zeɪʃn] *noun* action of organizing a company in a different way (as in the USA, when a bankrupt company applies to be treated under Chapter 11 to be protected from its creditors while it is being reorganized)

repair [rɪ'peə] **1** *noun* **(a)** mending something which is damaged; *the landlord carried out repairs to the roof*; *the bill for repairs to the car came to £250* **(b)** state of **repair** = physical condition of something; *the house was in a bad state of repair when he bought it* **2** *verb* to mend something which is damaged or broken; **full repairing lease** = lease where the tenant has to pay for all repairs to the property

repairer [rɪ'peərə] *noun* person who repairs; **repairer's lien** = right of someone who has been carrying out repairs to keep the goods until the repair bill has been paid

repatriate [riː'pætrɪeɪt] *verb* to force someone to leave the country he is living in and go back to his own country

repatriation [riːpætri'eɪʃn] *noun* **(a)** forcing someone to return to his own country **(b)** return of foreign investments, profits, etc., to the home country of their owner

repeal [rɪ'piːl] **1** *noun* doing away with a law so that it is no longer valid; *MPs are pressing for the repeal of the Immigration Act* **2** *verb* to do away with (a law); *the Bill seeks to repeal the existing legislation*; *Member States must repeal national legislation which conflicts with Community legislation*

> COMMENT: since the UK does not have a written constitution, all EC law has to be incorporated into UK law by acts of Parliament. Since no act of one parliament can be considered binding on another parliament, these acts can in theory be repealed by subsequent parliaments. No parliament can bind subsequent parliaments to the principle of the supremacy of EC law

repeat [rɪ'piːt] *verb* **to repeat an offence** = to commit an offence again

repetition [repɪˈtɪʃn] *noun* act of repeating something; *repetition of a libel is an offence*

replevin [rɪˈplevɪn] *noun* action brought to obtain possession of goods which have been seized, by paying off a judgment debt

reply [rɪˈplaɪ] **1** *noun* (i) written statement by a claimant in a civil case in answer to the defendant's defence (the reply must be filed at the same time as the claimant files his allocation questionnaire); (ii) speech by prosecution counsel or counsel for the claimant which answers claims made by the defence; **right of reply** = right of someone to answer claims made by an opponent; *he demanded the right of reply to the newspaper allegations* **2** *verb* to answer claims made by an opponent; to give an opposing view in a discussion

report [rɪˈpɔːt] **1** *noun* **(a)** statement describing what has happened or describing a state of affairs; *to make a report or to present a report or to send in a report; the court heard a report from the probation officer; the chairman has received a report from the insurance company;* **the company's annual report** *or* **the chairman's report** *or* **the directors' report** = document sent each year by the chairman of a company or the directors to the shareholders, explaining what the company has done during the year; **confidential report** = secret document which must not be shown to other than a few named persons; **Law Reports** = collection of reports of cases which are legal precedents; **progress report** = document which describes what progress has been made; **the treasurer's report** = document from the honorary treasurer of a society to explain the financial state of the society to its members **(b) a report in a newspaper** *or* **a newspaper report** = article or news item; *can you confirm the report that charges are likely to be brought?* **(c)** official document from a government committee; *the government has issued a report on the problems of inner city violence* **2** *verb* to make a statement describing something; *the probation officer reported on the progress*

of the two young criminals; he reported the damage to the insurance company; we asked the bank to report on his financial status; **reporting restrictions** = restrictions on information about a case which can be reported in newspapers; **reporting restrictions were lifted** = journalists were allowed to report details of the case

reported case [rɪˈpɔːtɪd ˈkeɪs] *noun* case which has been reported in the Law Reports because of its importance as a precedent

Report Stage [rɪˈpɔːt ˈsteɪdʒ] *noun* stage in the discussion of a Bill in the House of Commons, where the amendments proposed at Committee Stage are debated by the whole House of Commons

repossess [riːpəˈzes] *verb* to take back an item which someone is buying under a hire-purchase agreement or a property which someone is buying under a mortgage (because the purchaser cannot continue the repayments)

repossession [riːpəˈzeʃn] *noun* act of repossessing, such as taking possession of a mortgaged property where the purchaser cannot continue the mortgage repayments

represent [reprɪˈzent] *verb* **(a)** to state or to show; *he was represented as a man of great honour* **(b)** to act on behalf of someone; *the defendant is represented by his solicitor* **(c)** to be the elected representative of an area (in Parliament or on a council); *he represents one of the Northern industrial constituencies*

representation [reprɪzenˈteɪʃn] *noun* **(a)** statement, especially a statement made to persuade someone to enter into a contract; **false representation** = offence of making a wrong statement which misleads someone **(b) to make representations** = to complain **(c)** being represented by a lawyer; **the applicant had no legal representation** = he had no lawyer to represent him in court **(d)** system where the people of a country elect representatives to a Parliament which governs the country;

the **Representation of the People Act** = Act of Parliament which states how elections must be organized; *see also* PROPORTIONAL

representative [reprɪ'zentətɪv] *noun* **(a)** person who represents another person; *the court heard the representative of the insurance company*; **lay representative** = any person representing someone in a case in the small claims track who is not a solicitor, barrister or legal executive; **legal representative** = barrister, solicitor, or legal executive, who acts on behalf of a party in a case; **personal representative** = person who is the executor of a will or who is the administrator of the estate of a deceased person **(b)** *US* member of the lower house of Congress; **House of Representatives** = lower house of the American Congress (NOTE: a Representative is also referred to as a **Congressman**)

reprieve [rɪ'priːv] **1** *noun* temporarily stopping the carrying out of a sentence or court order **2** *verb* to stop a sentence or order being carried out; *he was sentenced to death but was reprieved by the president*

reprimand ['reprɪmɑːnd] **1** *noun* official criticism; *the police officer received an official reprimand after the inquiry into the accident* **2** *verb* to criticize someone officially; *he was reprimanded by the magistrate*

reproduction [riːprə'dʌkʃn] *noun* making a copy of something; *the reproduction of copyright material without the permission of the copyright holder is banned by law*; **mechanical reproduction rights** = right to make a recording of a piece of music, right to make a copy of a printed document by photographing it (against payment of a fee)

republic [rɪ'pʌblɪk] *noun* state which is not a monarchy, but which is governed by elected representatives headed by a President; *Singapore was declared a republic in 1965*; *most republics have Presidents as head of state*

republican [rɪ'pʌblɪkən] *adjective* **(a)** referring to a republic **(b)** believing in the idea of a republic; *some members of the Opposition have republican sympathies*

republication [riːpʌblɪ'keɪʃn] *noun* action of republishing a will

republish [riː'pʌblɪʃ] *verb* to make an existing will valid again from the date of republication (this makes possessions acquired since the will was originally made fall within the dispositions of the will)

repudiate [rɪ'pjuːdieɪt] *verb* to refuse to accept; **to repudiate an agreement** *or* **a contract** = to refuse to perform one's obligations under an agreement or contract

repudiation [rɪpjuːdi'eɪʃn] *noun* **(a)** refusal to accept **(b)** refusal to perform one's obligations under an agreement or contract

reputable ['repjutəbl] *adjective* with a good reputation; *we use only reputable carriers*; *a reputable firm of accountants*

reputation [repju'teɪʃn] *noun* opinion of someone or something held by other people; *company with a reputation for quality*; *he has a reputation for being difficult to negotiate with*

request [rɪ'kwest] **1** *noun* asking for something to be done; *the party was served a written request for further information*; **letter of request** = ROGATORY LETTER **2** *verb* to ask for something; **requesting state** = state which is seeking the extradition of someone from another state

require [rɪ'kwaɪə] *verb* to ask for or to demand something; *to require a full explanation of expenditure*; *the law requires you to submit all income to the tax authorities*; *the Bill requires social workers to seek the permission of the juvenile court before taking action*

requirement [rɪ'kwaɪəmənt] *noun* what is needed; *see also* PUBLIC SECTOR

requisition [rekwɪ'zɪʃn] **1** *noun* **requisition on title** = asking the vendor of a property for details of his title to the property **2** *verb* to take (private property) into the ownership of the state for the state to use; *the army requisitioned all the trucks to carry supplies*

res [reɪz] *Latin word meaning* 'thing' or 'matter'

resale ['riːseɪl] *noun* selling goods again, after buying them (as when a retailer sells goods he has bought from a wholesaler)

resale price maintenance (RPM)
['riːseɪl 'praɪs 'meɪntnəns] *noun* system where the price for an item is fixed by the manufacturer and the retailer is not allowed to sell it for a lower price

> COMMENT: this system applies in the UK to certain products only, such as newspapers

rescind [rɪ'sɪnd] *verb* to annul or to cancel; *to rescind a contract or an agreement; the committee rescinded its earlier resolution on the use of council premises*

rescission [rɪ'sɪʃn] *noun* **(a)** cancellation of a contract **(b)** *US* item in an appropriation bill which cancels money previously appropriated but not spent

rescue ['reskjuː] *verb* to save someone from injury or death

> COMMENT: if a rescuer is injured while rescuing someone from danger caused by the defendant's negligence, the defendant is liable for damages to the rescuer as well as to the person rescued

reservation [rezə'veɪʃn] *noun* keeping something back; **reservation of title clause** = clause in a contract whereby the seller provides that title to the goods does not pass to the buyer until the buyer has paid for them; *see also* ROMALPA CLAUSE

reserve [rɪ'zɜːv] **1** *noun* **(a)** money from profits not paid as dividend, but kept back by a company in case it is needed for a special purpose; **bank reserves** = cash and securities held by a bank to cover deposits; **cash reserves** = a company's reserves in cash deposits or bills kept in case of urgent

need; **contingency reserve** *or* **emergency reserve** = money set aside in case it is needed urgently; **reserve for bad debts** = money kept by a company to cover debts which may not be paid; **hidden reserves** = illegal reserves which are not declared in the company's balance sheet; **reserve fund** = profits in a business which have not been paid out as dividend but which have been ploughed back into the business **(b)** **reserve currency** = strong currency held by other countries to support their own weaker currencies; **currency reserves** = foreign money held by a government to support its own currency and to pay its debts; **a country's foreign currency reserves** = a country's reserves in currencies of other countries **(c)** **in reserve** = kept to be used at a later date **(d)** **reserve (price)** = lowest price which a seller will accept at an auction; *the painting was withdrawn when it did not reach its reserve* **2** *verb* **(a)** to reserve a room *or* a table *or* a seat = to book a room, table, seat; to ask for a room, table or seat to be kept free for you; *I want to reserve a table for four people; can your secretary reserve a seat for me on the train to Glasgow?* **(b)** to keep back; **to reserve one's defence** = not to present any defence at a preliminary hearing, but to wait until full trial; **to reserve judgment** = not to pass judgment immediately, but keep it back until later so that the judge has time to consider the case; **to reserve the right to do something** = to indicate that you consider that you have the right to do something, and intend to use that right in the future; *he reserved the right to cross-examine witnesses; we reserve the right to appeal against the tribunal's decision*

res gestae [reɪz 'dʒestaɪ] *Latin phrase meaning* 'things which have been done'

reside [rɪ'zaɪd] *verb* to live in a place; *(in the EU)* **right to reside** = one of the fundamental rights of EU citizens and workers, the right of any EU citizen to live in another EU state

residence ['rezɪdəns] *noun* **(a)** place where someone lives; *he has a country* *residence where he spends his weekends* **(b)** act of living or operating officially in a country; **residence permit** = official document allowing a foreigner to live in a country; *he has applied for a residence permit*; *she was granted a residence permit for one year*

COMMENT: in the European Union, a residence permit is a document which permits the holder to live in a country while not being a citizen of that country. Normally a residence permit is valid for five years and can be renewed automatically. A residence permit is not withdrawn if the person becomes unemployed involuntarily (if a worker gives up his job and makes no effort to find another, his residence permit may be withdrawn)

resident ['rezɪdənt] **1** *adjective* living or operating in a country; *the company is resident in France*; **person ordinarily resident in the UK** = person who normally lives in the UK; **resident alien** = alien who has permission to live in a country without having citizenship **2** *noun* **(a)** person living in a country; **non-resident** = person or company which is not officially resident in a country; *he has a non-resident account with a French bank*; *she was granted a non-resident visa* **(b)** (i) title of a diplomat of lower rank than an Ambassador, living in a foreign country; (ii) governor of a colony

residual [rɪ'zɪdjuəl] *adjective* remaining after everything else has gone

residuary [rɪ'zɪdjuəri] *adjective* referring to what is left; **residuary body** = body set up to administer the ending of a local authority and to manage those of its functions which have not been handed over to other authorities; **residuary devisee** = person who receives the rest of the land when the other bequests have been made; **residuary estate** = (i) estate of a dead person which has not been bequeathed in his will; (ii) what remains of an estate after the debts have been paid and bequests have been made; **residuary legatee** = person who receives the rest of the personal property after specific legacies have been made

residue ['rezɪdju:] *noun* what is left over, especially what is left of an estate after debts and bequests have been made; *after paying various bequests the residue of his estate was split between his children*

resign [rɪ'zaɪn] *verb* to leave a job; *he resigned from his post as treasurer*; *he has resigned with effect from July 1st*; *she resigned as Education Minister*

resignation [rezɪg'neɪʃn] *noun* act of giving up a job; *the newspaper published the Minister's letter of resignation and the Prime Minister's reply*; *he wrote his letter of resignation to the chairman*; **to hand in** *or* **to give in** *or* **to send in one's resignation** = to resign from a job

COMMENT: MPs are not allowed to resign their seats in the House of Commons. If an MP wants to leave the House, he has to apply for an office of profit under the Crown, such as the Stewardship of the Chiltern Hundreds, which will disqualify him from membership of the House of Commons

res ipsa loquitur ['reɪz 'ɪpsə 'lɒkwɪtə] *Latin phrase meaning* 'the matter speaks for itself': situation where the facts seem so obvious, that it is for the defendant to prove he was not negligent, rather than for the claimant to prove his claim

resist [rɪ'zɪst] *verb* to fight against something, not to give in to something; *the accused resisted all attempts to make him confess*; *the company is resisting the takeover bid*; **resisting arrest** = offence of refusing to allow oneself to be arrested

res judicata ['reɪz dʒu:dɪ'kætə] *Latin phrase meaning* 'matter on which a judgment has been given'

resolution [rezə'lu:ʃn] *noun* **(a)** action of solving a dispute; *the aim of the small claims track is the rapid resolution of disputes* **(b)** decision taken at a meeting of the United Nations Security Council **(c)** *US* **joint resolution** = Bill passed by both

House and Senate, sent to the President for signature to become law **(d)** decision taken at a meeting, especially a meeting of shareholders; **to put a resolution to a meeting** = to ask a meeting to approve a resolution; **ordinary resolution** = decision which is taken by a majority vote of shareholders; **extraordinary** *or* **special resolution** = resolution (such as a change to the articles of a company) which requires the holders of 75% of the shares to vote for it

COMMENT: there are three types or resolution which can be put to an AGM: the 'ordinary resolution', usually referring to some general procedural matter, and which requires a simple majority of votes; and the 'extraordinary resolution' and 'special resolution', such as a resolution to change a company's articles of association in some way, both of which need 75% of the votes before they can be carried

resort [rɪˈzɔːt] **1** *noun* **court of last resort** = highest court from which no appeals are allowed; **lender of the last resort** = central bank which lends money to commercial banks **2** *verb* **to resort to** = to come to use; *he had to resort to threats of court action to get repayment of the money owing*; *workers must not resort to violence in industrial disputes*

respect [rɪˈspekt] *noun* **with respect to** *or* **in respect of** = concerning; *his right to an indemnity in respect of earlier disbursements*; *the defendant counterclaimed for loss and damage in respect of a machine sold to him by the claimant*

respondeat superior [rɪˈspɒndeɪæt suˈpɪərɪɔː] *Latin phrase meaning* 'let the superior be responsible': rule that a principal is responsible for actions of the agent or the employer for actions of the employee

respondent [rɪˈspɒndənt] *noun* (i) the other side in a case which is the subject of an appeal; (ii) person against whom an order is sought (by an application notice);

(iii) person who answers a petition, especially one who is being sued for divorce; *see also* CO-RESPONDENT

response [rɪˈspɒns] *noun* reply, especially a reply to a written request for further information

responsibility [rɪspɒnsəˈbɪlɪti] *noun* **(a)** duty, thing which you are responsible for doing; *he finds the responsibilities of being managing director too heavy*; *keeping the interior of the building in good order is the responsibility of the tenant* **(b)** being responsible; *there is no responsibility on the company's part for loss of customers' property*; *the management accepts full responsibility for loss of goods in storage*; **collective responsibility** = doctrine that all members of a group (such as the British cabinet) are responsible together for the actions of that group; **age of criminal responsibility** = age at which a person is considered to be capable of committing a crime; **diminished responsibility** = state of mind of a criminal (inherited or caused by illness or injury) which means that he cannot be held responsible for a crime he has committed

responsible [rɪˈspɒnsɪbl] *adjective* **(a)** **responsible for** = directing, being in charge of or being in control of; *the tenant is responsible for all repairs to the building*; *the consignee is held responsible for the goods he has received on consignment*; *she was responsible for a series of thefts from offices* **(b)** **responsible to someone** = being under someone's authority; *magistrates are responsible to the Lord Chancellor* **(c)** **responsible government** = form of government which acts in accordance with the wishes of the people and which is accountable to Parliament for its actions; **a responsible job** = job where important decisions have to be taken or where the employee has many responsibilities

restitutio in integrum [restɪˈtuːtiəʊ ɪn ɪnˈtegrəm] *Latin phrase meaning* 'returning everything to the state as it was before'

restitution [restɪ'tjuːʃn] *noun* **(a)** giving back, the return of property which has been illegally obtained; *the court ordered the restitution of assets to the company*; **restitution order** = court order asking for property to be returned to someone **(b)** compensation or payment for damage or loss **(c)** *(in the EC)* **export restitution** = subsidies to European food exporters

restrain [rɪ'streɪn] *verb* **(a)** to control or to hold someone back; *the prisoner fought and had to be restrained by two policemen* **(b)** to tell someone not to do something; *the court granted the claimant an injunction restraining the defendant from breaching copyright*

restraining order [rɪ'streɪnɪŋ 'ɔːdə] *noun* court order which tells a defendant not to do something while the court is still taking a decision

restraint [rɪ'streɪnt] *noun* control; **pay restraint** *or* **wage restraint** = keeping increases in wages under control

restraint of trade [rɪ'streɪnt əv 'treɪd] *noun* **(i)** situation where a worker is not allowed to move to another job in the same trade (where the experience he has acquired with his present employer might prove useful); **(ii)** attempt by companies to fix prices, create monopolies or reduce competition, which could affect free trade

restriction [rɪ'strɪkʃn] *noun* limit, act of controlling; **to impose restrictions on imports** *or* **on credit** = to start limiting imports or credit; **to lift credit restrictions** = to allow credit to be given freely; **reporting restrictions** = restrictions on information about a case which can be reported in newspapers; **reporting restrictions were lifted** = journalists were allowed to report details of the case

restrictive [rɪ'strɪktɪv] *adjective* which limits; **restrictive covenant** = clause in a contract which prevents someone from doing something; **restrictive practices** = ways of working which exclude free competition in relation to the supply of goods or labour in order to maintain prices or wages; **Restrictive Practices Court** = court which decides in cases of restrictive practices

résumé ['reɪzumeɪ] *noun US* summary of a person's life story with details of education and work experience (NOTE: British English is **curriculum vitae**)

retail ['riːteɪl] *noun* sale of small quantities of goods to individual customers; **retail price** = price to the individual customer; *see also* WHOLESALE

retailer ['riːteɪlə] *noun* person who runs a retail business, selling goods to the public

retain [rɪ'teɪn] *verb* **(a)** to keep; *out of the profits, the company has retained £50,000 as provision against bad debts*; **retained income** = profit not distributed to the shareholders as dividend **(b) to retain a lawyer to act for you** = to agree with a lawyer that he will act for you (and pay him a fee in advance)

retainer [rɪ'teɪnə] *noun* **(a)** fee paid to a barrister **(b)** money paid in advance to someone so that he will work for you when required, and not for someone else; *we pay him a retainer of £1,000 per annum*

retiral [rɪ'taɪrəl] *noun US & Scottish* = RETIREMENT

retire [rɪ'taɪə] *verb* **(a)** to stop work and take a pension; *she retired with a £6,000 pension*; *the chairman of the company retired at the age of 65*; *the shop is owned by a retired policeman*; **retiring age** = age at which people retire (in the UK usually 65 for men and 60 for women) **(b)** to make a worker stop work and take a pension; *they decided to retire all staff over 50 years of age* **(c)** to come to the end of an elected term of office; *the treasurer retires after six years*; *two retiring directors offer themselves for re-election* **(d)** to go away from a court for a period of time; *the magistrates retired to consider their verdict*; *the jury retired for four hours*

retirement [rɪ'taɪəmənt] *noun* **(a)** act of retiring from work; **to take early retirement** = to leave work before the usual age; **retirement age** = age at which people retire (in the UK usually 65 for men and 60 for women); **retirement pension =** pension which someone receives when he or she retires; **retirement plan =** plan set up to provide a pension for someone when he or she retires; *US* **individual retirement account (IRA) =** private pension plan, where individuals can make contributions which are separate from a company pension plan (the British equivalent is a personal pension plan) **(b)** *(of a jury)* going out of the courtroom to consider their verdict

retrial [riː'traɪəl] *noun* new trial; *the Court of Appeal ordered a retrial*

retroactive [retrəʊ'æktɪv] *adjective* which takes effect from a time in the past; *they received a pay rise retroactive to last January*

retroactively [retrəʊ'æktɪvli] *adverb* going back to a time in the past

retrospective [retrə'spektɪv] *adjective* going back in time; *legislation is enacted with the presumption that it should not be retrospective*; **retrospective legislation =** Act of Parliament which applies to the period before the Act was passed; **with retrospective effect =** applying to a past period; *the tax ruling has retrospective effect*

retrospectively [retrə'spektɪvli] *adverb* in a retrospective way; *the ruling is applied retrospectively*

retry [riː'traɪ] *verb* to try a case a second time; *the court ordered the case to be retried*

return [rɪ'tɜːn] **1** *noun* **(a)** sending back; *he replied by return of post =* he replied by the next post service back; **return address =** address to send back something; **these goods are all on sale or return =** if the retailer does not sell them, he sends them back to the supplier, and pays only for the items sold **(b)** profit or income from money invested; **return on investment** *or* **on capital =** profit shown as a percentage of money invested; **rate of return =** amount of interest or dividend produced by

an investment, shown as a percentage **(c)** **official return =** official report or statement; **to make a return to the tax office** *or* **to make an income tax return =** to send a statement of income to the tax office; **to fill in a VAT return =** to complete the form showing VAT income and expenditure; **annual return =** form to be completed by each company once a year, giving details of the directors and the financial state of the company; **nil return =** report showing no sales, no income, no tax, etc. **(d)** election of an MP **2** *verb* **(a)** to make a statement; **to return income of £15,000 to the tax authorities =** to notify the tax authorities that you have an income of £15,000; *(of a jury)* **to return a verdict =** to state the verdict at the end of a trial; *the jury returned a verdict of not guilty* **(b)** to elect an MP for a constituency; *he was returned with an increased majority*

returning officer [rɪ'tɜːnɪŋ 'ɒfɪsə] *noun* official (usually a High Sheriff or mayor) who superintends a parliamentary election in a constituency, receives the nominations of candidates and announces the result of the vote

---

COMMENT: when a writ for an election is issued by the Lord Chancellor, the returning officer for each constituency must give notice of the election, and candidates may be nominated up to eight days after the writs are issued

---

reus ['reɪəs] *see* ACTUS REUS

revenue [revənjuː] *noun* money earned, income; **Inland Revenue,** *US* **Internal Revenue Service (IRS) =** government department dealing with tax; *to make a declaration to the Inland Revenue*; **revenue officer =** person working in a government tax office

reversal [rɪ'vɜːsl] *noun* **(a)** change of a decision to the opposite; *the reversal of the High Court ruling by the Court of Appeal* **(b)** change from being profitable to unprofitable; *the company suffered a reversal in the Far East*

reverse [rɪ'vɜːs] **1** *adjective* opposite, in the opposite direction; **reverse takeover =** takeover where the company which has been taken over ends up owning the company which has taken it over; **reverse charge call =** telephone call where the person receiving the call agrees to pay for it **2** *verb* to change a decision to the opposite one; *the Appeal Court reversed the decision of the High Court*

reversion [rɪ'vɜːʃn] *noun* return of property to an original owner when a lease expires; **he has the reversion of the estate =** he will receive the estate when the present lease ends or when the present owner dies

reversionary [rɪ'vɜːʃnri] *adjective* (property) which passes to another owner on the death of the present one; **reversionary annuity =** annuity paid to someone on the death of another person; **reversionary right =** right of a writer's heir to his copyrights after his death; *see also* REMAINDER

revert [rɪ'vɜːt] *verb* to go back to the previous state or owner; *the property reverts to its original owner in 2010*

review [rɪ'vjuː] **1** *noun* general examination of something again; *to conduct a review of sentencing policy*; *the coroner asked for a review of police procedures*; **financial review =** examination of an organization's finances; **judicial review =** review by a higher court of the actions of a lower court or of an administrative body; **wage review** *or* **salary review =** examination of salaries or wages in a company to see if the workers should earn more **2** *verb* to examine something generally; *a committee has been appointed to review judicial salaries*; *the High Court has reviewed the decision*

revise [rɪ'vaɪz] *verb* to change (a text or a decision) after considerable thought; *the judge revised his earlier decision not to consider a submission from defence counsel*

revision [rɪ'vɪʒn] *noun* act of changing something; *the Lord Chancellor has proposed a revision of the divorce procedures*

revival [rɪ'vaɪvl] *noun* making valid again a will that has been revoked but not destroyed

revive [rɪ'vaɪv] *verb* to make a revoked will become valid again

revocable ['revəkbl] *adjective* which can be revoked (NOTE: the opposite is irrevocable)

revocandi [revə'kændi] *see* ANIMUS

revocation [revə'keɪʃn] *noun* cancelling or annulment (of permission, right, agreement, offer or will)

COMMENT: a will may be revoked by marriage, by writing another will which changes the dispositions of the first one, or by destroying the will intentionally

revoke [rɪ'vəʊk] *verb* to cancel or to annul (a permission, right, agreement, offer or will); *to revoke a clause in an agreement*; *the treaty on fishing rights has been revoked*

reward [rɪ'wɔːd] *noun* payment given to someone who does a service (especially someone who finds something which has been lost or who gives information about something); *she offered a £50 reward to anyone who found her watch*; *the police have offered a reward for information about the man seen at the bank*

Rex [reks] *Latin word meaning* 'the King': the Crown or state, as a party in legal proceedings (NOTE: in written reports, usually abbreviated to **R: the case of** *R. v. Smith*)

rfp = REASONABLE FINANCIAL PROVISION

rider ['raɪdə] *noun* **(a)** additional clause (to a contract or report) **(b)** *US* clause attached to a bill, which may have nothing to do with the subject of the bill, but which the sponsor hopes to get passed into law more easily in this way

riding ['raɪdɪŋ] *noun (in Canada)* constituency, the area of the country represented by an MP

rig [rɪg] *verb* to arrange (an election) so that a particular candidate wins; *the Opposition claimed that the election had been rigged*; *see also* BALLOT-RIGGING

right [raɪt] *noun* **(a)** legal entitlement to something; *right of renewal of a contract*; *she has a right to the property*; *he has no right to the patent*; *the staff have a right to know what the company is doing*; **civil rights** = rights and privileges of each individual according to the law; **conjugal rights** = rights of a husband and wife in relation to each other; **constitutional right** = right which is guaranteed by the constitution of a country; **foreign rights** = legal entitlement to sell something in a foreign country; **human rights** = rights of individual men and women to basic freedoms, such as freedom of speech, freedom of association; **right to strike** = general right of workers to stop working if they have a good reason for it; **right of way** = legal title to go across someone else's property; *see also* AUDIENCE, BILL OF RIGHTS **(b)** **rights issue** = giving shareholders the right to buy more shares at a lower price than the current market price

rightful ['raɪtful] *adjective* legally correct; **rightful claimant** = person who has a legal claim to something; **rightful owner** = legal owner

rigor mortis ['rɪgə 'mɔːtɪs] *Latin phrase* meaning 'stiffening of the dead': state where a dead body becomes stiff some time after death, and which can allow a pathologist to estimate the time of death in some cases

ring [rɪŋ] **1** *noun* group of people who try to fix the prices paid at an auction so as not to compete with each other, so making a large profit by holding a secret auction afterwards with only the members of the group as bidders **2** *verb* to alter chassis or

engine numbers on a car, so as to falsify its origin

riot ['raɪət] **1** *noun* notifiable offence when three or more people meet illegally and plan to use force to achieve their aims or to frighten the public **2** *verb* to form an illegal group to use force

rioter ['raɪətə] *noun* person who takes part in a riot; *rioters attacked the banks and post offices*

riotous assembly ['raɪətəs ə'sembli] *noun* formerly, a meeting of twelve or more people who come together to use force to achieve their aims or to frighten other people

riparian [rɪ'peəriən] *adjective* referring to the bank of a river; **riparian rights** = rights of people who own land on the bank of a river (usually the right to fish in the river)

risk [rɪsk] *noun* **(a)** possible harm, loss or chance of danger; **to run a risk** = to be likely to suffer harm; *in allowing him to retain his passport, the court runs the risk that the accused may try to escape to the USA where he has friends*; **at owner's risk** = situation where goods shipped or stored are the responsibility of the owner, not of the shipping company or storage company **(b)** loss or damage against which you are insured; **fire risk** = situation or materials which could start a fire; **he is a bad risk** = it is likely that an insurance company will have to pay out compensation as far as he is concerned; *he is likely to die soon, so is a bad risk for an insurance company*

road tax ['rəud 'tæks] *noun* annual tax levied on cars and other vehicles

rob [rɒb] *verb* to steal something from (someone), usually in a violent way; *they robbed a bank in London and stole a car to make their getaway*; *the gang robbed shopkeepers in the centre of the town* (NOTE: **robbing - robbed**. Note also that you rob someone **of** something)

robber ['rɒbə] *noun* person who robs people

robbery ['rɒbri] *noun* **(a)** offence of stealing something from someone using force or threatening to use force; **robbery with violence** = stealing goods and harming someone at the same time **(b)** act of stealing something with violence; *he committed three petrol station robberies in two days*

rogatory letter ['rɒgətri 'letə] *noun* letter of request, a letter to a court in another country, asking for evidence to be taken from someone under that court's jurisdiction

roll [rəʊl] *noun* list of names (which used to be written on a long roll); **Roll of Solicitors** = list of admitted solicitors; **he was struck off the roll** = he was banned from practising as a solicitor; **Master of the Rolls** = senior judge who presides over the Court of Appeal, and is also responsible for admitting solicitors to the Roll of Solicitors

roll over ['rəʊl 'əʊvə] *verb* **to roll over credit** = to make credit available over a continuing period

Romalpa clause [rə'mælpæ 'klɔːz] *noun* clause in a contract, whereby the seller provides that title to the goods does not pass to the buyer until the buyer has paid for them

> COMMENT: called after the case of *Aluminium Industrie Vaassen BV v. Romalpa Ltd*

Roman law ['rəʊmən 'lɔː] *noun* laws which existed in the Roman Empire

> COMMENT: Roman law is the basis of the laws of many European countries but has had only negligible and indirect influence on the development of English law

Rome Convention ['rəʊm kən'venʃn] *noun* copyright convention signed in Rome, covering the rights of record producers, musical performers, broadcasters and television companies, etc.

root of title ['ruːt əv 'taɪtl] *noun* basic title deed which proves that the vendor has the right to sell the property

ROR *US* = RELEASE ON RECOGNIZANCE

rotation [rəʊ'teɪʃn] *noun* taking turns; **to fill the post of chairman by rotation** = each member of the group is chairman for a period then gives the post to another member; **two directors retire by rotation** = two directors retire because they have been directors longer than any others, but can offer themselves for re-election

rotten borough ['rɒtn 'bʌrə] *noun* formerly, a borough where there were very few eligible voters to elect the MP; *see also* POCKET BOROUGH

rough justice [rʌf 'dʒʌstɪs] *noun* legal processes which are not always very fair

rout [raʊt] *noun* offence of gathering together of people to do some unlawful act

royal ['rɔɪəl] *adjective* referring to a king or queen; **Royal Assent** = signing of a Bill by the Queen, confirming that the Bill is to become law as an Act of Parliament; **by Royal Command** = by order of the Queen or King; **Royal Commission** = group of people specially appointed by a minister to examine and report on a major problem; **the Royal Family** = the family of a king or queen; **Royal pardon** = pardon whereby a person convicted of a crime is forgiven and need not serve a sentence; **Royal prerogative** = special right belonging to a king or queen (such as the right to appoint ministers or to prorogue Parliament)

Royal Courts of Justice (RCJ)
['rɔɪəl 'kɔːts əv 'dʒʌstɪs] *noun* central civil court in London, where serious claims covering fatal accidents, professional negligence, defamation, and claims against the police are heard

royalist ['rɔɪəlɪst] *noun* person supporting rule by a king or queen

royalty ['rɔɪlti] *noun* money paid to an inventor, writer, the owner of land for the right to use his property (usually a certain percentage of sales, or a certain amount per sale); *oil royalties make up a large proportion of the country's revenue*; *he is receiving royalties from his invention*

rozzer ['rɒzə] *noun (informal)* policeman

RPM ['aː 'piː 'em] = RESALE PRICE MAINTENANCE

RSC ['aː 'es 'siː] = RULES OF THE SUPREME COURT

rule [ruːl] **1** *noun* **(a)** general order of conduct which says how things should be done (such as an order governing voting procedure in Parliament or Congress); *the debate followed the rules of procedure used in the British House of Commons*; **company rules (and regulations)** = general way of working in a company; **to work to rule** = to work strictly according to the rules agreed by the company and union, and therefore to work very slowly; **Judges' Rules** = informal set of rules governing how the police should act in questioning suspects; **Rules of the Supreme Court (RSC)** = rules governing practice and procedure in the Supreme Court; *see also* CIVIL PROCEDURE RULES, COUNTY COURT RULES, WHITE BOOK; **Ten Minute Rule** = rule in the House of Commons, where an ordinary MP can introduce a Bill with a short speech, and if the Bill is passed on a vote, it can proceed to the Second Reading stage; *the Bill was proposed under the Ten Minute Rule*; *see also* GOLDEN RULE, LITERAL RULE, MISCHIEF RULE **(b)** *US* special decision made by the Rules Committee which states how a particular bill should be treated in the House of Representatives; **closed rule** *or* **gag rule** = rule which limits the time for discussion of a bill **(c)** way in which a country is governed; *the country has had ten years of military rule*; **the rule of law** = principle of government that all persons and bodies and the government itself are equal before and answerable to the law and that no person shall be punished without trial **(d)** decision made by a court; **Rule in Rylands v. Fletcher** = rule that when a person brings a dangerous thing (substance or animal) to

his own land, and the dangerous thing escapes and causes harm, then that person is absolutely liable for the damage caused **2** *verb* **(a)** to give an official decision; *we are waiting for the judge to rule on the admissibility of the defence evidence*; *the commission of inquiry ruled that the company was in breach of contract* **(b)** to be in force or to be current; *prices which are ruling at the moment* **(c)** to govern (a country); *the country is ruled by a group of army officers*

ruler ['ruːlə] *noun* person who governs or controls a country or part of a country

ruling ['ruːlɪŋ] **1** *adjective* **(a)** in power or in control; *the ruling Democratic Party*; *the actions of the ruling junta have been criticized in the press* **(b)** most important; in operation at the moment, current; *the ruling consideration is one of cost*; *we will invoice at ruling prices* **2** *noun* decision (made by a judge, magistrate, arbitrator or chairman, etc.); *the MPs disputed the Speaker's ruling*; *according to the ruling of the court, the contract was illegal*

run [rʌn] **1** *noun* **(a)** making a machine work; **a cheque run** = series of cheques processed through a computer; **a computer run** = period of work of a computer; **test run** = trial made of a machine or a work process **(b)** rush to buy something; **a run on the bank** = rush by customers to take deposits out of a bank which they think may close down; **a run on the pound** = rush to sell pounds and buy other currencies **2** *verb* **(a)** to be in force; *the lease runs for twenty years*; *our lease has only six months to run*; **a covenant which runs with the land** = covenant which is attached to an estate and has to be obeyed by each new owner of the estate when it changes hands **(b)** to amount to; *the costs ran into thousands of pounds* **(c)** to offer oneself as a candidate in an election; *he is running for president*; *he had no hope of winning the nomination, so he decided not to run*; **running mate** = person who stands for election with another more important candidate (as when two candidates offer themselves for two posts, i.e. for President and Vice-President) (NOTE: **running - ran - has run**)

runner ['rʌnə] *noun (slang)* **(a)** member of a gang of pickpockets who takes the items stolen and runs away with them to a safe place **(b) to do a runner** = to runaway, to jump bail

run-up ['rʌnʌp] *noun* **run-up to an election** = period before an election; *in the run-up to the General Election, opinion polls were forecasting heavy losses for the government*

rustle [rʌsl] *verb* to steal livestock (especially cows and horses)

rustler ['rʌslə] *noun* person who steals livestock; *a cattle rustler*

rustling ['rʌslɪŋ] *noun* crime of stealing cattle or horses

Ss

sabotage ['sæbətɑːʒ] *noun* malicious damage done to machines or equipment; *several acts of sabotage were committed against radio stations* (NOTE: no plural; for the plural say **acts of sabotage**)

sack [sæk] **1** *noun* **(a)** large bag made of strong cloth or plastic; *the burglars carried a sack of clocks from the shop* **(b) to get the sack** = to be dismissed from a job **2** *verb* **to sack someone** = to dismiss someone from a job; *he was sacked after being late for work*

sacking ['sækɪŋ] *noun* dismissal from a job; *the union protested against the sackings*

safe [seɪf] **1** *noun* heavy metal box which cannot be opened easily, in which valuable documents, money, etc., can be kept; *put the documents in the safe*; *we keep the petty cash in the safe*; **fire-proof safe** = safe which cannot be harmed by fire; **night safe** = safe in the outside wall of a bank, where money and documents can be deposited at night, using a special door; **wall safe** = safe fixed in a wall **2** *adjective* **(a)** out of danger; **keep the documents in a safe place** = in a place where they cannot be stolen or destroyed; **safe keeping** = being looked after carefully; *we put the documents into the bank for safe keeping* **(b) safe investments** = shares, etc., which are not likely to fall in value; **safe seat** = seat where the Member of Parliament has a large majority and is not likely to lose the seat at an election; *compare* MARGINAL **(c)** (judgment of a court) which is well-based and is not likely to be quashed on appeal; *the court of appeal found that*

the original conviction was not safe; *see also* UNSAFE

safe deposit ['seɪf dɪ'pɒzɪt] *noun* safe in a bank vault where you can leave jewellery or documents

safe deposit box ['seɪf dɪ'pɒzɪt 'bɒks] *noun* small box which you can rent to keep jewellery or documents in a bank's safe

safeguard ['seɪfgɑːd] **1** *noun* protection; *the proposed legislation will provide a safeguard against illegal traders* **2** *verb* to protect; *the court acted to safeguard the interests of the shareholders*

safety ['seɪfti] *noun* **(a)** being free from danger or risk; **Health and Safety at Work Act** = Act of Parliament which regulates what employers must do to make sure that their employees are kept healthy and safe at work; **safety margin** = time or space allowed for something to be safe; **to take safety precautions** *or* **safety measures** = to act to make sure something is safe; **safety regulations** = rules to make a place of work safe for the workers **(b) fire safety** = making a place of work safe for the workers in case of fire; **fire safety officer** = person in a company responsible for seeing that the workers are safe if a fire breaks out

sale [seɪl] *noun* **(a)** act of selling or of transferring an item or a property from one owner to another in exchange for a consideration, usually in the form of money; **forced sale** = selling something because a court orders it or because it is the only way to avoid insolvency; **sale and**

lease-back = situation where a company sells a property to raise cash and then leases it back from the purchaser; **sale or return** = system where the retailer sends goods back if they are not sold, and pays the supplier only for goods sold; **bill of sale** = (i) document which the seller gives to the buyer to show that a sale has taken place; (ii) document given to a lender by a borrower to show that the lender owns a property as security for a loan; **conditions of sale** *or* **terms of sale** = list of terms under which a sale takes place (such as discounts and credit terms); **Sale of Goods Act** = Act of Parliament which regulates the selling of goods (but not land, copyrights, patents, etc.); *the law relating to the sale of goods is governed by the Sale of Goods Act* (b) **for sale** = ready to be sold; **to offer something for sale** *or* **to put something up for sale** = to announce that something is ready to be sold; *they put the factory up for sale*; *his shop is for sale*; *these items are not for sale to the general public* (c) **sales** = money received for selling something, number of items sold; **sales conference** *or* **sales meeting** = meeting of sales managers, representatives, advertising staff, etc, to discuss results and plan future sales; **sales department** = section of a company which deals in selling the company's products or services; **domestic sales** *or* **home sales** = sales in the home market; **sales figures** = total sales, or sales broken down by category; **forward sales** = sales (of shares, commodities or foreign exchange) for delivery at a later date; **sales tax** = tax to be paid on each item sold (d) selling of goods at specially low prices; *the shop is having a sale to clear old stock*; *the sale price is 50% of the normal price*; **half-price sale** = sale of items at half the usual price; **the sales** = period when major stores sell many items at specially low prices

salvage ['sælvɪdʒ] **1** *noun* (a) right of a person who saves a ship from being wrecked or cargo from a ship which has been wrecked, to receive compensation; **salvage agreement** = agreement between the captain of a sinking ship and a salvage crew, giving the terms on which the ship

will be saved; **salvage (money)** = payment made by the owner of a ship or a cargo to the person who has saved it from being destroyed or wrecked; **salvage vessel** = ship which specializes in saving other ships and their cargoes (b) goods saved from a wrecked ship, from a fire, etc.; *a sale of flood salvage items* **2** *verb* to save goods or a ship from being wrecked; *we are selling off a warehouse full of salvaged goods*

sample ['sɑːmpl] **1** *noun* small part of something taken to show what the whole is like; *they polled a sample group of voters*; **blood sample** *or* **urine sample** = small amount of blood or urine taken from someone to be tested **2** *verb* to take a small part of something and examine it; *the suspect's urine was sampled and the test proved positive*

sanction ['sæŋkʃn] **1** *noun* (a) official permission to do something; *you will need the sanction of the local authorities before you can knock down the office block*; *the payment was made without official sanction from a country* (b) *(in civil cases)* punishment by a court for failure to comply with an order; if the sanction is payment of costs, the party in default may obtain relief by appealing (c) punishment for an act which goes against what is normally accepted behaviour; **(economic) sanctions** = restrictions on trade with a country in order to influence its political situation or in order to make its government change its policy; *to impose sanctions on a country or to lift sanctions* **2** *verb* to approve or to permit (officially); *the board sanctioned the expenditure of £1.2m on the development plan*

sane [seɪn] *adjective* mentally well; *was he sane when he made the will?*

sanity ['sænɪti] *noun* being mentally well

sans frais ['sænz 'freɪs] *French phrase meaning* 'with no expense'

sans recours ['sænz rə'kuːəs] *French phrase meaning* 'with no recourse': used to show that the endorser of a bill (as an agent acting for a principal) is not responsible for paying it

satisfaction [sætɪsˈfækʃn] *noun* (i) acceptance of money or goods by an injured party who then cannot make any further claim; (ii) payment or giving of goods to someone in exchange for that person's agreement to stop a claim; **accord and satisfaction** = payment by a debtor of a debt or part of a debt, or the performing by a debtor of some act or service which is accepted by the creditor in full settlement, so that the debtor can no longer be sued; **memorandum of satisfaction** = document showing that a company has repaid a mortgage or charge

satisfy [ˈsætɪsfaɪ] *verb* (a) to convince someone that something is correct; *when opposing bail the police had to satisfy the court that the prisoner was likely to try to leave the country* (b) to fulfil or to carry out fully; *has he satisfied all the conditions for parole?*; *the company has not satisfied all the conditions laid down in the agreement*; *we cannot produce enough to satisfy the demand for the product*

scaffold [ˈskæfəʊld] *noun* raised platform on which executions take place

scale [skeɪl] **1** *noun* (a) system which is classified into various levels; **scale of charges** *or* **scale of prices** = list showing various prices; **fixed scale of charges** = rate of charging which does not change; **scale of salaries** *or* **salary scale** = list of salaries showing different levels of pay in different jobs in the same company (b) **large scale** *or* **small scale** = working with large or small amounts of investment, staff, etc.; **to start in business on a small scale** = to start in business with a small staff, few products or little investment; **economies of scale** = making a product more cheaply by producing it or buying it in large quantities; *(in the EU)* **test of scale** = test to show if an action is more effective when taken by the Community as opposed to a Member State (one of the tests to decide on subsidiarity); *compare* EFFECTIVENESS **2** *verb* **to scale down** *or* **to scale up** = to lower or to increase in proportion

scam [skæm] *noun (informal)* case of fraud

schedule [ˈʃedjuːl *US* ˈskedʒuːl] **1** *noun* (a) timetable, a plan of time drawn up in advance; **to be ahead of schedule** = to be early; **to be on schedule** = to be on time; **to be behind schedule** = to be late; *the Bill is on schedule*; *the Second Reading was completed ahead of schedule*; *I am sorry to say that we are three months behind schedule*; *the managing director has a busy schedule of appointments*; *his secretary tried to fit me into his schedule* (b) additional documents attached to a contract; *schedule of markets to which a contract applies*; *see the attached schedule or as per the attached schedule*; *the schedule before referred to* (c) list; *we publish our new schedule of charges* (d) **tax schedules** = six types of income as classified in the Finance Acts for British tax; **Schedule A** = schedule under which tax is charged on income from land or buildings; **Schedule B** = schedule under which tax is charged on income from woodlands; **Schedule C** = schedule under which tax is charged on profits from government stock; **Schedule D** = schedule under which tax is charged on income from trades or professions, interest and other earnings not derived from being employed; **Schedule E** = schedule under which tax is charged on income from salaries, wages or pensions; **Schedule F** = schedule under which tax is charged on income from dividends (e) *for the schedules applying to drugs, see* COMMENT *at* DRUG **2** *verb* (a) to list officially; *scheduled prices or scheduled charges* (b) to plan the time when something will happen; *the building is scheduled for completion in May*

scheme of arrangement [ˈskiːm əv əˈreɪnʒmənt] *noun* scheme drawn up by an individual to offer ways of paying his debts, and so avoid bankruptcy proceedings

scope [skəʊp] *noun* limits covered by something; *the question does not come within the scope of the authority's powers*; *the Bill plans to increase the scope of the tribunal's authority*

screen [skri:n] **1** *noun* glass surface on which computer information, TV pictures, etc., can be shown **2** *verb* **to screen candidates** = to examine candidates to see if they are completely suitable

screening ['skri:nɪŋ] *noun* **the screening of candidates** = examining candidates to see if they are suitable

screw [skru:] *noun (slang)* prison warder

scrip [skrɪp] *noun* certificate showing that someone owns shares in a company; **scrip issue** = new shares given free to shareholders

scuttle ['skʌtl] *verb* to sink a ship deliberately (by cutting holes in the bottom)

seal [si:l] **1** *noun* **(a)** piece of wax or red paper attached to a document to show that it is legally valid; stamp printed or marked on a document to show that it is valid; **common seal** *or* **company's seal** = metal stamp which every company must possess, used to stamp documents with the name of the company to show they have been approved officially; *to attach the company's seal to a document*; **contract under seal** = contract which has been signed and legally approved with the seal of the company or the person entering into it **(b)** mark put on a document by a court to show that it has been correctly issued by that court; *the document bears the court's seal and is admissible in evidence* **(c)** piece of paper, metal or wax attached to close something, so that it can be opened only if the paper, metal or wax is removed or broken; *the seals on the ballot box had been tampered with*; **customs seal** = seal attached by customs officers to a box, to show that the contents have passed through customs **2** *verb* **(a)** to close something tightly; *the computer disks were sent in a sealed container*; **sealed envelope** = envelope where the back has been stuck down to close it; *the information was sent in a sealed envelope*; **sealed tenders** = tenders sent in sealed envelopes, which will all be opened together at a certain time; *the company has asked for sealed*

bids for the warehouse **(b)** *(of a court)* to attach a mark to a document to show that it has been issued by that court; *a court must seal a claim form when it is issued* **(c)** to attach a seal; to stamp something with a seal; *customs sealed the shipment*; **sealed instrument** = document which has been signed and sealed

seal off ['si:l 'ɒf] *verb* to put barriers across a street or an entrance to prevent people from going in or out; *police sealed off all roads leading to the courthouse*

search [sɜ:tʃ] **1** *noun* **(a)** examining a place to try to find something; **search order** = order by a court in a civil case allowing a party to inspect and photocopy or remove a defendant's documents, especially where the defendant might destroy evidence (the search should be done in the presence of an independent solicitor) (NOTE: since the introduction of the new Civil Procedure Rules in April 1999, this term has replaced **Anton Piller order**); **search warrant** = official document signed by a magistrate allowing the police to enter premises and look for persons suspected of being criminals, objects which are believed to have been stolen or dangerous or illegal substances; **power of search** = authority to search premises, which is given to the police and certain other officials, such as Customs and Excise officers; *see also* STRIP SEARCH **(b)** **searches** = examination of records by the lawyer acting for someone who wants to buy a property, to make sure that the vendor has the right to sell it **2** *verb* to examine a place or a person to try to find something, to look inside something to see what is there; *the agent searched his files for a record of the sale*; *all drivers and their cars are searched at the customs post*; *the police searched the area round the house for clues*; **to stop and search** = to stop a person in a public place and search them for weapons, implements used for burglary, stolen articles, etc.

seat [si:t] *noun* **(a)** chair; *seats have been placed on the platform for the members of the council*; *Opposition MPs left their seats and walked out of the chamber in* *protest*; **seat belt** = belt attached to a seat in a car, plane, etc., which protects a person sitting in the seat from injury if an accident occurs (wearing of seat belts is obligatory) **(b)** (i) membership of the House of Commons, the state of being an MP; (ii) constituency; (iii) membership of a committee; *he lost his seat in the general election*; *this is a safe Tory seat*; *marginal seats showed a swing away from the government*; *the union has two seats on the general council*; *see also* EURO-SEAT

COMMENT: in the British House of Commons, the seats are arranged in rows facing each other across the chamber, with the table in between the front benches and the Speaker's chair at the end. In other legislative chambers (as in the French National Assembly), the seats are arranged in a semi-circle facing the rostrum with the seat of the President of the Assembly behind it

secede [sɪ'si:d] *verb* to break away from an organization or a federation; *the American colonies seceded from Great Britain in 1776 and formed the USA*

secession [sə'seʃn] *noun* act of seceding

second ['sekənd] **1** *adjective* coming after the first; *he came second in the contest for deputy leader*; *we will now deal with the second item on the agenda* **2** *verb* **to second a motion** *or* **a candidate** = to agree to support a motion after it has been proposed by the proposer, but before a vote is taken; *the motion is proposed by Mr Smith, seconded by Mr Jones*; *the name of Mr Brown has been proposed for the post of treasurer, who is going to second him?*

secondarily ['sekəndrəli] *adverb* in second place; *the person making a guarantee is secondarily liable if the person who is primarily liable defaults*; *see also* PRIMARILY

secondary ['sekəndri] *adjective* second in importance; **secondary banks** = companies which provide money for hire-purchase deals; **secondary evidence** = evidence which is not the main proof (such as copies of documents, not the original documents themselves) (secondary evidence can be admitted if there is no primary evidence available); **secondary action** *or* **secondary picketing** = picketing of another factory or place of work, which is not directly connected with a strike, to prevent it supplying a striking factory or receiving supplies from it; *(in the EU)* **secondary legislation** = legislation passed by the EU, as opposed to primary legislation passed by the Member States; *see also* PRIMARY

second ballot ['sekənd 'bælət] *noun* electoral system used in France and other countries, in which if a candidate does not get 50% of the votes, a second ballot is held a short time later, with the lowest candidate or candidates removed from the list

second degree murder ['sekənd dɪ'gri: 'mɜ:də] *noun US* murder without premeditation and not committed at the same time as rape or robbery

seconder ['sekəndə] *noun* person who seconds a proposal; *Mr Brown has been proposed by Mr Jones, and Miss Smith is his seconder*; *the motion could not be put, because the proposer could not find a seconder for it*

second mortgage ['sekənd 'mɔ:gɪdʒ] *noun* further mortgage on a property which is already mortgaged (the first mortgage still has prior claim)

Second Reading ['sekənd 'ri:dɪŋ] *noun* **(a)** detailed presentation of a Bill in the House of Commons by the responsible minister, followed by a discussion and vote **(b)** *US* detailed examination of a Bill in the House, before it is passed to the Senate

secret ['si:krət] **1** *adjective* (something) which is hidden or not known by many people; *the chief negotiator kept the report secret from the rest of the government team*; *they signed a secret deal with their main competitor*; **secret ballot** = election in which the voters vote in secret; *the new act stipulates that elections* *to union office shall be by secret ballot of members*; **in secret** = without telling anyone; *the rebel leader met the chief of police in secret*; *he photographed the plans of the new missile in secret*; **in secret session** = meeting when only members are allowed to be present, with no journalists, and sometimes with no officials; *the Committee met in secret session*; *the Council went into secret session to discuss the appointment of the new Chief Executive* **2** *noun* something which is kept hidden from most people; **to keep a secret** = not to tell someone a secret which you know; **official secret** = piece of information which is classified as important to the state, and which it is a crime to reveal; **Official Secrets Act** = Act of Parliament governing the publication of secrets relating to the state

secretariat [sekrǝ'teǝriǝt]   *noun* important office and the officials who work in it; *the United Nations secretariat*

secretary ['sekrǝtri] *noun* **(a)** person who types letters, files documents or arranges meetings, etc., for someone; *my secretary deals with visitors*; *his secretary phoned to say he would be late*; **legal secretary** = secretary in a firm of solicitors, in the legal department of a company, etc. **(b)** official of a company or society; **company secretary** = person who is responsible for a company's legal and financial affairs; **honorary secretary** = person who keeps the minutes and official documents of a committee or club, but is not paid a salary **(c)** Secretary of State, a member of the government in charge of a department; *the Education Secretary*; *the Foreign Secretary*; *UK* **Chief Secretary to the Treasury** = senior member of the government under the Chancellor of the Exchequer; *US* **Secretary of the Treasury** *or* **Treasury Secretary** = senior member of the government in charge of financial affairs **(d)** senior civil servant; **Permanent Secretary** = chief civil servant in a government department or ministry (NOTE: in Canada called **Deputy Minister.** Permanent Secretaries are appointed by the Prime Minister and are responsible to the Secretary of State in

charge of the relevant department; see also COMMENT below); **the Cabinet Secretary** *or* **Secretary to the Cabinet** = head of the Cabinet Office (and also of the British Civil Service), who attends cabinet meetings; **Private Secretary** = civil servant attached personally to a Secretary of State or Prime Minister, who acts as the link between the minister and the department; **Parliamentary Private Secretary** = young MP attached personally to a Secretary of State or Prime Minister, who acts as a general helper in Parliament; *US* **Secretary to the Senate** = head of the administrative staff in the Senate

Secretary-General ['sekrǝtri'dʒenrǝl] *noun* main administrator in a large organization (such as the United Nations or a political party)

Secretary of State ['sekrǝtri ǝv 'steɪt] *noun* **(a)** *GB* member of the government in charge of a department **(b)** *US* senior member of the government in charge of foreign affairs; *see also notes at* FOREIGN, MINISTER **(c)** *(in Canada)* government minister with general responsibilities for publications, broadcasting and the arts

COMMENT: the uses of the words **Secretary** and **Secretary of State** are confusing: **1.** In the UK, a Secretary of State is the head of a government department, usually a Cabinet Minister. Other members of the government, though not in the Cabinet, are Parliamentary Secretaries or Parliamentary Under-Secretaries of State, who are junior ministers in a department. Finally the Parliamentary Private Secretary is a Secretary of State's main junior assistant in Parliament **2.** In the USA, the Secretary of State is the person in charge of the Department of State, which is concerned with foreign policy. The equivalent in most other countries is the Foreign Minister (Foreign Secretary in the UK). Other heads of department in the US government are called simply Secretary: Secretary for

Defense or Defense Secretary **3**. In the British civil service, a government department is headed by a Permanent Secretary, with several Deputy Secretaries and Under-Secretaries. They are all government employees and are not MPs. Also a civil servant is a Secretary of State's Private Secretary, who is attached to the minister personally, and acts as his link with the department. The British Civil Service formerly used the titles Permanent Secretary, Deputy Secretary, Assistant Secretary and Principal Secretary as grades, but these have now been replaced by a system of numbers (G1, G2, G3, etc.) **4**. Both in the UK and USA, the word Secretary is used in short forms of titles with the name of the department. So, the Secretary of State for Education and Science in the UK, and the Secretary for Education in the USA are both called Education Secretary for short. In the USA, the word Secretary can be used as a person's title: Secretary Smith

section ['sekʃn] *noun* **(a)** department in an office; **passport section** = part of an embassy which deals with passport enquiries; **legal section** = department dealing with legal matters in a company **(b)** part of an Act of Parliament or bylaw; *he does not qualify for a grant under section 2 of the Act* (NOTE: when referring to a section of an act, it is abbreviated to **s: s 24 LGA**)

sector ['sektə] *noun* general area of business; **private sector** = all companies which are owned by private shareholders, not by the state; **public sector** = nationalized industries and services; **public sector borrowing requirement (PSBR)** = amount of money which a government has to borrow to pay for its own spending

secure [sɪ'kjuːə] **1** *adjective* **(a)** safe, which cannot change; **secure job** = job from which you are not likely to be made redundant; **secure investment** = investment where you are not likely to lose money; **secure tenant** = tenant of a local authority who has the right to buy the

freehold of the property he rents at a discount **(b)** safe, not likely to be opened; *the documents should be kept in a secure place*; *the police and army have made the border secure* **2** *verb* **to secure a loan** = to pledge a property or other assets as a security for a loan

secured [sɪ'kjuːəd] *adjective* **secured creditor** = person who is owed money by someone, and holds a mortgage or charge on that person's property as security; **secured debts** = debts which are guaranteed by assets; **secured loan** = loan which is guaranteed by the borrower giving valuable property as security

securities [sɪ'kjuːrɪtiz] *plural noun* (i) investments in stocks and shares; (ii) certificates to show that someone owns stock; **gilt-edged securities** *or* **government securities** = British government stock; **the securities market** = Stock Exchange, place where stocks and shares can be bought or sold; **securities trader** = person whose business is buying and selling stocks and shares

security [sɪ'kjuːrəti] *noun* **(a)** being safe, not likely to change; **security of employment** = feeling by a worker that he has the right to keep his job until he retires; **security of tenure** = right to keep a position or rented accommodation, provided that certain conditions are met **(b)** being protected; **airport security** = actions taken to protect aircraft and passengers against attack; **office security** = protecting an office against theft of equipment, personal property or information; **security guard** = person whose job is to protect money, valuables or an office against possible theft or damage; **top security prison** = prison with very strict security where category 'A' prisoners are kept **(c)** being secret; **security in this office is nil** = nothing can be kept secret in this office; **security printer** = printing company which prints paper money, secret government documents, etc. **(d)** **social security** = money or help provided by the government to people who need it; *he lives on social security payments*; **Department of Health and Social Security** = civil service department which is in charge of the National Health Service, state benefits, insurance and pensions **(e)** guarantee that someone will repay money borrowed; **to stand security for someone** = to guarantee that if the person does not repay a loan, you will repay it for him; *to give something as security for a debt*; *to use a house as security for a loan*; *the bank lent him £20,000 without security*

Security Council [sɪˈkjuːrɪti ˈkaunsəl] *noun* permanent ruling body of the United Nations, with the responsibility for preserving international peace

COMMENT: the Security Council has fifteen members, five of which (USA, Russia, UK, France and China) are permanent members, the other ten being elected by the General Assembly for periods of two years. The five permanent members each have a veto over the decisions of the Security Council

security for costs [sɪˈkjuːrɪti fə ˈkɒsts] guarantee that a party in a dispute will pay costs; *the master ordered that the claimant should deposit £2,000 as security for the defendant's costs*

COMMENT: where a foreign claimant or a company which may become insolvent brings proceedings against a defendant, the defendant is entitled to apply to the court for an order that the proceedings be stayed unless the claimant deposits money to secure the defendant's costs if the claimant fails in his action

sedition [sɪˈdɪʃn] *noun* crime of doing acts or speaking or publishing words which bring the royal family or the government into hatred or contempt and encourage civil disorder

COMMENT: sedition is a lesser crime than treason

seditious [sɪˈdɪʃəs] *adjective* which provokes sedition; **seditious libel** = offence of publishing a libel with seditious intent

seek [siːk] *verb* **(a)** to ask for; *they are seeking damages for loss of revenue*; *the applicant sought judicial review to quash the order*; *the Bill requires a social worker to seek permission of the Juvenile Court*; *a creditor seeking a receiving order under the Bankruptcy Act*; **to seek an interview** = to ask if you can see someone; *she sought an interview with the minister* **(b)** to look for someone or something; *the police are seeking a tall man who was seen near the scene of the crime*; *two men are being sought by the police* **(c)** to try to do something; *the local authority is seeking to place the ward of court in accommodation* (NOTE: **seeking - sought - has sought** [sɔːt])

segregate [ˈsegrəgeɪt] *verb* to separate or to keep apart, especially to keep different races in a country apart; *single-sex schools segregate boys from girls*

segregation [segrɪˈgeɪʃn] *noun* **racial segregation** = keeping different races apart

seised [siːzd] *adjective* **seised of a property** = being legally in possession of property

seisin [ˈsiːzɪn] *noun (feudal law)* possession of land

seize [siːz] *verb* to take hold of something, to take possession of something; *the customs seized the shipment of books*; *his case was seized at the airport*; *the court ordered the company's funds to be seized*

seizure [ˈsiːʒə] *noun* taking possession of something; *the court ordered the seizure of the shipment or of the company's funds*

select [sɪˈlekt] **1** *adjective* of top quality, specially chosen; *our customers are very select*; *a select group of clients* **2** *verb* to choose; *three members of the committee have been selected to speak at the AGM*; *he has been selected as a candidate for a Northern constituency*

Select Committee [sɪˈlekt kəˈmɪtiː] *noun (in the House of Commons)* special committee (with members representing various political parties) which examines the work of a ministry or a particular problem in the House of Commons; *(in Congress)* committee set up for a special purpose, usually to investigate something; **ad hoc Select Committee** = Select Committee set up to examine a special case or problem; **departmental Select Committee** = Select Committee set up to examine the work of a government department; **sessional Select Committee** = Select Committee set up at the beginning of each session of parliament; *the Select Committee on Defence or the Defence Select Committee*

COMMENT: the main sessional Select Committees are: **the Committee of Privileges** which considers breaches of parliamentary privilege; **the Committee of the Parliamentary Commissioner** which considers the reports of the Ombudsman; **the Public Accounts Committee** which examines government expenditure. The departmental select committees are: **Agriculture, Culture, Media and Sport, Defence, Education and Employment, Environment, Foreign Affairs, Health, Home Affairs, Northern Ireland, Scottish Affairs, Social Security, Science and Technology, Trade and Industry, Treasury, Welsh Affairs**

selection [sɪˈlekʃn] *noun* (i) choice; (ii) person or thing which has been chosen; **selection board** *or* **selection committee** = committee which chooses a candidate for a job; **selection procedure** = general method of choosing a candidate for election or for a job; *see also* DESELECT, DESELECTION

self-defence [ˈselfdɪˈfens] *noun* trying to protect yourself when attacked; *he pleaded that he had acted in self-defence when he had hit the mugger*

COMMENT: this can be used as a defence to a charge of a crime of violence, where the defendant pleads that his actions were attributable to

defending himself rather than to a desire to commit violence

self-determination

[ˈselfdɪtɜːmɪˈneɪʃn] *noun* free choice by the people of a country as to which country (including their own) should govern them; *countries with powerful neighbours have to fight for the right to self-determination*

self-government *or* **self-rule**

[ˈselfˈɡʌvənmənt *or* ˈselfˈruːl] *noun* control of a country by its own government, free from foreign influence

self-incrimination

[ˈselfɪnkrɪmɪˈneɪʃn] *noun* act of incriminating yourself, of saying something which shows you are guilty; **right against self-incrimination** = right not to say anything, when questioned by the police, in case you may say something which could incriminate you (NOTE: for the equivalent in the USA, see **Fifth Amendment**)

self-sufficiency [ˈselfsəˈfɪʃnsi] *noun* being self-sufficient; *we aim to achieve self-sufficiency in energy by 2010*

self-sufficient [ˈselfsəˈfɪʃnt] *adjective* able to provide for oneself; *the country is self-sufficient in oil*

sell [sel] *verb* to transfer the ownership of property to another person in exchange for money; *they tried to sell their house for £100,000; to sell something on credit; her house is difficult to sell; their products are easy to sell*; **to sell forward** = to sell foreign currency, commodities, etc., for delivery at a later date (NOTE: **selling - sold - has sold**)

seller [ˈselə] *noun* **(a)** person who sells; *there were few sellers in the market, so prices remained high*; **seller's market** = market where the seller can ask high prices because there is a large demand for the product **(b)** thing which sells; *this book is a good seller*; **best-seller** = item (especially a book) which sells very well

selling [ˈselɪŋ] *noun* **direct selling** = selling a product direct to the customer without going through a shop; **mail-order**

selling = selling by taking orders and supplying a product by post; **selling price** = price at which someone is willing to sell

semble ['sembl] *French word meaning* 'it appears': word used in discussing a court judgment where there is some uncertainty about what the court intended

senate ['senət] *noun* **(a)** upper house of a legislative body; *France has a bicameral system: a lower house or Chamber of Deputies and a upper house or Senate* **(b)** the upper house of the American Congress; *the US Senate voted against the proposal; the Secretary of State appeared before the Senate Foreign Relations Committee* **(c)** ruling body (of a university, college, etc.)

senator ['senətə] *noun* member of a senate (NOTE: written with a capital letter when used as a title: **Senator Jackson**)

senatorial [senə'tɔːriəl] *adjective* referring to the senate or to senators; **senatorial courtesy** = acknowledgement of the importance of the Senate (as in the convention that the President consults senators about appointments to federal posts in their states)

COMMENT: the US Senate has 100 members, each state electing two senators by popular vote. Bills may be introduced in the Senate, with the exception of bills relating to finance. The Senate has the power to ratify treaties and to confirm presidential appointments to federal posts

sender ['sendə] *noun* person who sends a letter, parcel or message

senior ['siːnjə] *adjective* older; more important; (worker) who has been employed longer than another; **senior manager** *or* **senior executive** = manager or director who has a higher rank than others; **senior partner** = partner who has a large part of the shares in a partnership; **John Smith, Senior** = the older John Smith (i.e. the father of John Smith, Junior)

seniority [siːni'ɒrəti] *noun* being older or more important; being longer in a job than someone else, often a reason for a

worker to earn more pay than another, even if the two jobs are the same; **the managers were listed in order of seniority** = the manager who had been an employee the longest or the manager with the most important job was put at the top of the list

sentence ['sentəns] **1** *noun* legal punishment given by a court to a convicted person; *he received a three-year jail sentence; the two men accused of rape face sentences of up to six years in prison*; **to pass sentence on someone** = to give someone the official legal punishment; *the jury returned a verdict of manslaughter and the judge will pass sentence next week*; **concurrent sentence** = sentence which takes place at the same time as another; **consecutive sentences** = two sentences which follow one after the other; **custodial sentence** = sentence which involves sending someone to prison; **suspended sentence** = sentence of imprisonment which a court orders shall not take effect unless the offender commits another crime **2** *verb* to give (someone) the official legal punishment; *the judge sentenced him to six months in prison or he was sentenced to six months' imprisonment; the accused was convicted of murder and will be sentenced next week*; *compare* CONVICT

sentencer ['sentənsə] *noun* person (such as a judge) who can pass a sentence on someone

separate property ['seprət 'prɒpəti] *noun* US property owned by a husband and wife before their marriage (as opposed to 'community property')

separation [sepə'reɪʃn] *noun* **(a)** agreement between a man and his wife to live apart from each other; **judicial** *or* **legal separation** = legal separation of man and wife, ordered by the court, where each becomes separated, but neither is allowed to marry again because they are not divorced **(b)** *US* leaving a job (resigning, retiring, or being fired or made redundant) **(c)** keeping separate; **separation of powers** = system in which the power in a state is separated between the legislative body which passes laws, the judiciary which enforces the law, and the executive which runs the government

---

COMMENT: in the USA, the three parts of the power of the state are kept separate and independent: the President does not sit in Congress; Congress cannot influence the decisions of the Supreme Court, etc. In the UK, the powers are not separated, because Parliament has both legislative powers (it makes laws) and judicial powers (the House of Lords acts as a court of appeal); the government (the executive) is not independent and is responsible to Parliament which can outvote it and so cause a general election. In the USA, members of government are not members of Congress, though their appointment has to be approved by Senate; in the UK, members of government are usually Members of Parliament, although some are members of the House of Lords

---

separatism ['seprətɪzm] *noun* belief that a part of a country should become separate and independent from the rest

separatist ['seprətɪst] **1** *adjective* referring to separatism; *the rise of the separatist movement in the south of the country* **2** *noun* person who believes that part of the country should become separate and independent

seq [sek] *see* ET SEQ

sequester *or* **sequestrate**
[sɪ'kwestə *or* 'siːkwəstreɪt] *verb* to take and keep (property) because a court has ordered it

sequestration [siːkwə'streɪʃn] *noun* taking and keeping of property on the order of a court, especially seizing property from someone who is in contempt of court; *his property has been kept under sequestration*

sequestrator ['siːkwəstreɪtə] *noun* person who takes and keeps property on the order of a court

sergeant ['sɑːdʒənt] *noun* **(police)** sergeant = rank in the police force above constable and below inspector; *US* Sergeant at Arms = *see* SERJEANT AT ARMS

seriatim [sɪəri'eɪtɪm] *Latin word meaning* 'one after the other in order'

serious ['sɪəriəs] *adjective* bad, important; *he faces six serious charges*; *she claims there has been a serious miscarriage of justice*

Serious Fraud Office (SFO)
['sɪəriəs 'frɔːd 'ɒfɪs] *noun* government department in charge of investigating major fraud in companies

Serjeant ['sɑːdʒənt] *see* COMMON SERJEANT

Serjeant at Arms ['sɑːdʒənt ət 'ɑːmz] *noun* official of the House of Commons or House of Representatives who keeps order in the House, makes sure that no one enters the chamber unless invited to do so, and ejects members if asked to do so by the Speaker; he also carries the mace in procession, and places it on the table at the beginning of each sitting (NOTE: the spelling **Sergeant at Arms** is used in the US House of Representatives)

servant ['sɜːvənt] *noun* **(a)** person who is employed by someone; **civil servant** = person who works in the civil service; **master and servant** = employer and employee; **the law of master and servant** = employment law **(b)** person who is paid to work in someone's house

serve [sɜːv] *verb* **(a)** to spend time in prison after being sentenced to imprisonment; *he served six months in a local jail*; *she still has half her sentence to serve* **(b)** to deal with (a customer), to do a type of work; **to serve articles** = to work as an articled clerk in a solicitor's office; **to serve a customer** = to take a customer's order and provide what he or she wants; **to serve in a shop** *or* **in a restaurant** = to deal with customers' orders; **to serve on a jury** = to be a juror **(c)** to deliver a document to someone officially; **to serve someone with**

a writ *or* to serve a writ on someone = to give someone a writ officially, so that he has to obey it

server ['sɜːvə] *noun* **process-server** = person employed to serve legal documents

service ['sɜːvɪs] *noun* **(a) service (of process)** *or* **personal service** = delivery of a document (such as a writ or summons) to someone in person or to his legal representative; **address for service** = address where court documents (such as pleadings) can be sent to a party in a case; **to acknowledge service** = to confirm that a legal document (such as a writ) has been received; **acknowledgement of service** = document whereby a defendant confirms that a claim form or other legal document has been received and that he intends to contest the claim; **service by an alternative method** = serving a legal document on someone other than by the legally prescribed method, for example by posting it to the last known address, or by advertising (NOTE: since the introduction of the new Civil Procedure Rules in April 1999, this term has replaced **substituted service**) **(b)** duty to do work for someone; **contract of service** *or* **service contract** = contract between employer and employee showing all conditions of work; **community service order** = punishment where a convicted person is sentenced to do unpaid work in the local community; **jury service** = duty which each citizen has of serving on a jury if asked to do so; **service charge** = (i) charge made by a landlord to cover general work done to a property (cleaning of the stairs, collection of rubbish, etc.); (ii) charge made in a restaurant for serving the customer **(c) civil service** = organization and personnel which administers a country under the direction of the government

COMMENT: the Civil Procedure Rules give five methods of service of documents: (i) personal service (ie., physically to a person himself); (ii) by first-class post; (iii) by sending or leaving the document at an address for service; (iv) by sending the document through a document exchange; (v) by fax or other electronic means, though this method is only used in certain circumstances, such as sending documents to a legal representative. Note also that under the new rules, documents are prepared and usually served by the court itself and not by one or other of the parties concerned

servient ['sɜːviənt] *adjective* which is less important; **servient owner** = owner of land over which someone else (the dominant owner) has a right to use a path; **servient tenement** = land over which the owner (the servient owner) grants an easement to the owner (the dominant owner) of another property (the dominant tenement)

servitude ['sɜːvɪtjuːd] *noun* **penal servitude** = former punishment by imprisonment with hard labour

session ['seʃn] *noun* **(a)** meeting, the period when a group of people meets; *the morning session will be held in the conference room*; **opening session** *or* **closing session** = first part, last part of a conference; **closed session** = meeting which is not open to the public or to newspaper reporters; **plenary session** = full session (of a congress) with all delegates present **(b)** period when Parliament is meeting; *the government is planning to introduce the Bill at the next session of Parliament* **(c) Court of Session** = highest civil court in Scotland

COMMENT: the Parliamentary session starts in October with the Opening of Parliament and the Queen's Speech. It usually lasts until August. In the USA, a new congressional session starts on the 3rd of January each year

sessions ['seʃnz] *plural noun* court; **petty sessions** = Magistrates' Court; **special sessions** = Magistrates' Court for a district which is held for a special reason (such as to deal with terrorists)

set [set] *noun* **set (of chambers)** = series of offices for a group of barristers who work together **2** *verb* to put, to fix; *the court set a timetable for the hearings* (NOTE: **setting - has set**)

set aside ['set ə'saɪd] *verb* to decide not to apply a decision, to decide to cancel an order, judgment or a step taken by a party in proceedings; *the arbitrator's award was set aside on appeal*

set down ['set 'daʊn] *verb* to arrange for a trial to take place by putting it on one of the lists of trials; *pleadings must be submitted to the court when the action is set down for trial*

set forth ['set 'fɔːθ] *verb* to put down in writing; *the argument is set forth in the document from the European Court*

set-off ['setɒf] *noun* counterclaim by a defendant which should be deducted from the sum being claimed by the claimant

set out ['set 'aʊt] *verb* **(a)** to put down in writing; *the claim is set out in the enclosed document*; *the figures are set out in the tables at the back of the book* **(b)** to try to do something; *counsel for the prosecution has set out to discredit the defence witness*

settle ['setl] *verb* **(a) to settle an account** = to pay what is owed; **to settle a claim** = to agree to pay what is asked for; *the insurance company refused to settle his claim for storm damage*; **the two parties settled out of court** = the two parties reached an agreement privately without continuing the court case **(b) to settle property on someone** = to arrange for land to be passed to trustees to keep for the benefit of future owners **(c)** to write out in final form; *counsel is instructed to settle the defence*

settled land ['setld 'lænd] *noun* land which is subject of a settlement

settlement ['setlmənt] *noun* **(a)** payment of an account; **settlement day** = day when accounts have to be settled; **our basic discount is 20% but we offer an extra 5% for rapid settlement** = we take a further 5% off the price if the customer pays quickly; **settlement in cash** *or* **cash settlement** = payment of an invoice in

cash, not by cheque **(b)** agreement after an argument; **to effect a settlement between two parties** = to bring two parties together to make them agree; **to accept something in full settlement** = to accept money or service from a debtor and agree that it covers all the claim **(c)** arrangement where land is passed to trustees to keep for the benefit of future owners; **marriage settlement** = arranging for property to be passed to a person who is getting married **(d) convict settlement** = prison camp where convicts are sent

settle on ['setl 'ɒn] *verb* to leave property to someone when you die; *he settled his property on his children*

settlor ['setlə] *noun* person who settles property on someone

sever ['sevə] *verb* to split off from the rest; *the property was severed from the rest of his assets and formed a specific legacy to his friend*

severable ['sevrəbl] *adjective* which can be divided off from the rest; *the deceased's severable share of a joint property*

several ['sevrl] *adjective* **(a)** more than a few, some; *several judges are retiring this year*; *several of our clients have received long prison sentences* **(b)** separate; **several tenancy** = holding of property by several persons, each separately and not jointly with any other person; **joint and several liability** = situation where two or more parties share a single liability, and each party is also liable for the whole claim

severally ['sevrli] *adverb* separately or not jointly; **they are jointly and severally liable** = they are liable both together as a group and as individuals

severance ['sevrəns] *noun* **(a)** ending of a joint tenancy **(b)** ending of a contract of employment; **severance pay** = money paid as compensation to someone who is losing his job

sexual ['sekʃuəl] *adjective* relating to the two sexes; **sexual discrimination** *or* **sex discrimination** *or* **discrimination on**

grounds of sex = treating men and women in different ways, implying that one is less important than the other; **sexual intercourse** = sexual act between man and woman; *it is an offence to have sexual intercourse with a girl under sixteen years of age*; **sexual offences** = criminal acts where sexual intercourse takes place (such as rape, incest)

SFO ['es 'ef 'əʊ] = SERIOUS FRAUD OFFICE

shadow ['ʃædəʊ] *adjective* the Shadow Cabinet = senior members of the Opposition who cover the areas of responsibility of the actual Cabinet, and will form the Cabinet if their party is elected to government; *the shadow Minister for the Environment*; *the shadow spokesman on energy matters*

shady ['ʃeɪdi] *adjective* not honest; *a shady deal*

sham [ʃæm] *adjective* false or not true; **sham marriage** = form of marriage arranged for the purpose of acquiring the nationality of the spouse or for other reasons

share [ʃeə] *noun* one of many parts into which a company's capital is divided, owned by shareholders; *he bought a block of shares in Marks and Spencer*; *shares fell on the London market*; *the company offered 1.8m shares on the market*; **'A' shares** = ordinary shares with limited voting rights; **'B' shares** = ordinary shares with special voting rights; **deferred shares** = shares which receive a dividend only after all other dividends have been paid; **ordinary shares** = normal shares in a company, which have no special benefits or restrictions; **preference shares** = shares (often with no voting rights) which receive their dividend before all other shares and are repaid first (at face value) if the company is liquidated; **share capital** = value of the assets of a company held as shares; **share certificate** = document proving that someone owns shares; **share issue** = selling new shares in a company to the public

shareholder ['ʃeəhəʊldə] *noun* person who owns shares in a company; **shareholders' equity** = ordinary shares owned by shareholders in a company; **majority** *or* **minority shareholder** = person who owns more than or less than half the shares in a company; *the solicitor acting on behalf of the minority shareholders* (NOTE: American English is **stockholder**)

shareholding ['ʃeəhəʊldɪŋ] *noun* group of shares in a company owned by one person; **a majority shareholding** *or* **a minority shareholding** = group of shares which are more or less than half the total (NOTE: American English is **stockholding**)

sharp [ʃɑːp] *adjective* **(a)** sudden; *a sharp rise in crimes of violence*; *a sharp drop in prices* **(b) sharp practice** = way of doing business which is not honest, but not illegal

sharper ['ʃɑːpə] *noun* **card sharper** = person who makes a living by cheating at cards

sheriff ['ʃerɪf] *noun* **(a)** *US* official in charge of justice in a county (NOTE: at federal level, the equivalent is a **marshal**); **sheriff's sale** = public sale of the goods of a person whose property has been seized by the courts because he has defaulted on payments **(b)** *UK* **(High) Sheriff** = official appointed as the government's representative in a county, responsible for executing court decisions, such as sending in bailiffs to seize property and acting as returning officer in parliamentary elections **(c)** *(in Scotland)* chief judge in a district; **Sheriff Court** = court presided over by a sheriff

ship [ʃɪp] **1** *noun* large boat for carrying passengers and cargo on the sea; **to jump ship** = to leave the ship on which you are working and not come back **2** *verb* to send goods (but not necessarily on a ship); *to ship goods to the USA*; *we ship all our goods by rail*; *the consignment of cars was shipped abroad last week*

shipment ['ʃɪpmənt] *noun* sending of goods, goods sent; **consolidated shipment**

= goods from different companies grouped together into a single shipment; **drop shipment** = delivery of a large order from a producer direct to a customer's shop or warehouse, without going through an agent

shipper ['ʃɪpə] *noun* person who sends goods or who organizes the sending of goods for other customers

shipping ['ʃɪpɪŋ] *noun* sending of goods; **shipping agent** = company which specializes in the sending of goods; **shipping company** *or* **shipping line** = company which owns ships; **shipping instructions** = details of how goods are to be shipped and delivered; **shipping note** = note which gives details of goods being shipped

shipwreck ['ʃɪprek] *noun* action of sinking or badly damaging a ship

shire ['ʃaɪə] *noun* former name for a county in Britain (still used in the county names: Buckinghamshire, Berkshire, etc.); **the shires** = the rural counties in the centre of England; *the Tory Party is very strong in the shires; we have to make sure that we do not lose the support of the shire voters*

shop [ʃɒp] **1** *noun* **(a)** place where goods are stored and sold (usually to the general public); *he has bought a shoe shop in the centre of town; she opened a women's wear shop; all the shops in the centre of town close on Sundays*; **retail shop** = shop where goods are sold only to the public **(b)** place where goods are made; **machine shop** = place where working machines are kept; **repair shop** = small factory where machines are repaired **(c)** **closed shop**, *US* **union shop** = system where a company agrees to employ only union members in certain jobs **2** *verb* **(a) to shop (for)** **something** = to look for things in shops **(b)** *(slang)* to give information about someone to the police; *he was shopped to the police by the leader of the other gang* (NOTE: **shopping - shopped**)

shoplifter ['ʃɒplɪftə] *noun* person who steals goods from shops; *at Christmas time*

gangs of shoplifters target the stores in Oxford Street

shoplifting ['ʃɒplɪftɪŋ] *noun* offence of stealing goods from shops, by taking them when the shop is open and not paying for them

Short Cause List ['ʃɔːt 'kɔːz 'lɪst] *noun* cases to be heard in the Queen's Bench Division which the judge thinks are not likely to take very long to hear

shorthand ['ʃɔːthænd] *noun* system of taking notes quickly by writing signs instead of letters; *the court proceedings were taken down in shorthand; the reporters could take notes in shorthand*; **shorthand writer** = person who takes down in shorthand evidence or a judgment given in court

shorthold tenancy   ['ʃɔːthəʊld 'tenənsi] *noun* protected tenancy for a limited period of less than five years

short sharp shock ['ʃɔːt 'ʃɑːp 'ʃɒk] *noun* formerly, a type of treatment for young offenders where they were subjected to harsh discipline for a short period in a detention centre

short title ['ʃɔːt 'taɪtl] *noun* usual name by which an Act of Parliament is known

show [ʃəʊ] **1** *noun* **(a)** exhibition or display of goods or services for sale; *motor show; computer show* **(b)** **show of hands** = way of casting votes where people show how they vote by raising their hands; *the motion was carried on a show of hands* **2** *verb* to make something be seen; **to show a gain** *or* **a fall**; **to show a profit** *or* **a loss**; **to show cause** = to appear before a court to show why an order nisi should not be made absolute (NOTE: **showing - showed - has shown**)

shrink-wrap licence *or* **license** ['ʃrɪŋkˈræp 'laɪsəns] *noun* manufacturer's licence applied to software sold to a customer under which the manufacturer grants only limited warranty over the product

COMMENT: in general, the customer does not own the software he has bought, and the manufacturer has no liability for damages consequent on using the product

SI = STATUTORY INSTRUMENT

sic [sɪk] *noun* used to show that this was the way a word was actually written in the document in question; *the letter stated : 'my legal adviser intends to apply for attack (sic) of earnings'*

sign [saɪn] **1** *noun* advertising board; notice which advertises something **2** *verb* to write your name in a special personal way on a document to show that you have written it or approved it; *to sign a letter or a contract or a document or a cheque; the letter is signed by the managing director; the cheque is not valid if it has not been signed by the finance director*

signatory [ˈsɪɡnətri] *noun* person who signs a contract, etc.; *you have to get the permission of all the signatories to the agreement if you want to change the terms*

signature [ˈsɪɡnətʃə] *noun* **(a)** name written in a special way by someone, which identifies that person; *the contract has been engrossed ready for signature; a pile of letters waiting for the managing director's signature; a will needs the signature of the testator and two witnesses; all the company's cheques need two signatures* **(b)** electronic signature = electronic text or symbols attached to a document which act in a similar way to a handwritten signature, in that they prove the authenticity of the document

silence [ˈsaɪləns] *noun* not speaking; *the accused maintained silence throughout the trial*; **right of silence** = right of an accused not to say anything when charged with a criminal offence

silent [ˈsaɪlənt] *adjective* **(a)** not talking, not making any noise; *the prisoner remained silent throughout the proceedings*; *US* silent partner = SLEEPING PARTNER **(b)** which does not mention; *if an order is silent as to*

costs, no party is entitled to costs relating to that order

silk [sɪlk] *noun (informal)* **a silk** = a Queen's Counsel; **to take silk** = to become a QC

similiter [sɪˈmɪlɪtə] *Latin word meaning* 'similarly' or 'in a similar way'

simple [ˈsɪmpl] *adjective* not complicated, not difficult to understand; *the case appears to be a simple one; it was a simple misunderstanding of the government regulations*; **simple interest** = interest calculated on the capital only, and not added to it; **simple contract** = contract which is not under seal, but is made orally or in writing; *see also* FEE, MAJORITY

sine die [ˈsɪniː ˈdiːeɪ] *Latin phrase meaning* 'with no day'; **the hearing was adjourned sine die** = the hearing was put off to a later date without saying when it would start again

sine qua non [ˈsɪni kwɑː ˈnɒn] *Latin phrase meaning* 'without which nothing': condition without which something cannot work; *agreement by the management is a sine qua non of all employment contracts*

single chamber [ˈsɪŋɡl ˈtʃeɪmbə] *noun* legislature with only one chamber (as in New Zealand and Nebraska); *see also* UNICAMERAL

single transferable vote (STV)
[ˈsɪŋɡl trænzˈfɜːrəbl ˈvəʊt] *noun* electoral system where all the candidates are listed, and the elector gives them numbers according to his or her preference

COMMENT: the total votes are counted to show how many votes a candidate needs to be elected (the electoral quota). Candidates with more than the electoral quota of first preference votes are automatically elected, and their second preference votes are passed to other candidates, and so on until the full number of candidates have the required quota and so are elected

sinking fund ['sɪŋkɪŋ 'fʌnd] *noun* fund built up out of amounts of money put aside regularly to meet a future need

sit [sɪt] *verb* **(a)** to meet; *no one can enter the Council Chamber when the committee is sitting*; *the court sat from eleven to five o'clock* **(b)** to be an MP; *she sat for a London constituency for ten years*; *the sitting MP was re-elected with a comfortable majority* **(c)** to sit on the bench = to be a magistrate

sitting ['sɪtɪŋ] *noun* **(a)** meeting of Parliament, of a court or of a tribunal **(b)** sittings = periods when courts sit

COMMENT: a Parliamentary sitting usually starts at 2.30 p.m. (11 a.m. on Fridays) and lasts until about midnight. All-night sittings happen occasionally, usually when Parliament is discussing very important or controversial matters. There are four sittings in the legal year: **Michaelmas, Hilary, Easter** and **Trinity**

situate *or* **situated** ['sɪtjʃueɪt] *adjective* in a certain place; *a freehold property situate in the borough of Richmond*

skeleton ['skelɪtən] *noun* **(a)** all the bones which make up a body; the basic details of something; **skeleton (argument)** = brief summary of the basis of an appeal filed within a short period after the judgment, or a summary of the defence against an appeal, lodged shortly after the appeal has been filed **(b)** **skeleton key** = key which will fit several different doors in a building

slander ['slɑːndə] **1** *noun* untrue spoken statement which damages someone's character; **action for slander** *or* **slander action** = case in a law court where someone says that another person had slandered him **2** *verb* **to slander someone** = to damage someone's character by saying untrue things about him; *compare* LIBEL

slanderous ['slɑːndrəs] *adjective* which could be slander; *he made*

slanderous statements about the Prime Minister on television

slate [sleɪt] *noun* list of candidates for a position; *the Democratic slate in the state elections*

sleeping partner ['sliːpɪŋ 'pɑːtnə] *noun* partner who has shares in a business but does not work in it (NOTE: American English is **silent partner**)

slip [slɪp] *noun* **(a)** small piece of paper, especially a note of the details of a marine insurance policy; **compliments slip** = piece of paper with the name of the company printed on it, sent with documents, gifts, etc., instead of a letter **(b)** mistake; *he made a couple of slips in calculating the discount*; **slip rule** = name for one of the Rules of the Supreme Court allowing minor errors to be corrected on pleadings

slip law ['slɪp 'lɔː] *noun US* law published for the first time after it has been approved, printed on a single sheet of paper, or as a small separate booklet

small [smɔːl] *adjective* **small ads** = short private advertisements in a newspaper (selling small items, asking for jobs, etc.); **small claim** = claim for less than £5000; **small claims court** = a court which deals with disputes over small amounts of money

small claims track ['smɔːl 'kleɪmz 'træk] *noun* case management system which applies to claims under £5,000

COMMENT: the aim of the small claims track is to deal with disputes as rapidly as possible, especially where the litigants appear in person. Lawyers are discouraged, but lay representatives can appear. There is only a limited right of appeal in this track

small-scale ['smɔːl'skeɪl] *adjective* (business) working in a small way, with few staff and not much money

smuggle ['smʌgl] *verb* to take goods into or out of a country without declaring them to the customs; *they had to smuggle the spare parts into the country*

smuggler ['smʌglə] *noun* person who smuggles

smuggling ['smʌglɪŋ] *noun* offence of taking goods illegally into or out of a country, without paying any tax; *he made his money in arms smuggling*

social ['səuʃl] *adjective* referring to society in general; *the government dealt carefully with many of the social problems of the day*; **social democracy =** belief that social change should be instituted by democratic means; **social ownership =** public ownership, situation where an industry is nationalized and run by a board appointed by the government; **social security =** money or help provided by the government to people who need it; **social services =** department of a local or national government which provides services, such as health care, advice, money, for people who need help; **social worker =** person who works in a social services department, visiting and looking after people who need help

sodomy ['sɒdəmi] = BUGGERY

soft [sɒft] *adjective* **soft currency =** currency of a country with a weak economy, which is cheap to buy and difficult to exchange for other currencies; **soft loan =** loan (from a company or a government) with no interest payable

sole [səul] *adjective* only; **sole owner** *or* **sole proprietor =** person who owns a business on his own, with no partners; **sole trader =** person who runs a business by himself; *see also* FEME

solemn ['sɒləm] *adjective* **solemn and binding agreement =** agreement which is not legally binding, but which all parties are supposed to obey

solicit [sə'lɪsɪt] *verb* **(a)** **to solicit orders =** to ask for orders, to try to get people to order goods **(b)** to ask for something immoral, especially to offer to provide sexual intercourse for money

soliciting [sə'lɪsɪtɪŋ] *noun* offence of offering to provide sexual intercourse for money

solicitor [sə'lɪsɪtə] *noun (in England and Wales)* lawyer who has passed the examinations of the Law Society and has a valid certificate to practise and who gives advice to members of the public and acts for them in legal matters, and who may have right of audience in certain courts; **to instruct a solicitor =** to give orders to a solicitor to act on your behalf; **duty solicitor =** local solicitor who is on duty at a magistrates' court and can be contacted at any time by a party who is appearing in that court or who has been taken to a police station under arrest or for questioning; **the Official Solicitor =** solicitor who acts in the High Court for parties who have no one to act for them, usually because they are under a legal disability; **the Treasury Solicitor =** the solicitor who is the head of the Government's legal department in England and Wales and legal adviser to the Cabinet Office and other government departments

COMMENT: solicitors who have qualified as barristers can be appointed as part-time judges, and can speak before the Court of Appeal and the House of Lords

Solicitor-General [sə'lɪsɪtə'dʒenrl] *noun* one of the law officers, a Member of the House of Commons and deputy to the Attorney-General; **Solicitor-General for Scotland =** junior law officer in Scotland

solitary confinement ['sɒlɪtri kən'faɪnmənt] *noun* being kept alone in a cell, without being able to see or speak to other prisoners; *he was kept in solitary confinement for six months*

solus agreement ['səuləs ə'gri:mənt] *noun* agreement where one party is linked only to the other party, especially an agreement where a retailer buys all his stock from a single supplier

solvent ['sɒlvənt] **1** *adjective* having enough money to pay debts; *when he bought the company it was barely solvent*

2 *noun* powerful glue; **solvent abuse** = sniffing solvent, which acts as a hallucinatory drug

solvency ['sɒlvənsi] *noun* being able to pay all debts; *see also* INSOLVENCY

sought [sɔ:t] *see* SEEK

sound [saʊnd] *adjective* reasonable, which can be trusted; *the company's financial situation is very sound*; *the solicitor gave us some very sound advice*; *the evidence brought forward by the police is not very sound*; **of sound mind** = sane, mentally well; *he was of sound mind when he wrote the will*

soundness ['saʊndnəs] *noun* being reasonable; *the soundess of the solicitor's advice*

source ['sɔ:s] *noun* place where something comes from; *source of income*; *you must declare income from all sources to the Inland Revenue*; **income which is taxed at source** = where the tax is removed before the income is paid

South-Eastern Circuit ['saʊθ'i:stən 'sɜ:kɪt] *noun* one of the six circuits of the Crown Court to which barristers belong, with its centre in London

sovereign ['sɒvrɪn] **1** *noun* **(a)** king or queen; *the sovereign's head appears on coins and stamps* **(b)** head of state; *the protection given to a foreign sovereign* **2** *adjective* **(a)** having complete freedom to govern itself; **sovereign state** = independent country which governs itself **(b) sovereign immunity** = immunity of a foreign head of state or former head of state from prosecution outside his country for crimes committed inside his country in the course of exercising his public function

sovereign rights ['sɒvrɪn 'raɪts] *noun* *(in the EU)* rights of a state, which are limited by the application of Community law

sovereignty ['sɒvrɪnti] *noun* power to govern; **to have sovereignty over a territory** = to have power to govern a territory; *two neighbouring states claimed*

sovereignty over the offshore islands; **the sovereignty** *or* **supremacy of Parliament** = unlimited right of Parliament to make or undo laws (a principle which is at variance with EC laws)

Speaker ['spi:kə] *noun* person who presides over a meeting of a parliament; **discussions held behind the Speaker's chair** = informal discussions between representatives of opposing political parties meeting on neutral ground away from the floor of the House (NOTE: MPs address the Speaker as **Mr Speaker** *or* **Madam Speaker**)

COMMENT: in the House of Commons, the speaker is an ordinary Member of Parliament chosen by the other members; the equivalent in the House of Lords is the Lord Chancellor. In the US Congress, the speaker of the House of Representatives is an ordinary congressman, elected by the other congressmen; the person presiding over meetings of the Senate is the Vice-President

special ['speʃl] *adjective* different, not normal; referring to one particular thing; *he offered us special terms*; *the car is being offered at a special price*; **special agent** = (i) person who represents someone in a particular matter; (ii) person who does secret work for a government; **Special Branch** = department of the British police which deals with terrorism; **special constable** = part-time policeman who works mainly at weekends or on important occasions; **special damages** = damages awarded by a court to compensate for a quantifiable loss (such as the expense of repairing something); **special deposits** = large sums of money which banks have to deposit with the Bank of England; **special procedure** = special system for dealing quickly with undefended divorce cases whereby the parties can obtain a divorce without the necessity of a full trial; **special sessions** = magistrates' courts held for a particular reason (such as to deal with terrorists); *US* **special session** = session of Congress convened by the President to discuss an important matter, after Congress has been adjourned sine die

special resolution ['speʃl rezə'lu:ʃn] *noun* resolution of the members of a company which is only valid if it is approved by 75% of the votes cast at a meeting

COMMENT: 21 days' notice that special resolution will be put to a meeting must be given. A special resolution might deal with an important matter, such as a change to the company's articles of association, a change of the company's name, or of the objects of the company

specialty contract ['speʃlti 'kɒntrækt] *noun* contract made under seal

specific [spə'sɪfɪk] *adjective* particular, relating to one particular thing; **specific performance** = court order to a party to carry out his obligations in a contract

specification [spesɪfɪ'keɪʃn] *noun* details of what is needed or of what is to be supplied; **patent specification** = full details of an invention which is the subject of a patent application

specify ['spesɪfaɪ] *verb* to state clearly what is needed; *to specify full details of the grounds for complaint*; *the contract specifies that the goods have to be delivered to London*

specimen ['spesɪmən] *noun* thing which is given as a sample; **to give specimen signatures on a bank mandate** = to write the signatures of all people who can sign cheques on an account so that the bank can recognize them

speech [spi:tʃ] *noun* (a) speaking, the ability to talk; **freedom of speech** = being able to say what you want without being afraid of prosecution, provided that you do not break the law (b) talk given in public; *to make a speech in Parliament*; *counsel's closing speech to the jury*; *the Chancellor's Budget Speech lasted two hours*; **Queen's Speech** = speech made by the Queen at the opening of a session of Parliament which outlines the government's plans for legislation; **the Debate on the Queen's Speech** = first debate of a new session of Parliament, the motion being to present an address of thanks to the Queen, but the debate in fact being concerned with the Government's legislative programme as outlined in the speech

speeding ['spi:dɪŋ] *noun* offence committed when driving a vehicle faster than the speed limit; *he was booked for speeding*

spent conviction ['spent kən'vɪkʃn] *noun* previous conviction for which an accused person has been sentenced in the past and which must not be referred to in open court

sphere of influence ['sfɪə əv 'ɪnfluəns] *noun* area of the world where a very strong country can exert powerful influence over other states; *some Latin American states fall within the USA's sphere of influence*

spiritual ['spɪrɪtʃuəl] *adjective* **Lords Spiritual** = archbishops and bishops sitting in the House of Lords

spoil [spɔɪl] *verb* to ruin, to make something bad; *half the shipment was spoiled by water*; *the company's results were spoiled by the last quarter*; **spoilt ballot paper** = voting paper which has not been filled in correctly by the voter (NOTE: **spoiling - spoiled** *or* **spoilt**)

spoils of war ['spɔɪlz əv 'wɔ:] *plural noun* goods or valuables taken by an army from an enemy

spokesman ['spəʊksmən] *noun* man who speaks in public on behalf of a group; *a White House spokesman denied the news report*; *a government spokesman in the House of Lords revealed that discussions had been concluded on the treaty*

spokeswoman ['spəʊkswʊmən] *noun* woman who speaks in public on behalf of a group

spokesperson ['spəʊkspɜːsən] *noun* person who speaks in public on behalf of a group (NOTE: the word **spokesperson** is now often used, as it avoids making a distinction between men and women)

sponsor ['spɒnsə] **1** *noun* **(a)** person or group (such as a trades union) which sponsors an MP **(b)** MP who proposes a Bill in the House of Commons **2** *verb* **(a)** **to sponsor an MP** = to pay part of the election expenses of an MP, and contribute to his local party's funds (for which the MP is expected to represent the sponsor's interests in Parliament) **(b)** to propose a Bill in the House of Commons

sponsorship [s'pɒnsəʃɪp] *noun* act of sponsoring; *sponsorship of two MPs cost the union several thousand pounds*

spouse [spaʊz] *noun* husband or wife; person who is married to another person; **surviving spouse** = living husband or wife of a person who has died (normally the beneficiary of the estate, even if the dead person died intestate; if there are living children, then the spouse takes the personal chattels, a statutory sum as legacy, and interest in half the remaining estate)

springing use ['sprɪŋɪŋ 'juːs] *noun* use which will come into effect if something happens in the future

spy [spaɪ] **1** *noun* person who tries to find out secrets about another country; *he spent many years as a spy for the enemy*; *he was arrested as a spy* **2** *verb* **(a)** to watch another country secretly to get information; *she was accused of spying for the enemy* **(b)** to see; **I spy strangers** = words said by an MP when he wants to tell the Speaker to clear the public galleries

squad [skwɒd] *noun* **(a)** special group of police; **the Drug Squad** = section of the police force which investigates crime related to drugs; **the Fraud Squad** = department of a police force which deals with cases of fraud; **the Homicide Squad** *or* **Murder Squad** = department of a police force which deals with cases of murder **(b)** special group of soldiers or workers; **firing squad** = group of soldiers who execute someone by shooting

squad car ['skwɒd 'kɑː] *noun* police patrol car

squat [skwɒt] *verb* to occupy premises belonging to another person unlawfully and without title or without paying rent (NOTE: **squatting - squatted**)

squatter ['skwɒtə] *noun* person who squats in someone else's property; **squatter's rights** = rights of a person who is squatting in another person's property to remain in unlawful possession of premises until ordered to leave by a court

COMMENT: if a squatter has lived on the premises for a long period (over 12 years) and the owner has not tried to evict him or her, he or she may have rights over the premises

squeal [skwiːl] *verb (slang)* to inform the police about other criminals

squire ['skwaɪə] *noun US* local legal official, such as a magistrate

stakeholder ['steɪkhəʊldə] *noun* **(a)** person who holds money impartially (such as money deposited by one of the parties to a wager) until he has to give it up to another party **(a)** person who has a stake in a business, such as a shareholder, an employee, a supplier, etc.

stamp [stæmp] **1** *noun* **(a)** (i) device for making marks on documents; (ii) mark made in this way; *the invoice has the stamp 'Received with thanks' on it*; *the customs officer looked at the stamps in his passport*; **date stamp** = stamp with rubber figures which can be moved, used for marking the date on documents; **rubber stamp** = stamp made of hard rubber cut to form words **(b)** small piece of gummed paper which you buy from a post office and stick on a letter or parcel to pay for the postage; *a postage stamp*; *a £1 stamp* **(c)** **stamp duty** = tax on legal documents (such as the conveyance of a property to a new owner or the contract for the purchase of shares) **2** *verb* **(a)** to mark a document with a stamp; *to stamp an invoice 'Paid'*;

the documents were stamped by the customs officials **(b)** to put a postage stamp on (an envelope, etc.); **stamped addressed envelope** = envelope with your own address written on it and a stamp stuck on it to pay for the return postage

stand [stænd] **1** *noun* **(a)** active campaign against something; *the government's stand against racial prejudice* **(b)** position of an official body or person on a question (either for or against); *the police chief criticized the council's stand on law and order* **(c) witness stand** = witness box, place in a courtroom where the witnesses give evidence; **to take the stand** = to go into the witness box to give evidence **2** *verb* **(a)** to offer oneself as a candidate in an election; *he stood as a Liberal candidate in the General Election; he is standing against the present deputy leader in the leadership contest; she was persuaded to stand for parliament; he has stood for office several times, but has never been elected* **(b)** to exist, to be in a state; *the House stands adjourned; the report stood referred to the Finance Committee* (NOTE: **stands - stood**)

standard ['stændəd] **1** *noun* normal quality or normal conditions against which other things are judged; **standard of living** *or* **living standards** = quality of personal home life (such as amount of food or clothes bought, size of family car); **production standards** = quality of production; **up to standard** = of acceptable quality; **gold standard** = attaching of the value of a currency to value of a quantity of gold **2** *adjective* normal or usual; *the standard charge for consultation is £50; we have a standard charge of £25 for a thirty minute session*; **standard agreement** *or* **standard contract** = normal printed contract form; **standard form contract** = contract which states the conditions of carrying out a common commercial arrangement (such as chartering a ship); **standard letter** = letter which is sent with only minor changes to various correspondents; **standard rate** = basic rate of income tax which is paid by

most taxpayers, basic rate of VAT which is levied on most goods and services

stand down ['stænd 'daʊn] *verb* to withdraw your name from an election; *the wife of one of the candidates is ill and he has stood down*

standi ['stændaɪ] *see* LOCUS

stand in for ['stænd 'ɪn fə] *verb* to take the place of someone; *Mr Smith is standing in for the chairman who is away on holiday*

standing ['stændɪŋ] **1** *adjective* permanent; **standing committee** = (i) permanent committee which always examines the same problem; (ii) committee of Members of Parliament which examines in detail Bills which are not passed to other committees; *see also* AD HOC **2** *noun* **(a) long-standing customer** *or* **customer of long standing** = person who has been a customer for many years **(b)** good reputation; *the financial standing of a company*; **company of good standing** = very reputable company

standing order ['stændɪŋ 'ɔːdə] *noun* **(a)** order written by a customer asking a bank to pay money regularly to an account; *I pay my subscription by standing order*; *compare* DIRECT DEBIT **(b) standing orders** = rules or regulations which regulate conduct in any body, such as the House of Commons, an army camp or a police station

stand over ['stænd 'əʊvə] *verb* to adjourn; *the case has been stood over to next month*

Star Chamber ['stɑː 'tʃeɪmbə] *noun* **(a)** formerly, a royal court which tried cases without a jury **(b)** recently, cabinet committee which examines the spending proposals of government departments

stare decisis ['stɑːreɪ dɪ'saɪsɪs] *Latin phrase meaning* 'stand by preceding decisions': principle that courts must abide by precedents set by judgments made in higher courts

state [steɪt] **1** *noun* **(a)** independent country; semi-independent section of a federal country (such as the USA); **to turn state's evidence** = to confess to a crime and then act as a witness against the other criminals involved in the hope of getting a lighter sentence; *see also* SECRETARY OF STATE **(b)** government of a country; **offence against the state** = act of attacking the lawful government of a country; **state enterprise** = company run by the state; *the bosses of state industries are appointed by the government*; **state ownership** = situation where an industry is nationalized; **state school** = school run by a local authority and paid for with public money **2** *verb* to say clearly; *the document states that all revenue has to be declared to the tax office*; **case stated** = statement of the facts of a case which has been heard in a lower court, drawn up so that a higher court can decide on an appeal; *he appealed by way of case stated*; *the Appeal Court dismissed the appeal by way of case stated*

state-controlled [steɪtkən'trəʊld] *adjective* run by the state; *state-controlled television*

State Department ['steɪt dɪ'pɑːtmənt] *noun* US government department dealing with relations between the USA and other countries; *see note at* FOREIGN

stateless person ['steɪtləs 'pɜːsən] *noun* person who is not a citizen of any state

statement ['steɪtmənt] *noun* **(a)** saying something clearly; **to make a statement** = to give details of something to the press or to the police; *(of a Member of Parliament)* **to make a statement to the House** = to tell the House of Commons that you have done something wrong, to explain your actions to the House; **to make a false statement** = to give wrong details; **statement of affairs** = official statement made by a bankrupt or an insolvent company, listing their assets and liabilities; **Statement of Means** = statement showing the financial position of the claimant, attached to an application for Legal Aid **(b)** *(in a civil court)* **statements of case** = documents relating to a claim, including the claim form, the particulars of claim, the defence and counterclaim, the reply and the defence to the counterclaim (NOTE: since the introduction of the new Civil Procedure Rules in April 1999, this term has replaced **pleadings**); **statement of claim** = pleading containing details of a claimant's case and the relief sought against the defendant (NOTE: since the introduction of the new Civil Procedure Rules in April 1999, this term has been replaced by **particulars of claim**); **statement of truth** = statement attached to a claim form or the particulars of claim by which the claimant or defendant states that he believes that the facts given are true (if it can be proved that he signed the statement without believing it to be true, he is guilty of contempt of court); **statement of value** = document filed by the claimant as part of his claim, detailing the value of the claim, or a document filed by the defendant giving his estimate of value in reply to the claim **(c)** **financial statement** = document which shows the financial situation of a company; *the accounts department have prepared a financial statement for the shareholders*; **bank statement** = written document from a bank showing the balance of an account; **monthly** *or* **quarterly statement** = statement which is sent every month or every quarter by the bank; **statement of account** = list of invoices and credits and debits sent by a supplier to a customer at the end of each month

state-owned ['steɪt'əʊnd] *adjective* owned by the state

statesman ['steɪtsmən] *noun* important political leader or representative of a country; *several statesmen from Western countries are meeting to discuss defence problems*

statesmanlike ['steɪtsmənlaɪk] *adjective* wise or skilful, like a good statesman

statesmanship ['steɪtsmənʃɪp] *noun* ability of being a good statesman

station [steɪʃn] *noun* **(police) station** = building where the police have their local offices; *six demonstrators were arrested and taken to the police station; he spent the night in the station cells*

stationer ['steɪʃnə] *noun* person who makes or supplies paper, pens, typewriter ribbons, etc.; **law stationer** = person who specializes in supplying stationery to legal firms

stationery ['steɪʃnri] *noun* office supplies for writing, such as paper, typewriter ribbons, pens, etc.; *legal stationery supplier; shop selling office stationery*; **continuous stationery** = paper made as a long sheet used in computer printers

statistical [stə'tɪstɪkl] *adjective* referring to statistics, based on figures; **statistical discrepancy** = amount by which two sets of figures differ

statistician [stætɪ'stɪʃn] *noun* person who prepares and analyzes statistics

statistics [stə'tɪstɪks] *plural noun* study of facts in the form of figures; *he asked for the birth statistics for 1998; council statistics show that the amount of rented property in the borough has increased; government trade statistics show that exports to the EC have fallen over the last six months*; **vital statistics** = figures dealing with births, marriages and deaths in a district

status [steɪtəs] *noun* (a) importance or position in society; **loss of status** = becoming less important in a group; **status inquiry** = checking on a customer's credit rating (b) **legal status** = legal identity of a person or body (such as a company or partnership)

status quo ['steɪtəs 'kwəʊ] *noun* state of things as they are now; *the contract does not alter the status quo*; **status quo ante** = the situation as it was before; *see also* IN STATU QUO

statute ['stætjuːt] *noun* established written law, especially an Act of Parliament; **statute book** = all laws passed by Parliament which are still in force; **statute of limitations** = law which allows only a certain amount of time (usually six years) for someone to start legal proceedings to claim property or compensation for damage, etc.

statute-barred ['stætjuːt'bɑːd] *adjective* which cannot take place because the time laid down in the statute of limitations has expired

statutorily ['stætʃʊtrɪli] *adverb* by statute; *a statutorily protected tenant*

statutory ['stætʃʊtri] *adjective* fixed by law or by a statute; *there is a statutory period of probation of thirteen weeks; the authority has a statutory obligation to provide free education to all children; powers conferred on an authority by the statutory code*; **statutory books** = official registers which a company must keep; **statutory declaration** = (i) statement made to the Registrar of Companies that a company has complied with certain legal conditions; (ii) declaration signed and witnessed for official purposes; **statutory duty** = duty which someone must perform and which is laid down by statute; **statutory holiday** = holiday which is fixed by law; **statutory instrument (SI)** = order (which has the force of law) made under authority granted to a minister by an Act of Parliament; **statutory trust** = holding property on behalf of the issue of a person who has died intestate; **statutory undertakers** = bodies formed by statute and having legal duties to provide services (such as gas, electricity, water); **statutory will** = will made on behalf of a mentally ill person on the instructions of the Court of Protection; *see* LEGACY

stay [steɪ] **1** *noun* temporary stopping of an order made by a court; **stay of execution** = temporary prevention of someone from enforcing a judgment; *the court granted the company a two-week stay of execution; the stay was extended for a further four weeks*; **stay of proceedings** = stopping of a case which is being heard; *proceedings will continue when the stay is lifted* **2** *verb* to stop (an action) temporarily; *the defendant made an application to stay the proceedings* *until the claimant gave security for costs; one of the parties asked for the action to be stayed for a month to allow for a settlement to be attempted*

steal [sti:l] *verb* to take something which does not belong to you; *two burglars broke into the office and stole the petty cash; one of our managers left to form his own company and stole the list of our clients' addresses; one of our biggest problems is stealing in the wine department*; **stolen goods** = goods which have been stolen; **handling** *or* **receiving stolen goods** = offence of dealing with goods (receiving them or selling them) which you know to have been stolen (NOTE: **stealing - stole - has stolen**. Note also that you steal things **from** someone)

stealing ['sti:lɪŋ] *noun* crime of taking property which belongs to someone else; **going equipped for stealing** = notifiable offence of carrying tools which could be used for burglary

steaming ['sti:mɪŋ] *noun* offence committed by a group of youths, usually unarmed, who rush down a street, through a department store, etc., stealing items and harassing people as they go past

stenographer [stə'nɒɡrəfə] *noun* official person who can write in shorthand and so take records of what is said in court

step- [step] *prefix* showing a family relationship through a parent who has married again; **stepfather** = man who has married a child's mother, but is not the natural father of the child; **stepmother** = woman who has married a child's father, but is not the natural mother of the child

stipendiary magistrate
[staɪ'pendiəri 'mædʒɪstreɪt] *noun* magistrate who is a qualified lawyer and who receives a salary (as opposed to an unpaid Justice of the Peace) (NOTE: now called **District Judge** *or* **Senior District Judge**)

COMMENT: a stipendiary magistrate usually sits alone

stipulate ['stɪpjuleɪt] *verb* to demand that a condition be put into a contract; *to stipulate that the contract should run for five years; to pay the stipulated charges; the company failed to pay on the stipulated date or on the date stipulated in the contract; the contract stipulates that the seller pays the buyer's legal costs*

stipulation [stɪpju'leɪʃn] *noun* condition in a contract

stir [stɜ:] *noun (slang)* prison

stirpes ['stɜ:pi:z] *see* PER STIRPES

stirpital ['stɜ:pɪtl] *adjective* referring to an entitlement which is divided among branches of a family rather than among individuals; *the judge placed a stirpital construction on the rule that children of a deceased person dying intestate must bring interest received from that person into hotchpot*

stock [stɒk] **1** *noun* **(a)** quantity of raw materials; *we have large stocks of oil or coal; the country's stocks of butter or sugar* **(b)** quantity of goods for sale; **opening stock** = details of stock at the beginning of an accounting period; **closing stock** = details of stock at the end of an accounting period; **stock control** = making sure that enough stock is kept and that quantities and movements of stock are noted; **stock valuation** = estimating the value of stock at the end of an accounting period; **to buy a shop with stock at valuation** = to pay for the stock the same amount as its value, as estimated by an independent valuer **(c) in stock** *or* **out of stock** = available or not available in the warehouse or store **(d) stocks and shares** = shares in ordinary companies; **stock certificate** = document proving that someone owns shares in a company; **dollar stocks** = shares in American companies; **government stocks** = government securities; **loan stock** = money lent to a company at a fixed rate of interest; *US* **common stock** = ordinary shares in a company giving the shareholders the right to vote at meetings and receive a dividend (NOTE: British English is **ordinary shares**) **2**

verb to hold goods for sale in a warehouse or store

stockbroker ['stɒkbrəukə] *noun* person who buys or sells stocks and shares for clients; **stockbroker's commission** = payment to a broker for a deal carried out on behalf of a client

stockbroking ['stɒkbrəukɪŋ] *noun* trade of dealing in shares for clients; *a stockbroking firm*

Stock Exchange ['stɒk ɪks'tʃeɪndʒ] *noun* place where stocks and shares are bought and sold; *he works on the Stock Exchange*; *shares in the company are traded on the Stock Exchange*; **Stock Exchange listing** = official list of shares which can be bought or sold on the Stock Exchange

stockholder ['stɒkhəuldə] *noun* person who holds shares in a company

stockholding ['stɒkhəuldɪŋ] *noun* shares in a company held by someone

stock market ['stɒk 'mɑːkɪt] *noun* place where shares are bought and sold; *stock market price or price on the stock market*; **stock market valuation** = value of shares based on the current market price

stop and search *US* **stop and frisk** ['stɒp ən 'sɜːtʃ] *noun* power held by a police officer to stop anyone and search them, even though there is no evidence that the person has committed any offence

straight [streɪt] *adjective* direct, not dishonest; **to play straight** *or* **to act straight with someone** = to act honestly with someone; **to go straight** = to stop criminal activities

stranger ['streɪnʒə] *noun* person who is not an MP but is allowed into the public gallery or the press gallery as a visitor; **strangers' gallery** = gallery for visitors in the House of Commons or House of Lords; *see also* SPY

strict [strɪkt] *adjective* exact; *in strict order of seniority*; *to follow a strict interpretation of the rules*; **strict liability**

= total liability for an offence which has been committed (whether you are at fault or not)

strife [straɪf] *noun* violent public arguments and disorder; **civil strife** = trouble when gangs of people fight each other

strike [straɪk] **1** *noun* **(a)** stopping of work by the workers (because of lack of agreement with management or because of orders from a union); **general strike** = strike of all the workers in a country; **official strike** = strike which has been approved by the union; **protest strike** = strike in protest at a particular grievance; **token strike** = short strike to show that workers have a grievance; **unofficial strike** = strike by local workers, which has not been approved by the union as a whole **(b) to take strike action** = to go on strike; **strike ballot** *or* **strike vote** = vote by workers to decide if a strike should be held; **strike call** = demand by a union for a strike; **no-strike agreement** *or* **no-strike clause** = (clause in an) agreement where the workers say that they will never strike; **strike fund** = money collected by a trade union from its members, used to pay strike pay; **strike pay** = money paid to striking workers by their trade union during a strike **(c) to come out on strike** *or* **to go on strike** = to stop work; *the office workers are on strike for higher pay*; **to call the workers out on strike** = to tell the workers to stop work **2** *verb* **(a)** to stop working because there is no agreement with management; *to strike for higher wages or for shorter working hours*; *to strike in protest against bad working conditions*; **to strike in sympathy with the postal workers** = to strike to show that you agree with the postal workers who are on strike **(b)** to hit (someone); *two policemen were struck by bottles*; *he was struck on the head by a cosh* **(c) to strike from the record** = to remove words from the written minutes of a meeting because they are incorrect or offensive; *the chairman's remarks were struck from the record* (NOTE: **striking - struck**)

strike off ['straɪk 'ɒf] *verb* to delete or to remove (a word from a text, a name from a list); **to strike someone off the rolls** = to stop a solicitor from practising by removing his name from the list of solicitors

strike out ['straɪk 'aʊt] *verb* **(a)** to delete or to remove (a word from a text, a name from a list); *US* **to strike out the last word** = way of getting permission of the chair to speak on a question, by moving that the last word of the amendment or section being discussed should be deleted **(b)** *(in civil law)* to order something written to be deleted, so that it no longer forms part of the case; *to strike out a pleading or a statement of case; a party can apply for a statement of case to be struck out if it is not verified; a court may strike out a statement of case if it appears that the statement shows no grounds for bringing the claim*

strip search ['strɪp 'sɜːtʃ] *noun* searching of a person after he or she has removed their clothes (strip searches should be carried out by a doctor or nurse, or at least by a police officer of the same sex as the person being searched)

strongbox ['strɒŋbɒks] *noun* safe, heavy metal box which cannot be opened easily, in which valuable documents, money, etc., can be kept

strongroom ['strɒŋruːm] *noun* special room (in a bank) where valuable documents, money, gold, etc., can be kept

STV = SINGLE TRANSFERABLE VOTE

sub- [sʌb] *prefix* under; less important; **sub-agency** = small agency which is part of a large agency; **sub-agent** = person who is in charge of a sub-agency; **sub-committee** = small committee which reports on a special subject to a main committee; *he is chairman of the Finance Sub-Committee*

sub-clause ['sʌbklɔːz] *noun* part of a clause in a Bill being considered by

Parliament, which will become a sub-section when the Bill becomes an Act

subcontract 1 [sʌb'kɒntrækt] *noun* contract between the main contractor for a whole project and another firm who will do part of the work; *they have been awarded the subcontract for all the electrical work in the new building; we will put the electrical work out to subcontract* 2 [sʌbkən'trækt] *verb* to agree with a company that they will do part of the work for a project; *the electrical work has been subcontracted to Smith Ltd*

subcontractor [sʌbkən'træktə] *noun* company which has a contract to do work for a main contractor

subject ['sʌbdʒɪkt] *noun* **(a)** what something is concerned with; *the subject of the action was the liability of the defendant for the claimant's injuries* **(b)** person who is a citizen of a country and bound by its laws; *he is a British subject; British subjects do not need visas to visit countries in the European Union*; **liberty of the subject** = right of a citizen to be free unless convicted of a crime which is punishable by imprisonment

subject to ['sʌbdʒɪkt tʊ] *adjective* **(a)** depending on; **the contract is subject to government approval** = the contract will be valid only if it is approved by the government; **agreement** *or* **sale subject to contract** = agreement or sale which is not legal until a proper contract has been signed; **offer subject to availability** = the offer is valid only if the goods are available **(b)** which can receive; **these articles are subject to import tax** = import tax has to be paid on these articles

sub judice [sʌb 'dʒuːdəsi] *Latin phrase* meaning 'under the law': being considered by a court and so not decided (cases which are 'sub judice' cannot be mentioned in the media or in Parliament if the mention is likely to prejudice the trial, and so would constitute contempt of court); *the papers cannot report the case because it is still sub judice*

sublease 1 ['sʌbliːs] *noun* lease from a tenant to another tenant **2** [sʌb'liːs] *verb* to lease a leased property from another tenant; *they subleased a small office in the centre of town*

sublessee [sʌble'siː] *noun* person or company which holds a property on a sublease

sublessor [sʌble'sɔː] *noun* tenant who lets a leased property to another tenant

sublet [sʌb'let] *verb* to let a leased property to another tenant; *we have sublet part of our office to a financial consultancy* (NOTE: **subletting - sublet - has sublet**)

submission [səb'mɪʃn] *noun* pleading an argument in court; *the court heard the submission of defence counsel that there was no case to answer or in the submission of defence counsel, there was no case to answer*

submit [səb'mɪt] *verb* **(a)** to put (something) forward to be examined; *to submit a proposal to the committee*; *he submitted a claim to the insurers* **(b)** to plead an argument in court; *counsel submitted that the defendant had no case to answer*; *it was submitted that the right of self-defence can be available only against unlawful attack* **(c)** to agree to be ruled by something; *he refused to submit to the jurisdiction of the court* (NOTE: **submitting - submitted**)

subornation of perjury [səbɔː'neɪʃn əv 'pɜːdʒri] *noun* offence of getting someone to commit perjury

subpoena [sə'piːnə] **1** *noun* court order requiring someone to appear in court; **subpoena ad testificandum** = court order requiring someone to appear as a witness; **subpoena duces tecum** = court order requiring someone to appear as a witness and bring with him documents relevant to the case (NOTE: since the introduction of the new Civil Procedure Rules in April 1999, these terms have been replaced by **witness summons**) **2** *verb* to order someone to

appear in court; *the finance director was subpoenaed by the prosecution*

subrogation [sʌbrəʊ'geɪʃn] *noun* legal principle whereby someone stands in the place of another person and acquires that person's rights and is responsible for that person's liabilities

subscribe [səb'skraɪb] *verb* **(a)** to **subscribe to a magazine** = to pay for a series of issues of a magazine **(b)** to **subscribe for shares** = to apply to buy shares in a new company

subscriber [səb'skraɪbə] *noun* person who subscribes (to a magazine, for shares in a new company); **subscriber shares** = the first shares issued when a new company is formed

sub-section ['sʌb'sekʃn] *noun* part of a section of a document, such as an Act of Parliament; *you will find the information in sub-section 3 of Section 47*

subsequent ['sʌbsɪkwənt] *adjective* which follows because of something; **condition subsequent** = condition which says that a contract will be modified or annulled if something is not done

subsidiarity [səbsɪdi'ærɪti] *noun (in the EU)* principle that the Community shall only decide on matters which are better decided at Community level than at the level of the individual Member States and that other matters shall be left to each Member State to decide; subsidiarity only operates in those areas where the Community does not have exclusive jurisdiction

subsidiary [sʌb'sɪdiəri] *adjective* less important than, depending on (something); *he faces one serious charge and several subsidiary charges arising out of the main charge*; **subsidiary company** = company which is owned by a parent company; **subsidiary motion** = motion which is attached to a substantive motion

subsidize ['sʌbsɪdaɪz] *verb* to help by giving money; *the government has refused to subsidize the car industry*; **subsidized accommodation** = cheap accommodation which is partly paid for by an employer or a local authority, etc.

subsidy [sʌbsɪdi] *noun* **(a)** money given to help something which is not profitable; *the industry exists on government subsidies; the government has increased its subsidy to the car industry* **(b)** money given by a government to make a product cheaper

substance [ˈsʌbstəns] *noun* **(a)** material; **dangerous substance** = material which may cause harm to someone **(b)** real basis of a report or argument; *there is no substance to the stories about his resignation*

substandard [sʌbˈstændəd] *adjective* not of the necessary quality to meet a standard

substantial [sʌbˈstænʃl] *adjective* large or important; **she was awarded substantial damages** = she received a large sum of money as damages; **to acquire a substantial interest in a company** = to buy a large number of shares in a company

substantive [səbˈstæntɪv] *adjective* real or actual; **substantive law** = all laws, including common law and statute law, which deal with legal principles (as opposed to procedural law which refers to the procedure for putting law into practice); **substantive motion** = motion which is complete in itself; **substantive offence** = offence which has actually taken place

substitute [ˈsʌbstɪtjuːt] **1** *noun* **(a)** person or thing which takes the place of someone or something else **(b)** *US* motion introduced in place of the business being discussed, which has the effect of killing the original motion **2** *verb* **(a)** to take the place of something else; **substituted service** = serving a legal document on someone other than by the legally prescribed method, for example by posting it to the last known address, or by advertising in the press (NOTE: since the introduction of the new Civil Procedure Rules in April 1999, this term has been replaced by

service by an alternative method) **(b)** to put something in the place of something else; *they made an application to substitute a party, but the claimant refused his consent*

substitution [sʌbstɪˈtjuːʃn] *noun* putting something in the place of something else; *the substitution of a party may take place if the court agrees that the original party was named by mistake*

substitutionary [sʌbstɪˈtjuːʃənri] *adjective* acting as a substitute; *he made a will leaving everything to his wife, but with the substitutionary provision that if she died before him, his estate devolved on their children*

subtenancy [sʌbˈtenənsi] *noun* agreement to sublet a property

subtenant [sʌbˈtenənt] *noun* person or company to which a property has been sublet

subversive [səbˈvɜːsɪv] *adjective* which acts secretly against the government; *the police is investigating subversive groups in student organizations*

succeed [səkˈsiːd] *verb* to follow, especially to take the place of someone who has retired or died; **to succeed to a property** = to become the owner of a property by inheriting it from someone who has died

success fee [səkˈses ˈfiː] *noun* conditional fee, a lawyer's fee which is only paid if the case has been successful

succession [səkˈseʃn] *noun* acquiring property or title from someone who has died; **law of succession** = laws relating to how property shall pass to others when the owner dies; **intestate succession** = rules which apply when someone dies without having made a will

successor [səkˈsesə] *noun* person who takes over from someone; *Mr Smith's successor as chairman will be Mr Jones*

sue [suː] *verb* to take someone to court, to start legal proceedings against someone to get compensation for a wrong; *to sue someone for damages*; *he is suing the company for £50,000 compensation*

sufferance ['sʌfrəns] *noun* agreement to something which is not stated, but assumed because no objection has been raised; *he has been allowed to live in the house on sufferance*; **tenancy at sufferance** = situation where a previously lawful tenant is still in possession of property after the termination of the lease

suffrage ['sʌfrɪdʒ] *noun* right to vote in elections; **universal suffrage** = right of all citizens to vote

suggestion box [sə'dʒestʃn 'bɒks] *noun* place in a company where members of staff can put forward their ideas for making the company more efficient and profitable

suicide ['suːɪsaɪd] *noun* (a) act of killing yourself; *the police are treating the death as suicide, not murder*; **to commit suicide** = to kill yourself; *after shooting his wife, he committed suicide in the bedroom*; **suicide pact** = agreement between two or more people that they will all commit suicide at the same time (b) person who has committed suicide

COMMENT: aiding suicide is a notifiable offence

sui generis ['suːaɪ 'dʒenərɪs] *Latin phrase meaning* 'of its own right': (thing) which is in a class of its own

sui juris ['suːaɪ 'dʒuərɪs] *Latin phrase meaning* 'in one's own right': (person) who is able to make contracts and sue others or be sued himself; *compare* ALIENI JURIS

suit [suːt] *noun* civil legal proceedings, lawsuit; *US* **class suit** = legal action brought on behalf of several people

sum [sʌm] **1** *noun* (a) quantity of money; *a sum of money was stolen from the personnel office*; *he lost large sums on the Stock Exchange*; *she received the sum of £500 in compensation*; **the sum insured** = the largest amount which an insurer will pay under the terms of an insurance; **lump sum** = money paid in one payment, not in several small payments (b) total of a series of figures added together **2** *verb (of a judge)* **to sum up** = to speak at the end of a trial and review all the evidence and arguments for the benefit of the jury (NOTE: **summing - summed**)

summarily ['sʌmərəli] *adverb* immediately; *magistrates can try a case summarily or refer it to the Crown Court*

summary ['sʌmri] **1** *noun* short account of what has happened or of what has been written; *the chairman gave a summary of his discussions with the German delegation*; *the police inspector gave a summary of events leading to the raid on the house*; **case summary** = short document (not more than 500 words) prepared by the claimant to help the court understand what the case is about **2** *adjective* which happens immediately; **summary arrest** = arrest without a warrant; **summary conviction** = conviction by a magistrate sitting without a jury; **summary dismissal** = dismissal of an employee without giving the notice stated in the contract of employment; **summary judgment** = immediate judgment of a case without a trial (this can be decided by the court itself or can be applied for by a party when he believes the other party has no real chance of succeeding with the case); **summary jurisdiction** = power of a magistrates' court to try a case without a jury or to try a case immediately without referring it to the Crown Court; **summary offence** = minor crime which can be tried only in a magistrates' court; **summary trial** = trial of a petty offence by magistrates

summing up ['sʌmɪŋ 'ʌp] *noun* speech by the judge at the end of a trial, where he reviews all the evidence and arguments and notes important points of law for the benefit of the jury (NOTE: American English is **instructions**)

summit ['sʌmɪt] *noun* meeting between heads of state or between superpower leaders; *(in the EU)* **summit conference** =

meeting of two or more heads of government; *the summit conference or summit meeting was held in Helsinki; the matter will be discussed at next week's summit of the EC leaders*

summitry ['sʌmɪtri] *noun* diplomacy as carried on in summit meetings

summon ['sʌmən] *verb* to call someone to come; *he was summoned to appear before the committee*

summons ['sʌmənz] *noun* official command from a court requiring someone to appear in court to be tried for a criminal offence or to defend a civil action; *he tore up the summons and went on holiday to Spain*; **judgment summons** = summons by a court ordering a judgment debtor to pay or to go to prison; **originating summons** = summons whereby a legal action is commenced (usually in the Chancery Division of the High Court in cases relating to land or the administration of an estate); **witness summons** = court order requiring someone to appear as a witness (and if necessary bring with him documents relevant to the case) (NOTE: since the introduction of the new Civil Procedure Rules in April 1999, this term has replaced **subpoena ad testificandum** and **subpoena duces tecum**); **writ of summons** = document which starts a legal action in the High Court

supergrass ['su:pəgrɑ:s] *noun (slang)* person (usually a criminal) who gives information to the police about a large number of criminals

superintendent [su:pən'tendənt] *noun* person in charge; **(police) superintendent** = high rank in a police force, above Chief Inspector and below Chief Superintendent

supervision order [su:pə'vɪʒn 'ɔ:də] *noun* court order for a young offender to be placed under the supervision of the probation service

supplemental [sʌplɪ'mentl] *adjective* which is additional to something; *US* **supplemental appropriations** = extra

appropriation of money passed later than the normal appropriation bill, but still within the same fiscal year

supplementary [sʌplɪ'mentri] *adjective* which is additional; **supplementary questions** *or* **supplementaries** = questions asked by an MP or councillor after a main written question has been answered, used to try to catch a Minister or council committee chairman by surprise or to embarrass them

supply [sə'plaɪ] *noun* providing something which is needed; **money supply** = amount of money which exists in a country; **Supply Bill** = Bill for providing money for government requirements; **supply price** = price at which something is provided; **supply and demand** = amount of a product which is available at a certain price and the amount which is wanted by customers at that price; **the law of supply and demand** = general rule that the amount of a product which is available is related to the needs of the possible customers

support price [sə'pɔ:t 'praɪs] *noun* price *(in the EU)* at which a government will buy farm produce to stop the price from falling

suppress [sə'pres] *verb* to hide documents; to prevent evidence being given

suppressio veri [sə'presiəu 'veraɪ] *Latin phrase meaning* 'suppressing the truth': act of not mentioning some important fact

supra ['su:prə] *adverb* above, see above

supremacy [su:'preməsi] *noun* **(a)** being in an all-powerful position; **the supremacy of Parliament** = situation of the British Parliament which can both pass and repeal laws **(b)** *(in the EU)* primacy, one of the twin pillars of EC law, by which Community law cannot be overridden by national laws even if the national laws existed before the EC law; it is based on all forms of Community law, ie. treaty articles, community acts or agreements with third parties

supreme court [sə'priːm 'kɔːt] *noun* (a) Supreme Court (of Judicature) = highest court in England and Wales, consisting of the Court of Appeal and the High Court of Justice (b) highest federal court in the USA and other countries

surcharge ['sɜːtʃɑːdʒ] *noun* (a) extra charge; **import surcharge** = extra charge on imported goods (b) penalty for incurring expenditure without authorization

surety ['ʃɔːrəti] *noun* (a) person who guarantees that someone will do something, especially by paying to guarantee that someone will keep the peace; *to stand surety for someone* (b) money, deeds or share certificates, etc., deposited as security for a loan

surrender [sə'rendə] 1 *noun* (a) giving up a right or power (b) giving up of an insurance policy before the contracted date for maturity; **surrender value** = money which an insurer will pay if an insurance policy is given up before it matures 2 *verb* to give in a document, to give up a right; *the contract becomes null and void when these documents are surrendered*; *the court ordered him to surrender his passport*; **to surrender a policy** = to give up an insurance

surrogate ['sʌrəgeit] *noun* person appointed to act in place of someone else; **surrogate mother** = woman who has a child by artificial insemination for a couple where the wife cannot bear children, with the intention of handing the child over to them when it is born

surveillance [sə'veiləns] *noun* watching someone carefully to get information about what he is doing; *the diplomats were placed under police surveillance*; *surveillance at international airports has been increased*; **surveillance device** = bugging device; **electronic surveillance** = surveillance using hidden microphones, etc.

survive [sə'vaiv] *verb* to live longer than another person; *he survived his wife*; *she is survived by her husband and three children*; *he left his estate to his surviving relatives* = to the relatives who were still alive

survivor [sə'vaivə] *noun* someone who lives longer than another person

survivorship [sə'vaivəʃip] *noun* (a) state of being the survivor of two or more people who hold a joint tenancy on a property (b) *(also* **right of survivorship**) right of the survivor of a joint tenancy to the estate, rather than the heirs of the deceased tenant (NOTE: the right of survivorship is also called by its Latin name: **jus accrescendi**)

SUS law ['sʌs 'lɔː] *noun (formerly)* law which allowed the police to stop and arrest a person whom they suspected of having committed an offence

suspect 1 ['sʌspekt] *noun* person whom the police think has committed a crime; *the police have taken six suspects into custody*; *the police are questioning the suspect about his movements at the time the crime was committed* 2 [sə'spekt] *verb* to believe that someone has done something; *he was arrested as a suspected spy*; *the police suspect that the thefts were committed by a member of the shop's staff*; *she was suspected of carrying drugs* (NOTE: you suspect someone **of** committing a crime)

suspend [sʌ'spend] *verb* (a) to stop (something) for a time; *we have suspended payments while we are waiting for news from our agent*; *the hearings have been suspended for two weeks*; *work on the preparation of the case has been suspended*; *the management decided to suspend negotiations*; **suspended sentence** = sentence of imprisonment which a court orders shall not take effect unless the offender commits another crime (b) to stop (someone) working for a time; *he was suspended on full pay while the police investigations were proceeding* (c) to punish an MP or council member by refusing to allow him to attend sittings or meetings; to punish a student by refusing to allow him to attend school or college; *John Brown, MP, was named by the Speaker and suspended*; *three boys were suspended from school for fighting*

suspension [sʌ'spenʃn] *noun* **(a)** stopping something for a time; *suspension of payments*; *suspension of deliveries* **(b)** stopping an MP or council member from attending sittings or meetings for a time; *the suspension of an MP*

COMMENT: when an MP is 'named' by the Speaker, the House will vote to suspend him. Suspension is normally for five days, though it may be for longer if the MP is suspended twice in the same session of Parliament

suspicion [sə'spiʃn] *noun* on suspicion = feeling that someone has committed a crime; *he was arrested on suspicion of being an accessory to the crime*

suspicious [sə'spiʃəs] *adjective* which makes someone suspect; *the police are dealing with the suspicious package found in the car*; *suspicious substances were found in the man's pocket*

swear [sweə] *verb* to make an oath, to promise that what you will say will be the truth; *he swore to tell the truth*; **'I swear to tell the truth, the whole truth and nothing but the truth'** = words used when a witness takes the oath in court (NOTE: **swearing - swore - has sworn**)

swear in ['sweə 'in] *verb* to make someone take an oath before taking up a position; *he was sworn in as a Privy Councillor*; **swearing-in** = act of making someone take an oath before taking up a position

swindle ['swindl] **1** *noun* illegal deal in which someone is cheated out of his money **2** *verb* to cheat someone out of his money; *he made £50,000 by swindling small shopkeepers*; *the gang swindled the bank out of £1.5m*

swindler ['swindlə] *noun* person who swindles

syllabus ['siləbəs] *noun* US headnote giving a short summary of a case

syndicalism ['sindikəlizm] *noun* type of socialism, where property and control of industry is in the hands of the trades unions in each industry (as opposed to strict socialism, where the control of industry is in the hands of the state)

Tt

tabs ['tæbz] *plural noun* bands of white cloth worn by a barrister round his neck, instead of a tie

table ['teɪbl] **1** *noun* **(a)** conference table *or* negotiating table = table around which people sit to negotiate; **round table conference** = conference with a round table, showing that each party at the meeting is of equal status with the rest; *the government is trying to get the rebel leaders to come to the conference table* **(b)** long table in the centre of the House of Commons between the two front benches (the Serjeant at Arms places the mace on the table when the business of the House begins; the two despatch boxes for main speakers from either party are also on the table) **(c) to lay a bill on the table** = (i) to present a bill to the House of Commons for discussion; (ii) *US* to kill debate on a bill in the House of Representatives; *US* **to let a bill lie on the table** = not to proceed with discussion of a bill, but to hold it over to be debated later **(d)** list of figures or facts set out in a list; **table of contents** = list of contents in a book; **actuarial tables** = lists showing how long people of certain ages are likely to live, used to calculate life assurance premiums; **Table A, B, C, D, E** = specimen forms for setting up companies, set out in the Companies Act; *see* A, B, C, D, E **2** *verb* to put items of information on the table before a meeting; *the report of the finance committee was tabled*; **to table a motion** = (i) to put forward a proposal for discussion by putting details of it on the table at a meeting; (ii) *US* to remove a motion from consideration for an indefinite period

tacit ['tæsɪt] *adjective* agreed but not stated; *he gave the proposal his tacit approval*; *the committee gave its tacit agreement to the proposal*

tack [tæk] **1** *noun* (*in Scotland*) lease **2** *verb* to add a first and second mortgage together

tactical voting ['tæktɪkl 'vəutɪŋ] *noun* way of voting, which aims not at voting for the candidate you want to win, but at voting in such a way as to prevent the candidate who you do not want to win from being elected

COMMENT: in a case where the three candidates A, B and C, have 47%, 33% and 20% of the vote according to an opinion poll, C's supporters might all vote for B, to prevent A winning

tail [teɪl] *see* FEE

take [teɪk] **1** *noun* money received in a shop **2** *verb* **(a)** to receive, to get; (*of a lawyer*) **to take instructions** = to ask your client how he wishes the lawyer to deal with something; *when the defence offered £1,000, the claimant's solicitor said he would take his client's instructions* **(b)** to do a certain action; **to take the chair** = to be chairman of a meeting; *in the absence of the chairman his deputy took the chair*; **to take someone to court** = to sue someone, to start civil proceedings against someone* (NOTE: **taking - took - has taken**)

take in ['teɪk 'ɪn] *verb* to trick or to swindle (someone); *we were taken in by his promise of quick profits*

take out ['teɪk 'aut] *verb* **to take out a patent for an invention** = to apply for and receive a patent; **to take out insurance against theft** = to pay a premium to an insurance company, so that if a theft takes place the company will pay compensation

take over ['teɪk 'əʊvə] *verb* **(a)** to start to do something in place of someone else; *Miss Black took over from Mr Jones on May 1st*; *the new chairman takes over on July 1st*; **the take-over period is always difficult** = the period when one person is taking over work from another **(b) to take over a company** = to buy a business by offering to buy most of its shares; *the buyer takes over the company's liabilities*; *the company was taken over by a large international corporation*

takeover ['teɪkəʊvə] *noun* buying a business; **takeover bid** *or* **offer** = offer to buy all or a majority of the shares in a company so as to control it; **to make a takeover bid for a company** = to offer to buy most of the shares in a company; **to withdraw a takeover bid** = to say that you no longer offer to buy most of the shares in a company; **the company rejected the takeover bid** = the directors recommended that the shareholders should not accept the offer; *the disclosure of the takeover bid raised share prices*; **Takeover Panel** = non-statutory body which examines takeovers and applies the City Code on Takeovers and Mergers; **contested takeover** = takeover where the board of the company being bought do not recommend the bid, and try to fight it

talaq ['tælæk] *noun* Islamic form of divorce, where the husband may divorce his wife unilaterally by an oral declaration made three times

talk out ['tɔːk 'aʊt] *verb* to go on talking in a debate, so that the time runs out before the vote can be taken; *the bill was talked out and so fell*

tamper ['tæmpə] *verb* **to tamper with something** = to change something or to act in such a way that something does not work; *the police were accused of tampering with the evidence*; *the charges state that he had tampered with the wheels of the victim's car*

tangible ['tændʒɪbl] *adjective* **tangible assets** *or* **property** = assets which are visible (such as machinery, buildings, furniture, jewellery, etc.)

Taoiseach ['tiːʃək] *noun* Prime Minister of the Republic of Ireland

tariff ['tærɪf] *noun* **(a) customs tariffs** = tax to be paid for importing or exporting goods; **tariff barriers** = customs duty intended to make imports more difficult; *to impose tariff barriers on or to lift tariff barriers from a product*; **protective tariff** = tariff which aims to ban imports to prevent competition with local products **(b)** minimum period of time which a life prisoner must serve in prison

tax [tæks] **1** *noun* **(a)** money taken compulsorily by the government or by an official body to pay for government services; **capital gains tax (CGT)** = tax on capital gains; **capital transfer tax (CTT)** = tax on gifts or bequests of money or property; **excess profits tax** = tax on profits which are higher than what is thought to be normal; **income tax** = tax on salaries and wages; **land tax** = tax on the amount of land owned; **sales tax** = tax paid on each item sold; **Value Added Tax (VAT)** = tax on goods and services, added as a percentage to the invoiced sales price **(b) ad valorem tax** = tax calculated according to the value of the goods taxed; **back tax** = tax which is owed; **basic rate tax** = lowest rate of income tax; **to levy a tax** *or* **to impose a tax** = to make a tax payable; *the government has imposed a 15% tax on petrol*; **to lift a tax** = to remove a tax; **tax allowances** *or* **allowances against tax** = part of one's income which a person is allowed to earn and not pay tax on; **tax avoidance** = trying (legally) to minimize the amount of tax to be paid; **tax code** = number given to indicate the amount of tax allowances a person has; **tax concession** = allowing less tax to be paid; **tax consultant** *or* **tax adviser** = person who gives advice on tax problems; *US* **tax court** = tribunal which hears appeals from taxpayers against the Internal Revenue Service; **tax credit** = part of a dividend on which the company has already paid tax, so that the shareholder is not taxed on it again; **tax deductions** = (i) money removed from a salary to pay tax; (ii) *US* business expenses which can be claimed against tax; **tax deducted at source** = tax which is removed from a salary, interest payment or dividend payment before the money is paid out; **tax evasion** = illegally trying not to pay tax; **tax exemption** = (i) being free from payment of tax; (ii) *US* part of income which a person is allowed to earn and not pay tax on; **tax haven** = country where taxes levied on foreigners or foreign companies are low; **tax holiday** = period when a new business is exempted from paying tax; **tax inspector** *or* **inspector of taxes** = official of the Inland Revenue who examines tax returns and decides how much tax someone should pay; **tax loophole** = legal means of not paying tax; **tax planning** = planning one's financial affairs so that one pays as little tax as possible; **tax relief** = allowing someone not to pay tax on certain parts of his income; **tax return** *or* **tax declaration** = completed tax form, with details of income and allowances; **double tax treaty** = treaty between two countries so that citizens pay tax in one country only; **tax year** = twelve month period on which taxes are calculated (in the UK, 6th April to 5th April of the following year) **2** *verb* **(a)** to make someone pay a tax, to impose a tax on something; *to tax businesses at 50%*; *income is taxed at 29%*; *these items are heavily taxed* **(b)** to have the costs of a legal action assessed by the court; *the court ordered the costs to be taxed if not agreed*; **taxed costs** = amount of costs (which may vary) awarded in legal proceedings by the costs judge **(c)** to assess the bill presented by a Parliamentary agent; **taxing officer** = person appointed by the House of Commons to assess the charges presented by a Parliamentary agent

taxable ['tæksəbl] *adjective* which can be taxed; **taxable items** = items on which a

tax has to be paid; **taxable income** = income on which a person has to pay tax

taxation [tæk'seɪʃn] *noun* **(a)** act of taxing; **direct taxation** = taxes (such as income tax) which are paid direct to the government out of earnings or profit; **double taxation** = taxing the same income twice; **double taxation treaty** = treaty between two countries that citizens pay tax in one country only **(b) taxation of costs** = formerly, the assessment of the costs of a legal action by the Taxing Master (NOTE: since the introduction of the new Civil Procedure Rules in April 1999, this term has been replaced by **assessment of costs**)

tax-deductible ['tæksdɪ'dʌktɪbl] *adjective* which can be deducted from an income before tax is calculated; **these expenses are not tax-deductible** = tax has to be paid on these expenses

tax-exempt ['tæksɪg'zempt] *adjective* (person or organization) not required to pay tax; (income or goods) which are not subject to tax

tax-free ['tæks'fri:] *adjective* on which tax does not have to be paid

Taxing Master ['tæksɪŋ 'mɑːstə] *noun* official of the Supreme Court who assesses the costs of a court action (NOTE: since the introduction of the new Civil Procedure Rules in April 1999, this term has been replaced in some contexts by **costs judge)**

taxpayer ['tækspeɪə] *noun* person or company which has to pay tax; *basic taxpayer or taxpayer at the basic rate*

tax point ['tæks 'pɔɪnt] *noun* **(a)** date when goods are supplied and VAT is charged **(b)** date at which a tax begins to be applied

TD ['ti: 'di:] = TEACHTA DALA member of the Irish Dáil

Teachta Dala ['tɪæχtə 'dælə] *noun* member of the Irish Dáil

technical ['teknɪkl] *adjective* referring to a specific legal point, using a strictly legal interpretation; *nominal damages* *were awarded as the harm was judged to be technical rather than actual*

technicality [teknɪ'kælətɪ] *noun* special interpretation of a legal point; *the Appeal Court rejected the appeal on a technicality*

teleological [tiːliə'lɒdʒɪkl] *adjective* referring to the final purpose of something; *the ECJ uses a teleological approach to legislation*

telephone hearing ['telɪfəʊn 'hɪərɪŋ] *noun* hearing conducted by telephone, using a telephone conferencing system; such hearings are recorded on tape

teller ['telə] *noun* (a) member who counts the votes in the House of Commons or House of Representatives (b) bank clerk

COMMENT: when a division is called in the House of Commons, the Speaker appoints four MPs as tellers, two for the motion and two against. They do not vote, but check the other MPs as they pass through the division lobbies

tem [tem] *see* PRO TEM

Temple ['templ] *see* INNER TEMPLE, MIDDLE TEMPLE

temporary ['tempri] *adjective* which lasts only a short time; *he was granted a temporary injunction*; *the police took temporary measures to close the street to traffic*; *she has a temporary job or temporary post with a firm of solicitors*; **temporary employment** = full-time work which does not last for more than a few days or months; **temporary injunction** = injunction which is granted until a case comes to court; **temporary staff** = staff who are appointed for a short time

tenancy ['tenənsɪ] *noun* (a) agreement by which a person can occupy a property; (b) period during which a person has an agreement to occupy a property; **joint tenancy** = situation where two or more persons acquire interests in a property together where, if one of the joint tenants dies, his share goes to the others who

survive him; **long tenancy** = tenancy for a period of more than 21 years; **several tenancy** = holding of property by several persons, each separately and not jointly with any other person; **protected tenancy** = tenancy where the tenant is protected from eviction; **tenancy in common** = situation where two or more persons jointly hold a property and each can leave his interest to his heirs when he dies; **tenancy at will** = situation where the owner of a property allows a tenant to hold it for as long as either party wishes (c) period during which a barrister occupies chambers

tenant ['tenənt] *noun* person or company which rents a house, flat or office in which to live or work; *the tenant is liable for repairs*; **tenant at will** = tenant who holds a property at the will of the owner; **tenant for life** = person who can occupy a property for life; **secure tenant** = tenant of a local authority who has the right to buy the freehold of the property he rents at a discount; **sitting tenant** = tenant who is living in a house when the freehold or lease is sold

tender ['tendə] **1** *noun* (a) offer to work for a certain price; **to put a project out to tender** *or* **to ask for** *or* **to invite tenders for a project** = to ask contractors to give written estimates for a job; **to put in a tender** *or* **to submit a tender** = to make an estimate for a job; **to sell shares by tender** = to ask people to offer in writing a price for shares; **sealed tenders** = tenders sent in sealed envelopes which will all be opened together at a certain time (b) **tender before claim** = defence that the defendant offered the claimant the amount of money claimed before the claimant started proceedings against him (NOTE: also called **defence before claim**) (c) **legal tender** = coins or notes which can be legally used to pay a debt (small denominations cannot be used to pay large debts) **2** *verb* (a) **to tender for a contract** = to put forward an estimate of cost for work to be carried out under contract; *to tender for the construction of a hospital* (b) **to tender one's resignation** = to give in one's resignation

tenderer ['tendərə] *noun* person or company which tenders for work; *the company was the successful tenderer for the project*

tenement ['tenəmənt] *noun* **(a)** property which is held by a tenant; **dominant tenement** = land which has been granted an easement over another property; **servient tenement** = land whose owner grants an easement to the owner of the dominant tenement **(b)** *(in Scotland)* building which is divided into rented flats

tenens ['tenenz] *see* LOCUM

Ten Minute Rule ['ten 'mɪnɪt 'ruːl] *noun* standing order in the House of Commons, where an ordinary MP can introduce a Bill with a short speech, and if the Bill is passed on a vote, it can proceed to the Second Reading stage; *the Bill was proposed under the Ten Minute Rule*

tenure ['tenjə] *noun* **(a)** right to hold property or a position; **security of tenure** = right to keep a job or rented accommodation provided certain conditions are met; **land tenure** = way in which land is held (such as leasehold) **(b)** time when a position is held; *during his tenure of the office of chairman*

term [tɜːm] *noun* **(a)** period of time; *the term of a lease*; *the term of the loan is fifteen years*; *to have a loan for a term of fifteen years*; *during his term of office as chairman*; **term deposit** = money invested for a fixed period which gives a higher rate of interest than normal; **term insurance** = life assurance which covers a person's life for a fixed period of time; **term loan** = loan for a fixed period of time; **term of years** = fixed period of several years (of a lease); **term shares** = type of building society deposit for a fixed period of time at a higher rate of interest; **fixed term** = period which is fixed when a contract is signed and which cannot be changed afterwards; **short-term** = for a period of months; **long-term** = for a long period of time; **medium-term** = for a period of one or two years **(b)** **term** *or* **terms** = conditions or duties which have to be carried out as part

of a contract, arrangements which have to be agreed before a contract is valid; *he refused to agree to some of the terms of the contract*; *by or under the terms of the contract, the company is responsible for all damage to the property*; **terms of payment** *or* **payment terms** = conditions for paying something; **terms of sale** = agreed ways in which a sale takes place (such as discounts and credit terms); **cash terms** = lower terms which apply if the customer pays cash; **implied term** = term in a contract which is not clearly set out in the contract (as opposed to an express term); **implied terms and conditions** = terms and conditions which are not written in a contract, but which are legally taken to be present in the contract; **trade terms** = special discount for people in the same trade **(c)** part of a legal or university year (the four law terms are Easter, Hilary, Michaelmas and Trinity); *the autumn term starts in September* **(d)** **terms of employment** = conditions set out in a contract of employment; **terms of reference** = areas which a committee or an inspector can deal with; *under the terms of reference of the committee it can only investigate complaints from the public*; *the tribunal's terms of reference do not cover traffic offences* **(e)** word or phrase which has a particular meaning; *counsel used several technical terms which the prisoner didn't understand*

terminable ['tɜːmɪnəbl] *adjective* which can be terminated

terminate ['tɜːmɪneɪt] *verb* **(a)** to end (something), to bring (something) to an end; *to terminate an agreement*; *his employment was terminated* **(b)** to come to an end; *an offer terminates on the death of the offeror*

termination [tɜːmɪ'neɪʃn] *noun* **(a)** bringing to an end; *the termination of an offer or of a lease*; *to appeal against the termination of a foster order*; **termination clause** = clause which explains how and when a contract can be terminated **(b)** *US* leaving a job (resigning, retiring, or being fired or made redundant)

territorial [terɪˈtɔːrɪəl] *adjective* referring to land; **territorial claims** = claims to own land which is part of another country; **territorial waters** = sea waters near the coast of a country, which are part of the country and governed by the laws of that country; **outside territorial waters** = in international waters, where a single country's jurisdiction does not run

territoriality [terɪtɔːriˈæləti] *noun* principle that a country has jurisdiction only over its own territory; *see also* EXTRA-

territory [ˈterɪtri] *noun* area of land (ruled by a government); *their government has laid claim to part of our territory*

terrorism [ˈterərɪzm] *noun* violent action (such as assassination or bombing) committed for political reasons; *the act of terrorism was condemned by the Minister of Justice*

terrorist [ˈterərɪst] *noun* person who commits a violent act for political reasons; *the bomb was planted by a terrorist group or by a group of terrorists; six people were killed in the terrorist attack on the airport*

test [test] **1** *noun* **(a)** examination to see if something works well or is possible; **test certificate** = certificate to show that something has passed a test; **control test** = test to decide if someone is an employee or is self-employed (used for the purposes of tax assessment); **feasibility test** = test to see if something is possible **(b) test case** = legal action where the decision will fix a principle which other cases can follow **2** *verb* to examine something to see if it is working well; *to test a computer system*

testament [ˈtestəmənt] *noun* **last will and testament** = will, document by which a person says what he wants to happen to his property when he dies

testamentary [testəˈmentəri] *adjective* referring to a will; **testamentary disposition** = passing of property to someone in a will; **testamentary freedom** = freedom of a person to dispose of his property in his will as he wants

testamentary capacity [testəˈmentəri kəˈpæsəti] *noun* legal ability of someone to make a will

> COMMENT: a testator must be able to make a will: he must be of sound mind (ie, must know what he is doing, what property he has, and who he is leaving it to), he must approve of the will (for example, in cases where a will is prepared for a testator by someone else), he must be acting freely (not coerced by anyone else, not tricked into making a fraudulent will)

testate [ˈtesteɪt] *adjective* having made a will; *did he die testate?*; *see also* INTESTATE

testator [teˈsteɪtə] *noun* man who has made a will

testatrix [teˈsteɪtrɪks] *noun* woman who has made a will

testify [ˈtestɪfaɪ] *verb* to give evidence in court

testimonium clause [testɪˈməʊnɪəm ˈklɔːz] *noun* last section of a will or conveyance, etc., which shows how it has been witnessed

> COMMENT: the testimonium clause usually begins with the words: 'in witness whereof I have set my hand '

testimony [ˈtestɪməni] *noun* oral statement given by a witness in court about what happened; *she gave her testimony in a low voice*

TEU = TREATY ON EUROPEAN UNION

text [tekst] *noun* written part of something; *he wrote notes at the side of the text of the agreement*; **text processing** = working with words, using a computer to produce, check and change documents, contracts, reports, letters, etc.

textbook [ˈtekstbʊk] *noun* book of legal commentary which can be cited in court

theft [θeft] *noun* **(a)** crime of stealing, taking of property which belongs to someone else with the intention of depriving that person of it; *we have brought in security guards to protect the store against theft*; *the company is trying to reduce losses caused by theft*; *to take out insurance against theft*; **petty theft** = stealing small items or small amounts of money (NOTE: no plural in this meaning) **(b)** act of stealing; *there has been a wave of thefts from newsagents*

COMMENT: types of theft which are notifiable offences are: theft from the person of another; theft in a dwelling; theft by an employee; theft of mail, pedal cycle or motor vehicle; theft from vehicles, from a shop or from an automatic machine or meter

there- [ðeə] *prefix* that thing (NOTE: the following words formed with **there-** are frequently used in legal documents)

thereafter [ðeəˈɑːftə] *adverb* after that

thereby [ðeəˈbaɪ] *adverb* by that

therefor [ðeəˈfɔː] *adverb* for that

therefrom [ðeəˈfrɒm] *adverb* from that

therein [ðeəˈɪn] *adverb* in that

thereinafter [ðeəɪnˈɑːftə] *adverb* afterwards listed in that document

thereinbefore [ðeəɪnbɪˈfɔː] *adverb* mentioned before in that document

thereinunder [ðeəɪnˈʌndə] *adverb* mentioned under that heading

thereof [ðeəˈɒv] *adverb* of that; **in respect thereof** = regarding that thing

thereto [ðeəˈtuː] *adverb* to that

theretofore [ðeətuˈfɔː] *adverb* before that time

therewith [ðeəˈwɪð] *adverb* with that

thief [θiːf] *noun* person who steals or who takes property which belongs to someone else; *thieves broke into the office and stole the petty cash*; **petty thief** = person who steals small items or small amounts of money (NOTE: plural is **thieves**)

third party [ˈθɜːd ˈpɑːti] *noun* any person other than the two main parties involved in proceedings or a contract; the other person involved in an accident; **third-party insurance** = insurance which pays compensation if someone who is neither the insured person nor the insurer incurs loss or injury; **third party notice** = pleading served by a defendant on another party joining that party to an existing court action; **third party proceedings** = introduction of a third party into a case by the defendant, or by the claimant in the case of a counterclaim (NOTE: the American equivalent is **impleader**); **the case is in the hands of a third party** = the case is being dealt with by someone who is not one of the main interested parties; *see also* PARTY

Third Reading [ˈθɜːd ˈriːdɪŋ] *noun* final discussion and vote on a Bill in Parliament

threat [θret] *noun* words (spoken or written) which say that something unpleasant may happen to someone, and which frighten that person

threaten [ˈθretn] *verb* to warn someone that unpleasant things may happen to him; *he threatened to take the tenant to court or to have the tenant evicted*; *she complained that her husband had threatened her with a knife*; **threatening behaviour** = acting in a way which threatens someone

throne [θrəʊn] *noun* special chair for a King or Queen; **speech from the throne** = QUEEN'S SPEECH

ticket [ˈtɪkɪt] *noun US* a party's list of candidates for election to political office; *he ran for governor on the Republican ticket*

tied cottage [ˈtaɪd ˈkɒtɪdʒ] *noun* house owned by an employer and let to an employee for the period of his employment

time [taɪm] *noun* **(a)** period when something takes place (such as one hour, two days, fifty minutes); **computer time** = time when a computer is being used (paid for at an hourly rate); **real time** = time when a computer is working on the processing of data while the problem to which the data refers is actually taking place; **time charter** = agreement to charter a ship for a fixed period; **time policy** = marine insurance policy which runs for a fixed period of time; **time immemorial** = from before 1189, the date from which events are supposed to be remembered; **time summons** = summons issued to apply to the court for more time in which to serve a pleading; **extension of time** = extra time allowed in which to serve a pleading or to take a step in a court action **(b)** system of hours on the clock; **Summer Time** *or* **Daylight Saving Time** = system where clocks are set back one hour in the summer to take advantage of the longer hours of daylight; **Standard Time** = normal time as in the winter months **(c)** period before something happens; **time limit** = period during which something should be done; **to keep within the time limits** *or* **within the time schedule** = to complete work by the time stated; **time lock** = lock which will open only at a certain time of day (as in a bank vault)

time-bar ['taɪmbɑː] *verb* to stop someone doing something (such as exercising a right) because a set time limit has expired (NOTE: **time-barring - time-barred**)

timetable ['taɪmteɪbl] *noun* printed list which shows the times of court cases, of trains leaving, etc.; **trial timetable** = detailed timetable of a hearing, set out in the listing directions, including the length of time allowed for speeches, for cross-examination of witnesses, etc.; *(see also* **FAST TRACK** *for a typical timetable for a fast track case)*

tip off ['tɪp 'ɒf] *verb (informal)* **to tip someone off** = to warn someone; *we think he tipped the burglars off that the police were outside*; *she tipped them off that a police investigation was about to take place* (NOTE: **tipping - tipped**)

tip-off ['tɪpɒf] *noun (informal)* piece of useful information, given secretly; *acting on a tip-off from a member of the public, customs officials stopped the truck*; *the*

police received a tip-off about a bomb in the building; *the police raided the club after a tip-off from the driver of a taxi*

tipstaff ['tɪpstɑːf] *noun* official of the Supreme Court who is responsible for arresting persons in contempt of court

title ['taɪtl] *noun* **(a)** (i) right to hold goods or property; (ii) document proving a right to hold a property; *she has no title to the property*; *he has a good title to the property*; **title deeds** = document showing who is the owner of a property; **absolute title** = land registered with the Land Registry, where the owner has a guaranteed title to the land (absolute title also exists to leasehold land, giving the proprietor a guaranteed valid lease); **to have a clear title to something** = to have a right to something with no limitations or charges; **good title** = title to a property which gives the owner full rights of ownership; **possessory title** = title to land acquired by occupying it continuously (usually for a period of twelve years); **qualified title** = title to a property which is not absolute as there is some defect **(b)** name of a bill which comes before Parliament, name of an Act of Parliament; **full title** *or* **long title** = complete title of an Act of Parliament; **short title** = usual title of an Act of Parliament

token ['təʊkn] *noun* thing which acts as a sign; **token charge** = small charge which does not cover the real costs; *a token charge is made for heating*; **token payment** = small payment to show that a payment is being made; **token rent** = very low rent payment to show that a rent is being asked; **token strike** = short strike to show that workers have a grievance

toll [təʊl] **1** *noun* payment made for using a road, bridge or ferry **2** *verb US* to suspend a law for a period

tort [tɔːt] *noun* civil wrong done by one person to another and entitling the victim to claim damages; **action in tort** = action brought by a claimant who has suffered damage or harm caused by the defendant;

proceedings in tort = court action for damages for a tort

tortfeasor [tɔːtˈfiːzə] *noun* person who has committed a tort; **joint tortfeasors** = two people who together commit a tort

tortious [ˈtɔːʃəs] *adjective* referring to a tort; **tortious act** = a wrong, an act which damages someone; **tortious liability** = liability for harm caused by a breach of duty

torture [ˈtɔːtʃə] *verb* to hurt someone badly so as to force him or her to give information

torturer [ˈtɔːtʃərə] *noun* person who tortures

totalitarian [təʊtælɪˈteəriən] *adjective* (*often as criticism*) having total power and not allowing any opposition or any personal freedom; *a totalitarian state*; *the totalitarian regime of the junta*

totalitarianism [təʊtælɪˈteəriənɪzm] *noun* (*usually as criticism*) political system in which the state has total power over its citizens; *many extreme right-wing or left-wing governments have been accused of practising totalitarianism*

total loss [ˈtəʊtl ˈlɒs] *noun* (*insurance*) **actual total loss** = loss where the thing insured has been destroyed or damaged beyond repair; **constructive total loss** = loss where the thing insured has been thrown away as it is likely to be irreparable; **the cargo was written off as a total loss** = the cargo was so badly damaged that the insurers said it had no value

toties quoties [ˈtəʊʃiːz ˈkwəʊʃiːz] *Latin phrase meaning* 'as often as necessary'

totting up [ˈtɒtɪŋ ˈʌp] *noun* adding previous convictions for traffic offences to a present conviction (each conviction entails the endorsement of the driver's licence and he may be disqualified if all the endorsements are added together)

tot up [ˈtɒt ˈʌp] *verb* to add up

town [taʊn] *noun* large group of houses and other buildings which is the place where many people live and work; **Town Clerk** = formerly the title of the chief administrator of a town, now usually called Chief Executive; **town planner** = person who supervises the design of a town, the way the streets and buildings in a town are laid out and the land in a town used; **town planning** = supervising the design of a town, the use of land in a town

township [ˈtaʊnʃɪp] *noun* (**a**) (*in North America*) small town which is a local government centre (**b**) (*in South Africa*) town outside the main urban areas, inhabited one especially by blacks during the apartheid era

trace [treɪs] *verb* to follow, to look for someone or something; *we have traced the missing documents*; *the police traced the two men to a hotel in London*; **tracing action** = court action begun to trace money or proceeds of a sale

track [træk] *noun* way which a case follows when managed by the court; *the three management tracks are the small claims track, the fast track and the multi-track*

trade [treɪd] **1** *noun* (**a**) business of buying and selling; **export trade** *or* **import trade** = the business of selling to other countries or buying from other countries; **home trade** = trade in the country where a company is based (**b**) **fair trade** = international business system where countries agree not to charge import duties on certain items imported from their trading partners; **free trade** = system where goods can go from one country to another without any restrictions; **free trade area** = group of countries practising free trade; **trade agreement** = international agreement between countries over general terms of trade; **trade description** = description of a product to attract customers; **Trade Descriptions Act** = Act of Parliament which limits the way in which products can be described so as to protect customers from wrong descriptions made by the makers of the products; **trade**

directory = book which lists all the businesses and business people in a town; **trade dispute** = (i) international dispute over trade matters; (ii) dispute between management and workers over conditions of employment or union membership; **trade fixtures** = equipment attached to a property by a tenant so that he can exercise his trade (he can remove them at the end of his tenancy); **to ask a company to supply trade references** = to ask a company to give names of traders who can report on the company's financial situation and reputation **(c)** people or companies dealing in the same type of product; *he is in the secondhand car trade*; *she is very well known in the clothing trade*; **trade association** = group which joins together companies in the same type of business **2** *verb* to buy and sell, to carry on a business; *to trade with another country*; *to trade on the Stock Exchange*; *the company has stopped trading*; *he trades under the name 'Eeziphitt'*

trademark *or* **trade mark** *or* **trade name** ['treɪdmɑːk *or* 'treɪd 'neɪm] *noun* registered trade mark = particular name, design, etc., which identifies a product, has been registered by the maker, and which cannot be used by other makers; *you cannot call your beds 'Softn'kumfi' - it is a registered trademark*

COMMENT: trade marks cover letters or numbers in various combinations, logos, shapes and colours in distinctive designs; also sounds (as in advertising jingles)

trader ['treɪdə] *noun* person who does business; **commodity trader** = person whose business is buying and selling commodities; **free trader** = person who is in favour of free trade; **sole trader** = person who runs a business, usually by himself, but has not registered it as a company

trade union *or* **trades union** ['treɪd 'juːnɪən] *noun* organization which represents workers, who are its members, in discussions about wages and conditions of employment with employers; *they are members of a trade union or they are trade union members*; *he has applied for trade union membership or he has applied to join a trade union*; **Trades Union Congress (TUC)** = central organization for all British trade unions (NOTE: although **Trades Union Congress** is the official name for the organization, **trade union** is commoner than **trades union**); *(in the EU)* **trade union membership** = being a member of a trade union (workers who are nationals of other EU states have the same rights as nationals of the state in which they are working as regards membership of trade unions)

trading ['treɪdɪŋ] *noun* carrying on a business; **fair trading** = way of doing business which is reasonable and does not harm the consumer; **Office of Fair Trading** = government department which protects consumers against unfair or illegal business practices; **fraudulent trading** = carrying on the business of a company while knowing that the company is insolvent; **Trading Standards Department** = department of a council which deals with weighing and measuring equipment used by shops, and other consumer matters (NOTE: also called the **Weights and Measures Department**); **trading standards officer** = official in charge of a council's Trading Standards Department

traffic ['træfɪk] **1** *noun* cars or other vehicles travelling on the road; **traffic offences** = offences committed by drivers of vehicles; **traffic police** = section of the police concerned with problems on the roads; **traffic warden** = official whose duty is to regulate the traffic under the supervision of the police, especially to deal with cars which are illegally parked **2** *verb* **to traffic in something** = to buy and sell something illegally; *he was charged with trafficking in drugs or with drug trafficking* (NOTE: **trafficking - trafficked**)

train [treɪn] *verb* to teach someone a skill or a profession; *he is a trained accountant*; *the director is American-trained*; **day training centre** = centre where young offenders attend courses as part of their probation; **training contract** = contract under which a trainee works in a solicitor's office to learn the law (NOTE: this term has officially replaced **articles**)

trainee [treɪˈniː] *noun* young person who is learning a skill; **trainee solicitor** = young person who is contracted to work in a solicitor's office for some years to learn the law (NOTE: this term has officially replaced **articled clerk**)

transact [trænˈzækt] *verb* **to transact business** = to carry out a piece of business

transaction [trænˈzækʃn] *noun* **business transaction** = piece of business, buying or selling; **cash transaction** = transaction paid for in cash; **a transaction on the Stock Exchange** = purchase or sale of shares on the Stock Exchange; *the paper publishes a daily list of Stock Exchange transactions*; **exchange transaction** = purchase or sale of foreign currency; **fraudulent transaction** = transaction which aims to cheat someone

transcript [ˈtrænskrɪpt] *noun* record (written out in full) of something noted in shorthand; *the judge asked for a full transcript of the evidence*; *transcripts of cases are available in the Supreme Court Library*

transfer 1 [ˈtrænsfə] *noun* **(a)** moving someone or something to a new place; **transfer of property** *or* **transfer of shares** = moving the ownership of property or shares from one person to another; **bank transfer** = moving money from a bank account to an account in another country; **capital transfer tax** = tax on the transfer of capital or assets from one owner to another; **credit transfer** *or* **transfer of funds** = moving money from one account to another; **deed of transfer** = agreement which transfers the ownership of shares; **stock transfer form** = form to be signed by the person transferring shares to another **(b)** moving the hearing of a case to another court **2** [trænsˈfɜː] *verb* to pass to someone else

transferable [trænsˈfɜːrəbl] *adjective* which can be passed to someone else; **the**

season ticket is not transferable = the ticket cannot be given or lent to someone else to use; **single transferable vote** = voting system in proportional representation where each voter votes for the candidates in order of preference, and his vote is transferred to the next candidate if his first choice is not elected

transferee [trænzfəˈriː] *noun* person to whom property or goods are transferred

transferor [trænzfəˈrɔː] *noun* person who transfers goods or property to another

transit [ˈtrænzɪt] *see* IN TRANSIT

transparency [trænzˈpærənsi] *noun* being open and easy to understand; *too many different decision-making processes can cause a lack of transparency*

transparent [trænzˈpærənt] *noun* **(a)** which is completely obvious; *his explanation was a transparent lie* **(b)** clear and open about official actions; *the government insists on the importance of all its actions being transparent*

traverse [trəˈvɜːs] *noun* denial in a pleading by one side in a case that the facts alleged by the other side are correct

treason [ˈtriːzn] *noun* a notifiable offence, the crime of betraying one's country, usually by helping the enemy in time of war; *he was accused of treason*; *three men were executed for treason*; *the treason trial lasted three weeks*; **high treason** = formal way of referring to treason; **misprision of treason** = crime of knowing that treason has been committed and not reporting it; **treason felony** = notifiable offence of planning to remove a King or Queen, or of planning to start a war against the United Kingdom

treasonable [ˈtriːznəbl] *adjective* which may be considered as treason; *he was accused of making treasonable remarks*

treasure [ˈtreʒə] *noun* gold, silver or jewels, especially when found or stolen; *thieves broke into the palace and stole the king's treasure*

treasure trove ['treʒə 'trəuv] *noun* treasure which has been hidden by someone in the past and has now been discovered

COMMENT: formerly, any treasure found was declared to the coroner, who decided if it was treasure trove. If it was declared treasure trove, it belonged to the state, though the person who found it usually got a reward equal to its market value. Since 1997 there is a new Treasure Act regarding treasure. The word now covers objects made of at least 10% gold or silver and over 300 years old, whether they have been buried intentionally or simply lost. It also covers other items of value such as pottery. Anyone finding treasure still has to report it to the local coroner, but they will only receive a reward if a museum wants to acquire the object. The reward is based on an independent expert's valuation. The owner of the land where the object was found is now also eligible for a reward

treasurer ['treʒərə] *noun* **(a)** person who looks after the money or finances of a club or society, etc.; **honorary treasurer** = treasurer who does not receive any fee **(b)** main financial manager of a large company

treasury ['treʒəri] *noun* **the Treasury** = government department which deals with the country's finance; **the Treasury Benches** = front benches in the House of Commons where the government ministers sit; **Treasury Bill** = short-term bill of exchange which does not give any interest and is sold by the government at a discount through the central bank (in the UK, their term varies from three to six months; in the USA, they are for 91 or 182 days, or for 52 weeks. In American English they are also called 'Treasuries' or 'T-bills'); **treasury bonds** = bonds issued by the Treasury of the USA; **Treasury counsel** = barrister who pleads in the Central Criminal Court on behalf of the Director of Public Prosecutions; **the Treasury Solicitor** = the solicitor who is the head of the Government's legal department in England

and Wales and legal adviser to the Cabinet Office and other government departments; *US* **Secretary to the Treasury** *or* **Treasury Secretary** = member of the government in charge of finance

COMMENT: in most countries, the government's finances are the responsibility of the Ministry of Finance, headed by the Finance Minister. In the UK, the Treasury is headed by the Chancellor of the Exchequer

treat [triːt] *verb* to deal with someone, to negotiate; **invitation to treat** = asking someone to make an offer to buy (as by putting items for sale in a shop window)

treaty ['triːti] *noun* **(a)** written legal agreement between countries; *commercial treaty*; *cultural treaty*; **Treaty of Accession** = treaty whereby the UK joined the EC; **Treaty of Rome** = treaty which established the EC in 1957 **(b)** agreement between individual persons; **to sell (a house) by private treaty** = to sell (a house) to another person not by auction

Treaty on European Union (TEU) ['triːti ɒn juərə'piːən 'juːnjən] *noun* treaty which created the European Union, with three main pillars: the European Community, the Common Foreign and Security Policy, and the Common Home Affairs and Justice Policy

COMMENT: the TEU established a committee of the regions; the Court of Auditors became part of the Community; more emphasis was put on cooperation in culture, education, etc.; the European Parliament had a greater role than before; capital can move freely between Member States

trespass ['trespəs] **1** *noun* tort of interfering with the land or goods of another person (note that trespass on someone's property is not a criminal offence); **trespass to goods** = tort of harming, stealing or interfering with goods which belong to someone else; **trespass to land** = tort of interfering with, going on someone's property or putting things or animals on someone's property without permission; **trespass to the person** = tort of harming someone by assault or false imprisonment **2** *verb* to offend by going on to property without the permission of the owner

trespasser ['trespesə] *noun* person who commits trespass by going onto land without the permission of the owner

triable ['traɪəbl] *adjective* (offence) for which a person can be tried in a court; **offence triable either way** = offence which can be tried before the Magistrates' Court or before the Crown Court

trial ['traɪəl] *noun* **(a)** criminal or civil court case heard before a judge; *the trial lasted six days*; *the judge ordered a new trial when one of the jurors was found to be the accused's brother*; **he is on trial** *or* **is standing trial for embezzlement** = he is being tried for embezzlement; **to commit someone for trial** = to send someone to a court to be tried; **trial bundle** = all the documents brought together by the claimant for a trial, indexed and in a ring binder; **trial judge** = judge who is hearing a trial; **trial timetable** = detailed timetable of a hearing, set out in the listing directions, including the length of time allowed for speeches, etc. for cross-examination of witnesses, etc. **(b)** test to see if something is good; **on trial** = being tested; *the product is on trial in our laboratories*; **trial period** = time when a customer can test a product before buying it; **trial sample** = small piece of a product used for testing; **free trial** = testing of a machine or product with no payment involved **(c)** **trial balance** = draft adding of debits and credits to see if they balance

tribunal [traɪ'bjuːnl] *noun* a court; especially a specialist court outside the judicial system which examines special problems and makes judgments; **industrial tribunal** = court which can decide in disputes between employers and employees; **Lands Tribunal** = court which deals with compensation claims relating to land; **military tribunal** = court made up of army officers which examines military problems; **rent tribunal** = court which adjudicates in disputes about rents, and can award a fair rent

trick [trɪk] **1** *noun* clever act to make someone believe something which is not true; **confidence trick** = business where someone gains another person's confidence and then tricks him **2** *verb* to get money or property by making someone believe something which is not true; *the gang tricked the bank manager into giving them the keys of the vault*; *they tricked the old lady out of £25,000*

trickster ['trɪkstə] *noun* **confidence trickster** = person who carries out a confidence trick on someone

trier of fact ['traɪə əv 'fækt] *noun US* a person, such as a member of a jury, whose job it is to find out true facts about a case

Trinity ['trɪnɪti] *noun* one of the four sittings of the law courts; one of the four law terms

Trinity House ['trɪnɪti 'haʊs] *noun* body which superintends lighthouses and pilots in some areas of the British coast

trough [trɒf] *noun* low point in the economic cycle

trove [trəʊv] *see* TREASURE

trover ['trəʊvə] *noun* action to recover property which has been converted, goods which have been taken or passed to other parties

true [truː] *adjective* correct or accurate; **true bill** = verdict by a grand jury that an indictment should proceed; **true copy** = exact copy; *I certify that this is a true copy*; *the document has been certified as a true copy*

trust [trʌst] **1** *noun* **(a)** being confident that something is correct, will work, etc.; **we took his statement on trust** = we accepted his statement without examining it to see if it was correct **(b)** duty of looking after goods, money or property which someone (the beneficiary) has passed to you (the trustee); *he left his property in trust for his grandchildren*; **breach of**

trust = failure on the part of a trustee to act properly in regard to a trust; **position of trust** = job where an employee is trusted by his employer to look after money, confidential information, etc.; **constructive trust** = trust arising by reason of a person's behaviour; **implied trust** = trust which is implied by the intentions of the parties; **trust for sale** = trust whereby property is held but can be sold and the money passed to the beneficiaries **(c)** management of money or property for someone; *they set up a family trust for their grandchildren; US* trust company = organization which supervises the financial affairs of private trusts, executes wills, and acts as a bank to a limited number of customers; **trust deed** *or* **instrument** = document which sets out the details of a trust; **trust fund** = assets (money, securities, property) held in trust for someone; **discretionary trust** = trust where the trustees decide when and how much money is to be paid to the beneficiaries; **investment trust** = company whose shares can be bought on the Stock Exchange and whose business is to make money by buying and selling stocks and shares; **unit trust** = organization which takes money from investors and invests it in stocks and shares for them under a trust deed **(d)** *US* small group of companies which control the supply of a product **(e)** **trust territory** = territory which is being administered by another country under a trusteeship agreement **2** *verb* **to trust someone with something** = to give something to someone to look after; *can he be trusted with all that cash?*

trustee [trʌˈstiː] *noun* **(a)** person who has charge of money or property in trust, person who is responsible for a family trust; *the trustees of the pension fund;* **trustee in bankruptcy** = person who is appointed by a court to run the affairs of a bankrupt and pay his creditors; **Public Trustee** = official who is appointed as a trustee of a person's property **(b)** country appointed by the United Nations to administer another country

trusteeship [trʌˈstiːʃɪp] *noun* position of being a trustee; *the territory is under United Nations trusteeship*

trusty [ˈtrʌsti] *noun (slang)* prisoner who is trusted by the prison warders

Truth in Lending Act [ˈtruːθ ɪn ˈlendɪŋ ˈækt] US Act of 1969, which forces lenders to state the full terms of their interest rates to borrowers

try [traɪ] *verb* to hear a civil or criminal trial; *he was tried for murder and sentenced to life imprisonment; the court is not competent to try the case*

TUC [ˈtiː ˈjuː ˈsiː] = TRADES UNION CONGRESS

turn [tɜːn] **1** *noun* profit or commission **2** *verb* to change direction or to go round in a circle; **to turn Queen's evidence,** *US* **to turn state's evidence** = to confess to a crime and then act as witness against the other criminals involved in the hope of getting a lighter sentence

turnkey operation [ˈtɜːnkiː ɒpəˈreɪʃn] *noun* contract where a company takes all responsibility for building, fitting and staffing for a building (such as a school, hospital or factory) so that it is completely ready for the purchaser to take over at an agreed date

turn over [ˈtɜːn ˈəʊvə] *verb* to have a certain amount of sales; *we turn over £2,000 a week*

turnover [ˈtɜːnəʊvə] *noun* **(a)** *GB* amount of sales; *the company's turnover has increased by 235%; we based our calculations on last year's turnover* **(b)** staff turnover *or* turnover of staff = changes in staff, when some leave and others join **(c)** *US* number of times something is used or sold in a period (usually one year), expressed as a percentage of a total

twin [twɪn] *verb* **to twin a town with another town** = to arrange a special relationship between a town in one country and a similar town in another country; *Richmond is twinned with Fontainebleau*

twinning [twɪnɪŋ] *noun* special arrangement between a town in one country and one of similar size or situation in another country; *the district council's town-twinning committee decided that Epping should be twinned with Eppingen in Germany*

two-party system [ˈtuːˈpɑːti ˈsɪstəm] *noun* political system in many countries, where there are only two political parties (or only two very large parties), with the result that any smaller party finds it impossible to get enough votes to form a government; *see also* ONE-PARTY

Uu

uberrimae fidei [uː'berɪmiː 'faɪdeɪ] *Latin phrase meaning* 'of total good faith': state which should exist between parties to certain types of legal relationship (such as partnerships or insurance); *an insurance contract is uberrimae fidei*

UCC ['juː 'siː 'siː] = UNIVERSAL COPYRIGHT CONVENTION

UDI ['juː 'diː 'aɪ] = UNILATERAL DECLARATION OF INDEPENDENCE

ulterior motive [ʌl'tɪərɪə 'məʊtɪv] *noun* reason for doing something which is not immediately connected with the action, but is done in anticipation of its result, and so is an act of bad faith

ultimate ['ʌltɪmət] *adjective* last or final; **ultimate consumer** = the person who actually uses the product; **ultimate owner** = real or true owner

ultimatum [ʌltɪ'meɪtəm] *noun* final demand, a proposal to someone that unless he does something within a period of time, action will be taken against him; *the union officials argued among themselves over the best way to deal with the ultimatum from the management* (NOTE: plural is **ultimatums** or **ultimata**)

ultra- ['ʌltrə] *prefix meaning* extreme or extremely; **ultra-leftist** = extremely left-wing

ultra vires ['ʌltrə 'vaɪriːz] *Latin phrase meaning* 'beyond powers'; **their action was ultra vires** = they acted in a way which exceeded their legal powers; *see* INTRA VIRES

umpire ['ʌmpaɪə] *noun* person called in to decide when two arbitrators cannot agree

unadmitted [ʌnəd'mɪtɪd] *adjective* (member of staff of a solicitor's office) who has not been admitted as a solicitor

unanimous [juː'nænɪməs] *adjective* where everyone votes in the same way; *there was a unanimous vote against the proposal*; *they reached unanimous agreement*; **unanimous verdict** = verdict agreed by all the jurors; *the jury reached a unanimous verdict of not guilty*

unanimously [juː'nænɪməsli] *adverb* with everyone agreeing; *the appeal court decided unanimously in favour of the defendant*

unascertained [ʌnæsə'teɪnd] *adjective* not identified; *title to unascertained goods cannot pass to the buyer until the goods have been ascertained*

unborn [ʌn'bɔːn] *adjective* (child) which is still in its mother's body and has not yet been born

unchallenged [ʌn'tʃæləndʒd] *adjective* (evidence) which has not been challenged

unclean [ʌn'kliːn] *see* CLEAN HANDS

unconditional [ʌnkən'dɪʃnl] *adjective* with no conditions attached; *unconditional acceptance of the offer by the board*; *on the claimant's application for summary judgment the master gave the defendant unconditional leave to defend*; **the offer went unconditional last Thursday** = the takeover bid was accepted by the majority of the shareholders and therefore the conditions attached to it no longer apply

unconfirmed [ˌʌnkən'fɜːmd] *adjective* which has not been confirmed; *there are unconfirmed reports that a BBC reporter has been arrested*

unconstitutional [ˌʌnkɒnstɪ'tjuːʃnl] *adjective* **(a)** which is not according to the constitution of a country; *legislation which is contrary to European Community regulations is declared unconstitutional; the Appeal Court ruled that the action of the Attorney-General was unconstitutional* **(b)** which is not allowed by the rules of an organization; *the chairman ruled that the meeting was unconstitutional*

uncontested [ˌʌnkən'testɪd] *adjective* which is not contested or defended; *an uncontested divorce case or election*

uncrossed cheque ['ʌnkrɒst 'tʃek] *noun* cheque which does not have two lines across it and can be exchanged for cash anywhere

undefended [ˌʌndɪ'fendɪd] *adjective* (case) where the defendant does not acknowledge service and does not appear at the court to defend the case; *an undefended divorce case*

under ['ʌndə] *preposition* controlled by, according to; *regulations under the Police Act; under the terms of the agreement, the goods should be delivered in October; he is acting under rule 23 of the union constitution; she does not qualify under section 2 of the 1979 Act; a creditor seeking a receiving order under the Bankruptcy Act 1974*

undercover agent [ˌʌndəkʌvə 'eɪdʒənt] *noun* secret agent, agent acting in disguise

underlease ['ʌndəliːs] *noun* lease from a tenant to another tenant

underlet ['ʌndəlet] *verb* to let a property which is held on a lease

undermentioned [ˌʌndə'menʃnd] *adjective* mentioned lower down in a document

Under-Secretary (of State) [ˌʌndə'sekrətri əv 'steɪt] *noun* **Parliamentary Under-Secretary (of State)** = junior member of a government working in a government department under the Secretary of State and Ministers of State

undersheriff ['ʌndəʃerɪf] *noun* person who is second to a High Sheriff and deputizes for him

undersigned [ˌʌndə'saɪnd] *noun* person who has signed a letter; **we, the undersigned** = we, the people who have signed below (NOTE: can be singular or plural)

understanding [ˌʌndə'stændɪŋ] *noun* private agreement; *the two parties came to an understanding about the division of the estate;* **on the understanding that** = on condition that, provided that; *we accept the terms of the contract, on the understanding that it has to be ratified by the full board*

undertake [ˌʌndə'teɪk] *verb* to promise to do something; *to undertake an investigation of the fraud; the members of the jury have undertaken not to read the newspapers; he undertook to report to the probation office once a month* (NOTE: undertaking - undertook - has undertaken)

undertaking [ˌʌndə'teɪkɪŋ] *noun* **(a)** business; *a commercial undertaking* **(b)** (legally binding) promise; *they have given us a written undertaking that they will not infringe our patent; the judge accepted the defendant's undertaking not to harass the claimant*

undertenant [ˌʌndə'tenənt] *noun* person who holds a property on an underlease

underworld ['ʌndəwɜːld] *noun* world of criminals; *the police has informers in the London underworld; the indications are that it is an underworld killing*

underwrite [ˌʌndəˈraɪt] *verb* **(a)** to accept responsibility for; **to underwrite a share issue** = to guarantee that a share issue will be sold by agreeing to buy all shares which are not subscribed; *the issue was underwritten by three underwriting companies*; **to underwrite an insurance policy** = to accept liability for the payment of compensation according to the policy **(b)** to agree to pay for costs; *the government has underwritten the development costs of the building* (NOTE: underwriting - underwrote - has underwritten)

underwriter [ˈʌndəraɪtə] *noun* **(a)** person who underwrites a share issue **(b)** person who accepts liability for an insurance; **Lloyd's underwriter** = member of an insurance group at Lloyd's who accepts to underwrite insurances; **marine underwriter** = person who insures ships and their cargoes

undesirable alien [ˌʌndɪˈzaɪrəbl ˈeɪliən] *noun* person who is not a citizen of the country, and who the government considers should not be allowed to stay in the country; *he was deported as an undesirable alien*

undischarged bankrupt [ˌʌndɪsˈtʃɑːdʒd ˈbæŋkrʌpt] *noun* person who has been declared bankrupt and has not been released from that state

undisclosed [ˌʌndɪsˈkləʊzd] *adjective* not identified; **undisclosed principal** = principal who has not been identified by his agent

> COMMENT: the doctrine of the undisclosed principal means that the agent may be sued as well as the principal if his identity is discovered

undue influence [ʌnˈdjuː ˈɪnfluəns] *noun* wrong pressure put on someone which prevents that person from acting independently

unemployment [ˌʌnɪmˈplɔɪmənt] *noun* absence of work; *the unemployment figures or the figures for unemployment are rising*; **unemployment benefit** = money paid by the government to someone who is unemployed

unenforceable [ˌʌnɪnˈfɔːsəbl] *adjective* (contract or right) which cannot be enforced

unequivocal [ˌʌnɪˈkwɪvəkl] *adjective* clear, not ambiguous

unfair [ʌnˈfeə] *adjective* which is not fair, not just; **unfair competition** = trying to do better than another company by using methods such as importing foreign goods at very low prices or by wrongly criticizing a competitor's products; **unfair contract term** = term in a contract which is held by law to be unjust; **unfair dismissal** = removing someone from a job by an employer who appears not to be acting in a reasonable way (i.e., as by dismissing someone who wants to join a union)

> COMMENT: an employee can complain of unfair dismissal to an industrial tribunal

unfit [ʌnˈfɪt] *adjective* **unfit to plead** = not mentally capable of standing trial

uni- [ˈjuːni] *prefix* meaning single

unicameral [juːniˈkæmərl] *adjective* (system of parliament) where there is only one legislative chamber (as in New Zealand and Nebraska); *see also* BICAMERAL

unilateral [juːniˈlætərl] *adjective* on one side only, done by one party only; *they took the unilateral decision to cancel the contract*; **Unilateral Declaration of Independence (UDI)** = act whereby a colony declares itself independent without the agreement of the colonial power; **unilateral nuclear disarmament** = decision by one country to stop storing or making nuclear weapons, regardless of what other countries may do; *compare* BILATERAL

unilaterally [juːniˈlætərli] *adverb* by one party only; *they cancelled the contract unilaterally*

unincorporated association
[ʌnɪnˈkɔːpəreɪtɪd əsəusiˈeɪʃn] *noun* group of people (such as a club or partnership) which is not legally incorporated

uninsured [ʌnɪnˈʃʊəd] *adjective* with no valid insurance; *the driver of the car was uninsured*

union [ˈjuːnɪən] *noun* (a) state of being linked together, as the linking of independent states into a federation; **the States of the Union** = the states joined together to form the United States of America; **State of the Union message** = annual speech by the President of the USA which summarizes the political situation in the country; **Union Calendar** = *see* CALENDAR (b) **trade union** *or* **trades union,** *US* **labor union** = organization which represents workers who are its members in discussions with management about wages and conditions of work; **union agreement** = agreement between a management and a trade union over wages and conditions of work; **union dues** *or* **union subscription** = payment made by workers to belong to a union; **union recognition** = act of agreeing that a union can act on behalf of staff in a company; *US* **union shop** = system where a company agrees to employ only union members in certain jobs (NOTE: British English is **closed shop**) (c) **customs union** = agreement between several countries that goods can go between them without paying duty, while goods from other countries have special duties charged on them

unionist [ˈjuːnɪənɪst] *noun* (a) member of a trade union (b) person who supports a political union of states or parties

unionized [ˈjuːnɪənaɪzd] *adjective* (company) where the members of staff belong to a trade union

United Kingdom (UK) [juːˈnaɪtɪd ˈkɪŋdəm] *noun* independent country, formed of England, Wales, Scotland and Northern Ireland; *he came to the UK to study*; *does she have a UK passport?*; *is he a UK citizen?*

United Nations *or* **United Nations Organization (UNO** *or* **UN)** [juːˈnaɪtɪd ˈneɪʃnz] *noun* international organization including almost all sovereign states in the world, where member states are represented at meetings; *see also* GENERAL ASSEMBLY, SECURITY COUNCIL

United States of America (USA) [juːˈnaɪtɪd ˈsteɪts əv əˈmerɪkə] *noun* independent country, a federation of states (originally thirteen, now fifty) in North America; **the United States Code** = book containing all the permanent laws of the USA, arranged in sections according to subject, and revised from time to time

> COMMENT: the federal government (based in Washington D.C.) is formed of a legislature (the Congress) with two chambers (the Senate and House of Representatives), an executive (the President) and a judiciary (the Supreme Court). Each of the fifty states making up the USA has its own legislature and executive (the Governor) as well as its own legal system and constitution

universal [juːnɪˈvɜːsəl] *adjective* which applies everywhere or to everyone; **universal franchise** *or* **suffrage** = right to vote which is enjoyed by all adult members of the population

Universal Copyright Convention (UCC) [juːnɪˈvɜːsəl ˈkɒpiraɪt kənˈvenʃn] *noun* international agreement on copyright set up by the United Nations in Geneva in 1952; *see also the comment at* COPYRIGHT

> COMMENT: both the Berne Convention of 1886 and the UCC were drawn up to try to protect copyright from pirates; under the Berne Convention, published material remains in copyright until 50 years after the death of the author and for 25 years after publication under the UCC. In both cases, a work which is copyrighted in one country is automatically covered by the copyright legislation of all countries signing the convention

unjust [ʌn'dʒʌst] *adjective* not just, not fair

unlawful [ʌn'lɔːfəl] *adjective* (act) which is against the law; **unlawful sexual intercourse** = sexual intercourse with someone who is under the age of consent, etc.; **unlawful assembly** = notifiable offence when three or more people come together to commit a breach of the peace or other crime; *(in a coroner's court)* **verdict of unlawful killing** = verdict that a person's death was murder or manslaughter

unless order [ʌn'les 'ɔːdə] *noun* order that a statement of claim will be struck out if a party does not comply with the order

unlimited [ʌn'lɪmɪtɪd] *adjective* with no limits; *the bank offered him unlimited credit*; **unlimited company** = company where the shareholders have no limit as regards liability; **unlimited liability** = situation where a sole trader or each single partner is responsible for all the firm's debts with no limit at the amount each may have to pay

unliquidated claim [ʌn'lɪkwɪdeɪtɪd 'kleɪm] *noun* claim for unliquidated damages

unliquidated damages [ʌn'lɪkwɪdeɪtɪd 'dæmɪdʒɪz] *plural noun* damages which are not for a fixed amount of money but are awarded by a court as a matter of discretion depending on the case

> COMMENT: torts give rise to claims for unliquidated damages

unmarried [ʌn'mærɪd] *adjective* (person) who is not married

unofficial [ʌnə'fɪʃl] *adjective* not official; **unofficial strike** = strike by local workers which has not been approved by the union as a whole

unofficially [ʌnə'fɪʃəli] *adverb* not officially; *the tax office told the company, unofficially, that it would be prosecuted*

unopposed [ʌnə'pəuzd] *adjective* (motion) with no one voting against; (proceedings) which have not been opposed; *the Bill had an unopposed second reading in the House*

unparliamentary [ʌnpɑːlə'mentri] *adjective* not suitable for Parliament; **unparliamentary language** = words used in Parliament which are considered to be rude, and which the Speaker may ask the MP to withdraw

> COMMENT: various terms of abuse are considered unparliamentary, in particular words which suggest that an MP has not told the truth. In a recent exchange in the House of Commons, a Member called others 'clowns' and 'drunks'; the Deputy Speaker said: 'Order. That is unparliamentary language, and I must ask the hon. Member to withdraw'. Another recent example occurred when an MP said: 'if the hon. Member were honest, I suspect that he would have to do the same'. *Mr. Speaker:* 'Order. All hon. Members are honest.'

unprecedented [ʌn'presɪdəntɪd] *adjective* which has no precedent, which has not happened before; *in an unprecedented move, the tribunal asked the witness to sing a song*

unprofessional conduct [ʌnprə'feʃnl 'kɒndʌkt] *noun* way of behaving which is not suitable for a professional person, which goes against the code of practice of a profession

unquantifiable [ʌnkwɒntɪ'faɪəbl] *adjective* (damage or loss) which cannot be quantified

unreasonable [ʌn'riːznəbl] *adjective* not reasonable, (action) which no reasonable person would take; **unreasonable conduct** = actions by a spouse which are not reasonable and which show that a marriage has broken down

unreasonably [ʌn'riːznəbli] *adverb* in a way which is not reasonable or which cannot be explained; *approval of any loan will not be unreasonably withheld*

unredeemed pledge [ʌnrɪ'diːmd 'pledʒ] *noun* pledge which the borrower has not claimed back by paying back his loan

unregistered [ʌnˈredʒɪstəd] *adjective* (land) which has not been registered

unreliable [ʌnrɪˈlaɪəbl] *adjective* which cannot be relied on; *the prosecution tried to show that the driver's evidence was unreliable*; *the defence called two witnesses and both were unreliable*

unreported [ʌnrɪˈpɔːtɪd] *adjective* **(a)** not reported to the police; *there are thousands of unreported cases of theft* **(b)** not reported in the Law Reports; *counsel referred the judge to a number of relevant unreported cases*

unsafe [ʌnˈseɪf] *adjective* (judgment) which does not stand up in law and may be quashed on appeal

unsecured [ʌnsɪˈkjʊəd] *adjective* **unsecured creditor** = creditor who is owed money, but has no mortgage or charge over the debtor's property as security; **unsecured debt** = debt which is not guaranteed by assets; **unsecured loan** = loan made with no security

unsolicited [ʌnsəˈlɪsɪtɪd] *adjective* which has not been asked for; *an unsolicited gift*; **unsolicited goods** = goods which are sent to someone who has not asked for them, suggesting that he might like to buy them

unsolved [ʌnˈsɒlvd] *adjective* (crime) which has not been solved

unsound [ʌnˈsaʊnd] *adjective* **persons of unsound mind** = people who are not sane

unsworn [ʌnˈswɔːn] *adjective* which has not been made on oath; *an unsworn statement*

unwritten [ʌnˈrɪtn] *adjective* **unwritten agreement** = agreement which has been reached orally (such as in a telephone conversation) but has not been written down; **unwritten law** = rule which is established by precedent

uphold [ʌpˈhəʊld] *verb* to keep in good order; **to uphold the law** = to make sure that laws are obeyed; **to uphold a sentence** = to reject an appeal against a sentence; *the Appeal Court upheld the sentence* (NOTE: **upholding - upheld**)

uplift [ˈʌplɪft] *noun* part of a conditional fee agreement, an extra fee (in addition to the normal fees) paid by a client to a lawyer if the case is won

upper house *or* **upper chamber** [ˈʌpə ˈhaʊs *or* ˈtʃeɪmbə] *noun* more important of the two houses or chambers in a bicameral system; *after being passed by the legislative assembly, a bill goes to the upper house for further discussion* (NOTE: opposite is **lower house**); *see COMMENT at* LOWER

urine [ˈjʊərɪn] *noun* waste water from the body; **urine test** = test of a sample of a person's urine to see if it contains drugs or alcohol

usage [ˈjuːzɪdʒ] *noun* **(a)** custom, way in which something is usually done **(b)** how something is used

use [juːs] *noun* **(a)** land held by the legal owner on trust for a beneficiary **(b)** **change of use** = order allowing a property to be used in a different way (such as a dwelling house to be used as a business office, a shop to be used as a factory); **land zoned for industrial use** = land where planning permission has been given to build factories

user [ˈjuːzə] *noun* person who uses something; **end user** = person who actually uses a product; **user's guide** *or* **handbook** = book showing someone how to use something; **registered user** = person or company which has been given official permission to use a registered trademark

user-friendly [ˈjuːzəˈfrendli] *adjective* which a computer user finds easy to work; *these programs are really user-friendly*

usher [ˈʌʃə] *noun* person who guards the door leading into a courtroom and maintains order in court

usufruct ['juːzufrʌkt] *noun* right to enjoy the use or the profit of the property or land of another person

usurp [juˈzɜːp] *verb* to take and use a right which is not yours (especially to take the throne from a rightful king)

usurpation [juːzɜːˈpeɪʃn] *noun* taking and using a right which is not yours

usurper [juːˈzɜːpə] *noun* person who usurps power; *the army killed the usurper and placed the king back on his throne again*

usury ['juːʒri] *noun* lending money at very high interest

utter ['ʌtə] *verb* to use a forged document criminally; **forgery and uttering** = notifiable offence of forging and then using an official document (such as a prescription for drugs)

Vv

v. ['vɜːsəs] = VERSUS against (NOTE: titles of cases are quoted as *Hills v. The Amalgamated Company Ltd; R. v. Smith*)

vacant ['veɪkənt] *adjective* empty, not occupied; **vacant possession** = being able to occupy a property immediately after buying it because it is empty; *the house is for sale with vacant possession*; situations **vacant** *or* appointments **vacant** = list (in a newspaper) of jobs which are available

vacantia [və'kæntiə] *see* BONA VACANTIA

vacate [və'keɪt] *verb* to **vacate the premises** = to leave premises, so that they become empty

vacation [və'keɪʃn] *noun* (a) *GB* period when the courts are closed between sittings, period of university holidays (b) *US* holiday, period when people are not working

vagrancy ['veɪgrənsi] *noun* being a vagrant; *he was charged with vagrancy*

vagrant ['veɪgrənt] *noun* person who goes about with no work and no place to live

valid ['vælɪd] *adjective* (a) which is acceptable because it is true; *that is not a valid argument or excuse* (b) which can be used lawfully; *the contract is not valid if it has not been witnessed*; *a ticket which is valid for three months*; *he was carrying a valid passport*

validate ['vælɪdeɪt] *verb* (a) to check to see if something is correct; *the document was validated by the bank* (b) to make (something) valid; *the import documents have to be validated by the customs officials*

validation [vælɪ'deɪʃn] *noun* act of making something valid

validity [və'lɪdɪti] *noun* being valid; *a national court can ask the ECJ for a ruling about the validity of a Community act*; **period of validity** = length of time for which a document is valid

valorem [və'lɔːrəm] *see* AD VALOREM

valuable ['væljʊbl] *adjective* which is worth a lot of money; **valuable consideration** = something of value (such as money) which is passed from one party (the promisee) to another (the promisor) as payment for what is promised; **valuable property** *or* **valuables** = personal items which are worth a lot of money

valuation [væljʊ'eɪʃn] *noun* estimate of how much something is worth; *to ask for a valuation of a property before making an offer for it*; **stock valuation** = estimating the value of stock at the end of an accounting period

value ['væljuː] **1** *noun* amount of money which something is worth; *he imported goods to the value of £250*; *the fall in the value of the dollar*; *the valuer put the value of the stock at £25,000*; **asset value** = value of a company calculated by adding together all its assets; **book value** = value as recorded in the company's accounts; **declared value** = value of goods entered on a customs declaration form; **face value** *or* **nominal value** = value written on a coin, banknote or share; **market value** = value of an asset, of a product or of a company, if sold today; **surrender value** = money which an insurer will pay if an insurance policy is given up before maturity date **2** *verb* to estimate how much money something is worth; *goods valued at £250*; *he valued the stock at £25,000*; *we are having the jewellery valued for insurance*; **valued policy** = marine insurance policy where the value of what is insured is stated

Value Added Tax (VAT)   ['væljuː 'ædɪd 'tæks] *noun* tax imposed as a percentage of the invoice value of goods and services

valuer ['væljuə] *noun* person who values property for insurance purposes

vandal ['vændəl] *noun* person who destroys property, especially public property, wilfully; *vandals have pulled the telephones out of the call boxes*

vandalism ['vændəlɪzm] *noun* wilful destruction of property

vandalize ['vændəlaɪz] *verb* to destroy property wilfully; *none of the call boxes work because they have all been vandalized*

variable ['veəriəbl] *adjective* which changes; **variable costs** = costs of producing a product or service which change according to the amount produced

variance ['veəriəns] *noun* difference; **budget variance** = difference between the cost as estimated for the budget and the actual cost incurred

variation [veəri'eɪʃn] *noun* (a) amount by which something changes; **seasonal variations** = changes which take place because of the seasons (b) change in conditions; *the petitioner asked for a variation in her maintenance order*

vary ['veəri] *verb* to change; *the court has been asked to vary the conditions of the order*; *demand for social services varies according to the weather*

VAT [væt] = VALUE ADDED TAX

vault [vɒlt] *noun* underground strongroom usually built under a bank

VC = VICE CHANCELLOR

vendee [ven'diː] *noun* person who buys

vendible ['vendəbl] *adjective* able to be sold; *for a patent application to succeed, the product being patented must be vendible*

vendor ['vendə] *noun* (a) person who sells; *the solicitor acting on behalf of the vendor* (b) **street vendor** = person who sells food or small items in the street

venue ['venjuː] *noun* place where a meeting or hearing is held; **mistake in venue** = starting legal proceedings in the wrong court

verbal ['vɜːbl] **1** *adjective* using spoken words, not writing; **verbal agreement** = agreement which is spoken (such as over the telephone); **verbal evidence** = evidence given by a witness speaking in court (as opposed to non-verbal evidence such as photographs or maps); **verbal warning** = stage in warning a worker that his work is not satisfactory (followed by a written warning, if his work does not improve) **2** *verb* to use threatening words when interviewing a suspect

verbally ['vɜːbəli] *adverb* using spoken words, not writing; *they agreed to the terms verbally, and then started to draft the contract*

verbals ['vɜːblz] *noun (informal)* words spoken to a police officer by a suspect

verbatim [vɜː'beɪtɪm] *adjective & adverb* in the exact words; *a verbatim transcript of the trial*; *Hansard provides a verbatim account of the proceedings of the House of Commons*

verdict ['vɜːdɪkt] *noun* (a) decision of a jury or magistrate; **to bring in** *or* **to return a verdict** = to state a verdict at the end of a trial; *the jury brought in* or *returned a verdict of not guilty*; **to come to a verdict** *or* **to reach a verdict** = to decide whether the accused is guilty or not; *the jury took two hours to reach their verdict*; **majority verdict** = verdict agreed by at least ten of the twelve jurors (b) decision reached by a coroner's court; *the court returned a verdict of death by misadventure*; **open verdict** = verdict in a coroner's court which does not decide how a person died; *the court recorded an open verdict on the dead policeman*

versa ['vɜːsə] *see* VICE VERSA

versus ['vɜːsəs] *preposition* against (NOTE: usually abbreviated to **v.** as in **the case of** *Smith v. Williams)*

vest [vest] *verb* to transfer to someone the legal ownership and possession of land or of a right; *the property was vested in the trustees* (NOTE: you vest something **in** *or* **on** someone)

vested interest ['vestɪd 'ɪntrəst] *noun* interest in a property which will come into a person's possession when the interest of another person ends

vested remainder ['vestɪd rɪ'meɪndə] *noun* remainder which is absolutely vested in a person

vesting assent ['vestɪŋ ə'sent] *noun* document which vests settled land on a tenant for life

vesting order ['vestɪŋ 'ɔːdə] *noun* court order which transfers property

vet [vet] *verb* to examine someone or a document carefully to see if there is any breach of security; *all applications are vetted by the Home Office*; **positive vetting** = thorough examination of a person before that person is allowed to work with classified information (NOTE: **vetting - vetted)**

veto ['viːtəʊ] **1** *noun* ban or order not to allow something to become law, even if it has been passed by a parliament; *the President has the power of veto over Bills passed by Congress*; *the UK used its veto in the Security Council* **2** *verb* to ban something, to order something not to become law; *the resolution was vetoed by the president*; *the council has vetoed all plans to hold protest marches in the centre of town*

COMMENT: in the United Nations Security Council, each of the five permanent members has a veto. In the USA, the President may veto a bill sent to him by Congress, provided he does so within ten days of receiving it. The bill then returns to Congress for further discussion, and the President's veto can be overridden by a two-thirds majority in both House of Representatives and Senate

vexatious [vek'seɪʃəs] *adjective* annoying, done in order to annoy; **vexatious action** *or* **litigation** = case brought in order to annoy the defendant; **vexatious litigant** = person who frequently starts legal actions to annoy people and who is barred from bringing actions without leave of the court

viable ['vaɪəbl] *adjective* which can work; **not commercially viable** = not likely to make a profit; **viable alternative** = different proposal which may work

vicarious [vɪ'keəriəs] *adjective* not direct, not personally interested; **vicarious performance** = performance of a contract where the work has been done by a third party; **vicarious liability** = liability of one person for torts committed by someone else, especially the liability of an employer for acts committed by an employee in the course of his work

COMMENT: if the employee is on a frolic of his own, the employer may not be liable

vicariously [vɪ'keəriəsli] *adverb* not directly

vice ['vaɪsi] *Latin word meaning* 'in the place of'; *was present: Councillor Smith (vice Councillor Brown)*

vice- [vaɪs] *prefix* deputy, second in command; *he is the vice-chairman of an industrial group*; *she was appointed to the vice-chairmanship of the committee*

Vice Chancellor (VC) ['vaɪs 'tʃɑːnsələ] *noun* senior judge in charge of the Chancery Division of the High Court

vice-consul ['vaɪs'kɒnsəl] *noun* diplomat with a rank below consul

Vice-President ['vaɪs'prezɪdənt] *noun* deputy to a president

COMMENT: in the USA, the Vice-President is the president (i.e. the chairman) of the Senate. He also succeeds a president if the president dies in office (as Vice-President Johnson succeeded President Kennedy)

vice versa ['vaɪsə 'vɜːsə] *Latin phrase* meaning 'reverse position': in the opposite way; *the responsibilities of the employer towards the employee and vice versa*

victim ['vɪktɪm] *noun* person who suffers a crime or a wrong; *the mugger left his victim lying in the road; he was the victim of a con trick; the accident victims or victims of the accident were taken to hospital*

victimless crime ['vɪktɪmləs 'kraɪm] *noun* crime where there is no obvious victim, such as drug pushing or prostitution

vide ['vɪdi] *Latin word meaning* 'see': used in written texts to refer to another reference

videlicet [vɪ'diːlɪset] *Latin word meaning* 'that is' (NOTE: usually abbreviated to **viz)**

video conferencing ['vɪdiəʊ 'kɒnfərənsɪŋ] *noun* system of conducting a hearing using closed-circuit television, the hearing is recorded on tape

Vienna Conventions [vi'enə kən'venʃənz] *noun* conventions signed in Austria, generally relating to international treaties and the rights of diplomats

view [vjuː] **1** *noun* way of thinking about something; **to take a view on something =** to have an opinion about something; **to take the view that =** to decide that, to have the opinion that; *the court takes the view that the defendant did not publish the defamation maliciously;* **to take the long view =** to plan for a long period before your current investment will become profitable;

in view of = because of; *in view of the age of the accused the magistrates gave him a suspended sentence* **2** *verb* to look at; **viewing the scene =** visit by a judge and jury to the place where a crime was committed

villain ['vɪlən] *noun* GB *(informal)* criminal; *the job of the policeman is to catch villains*

villainy ['vɪləni] *noun* wilful illegal act

violate ['vaɪəleɪt] *verb* to break a rule or a law; *the council has violated the planning regulations; the action of the government violates the international treaty on commercial shipping; the legislation was inapplicable in this case, and the country had not violated the Treaty*

violation [vaɪə'leɪʃn] *noun* act of breaking a rule; *the number of traffic violations has increased; the court criticized the violations of the treaty on human rights;* **in violation of a rule =** breaking a rule; *the government has acted in violation of its agreement*

violence ['vaɪələns] *noun* action using force; **robbery with violence =** robbery where force is used against people or property; **violence against the person =** one of the types of notifiable offence (such as murder or assault) against people

violent ['vaɪələnt] *adjective* using force; *a violent attack on the police;* **the prisoner became violent =** the prisoner tried to attack

virement ['vaɪəmənt] *noun* transfer of money from one account to another or from one section of a budget to another; *the council may use the virement procedure to transfer money from one area of expenditure to another*

vires ['vaɪriːz] *see* INTRA VIRES, ULTRA VIRES

virtue ['vɜːtjuː] *noun* particular goodness of character; good quality; **by virtue of =** as a result of; *he's eligible for British citizenship by virtue of his father who was born in Newcastle*

virtute officii [vɜːˈtuːti ɒˈfisii] *Latin phrase meaning* 'because of his office'

vis major [ˈvɪs ˈmeɪdʒə] *Latin words meaning* 'superior force': force of people or of nature (such as a revolution or an earthquake) which cannot be stopped

visa [ˈviːzə] *noun* special document or special stamp in a passport which allows someone to enter a country; *you will need a visa before you go to China*; *he filled in his visa application form*; **entry visa** = visa allowing someone to enter a country; **multiple entry visa** = visa allowing someone to enter a country many times; **tourist visa** = visa which allows a person to visit a country for a short time on holiday; **transit visa** = visa which allows someone to spend a short time in one country while travelling to another country

visitor [ˈvɪzɪtə] *noun* person who goes to see someone for a short time; **visitor's visa** = visa which allows a person to visit a country for a short time; **prison visitor** = member of a board of visitors appointed by the Home Secretary to visit, inspect and report on conditions in each prison

vital statistics [ˈvaɪtl stəˈtɪstɪks] *noun* statistics dealing with births, marriages and deaths in a town or district

viva voce [ˈvaɪvə ˈvəʊtʃi] *Latin phrase meaning* 'orally', 'by speaking'

vivos [ˈvaɪvəʊs] *Latin word meaning* 'living people'; **gift inter vivos** = present given by one living person to another

viz [viz *or* ˈneɪmli] *see* VIDELICET

void [vɔɪd] **1** *adjective* not legally valid, not having any legal effect; **void marriage** = marriage which is declared not to have had any legal existence; **the contract was declared null and void** = the contract was said to be no longer valid **2** *verb* **to void a contract** = to make a contract invalid

voidable [ˈvɔɪdəbl] *adjective* which can be made void

COMMENT: a contract is void where it never had legal effect, but is voidable if it is apparently of legal effect and remains of legal effect until one or both parties take steps to rescind it

volenti non fit injuria [vəˈlenti nɒn fit ɪnˈdʒʊəriə] *Latin phrase meaning* 'there can be no injury to a person who is willing': rule that if someone has agreed to take the risk of an injury he cannot sue for it (as in the case of someone injured in a boxing match)

volition [vəˈlɪʃn] *noun* will to do something; **of your own volition** = because you decide to do something yourself; *she gave up her job of her own volition*

voluntary [ˈvɒləntri] *adjective* **(a)** done without being forced or without being paid; **voluntary confession** = confession made by an accused person without being threatened or paid; **voluntary disposition** = transfer of property without any valuable consideration; **voluntary liquidation** *or* **winding up** = situation where a company itself decides it must close and sell its assets; **voluntary redundancy** = situation where a worker asks to be made redundant, usually in return for a payment; *(in the EU)* **voluntary unemployment** = situation where a worker resigns from his job of his own free will and does not look for another; *compare* INVOLUNTARY **(b)** without being paid a salary; **voluntary organization** = organization which has no paid staff

volunteer [vɒlənˈtɪə] **1** *noun* **(a)** person who gives or receives property without consideration **(b)** person who offers to do something without being forced **2** *verb* **(a)** to offer information without being asked; *he volunteered the information that the defendant was not in fact a British subject* **(b)** to offer to do something without being forced; *six men volunteered to go into the burning house*

vote [vəʊt] **1** *noun* marking a paper, holding up your hand, etc., to show your opinion or to show who you want to be elected; **to take a vote on a proposal** *or* **to put a proposal to the vote** = to ask people present at a meeting to say if they agree or do not agree with the proposal; **block vote** = casting of a large number of votes at the same time (such as of trade union members) by a person who has been delegated by the holders of the votes to vote for them in this way; **casting vote** = vote used by the chairman in the case where the votes for and against a proposal are equal; *the chairman has the casting vote*; *he used his casting vote to block the motion*; **popular vote** = vote of all the people in a country; **the president is elected by popular vote** = the president is elected by a majority of all the people in a country; **postal vote** = election where the voters send in their voting papers by post; **vote of censure** *or* **censure vote** = vote which criticizes someone, especially a vote which criticizes the government in the House of Commons; **vote of no confidence** = vote to show that a person or group is not trusted; *the chairman resigned after the vote of no confidence in him was passed by the AGM* **2** *verb* to show an opinion by marking a paper or by holding up your hand at a meeting; *the meeting voted to close the factory*; *52% of the members voted for Mr Smith as chairman*; **to vote for a proposal** *or* **to vote against a proposal** = to say that you agree *or* do not agree with a proposal; **two directors were voted off the board at the AGM** = the AGM voted to dismiss two

directors; **she was voted on to the committee** = she was elected a member of the committee

vote down [vəʊt 'daʊn] *verb* **to vote down** = to defeat a motion; *the proposal was voted down*

vote in ['vəʊt 'ɪn] *verb* **to vote someone in** = to elect someone; *the Tory candidate was voted in*

vote out ['vəʊt 'aʊt] *verb* **to vote someone out** = to make someone lose an election; *the government was voted out of office within a year*

voter ['vəʊtə] *noun* person who votes

voting ['vəʊtɪŋ] *noun* act of making a vote; **voting paper** = paper on which the voter puts a cross to show for whom he wants to vote; **voting rights** = rights of shareholders to voting at company meetings; **non-voting shares** = shares which do not allow the shareholder to vote at company meetings

vouch for ['vaʊtʃ 'fɔː] *verb* to state that you believe something is correct, to say that you take responsibility for something; *I cannot vouch for the correctness of the transcript of proceedings*

voucher [vaʊtʃə] *noun* paper which entitles the bearer to receive something

Ww

wager ['weɪdʒə] **1** *noun* bet, the amount deposited when you risk money on the result of a race, a game or an election **2** *verb* to bet, to risk money on the possibility of something happening; *he wagered £100 on the result of the election*

> COMMENT: a wager will not normally be enforced by a court under English law

waive [weɪv] *verb* to give up (a right); *he waived his claim to the estate*; **to waive a payment** = to say that payment is not necessary

waiver ['weɪvə] *noun* voluntarily giving up (a right), removing the conditions (of a rule); *if you want to work without a permit, you will have to apply for a waiver*; **waiver clause** = clause in a contract giving the conditions under which the rights in the contract can be given up

Wales and Chester Circuit ['weɪlz ən 'tʃestə 'sɜːkɪt] *noun* one of the six circuits of the Crown Court to which barristers belong, with its centre in Cardiff

walking possession ['wɔːkɪŋ prə'seʃn] *noun* temporary possession of a debtor's goods taken by a bailiff or sheriff until they can be sold to satisfy execution

war [wɔː] *noun* situation where one country fights another; *the two countries are at war*; **to declare war on a country** = to state officially that a state of war exists between the two countries; **civil war** = situation inside a country where groups of armed people fight against each other or fight against the government; **prisoner of war** = member of the armed forces captured and put in prison by the enemy in time of war; **war crimes** = criminal acts committed by a country, or by people in positions of power during time of war

ward [wɔːd] **1** *noun* **(a)** division of a town or city for administrative purposes; **an electoral ward** = area of a town represented by a councillor on a local council; *Councillor Smith represents Central Ward on the council* **(b)** minor protected by a guardian; *Mr Jones acting on behalf of his ward, Miss Smith* **(c)** minor protected by a court; **ward of court** = minor under the protection of the High Court; *the High Court declared the girl ward of court, to protect her from her uncle who wanted to take her out of the country* **2** *verb* to make a child a ward; *the court warded the girl*

warden ['wɔːdən] *noun* **(a)** person who is in charge of an institution **(b)** *US* head of a prison (NOTE: the British equivalent is **prison governor**) **(c)** person who sees that rules are obeyed; **traffic warden** = official whose duty is to regulate the traffic under the supervision of the police, especially to deal with cars which are illegally parked

warder ['wɔːdə] *noun* guard in a prison

wardship ['wɔːdʃɪp] *noun* being in charge of a ward; the power of a court to take on itself the rights and responsibilities of parents in the interests of a child; *the judge has discretion to exercise the wardship jurisdiction*

warehouse ['weəhaʊs] **1** *noun* large building where goods are stored; **bonded warehouse** = warehouse where goods are stored until excise duty has been paid **2** *verb* to store (goods) in a warehouse

warehousing ['weəhaʊzɪŋ] *noun* act of storing goods; **warehousing costs are rising rapidly**; **warehousing in bond =** keeping imported goods in a warehouse without payment of duty, either to be exported again, or for sale into the country when the duty has been paid

warrant ['wɒrənt] *noun* **(a)** official document from a court which allows someone to do something; **to issue a warrant for the arrest of someone** *or* **to issue an arrest warrant for someone =** to make out and sign an official document which authorizes the police to arrest someone; **bench warrant =** warrant issued by a court for the arrest of an accused person who has not appeared to answer charges; **search warrant =** official document signed by a magistrate allowing the police to enter and search premises; **warrant of committal** *or* **committal warrant =** court order sending a convicted person to prison; **warrant of execution =** warrant issued by a court which gives the bailiffs or sheriffs the power to seize goods from a debtor in order to pay his debts **(b)** official document authorizing the payment of money; *a dividend warrant*

warrantee [wɒrən'tiː] *noun* person who is given a warranty

warrantor [wɒrən'tɔː] *noun* person who gives a warranty

warranty ['wɒrənti] *noun* **(a)** guarantee; *the car is sold with a twelve-month warranty*; *the warranty covers spare parts but not labour costs*; **limited warranty =** warranty over a product which is limited in some way (ie. it is valid only for a certain period of time, or only under certain conditions of use) **(b)** contractual term which is secondary to the main purpose of the contract; **breach of warranty =** failing to do something which is a part of a contract **(c)** statement made by an insured person which declares that the facts stated by him are true

wash sale ['wɒʃ 'seɪl] *noun* buying stock and selling it almost immediately, to give the impression that business is good

wastage ['weɪstɪdʒ] *noun* things which have been wasted; **natural wastage =** losing workers because they resign or retire, not through redundancies or dismissals

waste [weɪst] **1** *noun* permanent damage done to land which diminishes its value **2** *verb* to use more of something than you need; *we turned off all the heating so as not to waste energy*; **wasted costs order =** order by a court that a party has to pay the costs involved in a case which has to be postponed because the party's representative is badly prepared or incompetent

watch [wɒtʃ] *noun* group of people who patrol the streets to maintain law and order; **watch committee =** committee of a local authority which supervises the policing of an area; **neighbourhood watch =** system where the residents in an area are encouraged to look out for criminals and help the police

watchdog (body) ['wɒtʃdɒg 'bɒdi] *noun* **(a)** body which sees that the law is obeyed; *the Commission acts as the watchdog for competition law* **(b)** body which watches something (especially government departments or commercial firms) to see that regulations are not being abused

way [weɪ] *noun* **(a)** act of going; **right of way =** right to go lawfully along a path on another person's land **(b)** manner of doing something; **Committee of Ways and Means =** committee of the whole House of Commons which examines a Supply Bill

weak [wiːk] *adjective* not strong; **weak case =** criminal case where the evidence against the accused is not strong

weapon ['wepn] *noun* **dangerous** *or* **offensive weapon =** item (such as a gun or knife) which can be used to harm someone physically; **carrying offensive weapons =** offence of holding a weapon or something (such as a bottle) which could be used as a weapon

wear and tear ['weə ən 'teə] *noun* **fair wear and tear** = acceptable damage caused by normal use; *the insurance policy covers most damage but not fair wear and tear to the machine*

Weekly Law Reports (WLR) ['wiːkli 'lɔː rɪ'pɔːts] *plural noun* regular reports of cases published by the Council of Law Reporting

welfare ['welfeə] *noun* comfort, being well cared for; *it is the duty of the juvenile court to see to the welfare of children in care*; **education welfare officer** = social worker who looks after schoolchildren, and deals with attendance and family problems; **welfare state** = state which spends a large amount of money to make sure that its citizens are well looked after

Western Circuit ['westən 'sɜːkɪt] *noun* one of the six circuits of the Crown Court to which barristers belong, with its centre in Bristol

Westminster ['wesmɪnstə] *noun* city, part of London, where the Houses of Parliament are situated; **the Palace of Westminster** = the Houses of Parliament, the building where the Commons and Lords meet (NOTE: often used to mean Parliament in general: **the news was greeted with surprise at Westminster; MPs returned to Westminster after the summer recess; rumours are current in Westminster that the plan will be defeated**)

whatsoever [wɒtsəu'evə] *adjective* of any sort; *there is no substance whatsoever in the report*; *the police found no suspicious documents whatsoever* (NOTE: always used after a noun and after a negative)

where- [weə] *prefix* which thing (NOTE: the following words formed from **where-** are frequently used in legal documents)

whereas [weə'æz] *conjunction* as the situation is stated, taking the following fact into consideration; *whereas the property is held in trust for the appellant*; *whereas the contract between the two parties*

stipulated that either party may withdraw at six months' notice

whereby [weə'baɪ] *adverb* by which; *a deed whereby ownership of the property is transferred*

wherein [weə'ɪn] *adverb* in which; *a document wherein the regulations are listed*

whereof [weə'ɒv] *adverb* of which; **in witness whereof I sign my hand** = I sign as a witness that this is correct

whereon [weə'ɒn] *adverb* on which; *land whereon a dwelling is constructed*

wheresoever [weəsəu'evə] *adverb* in any place where; *the insurance covering jewels wheresoever they may be kept*

whip [wɪp] *noun* **(a)** MP who controls the attendance of other MPs of his party at the House of Commons, who makes sure that all MPs vote; **Chief Whip** = main whip, who organizes the other whips; *the Government Chief Whip made sure the MPs were all present for the vote; US* **majority whip** *or* **minority whip** = assistants to majority or minority leaders in the House or Senate, whose responsibility is to make sure the members of his party vote **(b)** instruction given by a whip to other MPs, telling them which business is on the agenda and underlining items where a vote may be taken; **three line whip** = strict instructions to MPs to vote as the whips tell them (by underlining the item on the agenda three times)

White Book ['waɪt 'bʊk] *noun* book containing the Rules of the Supreme Court and a commentary on them

white collar crime ['waɪt 'kɒlə 'kraɪm] *noun* crimes committed by business people or office workers (such as embezzlement, computer fraud, insider dealings)

Whitehall ['waɪthɔːl] *noun* street in London, where several ministries are situated (NOTE: used to refer to the Government or more particularly to the civil service: **Whitehall sources suggest that the**

plan will be adopted; there is a great deal of resistance to the idea in Whitehall)

White House ['waɪt 'haʊs] *noun* building in Washington D.C., where the President of the USA lives and works; *see also* OVAL OFFICE (NOTE: also used to mean the President himself, or the US government: **White House officials disclaimed any knowledge of the letter; the White House press secretary has issued a statement**)

White Paper ['waɪt 'peɪpə] *noun GB* report issued by the government as a statement of government policy on a particular problem, often setting out proposals for changes to legislation for discussion before a Bill is drafted; *compare* GREEN PAPER

whole [həʊl] *adjective* complete or total; **of the whole blood =** relationship whereby a person is related to someone by two common ancestors; **Committee of the Whole House =** the House of Commons acting as a committee to examine the clauses of a Bill; *US* **Committee of the Whole =** committee formed of at least one hundred members of the House of Representatives, which discusses a bill which has already been debated in Committee

COMMENT: in both the House of Commons and House of Representatives, when the House becomes a Committee of the Whole the speaker leaves the chair and his place is taken by a chairman

whole-life insurance *or* **whole-life policy** ['həʊl'laɪf] *noun* insurance or policy where the insured person pays a fixed premium each year and the insurance company pays a sum when he or she dies

wholesale ['həʊlseɪl] *noun & adverb* buying goods direct from the producers and selling in large quantities to traders who then sell in smaller quantities to the general public; **wholesale dealer =** person who buys in bulk from producers and sells to retailers

wholesaler ['həʊlseɪlə] *noun* person who buys goods in bulk from producers and sells them to retailers

wholly-owned subsidiary ['həʊli'əʊnd sʌb'sɪdiəri] *noun* company which is owned completely by another company

wilful *US* **willful** ['wɪlfʊl] *adjective* (person) who is determined to do what he wants, (act) which is done because someone wants to do it, regardless of the effect it may have on others; **wilful misconduct =** behaviour which may harm someone and which is known to be wrong; **wilful murder =** murder which is premeditated; **wilful neglect =** intentionally not doing something which it is your duty to do

wilfully ['wɪlfəli] *adverb* done because someone wants to do it, regardless of the effect on others; *he wilfully set fire to the building*

will [wɪl] *noun* (a) *(formal)* **last will and testament =** legal document by which a person gives instructions to his executors as to how his property should be disposed of after he dies; *he wrote his will in 1964; according to her will, all her property is left to her children*; **holograph will =** will, written out by hand, and not necessarily witnessed; **nuncupative will =** unwritten will stated in the presence of a witness (such as by a soldier in time of war); *see also* BEQUEST, DEVISE, LEGACY **(b)** wishing or wanting to do something; **tenancy at will =** situation where the owner of a property allows a tenant to occupy it as long as either party wishes

COMMENT: to make a valid will, a person must be of age and of sound mind; normally a will must be signed and witnessed in the presence of two witnesses who are not interested in the will. In English law there is complete freedom to dispose of one's property after death as one wishes. However, any dependant may apply for provision to be made out of the estate of a deceased under the

Inheritance (Provision for Family and Dependants) Act

winding up ['waɪndɪŋ 'ʌp] *noun* liquidation, closing of a company and selling its assets; **compulsory winding up order** = order from a court saying that a company must be wound up; **voluntary winding up** = situation where a company itself decides it must close down; **winding up petition** = application to a court for an order that a company be put into liquidation

window ['wɪndəʊ] *noun* **(a)** opening in a wall, door, etc., which is filled with glass; *the burglar must have got in through the bathroom window* **(b)** **window of opportunity** = short moment when the conditions for something are especially favourable; **trial window** = period of three weeks during which a trial is scheduled to take place

wind up ['waɪnd 'ʌp] *verb* **(a)** to end (a meeting); *he wound up the meeting with a vote of thanks to the committee* **(b)** to **wind up a company** = to put a company into liquidation; *the court ordered the company to be wound up* (NOTE: **winding - wound - has wound**)

winner takes all ['wɪnə 'teɪks 'ɔːl] voting system where the candidate with most votes wins; *see also* FIRST-PAST-THE-POST

wiretapping ['waɪətæpɪŋ] *noun* action of bugging a telephone line, so as to listen to the conversations

with costs ['wɪð 'kɒsts] *adverb* **judgment for someone with costs** = judgment that the party's plea was correct and that all the costs of the case should be paid by the other party

withdraw [wɪð'drɔː] *verb* **(a)** to take back a charge, an accusation or a statement; *the prosecution has withdrawn the charges against him*; *the opposition MPs forced the minister to withdraw his statement*; *the chairman asked him to withdraw the remarks he had made about the finance director* **(b)** to take (money)

out of an account; *to withdraw money from the bank or from your account*; *you can withdraw up to £50 from any bank on presentation of a banker's card* **(c)** to take back (an offer); **one of the company's backers has withdrawn** = he stopped supporting the company financially; *to withdraw a takeover bid* (NOTE: **withdrawing - withdrew - has withdrawn**)

withdrawal [wɪð'drɔːl] *noun* removing money from an account; **withdrawal without penalty at seven days' notice** = money can be taken out of a deposit account, without losing any interest, provided that seven days' notice has been given

withhold [wɪθ'həʊld] *verb* to keep back, not to give (information); *he was charged with withholding information from the police*; *approval of any loan will not be unreasonably withheld*

within [wɪð'ɪn] *preposition* inside; *the case falls within the jurisdiction of the court*; *he was within his rights when he challenged the statement made by the police officer*

without [wɪ'ðaʊt] *preposition*; **without prejudice** = phrase spoken or written in letters when attempting to negotiate a settlement, meaning that the negotiations cannot be referred to in court or relied upon by the other party if the discussions fail; **without reserve** = sale at an auction where an item has no reserve price

witness ['wɪtnəs] **1** *noun* **(a)** person who sees something happen or who is present when something happens; **to act as a witness to a document** *or* **a signature** = to sign a document to show that you have watched the main signatory sign it; *the contract has to be signed in the presence of two witnesses*; **in witness whereof** = first words of the testimonium clause, where the signatory of the will or contract signs **(b)** person who appears in court to give evidence; **defence witness** *or* **witness for the defence** = person who is called to court to give evidence which helps the case of the defendant or of the accused;

prosecution witness *or* **witness for the prosecution** = person called by the prosecution side to give evidence against the defendant or the accused; **adverse witness** = witness whose evidence is not favourable to the side which has called him; **expert** *or* **professional** *or* **skilled witness** = witness who is a specialist in a subject and is asked to give his or her opinion on technical matters; **witness of fact** = person who gives evidence to say that facts in a claim are true; **witness box,** *US* **witness stand** = place in a courtroom where the witnesses give evidence; **witness statement** = written statement made by a witness and signed, containing evidence which he or she will make orally in court; **witness summary** = short document which summarizes the evidence which will be in a witness statement, or which lists points which a witness will be questioned on in court; **witness summons** = court order requiring someone to appear as a witness (and if necessary bring with him documents relevant to the case) (NOTE: since the introduction of the new Civil Procedure Rules in April 1999, this term has replaced **subpoena ad testificandum** and **subpoena duces tecum**) **2** *verb* to sign (a document) to show that you guarantee that the other signatures on it are genuine; *to witness an agreement or a signature*; **'now this deed witnesseth'** = words indicating that the details of the agreement follow

WLR = WEEKLY LAW REPORTS

Woolsack ['wʊlsæk] *noun* seat of the Lord Chancellor in the House of Lords

word [wɜːd] **1** *noun* **(a)** separate item of speech or writing; **word processing** = working with words, using a computer to produce, check and change texts, letters, contracts, etc.; **words of art** = words that have a special meaning in law **(b) to give one's word** = to promise; *he gave his word that the matter would remain confidential* **2** *verb* to put something into words; *the contract was incorrectly worded*

wording ['wɜːdɪŋ] *noun* series of words; *did you understand the wording of the contract?*

worker ['wɜːkə] *noun* person who is employed, even if in a part-time capacity

COMMENT: in the European Union, to be classified as a worker, a person has to perform services for an employer and to receive payment for those services; this includes trainees who may not receive a full normal salary, and it includes those who work for no pay as part of a cooperative

works [wɜːks] *noun* building; **clerk of works** = official who superintends the construction of a building

wound [wuːnd] **1** *noun* cut done to the skin of a person; *she has a knife wound in her leg* **2** *verb* to injure or to hurt someone in such a way that his skin is cut; *he was wounded in the fight*; **wounding with intent** = offence of injuring someone, especially when trying to avoid arrest

WPC ['dʌbljuː 'piː 'siː] = WOMAN POLICE CONSTABLE

wreck [rek] **1** *noun* **(a)** (i) action of sinking or badly damaging a ship; (ii) ship which has sunk or which has been badly damaged and cannot float; *they saved the cargo from the wreck*; *oil poured out of the wreck of the ship* **(b)** company which has become insolvent; *he managed to save some of his investment from the wreck of the company*; *investors lost thousands of pounds in the wreck of the investment company* **2** *verb* to damage badly or to ruin; *they are trying to salvage the wrecked ship*; *the defence case was wrecked by the defendant's behaviour in court*

writ [rɪt] *noun* **(a) writ (of summons)** = legal document which begins an action in the High Court; *the company issued a writ to prevent the trade union from going on strike*; *he issued writs for libel in connection with allegations made in a Sunday newspaper*; **to serve someone with a writ** = to give someone a writ officially, so that he has to defend it or allow judgment to be taken against him; **writ of habeas corpus** = writ to obtain the release of someone who has been unlawfully held in prison or in police custody, or to make the person holding a prisoner appear in court to explain why he is being held **(b)** legal action to hold a by-election; **to move a writ** = to propose in the House of Commons that a by-election should be held; **writ of summons** = notice from the Lord Chancellor asking a peer to attend the House of Lords

write in ['raɪt 'ɪn] *verb US* to write the name of a candidate in a space on the voting paper; **write-in candidate** = candidate whose name has been written by the voters on their voting papers

written application ['rɪtn æplɪ'keɪʃn] *noun (in the EU)* the first part of proceedings in the ECJ, where an applicant makes a written application, against which the defendant may reply in writing (the papers will then be examined by the judge rapporteur and one of the Advocates General, before moving on to oral hearings)

wrong [rɒŋ] *noun* act against natural justice, act which infringes someone else's right; *civil wrongs against persons or property are called 'torts'*

wrongdoer ['rɒŋduːə] *noun* person who commits an offence

wrongdoing ['rɒŋduːɪŋ] *noun* bad behaviour, actions which are against the law

wrongful ['rɒŋfʊl] *adjective* unlawful; **wrongful dismissal** = removing someone from a job for a reason which does not justify dismissal and which is in breach of the contract of employment

COMMENT: an employee can complain of wrongful dismissal to the County Court

wrongfully ['rɒŋfəli] *adverb* in an unlawful way; *he claimed he was wrongfully dismissed; she was accused of wrongfully holding her clients' money*

wrongly ['rɒŋli] *adverb* not correctly, badly; *he wrongly invoiced Smith Ltd for £250, when he should have credited them with the same amount*

Xx Yy Zz

Yard [jɑːd] *noun* Scotland Yard *or* the Yard = headquarters of the Metropolitan Police in London

year [jɜː] *noun* period of twelve months; **calendar year** = year from January 1st to December 31st; **financial year** = the twelve month period for a firm's accounts; **fiscal year** *or* **tax year** = twelve month period on which taxes are calculated (in the UK it is April 6th to April 5th of the following year); **Parliamentary year** = year of a session of Parliament, running from the Opening of Parliament in September to the summer recess in August; **year end** = the end of the financial year, when a company's accounts are prepared; *the accounts department has started work on the year-end accounts*

year and a day rule [ˈjɜː ənd ə ˈdeɪ ˈruːl] *noun* ancient rule that a person could not be convicted of murder if the victim died more than 366 days after the attack

COMMENT: the rule was abolished in 1996, as it had come to be used as a defence in cases of work-related deaths, such as from asbestosis or radiation, which may occur many years after the first contamination

yellow dog contract [ˈjeləu ˈdɒg ˈkɒntrækt] *noun US* contract of employment where the employee is forbidden to join a trade union

yield [jiːld] **1** *noun* money produced as a return on an investment **2** *verb* to produce interest or dividend; *the bonds yield 8%*

young offender *US* **youthful offender** [ˈjʌŋ əˈfendə] *noun* person aged between seventeen and twenty years of age who has committed an offence; **Young Offender Institution** = centre where young offenders are sent for training if they have committed crimes which would normally be punishable by a prison sentence (NOTE: formerly called a **Borstal**)

young person [ˈjʌŋ ˈpɜːsən] *noun* person over fourteen years of age, but less than seventeen

youth [juːθ] *noun* young man, young person; **Youth Court** = court (formerly called the Juvenile Court) which tries offenders between the ages of 10 and 18; **youth custody order** = sentence sending a young person to detention in a special centre

zebra crossing [ˈzebrə ˈkrɒsɪŋ] *noun* place in a street marked with white lines, where pedestrians can cross and have right of way

zero [ˈzɪərəu] *noun* nought, the number 0; *the code for international calls is zero zero (00)* **zero inflation** = inflation at 0%

zero-rated [ˈzɪərəuˈreɪtɪd] *adjective* (item) which has a VAT rate of 0%

zero-rating [ˈzɪərəuˈreɪtɪŋ] *noun* rating an item at 0% VAT

zip code [ˈzɪp ˈkəud] *noun US* series of numbers used to represent the area or part of a city or town where an address is situated (NOTE: British English is **post code**)

zipper clause [ˈzɪpə ˈklɔːz] *noun US* standard clause in a contract of employment, which tries to prevent any discussion of employment conditions during the life of the agreement

zone [zəun] *verb* to order that land in a district shall be used only for one type of building; *the land is zoned for industrial use*

zoning ['zəunɪŋ] *noun* order by a local council that land shall be used only for one type of building